The Gun Digest® Book of
.22 RIMFIRE
RIFLES • PISTOLS • AMMUNITION

by James E. House

©2005 Gun Digest

Published by

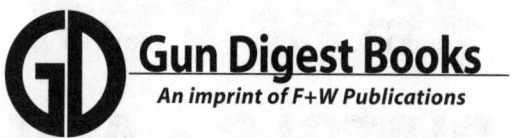Gun Digest Books
An imprint of F+W Publications

Our toll-free number to place an order or obtain
a free catalog is (800) 258-0929.

All rights reserved. No portion of this publication may be reproduced
or transmitted in any form or by any means, electronic or mechanical,
including photocopy, recording, or any information storage and
retrieval system, without permission in writing from the publisher,
except by a reviewer who may quote brief passages in a critical article
or review to be printed in a magazine or newspaper, or electronically
transmitted on radio, television, or the Internet.

Library of Congress Catalog Number: 2005928832
ISBN: 0-87349-908-5

Designed by Kara Grundman

Edited by Kevin Michalowski

Printed in the United States of America

PREFACE

Rimfire firearms are used throughout the world. They are used in competition, hunting, plinking, and protection. Some are very inexpensive while others represent the highest form of technical perfection and cost thousands of dollars. A rimfire firearm is the type of firearm most often used to introduce new shooters to shooting sports, but the seasoned hunter or competition may select a rimfire as the vehicle to develop and display shooting skill. In short, the rimfire is an everyday firearm for just about everyone.

Following the introduction of the 22 Winchester Magnum Rimfire in 1959 and the introduction and demise of the 5mm Remington Magnum in the early 1970s, the rimfire field was one which saw only incremental changes except perhaps for the development of the hyper velocity cartridges. Some new models of firearms were introduced and many others were discontinued, but there were no earth shaking developments. That changed dramatically in 2002 with the introduction of the 17 Hornady Magnum Rimfire and the situation is continuing to change rapidly. The 17 Mach 2 and 17 Aguila are here. There is even talk of yet another new 17 caliber cartridge. Ammunition has continued to evolve with several brands that were unknown not too many years ago becoming familiar names. The last few years have seen an enormous number of significant changes in the field of rimfire firearms and ammunition making this the most exciting time in many years with regard to products in this area of the shooting sports.

There have been others who have written books devoted to rimfire firearms and ammunition. Anyone who writes on a topic in any area builds on what others have done with an attempt to bring the field up to date. In that sense, this book is like others that have dealt with rimfire shooting sports. However, studying other writings has made it clear that each author has a particular outlook and system of values that are brought to bear on the content and organization of the material. As always, there is also the question of what to leave out and what to leave in. In writing this book, I have tried to communicate some of the observations and experience that have been accumulated over a period of 60 years. I have tried to make the material inviting, interesting, and informative. Wherever possible, I have also tried to make the material reflect the current status of the field in terms of product availability.

The field of activity involving the shooting of rimfires is too broad for every product to be listed and discussed. Some choice of topics to include must be made and this book certainly reflects the experience and point of view of the author. That is one reason why it is necessary to read works by several authors in order to be well versed on a subject. Consequently, I have included Appendix A which gives a list of books for further study. Some have balance of general and specific information that will be useful to both beginning and experienced rimfire shooters. It is the fervent hope of the author that this balance has been achieved.

No one writes a book such as this in isolation. In working on this book, it has been a great pleasure to gather information from discussions with many individuals. Special thanks are accorded in no particular order to Margaret Sheldon, Ed Goldshinsky, Sherry Kerr, Ron Herman, Mark Sheppard, Chris Erich, Curt Collins, Kevin Zumbrennen, Anthony Imperato, Andy Van Scyoc, Lisa Flaherty, Tony Aeschliman, Tim Achenbach, Joe Jones II, Rick Sanborn, Dino Longueira, and Ron Darnall. Friends and family members were called upon to provide firearms for testing and photography and in that connection it is a pleasure to acknowledge the assistance of Keith A. House, Ronald K. House, Larry W. House, and David Duley. Working with Kevin Michalowski, Joel Marvin, Steve Smith, and Debbie Bradley at Krause Publications has made the entire project a pleasant and rewarding experience that I hope to have again. Finally, the author would like to acknowledge the encouragement and assistance in this project given by his wife, Kathleen A. House, without whose efforts this project would not have been completed in the same form or time frame. She is also a good marksman. Thanks to all who have helped.

been included because they are classics even though they may be dated in their content. Also included as Appendix B is a list of suppliers and manufacturers where products that are useful to rimfire shooters can be found. Obviously, it is not possible to list every sporting goods store where these products are sold. Because rimfire shooters are often hunters, Appendix C has been included to make it easy to contact appropriate agencies to obtain information about hunting regulations in each state.

It is my opinion that some earlier books deal more with shooting in the form of stories about acquaintances, experiences, and occurrences than with the equipment and its evaluation. With its emphasis on rimfire rifles, pistols, ammunition, ballistics, sights, accessories, and performance of both current and vintage models, this book is intended to be a user's guide to rimfire firearms. Of course some "war stories" are related, but this is a book primarily about the equipment. Not every related topic can or should be covered, but the intent is to provide a

(Photo courtesy: U. S. Fish and Wildlife Service)

About the Author

James E. House has been involved with the shooting sports for well over half a century. During his early years, airguns and rimfire rifles formed the basis for his shooting. As a student at Southern Illinois University in Carbondale, he was a member of the Air Force ROTC rifle team. After receiving his Ph. D. from the University of Illinois, he spent 32 years as a faculty member and administrator at Illinois State University.

As an emeritus professor of chemistry, House has been active as an author. His books include titles on chemical kinetics, quantum mechanics, and a book on descriptive inorganic chemistry that was co-authored with his wife, Kathleen A. House.

Since his retirement, he and his wife have traveled extensively in the mountain states where they enjoy photography, camping, and shooting activities. He is the author of *American Air Rifles* (Krause Publications, 2001) and *CO_2 Pistols & Rifles* (Krause Publications, 2003). House has also written numerous articles that have appeared in publications such as *Gun World*, *The Varmint Hunter*, *The Backwoodsman*, *Predator Extreme*, *The Illinois Shooter*, and *Gun List*.

Contents

PREFACE 3

ABOUT THE AUTHOR 4

CHAPTER 1   **Development of Rimfire Ammunition** 8
Cartridge Development • 22 Winchester Rim Fire (WRF) • Other Early Rimfire Cartridges • Propellants and Primers • Hyper Velocity 22 Ammunition • 22 Winchester Magnum Rimfire (WMR) • 5mm Remington Magnum • 17 Hornady Magnum Rimfire (HMR) • 17 Mach 2 • 17 Aguila

CHAPTER 2   **Safe Shooting** 20
Devices and Programs • Safety Rules • Weapons and Image

CHAPTER 3   **The Rimfire Rifles** 32
Types of Actions • Calibers • Selection and Cost • Youth Rifles Selecting a Rimfire Varmint Rifle • Ancillaries

CHAPTER 4   **The Rimfire Handguns** 51
Practical Considerations • Revolver or Semiautomatic • Calibers Revolvers • Autoloaders • Thoughts on Selection • Ancillaries

CHAPTER 5   **Sights and Sighting** 65
Open Sights • Peep Sights • Scopes • Red Dot and Laser Sights

CHAPTER 6   **Rimfire Ammunition** 78
Selection • Projectiles • The 22 Short • The 22 Long • The 22 Long Rifle • The 22 Winchester Rim Fire (WRF) • The 22 Winchester Magnum Rimfire (WMR) • The 17 Hornady Magnum Rimfire (HMR) • The 17 Mach 2 • The 17 Aguila • Matching the Ammunition to the Target

CHAPTER 7   **Internal Ballistics for Beginners** 94
Ignition • Rim Thickness • Cartridge Weights • Firing Pin Impact • Pressure • Rimfire Rifle Velocities • Bullet Velocities from Handguns

CHAPTER 8   **External Ballistics for Beginners** 114
Forces on Projectiles • Trajectory • 22 Long Rifle • 22 Winchester Magnum Rimfire • 17 Hornady Magnum Rimfire • 17 Mach 2 and 17 Aguila • Ballistics Tables • Effect of Sight Height • Wind Deflection • Shooting Uphill and Downhill

CHAPTER 9	**Rimfire Hunting Tools**	**131**

What Rimfires Can Do • Terminal Effects • Penetration • Smash
• Shot Cartridges • Hitting the Target • Caliber Considerations
• Scopes for Rimfire Hunting • Field Accuracy

CHAPTER 10	**Rimfire Maintenance**	**152**

Tools • Techniques • Restore or Refinish? • Metal Finishing
• Wood Finishing

CHAPTER 11	**Choose A Rimfire for Tough Times**	**164**

Tough Times • Why a Rimfire? • Rifle or Handgun? • Rifle Choices
• Handgun Choices • Caliber • Ammunition

CHAPTER 12	**Accessories, Accuracy, and Competition**	**180**

Stocks • Barrels • Triggers • Sights • Accuracy • Holding Steady
• Competition

CHAPTER 13	**Evaluations of Some Current Rimfire Rifles**	**196**

The Study • Marlin 25N (925) • Ruger 10/22 Carbine
• Ruger 10/22 Target • Ruger 10/22 Rifle • Marlin 60
• Remington 597 • Thompson/Center Classic • Henry Lever Action
• Winchester 9422 • Ruger 77/22 • CZ 452 American (22 LR
• Ruger 77/22M • Ruger 77/17 • CZ 452 American (17 HMR)

CHAPTER 14	**Shooting Some Vintage Rimfire Rifles**	**223**

Winchester 90 • Browning SA-22 • Winchester 190 • Winchester 69A
• Ithaca Saddle Gun • Winchester 320 • Daisy 2201, 2202, and 2203
• Remington 541T • Anschutz 164

CHAPTER 15	**Evaluations of Some Current Rimfire Handguns**	**240**

Accuracy • Browning Buck Mark • Ruger Mark II • Ruger Super Single
Six Convertible • Ruger Mark II 22/45 • Smith & Wesson Model 22A
• Walther P22

CHAPTER 16	**Shooting Some Vintage Rimfire Handguns**	**260**

Colt Huntsman • Smith & Wesson 2206 • High Standard H-B
• Smith & Wesson K-22 • Smith & Wesson Model 34 Kit Gun
• Ruger Single Six • Colt Frontier Scout

APPENDIX A	**Suggestions for Further Reading**	**278**
APPENDIX B	**Sources for the Rimfire Shopper**	**281**
APPENDIX C	**Sources for Hunting Information**	**286**

Chapter 1

DEVELOPMENT OF RIMFIRE AMMUNITION

As you look at the rimfire section of the ammunition counter in a sporting goods store you will see stacks of boxes labeled 22 Long Rifle (LR), 22 Winchester Magnum Rimfire (WMR), and 17 Hornady Magnum Rimfire (HMR). If the store has a comprehensive line of ammunition, you may also see boxes of the new 17 Mach 2, 22 Short, 22 Long or perhaps those dinosaurs known as the 22 CB Short and 22 CB Long that live on for some reason. It is possible that you may also see a box or two of 22 Winchester Rim Fire (WRF), a cartridge that was introduced in 1890 along with the Winchester Model 90 pump rifle that was chambered for the cartridge. As this is being written, another 17-caliber cartridge or two are being marketed or are under development.

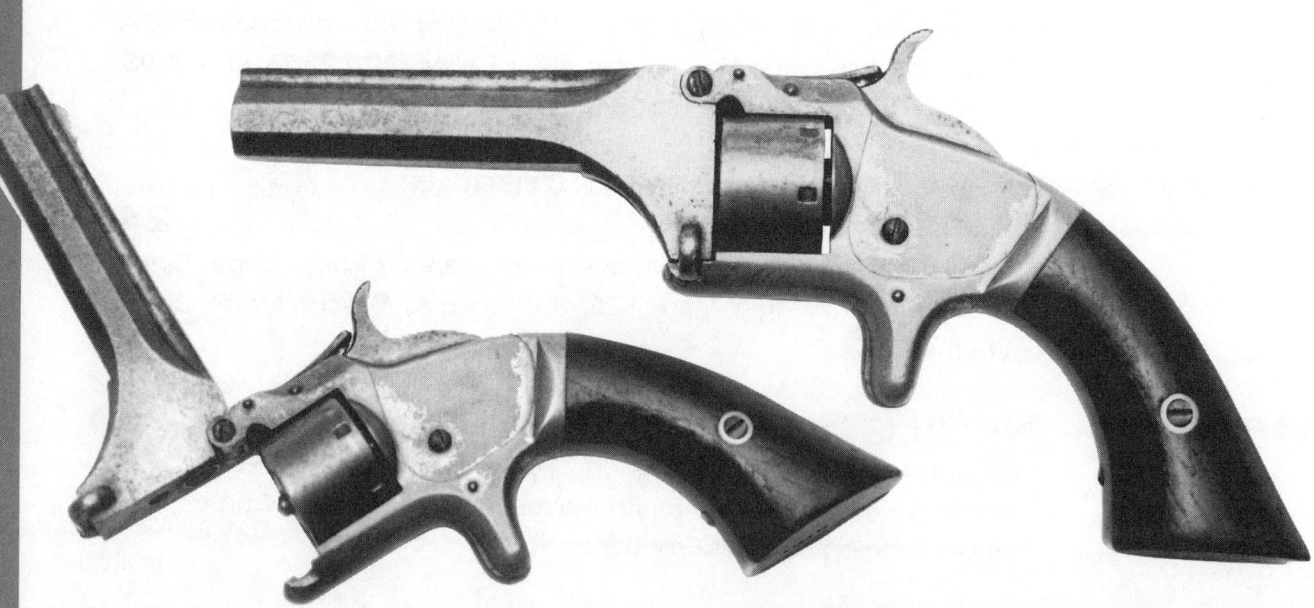

The frame of the Smith & Wesson opened at the bottom and was hinged at the top.

The Smith & Wesson No. 1 First Issue was the first revolver chambered for the 22 Short black powder cartridge. Shown here is a No. 1, Second Issue model.

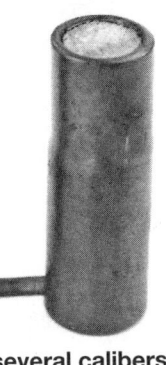

Pinfire cartridges were produced in several calibers including shotgun rounds.

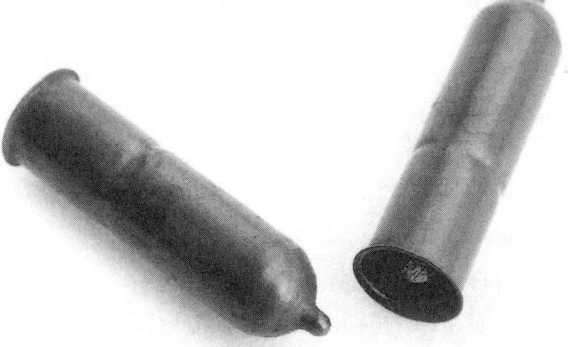

Teat fire cartridges were developed in the 1800s before rim fire cartridges were introduced.

If this list of approximately 10 cartridges makes it seem like there are many choices in rimfire calibers, look again. The 22 Short, Long, Long Rifle and the two CB rounds are all used in the 22 LR chamber. The 22 WMR is a separate caliber as are the 17 HMR and 17 Mach 2. We can ignore the 22 WRF for the moment. What we have is really a short list of rimfire cartridges most of which can be used in firearms of one caliber, but as we shall see it has not always been so. In this chapter, we will provide a brief history of rimfire ammunition and a description of some of the most significant obsolete and current rimfire cartridges.

Cartridge Development

One should not lose sight of the fact that developments in different areas of science and technology are interrelated. For example, it would not be possible to build a long-range rocket without developments in rocket fuel (which is a problem in chemical science). It was not possible to produce the atomic bomb until methods of enriching uranium were developed. The high performance of cartridges today is in great measure the result of improvements in propellants and metallurgy. Some of the basic principles involved in cartridge performance will be described in Chapter 7.

The four approaches to firing metallic cartridges are illustrated here. The cartridges illustrate (left to right) teatfire, pinfire, rimfire, and centerfire types.

A cartridge consists of a primer, propellant, projectile, and a case for these components. In order to ignite a propellant, some substance that explodes is needed. The cause of the explosion is actually percussion (crushing) that is the result of a spring-loaded striker (hammer or firing pin) changing positions at the time of firing. In order to have shot-to-shot uniformity (which results in accuracy), it is necessary to have the same amount of explosive (primer) ignited in the same way for each shot and have the same amount of propellant in each cartridge.

Early developments in muzzle-loading firearms included the flintlock and the caplock, which used a percussion cap. In the flintlock, the primer consisted of a small amount of fast-burning black powder of fine granulation (FFFFg) that was ignited by the sparks produced when a piece of flint struck a piece of steel known as the frizzen. The priming charge was held in the flash pan, which had a hole that led downward into the barrel where the main propellant charge was held. The gas resulting from the burning powder in the main charge provided the driving force to move the bullet down the bore.

As firearm technology developed, so did the chemistry of explosives. It was discovered that mercury fulminate exploded violently when it was struck. Therefore, percussion caps were produced which consisted of a small amount of mercury fulminate contained in a small copper cup that fitted over a hollow nipple. When the hammer fell and struck the cap, the mercury fulminate in the percussion cap exploded which ignited the powder charge as fire was directed from the primer into the barrel breech. The percussion cap was introduced in the early 1800s, and its use in muzzle loading rifles continues to the present time.

Caplock rifles of yesterday and today are relatively reliable devices. This author has fired many rounds through his muzzle loading rifles with only a few instances of misfiring or delayed firing (known as a hang fire). Loading a caplock rifle is a slow process because the powder charge must be measured and poured into the barrel and a projectile loaded on top of the charge. The process is slightly faster if the projectile is a "bullet" rather than a lead ball that is used with a lubricated cloth patch. New developments in muzzle loading make use of propellant that is compressed into pellets of known weight. One or more of these pellets can be dropped down the barrel and projectile loaded on this charge. It became apparent that producing a single unit containing the primer, propellant, and projectile that could be loaded in one operation would be a great convenience. That is exactly the impetus that led to the development of so-called metallic cartridges. However, there still remained the problem of where to place the primer in the cartridge and how to cause it to explode reliably to ignite the powder charge. Attempts to solve that problem led to several early designs in metallic cartridge ammunition.

Black powder had been in general use in muzzle loading firearms for many years so it was the propellant utilized in early metallic cartridges.

Black powder consists of a mixture of potassium nitrate (saltpeter), charcoal (carbon), and sulfur in the approximate percentages 75, 15, and 10, respectively. Burning rate of the propellant, which is designated by an "F" system, is controlled by the particle size. A granulation known as FFFFg (very fine, often referred to as "4F") is a very fast-burning form while a coarse granulation designated as Fg is comparatively slow burning. Black powder used most often in rifles is FFg (medium) while FFFg (fine) is used in handguns or rifles of small caliber.

One of the early designs for a self-contained cartridge is known as the pinfire, and it dates from about 1830 when Monsieur Casimir Le Facheux invented it in Paris. The cartridge contained a bullet, propellant (black powder), and a primer. However, the blow of the hammer was transmitted to the primer by means of a pin that stuck out of the side of the case at the rear. This meant that the cartridge had to be oriented in the chamber in such a way that the hammer would strike the pin to push it into the case to crush the primer. Although placing the cartridges in the firearm in the correct orientation made loading slow by today's standards, it was still rapid compared to loading a muzzle-loader. With pinfire cartridges, there was also the possibility that the protruding pin could be struck accidentally which could force it into the case causing the cartridge to fire. From the standpoint of safety, the pinfire left a lot to be desired. However, cartridges of this type were fairly popular in Europe and some shotguns employed this type of cartridge.

Another cartridge design consisted of a closed tube that contained the bullet and propellant with the primer being contained in a small protruding portion at the rear end of the tube. This type of cartridge, known as the Moore teat fire, was loaded into the front of the cylinder of a revolver with the teat at the rear where it could be struck by the hammer. The front end of the cartridge was flared to form a retaining flange that fit against the front of the cylinder. Cartridges of this design were produced in the mid-1800s. Because the protrusion that held the primer was located in the center of the cartridge head, it was actually a center fire design rather than a true rim fire.

Each of the early cartridge designs described above contained a primer that was sensitive to shock. Subsequent designs would also rely on shock or

The 41 Swiss (left) and 22 Short (right) illustrate the range of cartridges that were eventually produced in rimfire calibers.

percussion to cause the primer to explode, but the primer would be located differently in the cartridge. In 1845, a man named Louis N. Flobert in France loaded a round ball in a percussion cap and produced a small cartridge known as the 22 caliber BB (bulleted breech) cap. Power was the result of the primer since no powder was used. Some American versions of this cartridge employed a conical bullet (hence these were known as CB caps) that was loaded over a small powder charge. In 1851 at an exhibition in London, Horace Smith and Daniel B. Wesson became convinced that this cartridge design could be refined.

The rimfire cartridge was developed by producing a cartridge case with a flange or rim of larger diameter than the body by folding the rear of the case over on itself. The rim was hollow and allowed the priming mixture to be contained within it. The priming mixture was placed in the case while wet and spinning the case caused the mixture to fill the hollow rim. When the primer was dried, it then became sensitive to shock. Crushing the rim by a forward blow of the firing pin caused the primer contained within it to explode which in turn ignited the powder charge.

A short, self-contained 22 caliber cartridge called the Number One Cartridge (essentially identical to the 22 Short of today except for primer and propellant) was introduced in 1854 by Smith & Wesson for use in a small revolver. The revolver was designated as the Smith & Wesson Model 1 First Issue produced from 1857 to 1860. It was followed by the Model 1 Second Issue that was produced from 1860 to 1868 and the Third Issue from 1868-1881. All issues of the Model 1 had a hinge that connected the barrel to the top of the frame at the front end. It was opened by means of a latch at the bottom of the front edge of the frame that allowed the barrel to be tipped up so that the cylinder could be removed for loading and unloading. The cartridge employed a 29-grain bullet that was propelled by 3 to 4 grains of black powder contained in a case that was slightly longer than that of the BB cap. A patent was granted on August 8, 1854 for the rimfire cartridge that was the precursor of the 22 Short. While certainly no powerhouse, the 22 Short has been used as a target load for many years in firearms designed specifically for that cartridge. As strange as it may seem, the 22 Short was originally viewed as a self-defense load! In modern times, small semiautomatic pistols chambered for the 22 Short have been produced for concealed carry and self-defense. The 29-grain bullet from the 22 Short high-velocity load has a velocity of approximately 1,095 ft/sec while the 27-grain hollow-point bullet has a velocity that is a slightly higher.

Introduced in 1887, the 22 Long Rifle (LR) is by far the most popular rimfire cartridge. However, another 22 rimfire cartridge appeared in the 30-year interval between the introduction of the Short and the Long Rifle cartridges. That cartridge, the 22 Long, was introduced in 1871 and made use of a 29-grain bullet propelled by a charge of 5 grains of black powder. Like other 22 rimfires, it eventually became loaded with smokeless powder. The current 22 Long high-velocity cartridge produced by CCI has an advertised muzzle velocity of 1,215 ft/sec, which is about 100 ft/sec higher than the 22 Short. Any difference in power is more imagined than real, and there is no logical reason for the 22 Long to survive. Most of the ammunition companies have ceased production of the 22 Long.

When we come to the 22 LR we arrive at a cartridge that is the most popular and widely used metallic cartridge that exists. It is used throughout the world for recreation, competition, and hunting. The original load consisted of a 40-grain bullet and a 5-grain charge of black powder. Ammunition in 22 LR caliber is loaded in many parts of the world and in some instances to the highest level of technical perfection. The accuracy capability built into a competition rifle chambered for the 22 LR is matched by several types of ammunition that are specifically designed for competition at the highest level. Such ammunition is a far cry from the old black powder loads with corrosive priming that appeared in the 1880s. In later chapters, some of the characteristics of the modern "high-velocity" 22 LR loads will be described. The 22 LR uses a bullet of 0.223 inch diameter that has a short section that is smaller in diameter (the heel) that fits inside the case. The lubricated portion of the bullet is outside the case.

While the target shooter has special ammunition available, the hunter of small game and pests has not been left out. The 22 LR high-speed solid uses a 40-grain bullet that has a muzzle velocity of approximately 1,235 ft/sec while the 36- to 38-grain hollow-points are about 40 to 50 ft/sec faster. Other specialty loads will be described elsewhere in this chapter and in several later chapters. The 22 LR is in many ways the most useful cartridge in existence. A rifle or handgun chambered for this round can be used for many purposes.

22 Winchester Rim Fire (WRF)

In 1890, Winchester introduced a pump-action rifle that is quite possibly the most famous 22 pump rifle ever produced. Designated as the Model 1890 (also known as the Model 90 and some rifles are so marked), the rifle chambered either the 22 Short or a new rimfire cartridge known as the 22 Winchester Rim Fire (WRF) or Winchester Special. The 45-grain flat-point bullet was offered in several loads, some of which gave a velocity as high as 1,400 ft/sec. The original load consisted of 7.5 grains of black powder and it had a muzzle velocity of 1,100 to 1,200 ft/sec. Remington used essentially the same case loaded with a round-nose bullet as the 22 Remington Special. The 22 WRF was popular for many years, but because it offered little advantage over the 22 LR, its popularity declined as the 22 LR became more highly developed.

The 22 WRF case is larger in diameter than that of the 22 LR. As a result, a bullet of 0.224" diameter fits inside the case mouth without having a section of smaller diameter at the base. This is also the situation with the 22 Winchester Magnum Rimfire (WMR) which has almost identical dimensions as the 22 WRF except for length. Therefore, the 22 WRF cartridges can be fired in rifles chambered for the 22 WMR, and they provide a lower-powered (if not lower priced) alternative to the magnum round. In my bolt-action Ruger 77/22M, the CCI 22 WRF ammunition delivers excellent accuracy as will be described in Chapter 15.

Other Early Rimfire Cartridges

Although current rimfire cartridges are all 22 or 17 caliber, many of the rimfire cartridges of historical significance were of larger caliber. One of the most important rimfire developments was the 44 Henry cartridge developed by B. Tyler Henry. It has the distinction of being the chambering for the first successful lever-action rifle. Imagine the effect of a few Union soldiers firing Henry lever-action rifles, which had tubular magazines that held 15 cartridges, on the Confederate soldiers who were using single-shot muzzle-loading rifles! Ballistics of the 44 Henry were not impressive by today's standards (a 210-grain lead bullet propelled by a charge of 28 grains of black powder to give a velocity of 1,150 ft/sec), but the importance of rapid, sustained fire in military operations is obvious. The 44 Henry cartridge was in production from 1860 to 1934. Another large caliber rimfire cartridge used in the Civil War was

The 22 WRF (right) is a shorter cartridge than the 22 WMR (left) but has almost identical case dimensions except for length.

the 56 Spencer. Incidentally, the Henry lever-action was produced from 1860-1866 and was no doubt a driving force which led to the development of the Winchester 73 which used the center fire 44-40 cartridge.

Several other rimfire cartridges were developed about the same time as the 44 Henry. As is now the case with 22 caliber cartridges having different lengths, larger caliber "short" and "long" rimfire cartridges were common in the latter half of the 1800s. Examples include the 30 Short and Long; the 32 Extra Short, Short, and Long; the 38 Extra Short, Short, and Long; and the 41 Short and Long among others. Revolvers were often designed with cylinders to accept the shorter cartridges while the extra long types were most often used in single-shot rifles. They were, of course, loaded with black powder. Although there is no need to review the development of all of these cartridges individually, it is necessary to mention several of them in order to trace the evolution of the rimfire cartridge design. It is interesting to note that of the approximately 75 rimfire cartridges that existed in the late 1800s, only about 10 remained in production after WW II.

Two cartridges that were developed somewhat later were the 25 Stevens Short and 25 Stevens Long (sometimes referred to as simply the 25 Stevens) that were introduced around 1900. These cartridges were produced until 1942, and they were popular in rifles like the Stevens single-shot models. Firing a 65- to 67-grain bullet that was driven at approximately 1,200 ft/sec by a charge of 11 grains of black powder, the 25

It is easy to forget that rimfire cartridges were produced in shorter lengths for use in revolvers and longer versions for rifles in many calibers.

Note how the current 22 Short and Long Rifle have parallels in the 25 Short and Long cartridges of a century ago.

Stevens had a good reputation as a small game load. Compared to any of the 22 caliber rimfires, the larger diameter, heavier bullet of the 25 Stevens, which had a muzzle energy of approximately 208 ft lbs, dispatched many species more dependably. It would still be a useful cartridge, especially in a modern loading that would improve the ballistics.

Propellants and Primers

As the quest for better ammunition continued, it was recognized that black powder left a residue that attracted moisture and led to corrosion. Barrel life of the firearm was nowhere near as long as it is today. In the late 1890s, a new type of propellant was developed by making use of an entirely different type of chemistry. When cotton is nitrated with a mixture of nitric and sulfuric acids, the product is known as nitrocellulose, and it burns very rapidly when ignited. Moreover, the combustion produces very little smoke so this propellant is known as "smokeless" powder. This book is not the place for a review of propellant technology, but it should be mentioned that the burning rate of nitrocellulose can be controlled to a great extent by the particle size. Therefore, it is possible to produce nitrocellulose and tailor it for use in cartridges having different sizes. Another development in propellant technology resulted in a type of powder known as double-base powder. This type of propellant makes use of nitrocellulose to which has been added a small percentage of nitroglycerin. In addition to varying the particle size of the propellant, various additives are included to impart particular properties such as flowing ease, reduction of static electricity, flash reduction, etc. By controlling these characteristics, a large number of types of propellants have been developed with burning rates that vary enormously. Some propellants work best in small cases such as the 22 Short or 25 ACP while others perform best in large cases such as the 300 Winchester Magnum.

Even with the use of smokeless powder, the problem of corrosion persisted. The cause was the residue that was produced from the primer that was a mixture that contained potassium chlorate. Because of the resulting corrosion, primers containing potassium chlorate became known as corrosive primers. Some ammunition was loaded with primers containing mercury fulminate and after detonation the resulting mercury reacted with the brass case which caused it to be weakened and thus unsuitable for reloading. In 1927, Remington introduced Kleanbore primers that contained a type of priming mixture that was noncorrosive. In most modern ammunition, the primer contains an explosive known as lead styphnate, but recently primers have been developed that do not contain lead. The motivation behind this is to reduce the amount of lead that is present in the air when firearms are used on indoor ranges. For use in rimfire cartridges, the priming mixture contains 35 to 45 percent lead styphnate, 25 to 35 percent barium nitrate, 18 to 22 pecent ground glass, and 6 to 10 percent lead thiocyanate as well as some other minor constituents. The function of the ground glass is to make the mixture more sensitive to friction when crushed in the rim. On the negative side, the small amount of ground glass remaining in the bore increases the rate of wear so that even though soft lead bullets are used, the bore eventually shows the effects of erosion. A 22 LR barrel will not last indefinitely. One of the characteristics of lead styphnate is that its explosive character is destroyed by oil and some organic solvents. If oil seeps into a case, it may cause the round to misfire. This is one reason for the substantial crimp given to 22 rimfire ammunition, the other being that a heavy crimp is necessary to give the correct "pull" that results in uniform velocities.

Hyper-Velocity 22 Ammunition

Over the many years in which it has been produced, the 22 LR cartridge has undergone several changes. Most of these involved minor changes in velocity that resulted from the use of different powders or bullets of slightly different weight or shape. However, a radical departure from the norm occurred in 1977 when CCI introduced a round known as the Stinger. The new round utilized a 32-grain bullet that was driven by a heavier charge of powder that had a slower burning rate than the powder ordinarily used in 22 LR ammunition. To accommodate the larger powder charge, the case of the Stinger was made approximately one-tenth of an inch longer than the normal 22 LR case. The result was a round that produced a muzzle velocity of 1,640 ft/sec and a muzzle energy of 191 ft lbs. A flat trajectory resulted from the high bullet velocity so the effective range of the 22 rifle was increased. Owing to the high-velocity hollow-

Remington ammunition has featured Kleanbore priming for many years as shown on these boxes of 22 LR cartridges from the 1950s.

point bullet, the new round was explosive in its effect on small pests or unopened cans of pop. The term "hyper-velocity" is generally applied to 22 LR ammunition that produces very high velocity.

Very soon after the Stinger was introduced, Winchester began producing a type of hyper-velocity round known as the Xpediter. This load utilized a 29-grain hollow-point bullet with a muzzle velocity of 1,680 ft/sec which gives a energy of 182 ft lbs. Federal followed suit by introducing the Spitfire which employed a 33-grain bullet with a velocity of 1,500 ft/sec and an energy of 165 ft lbs. The Winchester Xpediter was discontinued after being available for a few years, and the current Federal hyper-velocity load is not designated as the Spitfire although the ballistics are unchanged from that round.

Remington entered the competitive field of hyper-velocity ammunition with two offerings. The Yellow Jacket features a 33-grain hollow-point bullet at 1,500 ft/sec giving a muzzle energy of 165 ft lbs while the Viper features a 36-grain truncated cone solid-point bullet at 1,410 ft/sec for an energy of 159 ft lbs. Aguila produces one other hyper-velocity round, and it drives a 30-grain bullet at an advertised velocity of 1,750 ft/sec to give 204 ft lbs of energy. However, the energy drops to only 93 ft lbs at a range of 100 yards. Another hyper-velocity round is the CCI Quik-Shok which uses a 32-grain bullet, but the bullet is designed so that it breaks into four pieces on impact. This produces a devastating effect on small varmints although penetration is generally less than with other types of ammunition.

Although the hyper-velocity ammunition gives dramatic effects at short ranges, the light bullets lose velocity more rapidly than do the heavier bullets used in conventional 22 LR ammunition. The result is that the remaining energy of the hyper-velocity ammunition is approximately equal to that of the slower rounds at a range of 100 yards or so. It is also generally true that hyper-velocity ammunition does not deliver the best accuracy in most rifles. There have been many reports published to verify that conclusion, and based on the results of tests conducted during this work it certainly true. Moreover, the longer cases of the Stinger and Quik-Shok pose a problem when used in rifles with so-called match-type chambers because the *case* engages the rifling just in front of the chamber. With match chambers, the rifling extends back to the front end of the chamber so the bullet engages the rifling as a round is chambered. The makers of some rifles having match chambers warn against using the Stinger ammunition in those rifles. Bullet diameter for the 22 Short, Long, and Long Rifle is 0.223 inch.

With all of these developments and those described in the following sections, there can be little doubt that this is an exciting time for the rimfire shooter. More details on the performance of today's rimfire cartridges will be presented in several later chapters in this book.

22 Winchester Magnum Rimfire (WMR)

As wonderful as the 22 LR is, there are situations where more power is called for. In 1959, Winchester responded to that need by developing a cartridge that utilizes a case that is 1.05 inches in length and has a slightly larger diameter head and body than the 22 LR case (0.291" vs. 0.275" and 0.241" vs. 0.225", respectively). Instead of using a bullet with a heel of smaller diameter that fits inside the case and a bullet that has the same diameter as the case, the new round used a 40-grain jacketed bullet of 0.224-inch diameter. This "magnum" rimfire is appropriately named the 22 Winchester Magnum Rimfire (WMR), and the advertised velocity is 1,910 ft/sec from a 24-inch barrel. With a muzzle energy of 310 ft lbs, the 22 WMR is still the most powerful rimfire cartridge available. From the 20-inch barrel of my Ruger 77/22M, the velocity at 10 feet from the muzzle is below the advertised value by about 75 ft/sec.

The main drawback to the 22 WMR has always been the cost of ammunition. Although some special

Three magnum rimfire cartridges are (left to right) the 17 HMR, the 5mm Remington, and 22 WMR. The 5mm Remington has been discontinued since the 1970s.

target ammunition in 22 LR may cost as much as $10 for a box containing 50 rounds, the cost of most of the ordinary types is only $2 to $3 per box. Some promotional ammunition in 22 LR can be bought for around $1 per box. Most of the types of ammunition in 22 WMR sell for $6.00 or more with the Remington Premier selling for around $10 per box. It is simply a fact of life that it costs around 12 to 20 cents per shot to fire a 22 WMR.

Being a larger and more powerful cartridge than the 22 LR, the 22 WMR could not be adapted to most actions that were designed specifically for the smaller cartridge. The actions had to be made slightly longer than those used on regular 22s, but very soon after the 22 WMR was introduced a large number of arms were available to chamber it. Winchester marketed the lever-action Model 9422M, and Ruger offered single-action revolvers with two cylinders, one in 22 LR and the other for the 22 WMR. Marlin, Savage, Anschutz, and others produced bolt-action rifles for the 22 WMR soon after its introduction. Currently, bolt-actions, lever-actions, and autoloaders are available in the magnum rimfire calibers as are many handguns (see Chapters 3 and 4).

The major complaint about the 22 WMR has centered on the subject of accuracy. It is popularly believed that the 22 WMR does not give accuracy that is quite the equal of that given by the 22 LR and some newer rimfire rounds. This perception may be in error, but that topic will be addressed more fully in later chapters.

5mm Remington Magnum

In 1970, Remington unveiled a rimfire magnum cartridge that offered even better performance than the 22 WMR. However, that cartridge deviated from the usual rimfire caliber because it was a 5mm or 20-caliber (actual bullet diameter is 0.2045"). The 5mm Remington Magnum cartridge produced 2,100 ft/sec with a ballistically efficient 38-grain bullet. As a result, the muzzle energy was 372 ft lbs, and the remaining energy also exceeded that of the 22 WMR at longer ranges. The 5mm Remington used a case that is slightly larger in diameter than that of the 22 WMR. Remington produced the Model 591 (box magazine) and Model 592 (tubular magazine) bolt-actions, but these were the only rifles produced for the 5mm Remington cartridge. Thompson/Center produced barrels chambered for the 5mm Remington to be used on the single shot pistols that they market. The 591 and 592 were discontinued in 1974 with a total of approximately 50,000 having been produced. The 5mm cartridges have become highly collectible with prices for a full box often being in the $50 to $75 range or more.

With greater energy and flatter trajectory than the 22 WMR, the 5mm Remington may well have been the best rimfire cartridge in modern times. Although the trajectory is not quite as flat as that of the 17 HMR with a 17-grain bullet, the 5mm Remington with its 38-grain bullet is a far more powerful cartridge. Part of the difficulty with the 5mm stemmed from the high pressure, which may have been as high as 35,000 lb/in^2. The high pressure caused the case to expand into the extractor notches, which necessitated some changes in the chamber, bolt face, and extractor grooves. Given the propellants available today, it is likely that the remarkable ballistics of the 5mm Remington could be produced with a somewhat lower pressure. Moreover, there are several rifles available today that could probably serve as platforms for the excellent 5mm Remington cartridge. The Ruger 77/22M, Anschutz, Remington 504, CZ 452, and Kimber models come to mind immediately. We can only hope that rifles and ammunition in this outstanding rimfire caliber become available once again. If not, a 20-caliber cartridge based on a necked down 22 WMR case but utilizing the superb Hornady V-Max polymer tipped bullets would be very interesting and useful. Given the fine rifles that are available in 22 WMR caliber, it should be a simple matter to produce a 20 caliber cartridge based on that case.

17 Hornady Magnum Rimfire (HMR)

Perhaps no other new cartridge has generated so many printed words in such a short time by so many writers as the 17 HMR. Introduced in 2002, the 17 HMR was the first new rimfire cartridge since the short-lived 5mm Remington. However, the 17 HMR certainly will not suffer a similar fate! The number of rifles and handguns available in 17 HMR caliber is very large. This is natural because the 17 HMR case is simply a 22 WMR case necked down to hold a 17-caliber bullet. Therefore, a firearm designed around the 22 WMR can be made into a 17 HMR simply by changing the barrel. Even the magazines that hold 22 WMR cartridges will feed 17 HMR cartridges. Because so many firearms in 22 WMR caliber were already in production, there are now many that are also produced in 17 HMR.

Nominal bullet diameter for the 17 HMR is 0.172". The original load consisted of a 17-grain Hornady V-Max polymer tipped bullet that was loaded to a velocity of 2,550 ft/sec giving an energy of 245 ft lbs. The well-shaped bullet has a ballistic coefficient of 0.125 so it holds velocity well which results in a rather flat trajectory that makes hits

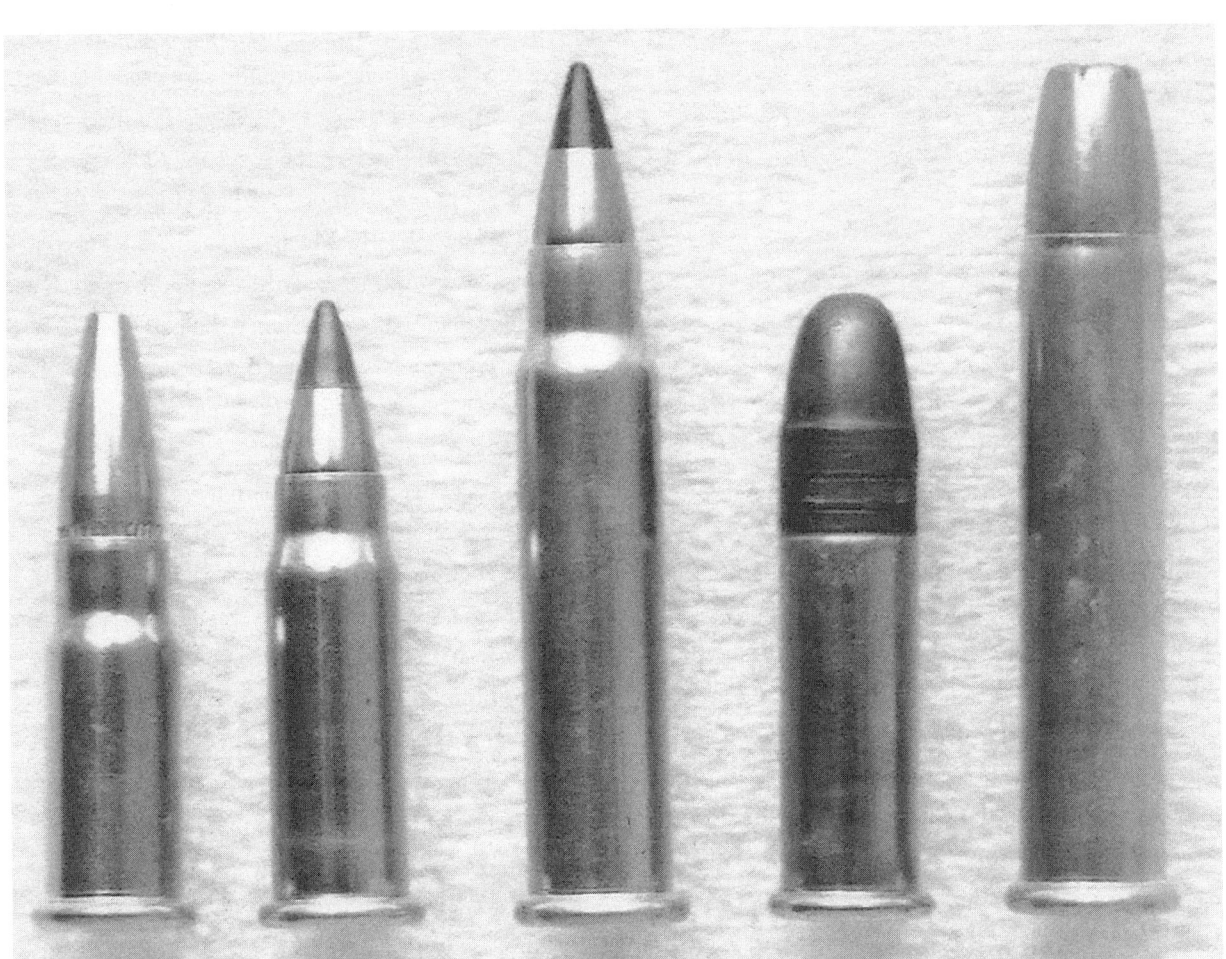

Calibers available to the rimfire shooter are (left to right) the 17 Aguila, 17 Mach 2, 17 HMR, 22LR, and 22 WMR. Although all are useful, each has its advantages and disadvantages.

Introduced in 2004, the 17 Mach 2 is gaining wide acceptance. Note the mention on the label of the "first production run" on this box.

Two cartridges that the author (and many others) would like to see brought back are the 5mm Remington (left) and the 25 Stevens (right).

on small pests possible out to 150 yards or more. Although many larger varmints have been taken with the 17 HMR, the cartridge is at its best when used on species like ground squirrels, crows, pigeons, and prairie dogs. Early reports by some writers described the use of the 17 HMR on species as large as coyotes, but many reports have also described failures of the tiny bullets on larger pests like groundhogs, foxes, and coyotes. One of the most interesting discussions on the 17 HMR is that by C. Rodney James which was published in *Gun Digest 2005*. In an article published in the February 2005 issue of *Predator Xtreme*, Ralph Lermayer has related some of his experiences on the failure of the 17 HMR as a cartridge for use on larger varmints. Recently, loads employing 20-grain hollow-point bullets having a muzzle velocity of 2,375 ft/sec have been introduced to reduce the explosive character. This ammunition may help reduce bullet fragmentation, but the tiny 17 HMR was never really intended for use on larger species of varmints. Nonetheless, the 17 HMR is a great little cartridge that gives outstanding accuracy, and we will have a lot to say about it in other chapters of this book. Incidentally, it was the development of suitable propellants that made the ballistics given by the 17 HMR possible. Had such propellants been available at the time the 5mm Remington was introduced, the 17 HMR might never have been developed.

17 Mach 2

The 17 HMR represents a 22 WMR case necked to hold 17-caliber bullets, but consider the potential of a 22 LR case necked to hold a 17-caliber bullet. An enormous number of rimfire rifles could become 17-caliber rifles simply by changing the barrels. In order to produce a cartridge that would hold enough powder to give a high velocity, the case used could be that of the CCI Stinger which is 0.700 inch long rather than 0.600 inch of the normal 22 LR. These procedures are exactly those used by Hornady and CCI to produce the 17 Mach 2, which launches a 17-grain bullet at 2,100 ft/sec (which is approximately twice the velocity of sound hence the name Mach 2).

However, there is a potential problem with simply changing the barrels on 22 LR semiautomatics. The new 17 Mach 2 burns more powder than a 22 LR so the chamber pressure remains high for a longer period of time. This causes the bolt to be driven to the rear at higher velocity than when 22 LR cartridges are fired. To keep the bolt from being driven back with enough force to damage the action, a heavier bolt must be used or a stronger recoil spring or both. There is no problem with bolt-action 22 LR rifles becoming 17 Mach 2 pieces, but in the case of autoloaders, changes other than merely switching barrels may be necessary.

Firing a 17-grain bullet with a muzzle velocity of 2100 ft/sec, the 17 Mach 2 produces a muzzle energy of 166 ft lbs. This is less power than that produced by some high performance 22 LR rounds so the 17

Mach 2 is a rifle for small pests. Accuracy as good as that produced by any rimfire is the strong point of the 17 Mach 2. With its flat trajectory, small pests are in danger out to around 125 yards when the shooter does his or her part. However, two of the last three boxes of 17 Mach 2 ammunition that I bought cost $6.99 each while the other was $5.99. This is approximately two or three times the cost of good quality 22 LR ammunition and is about the same as 22 WMR ammunition. The difference probably would not matter to a pest hunter, but it certainly would to the casual plinker.

17 Aguila

A recently introduced 17-caliber cartridge is known as the 17 Aguila. While the 17 Mach 2 utilizes the longer CCI Stinger case necked to hold a 0.172 caliber bullet, the 17 Aguila employs a 22 LR case of normal length. Powder capacity of the 17 Aguila is less than that of the 17 Mach 2 so a muzzle velocity of 1,850 ft/sec is produced with a 20-grain bullet (remaining velocity at 100 yards is 1,267 ft/sec). However, bolt-action rifles and most autoloaders that fire 22 LR cartridges can be converted to 17

Newest of the rimfire cartridges is the 17 Aguila, which is a 22 LR case necked to hold a 17 caliber bullet.

Aguila caliber simply by changing the barrels. Even though the 17 Aguila produces slightly lower velocity than the 17 HMR, the difference is not enough to make any practical difference in hunting use especially since the 17 Aguila uses a 20-grain bullet. Shots should be limited to somewhat shorter ranges with the 17 Aguila, but both are suitable for small game and small pests. The almost unknown 17 High Standard cartridge is apparently almost identical to the 17 Aguila.

Although several obsolete rimfire cartridges have been interesting and historically important, the choices available today make this the most exciting time in rimfire history. Hopefully this will become more apparent as you read this book.

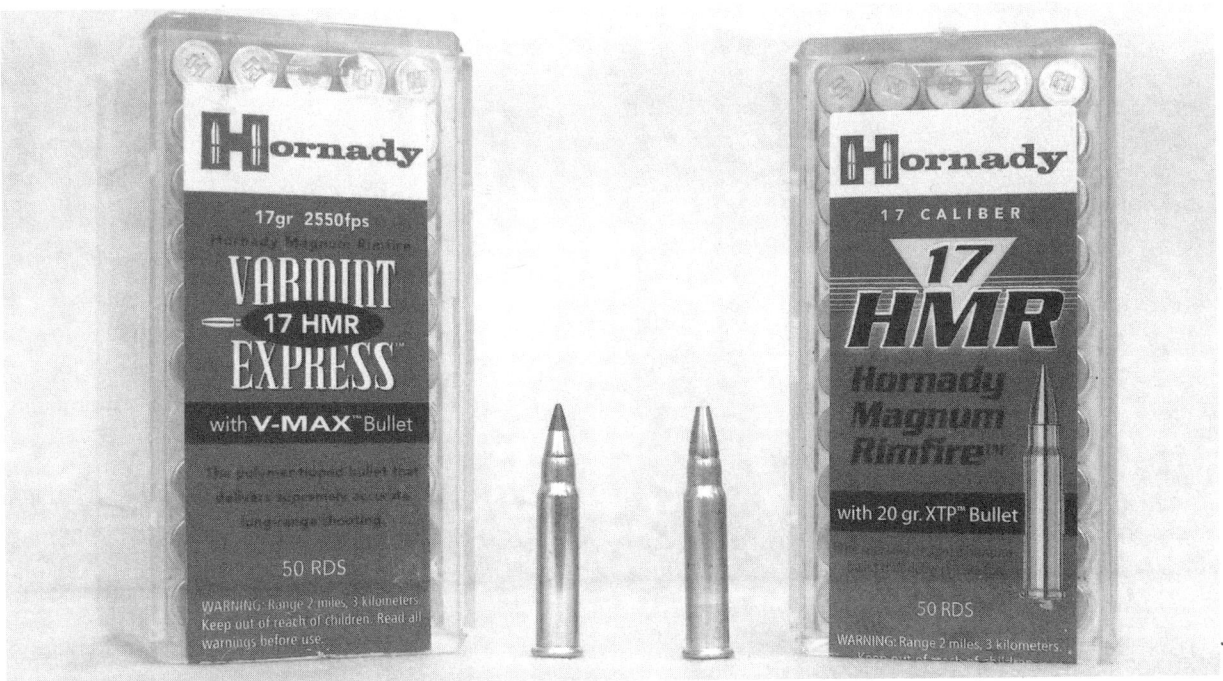

In 17 HMR, Hornady markets loads with a 17-grain polymer tipped bullet (left) or a 20-grain hollow-point (right).

Chapter 2
SAFE SHOOTING

Anything that launches projectiles has the potential to cause injury. This is not limited to slingshots, bows, airguns, or firearms. Golf balls, baseballs, and horseshoes have all caused fatalities. In baseball, batters wear helmets for a reason. Participants in other sports wear protective equipment. However, it is in the shooting sports that safety must be paramount. Firearms launch small projectiles at high velocity so they can travel great distances. In spite of this, it entirely possible to enjoy shooting sports for many years and fire tens of thousands of shots in complete safety even though the news media may routinely consider that anything involving a firearm is a high risk activity. In this chapter, we will describe some of the aspects of safety that shooters must follow in order to participate safely in shooting sports.

Aware of the safety issues related to the storage of firearms, Sturm, Ruger & Co. include a safety lock with most of their products.

Devices and Programs

We are at a point in time when shooting accidents are occurring at the lowest rate they have been for many years. There are several reasons for this welcome decline. First, currently produced rifles and pistols are manufactured with more safety features than ever before. Let me cite just one example. Older single-action revolvers can fire accidentally if dropped or the hammer is struck a blow because in some cases the firing pin is an integral part of the hammer and it rests against a cartridge. In other models, the firing pin is held permanently in the frame, but the hammer rests against the firing pin. In either of these types of single-action revolvers, the firing pin may be held away from the cartridge by a notch on the hammer (a so-called safety notch). That safety notch may not be adequate to keep the firing pin from striking the cartridge if a substantial blow to the hammer occurs. In order to carry such a revolver safely, it is necessary to keep an empty chamber in front of the firing pin. Old timers knew this and their revolvers were treated as "five shooters" rather than "six shooters."

Single-action revolvers are those that require cocking the hammer for each shot (which also rotates the cylinder) and this type has been popular for about 150 years. In 1973, Sturm, Ruger, & Company redesigned its single-action revolvers to produce the "new model" single-action. After the new model revolver is cocked, a transfer bar moves upward to a position between the hammer and the firing pin only as the trigger is pulled to the rear. Therefore, only if the trigger is pulled will the hammer strike the bar and transmit the blow to the firing pin. Neither accidentally dropping a new model revolver nor a blow to the hammer will cause it to fire because when the transfer bar is down, the hammer rests against the frame and it is not in contact with the firing pin. These "new model" revolvers can be carried safely with all six chambers loaded. This is just one example of the additional safety features that are found on some newer firearms.

While the situation described above is in reference to single-action revolvers, it also existed for some of the familiar lever action rifles with their visible, manually operated hammers. Most newer lever action rifles have safeties that block the hammer from moving forward to strike the firing pin if the hammer is struck by an accidental blow. Many models of bolt action rifles also have improved safeties. While most older bolt action rifles required the safety to be moved to the "off" position to open the bolt, many newer ones allow the bolt to be opened without having to disengage the safety. This is a great improvement because to open the action the shooter does not have to operate the bolt of a rifle that is in firing condition. Some bolt action rifles have indicators to show when the piece is cocked, but with others there is nothing visible to show whether the action is cocked or not. Today, most semiautomatic rifles and pistols have a device that holds the action open after the last shot has been fired. An increasing number of semiautomatic pistols have some sort of indicator that shows when there is a cartridge in the chamber. For example, on the new Ruger Mark III the loaded chamber indicator is a lever that runs along the left hand side of the frame and fits flush with the frame when the chamber is empty. When a round is chambered, the lever swings out of the frame slightly and a red dot on the top edge of the lever is visible.

All modern semiautomatic pistols chambered for rimfire cartridges have safeties. Usually they are levers located on the left hand side at the rear of the frame and are

Older single-action revolvers had to have the hammer at half cock in order to rotate the cylinder.

Many firearms are shipped with a "flag" in the chamber to show that no cartridge resides in the chamber. Shown here is a Smith & Wesson Model 22A.

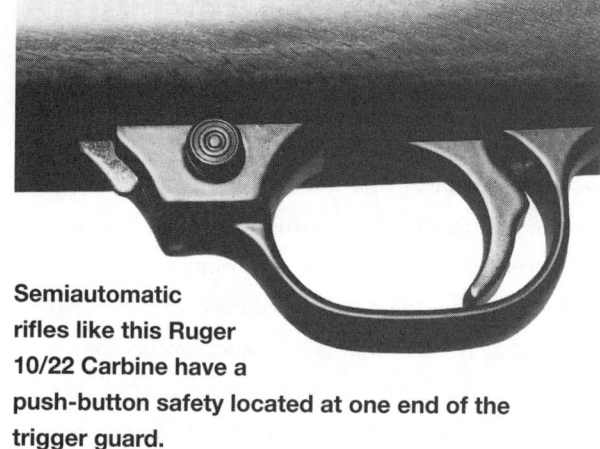

Semiautomatic rifles like this Ruger 10/22 Carbine have a push-button safety located at one end of the trigger guard.

operated by the thumb of the shooting hand. It is possible as a result of handling the firearm or removing it from a holster to cause this lever to be moved accidentally. Pistols of recent manufacture often have safeties that are better designed to prevent this from happening, and the possibility of litigation has caused most firearms marketed today to have triggers that require more force to discharge the piece than was the case a generation or two ago. These and other improvements in firearms have helped reduce accidents, but the most important aspect of safety is still the human mind.

While the changes in equipment have made the shooting sports safer, so have the training programs that have been conducted or sponsored by numerous organizations. The National Rifle Association (NRA) has conducted the Eddie Eagle GunSafe Program for many years, and more than 18 million of youngsters have received instruction in what to do when encountering a firearm as a result. More information on this program is available from the NRA Eddie Eagle Department at (800) 231-0752 or from the web site www.nrahq.org/safety/eddie/. According to the National Center for Health Statistics, fatal accidents from firearms in the pre-K through third grade age group has been reduced by more than two-thirds during the operation of this program.

The Boy Scouts of America includes instruction in shooting in many areas of the country. Other groups that are proactive with regard to shooting include 4-H and Future Farmers of America (FFA) groups. Many summer camps that are operated by civic and church groups for youngsters have instruction and practice in target shooting. Other companies and groups are concerned primarily with safe handling and shooting of airguns, and this activity is frequently a forerunner of shooting firearms. Daisy Outdoor Products has sponsored national BB and airgun competition for many years. Daisy also has a trailer that has been converted to a portable range that is used in various parts of the country to introduce boys and girls to shooting activities with airguns. Crosman Corporation also sponsors programs that are directed toward training and safe shooting.

With the emphasis on safety in shooting, most states require the completion of a hunter safety course for anyone under a certain age who wishes to get a hunting license. Certified instructors who make sure that the prospective hunter is familiar with proper handling and use of a firearm conduct these courses. Safety is a constant thing, not a sometime thing. Changes in equipment and training have led to a drastic reduction in firearm-related accidents, but further reductions are possible. Those of us involved in the shooting sports must constantly be concerned with the safety issues of our activities.

Rimfire rifles and pistols are at the same time some of the safest and most dangerous of firearms. Because of their having low noise and almost no recoil, they are convenient and pleasant to use. However, the same characteristics may also cause them to be taken lightly. This should never be the case! The author has served on a coroner's jury and seen first hand the incredible effect that can be produced by a bullet from a 22 rimfire. He has also used a rimfire to prepare large hogs and cattle for the butcher's block. A rimfire round can produce an enormous amount of damage!

A bullet from the lowly 22 LR rimfire can travel up to a mile and a bullet from the 17 HMR or 22 WMR can travel even farther. Because the velocity is relatively low, bullets from rimfire firearms (especially the 22 Short, Long and Long Rifle) are prone to ricochet badly. Shooting at almost any object on the ground will result in that familiar but horrible whine of a bullet on its way to somewhere else. Not only that, it may be going at some merry angle compared to the direction in which it was fired. The rimfire shooter must exercise good judgment and restraint. If you are engaged in the noble and time-honored pastime of hunting squirrels with a 22, remember that you may be able to fire at game in some directions but not others. If you miss that squirrel on a limb 40 yards away, the bullet is going to come down a long way from where you are. It may also strike a branch and ricochet in some uncontrollable and unknown direction.

The Thompson Center Classic has a hole through the rear of the trigger guard through which a special lock is placed.

A 22 LR looks tiny beside a 458 Winchester magnum cartridge. As a result of its small size, there is sometimes a tendency to take a 22 caliber firearm lightly.

A bullet from a rimfire can easily penetrate a 2x4 or several inches of flesh. I have performed almost every test imaginable, and the power produced by a cartridge that measures only one inch in length and costs as little as 2 cents is almost unbelievable. Not far from where this is being written, a man getting into a vehicle dropped a loaded 22 handgun, which struck the floor, discharged, and sent a bullet into his body. It penetrated several organs on its upward path and the man was killed. A rimfire has the power to be lethal from many directions, not only when a bullet hits "just right." All of the safety requirements for *any* firearm must be exercised in the use of a rimfire. A rimfire firearm is every bit as much a firearm as is a powerful rifle that is intended for hunting elephants. In fact, the story has been told of a shooter actually killing an elephant with a 22 LR!

Safety Rules

Many accidents are avoidable. Common sense and logic would prevent many situations from arising in which someone might be injured or killed. Millions of shooters have enjoyed their sport for many years without ever being involved in an accident. In terms of the number of man-hours involved and the very low incidence of accidents, shooting sports are safer than are many other types of activities. However, when an accident involving a firearm does occur, it is deemed a newsworthy item. Even a minor injury inflected by a firearm will get more press coverage than a broken spine that results from a skiing accident except when the injured party is someone famous. Those of us who are involved in any form of shooting sport must remember that there is a large, vocal segment of the population who does not believe that we even have the right to own and use a firearm. They believe that the Second Amendment is some sort of collective right that was intended for militias but not individuals. That is remarkable in view of the fact that the other rights specified in the Bill of Rights are *individual* rights. Historians of my acquaintance who specialized in constitutional history at the doctoral level and studied the papers of the writers of that time say that the documents made it clear that the citizens of this country would not be reduced to serfs. It was clearly their intention that law-abiding *individuals* would enjoy the freedom to own and use firearms lawfully.

While this may seem so elementary that there is no need to state it, read and follow all instructions in the owner's manual that came with your firearm! The manual may contain information regarding the operation of your firearm that you may not know even if you are an experienced shooter. Some firearms have particular features or characteristics that may have changed so that even experience with a similar model some years ago does not necessarily mean that the latest version operates in exactly the same way. I found recently when I was having trouble with a certain rifle that consulting the owner's manual showed me why. It was not a safety issue but rather involved convenience in operation of the rifle. In addition to information on safety, the owner's manual will give tips on maintenance of the firearm that can lead to long, trouble-free service. Correct procedures for loading, unloading, and handling firearms are important, and the owner's manual will give you the information you need to perform these functions correctly.

It is incumbent upon all shooters to use all means available to make the shooting sports as safe as possible. There are several rules that serve as a basis for conduct in the shooting sports, a sort of shooting etiquette. The list takes on several forms depending on who is drawing up the list, but the rules can be distilled to embody the following areas.

1. Treat every gun as if it were loaded.

Some gun handlers become sloppy when they "know" a gun isn't loaded. However, it is the "unloaded" gun that is sometimes involved in an accident. Never assume that a firearm is unloaded when you pick it up or someone hands it to you. With many firearms, there is no way to tell at a glance that there is not a round in the chamber. It may also be that there is a round in the magazine, and working the action may place that round in the chamber unknown to the person handling the gun. If this rule were always followed, it would prevent a firearm from being handled in a careless manner. The author knows of a case where a hole was drilled through a leg of a lamp table in a living room. The shooter thought his 22 rifle was unloaded and was attempting to release the spring tension on the firing pin by snapping it while aiming at a section of the table leg. It turned out that there was a round in the chamber, and a bullet was placed squarely through the table leg. Although his aim was good, his logic was defective. This type of mistake can lead to disaster. If the tension on the cocking mechanism is to be released, first insert a snap cap before pulling the trigger. If the piece is a bolt action rifle, raise the bolt handle, pull back on the trigger, and slowly move the bolt handle to the "down" position which allows the firing pin to move forward in a controlled manner. Treating every gun as if it were loaded has been translated by some to read "all guns are loaded." Always assume that this is so.

As a young lad, the author remembers being in the home of a relative and looking around in a bedroom. On the floor was a small revolver that did

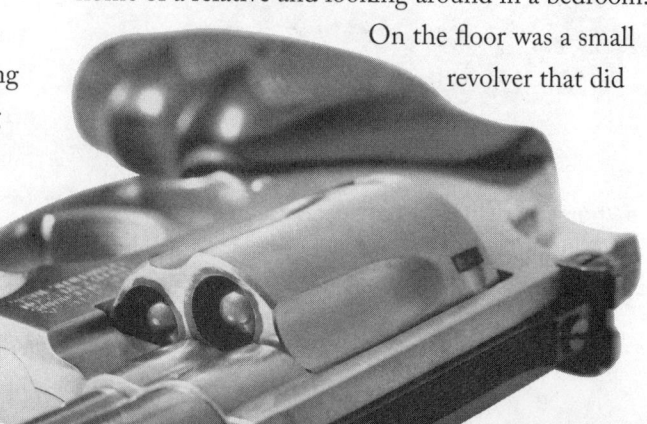

It is readily apparent that this revolver is loaded. This is one advantage of the revolver over the autoloader.

not look much different than the toy cap pistols that were so familiar at that age. However, when the revolver was picked up, the bullets in the cartridges were clearly visible from the front of the cylinder and the cartridge heads were visible at the rear. Having been around firearms a great deal it was immediately obvious that this was a real gun rather than some toy that had been left behind. Very carefully the revolver, a Smith & Wesson 32 Hand Ejector model, was placed where it was found. Someone who did not know better might have been involved in a tragic accident when finding a loaded revolver. Teaching youngsters about firearm safety (even those who live in homes where there are no firearms) is a worthwhile activity. Knowing and teaching about firearms is infinitely better than trying to isolate young, curious children so they will never have contact with a firearm. Sadly, it seems today that the approach taken by many individuals is to pretend that firearms are somehow evil and must be avoided.

Many years ago, I visited a gun shop that had handguns in a glass case. A Colt 1911 attracted my attention, and I asked to look at it. The owner handed the pistol over the case, and I held it carefully. Casually pulling back the slide, a loaded 45 ACP cartridge was ejected! With the action open, it was obvious that there were additional cartridges in the magazine. I carefully handed the pistol to the totally baffled owner. It seems as if the pistol had been placed in the case only a day or two earlier when the previous owner delivered it to the shop to consummate a trade that had been arranged earlier. Having examined the pistol at the time the trade was made, the owner assumed that the previous owner had unloaded the pistol before bringing it in for transfer. Never assume that any gun anywhere is unloaded.

2. Never allow a gun to point in an unsafe direction or point a gun at anything you would not shoot.

Firearms, especially handguns, are short enough that simply by moving an arm or turning one's body the muzzle may be pointed in a direction in which a shot should not be fired. Realizing that the firearm being handled may be loaded (and should always be treated as if it were!), the firearm must be controlled in such a way that the muzzle is *never* brought to point in a line that represents an unsafe shooting direction. Handguns should be manipulated with the muzzle pointing upward, action open, and finger off the trigger until it is safe to load the piece and assume a firing position. Rifles should be kept unloaded with the actions open and the muzzle pointed upward or in another safe direction depending on the circumstances. On ranges, special racks are usually available where all rifles are held in this condition. This writer has observed instances in which someone holding a firearm was spoken to by someone else. While turning toward the speaker, the person holding the firearm allowed the muzzle to sweep through an arc which brought the muzzle in line with another person. While holding a firearm, you must always be conscious of where a bullet would go if the piece discharged at any time. It is bad enough to have a firearm discharge accidentally under any circumstances, but it is much better to have it fire in a safe direction (in the air or down range) should such an event occur.

3. Always wear eye and ear protection.

While it is by no means a common occurrence, it is possible for the case rim to rupture when a rimfire firearm is discharged. The author has had it happen several times, and when it does hot gases as well as bits of powder and brass are ejected around the bolt face of the rifle (or out of the

Safe shooting requires the participant to wear eye and hearing protectors.

front or rear of the cylinder of a revolver) . These are sufficiently energetic to cause eye injuries. Even when the case rim does not rupture, the gap between the cylinder and barrel in a revolver can allow bits of unburned powder or lead shavings to escape. Modern rimfire ammunition is extremely good, but the author recently had four rounds of 22 LR target ammunition from the same box misfire. Moreover, two of these rounds misfired in each of two bolt action rifles. After waiting a short time with the muzzle remaining pointed at the target, the bolt was carefully opened and the round gently removed by pulling the bolt back. In such instances, it is possible for a "hang fire" round to detonate inside the open action causing all sorts of debris to be launched in all directions. If such an event happens, the shooter had better be wearing eye protection. Depending on the type of backstop being used, it is also possible that some small particles of the lead bullet may ricochet. Eyes are delicate and it is prudent to use every precaution possible to prevent eye injury. Participants in paintball sports are certainly aware of this requirement.

Most corrective eyeglasses are made with polycarbonate lenses which are impact resistant. If the shooter is wearing glasses, the majority of bits of debris will be deflected although most glasses do not provide any protection from the sides. Good shooting glasses need not be expensive. Some suppliers of firearms market shooting glasses under their own labels. For example, Remington and Smith & Wesson each offer several styles that are available from many suppliers of shooting-related products such as Cabela's. Prices range from $20-40 for most of these glasses. Inexpensive wrap around safety glasses are available which are intended for shooters of airguns. Glasses such as these are generally sufficient to afford eye protection when shooting rimfire firearms. The important thing is to get a rigid, transparent layer of plastic between your eyes and any flying objects or gases.

There was a time when hearing protection was not deemed necessary when firing a rimfire. True, the report is low compared to that from firearms of higher power, but it is sufficient to cause hearing loss, especially over an extended period of time. The author competed as a member of a small-bore rifle team for two years with firing conducted on an indoor range. He also has little hearing in his left ear (the one toward the muzzle), which is partially attributable to a lack of hearing protectors at that time. Rimfire firearms make a loud crack that is certainly capable of causing hearing loss. We know a lot more about these things now that we did 40 or 50 years ago, and hearing protectors are commonly used in occupations from airport workers to highway construction.

Although hearing protectors are available which cost as much as $200, it is not necessary to spend a lot of money to get adequate protection, especially when shooting rimfire firearms. My wife and I use Beretta Range Muffs that fold up to make a compact unit. These muffs are available from Cabela's for $24.99 with your choice of blue or black color. There are many other brands and styles available in the over the ear type of protector. The in the ear plug styles are also available and most are inexpensive.

Trigger locks are one way to keep a handgun secure. This lock requires a special key that has a most unusual shape to open it.

4. Do not shoot at a hard surface or water.

Almost anyone who has fired a rimfire firearm in the outdoors has heard the whine of a bullet that has been deformed but not stopped. It can happen when shooting at a pine cone and the bullet hits the target or a branch and goes off into space. It can happen when a bullet fired at a pop can makes contact with the ground and whines on its way. It will almost certainly happen if the bullet is fired at a target on the surface of water. The shooter of a rimfire firearm must anticipate that a ricochet is likely under these conditions. Most states prohibit shooting at targets on the surface of water. A bullet that is deflected during a ricochet may be capable of traveling a long distance because the velocity may not be reduced a great deal. Always be sure of your backstop or shoot in an area where there is nothing that can be damaged for a long distance if the bullet continues past the target.

5. Do not cross a fence or stream with a loaded gun.

Sometimes, it may not always be possible to pass an obstacle while constantly keeping the muzzle of a firearm pointing a safe direction. There is always the chance for a foot or hand to slip causing the shooter to assume some unsafe position while trying to regain control. It may also happen that the safety or hammer of the piece may contact the fence or some part of the anatomy and be moved. Any of these events can result in an unsafe situation. If it is necessary to pass some obstacle such as a fence, unload the firearm, leave the action open, and hand it to someone on the other side of the fence. If you are alone, place the empty firearm with the action open on the other side of the fence before you cross it. When crossing a stream, unload the firearm, open the action, and cross the stream safely before reloading. Having seen the foot of a hunter slip off a wet stone in the middle of a stream and the hunter go one way and the his rifle another, it can not be overemphasized that it is unsafe to cross a stream with a loaded firearm.

6. Keep every firearm unloaded until you are ready to shoot.

Some of the most unsafe situations involving firearms result from improperly storing and transporting them. Firearm safety requires that an encounter of a person with the firearm begins with an unloaded piece. Someone else in your home or vehicle may have access to the piece in your absence. That person may not know the characteristics of your particular firearm which could lead to accidental discharge if the piece is loaded. Some firearms have actions that can not be opened unless the safety is in the "off" position. If the firearm is loaded, taking the safety off prior to opening the action places it in the ready mode. Therefore, it is imperative that the firearm be unloaded so that the person handling it is not manipulating a firearm that can be discharged immediately and accidentally. An exception to this can be made if the firearm is being used for self defense, but it should be stored so that only the person to whom the firearm belongs has immediate access to it.

7. Transport only unloaded, cased firearms.

In almost every situation, it is unlawful to discharge a firearm from a vehicle on a highway. In the confines of a vehicle, handling a rifle or handgun can cause the muzzle to point at someone else or at your own body parts. It is difficult to keep the muzzle from pointing in a direction that violates rule No. 2 given above. Even if the firearm is cased, removing a loaded firearm from a gun case can be an unsafe practice. It is possible that while transporting the piece the safety may have become disengaged. For firearms having external hammers, the hammer may have become partially or fully cocked. It is all too easy under these conditions to accidentally discharge the firearm. In the state of Wyoming there were four gun related accidents during the 2003 hunting season. Two of them involved loaded firearms in vehicles.

State laws regarding transportation of firearms vary enormously. Some states allow firearms to be transported uncased and loaded while in other states transported firearms must be unloaded and cased. Even within certain states there are great difference. For example, some municipalities forbid the ownership of handguns. Travelers who are transporting a handgun in such areas even when it cased and unloaded may be considered to be in possession of an illegal firearm. In some states, firearms and ammunition cannot be transported in the same case. The point is that there are literally thousands of laws on the books that relate to firearms, their transportation, and their uses. It is your responsibility to know and obey the rules that apply in your locality.

8. Keep all guns stored unloaded and away from unauthorized persons.

We are at a point in time where certain jurisdictions require that all firearms in homes be stored in locked containers or with a trigger lock of some sort in place. The idea behind this is to prevent someone who does not know safe gun handling procedures from picking up a loaded gun and accidentally firing it. Firearms vary enormously in design. The author once handed his single-action revolver to a police officer who was fully qualified for duty with a semiautomatic pistol. The officer had no idea how a single-action revolver worked and thought it was some type of top-break model that had to be opened at the top for loading. Of course there was no lack of concern for keeping the muzzle pointed correctly or other safe handling rules. It was simply a matter of not knowing how the mechanism of a single-action revolver worked. Someone who is unfamiliar with firearms, especially children, may find it all too easy to move some button or knob and place the firearm in a "ready" mode. The tragedy of a child finding a loaded gun, pointing it in the wrong direction, and accidentally discharging the weapon is a scenario that can and does happen. It should not.

Numerous attempts are being made to make it more difficult for anyone other than the primary user of a firearm to operate it. Built in smart locks that use code or a small key that must be inserted are currently being utilized or developed. By incorporating such devices, the chance of someone other than the owner firing the piece when the owner is not around is reduced. Some of the rimfire models with built in locks include the Ruger Mark III and the Walther P22. Regardless of what safety devices are developed, the most effective safety device is a careful, well-trained person who exercises appropriate caution while handling a firearm.

9. Obey all range commands instantly.

Shooters of rimfire rifles and pistols often engage in formal or informal target shooting which may involve training sessions. This may occur at a range or in some other safe area with a suitable backstop. When firing is conducted on a range, it may be under the supervision of a range officer especially if it is a formal match carried out with time limitations. If this is the case, shooters are arranged at stations on the firing line with the firearms lying on a bench or table pointing toward the target area. When the target area is clear, the range officer may call, "Ready on the left? Ready on the right? Ready on the firing line! (pause) Commence firing!" At that point, the shooters are permitted to start firing the course. At the end of the time allowed, the range officer will announce, "Cease fire!" The course of fire is over at that time regardless of whether or not all competitors have fired the number of shots normally included in that course. As firing progresses, the range officer may issue other commands. Regardless of what these commands are or whether or not they involve you, obey all such commands instantly. In basketball, when a whistle sounds the ball is almost always lobbed toward the basket, but no shot is ever to be fired on a shooting range after a command to cease is given. It is entirely possible that the range officer has seen something that none of the shooters on the line has observed. At many clubs, there may be no range officer present, but the shooters follow the same rules. A "cold line" is observed with all weapons having actions open and magazines empty until all shooters are "ready" and the appropriate commands are given to allow the line to become "hot."

Benchrest shooting, one of the popular forms of target shooting, involves firing the rifle from a heavy bench with the rifle fully supported. The object of this type of shooting is to fire the shots into the smallest group possible although in some cases, firing is for score. All shooters must keep their firearms unloaded and with the actions open until they are actually on the firing line. In rimfire benchrest competition, bolt actions are to have the bolts removed when they are not actually being set up for firing. When any person is downrange from the benches, the rifles are to be removed from the benches and all shooters are to be away from the benches. Rifles that do not have removable bolts are to have a safety device (a safety flag) protruding from the open breech when they are resting on the benches and a person is downrange.

10. Never use a firearm when mental or motor skills are impaired.

It is a crime to operate a motor vehicle while under the influence of alcohol. Some medications can cause the user to become drowsy or sluggish, which are physiological effects that are not unlike those produced by alcohol. Anyone who has received any substance that reduces mental or motor skills should not use a firearm. Crisp mental action and physical motions are required to manipulate a firearm in a safe, efficient manner.

While spending a great deal of time in the Big Horn Mountains of Wyoming, the author and his wife became friends with one of the campground workers and his son, David. One summer, David had a friend, Josh, who came to the mountains to spend a week with him. Each afternoon, for the week of Josh's visit, it was customary to see the boys with their 22s heading out into the forest for an afternoon of adventure. It usually involved shooting a box of ammo at pine cones and pop cans that they took with them and brought back. If, as was usually the case, the boys came over to talk for a while before heading out, it was interesting to note that their rifles were unloaded, actions open, and muzzles pointing either straight up or down. They had faithfully learned the proper etiquette of handling firearms. The entire scene portrayed the very essence of our heritage and the legacy of the 22 rimfire. Watching David and Josh brought back memories from more than half a century earlier when my brother and I engaged in similar pursuits. There are those who wish to do away with such wonderful activities of others for their own misguided reasons. However, when, not if, this privilege is lost, America will be the poorer for it. Safe firearm handling may forestall our loss of this right assured by The Second Amendment.

Weapons and Image

Image is everything someone has said. If you do not believe it, watch a candidate for office as he meets with a group of business people or for a debate dressed in a black suit, white shirt, and red tie. Watch the same candidate as he meets with occupants of a nursing home or a group of farmers and note the difference in the candidate's attire. This is not a sexist observation because equivalent dress codes also exist for female candidates. Not long ago, as this is being written, a news report from the TV station in a city nearby gave the story of a homicide. As the announcer was talking, the graphic on the screen showed a handgun, the word "murder" and the outline of a body. You have probably seen such things before. However, in this instance, the victim had been stabbed to death! The desired connotation had nonetheless been conveyed to the viewers as they heard about a murder.

Let us look at one instance of how statistics and image are used in relation to reporting data regarding shooting sports. A recent study reported that an "estimated 21,840 injuries" resulting from nonpowder guns (air rifles, paintball pistols, and BB guns) were treated in the year 2000. That estimate may or may not be accurate, but the implication is that the number is known because it is not given as "over 20,000" which would clearly show that it is an *estimate*. As bad as the use of the use of the word "estimated" is, there was another factor in the report that was even worse. In the lead paragraph of the report was the phrase "…undermining the notion that such weapons are harmless…" Did you ever hear a baseball announcer say, "Jones dropped his weapon and headed for first base" during a baseball game? Is a baseball bat a weapon? Absolutely, if it is used as a weapon. What about a golf announcer making the statement, "Jones had a good swing with the weapon." Is a golf club a weapon? Absolutely, if it is used as a weapon. If you think these are absurd examples, what about watching a TV show on cooking only to hear the chef say, "Slice the cold dessert with a warm-bladed weapon." In this book, the only time the author will use the word "weapon" is in Chapter 11, which deals with some aspects of self-defense. It is true that the same shotgun that is used when hunting quail or 22 rifle used to hunt squirrels can be used as a weapon, but it is the use that determines what is a weapon. The person who "rode shotgun" on a stage coach had a short-barreled shotgun known as a coach gun that was indeed a weapon.

Once, while the author was shooting on a range at a military establishment, a worker there came by and noting my 22 caliber semiautomatic pistol remarked, "What a beautiful weapon." I was astonished because I regarded it as a device for punching holes in a piece of paper that was 50 feet away. That handgun was never used as a weapon. It is the contention of this author that in sporting circles the word "weapon" should generally be avoided because it conveys a negative connotation to nonshooters (who are all too numerous and a growing segment of the population).

In the 10-year period 1990-2000, the total number of deaths from nonpowder guns was 39 (approximately four per year), far fewer than those resulting from bicycle accidents which have been averaging about one death every six hours or up to almost 1,500 per year! According to the Consumer Product Safety Commission (CPSC), 36 children die annually by drowning in 5-gallon buckets! This does not include the hundreds more that drown in bathtubs, showers, toilets, etc. According to the same CPSC, children under the age of 5 die at a rate of approximately 150 per year as a result of playing with cigarette lighters (this does not include approximately 1,100 per year under age 15 who die in residential fires). Falls from open windows annually account for the deaths of approximately 18 persons under the age of 10. Note the lack of media coverage to some of the other types of accidents compared to those in the shooting sports. If the intent is really to reduce accidental injuries and deaths, there are far more fruitful areas in which to work than with the shooting sports. For example, each year, almost a million children are treated for injuries involving bicycles.

During the three score years of involvement in shooting sports by the author, there has been a drastic change in firearms and the presentation of information about them. If you pick up a copy of almost any magazine devoted to guns and shooting, you will see photos of firearms that have laser sights, flashlights attached (hunting at night is illegal under almost all conditions), and a red glow at the muzzle with streaks emanating from it. Often the holder of the firearm is dressed in black and wearing a mask. Such presentation of a firearm may have a place in military and law enforcement settings. However, if a nonshooter passing the magazine rack on his way to find a copy of *Financial Insight* or *Daydreamer's Quarterly* sees several magazines with these sinister looking firearms on the cover, he or she has a mental image generated which is likely transferred to all shooting sports. Never mind that the first Gold Medal given in the 2000 Olympics was won by Nancy Johnson in women's airgun competition. As this is being written, the so-called Assault Rifle Ban that was introduced in 1994 has just expired. That Act was placed in force in no small measure because of the image of certain firearms. Never mind that

The Thompson/Center Classic is shipped with a red flag that is attached to a plastic plug that inserts into the chamber.

the vast majority of such firearms were never used in criminal acts. Note that the news report described above used the word "weapon" as a descriptor for air rifles, paintball pistols, and BB guns. The first step in getting people on your side of an issue is to generate an image. In this case, the image of a "weapon" is being transferred to even BB guns and the paintball pistols used in a type of game or sport but not as weapons.

Another word that is used frequently in many shooting publications is the word "tactical." We read about tactical pistols, tactical flashlights, tactical knives, and tactical scopes. What sort of tactics? Squirrel hunting? Shooting groups to test accuracy? Shooting pop cans and pine cones? Tactical is the adjective form of the word "tactics" which my dictionary defines in one way as the science of maneuvering forces in combat. No wonder a nonshooter seeing a magazine that has listed the contents on the cover as articles on "tactical pistols" or "tactical knives" might think that the readers of such a magazine are (or want to be) members of some paramilitary group. There is nothing wrong with any of these "tactical" items, but they are not part of recreational or practice shooting unless the participant is training for tactics of a different sort.

Just as this is being written, the December 2004 issue of *The American Rifleman* arrived. It had a short story about an auction on eBay that had been pulled because the item being offered was believed to be related to assault weapons. It seems that the person whose item was for sale had used the descriptors "sniper" and "tactical" in reference to the item. It turned out that the item was a composite stock for a version of the popular bolt-action Remington Model 700 rifle that is sometimes referred to as a "tactical rifle." Someone associated with eBay believed that somehow the stock was for an assault rifle and it seems that the policy is not to offer for sale on eBay anything that is associated with such firearms. Had the words tactical and sniper terms not appeared in the ad, the item would have been just as legitimate as the stock that I bought on eBay for my Ruger 77/17 that is described elsewhere in this book. In view of what took place in the Washington, DC area in the recent past, it is probably best to avoid the use of the word "sniper" in sport shooting circles. Image may not be everything, but it obviously important to those who are not knowledgeable about shooting sports.

We who love (a word that is appropriate for this author who has used rimfire rifles for 60 years) sport shooting can help give a positive image to the shooting sports. The "study" cited above did not mention the fine work done by Daisy Outdoor Products in conducting the National BB Gun Competition because the intent was to emphasize how "dangerous" airguns are. Shooting sports in the Olympics are virtually never even mentioned in the TV coverage. We cannot expect balanced coverage of our sports in the mainstream media. A great deal of what is written in this section shows the personality, interest, and concerns of the writer. Almost all writing always does. It remains, however, that we can go a long way toward preserving the shooting sports by the image we present. In this book, the intent is going to be to present an image of shooting as a skill, a sport, and a science to be enjoyed safely by an enormous number of people.

Chapter 3

THE RIMFIRE RIFLES

This book was written to serve as a user's guide to rimfire rifles and pistols. Some readers are perhaps old hands in the rimfire game, but others may be newcomers. If you are a member of the former group, you may already have rimfire firearms and need this chapter only for reference. If you are a member of the latter group, this chapter will give you some insight into the factors to consider when you start evaluating the enormous number of rimfire firearms that are available in order to select the equipment for your own use or perhaps for use by another member of your family.

To operate a bolt-action, the handle must be lifted and the bolt withdrawn then pushed forward. Shown here is the famous Anschutz Model 64 action.

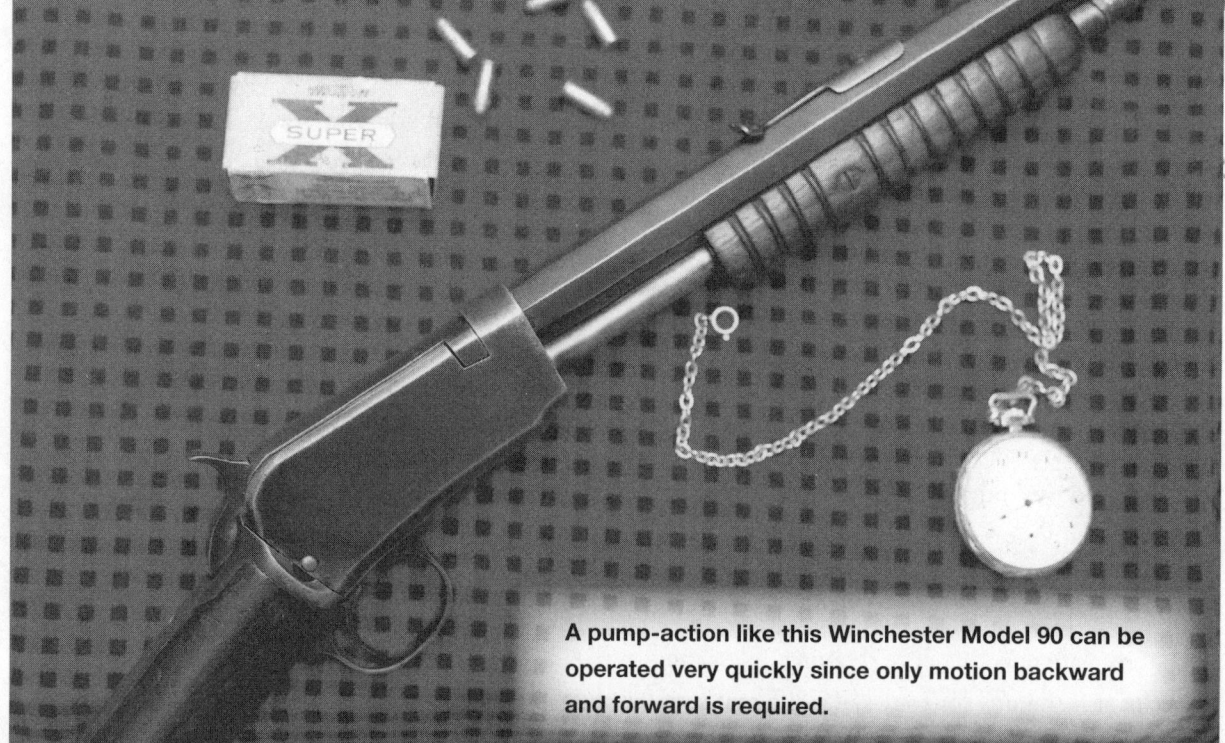

A pump-action like this Winchester Model 90 can be operated very quickly since only motion backward and forward is required.

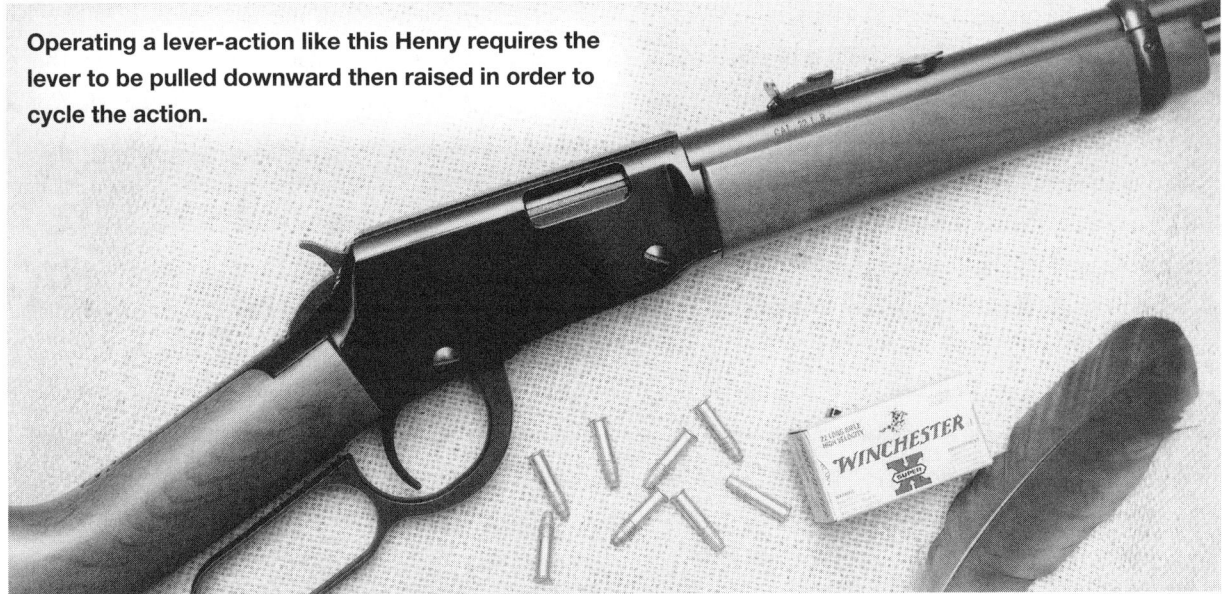

Operating a lever-action like this Henry requires the lever to be pulled downward then raised in order to cycle the action.

Before you select a rimfire firearm, it is necessary to decide what you intend to do with it. It is not unreasonable for a rimfire shooter who is buying a new rifle for serious varmint hunting or competition to spend a great deal of money. For these shooters, equipment at the cutting edge of performance is worth the investment. The rifles and pistols in this category are not made by the millions as are some of the low-end models. By the same token, it is not necessary to spend a great deal of money if all you are going to do is to take a youngster out to hunt squirrels or shoot pop cans. Rifles that perform well enough for this type of shooting do not cost a great deal of money.

In this chapter, a survey of the different types of rifles will be presented to give a general introduction to the rimfire field. Rifles are available with lever, pump, bolt, single-shot, and semiautomatic types of actions. Within certain limits, rifles having any of these types of actions may meet the performance requirements for the intended uses. However, you are not likely to find many lever-action or pump rifles that deliver tack-driving accuracy, but there are exceptions. Target rifles generally have bolt-actions although there are some very accurate semiautomatics. One of the first decisions to be made is that of the caliber of the rimfire rifle to be chosen.

For many years, the only choice was 22 LR, but that is not the case today.

Types of Actions

In order to fire a series of shots, some means must be available for reloading. The empty case must be removed and a loaded round placed in the chamber for the next shot. Sounds elementary, doesn't it? In principle it is, but how it is done often involves some sophisticated engineering and the fabrication of intricate mechanisms. As with most forms of human endeavor, approaches to solving the problem have been many and varied. Some of the earliest breech

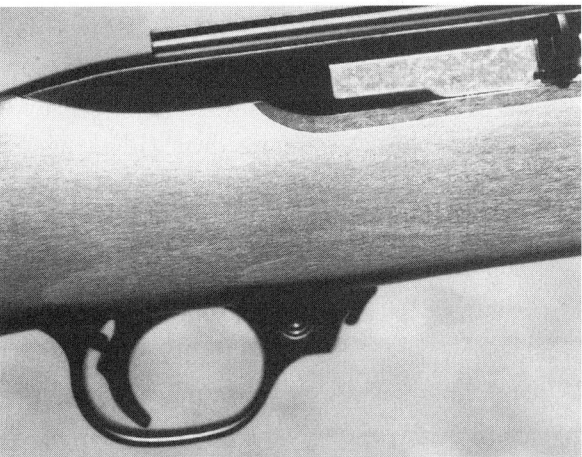

The Ruger 10/22 autoloader requires only pulling the trigger to fire successive shots.

loading rifles had some sort of block that moved upward behind the cartridge to hold it in place and at the same time placed the firing pin directly between the cartridge and the hammer. The hammer could be drawn back so that the sear engaged a notch to hold it in place. When the trigger was pulled, the sear disengaged letting the spring-driven hammer go forward to strike the firing pin that in turn struck the primer and fired the shot.

Most of the single-shot rifles that incorporate a moving locking block (either falling block or rolling block) have long since disappeared from the marketplace. In the late 1800s and early 1900s, there were numerous models of such rimfire rifles that were generally of a small-scale design. Replacing them were single-shot bolt-actions in which the bolt handle could be lifted out of its retaining notch and drawn back to open the chamber with the extractor pulling out the empty case. After a cartridge was placed in the chamber, pushing the bolt forward and turning the handle down into its locking notch closed the action. In some models, a cam moved the firing pin back to cock the action as the action was opened while in others the firing pin was held back by the sear as the action was closed. The first type is known as "cocks-on-opening" while the other is the "cocks-on-closing" type. In still other rifles, neither opening nor closing the bolt cocked the rifle. That was done after the action was closed by pulling back on a knob at the rear end of the bolt (the cocking piece).

Because most shooters would rather load several rounds at one time and then fire them without any further handling of ammunition, the "repeating rifle" was designed. In rimfire calibers, there are two common ways in which the cartridges are held. The first type of reservoir, located in front of the trigger, is a box in which the rounds are stacked vertically. When the bolt is drawn back, a cartridge moves upward so that when the bolt is pushed forward it takes the top round out of the magazine and moves it into the chamber. A variation of this type of magazine is one in which the cartridges are held in a box that allows them to stack around a spindle. The rotary magazines employed by many of the popular Ruger rimfire rifles are of this type. The second type of reservoir for cartridges is a long tube that is located under the barrel or less commonly inside the stock. Inside the tube is a spring-loaded follower that pushes the cartridges to the rear so that as the bolt is opened, a cartridge is moved into a position that allows the bolt carry it into the chamber as it is closed. Both of these types of magazines have been popular for many years.

Rather closely related to the bolt-action with a tubular magazine is the slide or pump-action. In this type of action, moving a handle located below and in front of the action backward causes the action to open and the empty case to be ejected then moving the handle forward pushes cartridge into the chamber. Because the magazine tube lies below the barrel, the cartridge must be moved upward by a carrier as the pump handle nears its rearmost position. Pump-action rifles having both external and internal hammers have been produced for many years.

Not too far removed from the pump-action is the lever-action in which the cartridges are also usually held in a tubular magazine. In this case, the cartridges are moved from the magazine to the chamber by operating a lever located behind the trigger. Pulling the lever down opens and cocks the action as the empty case is ejected. Pulling the lever back up pushes a cartridge into the chamber as the action is closed. The vast majority of lever-action rifles have external hammers.

In terms of the number of units sold, the most popular type of action for rimfire rifles is that known as the semiautomatic, self-loading, or auto-loading type. The bolt is held in the forward position by a strong spring known as the recoil spring. When the rifle is fired, the impulse transferred from the cartridge head to the bolt forces the bolt to the rear, which cocks the action. As the bolt is pushed forward by the recoil spring, it takes with it a cartridge from the magazine, which can be of either the vertical box, rotary, or tubular type. A rifle that operates this way is often called an "automatic", but this term strictly applies to a rifle type that fires the next shot simply by holding the trigger back. With the self-loading or semiautomatic rifle, loading is automatically accomplished after each shot, but the trigger must be released and pulled for each shot.

Each type of action has some advantages and disadvantages. The bolt-action is the slowest to operate because the shooter's hand must be removed from the grip, the handle grasped, the bolt turned and pulled back, then pushed forward and closed. With the pump and lever-actions, only a back and forth motion is required. With the autoloader, the trigger must be released and then pulled for the next shot. However, bolt-action rifles are generally more accurate, and as a result most accurate sporting and target rifles have that type action. Some target rifles are extremely accurate autoloaders. Today, the bolt-action and semiautomatic rifles are by far the most popular rimfires and there is an extensive selection of rifles of each type. Before making a selection, handle rifles having different types of actions and evaluate them in terms of your anticipated use. You may be surprised to find how far down the list of criteria that rate of fire ranks in terms of importance. If you want a rifle that is a real tack driver, you will probably select a bolt-action or one of the target autoloaders that are becoming more popular.

Except for length, the dimensions of the 22 WRF and the 22 WMR are almost identical.

Rimfire rifles are currently available in several calibers. Shown here (left to right) are the 17 Aguila, 17 Mach 2, 17 Hornady Rimfire Magnum, 22 Long Rifle, and the 22 Winchester Magnum Rimfire.

Calibers

Although there were once rimfire rifles available in several calibers, they are currently all either 17s or 22s. The 17 HMR, the 17 Mach 2, 17 Aguila and as this is written, perhaps even other 17 rimfires are becoming popular. However, the 22 Long Rifle (LR) is by far the most popular rimfire caliber. Both 22 LR firearms and ammunition are less expensive than those in any other caliber. Of course, the choice of caliber should be made based on the use to which the firearm is to be put.

Chapter 9 deals with using rimfire firearms for hunting and pest shooting. In that chapter, several factors regarding the suitability of the various rimfire calibers for specific purposes are briefly discussed. If you plan to do a lot of shooting or want to enjoy shooting for the lowest possible cost, there is no doubt that the 22 LR is the caliber of choice because of the lower cost involved. Also, the 22 LR generally gives better accuracy than the 22 Short except when the latter is fired in special target arms chambered specifically for that round. At one time, rifles chambered for the 22 Short were popular, but the choice of arms chambered specifically for the 22 Short is very limited now. Moreover, the cost of 22 Short ammunition now exceeds that of most 22 LR loads because of the difference in sales volume, and the 22 Short is not available in every corner store that sells only a few of the most popular types.

For many years, the 22 LR has been the choice of squirrel hunters when they are hunting in a location that allows a rifle to be used safely. Most rimfire rifles are capable of fine accuracy when the appropriate ammunition is used. It may take some testing with several types of ammunition to determine which

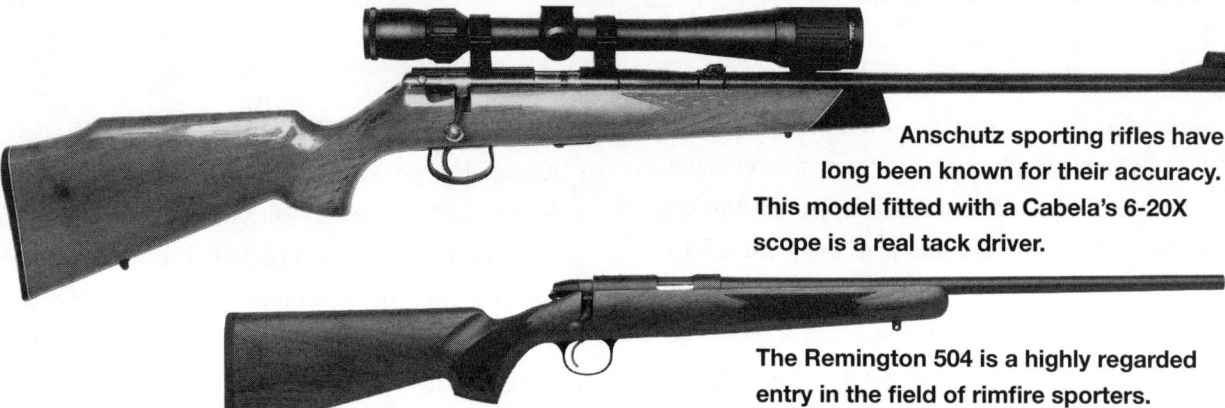

Anschutz sporting rifles have long been known for their accuracy. This model fitted with a Cabela's 6-20X scope is a real tack driver.

The Remington 504 is a highly regarded entry in the field of rimfire sporters.

types perform best in your rifle, but it pays dividends when you take a shot at a very small target that you wish to harvest cleanly. In my experience, shots at small game are usually no longer than 50 yards, and the 22 LR has plenty of power to harvest squirrels at that range. Generally, head shots are made in order to minimize meat damage so the target area is not much larger than an inch in diameter. Accuracy of the rifle/ammunition combination and shooting skill are the most important factors.

Frequently, someone writing either in an advertisement or an article mentions using the 22 WMR or 17 HMR for hunting small game. Either will certainly dispatch small game species, but head shots better be made if you want much left to eat. These high velocity rounds are explosive to small targets, especially at the ranges at which squirrels and rabbits are normally taken. The primary use of these magnum calibers is in taking larger species or taking small species at long range where their higher power and flatter trajectory are advantageous. Rabbits, squirrels, and treed raccoons do not require the use of a magnum rimfire. There is one advantage of the 22 WMR over the 17 HMR for small game hunting. Although the overall case length is shorter, the old cartridge known as the 22 Winchester Rim Fire (WRF) has almost identical head size and body taper as does the 22 WMR. Therefore, it is perfectly safe to fire 22 WRF ammunition in a rifle chambered for the 22 WMR. Because it is a specialty item having low sales volume, the cost of 22 WRF ammunition is about the same as it is for some of the lower cost (not premium) 22 WMR ammunition. The advantage of using the 22 WRF cartridges is that they feature a 45-grain bullet with a muzzle velocity of around 1,300 ft/sec so they are similar in power to a 22 LR high velocity round. This can be important when using a rifle chambered for the 22 WMR on edible game. The only factor to consider is whether the slightly shorter 22 WRF round is sufficiently accurate in your 22 WMR to justify its use. In my bolt-action Ruger 77/22M, the CCI 22 WRF gives outstanding accuracy. Five-shot groups average just over 0.6 inches at 50 yards so this gives me the flexibility to use ammunition of lower power in my 22 WMR without sacrificing accuracy. However, I must sight in with the 22 WRF ammunition because the point of impact at 50 yards is 5 or 6 inches lower than where the 22 WMR hits. The 17 HMR offers no such lower-powered option in ammunition.

As will be discussed in Chapter 9, varmint hunting with rimfire rifles is an entirely different matter since recovery of edible meat is not a factor. While you will almost certainly begin with a 22 LR, there are obvious advantages to the use of the 22 WMR and 17 HMR for the varmint hunter. Either will extend the range of a 22 LR by a considerable margin and will permit taking larger species. The 22 WMR is effective to about 125 to 150 yards while the flatter-shooting 17 HMR is effective to perhaps 150 to 175 yards with best performance of both calibers at or close to the lower end of the ranges mentioned. As we will now discuss, this performance comes at a price when the cost of ammunition is considered. In this regard, the 22 WMR has some advantage because all ammunition for the 17 HMR is of a "premium" type, which costs more than most of the 22 WMR types, which are not designated as premium ammunition. Although the topic will be discussed in detail in Chapter 9, the 22 WMR is better suited to taking larger species while the 17 HMR is better suited to taking smaller species at longer ranges. The logical approach is probably to choose a 22 LR for plinking and small game hunting then add a 17 HMR or 22 WMR if you wish to get more involved with varmint hunting using only rimfire rifles. However, many small bore enthusiasts do serious varmint hunting with rifles chambered for the 22 LR by limiting the ranges at which shots at game are taken and choosing rifles and ammunition that are capable of giving target-grade accuracy.

If the varmints you plan to hunt are small species such as ground squirrels and crows at ranges not to exceed 125 yards or so, the 17 Mach 2 may be the round you choose. With a muzzle velocity of approximately 2,100 ft/sec, the trajectory is quite flat out to about 125 yards making hits easy. Keep in mind that this is not a powerful round so its use should be confined to smaller species of varmints. Outstanding accuracy is reported with most rifles in this caliber so it would also function well for the squirrel hunter who is willing to pass up all but head shots. As this is written, the price of a box of 17 Mach 2 ammunition is approximately $6 to $7 for 50 rounds, which means that it is not much less expensive than that for the 17 HMR.

Selection and Cost

As with any field of endeavor, the cost of the available equipment varies enormously. Since handguns will be considered in Chapter 4, let us first discuss the selection and cost situation with respect to rimfire rifles and ammunition. Many years ago, firearms (and many other things) were subject to the so-called "fair trade" laws under which the prices were set by the manufacturer. Such laws were changed long ago, but manufacturers still publish price indicators. These are simply numbers that may serve as a basis for comparison between two different models or manufacturers. Keep in mind that there is a considerable difference between the manufacturer's suggested retail price (MSRP) and the actual retail price of any firearm. Currently, the very low end of the cost spectrum for rimfire rifles begins at a retail price of approximately $100 while at the upper end are models that sell for many times as much. The number of available models of rimfire rifles is enormous. In this section, only a quick overview of some of the available models and their approximate prices can be given, and manufacturer's catalogs or web sites should be studied to see all of the options available. Another good source of information is *Gun Digest*. This book contains a wealth of information in a single volume that is updated annually.

Most people usually own a firearm for a long

The Ruger 77/22 will handle almost any task required of a rimfire sporter.

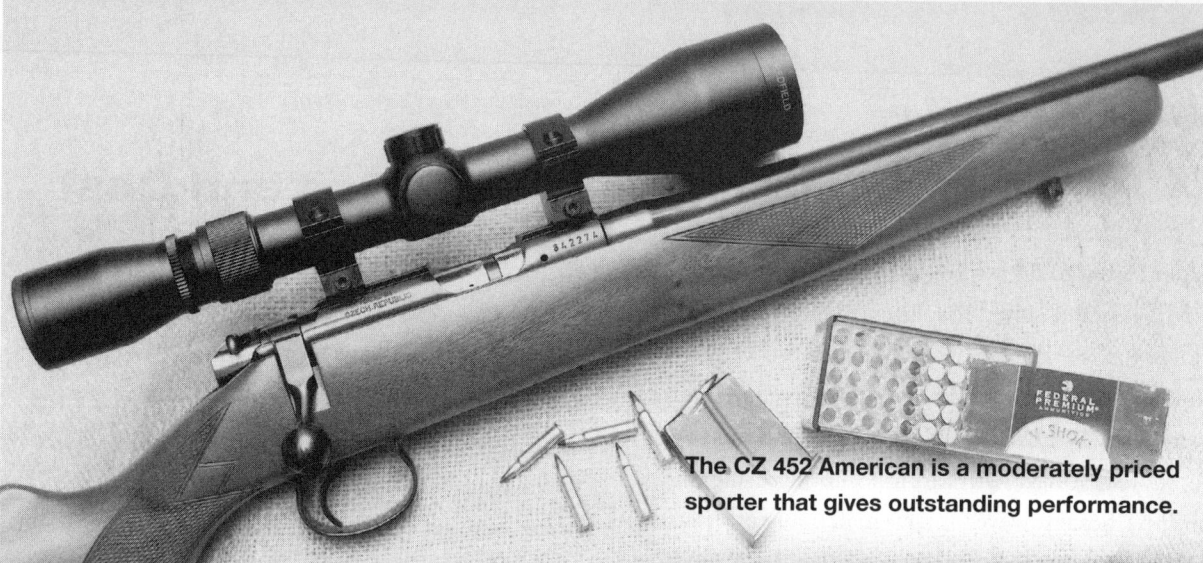

The CZ 452 American is a moderately priced sporter that gives outstanding performance.

period of time. Before deciding to buy any rifle, look at manufacturers' catalogs to try to limit your choices somewhat. Then, go to some stores and actually handle those rifles that interest you. You may find after handling a certain model that you especially like (or dislike) it. There may be some features or controls that attract (or annoy) you. The word "feel" is probably one of the most overused words, but it gives the correct connotation. The choice of a firearm is a personal matter and how a rifle "feels" is an important consideration.

We will now try to arrive at some basic ideas related to the selection of a rimfire rifle. First, consider the caliber. A wide selection that includes bolt-action, autoloaders, and lever-action rifles is available in all of the rimfire calibers (22 LR, 22 WMR, 17 Mach 2, 17 HMR, and 17 Aguila). In 22 LR, pump-action rifles are also available. If you are selecting the rifle for general use, the 22 LR should be your first choice. Another rifle in one of the rimfire magnum calibers can be added later if you get into varmint hunting. At that time, rifles with the whole range of action types can be considered again although you may want to select identical rifles in two calibers. To simplify matters, the selection process will be approached from the standpoint of cost.

If cost is no object and a price tag of over $600 to perhaps twice that figure is acceptable to you, a bolt-action sporting rifle is probably your best choice. For many years, the outstanding rifle of this type was the legendary Winchester Model 52 Sporter, but it is no longer available. Elegant bolt-action rimfire rifles are represented by models like the Cooper Model 57M, which is priced at approximately $1,200 and the Kimber Classic that sells for around $800 to $1,200. Some of the fine sporting rifles produced by Anschutz are also in this price range. In this upper price bracket at the present time, take your choice of the Anschutz Models 1712 or 1502, Cooper Model 57M, Kimber .22 Classic, or Sako Finnfire rifles. All are of superb quality and will give outstanding performance. For example, the Cooper Model 57M must shoot a five-shot group at 50 yards that measures 1/2-inch or less with premium match ammunition before it is shipped, and the Kimber Classic must give a group of 0.4-inches or smaller. Test groups are included with these rifles when they are shipped. These are rifles for the most discriminating small-bore enthusiast from both performance and appearance standpoints. Some of the models mentioned are available in 22 WMR, 17 HMR, and 17 Mach 2 as well as in 22 LR.

For many years, Anschutz rimfire rifles in sporter and more specialized target configurations have been built on their famous Model 54 and 64 bolt-actions. Anschutz target rifles have been consistent medal winners in international and Olympic competition. The two series of rifles are known as the 1700 and 1400/1500 series, respectively, depending on whether the action is the Model 54 or 64. Some of the target models have dominated small-bore competition, and the accuracy of both sporter and target rifles is outstanding. Models are offered with standard and heavy weight barrels. Receivers have grooves 11mm in width for attaching scope mounts, but they are also drilled and tapped for mounting scope bases, making it possible to use many types of scope rings. Keep in mind that except for a few of the Anschutz sporters, almost all of these high-end rifles are sold without sights so a scope must be added. The price of the scope and mounts may add a considerable amount to the cost of the rifle.

The new 22 LR Remington 504 has a list price of approximately $700 (but is usually found at retail for around $600), and a heavy-barrel version of the Remington 504 has been announced that will be available in 2005. Also available in 2005 will be a 17 HMR version. Although not tested for this project, the Remington 504 has received a considerable amount of praise from other writers. It is sold without sights.

When it comes to high-performance auto-loaders, the most highly regarded (and expensive) models are those produced by Volquartsen. Some of these rifles may sell for about as much as a Kimber or Cooper bolt-action. However, in terms of performance a Volquartsen is similarly placed.

If you are limited to the retail price range of approximately $300 to $500 but still want a bolt-action sporting rifle, consider the Ruger 77/22 and the CZ 452 American each of which is actually a series that includes several versions that have manufacturer suggested prices of approximately $595 and $420, respectively, depending on stock material and metal finish. The Ruger 77/22 has a list price of $595 (usually found at retail for around $425 to $450) and is available in four versions that include blued steel action and barrel combined with a walnut stock, stainless steel metal parts and composite stock with or without sights, and a low-luster stainless steel and laminated stock combinations. Information on the performance of the Ruger 77/22 will be given later in this book.

Outstanding bolt-action rifles are also available from Ceska Zbrojovka (CZ). The CZ 452 American features a well-shaped, checkered walnut stock, highly polished and blued metal parts, and true sporting rifle styling. They also have barrels that are threaded into the steel receivers. Several versions of the CZ 452 are available, but the typical retail price for the CZ 452 American is about $350 to $375. Evaluations on the performance of two of these fine CZ rifles in 22 LR and 17 HMR calibers are included in Chapter 13. Other versions of the CZ 452 series include the Lux, Varmint, Style, Silhouette, and FS, which differ in stock and barrel materials. The Varmint has a shorter barrel of heavier weight and a stock that is of a target shape. The Lux version features a longer barrel and a stock of European design, and the FS (full-stock) version has a full-length or Mannlicher style stock. Synthetic stocks are found on the Style which has nickel finished metal and the Silhouette which has blued metal.

This listing of options should show that Ruger and CZ bolt-action rifles are available in an array of models that allow a selection to suit almost any taste. Even though these rifles are priced below the models from Anschutz, Cooper, Kimber, and Sako, do not assume that they are drab in appearance. For most of us, the Ruger and CZ models represent stylish rifles that also deliver excellent performance. Of course, models are available in 22 LR, 22 WMR, 17 HMR, and 17 Mach 2 calibers. If you want to consider them as fine sporting rifles for shooters on a somewhat limited budget, it would not be inappropriate.

Rimfire shooters who favor lever-action rifles and want outstanding performance can choose the elegant Winchester 9422 Legacy.

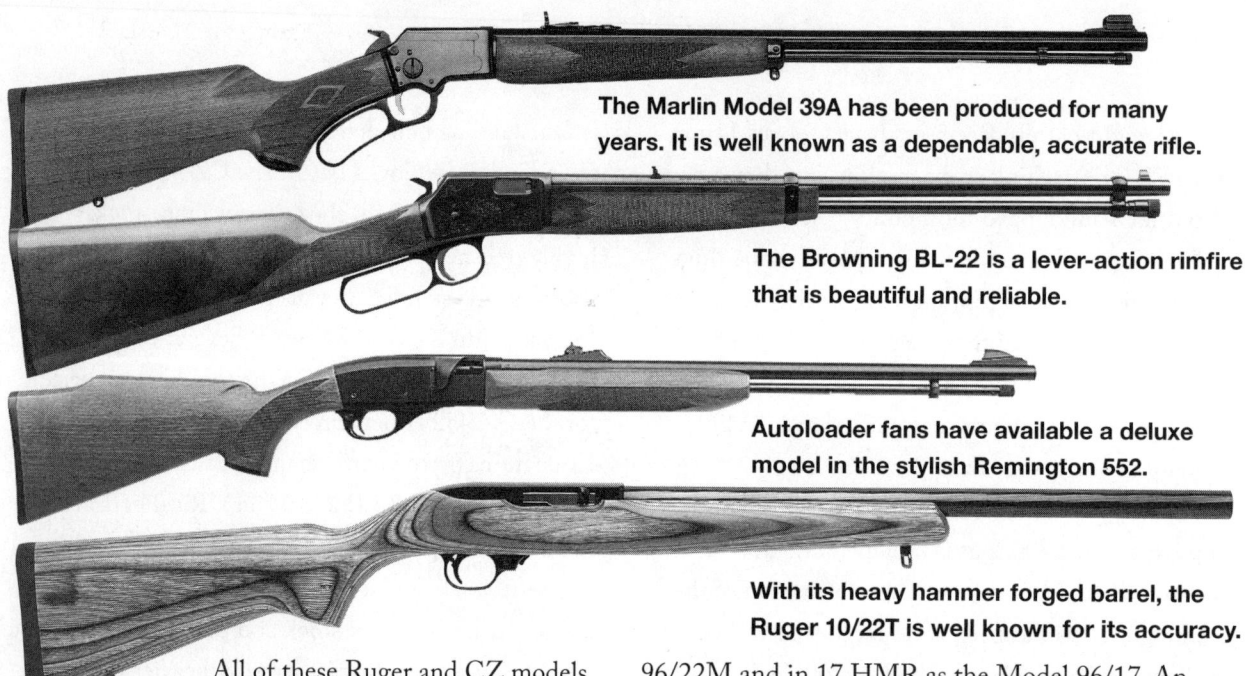

The Marlin Model 39A has been produced for many years. It is well known as a dependable, accurate rifle.

The Browning BL-22 is a lever-action rimfire that is beautiful and reliable.

Autoloader fans have available a deluxe model in the stylish Remington 552.

With its heavy hammer forged barrel, the Ruger 10/22T is well known for its accuracy.

All of these Ruger and CZ models are bolt-action repeaters. The CZ has a grooved receiver and can accept any of the popular scope mounts that clamp in these grooves. The Ruger has the integral base configuration that requires Ruger rings or those made by other companies that fit the curved notches that are milled into the Ruger receiver. Rings are supplied with the Ruger rifles so the slightly higher cost of the Ruger compared to the CZ is partially offset. Both the Ruger and CZ rifles have performed extremely well for me, and they are widely available.

Up to this point, the discussion of rifles in the $300 to $500 range has been concerned with bolt-action models, but it certainly should not be limited to that action type. Also in the $300 to $500 range are the Winchester 9422, Marlin 39A and Browning BL-22 lever-actions all of which are fine rifles for almost any sporting purpose. The Winchester 9422 and Marlin 39A (which has the distinction of being the rimfire long gun in longest production) have retail prices around $400 or slightly more. The Browning BL-22 sells for approximately the same price. Like other lever-actions, this rifle makes use of a tubular magazine held under the barrel and typifies the superb fit and finish for which Browning firearms are famous. The Ruger 96 lever-action, which has a receiver with a rounded profile with no external hammer, is produced in 22 WMR as the Model 96/22M and in 17 HMR as the Model 96/17. An evaluation of the Winchester 9422 is presented in Chapter 13.

A rather wide selection of autoloaders fall in the $300 to $500 range. Autoloaders include the Thompson/Center Classic, the Remington 552 BDL Speedmaster, and the some of the Browning Buck Mark models. Target type autoloaders in this price range include the Ruger 10/22T, T/C Benchmark, and Browning Buck Mark Target models. The Ruger 10/22T has a heavy, beautifully finished hammer-forged barrel and comes with no sights. With a blue barrel, the list price is $445 while the stainless steel version has a list price of $495. Retail prices are normally about $100 lower. Performance of the Ruger 10/22T is discussed in Chapter 13. For shooting that may involve low-level bench rest or silhouette competition, the choice would be a toss up between the Ruger 10/22T and the T/C Benchmark depending on personal preference. At 7.5 pounds without sights, the Ruger 10/22T and T/C Benchmark are somewhat heavy for general field use, but either would be an outstanding rifle for the hunter who likes to sit in the woods watching for squirrels. Keep in mind, there is a lot of personal preference in these *suggestions* (not necessarily to be taken as the author's *recommendations*), but they are based on experience with several of the rifles described.

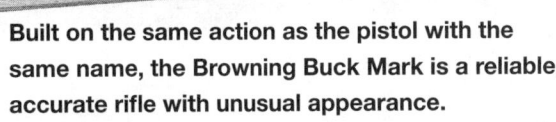

Built on the same action as the pistol with the same name, the Browning Buck Mark is a reliable, accurate rifle with unusual appearance.

The Thompson/Center Classic is known for outstanding accuracy. It is also one of the most elegant autoloaders available.

One of the most stylish autoloaders ever produced is the Browning Semi Automatic.

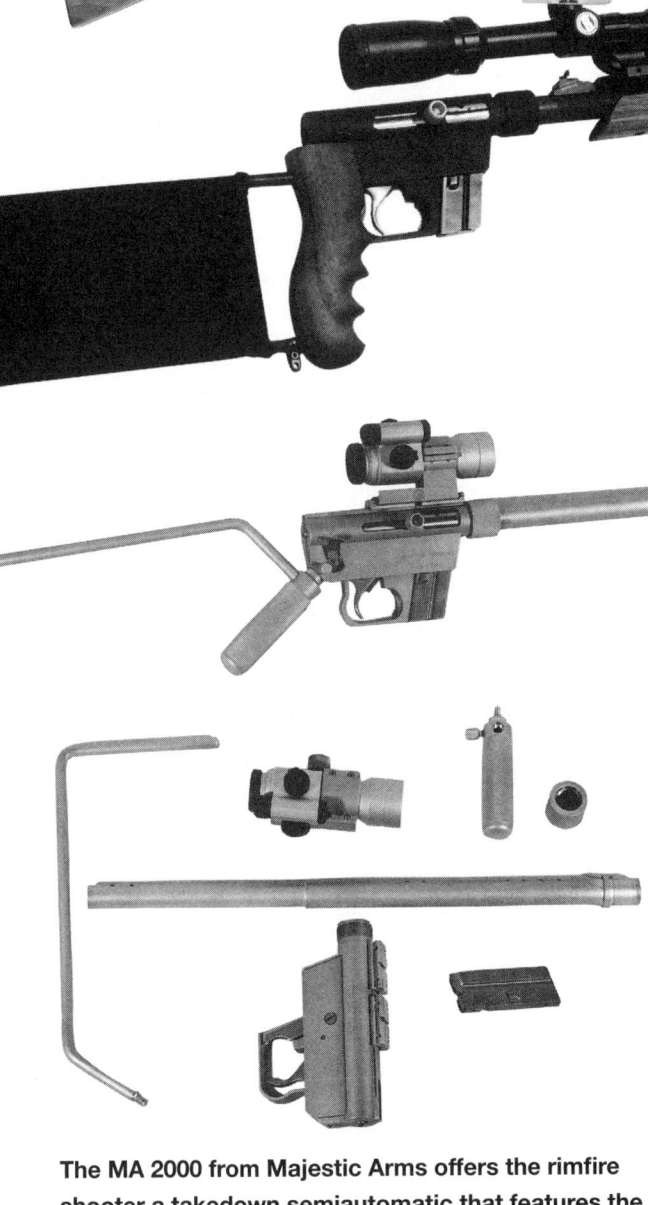

The MA 2000 from Majestic Arms offers the rimfire shooter a takedown semiautomatic that features the Aluma-Lite barrel that has a Lothar Walther insert.

The T/C Classic has a well-shaped and finished walnut stock and metal parts that are highly polished and blued. Unlike most other 22 LR autoloaders, the receiver is made of steel. It comes drilled and tapped for attaching Weaver-style scope bases (see Chapter 5). The 20-inch match-grade barrel is threaded into the receiver to provide rigid attachment that doubtless contributes to the high level of accuracy that this model exhibits. This is an elegant auto-loading sporting rifle that has a retail price around $300, and it has established an enviable reputation for accuracy as will be described in Chapter 13.

In addition to the Classic version, the T/C autoloader is also available with a stainless steel barrel and receiver combined with a black composite stock. This version, known as the Silver Lynx, is impervious to the elements and is a good choice for those hunters who encounter a wide variety of weather conditions. T/C also produces the 22 Benchmark which features a heavy barrel that is 18 inches long and a laminated hardwood stock giving a rifle that weighs almost 7 pounds without sights. A 10-round magazine is standard on the Benchmark. This is the target version of the Classic sporter, and both are known for their superb accuracy.

One of the best-known 22 LR autoloaders of all time is the Browning Semi-Auto 22 (known as the

The MA 4 allows the rimfire shooter to configure the rifle to fire 22 LR, 22 WMR, 17 Mach 2, or 17 HMR by interchanging four barrels and two bolts.

Model SA 22) which is one of the most streamlined rifles ever made. It utilizes a tubular magazine that is located in the stock so there is no magazine protruding from the bottom of the action or tube under the barrel. Also, empty cases are ejected from the bottom of the action so there are no cut out sections on the sides of the receiver. Left-handed shooters appreciate not having empty cases ejected across their faces from the right hand side of the receiver. Like most other Browning firearms, the Semi-Auto 22 is available in several grades that differ in the amount of engraving and inlay work. Known as Grade I, the lowest priced SA 22 has a list price of $519 while the elegant and ornate Grade VI has a list price of $1,112.

One of the most unusual 22 LR autoloaders is the MA 2000 from Majestic Arms, LTD. This rifle is a take-down model based on the action of the Henry U.S. Survival rifle to which has been fitted an Aluma-Lite barrel with a Lothar Walther insert (see Chapter 12). The wire, skeletonized stock has a nylon cover that functions as a storage bag for a cleaning kit and a spare magazine. The suggested price of the MA 2000 is $389.

In early 2005, Majestic Arms announced that in mid year a new rifle known as the MA 4 would be available. This unique rifle is designed so that the same receiver and stock can be used with four different barrels to make a system that will fire 22 LR, 22 WMR, 17 Mach 2, or 17 HMR cartridges. The barrel must be changed to adapt the rifle to each of these calibers, but two bolts accommodate the 22 WMR/17HMR and the 22LR/17 Mach 2 combinations. A wide variety of options exists with regard to types of stocks, sights, etc. Also known as the Majestic Arms Rimfire Rifle System (MARRS), the MA 4 has scope mounts on the barrel. As a result, even though the rifle is a take down model, the sights remain in permanent alignment with the bore. The MA 4 may represent a trend toward interchangeability and versatility for the rimfire shooter.

Suppose that you want to get a rimfire rifle that is capable of good performance, but your budget will not allow even a $250 retail price or you simply do not want to spend more for the rifle. In this category, there are a number of choices that will still allow you to go plinking, small game hunting, or varmint shooting successfully. Because rimfire rifles are part and parcel to inexpensive shooting, there is a broad range of rifles in this category. First, there are the numerous bolt-action repeaters (having either box or tubular magazines) from makers like Marlin, CZ, and Savage. These are sturdy, dependable rifles that normally give good accuracy (around 1-inch groups at 50 yards) when appropriate ammunition is used. It is the experience of this author that these lower-priced rifles frequently seem to show a greater difference in accuracy with the type of ammunition chosen than do bolt-action rifles like the Ruger 77/22 or the CZ 452 American. Testing several types of ammunition will usually allow you to find one or two types that perform very well in a specific rifle. For example in the tests, the bolt-action Marlin 25N (forerunner of the current Model 925) gave an average group size for five five-shot groups at 50 yards of only 0.78 inches with Wolf Match Target ammunition. The average group size was also under an inch when using CCI Green Tag and Federal Match Target ammunition. Several versions of the

The rimfire shooter who wants good performance at a rock bottom price need look no farther than the Marlin Model 925.

The Savage Mark II bolt-action rifle is a dependable, low cost model that gives performance beyond its price.

Savage bolt-action models known as the Mark II series provide excellent performance, and they are inexpensive rifles. The point is that even an inexpensive rifle may give performance which equals that of more expensive models if some testing is carried out to find the ammunition that performs best in that particular rifle. The CZ Basic, which has many of the features of the 452 American, is a low-cost bolt-action rifle that has a suggested price of only $240 and it should be available for a lower price at retail.

If a bolt-action is not your choice, other rifles in the under $250 price category include many that have other types of actions. Economically priced autoloaders that generally sell at retail for $150 to $200 include the Ruger 10/22 Carbine and the 10/22 Rifle, the Remington 597, the Marlin 60, Savage 64, and the Henry U.S. Survival rifle. Some of these models are available in several versions that differ in metal finish and stock configuration. In terms of units sold, these are the most popular rimfire rifles made.

For example, the legendary Ruger 10/22 autoloader is available for well under $250 in both the Carbine and Rifle versions. Savage offers the Model 64 series of autoloaders consisting of several versions that are available with different stock material and metal finishes. All of these are competent, dependable rifles that are adequate for informal rimfire sport shooting.

One of the most successful 22 LR autoloaders of all time is the Ruger 10/22 Carbine with about 4 million having been produced since it was introduced in 1964. This model is offered in several variants, but the most popular is that with a carbine style hardwood stock and 18.5-inch barrel. It has suggested price of $250 but is heavily discounted to a retail price of around $160 to $170 in many stores. New for 2004 is the 40th Anniversary model which has a large nickel silver medallion embedded in the stock.

It is difficult to imagine a better choice than the Ruger 10/22 Carbine autoloader if an inexpensive rifle with that type of action is desired. Moreover, once you have a 10/22, it is capable of being modified almost without limit. Such upgrades are not merely cosmetic because match grade barrels are popular options. The new Ruger 10/22 Rifle (shown on the cover of this book) has a list price of $275 and normally sells at retail for around $200 or so. This handsome rifle has all the desirable qualities of the legendary 10/22 Carbine but has a 20-inch barrel and far better styling. Also in this category is the Henry lever-action, which should be given serious consideration. The experience of the author is that the Henry lever-action will give accuracy at least as good as most inexpensive autoloaders, and it is light, compact, attractive, and classic in styling (see Chapter 13). As a 22 for woods roaming that costs under $200, it is hard to beat one of the Ruger 10/22 versions, the Marlin 60, or the Henry lever-action. They can be used very successfully for plinking pine cones or potting squirrels.

In the same general price range as the Ruger 10/22 Carbine is the Remington 597. This rifle is available in several variants that feature different metal finishes and stock materials. The weight and dimensions of the Remington 597 make it a convenient rifle to carry while hunting, and the matte finish and

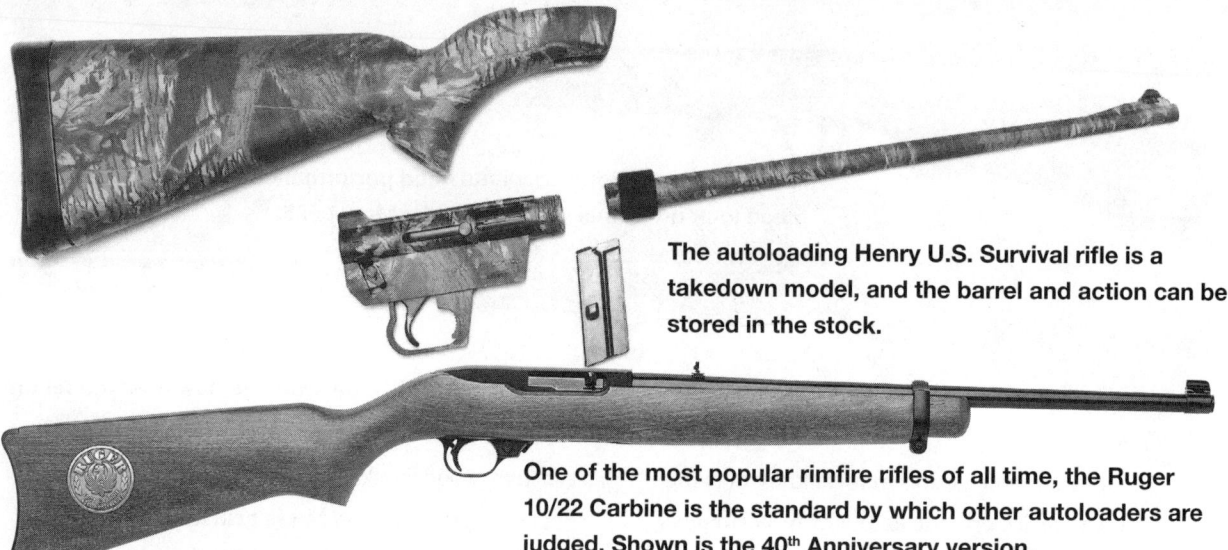

The autoloading Henry U.S. Survival rifle is a takedown model, and the barrel and action can be stored in the stock.

One of the most popular rimfire rifles of all time, the Ruger 10/22 Carbine is the standard by which other autoloaders are judged. Shown is the 40th Anniversary version.

synthetic stock render it resistant to harsh conditions

The autoloader that has been produced in greater numbers than any other is the Marlin Model 60 in its numerous versions. For about half of the $250 figure, it is possible to buy a Marlin Model 60 autoloader since one of the large "marts" regularly sells this model for around $115 to $120 in the blue and hardwood form. Versions having stainless steel metal parts and composite stocks are also available in the under $250 category. Almost any combination of barrel and stock from blue and hardwood to stainless steel and laminated is available in versions offered for this popular rifle. Getting one of these rifles and adding an inexpensive scope (see Chapter 5) enables a shooter to enjoy rimfire shooting with a minimum outlay of cash. One of the interesting facts about the Marlin 60 is that it has been produced for many years for sale not only carrying Marlin's name but also the names of other retailers such as Western Auto, Coast to Coast Hardware, etc. The Marlin Model 60 is one of the true classics among American 22s. We will have a great deal more to say about the Marlin Model 60 in Chapter 13.

Bolt-action rimfire rifles in the magnum calibers normally sell for approximately $20 to $25 more than the similar model in 22 LR. For example, the lowest priced variant of a Marlin Model 925 (22 LR) bolt-action has a retail price of around $150 while the 925M (22 WMR) and 917V (17 HMR) sell for around $170-$180. A similar situation exists for the Savage 93 series of rimfires. However, both Marlin and Savage also produce bolt-action rimfires that have heavy stainless steel barrels and laminated stocks that sell for approximately $100 more than the basic models. Performance of the Marlin bolt-action 22 LR will be described later in this book (see Chapter 13).

While the cost of a bolt-action rifle in one of the magnum calibers may be around $20-$25 higher than that of a comparable 22 LR, this is not the case for autoloaders. For example, the retail cost of a Ruger 10/22 Carbine semiautomatic may be around $160, but the cost of the rifles in magnum rimfire calibers is as much as $150 higher. The reason for this is that in the 22 LR caliber, the receiver can be made from cast aluminum. Because of the much higher power of the magnum calibers, the receiver must be made of steel, and the bolt assembly must be more massive to handle the stresses that occur during blow back of the action. Although they are similar in appearance and model numbers, the auto-loading magnum rifles and those in 22 LR are essentially different rifles. A similar situation exists for the Remington 597 autoloader in 22 LR compared to the magnum calibers.

Not only is the cost of the firearm important, but also the cost of ammunition must be considered. I just finished reading an article in which the author described his use of a 17 Mach 2 on "barnyard pests like sparrows and starlings." There is nothing wrong with such a practice, but it is massive overkill (not to mention expense) when an air rifle would work

Introduced in 2004, the Ruger 10/22 Rifle has a longer barrel and slimmer stock than the Carbine, but it has the same outstanding features.

The Remington 597 offers good performance at a reasonable price.

well on such species. With 17 Mach 2 ammunition selling for about $6 to $7 per box (about the same as 22 WMR), this is not my idea of rifle for use on sparrows and starlings. Occasionally, I see someone describe a rifle chambered for the 17 HMR as a "rifle for small game and plinking." Plinking to most people means shooting pine cones, pop cans, and an occasional starling. With the ammunition selling for $8 to $11 per box, I do not intend to use my 17 HMR for plinking when some promotional types of 22 LR can be found for as low as $1 per box! It is possible to buy 500 rounds of inexpensive 22 LR for about the same price as a box containing 50 rounds of 17 HMR. However, I do not intend to use the very inexpensive 22 LR ammunition for prairie dog shooting (unless it performs very well in my rifle).

As in the case of selecting an automobile, when it comes to selecting a firearm, personal preference plays an important role including with this author. I know one individual who used to stoutly proclaim, "I would rather walk than ride in a Ford!" In retrospect, I should have responded with, "Get out of my car!" I know another who insists, "Chevrolets are junk!" Well, we all have our preferences. The truth is that within the parameters of size, weight, and price most firearms are likely to prove satisfactory, and that is why many models have been produced by the millions. Even some inexpensive models have been passed down for a couple of generations and continue to function well.

Youth Rifles

Throughout the history of the 22 rimfire, it has been the caliber most often selected for the first firearm for youthful shooters. Single-shot rifles of smaller proportions became known as the "boys rifles" which were popular in the late 1800s and early 1900s. Although they were made in a variety of types, perhaps the most familiar was the falling block. This type of action has a lever located behind the trigger guard or as an extension of the trigger guard. When the lever is pulled downward, a block located behind the breech moves downward exposing the chamber into which a single cartridge is loaded. These rifles have a visible hammer with a safety notch but no other safety. One rifle of this type is the Stevens Favorite, which was one of the most popular models.

Recognizing the need for rifles appropriately scaled for boys and girls, so-called youth models are still being produced. One such model is the reintroduced Stevens Favorite Model 30G. It has a falling block action, and its 21-inch barrel can be obtained in 22 LR, 22 WMR, and 17 HMR calibers. Most of the youth models available today are single-shot bolt-action rifles that measure approximately 32 to 34 inches in length, have a length of pull of about 12 inches, and weigh 3.5 to 4.5 pounds. Historically a leader in the production of youth rifles, Savage has what is perhaps the most extensive line currently available. The Cub is a bolt-action single-shot that is 33 inches long, has a 16 1/8-inch barrel, and weighs 3.3 pounds. With a suggested price of $152, it has a hardwood stock and is sold with a rear peep sight. Savage also offers the Mark I as a full size rifle in several variations. The suggested price is approximately $180. The youth version, known as the Savage Mark I-G, measures 39.5 inches in length, has a 20.75-inch barrel, weighs 5.5 pounds, and has a suggested price of $147. A smooth bore version is available for shooting shot cartridges.

Marlin produces two youth rifles known as the Models 915 Y and 915 YS. These rifles are 33.5 inches in length, have 16.5-inch barrels, and weigh

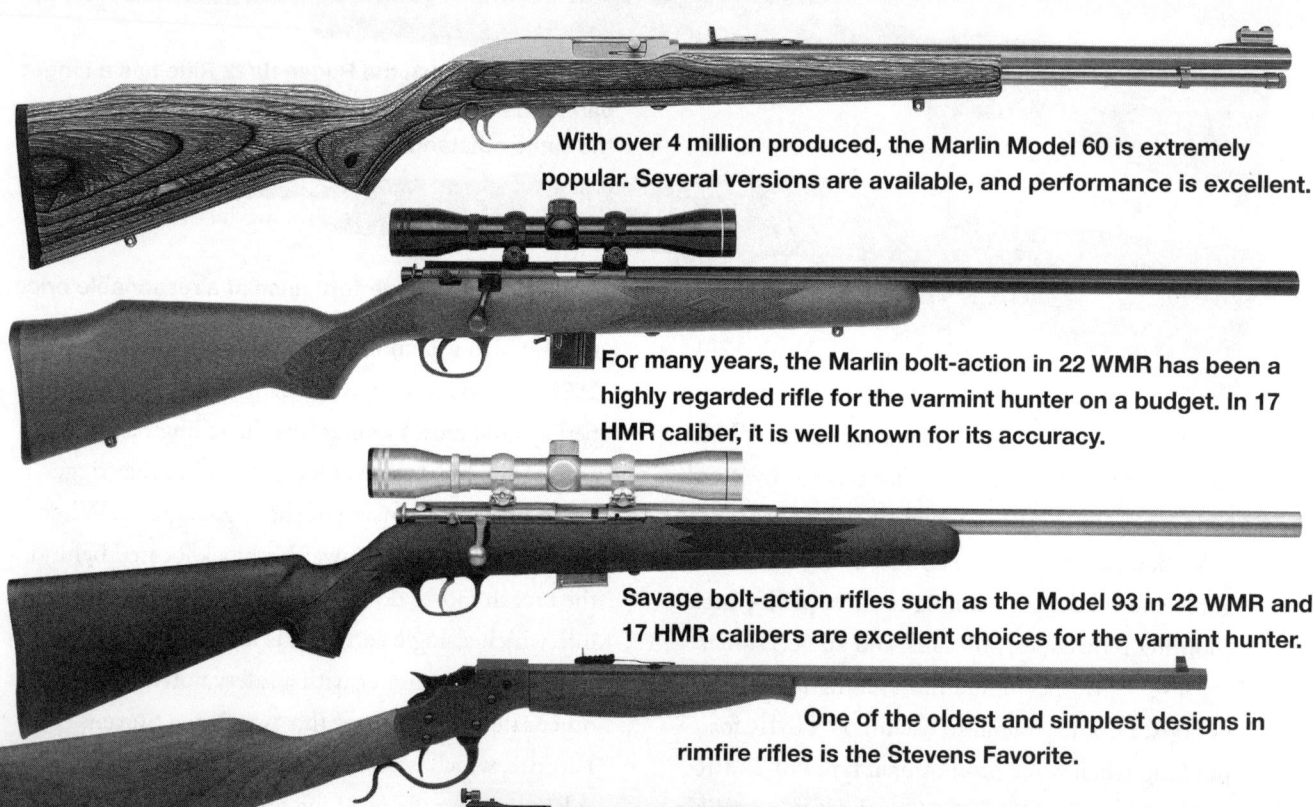

With over 4 million produced, the Marlin Model 60 is extremely popular. Several versions are available, and performance is excellent.

For many years, the Marlin bolt-action in 22 WMR has been a highly regarded rifle for the varmint hunter on a budget. In 17 HMR caliber, it is well known for its accuracy.

Savage bolt-action rifles such as the Model 93 in 22 WMR and 17 HMR calibers are excellent choices for the varmint hunter.

One of the oldest and simplest designs in rimfire rifles is the Stevens Favorite.

The single-shot bolt-action youth rifle is well represented by this Savage Cub which comes with a peep sight.

4.25 pounds. The YS version has a stainless steel barrel and action. The CZ Scout is the youth rifle from the famous Czech manufacturer. It measures 32.8 inches in length, has a 16.2-inch barrel, and weighs 4.0 pounds. The Scout is furnished with an adapter that replaces the magazine and makes the rifle a single-shot. However, the Scout will also accept the standard magazine used in the full-size rifle to convert it into a repeater when the shooter has progressed to that point. Another choice in the youth rifle line is the Henry Mini Bolt, which has a suggested price of $199.95, but it retails for less. This is a bolt-action single-shot made of stainless steel with a synthetic stock. On this rifle and some others of this general type, opening and closing the bolt does not cock the rifle. There is a knurled cocking piece at the rear of the bolt which must be drawn back to cock the rifle. Separate loading and cocking operations make shooting such a rifle a slow, deliberate process compatible with safe shooting. The overall length of the Henry Mini Bolt is only 30.25

inches and the barrel is 16.25 inches in length. Open sights on the Mini Bolt are made by Williams Gun Sight Company and feature fiber optic inserts (green on the rear sight and red on the front). Because the top of the receiver is split to allow clearance for the bolt handle, a scope can not be mounted on the little Henry.

One of the most interesting series of youth rifles is the Chipmunk series from Rogue Rifle Company. No less than 11 versions are available most of which differ in the barrel weight (sporter or target) and colors of the laminated stocks. Most of the versions are available in 22 LR, 22 WMR, and 17 HMR calibers. Four of the versions feature walnut stocks, two checkered and two plain. Models with heavy weight barrels have no sights installed while the standard weight barrels have sights attached with the rear sight being a peep sight. There is also a target model with adjustable length of pull and target style stock and sights. Almost any configuration of the little Chipmunk is available. All of the rifles are

The Marlin Model 915 offers many of the features of other Marlin bolt-action rifles in a single shot model of smaller size.

The Chipmunk rifles are single-shot models that are available in several styles. They are scaled specifically for small shooters.

This heavy barreled Chipmunk rifle with checkered walnut stock makes an elegant target rifle for a young shooter.

cocked manually by drawing back the cocking piece at the rear of the bolt.

In addition to the models described above, there are others available from other manufacturers. For many years, there were few choices available for a true youth rifle, but as in other areas of rimfire sports, this is an exciting time.

Selecting a Rimfire Varmint Rifle

Having dispensed with some suggestions for the selection of a rifle in 22 LR caliber, let us now suppose that you have identified varmint hunting as a developing passion and that you need to select a rimfire rifle to be used primarily for that work. Keep in mind that the varmint rifle must first and foremost be accurate. My suggestion is to consider carefully the types of varmints that you will hunt most. If the emphasis is to be on ground squirrels, crows, and small varmints up to the size of prairie dogs, I would select a rifle chambered for the 17 HMR. It shoots with a flatter trajectory than the 22 WMR, and because the ammunition is loaded with premium bullets, the *average* 17 HMR will deliver slightly better accuracy than the *average* 22 WMR. Because the bore in a 17 HMR barrel is so small, barrels have thicker walls than those on 22 WMR rifles which is one factor contributing to excellent accuracy. Experience has shown that there is not a great deal of difference in accuracy between 22 WMR and 17 HMR rifles as long as ammunition of identical quality is used in identical rifles. There is a belief, probably with some validity, that manufacturing tolerances are smaller for 17 HMR rifles and ammunition than with the 22 WMR.

The new 17 Mach 2 is developing a reputation as a cartridge that gives outstanding accuracy. Even barrels of normal diameter are stiff when the bore is so small and, 17 Mach 2 ammunition is loaded with premium bullets. These factors contribute to a high degree of accuracy. For taking small pests at ranges out to perhaps 125 yards or a bit farther, the 17 Mach 2 would work very well.

On the other hand, if the varmints are likely to include species as large as foxes or coyotes, the 22 WMR will be a better choice than either the 17 HMR or 17 Mach 2. The larger, heavier bullets hit with more authority, which is needed to anchor such species. Keep in mind that because the overall sizes of the 17 HMR and 22 WMR cartridge cases are similar, the same rifle action can be used as a platform for either. Only the barrel needs to be different and even the same magazine can be used with either cartridge. Therefore, in a specific model, the rifles are identical except for caliber. In terms of ammunition cost, the 17 Mach 2 and 22 WMR run in the range of $6-$7 per box while the 17 HMR is around $9-$11 per box.

Suggestions for specific arms in 17 HMR, 17 Mach 2, and 22 WMR run parallel to those given for 22 LR rifles. If your budget can accommodate a price tag of over $500 (perhaps well over $500), the Anschutz, Cooper, Kimber, Sako, and similar sporting rifles are elegant, and they give outstanding performance. Two of the outstanding new rifles in 17 Mach 2 are the Anschutz 1502 and 1702 which are built on the famous 64 and 54 actions, respectively. Remington has announced that the Model 504 bolt-action will be produced in 17 HMR caliber, and it should make a fine varmint rifle. Take your pick of these upper end models based on price, style, and availability. All are elegant rifles that give a high level of performance.

In the $300 to $500 price range, the experience of this author leads to the conclusion that two of the outstanding choices are the CZ 452 and Ruger 77/22M or 77/17. Both rifles are capable of excellent accuracy with perhaps a very small edge to the CZ. However, both the Ruger 77/22M and 77/17 can be fitted with aftermarket barrels having different configurations and other accessories. For example, a 17 HMR barrel can be fitted to a Ruger 77/22M action to change the caliber. In that sense, the Ruger is somewhat more versatile than the CZ. Lever-action and semiautomatic rifles in the magnum rimfire calibers that are intended primarily for varmint hunting do not excite me. True, they will give good performance, but most are unlikely to equal the accuracy of a good bolt-action and accuracy not rate of fire is what varmint hunting is all about. Notable exceptions are the autoloaders produced by Volquartsen, which are known for their superb accuracy, but these are more expensive. If you enjoy hunting with a lever-action rifle, by all means consider the Winchester 9422M and Henry in 22 WMR or 17 HMR caliber. Either is sufficiently accurate for taking varmints out to around 100 yards, and both are easily fitted with scopes since they have grooved receivers. Another, more modern lever-action is the Ruger Model 96 that is available in 22 WMR and 17 HMR calibers.

A number of options exist for the rimfire buyer who does not want to spend over $250 for a pest rifle chambered for the 22 WMR, 17 HMR, or 17 Mach 2. Outstanding among these are the bolt-action rifles from Marlin and Savage ,which typically give excellent accuracy. These are available with standard or heavy weight barrels that are blued or stainless steel. Stock options include hardwood, laminates, and composites. Price is determined by the variant selected, but the lowest price combinations start at approximately $170. As I write this, one of the Savage 17 HMR bolt-action models with standard weight blued barrel and a composite stock is on sale near here for $159.95. This is a lot of rifle for the money, and it enables a pest hunter to get equipped for hunting without taking out a mortgage. At an even lower price are the break-action single-shot rifles available from New England Firearms or Rossi. With a good scope in place, these are sturdy, dependable rifles that can perform well as pest rifles.

Ancillaries

After selecting a rifle, the majority of rimfire shooters will probably add other peripheral equipment to their outfits. Aftermarket barrels, stocks, triggers, and sights constitute a rather large industry, which will be covered in Chapters 5 and 12. While many rimfire shooters will not change the barrels or stocks on their rifles, there is no doubt that sights, especially scopes, will be necessary because an increasing number of fine rimfire rifles are being sold without sights. That is especially true of the models in 22 WMR and 17 HMR calibers which are intended for use at ranges up to 150 yards and includes some of the moderately priced Marlin and Savage rifles. It is unreasonable for most people to expect to hit a ground squirrel or crow at 150 yards with open sights. Therefore, the majority of rimfire shooters will make choices of scopes to mount on their rifles. Scope sights and mounts are discussed more fully in Chapter 5, but we will make some general comments here.

Several types of scopes are available that are intended specifically for use on rimfire rifles. Such scopes are adjusted optically to eliminate parallax at a range of 50 yards since this is a typical range for 22 LR rifles. Scopes intended for use on centerfire rifles are adjusted to be free of parallax at a range of 100 yards, and thus they will work equally well on rifles chambered for 22 WMR or 17 HMR. In fact, any scope that is suitable for use on center fire rifles will prove to be satisfactory on these magnum rimfires since they are often used at ranges comparable to those at which centerfire rifles are used. Some scopes are equipped with a focusing or adjustable objective (denoted as AO) so that they can be accurately focused on targets at varying distances. This is probably the best of all choices since focusing on a target corrects for parallax at the distance at which the scope is focused. Therefore, such a scope works equally well on all types of rimfire rifles.

As in the case of rifles, scopes are available in an enormous range of prices. Some of the elegant models that carry the most prestigious names sell for up to $1,000 or more. The average rimfire shooter should not be daunted by such figures because it is possible to get a very capable and satisfactory scope for a reasonable price. To some extent, the scope should match the rifle. It is not likely that a $50 scope will be found on a Cooper Model 57M sporting rifle that sells for over $1,000, and it is not likely that a $500 Kahles scope will be found on a Marlin 925 bolt-action, Henry lever-action, or Ruger 10/22 semiautomatic, all of which sell for well under $200. There is nothing wrong with a $500 scope on a $150 rifle, but it probably will not be set up that way in most cases.

Because scopes for centerfire rifles are satisfactory for use on 17 HMR and 22 WMR rifles, the range of available models is enormous. They are produced with fixed powers of magnification that include 2.5X, 4X, and 6X on up to target models of 24X, 32X, or higher magnification. Because of the advances in optics, zoom lenses for cameras have become more common than those of fixed focal length. This trend is also observed in scope sights. If you look at a catalog from a scope manufacturer, you will see that there are many more models available with variable magnification than there are of fixed power. Scopes with variable power are available in several ranges of magnification, but the 2.5-7X, 3-9X, 3-12X, and 4-16X are the most common although other ranges are available. Eye relief of scopes intended for use on centerfire rifles is around 3 inches or more, but rimfire rifles produce almost no recoil so that is never a problem.

Scopes made specifically for use on rimfire rifles (especially those in 22 LR caliber) are sometimes more compact and lighter in weight than those intended for use on centerfire rifles. This is reasonable since most rimfire rifles are slimmer and lighter in weight than most centerfire models. Many manufacturers produce so-called rimfire scopes in a wide range of prices, and to some extent the old caveat "you get what you pay for" applies to scopes. Large suppliers of outdoor equipment such as Cabela's and Scheels market scopes with their own brand labels. Two of the scopes in the Cabela's Pine Ridge line are a very nice 3-9X rimfire model that has a catalog price of $79.99 and a 4X model that sells for $49.99. These are good quality scopes that are representative of the lower priced models that provide good value and reliable service. When mated to a rimfire rifle of modest cost, the combination gives the shooter a rifle capable of fine performance. I have used two of the Pine Ridge scopes from Cabela's with complete satisfaction.

Tasco markets a line of scopes that includes 4X and 3-9X rimfire models that sell for under $50. BSA offers a 4X rimfire scope for under $30 including mount which is the model my brother mounted on his Remington 597 autoloader. Simmons offers

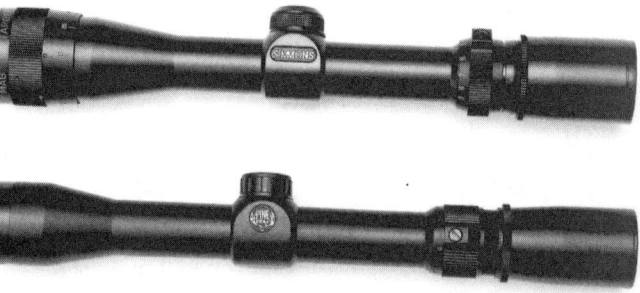

Two superb rimfire scopes are the 3-9X AO Simmons 1022 T (top) and the 2.5-7X Cablea's Pine Ridge (bottom).

several rimfire scope models although some differ only in finish. The popular 22 Mag series is available in 4X and 3-9X models for $50 or less at most retail outlets. Bushnell markets two popularly priced scopes for rimfire rifles, 4X and 3-9X models. The scopes mentioned are typical of the budget class of optics, but all are capable of enabling the shooter to get good performance from a rimfire rifle. While I may prefer a better scope, I have used a number of low priced scopes on my rimfires with complete satisfaction. If I could afford nothing better, I would mount one on my rifle, sight in carefully with ammunition that I know to shoot accurately in my rifle, and enjoy rimfire shooting.

Moving upward in price gives the rimfire shooter many more options. Weaver offers rimfire scopes in 4X, 2.5-7X, and 3-9X AO models with the first two selling for around $150 and the last for around $250 because of its AO feature. I have had experience with some of these scopes and they are superb. Simmons also offers a 3-9X AO scope appropriately known as the Model 1022T which is found for a retail price of approximately $140. It is a fine scope that will enable the rimfire shooter to enjoy a wide range of shooting activities. Another scope that I have found to be well-suited for use on a rimfire rifle is the Nikon Pro Staff 4X model which is corrected for parallax at 50 yards and is generally available for a retail price of about $100. Thompson/Center makes a superb 2.5-7X rimfire scope that sells for around $250. While many other scopes could be discussed, these are representative models in the mid-price range. Higher priced optics of outstanding quality are available from manufacturers like Burris, Leupold, Swarovski, and Zeiss. These outstanding products will meet or exceed any reasonable expectation for a scope.

Having discussed rifles and scopes does not mean that these are the only items that you will find useful in rimfire shooting. Except possibly for shooting from a bench, a sling should be considered as a necessary piece of equipment. Most rimfire rifles are sold with either swivels or studs for attaching them. Notable exceptions are the lever-action rifles and a few autoloaders including the Ruger 10/22 Rifle. However, it is possible to install swivels on these rifles. Front swivels that clamp around tubular magazines simplify that part of the problem for lever-actions and some autoloaders. A sling not only makes carrying the rifle easier, but also it is an aid to steady aiming under field conditions. The classic military sling is a two-part affair, but an adjustable nylon strap will suffice for most uses. A rifle with a composite stock will not look out of place with a nylon strap. On a fine sporting rifle with a checkered walnut stock, an elegant leather sling would be more appropriate.

One item that is closely related to the rimfire rifle is a case to carry it in. This is often given very little attention and almost any case that will hold the rifle is placed in service, but a fine case that fits properly is a good investment. Many cases simply are not proportioned well for a rimfire rifle, which is often shorter than a rifle in a centerfire caliber. Good cases are not expensive with many of the models with nylon shells selling for around $20 or so. If you are so inclined, a heavy canvas duck case with leather trim can be obtained for around $50 or so. Finally, if you expect travel by air with your rimfire rifle you will need a case that meets FAA requirements. Probably more shooters take centerfire rifles on long hunting trips by means of air travel, but it is not uncommon for the rimfire enthusiast to take his or her special rifle to competitive events or on that special prairie dog shoot. The lockable hard case that meets FAA requirements may become a necessity for such shooters.

The rifle, scope, and sling constitute the basic shooting unit. Other aftermarket options will be discussed in more detail in Chapter 12 and ammunition will be discussed in Chapter 6. To my knowledge, there has never been a time when the rimfire rifle shooter had such a wide selection of rifles and related items.

Chapter 4

THE RIMFIRE HANDGUNS

In Chapter 3, an overview was presented of many of the rimfire rifles that are currently available. In the case of rimfire handguns, the primary uses for many shooters involve recreational shooting in the form of plinking but handguns are often used for hunting and dispatching pests. Rimfire handguns are not normally the first choice for defensive purposes although they may certainly be used in that manner. There is also a great deal of interest in formal target shooting (both paper and silhouette targets) for which specialized high-end equipment is required (see Chapter 12). These uses for rimfire handguns will be considered separately.

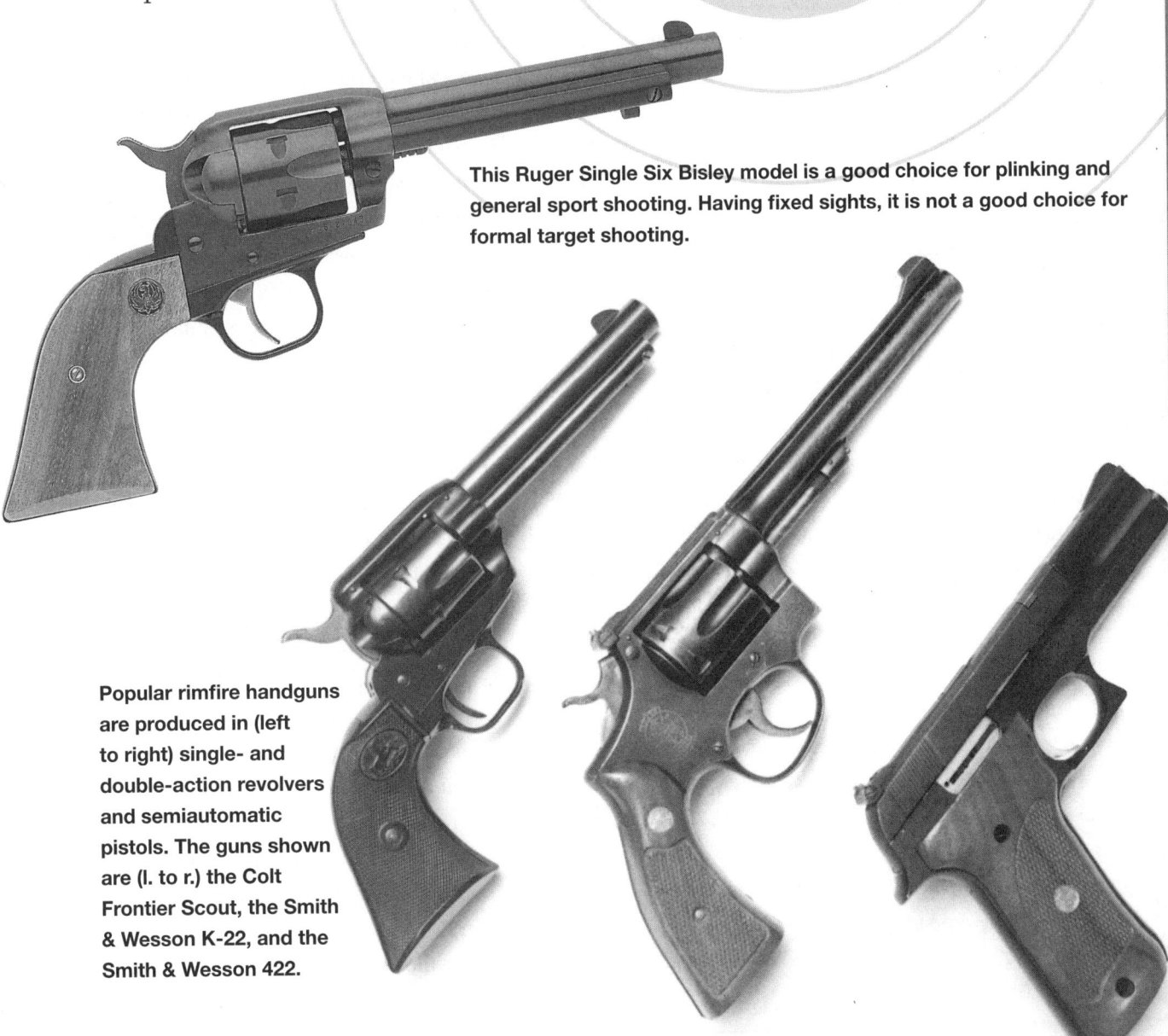

This Ruger Single Six Bisley model is a good choice for plinking and general sport shooting. Having fixed sights, it is not a good choice for formal target shooting.

Popular rimfire handguns are produced in (left to right) single- and double-action revolvers and semiautomatic pistols. The guns shown are (l. to r.) the Colt Frontier Scout, the Smith & Wesson K-22, and the Smith & Wesson 422.

Basically, rimfire handguns fall into the broad classifications as "sport" and "target" models. Sport models generally have shorter barrels and may not have adjustable sights or at least may have sights that are not as sophisticated as those on target models. Rimfire handguns intended for high level competition usually have rather long barrels and the best possible sights that are fully adjustable. Some of the most sophisticated target handguns are single shots that are designed for ultimate accuracy rather than rate of fire. Although revolvers were popular target handguns in the past, the majority of target pistols today are semiautomatics. In this chapter, a discussion of rimfire handguns is presented and some specific models are discussed, but it is not meant to be a catalog of all currently available models. For that type of coverage, consult the current edition of the *Gun Digest* or *Handguns 2005* (see Appendix A).

Before progressing to the subject of rimfire handguns, it is appropriate to make clear certain factors related to terminology. The inclusive term "handgun" applies to any firearm that can be fired with one hand. Long ago, the term "pistol" was used to describe such a piece, and the pistols of that period had a single chamber and a single barrel that was loaded from the muzzle. As firearm technology developed, it was soon observed that one shot was quite limiting in some situations so double barreled pistols were made. At that time, they were still loaded from the muzzle. Further developments led to "pistols with revolving chambers" which we would now call a "revolver", but they are still appropriately called pistols. Still later, pistols were developed that had one barrel and one chamber that could have several cartridges held in a magazine. While in some circles these and the single shot types are referred to as "pistols" and those with revolving chambers are called "revolvers", the historical use of the term "pistol" was in the same sense that the term "handgun" is now used. It was a global term used to describe a piece with any type of action. It may be supposed that the old song, "Pistol Packin' Mama" did not necessarily distinguish whether she had a semiautomatic or revolver! If I remember correctly, she had a 44 caliber, which indicates that it was of the "pistol with a revolving chamber" type.

Practical Considerations

Rimfire handguns are available that range from tiny derringers and revolvers to target pistols that are a foot long and weigh three pounds. One would neither choose the former for target shooting nor the latter for concealed carry. The choice of a rimfire handgun must be made with the primary end use in mind although there will certainly be some overlap possible. The selection may represent a compromise. For example, a rimfire handgun with a barrel of medium length and good sights could easily be suitable for informal target shooting as well as hunting. A rimfire handgun with a 3-inch barrel might serve for self-defense and pop can plinking. If a handgun with a 6-inch barrel and target sights is selected, it would serve well for small game hunting and formal target shooting. No one handgun is going to be the best choice for covering the entire spectrum of rimfire handgun shooting sports.

The principles involved in choosing a rimfire handgun are no different than those involved in choosing anything else. Personal preference weighs heavily in the decision as does intended use. A handgun for concealed carry should not have a long barrel and high, adjustable sights with sharp corners. A handgun for hunting squirrels or formal target shooting should not have a 3-inch barrel and fixed sights. The type of handgun should be matched to the functions it will perform. Fortunately, there is considerable overlap and one handgun can be used in a variety of ways even if some compromise is involved. For general sport use, the handgun chosen should have a barrel that is 4-6 inches long. Barrels shorter than 4 inches give short sight radius which makes accurate shooting more difficult while barrels longer than about 6 inches makes the piece too long for convenient carrying.

In recent years, the use of scopes on handguns has

become more common. The reason is quite simple; there is only one distance at which the shooter's eye can be focused. The target and the front and rear sights are at different distances from the eye so all cannot be in sharp focus simultaneously. In a scope, the crosshair or other type of reticule appears to be at the same distance as the target. It is simple to align the reticule on the target and squeeze off the shot. Just as in the case of rifles, the level of accuracy achieved with a handgun is much greater when a scope is used (see Chapter 15). While scopes are not part of the equipment allowed for formal target shooting, the hunter of pests and small game is under no such restrictions. A scope-sighted handgun can give outstanding accuracy which may equal that of some rifles. A brother of the author regularly hunts squirrels with a scoped Ruger Mark II 22/45. If you plan to engage in the growing sport of handgun hunting, you may wish to give some consideration to the ease of mounting a scope on the handgun you select. In this regard, the Smith & Wesson 22A and 22S Models are excellent because they are sold with a permanently attached scope rail in place. Only the scope and rings are needed to attach a scope.

Revolver or Semiautomatic

When one is choosing a rimfire handgun for plinking and pest control, the choice must first be made between revolver and semiautomatic. Revolvers come with one of two types of actions. A single-action revolver must be cocked manually for each shot while a double-action revolver can be fired simply by pulling the trigger. This action causes the cylinder to turn to place a fresh round under the firing pin while moving the hammer to the rear. When the trigger is pulled sufficiently far to the rear, the sear is released and the hammer falls causing the gun to fire. This action can be repeated to fire successive shots until the cylinder is empty. Any cartridge that fits correctly in the cylinder can be used. Therefore, Short, Long, Long Rifle and shot cartridges can be loaded in any cylinder that is designed to handle the 22 LR.

Single-action revolvers must be loaded one chamber at a time. On most current models, there is a loading gate at the rear of the cylinder on the right hand side that swings to the side to expose the chambers. A cartridge can be inserted in a chamber, the cylinder rotated to expose the next empty chamber and another cartridge inserted. The process is repeated until all chambers have been loaded. After the cartridges have been fired, the empty cases are removed by opening the loading gate and moving an ejector rod to the rear. This forces the empty case out of the back of the chamber. Rotating the cylinder to the next chamber and moving the ejector rod backward knocks out another empty case, etc. Loading and removing empty cases are slow processes with a single-action handgun.

Virtually all double-action revolvers of today have a cylinder that swings out of the frame on the left hand side. A latch, located on the left hand side of the frame behind the cylinder on most models, must be moved which unlocks the cylinder so it can be swung out of the frame. An ejector rod that is located at the front of the cylinder can be pushed backward which forces all of the empty cases out at the same time. As a result, loading and unloading are accomplished much faster than with a single-action revolver. However, for a great deal of sport shooting, rate of fire as determined by the speed of loading and unloading is of no importance.

Semiautomatic handguns hold cartridges in a magazine that is contained within the grip. In firing, the force generated by firing a round moves the slide to the rear against a strong recoil spring, and it also cocks the hammer (which may or may not be externally visible). The spring forces the slide forward, which allows it to engage

Semiautomatic pistols hold the removable magazine in the grip.

the top cartridge in the magazine forcing it into the chamber. Therefore, the semiautomatic is actually a self-loading handgun. Incidentally, it is sometimes found that a particular semiautomatic handgun will cycle more reliably with some types of ammunition than with others. You may have no way to test this before you buy the piece, but if you find that your pistol "jams" with some particular brand or type of ammunition, by all means try a few others before you assume that the pistol is defective. The experience of this author with several pistols that have been fired with a wide range of ammunition is that most rimfire pistols are remarkably forgiving with respect to type of ammunition used. Of course, 22 LR semiautomatic pistols will not function reliably with 22 Short, Long, or shot cartridges.

In order to ready a semiautomatic for firing, the magazine must be loaded with cartridges. There is a often great deal of difference in the ease of inserting cartridges into the magazines of different semiautomatic pistols. A long spring inside the magazine places pressure on the magazine follower, and the spring tension increases as each successive cartridge compresses the spring. The magazines of some pistols have a small button on the side that allows pressure to be applied to compress the magazine spring that way rather than by applying force from the top by pressing on the cartridges. Some magazines have buttons on both sides of the magazines so that the follower can be pulled downward and held there as cartridges are inserted. Check the magazine of any semiautomatic pistol that you consider buying to see how easily it can be loaded.

After a loaded magazine is inserted in the grip of the pistol, a cartridge must be moved from the magazine into the chamber. Pulling the slide fully

Moving a cartridge from the magazine to the chamber requires the slide to be drawn back and released.

to the rear and letting it go accomplishes this. The strong recoil spring forces the slide forward and as it moves, it takes with it the top cartridge from the magazine. Here a word of caution is needed. Some pistols allow the slide to be drawn to the rear only when the safety is in the "off" position. When the slide on such a pistol moves forward during the initial loading, the pistol is ready to fire! Other models allow all operations to be conducted with the safety in the "on" position, which is highly desirable. Generally, it is the older models that must have the safety off to operate the slide. It is an advantage to be able to open the slide with the safety on.

A great many semiautomatic handguns intended for plinking have sights that are not fully adjustable. It may be possible to move the rear sight laterally in its retaining notch, but there may be no provision for elevation adjustment. This may not be as bad as it sounds at first. Rimfire handguns for plinking are intended for use at short range. The targets may be no more than 10 to 15 yards, and at such distances small sighting errors are likely to be unnoticed. Moreover, the difference in point of impact caused by using different types of ammunition will be small enough that the average shooter will probably not notice the difference. Handguns having fixed sights are entirely practical for a lot of reasons. First, if the handgun is going to be carried in a holster, there is no possibility of changing sight settings by inserting or removing the gun from the holster. Second, fixed sights are sturdy enough that some bumps and scrapes can be endured without affecting the sight adjustment. That may not be the case with target pistols having precise, adjustable sights that are less robust. Third, at the average distance at which the handgun is used there may be no need to adjust the sights. Fourth, if you do not need adjustable sights on your pistol for its intended uses, there is no need to pay for them. High quality adjustable sights often add $20 to $50 to the cost.

Firing at a 4-inch black circle at 50 yards is an entirely different matter as is trying to take squirrels at ranges of 25 to 30 yards. In these cases, the handgunner is looking for all the accuracy possible and that means adjustable sights that are set for the type of ammunition being used at the appropriate range. The same fine handgun with adjustable sights makes an appropriate piece of equipment for target shooting as well as an effective tool for hunting small game and pests.

In summary, if you plan to shoot pine cones and pop cans at short range, almost any rimfire handgun will serve well. A low-end model with a short barrel and fixed sights will work just fine. If you want a handgun that you can use to hunt small game and pests or if you want to participate in more serious target shooting, a model having a longer barrel and adjustable sights is in order. Whether the handgun is a revolver or autoloader will be dependent on your personal preference. There is a wider choice available in the case of semiautomatics and they are more popular than revolvers today. It is the opinion of many, including this author, that the revolver is generally safer for inexperienced users. With an autoloader, the pistol is ready to fire just as quickly as the action cycles and puts a fresh round in the chamber. With a revolver, immediately after a shot the hammer is down and the chamber in line with it holds an empty case. A double-action revolver can be fired again by pulling the trigger, but the long, heavy double-action pull is required which is not likely to be accomplished by slight pressure applied by an inattentive shooter. This is not so with the autoloader which requires only light finger pressure to fire again.

A few single-shot handguns are available. One often sees an article dealing with "handgun" hunting in which a single-shot pistol having a barrel as long as 14 to 16 inches is used on a piece that is chambered for a cartridge that is normally used in centerfire rifles. These "handguns" may even have a bolt action or break action that is identical to that used on some models of rifles. The stock has been cut off and reshaped to give a pistol grip, but in reality these "pistols" are short rifles. They almost always have scope sights attached. Instead of "handgun" hunting, the sport is more appropriately called "hunting with a short rifle with the stock cut off" hunting. In order to effectively use a cartridge that is normally used in rifles, the barrels are of necessity longer than those used on handguns. In the area of rimfire handguns, there are a few single shot models and in calibers like 22 WMR and 17 HMR they are effective for hunting and pest control. As a handgun for the general uses for which rimfire handguns are appropriate, the single-shot is really a minor player in a big game.

Calibers

Along with the type of action, the choice of caliber needs to be made. In rimfire rifles, identical models are available in 22 LR, 22 WMR, and 17 HMR calibers and some are also available in 17 Mach 2. This is by no means the case with handguns, and comparable models are not always available. One outstanding exception is the Ruger Single Six convertible, which comes with one cylinder that chambers the 22 LR and another that chambers the 22 WMR. It is possible to offer a combination such as this even though the bullet diameter for the 22 LR is 0.223" while that for the 22 WMR is 0.224" and the small difference causes no problems. This is a single-action revolver that gives the shooter the choice between two power levels (and price levels in ammunition). Another manufacturer that offers a single-action revolver with two cylinders is Heritage. Some older Harrington and Richardson revolvers offer two cylinders and can be found on the secondary market.

One factor to consider when discussing handgun calibers is the

Rimfire handguns are produced in the (left to right) calibers 17 Mach 2, 22 LR, 17 HMR, and 22 WMR.

difference in velocity that results from the short handgun barrel compared to that of a rifle. The 22 LR develops maximum velocity while traveling approximately 16 inches in a rifle barrel. If the barrel is longer than about 18 inches, the velocity actually decreases slightly because of being slowed by friction. In a 6-inch handgun barrel, the velocity produced by a given load is somewhat lower than it is when the same load is fired in a rifle. In most cases, there is approximately 125 to 150 ft/sec difference between the velocity produced by a 6-inch barreled handgun and the velocity given by the same load in a rifle. Moreover, because there is a gap between the cylinder and barrel in a revolver (usually 0.002 to 0.008 inches), some gas escapes through this gap and is not used to push on the bullet. As a result, a revolver having a given barrel length generally gives lower velocity than that produced by a semiautomatic having the same barrel length and firing the same type of ammunition. Incidentally, barrel length of a revolver does not include the cylinder in the measurement. The barrel length for a semiautomatic is the distance from the breech to the muzzle.

The fraction by which the velocity from a handgun is lower than that given by a rifle depends on several factors. First, even with the same barrel length (which does not include the length of the cylinder), a revolver will generally give a velocity that is approximately 50 ft/sec lower than that of a semiautomatic. As will be discussed in Chapter 7, most types of ammunition give about the same velocity from a 6-inch barreled revolver as from a semiautomatic having a 4.5-inch barrel. Of course, the length of the gap between the cylinder and barrel has a significant effect. A gap of 0.003 inches results in less velocity loss than does a gap of 0.007 inches.

A semiautomatic with a 5.5-inch barrel will give approximately 50 ft/sec higher than one with a 4.5-inch barrel (see the table of velocities presented in Chapter 7). It should be remembered that there are other factors that influence bullet velocity from semiautomatic handguns. Dimensions of the chamber and bore as well as bore smoothness have some effect on velocity. Therefore, it is possible for a particular handgun with a 4-inch barrel to give velocities that are as high or higher than those from another specimen with a 4.5 or 5-inch barrel.

As a result of their using larger charges of slower burning powders, some of the hyper velocity loads in 22 LR suffer a greater loss than do ordinary cartridges when fired in handguns. This effect is even greater in 22 WMR and 17 HMR calibers which need longer barrels to allow the powder charges to burn efficiently. In a handgun with a 6-inch barrel, the 40-grain 22 WMR bullet that is driven to about 1,900 ft/sec in a rifle achieves only approximately 1,450 to 1,500 ft/sec which generates an energy of almost 200 ft lbs. Although energy this high does not make a 22 WMR handgun a better choice than most centerfire calibers for defensive uses, it is more effective than a 22 LR, 25 Auto, and some other low-powered calibers. While they cannot fire ammunition of any other caliber or accept another cylinder, there are several double-action revolvers available in 17 HMR caliber. With cylinder swapping options that exist for some single-action revolvers, a handgun in 17 HMR could use a cylinder chambered for the shorter 17 Mach 2 if one exists as an option. The 2005 Ruger catalog lists the 17 HMR/17 Mach 2 combination for the Single Six Hunter.

The Ruger Single Six Hunter has a 7.5-inch barrel. In 17 HMR caliber, the 17-grain bullets are given a muzzle velocity of approximately 2,000 ft/sec from a revolver barrel of this length. This represents a velocity that is about 600 ft/sec lower than the same load gives in a rifle. The 20-grain bullets, which are driven at 2,375 ft/sec from a rifle, achieve only 1,725 to 1,750 ft/sec from the handgun barrel. Much of the effectiveness of the 17 HMR that results from high velocity is lost in handguns. In fact, the velocity of the 17 HMR bullets from handguns almost exactly duplicates that from the 17 Mach 2 when fired from a rifle. While not equal to the performance of a 17 HMR rifle, the handguns offer flat trajectory when

The Ruger Bearcat is a small single-action revolver that makes a good trail gun. The small grip allows shooters with small hands to fire it comfortably.

Available in 22 LR, the Smith & Wesson Model 617 makes a good choice for any type of shooting. The same gun is available in 17 HMR and 22 WMR.

The Taurus double-action revolvers are available in blue or stainless steel. They are outstanding firearms at reasonable prices.

compared to any other handgun in a rimfire caliber. They are suitable for taking small game and varmints.

If you are selecting a handgun specifically for hunting small game and pests, you may wish to consider a piece chambered for one of the magnum calibers. However, since the primary use of a rimfire handgun is for pleasure and target use, the caliber that makes the most sense is the 22 LR. With a good handgun chambered for the 22 LR, you can do a lot of shooting because the cost of ammunition is so low. In some cases, the rimfire handgun is an understudy for a centerfire piece and the choice of handguns in 22 LR is very broad indeed. Because of this, it is possible in many cases to select a rimfire handgun that operates in much the same way as a centerfire model which makes training with the rimfire have some carryover value.

Revolvers

The most famous single-action revolver of all time is the legendary Colt Single-action Army, also known as the Peacemaker, which was introduced in 1873 and was for a time a military sidearm. From 1957 to 1977, Colt produced a scaled-down model known as the Frontier Scout that was chambered for the 22 LR, but it was also marketed later with a cylinder that chambered the 22 WMR. Although these models have been discontinued, they are frequently found as used guns. Single-action revolvers of the

Colt style (and Ruger single-actions made prior to 1973) allow a blow on the hammer to cause the revolver to fire. The firing pin makes direct contact with the cartridge. Even though the hammer can be moved back to engage a safety notch, this was not totally effective in keeping the firearm from being discharged. Accordingly, users of this "old style" revolver normally carried them with only five cartridges in the cylinder and an empty chamber below the hammer.

Ruger has offered the Single Six in 17 HMR caliber for a couple of years and in 2004 introduced the Single Six Hunter version which has a 7.5-inch heavy barrel. The top rib of the barrel has the curved grooves milled into it so Ruger scope rings can be attached, and it is also grooved for attaching the tip-off mounts. This handgun weighs about 45 ounces, and it is clearly intended for hunting small game and pests. It appears that this fine revolver will be made available with a second cylinder chambered for the 17 Mach 2 round. The Single Six Hunter is already available as a convertible model with 22 LR and 22 WMR cylinders.

By far the most commonly encountered single-action rimfire revolvers at the present time are the Ruger Single Six in its various forms and the small-scale revolver known as the Ruger Bearcat. All

Several years ago, the single-action Colt Frontier Scout revolvers were quite popular. Shown here are two fine examples of this model.

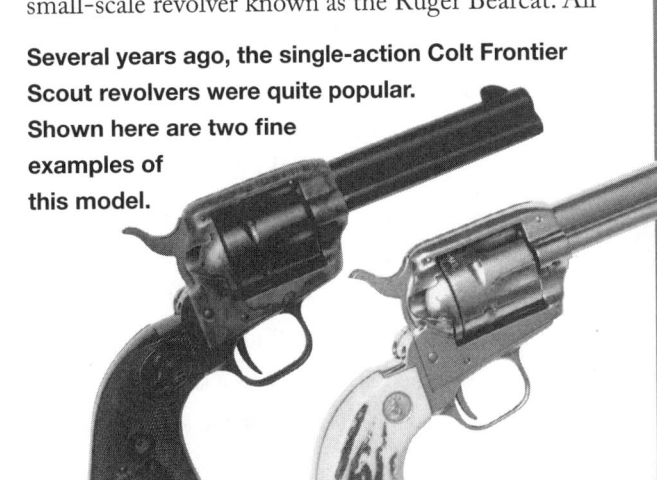

current Ruger single-action revolvers are designed to be carried with all chambers loaded because the hammer cannot strike the firing pin until the trigger is pulled causing a transfer bar to be moved into position to transit the blow from the hammer to the firing pin.

Many years ago, two of the most popular target revolvers were the double-action Colt Officer's Model Match and the Smith & Wesson Masterpiece, both of which were available in 22 LR. These fine revolvers were capable of outstanding performance even in formal competition. In addition to these models with 6-inch barrels, both Colt and Smith & Wesson produced target grade revolvers with 4-inch barrels that were intended to serve as companion pieces to the centerfire firearms carried on duty by many police officers. The Colt Diamondback was available in both 38 Special and 22 LR as was the Smith & Wesson Combat Masterpiece. None of these models is produced at this time. However, Smith & Wesson offers two types of double-action revolvers in 22 LR. The first is the Model 617 that is a full size revolver weighting 41 ounces and having a list price of $663. This stainless steel model with a full-length barrel lug can be considered as a modern replacement for the legendary K-22 Masterpiece target revolver. The Model 317 Airweight is a small frame eight-shot revolver that is available with a 3-inch or 1.88-inch barrel. Weights are only 11.9 or 10.5 ounces respectively. Large-frame revolvers are available in 17 HMR (Model 647) and 22 WMR (Model 648) from Smith & Wesson. In 17 HMR the barrel lengths are 8.38 and 12 inches with weights being over 50 ounces in each case. The 22 WRM is available with a 6-inch barrel length. List prices for these models are in the $650-$700 range. For defensive purposes, Smith & Wesson markets the Model 351 small-frame piece in 22 WMR that has a 1.88-inch barrel and weighs only 10.6 ounces.

Another fine double-action 22 revolver is the Ruger SP 101 which is available as a six-shot stainless steel model having adjustable sights. With a suggested price of $505, it represents the middle ground in the price range. This is a very sturdy revolver that weighs 34 ounces and has adjustable sights. It is an excellent choice for the backpacker and woods roamer. This model has recently been discontinued, but Ruger still has some warehoused, and it is still available from some dealers.

Taurus offers an extensive line of revolvers chambered in 22 LR, 17 HMR, and 22 WMR calibers. These include the Hunter (12-inch barrel, 56.8 ounces) and Tracker (6.5-inch barrel, 45.6 ounces) which are available in all three calibers. These models have list prices of approximately $400. In addition to these models built on large frames, there is also a series of rimfire revolvers that are built on medium frames that are available in a wide range of finishes, barrel lengths, etc. These models have list prices in the $350 range and weights run from 25 to 30 ounces.

Autoloaders

When it comes to autoloaders, the rimfire shooter has an enormous range of models from which to choose. Even if some of the classic models like the Colt Woodsman are no longer being produced, the spectrum of products available encompasses the Smith & Wesson Model 41, a high-level competition model, on one end and the diminutive Beretta Bobcat on the other. There are many models in between. The Smith & Wesson Model 41 is available in 5.5- and 7-inch barrel lengths with weights of 41 and 42 ounces and has a list price of $1,026. The Beretta Bobcat has a 2.4-inch barrel, weighs 11.8 ounces, and has a list price of $290. There is truly a rimfire autoloader for almost any taste.

Autoloaders from a particular manufacturer can often be considered as a family of related products that share many common features. For example, popular sport pistols include the Browning Buck Mark, which is available in numerous configurations from the long, heavy-barreled Silhouette competition model to a 4-inch barreled sport model that is

Ruger's Mark II Standard model is one of the most durable and dependable rimfire autoloaders made. It is also a beautiful piece.

For target or silhouette shooting, the Brown Buck Mark 5.5 Target is a superb choice. It is equipped with target sights and a scope rail.

The Smith & Wesson Model 41 is the premier autoloader for high-level target shooting.

intended as a camp, trail, or plinking model. The Buck Mark 5.5-inch barreled standard model comes with excellent sights that are fully adjustable and a trigger action that is about as good as that on almost any other mass-produced pistol. Having experience with two of these fine pistols, this author can attest to the fact that groups smaller than one-inch at 50 feet on an indoor range are the norm with factory sights when using appropriate ammunition. There is also a target version that has a 7.25-inch fluted barrel. List prices range from $279 for the camper model to $586 for the target model. The Silhouette version comes without sights but has an accessory rail for mounting optional sights.

Labeled by Ruger as "The number one 22 pistol in the world," the Ruger Mark II (and the recently introduced Mark III) may well be just that. The Ruger Mark II was introduced in 1982, but its forerunner was introduced in 1949 and the Ruger autoloader has been in production ever since. More than a dozen variants of this enormously popular pistol were available as the newer Mark III went into production. The Standard model comes in either blue or stainless versions with fixed sights and having list prices of $299 and $390, respectively. Available barrel lengths include 4.75 and 6 inches. Several target models are available including those known as Target, Government, and Competition models all of which have adjustable, target-style sights. List prices range from $365 to $555 depending on the specific version. These versions with adjustable sights are furnished drilled and tapped so that a Weaver-type scope base can be attached. One target model that is available in both blue and stainless steel is produced with a 10-inch bull barrel, and it weighs approximately 51 ounces. The Ruger autoloader has established an enviable reputation for reliability and durability in the more than half a century that it has been in production. The one-millionth pistol was produced in 1979 and total production is well over 3 million. Another successful autoloader from Ruger is the version known as the 22/45. This model features a polymer grip frame that has the size and angle that duplicate the feel of the famous Colt 1911.

After production of over 3 million Mark II pistols, the first Ruger Mark III pistols became available in 2004. Major changes include safety features like a loaded chamber indicator, a magazine disconnect, and a key lock system. Late in 2004, the stainless steel Mark III 678 Hunter model appeared that features a 6.88-inch fluted barrel. The receiver is drilled and tapped for attaching a scope rail that comes with the pistol. Another version of the Mark III is known as the Model 512, which has a blue finish and a 5.5-inch heavy barrel (list price $382-483 depending on features). The Model 22/45 (list price $305) is also being upgraded to become a Mark III. The final 1,000 of the Mark II pistols were shipped in November 2004 carrying the "One of One Thousand" logo on top of the receiver.

Kimber markets an autoloader that is a clone of the Colt 1911, and it is available in 22 LR and 17 Mach 2 calibers. The slide is made of aluminum in

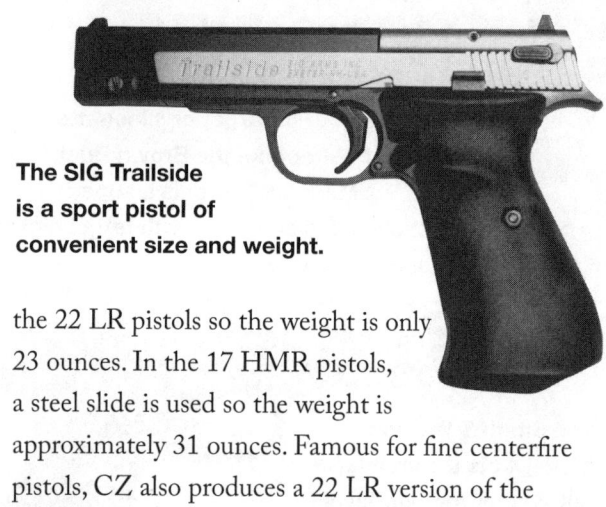

The SIG Trailside is a sport pistol of convenient size and weight.

With a 3.4-inch barrel, the Walther P22 is a compact, lightweight sport pistol.

the 22 LR pistols so the weight is only 23 ounces. In the 17 HMR pistols, a steel slide is used so the weight is approximately 31 ounces. Famous for fine centerfire pistols, CZ also produces a 22 LR version of the Model 75 known as the Cadet.

In addition to the Model 41 target model, Smith & Wesson has an extensive line of 22 LR pistols in the 22A and 22S series that is available in various finishes with barrel lengths of 4, 5.5, and 7 inches, and the barrels can be easily interchanged. The 22A models have alloy frames and weigh around 30 ounces. They have list prices in the $283-355 range depending on options selected. The 22S models are made with stainless steel barrels and frames which gives weights of over 40 ounces. All of the 22A and 22S versions have scope rails that accept Weaver-type rings so a wide variety of optional sighting equipment can be mounted, and the accuracy displayed by these fine pistols makes them suitable for hunting. With the wide selection of options in finish, grips, and other options available, almost any taste can be satisfied by one of the Smith & Wesson pistols.

Beretta markets an extensive series of pistols known as the Model U22 Neos. Barrel lengths of 4.5, 6, and 7.5 inches are available in several finishes. List prices are in the $310 to $365 range with the target version listed at $440. Beretta also produces the Model 87 Target, a high-quality piece that has a suggested price of $708. Another Beretta model that is more conventional in its appearance is the Cheetah, which comes with a choice of 3.8 or 4.4-inch barrels. The Cheetah can be fired in double-action mode for the first shot. Sigarms markets an interesting pistol known as the Trailside. It is available with 4.5 and 6-inch barrels with corresponding weights of 28 and 30 ounces. Retail prices are in the $350 to $400 range. High Standard has produced rimfire autoloaders for many years. Current models include several target versions known as the Victor, Trophy, Olympic, and Citation, which have retail list prices in the $750 to $800 range. These are pistols that have established an enviable reputation.

One of the recent additions to the lineup of 22 autoloaders is the Walther P22. This pistol is designed with the look and feel of the famous Walther P99 centerfire pistol that is widely used in law enforcement and military work. With a polymer frame, the basic P22, which has a 3.4-inch barrel, weighs only about 18 ounces. The target model, which has a 5-inch barrel and adjustable sights weighs approximately 20 ounces. Both models have many unique features one of which is a replaceable back strap that can be interchanged to alter the grip size. The P22 also comes with a built-in lock that requires a specially designed key to place the pistol in a firing configuration. Dual safety levers are mounted on the top of the receiver at the rear, but they do not function as decocking levers. Moreover, barrels of different length are interchangeable to convert a sport model into the target version.

There are also several compact pistols available in 22 LR that are intended for carry or defense. These include the tiny Beretta Bobcat with a 2.4-inch barrel and a weight of only about 11.5 ounces. The Bobcat has a list price of approximately $265. Taurus produces a small double-action-only (DAO) model known as the PT 22. It has a 2.75-inch barrel, weighs only 12.3 ounces, has a list price of slightly over $200.

Frequently, one reads on the chat room of some internet forum how the writer just loves a particular handgun. In the next post, another participant tells how his specimen of the same model jams frequently. It may be that the first writer owns a particularly good sample while the other got one made on Friday as they used to say. Part of the difference may lie in the types of ammunition being used in the two pistols. Certain types of pistols function much better with some types of ammunition than with others. For example, some older pistols were designed to handle standard-velocity loads by making use of a rather soft recoil spring. Modern high-velocity loads should not be used in such models. Still other pistols seem to function best with high velocity loads. Ammunition such as CCI Stinger and Quik-Shok is produced with a case length that is approximately 0.1 inch longer than the standard 22 LR case. It should come as no surprise that such ammunition might not feed reliably in certain semiautomatic pistols.

If a rimfire pistol fails to function flawlessly, there are four things to check in seeking a remedy for the situation. First, make sure that the action is clean and properly (but not overly!) lubricated. During firing, autoloaders have unburned powder deposited in the action that can result in enough gunk so that the bolt does not cycle smoothly. Second, check the loading ramp that leads into the chamber. It should be smooth and correctly shaped. Third, check the lips on the magazine. If a magazine is dropped on a hard surface, it is possible for the lips to become bent. Since this is the area from which the cartridges are fed into the chamber, the bent magazine may not allow the pistol to function correctly. Fourth, try different ammunition. Some variation in dimensions between types of ammunition is inevitable, and different types of lubricant may make a difference in feeding. If these simple factors do not solve the problem, have the pistol checked by a competent pistolsmith.

Thoughts on Selection

Gone are the superb Colt Match Target Woodsman and some of the High Standard pistols of many years ago. They are now highly prized as collectors' pieces. Even with the disappearance of these fine firearms, the rimfire handgunnner has a wealth of choices that includes both autoloaders and revolvers. What follows should not necessarily be taken as strongly as if they were recommendations. I am merely making some summary comments based on first-hand experience. For sporting purposes, it would be hard to fault the Ruger Single Six, especially with the extra cylinder in 22 WMR caliber. Such a handgun is suited to plinking, small game and pest shooting, and woods roaming. The Ruger single-actions are famous for their durability. In 17 HMR caliber (or 17 Mach 2 with the optional cylinder), a Single Six is a good choice for small varmints at long handgun ranges (although you will probably need a scope for taking varmints under such conditions), but it does not really fit the role of a plinking handgun, and it is far less versatile than the 22 LR/22 WMR version. The recently released Ruger Single Six Hunter has a built in rib that accepts Ruger rings for ease in scope mounting. The large frame Smith & Wesson double-action revolvers such as the Model 617 are superb handguns that can readily accept scope mounts. The Taurus revolvers represent excellent values as well. A handgun from any of these famous makers would make a superb choice for all around use.

The autoloader fan will find a wide selection of models in a broad spectrum of price ranges from which to make a selection. Before selecting any rimfire autoloading handgun, examine several models to determine how the size, weight, and handling characteristics compare. If an autoloader is your cup of tea, it is hard to imagine a more reliable, dependable rimfire handgun than the Ruger Standard model in either the Mark II (which is still in the display cases of many dealers) or the recently introduced Mark III configuration. As a plinking pistol for the outdoorsman, the Standard model is adequate, but one of the variants with adjustable sights would be a better choice if the pistol is to be used as a training piece for formal target shooting or for small game or pest shooting. Another excellent choice for general use would be one of the several versions of the Browning Buck Mark. In my experience, they are extremely accurate and reliable, and the Buck Mark Standard weighs only 32 to 33 ounces.

The Smith & Wesson 22S and 22A are available with either stainless steel or alloy frames with barrel lengths ranging from 4 to 7 inches so a sport, target, or hunting configuration can easily be achieved. The Beretta autoloaders provide alternatives at reasonable prices. Any of these autoloaders can have a scope attached for producing the ultimate in accuracy for hunting and pest shooting. For plinking and sport shooting, the Walther P22 would make a fine choice. With its light weight and small grip size, it would be a superb choice for women and younger shooters who may have small hands. Moreover, the grip size can be modified by changing the replaceable back strap insert, and it is a simple process to interchange barrels.

Although there is probably not a great difference in inherent accuracy between most of the models mentioned, there may be a considerable difference in trigger action and sights. These characteristics may allow you to shoot some handguns more accurately than others. As in the case of rifles and perhaps to an even greater extent, the choice of a handgun is a personal matter, and subjective factors play a large role in the enjoyment derived from using the piece. For example, one of the handgun designs that is extremely popular with many shooters is one that I do not like at all. If you were to handle such a pistol, you might find your emotions so stimulated that it would be your top choice. It is this type of preference that makes both single-action revolvers and semiautomatics immensely popular. They are many fine rimfire handguns available from which to make a good selection.

Ancillaries

The person who is getting equipped to enjoy the sport of rimfire handgun shooting will probably want items in addition to the handgun. While it is possible to enjoy such shooting with only a handgun and some ammunition, other items will be added to the shooter's kit if the sport becomes addictive. Most semiautomatic pistols are sold with two magazines included. If only one magazine is furnished, you should add another either to have as a spare in case something happens to one or just as a convenience. It is much easier to have two loaded magazines handy so that when one is empty it can be dropped out and the other inserted to continue shooting.

Probably the most frequent purchase by the handgunnner is a holster. Traditional material for constructing holsters is leather, but in recent years various synthetic materials have become widely used. There is little question in the minds of many purists that the leather holster is more attractive. However, it also requires more maintenance and the residual chemicals from the tanning process can lead to corrosion if the handgun is left in the leather for a long period of time. A friend recently showed me a fine old Swedish military pistol that he had left in its original holster for a long time. The bluing had been removed over large areas of the pistol by the chemicals in the leather thereby decreasing the value of the pistol considerably. The owner thought that since the holster came with the pistol that they should be stored together with the pistol inside. Leather also tends to become brittle with age unless treated with an appropriate solution to replace lost natural oils. It should be remembered that leather is also a material that is used to polish metals. If a leather holster fits loosely enough that the gun slides around in it, the bluing is

A fine leather holster like this one produce by Browning for the Buck Mark series is durable and attractive.

going to be worn off in short order at the contact points. Make sure that a leather holster is made for your specific handgun. It has become more popular to produce a compromise holster that fits a certain general handgun type such as "large-frame auto, 3.5- to 5-inch barrel." Do not settle for this type of holster without trying it with a handgun of the same model and barrel length as yours. If it fits well, it will be satisfactory. If not, keep looking or buy another type. One drawback to the leather holsters made for specific firearms is that they are expensive. It is not uncommon to find models that cost $50 to $75 or in some cases even more.

For many years, the author owned only a few leather holsters. As the cost of fine leather holsters escalated, nylon holsters became more popular. These are generally produced in several sizes each of which fits several handguns of similar dimensions. While this can present a problem with a leather holster, it is acceptable if the holster is made of nylon. If fact, the author has one pistol for which no leather holster could be found in the price range acceptable. The result was that a nylon holster produced by Gun Mate was selected and it worked so well that another of the same type was obtained for another hard to fit handgun. In addition to Gun Mate, there are several producers of fabric holsters some of which are Bianchi and Uncle Mike's. Nylon holsters require very little maintenance, they do not tend to rub off bluing, and they are inexpensive. Some of the very good models sell for $25 or less with some being available for $12 to $15.

Don't forget that you will have to transport your handgun both in a vehicle as well as in the field. Almost all states have requirements for transporting firearms in vehicles that require the piece to be in a closed case. Today, most handguns are shipped from the manufacturer in a foam padded plastic case or in a case that is molded to hold the gun securely. These containers are adequate for transporting the handgun and most have a hole where a lock can be attached to keep the case closed. A hard case made of aluminum

Red dot sights like this model from Simmons have become very popular for use on handguns. They offer some of the advantages of a scope are faster to use.

or other material is an inexpensive addition to the shooters kit.

In recent years, the development of handgun grips has made it possible for the shooter to change the grip of his or her pistol. In some cases, the grips may be desirable to enable the shooter to handle the piece better but in other cases the effect may be primarily cosmetic. There are special grips made of wood, staghorn, composites, rubber, or laminated materials. They may have finger grooves that provide a better grasp of the grip or they may be made with a non-slip surface. The rubber grips give an especially good feel, they are not slick, and they give a more pleasant feel in cold weather. Several manufacturers make grips of this type, but the grips from Hogue are very highly regarded. Pachmayr and Uncle Mike's are also producers of extensive lines of grips.

There was a time when the purchaser of a handgun had a choice of a "target" model with adjustable sights or a "sport" model with fixed sights. In many cases, the guns were identical except for barrel length and sights. If there is one aftermarket area that has expanded exponentially, it surely must be handgun sights, the majority of which are produced with increased visibility as the main feature. It is true that many handguns are equipped with fixed sights that make it impossible or difficult (which can usually be interpreted as expensive) to make a change in sighting equipment. However, there are optional sights for many handguns that have white dots on either side of the notch in the rear sight blade and on the back surface of the front sight. These dots make it easier to align the sights in dim light. Other sights have dots that glow in the dark to make it possible to see them in very dim light. In some cases, the rear sight has the square notch outlined with a white line and the front sight has a white or red insert that makes the sights more visible. In the very recent past, the fiber optic inserts have become quite popular. The front sight has an insert that lies along the top of the post while the rear sight has a fiber optic element embedded on either side of the notch. Such sights are visible in low light, but in some cases the top of the front sight does not have a square shape. For most handgun shooting, the square topped post front sight and adjustable rear sight with a square notch make a combination that is hard to beat.

Optical sights for handguns have become immensely popular in recent years. These include scope, red dot, and laser sights. While laser sights are useful for shooting at night or possibly in law enforcement and military applications, lasers are dangerous. The author recently saw two youngsters playing with a laser pointer. One was pointing the beam directly in the face of the other! The warnings on lasers are there for a reason. It might be appropriate to point out that laser surgery on the eye has become an important technique. The danger of lasers being used carelessly is real and significant. Laser sights will not be discussed further in this chapter.

If you are in the same age group as the author, it is easy to remember a time when a scope on a handgun was regarded as a novelty. That is not the case any more. Hunting for both small and large game with handguns has become much more common. Enhanced handgun performance has also been a factor because it is practical to shoot at targets at longer ranges that makes improved aiming devices more important. Mounting scopes on handguns is so common that some models are sold with scope rails in place. Others are available with integral ribs along the tops of the barrels where scope bases can be attached. For an enormous number of other models, aftermarket mounts are available. Most of the major scope manufacturers produce scopes specifically for use on handguns. The point is that a scope can be mounted on almost any handgun except the very small pocket pistols.

Although early handgun scopes were of very low magnification, the models currently available include fixed powers that may be as high as 8X, and scopes having variable magnification are quite popular. One of the scopes with which the author has had most experience is the superb Weaver 1.5 to 4X variable. Eye relief of scopes for use on handguns is normally 12 to 16 inches so that the piece can be held at arm's length and fired in the normal way for a handgun. There is no question that a scope on a handgun enables the shooter to make shots routinely that would have been impossible or accidental under other circumstances.

The so-called red dot sight has been produced for many years in one form or another. This sight has a red dot projected onto a lens, which the shooter then looks through to place the red dot on the target. The red dot is produced by battery power, and the intensity of the dot can be varied widely by means of a rheostat. The location of the red dot in relation to the point of impact can be adjusted by means of adjustment knobs just as in the case of a scope. Because of the way in which the optical system is designed, there is no problem of parallax so the shooter merely places the red dot on the target and squeezes off the shot. Red dot sights are available with dots that cover a specific area on the target. Those with 3 MOA and 4 MOA are probably the most popular. Elsewhere in this book, the evaluation of one of the fine Simmons red dot sights will be presented. Sights of this type can also be used on shotguns, muzzle-loaders, and rifles. In the mind of the author, the main disadvantage to the red dot sight is that it produces a large blob on top of an otherwise trim handgun. This is no problem for the hunter using a handgun, but it makes it impossible to carry the piece in a holster. Nevertheless, the red dot sight is very popular, and there is a great difference between the red dot sights available today and those early models of a generation ago.

Chapter 5
SIGHTS AND SIGHTING

In order to hit a target with a rifle, some sort of aim is required unless the target is very close. Hitting a pop can at 15 yards with a shotgun requires no more than pointing the gun at the can and firing. Hitting the can at that distance with a rifle bullet, while not difficult, requires a more accurate aim by making use of some sort of sighting equipment. Hitting a pop can at 100 yards requires even more accurate aiming. A pop can at 300 yards is a small target and hitting it requires very accurate aiming. Hitting a one-inch circle at 300 yards would require an extremely accurate aim and would be possible only when the rifle is equipped with appropriate sights (even if the rifle were accurate enough). To some extent, the level of accuracy desired will dictate the sighting equipment required. In this chapter, the types of sights most appropriate to rimfire firearms will be discussed.

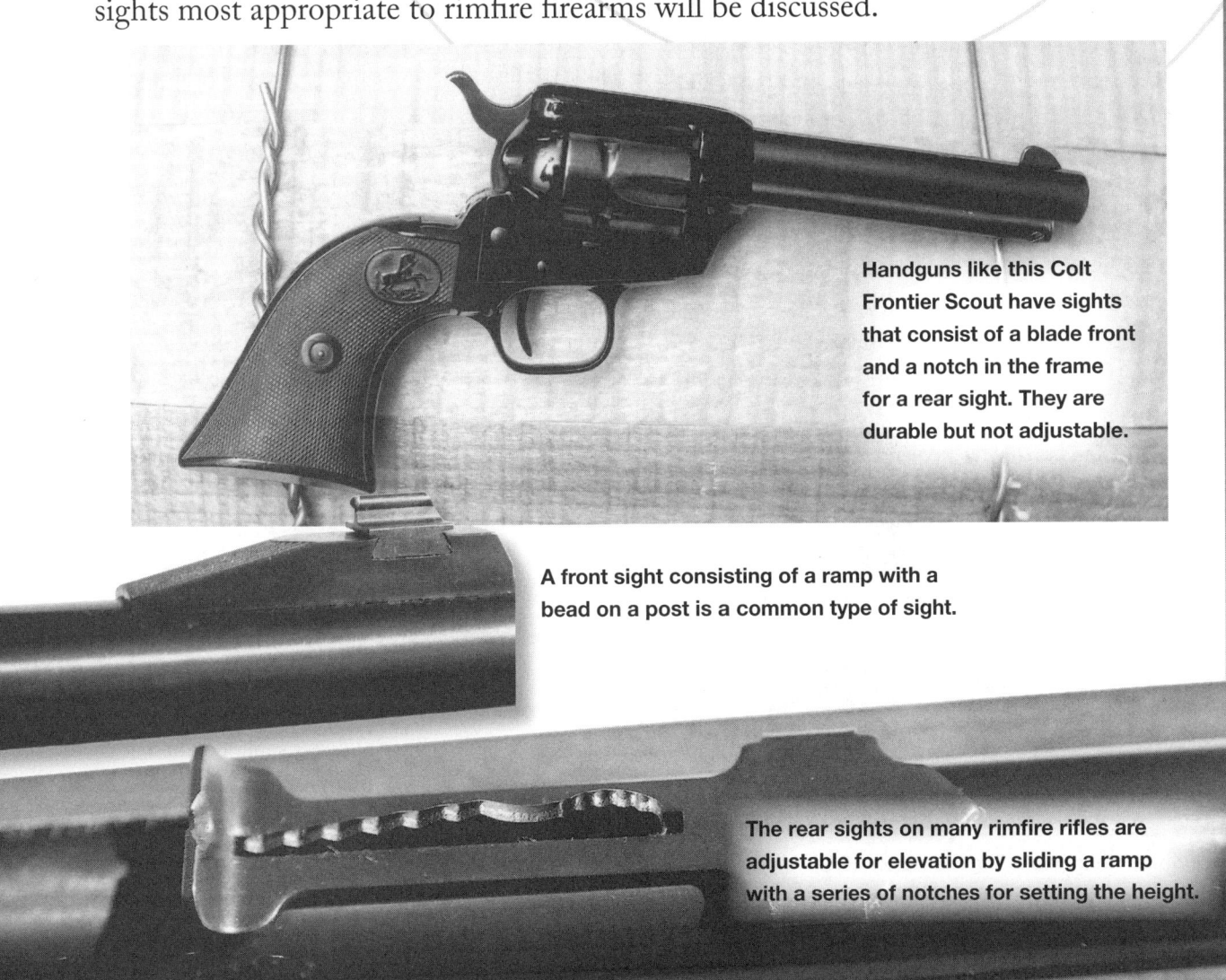

Handguns like this Colt Frontier Scout have sights that consist of a blade front and a notch in the frame for a rear sight. They are durable but not adjustable.

A front sight consisting of a ramp with a bead on a post is a common type of sight.

The rear sights on many rimfire rifles are adjustable for elevation by sliding a ramp with a series of notches for setting the height.

Sight pictures for open sights. In (a), a 6 o'clock hold is illustrated. If the sights are adjusted to hit the center of the bull as shown in (a), the bullet will hit below the center of the larger bull shown in (b). In (c), the sights are adjusted so that the top of the post is aligned with the center of the bull. In this way, the point of impact is at the top of the post which is useful for targets of different size and shape.

Open Sights

Aiming a rifle is accomplished by means of sights. Rifle sights have been made in a bewildering array of types over the centuries. In fact, acquiring old sighting equipment has become a passion for many collectors. Sights fall into two general categories, metallic and optical types. Metallic sights include the so-called open sight and the aperture or peep sight. Open sights often consist of a bead or post near the muzzle and a blade with a notch in it mounted near the rear end of the barrel. Aligning the post or bead front sight with the notch in the rear sight allows the barrel to be pointed at the target correctly. As will be discussed, there are numerous variations in open sights some of which are much better than others.

Aligning the sights on the target requires the shooter to establish simultaneously the relationship between three objects, the rear sight, the front sight, and the target. This relationship is known as the *sight picture*, and it must be the same for each shot if consistency is to be achieved. Suppose the rear sight

Some rifles, including the Ruger 10/22 and 77/22 have a folding rear sight.

has a square notch and the front sight consists of a post with a square top. Correct sighting requires that the post be placed in the notch so that the tops of both are in horizontal alignment. The front post must be centered in the notch in the rear sight with a small sliver of space on either side of the post. Next, the relationship between the top of the post and the target must be established. When the target is a black circle (the bull) on a piece of paper, the usual procedure is to have the sights adjusted so that the top of the post is positioned at the bottom edge of the bull. The problem with this arrangement is that if bulls having different sizes are fired at, the sights must be adjusted to compensate for the size difference otherwise the distance from the top of the post to the center of the bull is different and shots will strike either high or low relative to the center of the bull. The situation is even more difficult when the target may be a squirrel at 40 yards for one shot and a starling at 25 yards for the next. For this type of shooting, it is better to have the sights adjusted so that the point of impact coincides with the top of the post. Then, you can simply align the rear and front sights as described above and place the top of the post where you want the point of impact to be.

While the situation described deals with a rear sight with a square notch and a post front sight, the situation is similar when the rear sight has a "U" notch and the front sight is a bead. The sights should be adjusted so that the bead rests in the "U" and the top of the bead is used as the specific point to determine the alignment on the target. Most often found on rifles for plinking and hunting, the bead front sight is more difficult to place exactly on a paper target because of its rounded top. It is the experience of this author that the top edge of a circular bead becomes rather indistinct in dim light and tends to reflect light in direct sunlight. These conditions can lead to sighting errors, and they explain why a rifle sighted in correctly for one person may not prove to be correctly sighted in for another.

Almost all open sights have some provision for

adjustment. On many rimfire rifles, the rear sight blade can be moved up or down by sliding an elevator blade that is nothing more than a ramp that has a series of notches or steps. The elevator moves forward or backward in a slot cut in the rear sight. Notches cut in the sight elevator ramp hold the rear sight at a particular height. To raise the point of impact on the target, the rear sight is raised (elevated) which causes the muzzle to be raised in order to align the front sight in the rear sight notch. If the rifle is shooting high, the rear sight must be lowered to make the point of impact coincide with the point of aim. Note that *the rear sight must be moved in the direction in which the point of impact needs to be moved on the target* in order to sight in the rifle.

On many rimfire rifles (especially inexpensive ones), the rear sight is attached to the barrel by means of a dovetailed groove cut into the barrel. Lateral (horizontal) sight adjustment is known as the *windage* adjustment. The only way to move the sight laterally to adjust the point of impact is by sliding the entire sight. This requires tapping on the side of the sight base to move it in the groove. This needs to be done carefully in order to avoid marring the surface of the sight base and the barrel. For this purpose, the Lyman gunsmith's hammer is a useful tool. This small hammer has three interchangeable striking surfaces and a brass punch that is stored in the handle. The brass punch can be placed against the edge of the sight base and tapping it moves the rear sight laterally. A small amount of discoloration may occur as brass from the punch rubs off on the steel sight base, but it is usually easy to remove by rubbing briskly with an oily rag. If you do not have a special hammer for sight movement, you can get by with any small hammer and a small piece of brass rod having a diameter of about 1/8 or 3/16-inch diameter. Brass rods of this type are available at most hardware stores.

Another brief comment will be made here on the subject of tools although the subject will be discussed in greater detail in Chapter 10. A serious

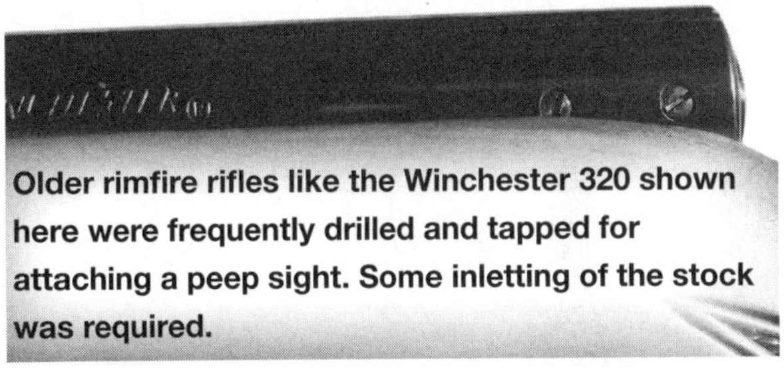

Older rimfire rifles like the Winchester 320 shown here were frequently drilled and tapped for attaching a peep sight. Some inletting of the stock was required.

Peep sights like the Lyman model shown here on a Winchester Model 69A Target rifle are widely used in target shooting.

shooter knows that mounting scopes or peep sights, and some firearm disassembly and adjustment are an integral part of the shooting activity. Keeping things tight is required even if other changes to the equipment are not being made. Nothing detracts from the appearance of a firearm more than screws that have been badly deformed by using improper screwdrivers. If you are serious about your firearms and keeping them in proper working order and looking good, invest in a set of gunsmith's screwdrivers. They are not expensive, and they provide a way of having the right tool for the job. In some cases, the bits are removable and store in the handle. Two of the most common kits are those available from Hoppe's and Pachmayr. These sets contain bits having blade, Phillips, and hex fittings. The Pachmayr set also has Torx bits.

Peep Sights

Like an open sight, an aperture or peep sight (sometimes referred to as a receiver sight) also makes use of a front sight consisting of a bead or blade. However, the rear sight is mounted on the receiver near

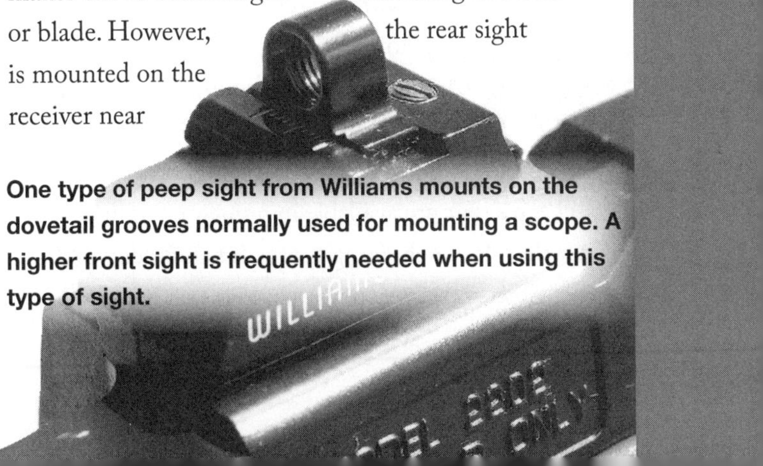

One type of peep sight from Williams mounts on the dovetail grooves normally used for mounting a scope. A higher front sight is frequently needed when using this type of sight.

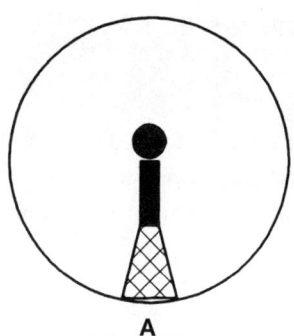 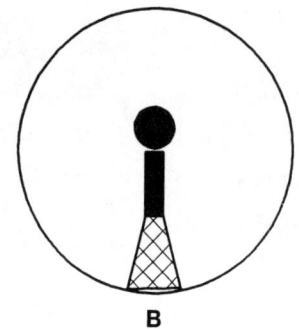 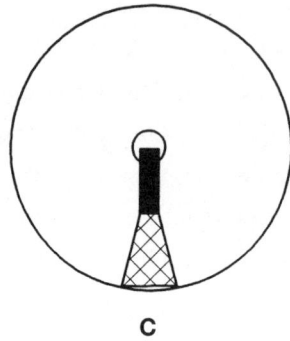

A   B   C

Figure A shows the sight picture for a 5 o'clock hold using a peep sight.
Figure B shows a 6 o'clock hold on a larger bull. If the rifle is sighted correctly as in Figure A, the shots will hit below the center of the larger bull.
Figure C shows the sight picture when the rifle is sighted to hit at the center of the bull. Shots will be centered regardless of the size of the bull.

the eye and has a small hole or aperture through which the shooter looks at the front sight and its relationship to the target. Because the human eye looks through a hole at the brightest point, the center of the aperture is naturally selected for looking at the front sight and where it is placed on the target. The shooter looks *through* the aperture rather than *at* it. With such a combination, it is possible to align the sights in relation to the target much more accurately than can be done with open sights. In fact, some types of competitive target shooting require the use of metallic sights, and when this is the case, it is a high quality aperture sight that is chosen. These sights have adjustment screws for moving the aperture laterally and vertically so precise sighting in is possible. Today, because of the availability of telescopic sights, aperture sights are much less popular now than they were in the past except for formal target shooting. They were once very popular on hunting rifles. Some of the peep sights for use on hunting rifles could be adjusted then the settings locked in by means of locking screws. Generally, target type peep sights have large knobs that are easy to grasp and turn so that they can be adjusted quickly without tools. Some of the most sophisticated aperture sights that are intended for high-level competition are elegant instruments that sell for $300-400. Fine accuracy is possible when using an aperture sight if the shooter has good vision.

Peep sights are available in numerous configurations for the various shooting sports. Small models are available that clamp in the grooves that are present on the receivers of most rimfire rifles. Other models attach by means of screws to the side of the receiver. In times past, many rimfire rifles came drilled and tapped for receiver sights as well as with grooved receivers for attaching scope mounts. An example of that type of rifle is the Winchester 320, which is shown in the photo. Other than target rifles, few models are now marketed with provision for attaching peep sights to the receivers by screws.

Generally, the receiver sight is somewhat higher than an open rear sight. Therefore, the front sight must also be higher than the usual bead sight found on most rimfire rifles. Peep sights are normally used in combination with a front sight on a ramp or with a special target type front sight. Some of the target front sights have interchangeable inserts so that the shooter sees a post or an aperture.

The sight picture when using a peep sight is an important consideration. With the human eye automatically locating the center of the aperture, the top of the front sight and its placement on the target are the primary concerns. Generally, the top of the front sight is located in the center of the aperture. Then, the rifle is aimed so that the top of the post rests on the target in one of two ways. In the first, the rifle is held so that the round bull sits on top of the post with a sliver of light between the post and the bull. The reason that the sighting is not so that the bull sits exactly on the post is that with the post and bull being black it is not easy to see just how far the post is riding up on the bull. Therefore, it is preferable that a very thin sliver of light separate the top of the post and the bull. In the second procedure, the sights are adjusted so that the point of impact coincides with the location of the top of the post on the target. If targets of different sizes are fired at, the shooter will know that the bullets will strike where the top of the post rests on the target. This procedure should be followed for any aperture sight that is to be used in hunting situations because of different sizes and shapes of the targets.

In competitive shooting, the target-style peep sight is usually used in conjunction with a high front sight that has a hood. Many such front sights have a series of inserts in the form of circular blades that can be changed to suit the situation. A set of these insert blades usually consists of several apertures of different diameter and one or more posts of varying widths. When viewed through the aperture of the receiver sight, the aperture in the front insert makes another ring that then surrounds the bull on the target. The result is a series of concentric rings that can be aligned very accurately to obtain high accuracy.

Scopes

Telescopic sights (usually referred to as "scopes") are not a recent development. Snipers used them as long ago as the Civil War. For many years, scopes were fraught with several problems. They were relatively expensive, relatively fragile, and subject to problems such as fogging (condensation of moisture inside the scope under cool, humid conditions). These problems have largely been solved and scopes are so common today that many rifles are sold with no iron sights in anticipation that a scope will be mounted on the rifle. Even a relatively inexpensive scope can be rugged, fog proof, and have accurate adjustments.

Inside a scope is some sort of reticle that is aligned on the target to give the aiming point. Reticles consist of crosshairs, dots, circles, or some combination of these. The scope is constructed so that the target and the reticle appear in the same optical plane. The shooter merely aligns the reticle on the target and squeezes the trigger. A scope is the simplest, and for most people, the most accurate type of sight available.

The fact that a scope magnifies the target enables the shooter to see it more clearly. Therein lies one of the great advantages of this type of sight. With a circular aperture and a front sight and target of regular shape, it is possible to obtain an accurate sight picture with a peep sight. However, such an arrangement does not allow the shooter to see better. When the target has an irregular shape (as in hunting), the ability to see the target larger and clearer is an enormous advantage.

Ammunition testing is best accomplished by making use of a scope of high magnification like the 6-24X Tasco being used here by the author's wife, Kathy.

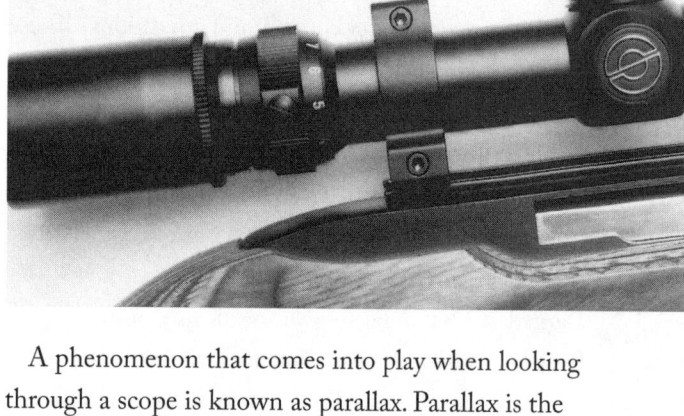

One of the superb optics for rimfire rifles is the Simmons 3-9X AO rimfire scope shown here mounted on a Ruger 10/22T.

A phenomenon that comes into play when looking through a scope is known as parallax. Parallax is the apparent movement of an object when the point of observation changes. It can be illustrated by the following procedure. With one arm extended, point your finger at an object and look at your finger and the object with one eye closed. Holding your arm stationary, look at the object with the other eye. Note how the object appears to have moved. What actually moved was the point of observation. When you look through a scope which has the reticle positioned on a target, the reticle may appear to move on the target as you move your eye from side to side. If so, the scope has parallax when the target at that distance.

Many people have trouble estimating distances with any degree of accuracy. They cannot tell whether an object is 50 or 90 feet away. There is a very elementary way that makes use of parallax to estimate the distance that separates you from an object. With your arm extended, point your finger at the object while looking at it with one eye closed. Close that eye and open the other. From the size of the object, estimate approximately how much it appears to move as you look at it first with one eye open and then the other. The object is approximately 10 times this distance from you. This procedure sounds crude (and it is), but you may be surprised how well you can estimate distance in this way after a little practice. There are numerous references distances that can be used. For example, most adults are approximately 5 to 6 feet tall. If you are estimating the distance to

The 6-20X Cabela's Outfitter scope features an adjustable objective.

some object with a person in your field of view, you can estimate the apparent movement of the object in relation to the height of the person. Suppose a paper target of normal size is located at some unknown distance from your shooting position. Try the procedure described above remembering that the target is probably about 1 foot in width. If it appears to move approximately a distance that is 10 times the size of the target (10 feet) when you observe it using each eye, it is probably about 100 feet away.

Scopes that are intended for use on center fire rifles are adjusted to have no parallax at a distance of 100 yards. A scope that is intended for use on a rimfire rifle is normally free of parallax at 50 yards. Some scopes that are designed for use on muzzle loaders or shotguns are parallax free at 75 yards. Unless the eye is positioned rather far from the axis of the scope, the parallax results in a very small error at normal rimfire ranges (25-100 yards). In my youth, I saw some very fine marksmanship demonstrated with a rimfire rifle that had a Weaver K4 scope mounted. That scope was intended for use on center fire rifles and was free of parallax at 100 yards.

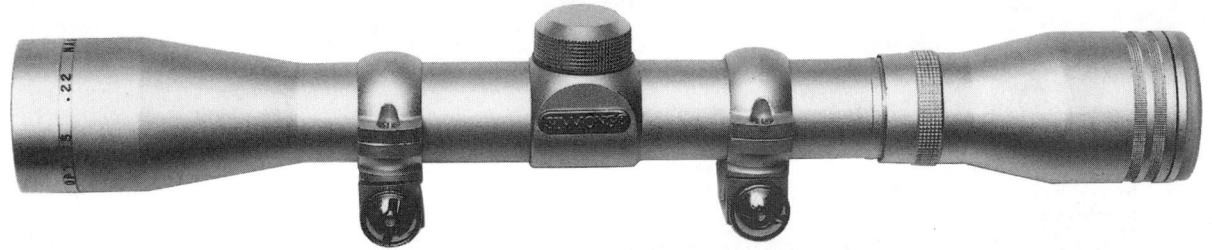

This Simmons 22 Mag scope is a 4X model that is available with a bright finish.

One type of scope has a front lens (objective) that can be rotated to focus the scope on targets at different distances. Scopes with an adjustable objective are designated by "AO" following the other description. For example, a scope designated as 2-7x32 AO is a variable scope with a magnification range of 2-7X and an adjustable objective of 32 mm diameter. Scopes of this type are advantageous for the rimfire shooter who may use the rifle on targets from 25 to 75 yards for the 22 LR or out to 150 yards if the rifle is a 17 HMR or 22 WMR because parallax can be eliminated at the range for which the scope is focused. However, such scopes tend to be rather expensive, but there are exceptions.

One characteristic of scopes that has not been mentioned to this point is that concerning the types of reticles. In the early days of scope use, the crosshair (fine wires) was by far the most common type of reticle. As time went on, it became clear that in dim light the fine wires were difficult to see, especially in a wooded area. Designers then produced scopes with reticles that consisted of a horizontal wire but instead of a vertical wire a tapered post was used. The idea behind this design was that the heavy post could be seen in dim light and if the rifle were sighted in so that the point of impact was at the top of the post, shots at game would be possible. Another type of reticle consists of a crosshair with a dot at the point of intersection. This is still a popular reticle with the size of the dot being determined by scope magnification and the anticipated targets. For example, high-powered scopes for use on varmints or targets have a very small dot. Scopes intended for use on large game are generally lower in magnification and have reticles with larger dots.

Scopes have also been produced that have a standard crosshair but an additional horizontal wire separated from the intersection by some specific amount that corresponds to a known distance at a given range. For example, the distance between the horizontal wires might represent six inches at a distance of 100 yards (which is equivalent to 12 inches at 200 yards, 18 inches at 300 yards, etc.). The idea behind this type of reticle is that it is possible to use the distance between the horizontal wires to estimate range. Suppose that a groundhog sitting vertically just fills the distance between the horizontal wires. If we assume that the groundhog has a height of 12 inches, then the range must be 200 yards. The successful use of this procedure requires the shooter to know the approximate size of the target being shot.

The fine crosshair reticle on some scopes can be difficult to see in wooded areas in dim light. Because of this, another approach to reticle design is the crosshair that has considerable thickness except near the intersection where the wires are thin. That way the outer portions of the reticle are easily seen and point the way to the fine crosshair which permits an

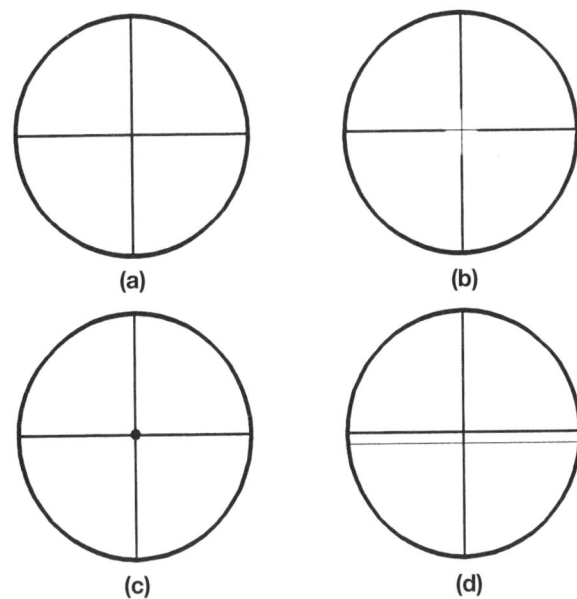

Types of reticules include (a) crosshair; (b) duplex; (c) crosshair with dot; and (d) range finder.

This fine Weaver 2.5-7X rimfire scope has adjustment knobs that require a coin to turn. Each click moves the point of impact 1/4 inch at 100 yards.

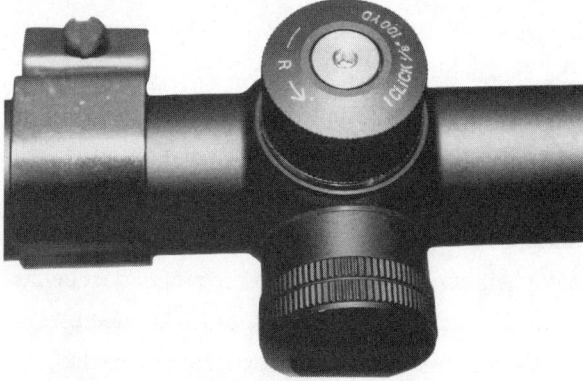

Adjustments on the Cabela's 6-24X AO are of the target type that can easily be turned by hand after the covers are removed. Each click represents 1/8 inch at 100 yards.

accurate aiming point. Sometimes known as duplex or dual-x reticles, they offer some of the better features of the standard crosshair while offering greater visibility. Almost all of the scopes that are intended for use on rimfire rifles (so-called rimfire scopes) have this type of reticle.

There are several other types of reticles some of which may be produced by only one manufacturer and not readily available on numerous types and brands of scopes. Almost all of the scopes owned by the author have either the duplex or fine crosshair type of reticle. The Weaver V-16 Classic was ordered specifically for testing purposes with the fine crosshair reticle because it permits the most accurate aim. Other scopes that are intended primarily for target shooting are offered with the fine crosshair reticles. For general use on rimfire rifles, the author could get along with no other type of reticle. It is the reticle that is found in some of my older scopes like the Weaver K4 and K6 models that were made in El Paso, Texas many years ago. These older models are not only collectible, but also excellent scopes for use on rimfire rifles. Several other scopes in my collection would have fine crosshair reticles if it were possible insert them easily. A Leupold Vari-X II 2.5-7X in my collection has a reticle that is very close to my idea of the perfect reticle. The reticle consists of a crosshair, but the wires are tapered so that where they cross the wires are very fine even though they get thicker toward the edges of the field of view. This reticle is easy to see in dim light, but the fine wires at the intersection permit a very accurate aim. Although several types of reticles have been described, there are numerous others that have been produced. It is rather like tread design on tires--almost endless in variety and each one better than all the rest. Even after using scopes having a variety of types of reticles, my favorite remains the standard crosshair type.

Another type of option exists with scopes made today. Although scopes were originally made with steel tubes that were polished and blued, it is now possible to buy scopes in other finishes. Almost all scopes have tubes that are made of "aircraft grade" aluminum, and cannot be blued by the processes used to blue steel. Instead, available finishes on scopes include gloss and matte black, nickel, and even camo. Therefore, it is possible to equip a rifle with a scope so that the finishes of the rifle and scope match. To my mind, rifles made of stainless steel look very good when the scope has the nickel finish. However, a camo finish on an optical device seems a little extreme to my conservative taste.

Turning knobs located on the scope turret makes adjustment of a scope for windage and elevation possible. Divisions are referred to as "clicks" and one click moves the point of impact a specific amount on the target. Of course, it is actually the point of aim that is being moved so that it coincides with the point where the barrel is sending the bullet. On most scopes, one click amounts to 1/4 inch of movement at 100 yards so it takes four clicks to make an adjustment of one inch. Other scopes have clicks that are equivalent to 1/2 inch at 100 yards

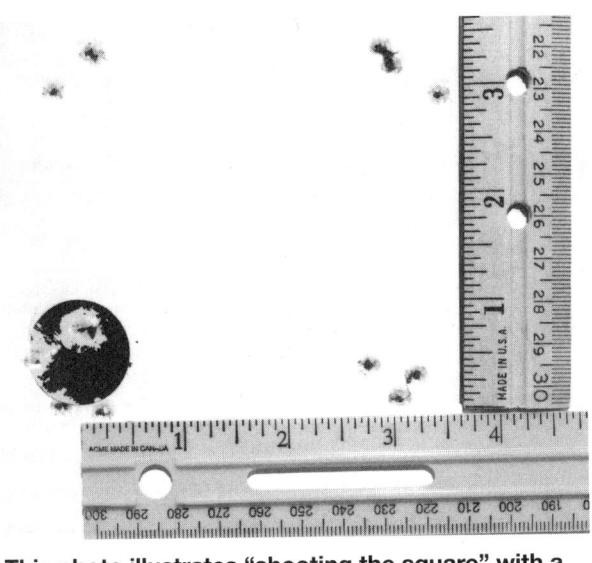

This photo illustrates "shooting the square" with a Weaver 2.5-7X rimfire scope in which 3-shot groups were fired at 50 yards as the scope was adjusted 24 clicks up, right, down, and left while aiming at the black dot. Note that the first three shots and the last three give a group of less than one inch after all adjustments have been made.

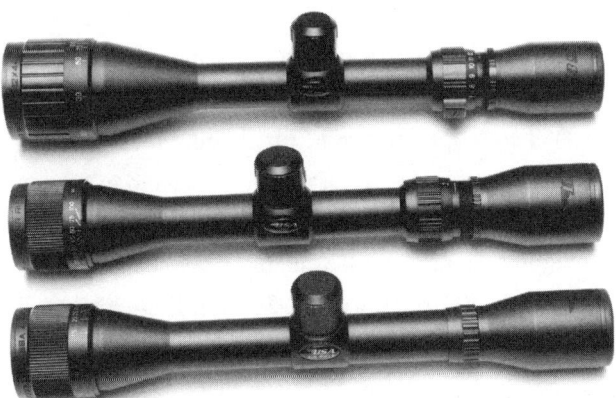

Although these BSA scopes are intended for use on air rifles, they work very well on rimfire rifles. Shown are (top to bottom) the 3-12X, 2-7X, and 4X models all of which have adjustable objectives.

This 0.4-inch group was fired at 50 yards with a Ruger 10/22T that was fitted with a Weaver 2.5-7X rimfire scope. One shot was fired at each power setting from 3X to 7X with no shift in the point of impact.

and some of the scopes intended mainly for target shooting have 1/8-inch clicks. These are usually the models that have high magnification. When selecting a scope for general use including plinking and small game or pest hunting, the magnitude of the adjustment produced by one click is unimportant. Most shooting with a rimfire will be conducted well inside of 100 yards, and at 50 yards one click moves the point of aim only one-half as much as it does at 100 yards. Thus, a scope that has 1/4-inch clicks at 100 yards has 1/8-inch clicks at 50 yards. If a rimfire rifle will produce one-inch groups at 50 yards, the group size itself measures eight clicks if the scope has 1/4-inch click adjustments. Only with extremely accurate target rifles and scopes of relatively high magnification does the amount of change produced by one click become important. The vast majority of scopes used on rimfire rifles have 1/4-inch clicks at 100 yards so it is actually not a problem to adjust the scope so that the point of impact and point of aim coincide to within the accuracy limit of the rifle.

Some scopes are constructed with adjustments that are measured in terms of minutes of angle (MOA) rather than in inches. A minute of angle is one-sixtieth of a degree. On a target at 100 yards, the distance represented by a change of one MOA at the firing point amounts to 1.047 inches. The difference between 1 MOA and 1 inch is so slight that it is insignificant in most instances. One click amounts to 0.250 inches in one case and 0.262 in the other. A very accurate rifle might produce groups measuring 1 inch at 100 yards. Moving the *average* point of impact (not that of any specific shot) exactly one inch or 1.047 inches will not cause any discernable difference. At 50 yards, it is even less important because one click represents 0.125 inch if four clicks equal one inch at 100 yards or 0.131 inch if four clicks represent one MOA.

The new Weaver Quad Lock comes in low, medium, and high versions. Four independent straps hold the scope to the bases of the rings.

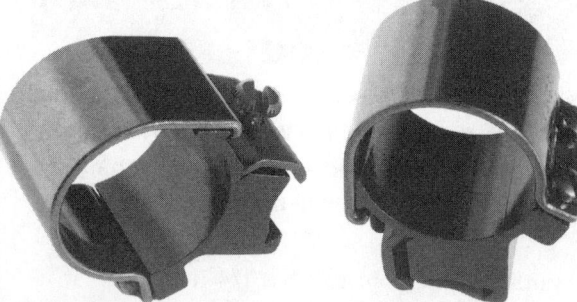

One of the most famous scope mounts for use on rimfire rifles is the Weaver Tip-Off mount that clamps in the grooves along the receiver.

The Leupold Rifleman mount shown here is sturdy and simple. Each part of the mount contains only two screws.

Of more importance than the magnitude of the correction produced by one click is the accuracy and reproducibility of the adjustments. In other words, does a change of four clicks produce a change of exactly one inch in point of impact? To test this, start with the rifle sighted in at 50 yards and fire a group of three or five shots. Next adjust the scope so that the point of impact is changed by some specific amount and shoot another group to see if the point of impact moves the expected distance from the first group.

One procedure for checking the accuracy of scope adjustments is known as shooting the square. In order to demonstrate this procedure, I took my Ruger 10/22T with a Weaver 2.5-7X rimfire scope in place and fired a three-shot group at 50 yards. Next, I adjusted the elevation by turning the knob 24 clicks to raise the point of impact. Since the scope has 1/4-inch clicks, that change should move the point of impact 6 inches at 100 yards or 3 inches at 50 yards. I then fired another three-shot group. The scope was then adjusted 24 clicks to move the point of impact three inches to the right and another three-shot group was fired. After adjusting the scope 24 clicks to shoot lower, another three-shot group was fired. Finally, adjustment was made for 24 clicks to the left, which would bring the point of impact back to the original position and three more shots were fired. The photo shows the results obtained. It is apparent that the point of impact at 50 yards was changed three inches by each of the 24-click adjustments. The final three shots merged nicely with the first three shots. This exercise demonstrated that the Weaver scope has adjustments that perform extremely accurately and reproducibly.

When scopes first came into common use, the magnification was almost always fixed and was usually 2.5, 4, or 6 power. Scopes having these magnifications are still available as are scopes having 8, 10, 16, 24, and 32X power. These high magnification scopes are generally labeled as target or varmint scopes. However, scopes having variable power are extremely popular now. Many magnification ranges will be observed from a casual examination of available scopes. Some of the most common are 2.5-7X, 3-9X, 4-12X, 4-16X, 6-24X, etc. On most scopes, rotating a ring located just in front of the eyepiece changes the magnification. Unless one has an extremely accurate rifle and is interested in extremely accurate bullet placement, most shooters will be well-served by a rimfire fitted with a 2.5-7X or 3-9X scope. It has been observed by many shooters that the scope is almost always set on the highest power available and left there.

There is always a question as to whether changing

The massive Beeman mount is extremely sturdy. It provides enough height for large scope objectives to clear the barrel.

Ruger scope mounts clamp in notches on the sides of the receivers. The tab in the base of each ring fits in a groove to prevent movement of the scope forward or backward.

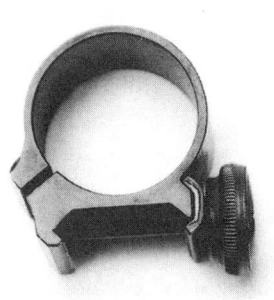 

Weaver-type bases attach to the receiver and the rings clamp to the bases.

the power of a scope might produce some change in the point of impact because the optical characteristics may be slightly different at different magnification. In order to test this, simply fire a group at 50 yards with the scope set on each magnification. I tested a Weaver 2.5-7X rimfire scope in this way. Using my Ruger 10/22T and SK Jagd. Standard Plus ammunition, I fired one shot with the scope set on 3, 4, 5, 6, and 7 power to produce the group shown in the photo. The group is simply a ragged hole that measures approximately 0.36 inches with no indication that the point of impact changes as the magnification is changed. This is the type of performance that characterizes a scope of good quality.

Most of the discussion presented has been directed toward the rifle shooter, but it need not be so. The makers of scopes and mounts have not ignored handgun shooters. Except for some of the small, short-barreled models, most of the popular handguns are amenable to mounting a scope. The major disadvantage of having a scope on a handgun is that it is no longer compact and convenient to carry. A special holster is needed to hold the scoped handgun, but this is not particularly troublesome to a hunter who is stalking or still-hunting in a woods. Some rimfire handguns are capable of outstanding accuracy, which can be achieved only when a scope is used. Most of the manufacturers mentioned in connection with rimfire scopes for rifles also have available models for use on handguns. In the case of handgun scopes, there is no distinction between those intended for use on center fire or rimfire handguns since they are generally used at similar ranges. There are many fine handgun scopes available from makers such as Simmons, Weaver, Leupold, Bushnell, and many others.

Because rimfire rifles produce almost no recoil, the majority of scope mounts have enough strength to hold a scope in place. Three scope-mounting systems are commonly used on rimfire rifles. First, the top of the receiver may have grooves for attaching scope mounts that clamp in the grooves. On rifles made in the U.S. or elsewhere for the U.S. market, the grooves are 3/8-inch (0.375 inch) apart but in other countries the groove separation is often 11mm (0.433 inch). Many clamp-on scope mounts have enough latitude in adjustment that they will work on rifles having grooves of either width. However, some mounts that are intended for use on rifles having the narrower grooves are held open farther by wider grooves so that when they are tightened there is a great deal of force on the movable side plate. When the locking screw is tightened sufficiently, that part of the mount can be bent because most of the inexpensive mounts made for use on rimfire rifles are made of aluminum. This can draw one end of the scope laterally out of alignment with the bore enough to make it impossible to sight in the scope. There are many sturdy clamp-on mounts available. One mount that has been marketed for many years is the Weaver Tip-Off mount. Made of steel, this is a proven, durable mount. Leupold produces the Rifleman mount that is made of aluminum, but it does not have a thin side section that can be bent during tightening. Another durable mount is made by Burris. It has a curved, movable side plate, but it is very sturdy. I have used all of these mounts with complete satisfaction.

Because some scopes have large diameter objectives, it is necessary to select a mount that holds the scope high enough to clear the barrel. One mount that will accomplish this is a mount available from Beeman that is intended for use on air rifles that produce heavy recoil. Although made of aluminum alloy, this massive mount is extremely sturdy and has enough latitude in adjustment to work well on rifles having 3/8-inch or 11mm grooves. This is the mount I choose when I want to mount my BSA 3-12 x 44 AO airgun scope on a rimfire rifle. It also provides enough height to allow most scopes to clear the open rear sight.

Mounting a scope on a pump rifle like this Winchester Model 90 is difficult because the top of the action moves and empty cases are ejected upward.

Although most rimfire rifles are produced with grooved receivers, some are produced with the receivers drilled and tapped to accept separate scope bases to which rings are attached. One type of scope base has long been known as the Weaver style base. The bases are made to properly fit only on specific rifles because of the differences in the shapes of the receivers. These bases are used in conjunction with rings available from Weaver and several other companies. The Thompson/Center Classic and the Remington 504 are designed with Weaver style bases. Some Anschutz rifles are produced with grooved receivers that are also drilled and tapped to accept Weaver style bases. This provides maximum versatility in scope mounting systems.

Ruger bolt action rimfire rifles have a unique proprietary scope mounting system. The receiver has milled notches and the scope rings have matching tabs that tighten in those notches. Transverse slots in the receiver accept small tabs that protrude from the bottom of the scope rings so that there is no possibility of the scope shifting forward or backward. Ruger rings are available in three heights (low, medium, and high) in both blue and stainless steel. Although Ruger supplies rings of its own making with its rifles, several other manufacturers also produce rings to fit Ruger rifles. Those that I have used with complete satisfaction include the models from Leupold and Warne.

Although grooved receivers are almost universal, a few rimfire rifles have no such provision for mounting a scope. For example, some pump action rifles have an open top action from which the breech block rises as the slide is operated. Such rifles eject empty cases upward and there is no way to attach a scope mount to the top of the action. However, the Henry pump rifle has a closed top receiver that is grooved to accept scope mounts. Because it ejects empty cases out of the side of the receiver, the Henry pump rifle can easily have a scope attached even though the rifle has an external hammer.

Red Dot and Laser Sights

In recent years, a type of optical sight known as a red dot sight has become available. Essentially, a red dot (red is used because it is quickly visible against almost any background) sight projects a battery powered red dot onto a lens. The sight is constructed so that when the shooter looks through the sight the dot can be placed on the target in much the same way as is the reticle of a scope. Moreover, when used correctly there is no parallax involved so sighting becomes as simple as moving the firearm so that the dot aligns with the target. In order to be useful in different lighting conditions, a rheostat is built in so that turning a dial can vary the brightness of the dot. Adjustments similar to those on scopes are provided so that the piece can be sighted in just as when a scope is used.

A red dot sight is usually mounted on a firearm in much the same way as a scope. One model that is available from Simmons is designed specifically for use on firearms having grooved receivers, and it comes with an integral mount that clamps directly in the grooves. However, in most cases, it is necessary to have a base or bases to which the red dot sight is attached. Because the Weaver-style base is so common, some red dot sights come with a rail along the bottom that can be attached to the base.

The basic idea behind the use of a red dot sight is that the bright dot can be located quickly on the target and there are only two things to align--the dot and the target. Obviously, the dot covers part of the target. For many of the more common sights, the coverage of the dot is three minutes of angle (3 MOA) while for others it may be 4 MOA. As a result, the red dot sight is not going to be used when firing

Brightness of the red dot is controlled by a rheostat that has eleven brightness settings.

Red dot sights are popular especially for use on handguns. This Simmons model is inexpensive but effective.

at a target 50 yards away to get the smallest group. It is a popular sight for International Practical Shooting Confederation (IPSC) events that involve speed and accuracy in handgun firing.

The word LASER is the acronym that comes from Light Amplification by Stimulated Emission of Radiation. Sure looks like a stupid name for a car doesn't it? In recent years, small lasers have been developed that project a red beam. It was inevitable that someone would come up with the idea that if the laser were attached to a firearm and adjusted so that the beam and the bullet path nearly coincide, the laser beam could be used in sighting. Moreover, the red beam can be seen in the dark so the sight would be effective for shooting in the dark. This has obvious advantages for law enforcement and military tactics and possibly for self-defense.

From my point of view, there is little justification for shooting a rimfire firearm in the dark. Recreational and sport shooting are not done in the dark. Target competition is conducted in daylight or on lighted ranges. However, the primary reason for my leaving laser sights to another forum deals with safety issues. Lasers are inherently dangerous and come with warning labels attached. When shined into an eye, there is no sensation of pain although irreparable damage is being done. Furthermore, the damage may be done very quickly. Laser pointers are very common and inexpensive. Having seen the complete ignorance demonstrated by children allowed to play with laser pointers, it seems incredible that we would want to mount a laser on a rimfire firearm of the type often used by young shooters. Laser sights have their place, but it is not on rimfire sporting firearms.

Chapter 6

RIMFIRE AMMUNITION

Modern manufacturing technology is the basis for the high quality rimfire ammunition available today. The basic materials of cartridge construction consist of lead, brass, nitrocellulose propellant, and lead styphnate in the primer, and this has been the situation for many years. However, the array of rimfire ammunition available today includes products that were not dreamed of only a few years ago. Having shot 22 rimfires for approximately 60 years, I am amazed at the variety of ammunition that is currently produced. In this chapter, we will give an overview of the ammunition offerings from many companies both domestic and foreign. How well I remember that when I was young a rimfire shooter bought the yellow box labeled Winchester, the green box labeled Remington, or the blue box labeled Federal. CCI did not begin to produce rimfire ammunition until 1963, but now produces an extensive line of products some of which are among the most innovative in the field. While some of the foreign producers were in business many years ago, their products were seldom seen. The situation now is quite different from what it was in my younger days.

Ammunition in rimfire calibers is available in many types that are designed for a wide range of uses.

Ammunition in 22 LR is produced all over the world.

The Sporting Arms and Ammunition Manufacturers Institute (known as SAAMI) provides standardization of ammunition so that specifications are uniform from one manufacturer to another. Test procedures are also standardized according to SAAMI specifications so that all ammunition makers are testing the same thing in the same way (barrel lengths, dimensions, etc.). Firearms are tested with overloads (proof loads), and SAAMI specifies those procedures as well as the standard dimensions for chambers and bores. If the specification for a 22 LR with a high-velocity load is a velocity of 1,255 ft/sec, that velocity, or one very close to it, is generally given by loads from other manufacturers. Sometimes there are minor variations because the hollow-point bullet produced by one company weights 37 grains while that from another firm weighs 38 grains. One finds that the performance data from most ammunition manufacturers is rather uniform. Of course, bullet designs, bullet lubricants, etc. vary from one company to another.

Rimfire ammunition is produced all over the world. There are literally hundreds of types loaded by dozens of loading companies both foreign and domestic. In this chapter, several specific types of ammunition will be described, but this is in no way a complete catalog of the offerings worldwide. Generally, if one manufacturer produces a particular load a different company will offer a similar product. In some ways, the products described in this chapter reflect wide availability rather than an attempt at being globally inclusive. In most cases, the types of ammunition described are those with which the author has had first hand experience. Some of the ideas discussed in this chapter will be revisited in later chapters because rimfire ammunition is a central theme in a book such as this.

Selection

In the history of rimfire ammunition presented in Chapter 1, a brief discussion of several of the currently popular calibers was given. In this section, we will give an overview of what the various ammunition manufacturers are producing in those calibers. Before we progress to a discussion of specific calibers, we need to present an overview of the types of rimfire ammunition currently being offered. An attempt has been made to reduce this information to a single table although the offerings of many manufacturers, especially foreign ones, were not studied. The summary of the types of rimfire ammunition available is presented in the accompanying table. Actual velocity data from testing and factors affecting velocity will be discussed in Chapter 7.

For many years, I did exactly what a large number of rimfire shooters do. I went to a couple of local stores in small towns and surveyed the ammunition available on the shelves. Eventually, as I perused the ammunition catalogs from several companies, it became apparent that there were many options that I had never considered. For example, there are some ammunition makers that produce a complete line of products while others may produce only two or three types. On the national scene, the best-known producers are CCI, Federal, Winchester, and Remington. On the other hand, large importers of foreign-made rimfire ammunition include Wolf, PMC, and Aguila among others. When added to offerings from the famous international makers like Lapua, RWS, Eley, CIL (Canada) and Baikal, it becomes apparent just how enormous the number of rimfire products has become. Most sporting goods stores will carry several types of rimfire ammunition, but you can be sure that many other types of cartridges are available.

The table contains an enormous amount of information, especially when you consider that there are actually a very large number of target loads manufactured around the world all of which utilize a 40-grain solid bullet with a muzzle velocity of around 1080 ft/sec and are thus represented by a single row in the table. In some cases, the entry is for a single load. For example, the Lapua Scoremax is unique in that it employs a 48-grain solid lead bullet. Similarly, the Aguila Sniper Subsonic (SSS) is loaded with a 60-grain solid bullet. Also included in the table is the 5mm Remington Magnum which is listed for comparison even though it has not been produced for almost 30 years. The author (among many others) certainly wishes it were still available and that new rifles were being produced in that excellent caliber. A casual glance at the data for that round shows that it gave impressive performance, but that subject will be explored in more detail elsewhere. With the table containing a summary of the relevant data for ammunition in each of the modern rimfire calibers, we will now progress to a discussion of each cartridge. As it turns out, the order of discussing the cartridges is in the order of their historical development as it progresses through the series from the 22 Short, Long, Long Rifle, WRF, and WMR calibers.

The Lapua Scoremax has a 48-grain bullet while the Aguila SSS utilizes a 60-grain projectile in a short case.

Projectiles

When I became a rimfire shooter, one had a choice of ammunition with solid round-nose bullets or hollow-points. There were two velocity levels, standard-velocity and high-velocity, but hollow-pointed bullets were usually available only in high-velocity rounds. If there were other options, I did not know about them for many years. Today, those early types of projectiles are still available, but so are many others. Standard-velocity ammunition is often used for target shooting. The author participated as a member of a very successful Air Force ROTC rifle team, and our equipment consisted of Winchester Model 52D target rifles and Federal standard-velocity ammunition. The loading companies have optimized the velocity of that load so that the bullets travel at velocities that are lower than the velocity of sound. As a projectile (or airplane) goes through the sound barrier, there are shock waves

A Summary of Rimfire Ammunition Types.*

Cartridge	Bullet type	Wt. gr.	Vel, ft/sec Muz./100 yd	E, ft lb Muz./100 yd	Notes
17 Aguila	JHP	20	1850/1353	152/81	A, PMC
17 Mach 2	JPT	17	2100/1510	166/88	H, CCI, E
17 HMR	JPT	17	2550/1900	245/135	E,H,F,R,CCI
17 HMR	JHP	20	2375/1775	250/140	H, CCI
5mm Rem. Magnum	JHP	38	2100/1606	372/217	R (obsolete)
22 Short CB	SRN	29	710/581	32/27	CCI
22 Short	SRN	29	830/679	44/30	CCI TGT.
22 Short	SRN	29	1095/903	77/52	A, CCI, R
22 Short	HP	27	1105/879	73/46	CCI
22 Long CB	SRN	29	710/581	32/22	CCI
22 Long	SRN	29	1215/922	95/55	CCI
22 Long	SRN	20	375/183	6/--	A Colibri
22 Long	SRN	20	500/---	11/---	A S. Colibri
22 Long Rifle	HP	38	1000/854	84/62	PMC Mod.
22 Long Rifle	HP	38	1050/901	93/69	R, E Sub.S.
22 Long Rifle	SRN	40	1050/---	98/---	Wolf MT
22 Long Rifle	SRN	40	1033/---	95/---	Wolf Match
22 Long Rifle	SRN	40	1080/930	105/75	Most Mfrs.
22 Long Rifle	SRN	40	1150/976	117/85	W T22
22 Long Rifle	HP	38	1280/1020	140/90	Most Mfrs.
22 Long Rifle	SRN	40	1255/1020	140/93	Most Mfrs.
22 Long Rifle	SRN	40	1312/1100	154/107	E
22 Long Rifle	HP	37.5	1312/1100	143/100	E
22 Long Rifle	HP	40	1280/1001	146/89	W P.P.
22 Long Rifle	STC	36	1410/1056	159/89	R Viper
22 Long Rifle	HPTC	33	1500/1075	165/85	R Yel.Jkt.
22 Long Rifle	HP	32	1640/1124	191/90	CCI Stgr.
22 Long Rifle	HP	40	1435/1112	183/110	CCI Vctr.
22 Long Rifle	SFP	40	1235/1015	135/91	CCI SGB
22 Long Rifle	HP	30	1750/1191	204/95	A
22 Long Rifle	SRN	30	1750/1191	204/95	A
22 Long Rifle	SRN	48	1040/---	117/---	L Scoremax
22 Long Rifle	SRN	60	950/802	120/86	A SSS
22 WRF	SFP	45	1300/1023	169/105	W
22 WRF	JHP	45	1300/1056	169/112	CCI
22 WMR	JHP	30	2200/1419	325/120	CCI, F
22 WMR	PT	33	2000/1495	293/164	R Premier
22 WMR	JHP	34	2120/1435	338/155	W Supreme
22 WMR	JHP	40	1910/1326	324/156	W, R,PMC, F
22 WMR	JHP	40	1875/1375	312/168	CCI
22 WMR	FMJ	40	1875/1375	312/168	CCI
22 WMR	FMJ	40	1910/1326	324/156	W, R,PMC, F
22 WMR	JHP	50	1650/1280	300/180	F

*In some cases such as that of the 40-grain round-nose 22 LR, the high-velocity load is listed as 1235, 1250, 1255, or 1260 depending on the manufacturer. These are not considered as constituting different loadings. Velocities for the standard-velocity 22 LR are given as 1050, 1070, 1080, or 1085 depending on the manufacturer.

Abbreviations: SRN=solid round-nose; SFP=solid flat point; HP=hollow point; STC=solid truncated cone; HPTC=hollow point truncated cone; JPT=jacketed polymer tip; JHP=jacketed hollow point; JSP=jacketed soft point; FMJ=full metal jacket; TGT=target; SSS=Sniper SubSonic.

Notes: Most Mfr. indicates that this load or one very similar to it is offered by most manufacturers. A=Aguila; CCI=CCI; E=Eley, F=Federal; H=Hornady; L=Lapua R=Remington; W=Winchester; PMC=PMC, Vctr.=Velocitor; Stgr.=Stinger; SGB=small game bullet; P.P.=power point; Mod=Moderator; MT=Match Target; Sub. S.= Subsonic.

Remington target loads represent a joint offering with Eley.

The CCI SGB cartridges offer the small game hunter a flat-pointed projectile for greater impact.

that build up on the nose. This causes some instability in the bullet's flight, which reduces accuracy. Consequently, 22 LR ammunition intended for target use is loaded to subsonic velocities. Minor variations may be present in the profiles of projectiles from different manufacturers. In some cases, the highest quality target ammunition offered by a company is really nothing more than lots of the standard-velocity load, which are particularly uniform. Just as the old Federal load showed me long ago, some of the most accurate ammunition tested in this work were the standard-velocity, solid bullet loads. A check of the results displayed in Chapter 13 will confirm this conclusion. In most of the rifles tested, the CCI Standard-velocity ammunition was very accurate with the Winchester T22 being very close in performance. These loads should always be tried when you are searching for ammunition that gives high accuracy at a lower cost than the ammunition used in high-level competition.

Also among the types of standard-velocity ammunition with the 40-grain solid point bullet that should be tried when searching for highest accuracy are CCI Green Tag and Federal Gold Medal Target (Federal product number 711B). Federal offered their Ultra Match ammunition for many years (which usually sold at retail for around $10 per box), but it has recently been discontinued along with the Gold Medal Match. The 711B load is a standard-velocity round, but it is essentially a target load that sells for a retail price of approximately $2.50 per box. This ammunition also exhibited outstanding accuracy in some of the rifles tested. Target ammunition is also available from Remington in the load known simply as Remington Target (product number 6122). In a liaison with the noted Eley company in

Hyper-velocity loads for the 22 LR have become popular. Shown here (left to right) are the CCI Stinger, Winchester Expediter, Federal Spitfire, Winchester Super-Max, Winchester Superspeed, Remington Yellow Jacket, and Remington Viper. Some of these are no longer available.

Although the velocity of the 60-grain bullet from the Aguila SSS load is low, it is a useful cartridge.

England, Remington markets three grades of target ammunition. These are the Target Rifle, Club Xtra, and Match EPS in the order of increasing quality (and price). This is really excellent ammunition for the target shooter. A wide variety of rimfire ammunition is available from PMC including Scoremaster and Match Rifle loads which have 40-grain round-nose solid bullets. Both of these gave good accuracy in the rifles tested as did the Wolf Match Target. The Wolf Match Target rimfire ammunition is made in Germany. We will have more to say about this load in Chapter 13. In addition to the products listed, outstanding ammunition is produced by RWS, Eley, Aguila, Lapua, and others. The problem is one of availability because you simply cannot walk into your local "mart" and find most of these brands. For almost all of the types mentioned above, the muzzle velocity is approximately 1,080 and 1,150 ft/sec.

Although the emphasis in this discussion has been with regard to accuracy, the standard-velocity 22 LR should also be considered a hunting load. The rationale is simply that such ammunition gives good accuracy (often superb accuracy) so it is easier to put the bullet in the desired location on the target. Strange as it may seem, standard-velocity bullets are not affected as much by wind as are the high-velocity ones. In my old Winchester 190 semiautomatic, the best accuracy obtained when several types of ammunition were tested was with the CCI Standard-velocity. The average group size using this load in both my Ruger 10/22 and 10/22T was well under an inch. With this type of accuracy, it is easy to perform sniping on pests and small game. Penetration by the relatively slow moving solid bullets is outstanding.

High-velocity ammunition is also produced with 40-grain solid bullets. In fact, this may be the most popular type, and prices cover a broad spectrum. Federal Champion (which was formerly known as Lightning) is currently available at one of the large "marts" for $0.98 per box. In the same price range are the Winchester Wildcat, Remington Thunderbolt, and the CCI Blaser. These price leader loads may perform well in some rifles, and they certainly should be tested to find out. If one or more of them give good accuracy in your rifle or handgun, by all means use them. I particularly like to shoot such ammunition in a handgun because gilt-edge accuracy is not particularly important given my abilities with a handgun.

Moving up in price, one finds the Federal, Winchester, Remington, CCI, PMC, and other brands loaded with the 40-grain bullets. Some brands have bullets that are copper plated rather than uncoated, lubricated lead. As with any other type of ammunition, the major concern is accuracy in your particular firearm. I never hesitate to choose any of these loads when I am sniping varmints or hunting small game as long as I have determined in advance how accurate they are in the rifle I am using. There is no substitute for the confidence that comes from firing consistently small groups with your rifle and ammunition.

Solid bullets are not always of the round-nose variety.

The CCI Stinger on the left has a case that is longer than that of the standard 22 LR.

CCI produces a load known as the SGB (Small Game Bullet) that contains a 40-grain flat point lead bullet. The flat point bullet produces a greater shock effect than that resulting from a round-nose bullet but without the destructive effect and with greater penetration than a hollow point gives. Moreover, this load has shown excellent accuracy in several rifles. Being a specialty load, the price is around $3.50 to $4.00 per box.

Aguila produces a load known as the SSS (SubSonic Sniper) that utilizes a 60-grain solid-point bullet. To produce a round having the SAAMI overall length for a 22 LR, the long bullet requires a shorter case than that normally used in 22 LR cartridges. Consequently, the SSS load may not function reliably in some rifle actions. Nominal muzzle velocity is only 950 ft/sec, but it gives excellent penetration. Some writers have reported that accuracy of this load may not be acceptable in all firearms. This is not surprising because with a rifling twist of one turn in 16 inches the slow moving, heavy bullet may not be adequately stabilized which could affect accuracy.

During the testing of a large quantity of ammunition comprising a considerable number of types, one load that the author had never used before became a favorite. The European firm, Lapua, produces some of the finest rimfire ammunition available. One type is known as Lapua Scoremax, and it is loaded with a 48-grain solid bullet. This load is intended for target use, specifically silhouette shooting in which a heavy blow is needed to knock over the metal animal. Not only is a heavy blow needed, the ammunition must deliver target-grade accuracy. As might be expected, such ammunition is not cheap, and I paid $8.00 per box for the Scoremax. This might sound incredibly high because it means shooting this ammunition costs as much as if you were shooting a 17 HMR or a 22 WMR, but you are actually getting a comparable level of performance. True, I do not use Scoremax for plinking pine cones, but to use half a box during a hunt is quite reasonable.

As was described briefly in Chapter 1, the hyper-velocity loads in 22 LR have become very popular. All make use of lighter bullets propelled by larger charges of slower-burning powders to achieve velocities of approximately 1,500 to 1,650 ft/sec. With hollow-point bullets at high-velocity, the hyper-velocity loads produce dramatic effects at short ranges. The point of impact of the bullets from hyper-velocity loads is frequently quite different from that of heaver, slower bullets from ordinary rounds. Do not buy a box of hyper-velocity ammunition and go hunting without sighting in your rifle with that ammunition. Accuracy has never been a strong point with hyper-velocity loads. Do some accuracy testing with this type of ammunition before you depend on it to bring home your next meal.

Another innovative bullet design from CCI is known as the Quik-Shok. Loaded in a longer case like that used for the Stinger, the Quik-Shok bullet weighs 32 grains and has a muzzle velocity of 1,640 ft/sec. However, the bullet is designed to break into four pieces on impact to maximize the devastation on pests. Like the lightweight bullets used in other hyper-velocity loads, the bullet used in the Quik-Shok loses its velocity rapidly.

The 22 Short

Being the original 22 rimfire, the 22 Short has the distinction of having been in continuous production longer than any other cartridge (disregarding BB and

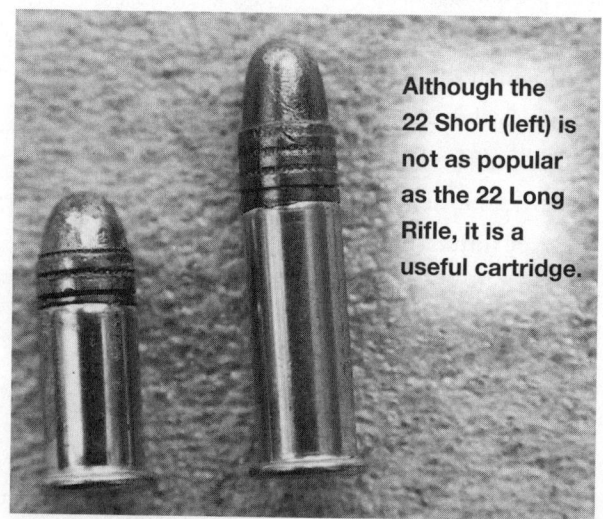

Although the 22 Short (left) is not as popular as the 22 Long Rifle, it is a useful cartridge.

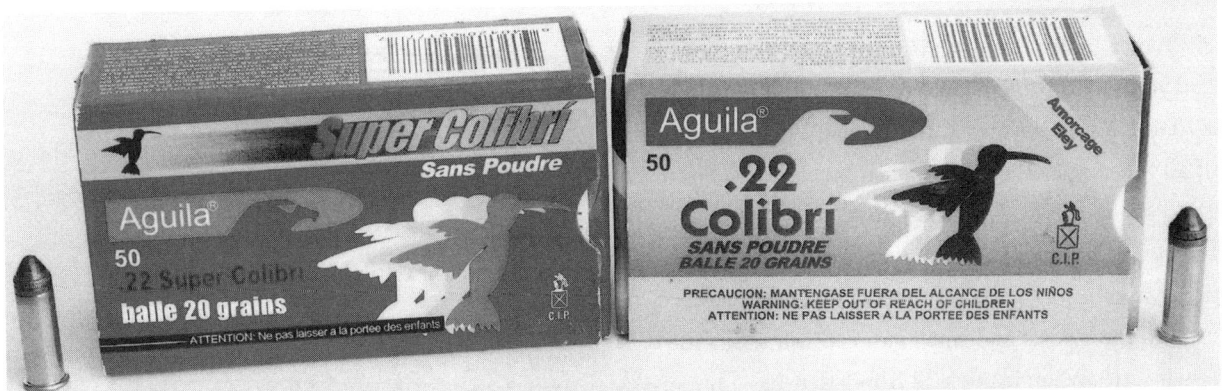

The Aguila Colibri and Super Colibri cartridges make use of 20-grain bullets that are propelled only by the priming.

CB caps which contain no powder). That span is approximately 150 years! However, the 22 Short is less popular now that it was in former times. About the only firearms produced specifically for the 22 Short today are some specialty target pistols and a couple of models of tiny auto-loading handguns. Many years ago, Winchester produced the Model 1890 pump rifle and the Model 74 autoloader chambered for the 22 Short only. Browning produced the sleek Model SA 22 autoloader in 22 Short. In some cases, these rifles were known as gallery specials because of their use in shooting galleries. The author can well remember how the county fair always had a shooting gallery, and how he once won a small lamp for knocking over some number of consecutive targets. As the world has become more civilized, such activities are no longer tolerated.

The use of the 22 Short in chambers designed for the 22 LR is often discouraged by someone on the grounds that the shorter cartridge will lead to corrosion that will make chambering the longer cartridge difficult. All I can say is that if it were to happen it would take a lot of firing of the 22 Short to cause a problem. All that is required is to brush out the residue with a nylon brush wet with a powder solvent. Having said that, it must be conceded that 22 Shorts fired in a 22 LR chamber do not normally give highest accuracy. The bullet from the shorter cartridge must jump some distance before it gets to the rifling, which usually is detrimental to accuracy. While this is a factor, there is another that is likely

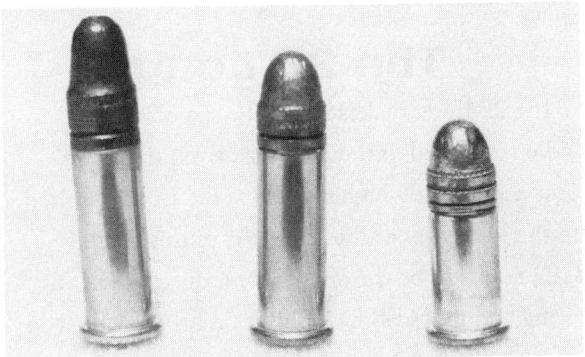

The 22 Long (middle) offers little power advantage over the 22 Short and generally does not give the accuracy of the 22 LR.

even more important. The stubby little 29-grain bullet used in the 22 Short requires less spin to stabilize in flight than does the longer 40-grain bullet used in a 22 LR. The rate of twist used in 22 LR barrels is one turn in 16 inches while the optimum twist for the 22 Short bullet is about 1 turn in 21 inches. Therefore, the short bullet is over stabilized in barrels with the faster twist. Firearms designed specifically for the 22 Short normally have the slower twist that is optimum for the cartridge.

Current offerings in the 22 Short are not nearly as extensive as are those for the 22 LR. Winchester, Remington, and CCI produce 22 Short ammunition with a 29-grain solid point bullet that has a nominal muzzle velocity of 1095 ft/sec and an energy of 77 ft lbs. Aguila, Eley, and RWS also produce 22 Short ammunition include some that is intended for target shooting. While this certainly looks puny, keep in mind that this is almost exactly the remaining energy given by a bullet from the 17 HMR at a range of 200 yards, and some people seem to think that it is a good load for coyotes at that range! When I think of all the species that I took with an old Winchester 1890 pump using 22 Shorts I vow never to take this round lightly. If an air rifle firing a 177 caliber pellet weighing 7.9 grains at 1000 ft/sec can be used to hunt pests and small game, think about the possibilities when using a 22 Short that has a bullet weighing almost four times as much traveling at the same velocity.

The 22 Long

The 22 Long makes use of the same 29-grain bullet as is used in the 22 Short. Even though it produces slightly higher velocity, the Long is suited to the same uses as the Short. As of this writing, CCI seems to be the only U.S. producer of the 22 Long and that load has a 29-grain solid bullet at an advertised muzzle velocity of 1,215 ft/sec and a muzzle energy of 95 ft lbs. Although most stores that sell rimfire ammunition do not carry the Long, there is little reason to try to find it because it is not a better cartridge than the 22 Short and does not even approach the 22 LR. One advantage, a minor one, is that the case length of the Long is identical to that of the Long Rifle so there is no likelihood that a ring can be produced in the chamber as a result of firing a cartridge having a shorter case.

Aguila produces two rounds, the Colibri and Super Colibri, which make use of the Long/Long Rifle case containing 20-grain bullets propelled only by the priming mixture (they are "*sans poudre*"). These are loaded to very low velocity and are intended for exterminating small vermin or shooting indoors in a suitable place with a suitable backstop. The Colibri and Super Colibri have essentially the same power as some airguns. The boxes of the lower-powered Colibri cartridges carry the warning that they are not for use in rifles because having such low power there is a chance that the bullet would become lodged in the barrel.

The 22 Long Rifle

If there is a universal cartridge, it surely must be the 22 Long Rifle. Loaded throughout the world, the 22 LR is a used for recreation, sport shooting, and hunting. It is also the basis for several shooting sports that are designed specifically for the use of rimfire firearms. Originally produced with a 40-grain lead bullet propelled by a charge of 5 grains of black powder, the 22 LR has undergone enormous changes over the lifetime of the cartridge which is almost six score years. The 22 LR has reached an almost unbelievable state of technical development, and the number of ammunition types is quite large. This discussion is rather an expansion of that presented earlier under the heading of projectiles.

Probably the most commonly encountered type of 22 LR ammunition (in terms of number of stores that carry it and the number of rounds expended annually) is the high-velocity load that utilizes a 40-grain solid bullet at a velocity of 1,225 to 1,275 depending on the manufacturer. Current offerings include the very economical Federal Champion, Remington Thunderbolt, CCI Blaser, and Winchester Wildcat varieties that are the promotional price leaders at right around $1.00 per box. However, the regular varieties of this loading that sell for $1.75 to $2.50 per box are also available from numerous manufacturers. The hollow point high-velocity load has a bullet that weights 36 to 38 grains and a muzzle velocity of approximately 1,275 ft/sec. These loads have been the mainstay of the small game hunter, pest shooter, and plinker for many years.

Another of the ubiquitous 22 LR loads is the 40-grain solid bullet loaded to so-called standard-velocity, which is

Remington hyper velocity rounds like the Viper (right) make use of a bullet which has a nose in the shape of a truncated cone.

around 1,050 to 1,100 ft/sec depending on the manufacturer. Prominent among this type of load are the Federal Gold Medal Target (Load No. 711B), Remington Target, CCI Standard Velocity, Wolf Match Target, and numerous others. Some of these types carry the designation as "target" loads even though they may not sell for a premium price as do the cartridges intended for high-level target shooting. The T22 from Winchester is of the standard-velocity type although with a velocity of 1,150 ft/sec the velocity is actually more of an intermediate between the high and standard-velocity rounds. Some rifles give accuracy with the standard-velocity ammunition that rivals that given with the highest quality target ammunition that is intended for competitive shooting. This will be clear from the test results presented in Chapter 13. The accuracy of standard-velocity ammunition comes as no surprise to the author after shooting competitively with it in a Winchester 52D.

At the upper end of the ammunition spectrum there are several types of ammunition that are intended for target competition at the highest levels. These include Federal Ultra Match, Eley Tenex, Lapua Midas, Winchester Supreme, and similar loads from other manufacturers. A price of around $10 per box is not unusual for ammunition of this degree of excellence. In many instances, the velocity matches that of the standard-velocity load, which makes it possible to practice with a lower cost round then to switch to the target loads for competition. Although the intended use of the high-priced target ammunition is for competitive shooting, many hunters using rimfire rifles choose to use this type of ammunition because of its outstanding accuracy. Careful, accurate bullet placement is more important than the additional 100 to 150 ft/sec velocity given by high-velocity loads. Having seen how some of my rifles perform with the standard-velocity and target cartridges, I have begun to consider them for small game hunting.

The competitive pistol shooter has available ammunition specifically intended for such purposes.

Shot cartridges have been popular for many years. The CCI load uses a plastic shot capsule while the Winchester and Remington varieties employ the crimped case.

The handgun shooter has not been forgotten. Several ammunition manufacturers such as RWS, CCI, and Eley produce 22 LR ammunition specifically for pistol competition. In fact, Eley produces a complete line of pistol ammunition.

There are a few types of 22 LR ammunition that deserve special mention. One of them is Lapua Scoremax which uses a 48-grain bullet at a nominal velocity of 1,040 ft/sec. Even at a rather low velocity, the heavy bullet gives outstanding impact and the accuracy is superb. Scoremax has become a favorite hunting load even though the cost of a box is approximately three times that of some of the ordinary types. The author is indebted to biathalon competitor Marc Sheppard of Altius Handcrafted Firearms, W. Yellowstone, Montana for introducing him to Scoremax and several other types of high-quality ammunition. Why am I impressed with Lapua Scoremax? First and foremost, in my bolt action Ruger 77/22 with an old Weaver K-10 scope, the *average* size for five 5-shot groups at 50 yards was only 0.60-inch and the smallest was only 0.46-inch! With this level of accuracy, I know that the target will be hit if I do my part. Second, the heavy 48-grain bullet gives real smash and penetration on

Although it is over a century old, the 22 WRF (right) is still available and can be fired in rifles chambered for the 22 WMR.

The two loads available for the 22 WRF are the Winchester (left), which has a 45-grain flat-point bullet and the CCI (right) which uses a 45-grain hollow-point bullet.

game. From the 22-inch barrel of my Ruger 77/22, the average velocity at 8 feet from the muzzle is 1,042 ft/sec, which corresponds to an energy of 117 ft lbs. Keep in mind that this is a bullet that is 20 percent heavier than the usual weight for solid 22 LR bullets, and as a result it is not as prone to deflection by wind.

Although I was reasonably well versed in the 22 LR ammunition scene, I would never have found Lapua Scoremax at the usual mass merchandisers. Such stores sell in quantity, usually with a low profit margin, rather than offering a comprehensive line of ammunition. Thanks to Mark Shepherd, I found out about a type of ammunition that has become one of my favorites. Therein lies one of the advantages of patronizing specialty shops owned and operated by experts in the field who have a wealth of knowledge. For the plinker who also participates in small game hunting and dispatching an occasional pest, it is not necessary to go to such lengths. However, the serious rimfire hobbyist realizes that improvements in accuracy and performance come small increments, which may mean special ammunition. For those seeking to get the most out of their equipment, all options will be explored.

Hyper-velocity ammunition has become quite popular in recent years. Following the introduction of the CCI Stinger in 1977, other types of cartridges appeared that made use of bullets weighing 29 to 35 grains pushed by larger charges of slower-burning powder. With velocities in the 1,500 to 1,700 range, the trajectory is less curved, and the lightweight bullets give explosive results on small game and varmints. One negative factor related to hyper-velocity ammunition is that accuracy is not always as good as with some of the more pedestrian loads. Of the hyper-velocity rounds, the Remington Yellow Jackets are the favorite of the author for several reasons. First, they do not have a case that is longer than the conventional 22 LR, which can engage the rifling in match type chambers. Second, they seem to give better accuracy in some of my rifles than other hyper-velocity loads. Third, the 33-grain bullet has enough mass to impart a significant blow while the large hollow cavity assures expansion.

Even with the desirable features of hyper-velocity loads, the fact remains that the lightweight bullets lose velocity rapidly so their advantage is lost if the range is about 75 yards or longer.

Although not listed in the table, 22 LR cartridges loaded with No. 12 shot are available for dispatching small vermin and birds at short (no, make that very short) ranges. Fired from a rifled barrel, the shot

The 17 HMR has been enormously successful. New ammunition offerings have appeared rapidly.

spreads quickly so that an effective pattern is not maintained beyond the range of a dozen or so feet. The CCI shot cartridges have the shot load contained in a plastic case that is loaded in the same manner as a bullet. Shot cartridges from other manufacturers have the shot load held a long case that is crimped at the top. Except for revolvers in which the shot cartridges work very well, shot cartridges must be used in a single-shot mode, and they may not eject reliably from autoloaders.

The 22 Winchester Rim Fire (WRF)

The 22 WRF was all but dead for many years. Rifles in that caliber were no longer being produced, and many shooters of the original Winchester Model 1890 pump had moved on to other rifles or the happy hunting ground. Finally, as is so often the case, it was discovered that a small residual demand for the cartridges persisted. Winchester responded with a manufacturing run of 22 WRF in 1986. Perhaps the users of 22 WMR firearms discovered that the 22 WRF cartridges performed respectably in their guns because the demand was such that Winchester is again offering the 22 WRF ammunition in its regular line of ammunition. In the seemingly never-ending expansion of their rimfire line, CCI also markets the 22 WRF loads. The specified diameter of the rim and case near the base is approximately 0.004-inch larger for the WRF than for the WMR. Such a small difference allows the shorter WRF case to chamber easily in WMR rifles. Bullet diameter for the WMR is 0.224-inch while that of the WRF is 0.226-inch. Having no tough jacket, the larger diameter bullet of the WRF swages to 0.224-inch readily and still gives accuracy that is acceptable for shooting small game and pests at moderate ranges.

The CCI load in 22 WRF consists of a 45-grain jacketed hollow-point bullet at a nominal velocity of 1,300 ft/sec, which produces 169 ft lbs of energy. At 50 yards, the velocity is 1,147 ft/sec and the energy is 132 ft lbs, and at 100 yards the values are 1,056 ft/sec and 112 ft lbs. A high-velocity 22 LR has a muzzle energy of about 135 ft lbs and a remaining energy at 100 yards of 91 ft lbs. Consequently, the 22 WRF is slightly more powerful than the 22 LR, but not enough to make much difference in practical terms.

Winchester's 22 WRF load consists of a 45-grain flat-nosed lead bullet that has a muzzle velocity of 1,300 ft/sec which gives an energy of 169 ft lbs. However, the bullet has a different shape than that used in the CCI version of the cartridge so the remaining velocity at 100 yards is 1,023 ft/sec and the energy at that distance is 105 ft lbs. With a bullet that is 5 grains heavier than most 22 LR solids, the 22 WMR is slightly better as a game load than is the 22 LR. Most rifles that are chambered for the 22 WRF will not quite equal the accuracy shown by 22 LR firearms especially since there are so many more options in ammunition for the 22 LR shooter to choose from.

The availability of 22 WRF ammunition enables shooters with vintage rifles to continue to use these arms. Quite by surprise I found that 22 WRF ammunition gives accuracy that is quite good in my Ruger 77/22M. Therefore, I now have a lower powered load, but I must sight in my rifle for it. There is no real cost savings since a box of the specialty 22 WRF sells for approximately the same price as a box of the more powerful 22 WMR.

The 22 Winchester Magnum Rimfire (WMR)

As we move upward in the ammunition hierarchy, we come to the 22 WMR. This round was introduced in 1959 to provide the varmint and small game hunter

Bullets loaded in 22 WMR ammunition include (left to right) the polymer-tipped, soft-point, and hollow-point styles.

with a round that extends the range and effectiveness of the 22 LR. With a 40-grain bullet that has a higher velocity at 100 yards than a similar weight bullet from the muzzle of a 22 LR, the 22 WMR is a powerful round. Muzzle energy of the 22 WMR is over twice that of a 22 LR high-velocity load. This is important for the varmint hunter, but it may well be massive overkill for the small game hunter who would like to have something left to cook. One possible exception, where legal, is the use of the 22 WMR on wild turkeys. Rabbits, squirrels, and opossums up trees are simply not that hard to kill. A standard-velocity 22 LR solid round or a hollow point will do the job very well when placed accurately. After all, hunting small game and pests with air rifles is becoming more common, and the vast majority of them do not have even the energy of a 22 Short! What is important is bullet placement.

As a varmint load, the 22 WMR is in a different league from the 22 LR. Varmints as large as fox or coyote are fair game for the 22 WMR as long as the range is reasonable (100 yards or so) and an accurate rifle is used. The 22 WMR is an excellent choice for groundhogs or marmots when the range is 125 yards or under. The original load for the 22 WMR as introduced by Winchester was a 40-grain jacketed hollow-point bullet loaded to almost 2,000 ft/sec. The current velocity is advertised as 1,910 ft/sec. Because of the explosive nature of the hollow-point bullet, a 40-grain bullet with a full metal jacket was offered. For many years, those constituted the choices of ammunition in 22 WMR produced by Winchester and CCI. Unlike the Winchester load, which uses a jacketed bullet, some manufacturers load 22 WRM ammunition with plated bullets. In most instances, these work just about as well as the jacketed bullets but may give less penetration.

As with other rimfire calibers, the choice of ammunition in 22 WMR has grown dramatically in recent years. Soon after the hyper-velocity loads in 22 LR were introduced, the 22 WMR was to experience the same evolution. Bullets as light as 30 grains were loaded to velocities in the 2,200 ft/sec range. Most of these bullets had gaping hollow-points so that they would blow up small varmints. However, they also lost velocity rapidly so that at a range of 100 yards, the remaining energy was only 120 to 130 ft lbs out of the 320 ft lbs produced at the muzzle. If the range extends to 125 yards or more, the trajectory is not much flatter than that of the 40-grain load, which starts out slower but retains velocity better. As stated elsewhere in this book, there is no free lunch.

In recent years, Winchester has opted for a lighter bullet at higher velocity, but chose to use a 34-grain hollow-point loaded to 2,120 ft/sec in the Supreme ammunition line. Because this bullet retains velocity better than the 30-grain loads, it gives a remaining energy at 100 yards that is virtually identical to that of the 40-grain load. However, the Winchester Supreme load employs a bullet that has a large cavity so it is not noted for deep penetration. Remington has taken a different approach by marketing the Premier load that utilizes a 33-grain Hornady V-Max polymer-tipped bullet. The nominal velocity is specified as 2,000 ft/sec, but my chronograph indicated a velocity closer to 2,200 ft/sec. Moreover, this load gives good accuracy in my Ruger 77/22M, and it does not produce quite the explosive effect of the lightweight hollow-points.

Going the other way in trying to improve the effectiveness of the 22 WMR cartridge in some situations, Federal produces a load utilizing a 50-grain hollow-point bullet loaded to a nominal velocity of 1,650 ft/sec although my chronograph indicates about 1,575 ft/sec at 8 feet from the muzzle of a 22-inch barrel. However, the 50-grain bullet holds its velocity well so the remaining energy at 100 yards exceeds that of any load having a bullet of 40 grains or less. True, the trajectory is more curved, but it is certainly flat enough for shooting varmints at 100 yards. If larger species like fox or coyote are your targets, try the 50-grain Federal load in your rifle. A 22 WMR load featuring the 50-grain Gold Dot bullet was offered by CCI for a few years, but it has recently been discontinued. Some is still available on dealers shelves.

Some critics of the 22 WMR have commented on the accuracy of this caliber. Having experimented with this caliber in three rifles over the years, my belief is that the problem is not with the caliber but rather with the cartridges. In some cases, plated bullets are asked to perform at near centerfire rifle velocities while in others, the bullets are jacketed but they are by no means premium bullets. The result is a combination that may not quite produce the accuracy expected. We will have a great deal more to say on this subject in later chapters. Some tests have given results reported by other authors indicating that in identical high quality rifles using premium ammunition there is nothing lacking in accuracy produced by the 22 WMR cartridge.

Another 22 WMR load that is useful is the shot cartridge produced by CCI. The plastic capsule holds 1/8-ounce of No. 12 shot and it will certainly take out a rodent or snake at short range. This load is particularly convenient to use in a revolver.

From the foregoing discussion, it can be seen that there is a wide range of ammunition for use in the 22 WMR. For a lower-powered alternative, even the 22 WRF can be used. In spite of the offerings, none of the manufacturers produces what I want. What I want someone to produce is a 22 WMR load that makes use of a 40-grain premium spitzer bullet with a polymer tip and a boat tail. The ballistic coefficient of such a bullet would be 0.15 to 0.18, which is much higher than any bullet now offered in 22 WMR ammunition. It is also much higher than any bullet that is offered (or probably will be offered) in 17 HMR because I have been told that experimental loads with 25-grain bullets cannot be driven fast enough to give an explosive effect. Therefore, 17 HMR loads with bullets having high enough weight to give a ballistic coefficient much over 0.125 are unlikely. Even if the muzzle velocity of this hypothetical 22 WMR load were only 1,850 ft/sec, the downrange performance would far exceed that of any 22 WMR or 17 HMR now available. Of the 303 ft lbs of energy it would produce at the muzzle, calculations indicate that 197 ft lbs would remain at 100 yards and 159 ft lbs would remain at 150 yards in contrast to the 139 and 102 ft lbs given by the 17 HMR at these ranges. Will such a 22 WMR load be produced? I do not know, but if it is I want a few boxes. I will also volunteer to conduct field trials for the manufacturer who produces it.

The 17 Hornday Magnum Rimfire (HMR)

The 17 Hornady Magnum Rimfire (abbreviated as HMR and sometimes given the nickname "hummer") is one the most written about cartridges of all time. In fact, it may even hold the title! We are, it seems, caught up in the velocity craze again, this time in the area of rimfire cartridges. I say "again" because such a craze existed many years ago when Roy Weatherby introduced the line of centerfire cartridges that constitute the Weatherby magnums. With large belted cases and free bored chambers, the velocities produced by the Weatherby magnums are high. As with any other area of human endeavor, there are newer series of cartridges that eclipse the Weatherby magnums. In the 17 HMR, a new standard for velocity produced by a rimfire cartridge was established. The case for the 17 HMR cartridge was formed by necking a 22 WMR case to hold a bullet of 0.172-inch diameter. A 17-grain polymer tipped bullet was driven to a velocity of 2,550 ft/sec. The trajectory of that bullet is much less curved than that of any fired from a 22 WMR cartridge.

Small bullets at high velocity expand violently or disintegrate on impact so reports of the

The 17 HMR is based on the 22 WMR case necked to hold 17 caliber bullets.

effects of the 17 HMR began to detail dramatic kills on everything from sparrows to coyotes. However, some writers also began to report that even on groundhogs the bullets sometimes blew up without penetrating sufficiently to drop the animal on the spot so they made it back to their holes. An increasing number of such reports began to appear and they somehow offset the reports of dramatic one-shot kills on coyotes at over 200 yards. The designers decided that a heavier bullet of different construction would be appropriate so a load featuring a 20-grain hollow-point bullet having a velocity of 2,375 ft/sec was produced. Such a load is offered as the CCI Game Point and the Hornady V-Max. These loads join the 17-grain polymer-tipped loads from Hornady, Federal, CCI, Winchester and Remington as well as the 17-grain hollow-point load from CCI. However, at this time all 17 HMR ammunition is produced by CCI.

With the sharp pointed bullet at high-velocity, the trajectory of the 17 HMR has little curvature so hits at long ranges (for a rimfire) are possible. Moreover, the bullets used in 17 HMR ammunition are of the premium "varmint bullet" type so accuracy of most 17 HMR rifles is outstanding which also contributes to scoring hits at long ranges. On the downside, the bullets are tiny so they are suitable only for smaller varmint species.

In terms of firearms, the 17 HMR was given a flying start because any firearm that could function with a 22 WMR could be altered to 17 caliber by means of a different barrel. Case and rim diameter and rim thickness is the same for both calibers. The number of firearms chambered for the 17 HMR is very large.

The 17 Mach 2

Necking down an existing case to hold a bullet of smaller diameter has long been an honorable pastime for cartridge designers. The 243 Winchester case is that of the 308 Winchester necked to hold a .243-inch bullet and a 25-06 Remington utilizes a 30-06 Springfield case necked to hold a .257-inch bullet. If necking the 22 WMR case to hold a 0.172-inch diameter bullet is successful, why not neck a 22 LR to hold a bullet of that diameter? While we are at it, let us use the case of the CCI Stinger since it is slightly longer than that of the 22 LR and then a slightly greater powder charge can be used. The result produced by Hornady is the cartridge known as the 17 Mach 2 so named because it gives a velocity that is close to twice the velocity of sound. This cartridge was also given a flying start because most firearms chambered for the 22 LR (and that is an enormous number!) can be made into 17 Mach 2 pieces simply by changing the barrel. There is a problem with certain autoloaders because the 17 Mach 2 uses a larger charge of slower-burning powder than the 22 LR. This results in the pressure staying high for a longer period of time causing the bolt to be driven back at a velocity that may exceed the design limit of the rifle and could damage the firearm.

As of this writing in late 2004, the only 17 Mach 2 load available is with a 17-grain Hornady V-Max polymer-tipped bullet that gives a muzzle velocity of 2,100 ft/sec which corresponds to an energy of 166 ft lbs. The ammunition is available from CCI and Hornady (both loaded by CCI) and Eley. With a velocity of 2,100 ft/sec, the trajectory is sufficiently flat to make hits on small targets possible at ranges up to 125 yards or so. At that range the velocity is 1,756 ft/sec and the energy 75 ft lb. Accuracy is reported to be superb for this cartridge, which should allow it to be an excellent choice for small pests.

The 17 Aguila

If necking a CCI Stinger case to hold a 0.172-inch bullet produced a useful cartridge, why not neck the standard length 22 LR case in the same way? That is precisely the origin of the cartridge that is known as the 17 Aguila. The load consists of a 20-grain hollow-point bullet that produces a nominal muzzle velocity of 1,850 ft/sec. This makes the 17 Aguila only slightly less powerful than the 17 Mach 2 and it

Both polymer-tipped and hollow-point bullets are loaded in 17 HMR caliber ammunition.

is suitable for the same purposes.

One advantage of the 17 Aguila is that since the powder charge is smaller than that used in the longer-cased 17 Mach 2, the pressure does not remain as high for as long a period so the back thrust on the bolt is lower. Accordingly, it is possible to add a barrel chambered for the 17 Aguila to most autoloader actions that work for the 22 LR. This is of no consequence for bolt-action rifles or revolvers in which the longer 17 Mach 2 works satisfactorily. Whether the 17 Aguila will achieve popularity anywhere near that of the 17 Mach 2 remains to be seen.

Matching the Ammunition to the Target

No one wishing to hunt bear with a 30-06 Springfield would go to a sporting goods store and say, "I want a box of .30-06 ammunition." If you did, you might be sold a box of 125-grain soft points (in former times it could have been 110-grain bullets) that are better suited to varmint hunting. The bear hunter would likely select one of the 30-06 loads with 165- to 180-grain bullets of premium construction. The rimfire shooter should also give some serious attention to the anticipated use of his or her firearm before accepting ammunition that is unsuitable.

If there is one aspect of rimfire ammunition availability that has changed over the years it is in having the ability to select a type of ammunition for specific purposes. This will be discussed in more detail in Chapter 9, but the general principles will be discussed here. It must be said at the outset, regardless of the type of ammunition and projectile, the primary requisite is being able to place that projectile in a location where it can achieve its potential effect. Accuracy is paramount in rimfire shooting. After all, that is what rifle shooting in the sporting sense is all about. It is why most of us try to select an accurate rifle and add sighting equipment to enable us to achieve that high degree of accuracy. So before you look at ballistics tables from ammunition manufacturers and decide that you want to use the XYZ Pest Popper on your next prairie dog shoot, by all means get a couple of boxes and do some testing. You may find that a four-inch group at 50 yards precludes your doing good work with your rifle even if the Pest Popper has a devastating blow.

Target shooters who shoot paper targets for score (silhouette shooting is a somewhat different matter) want the most accurate ammunition available. Power is not required and may even be detrimental in shooting paper targets. Trappers who may have to dispatch animals often use the least destructive load available. For such use, the lowly 22 Short works very well in either the solid or hollow point form. Pelt damage is to be kept to a minimum level. Varmint hunters want (and need) the most destructive rimfire load to prevent wounded animals from escaping. Fortunately there are rimfire cartridges that handle all of these chores.

Varmint and small game hunters can choose from several rimfire calibers. Shown here (left to right) are 17 Mach 2, the 17 HMR, 22 LR, and 22 WMR cartridges.

Chapter 7

INTERNAL BALLISTICS FOR BEGINNERS

Ballistics is the branch of science that deals with problems related to launching and motion of projectiles. *Internal* ballistics concerns the forces acting on the projectile and its motion during the firing process. *External* ballistics is the branch of science that deals with the motion of the projectile after it leaves the firing device. The more a shooter knows about ballistics, the better he or she will understand the performance of the chosen firearms and ammunition and how to use them effectively. In this chapter, the basic principles of internal ballistics will be presented, and Chapter 8 will deal with external ballistics along with some discussion of the performance characteristics of current rimfire ammunition.

A chronograph is an indispensable tool for the serious rimfire shooter. The author uses a Competition Electronics ProChrono model.

The science of internal ballistics involves the transformation of energy from one form into another. When the primer explodes, the powder is ignited and the chemical energy stored in the powder is converted into the kinetic energy of the bullet and heat that is transferred to the bullet and rifle. As a result of the powder being transformed into gaseous products and the expansion of the gas, the bullet increases in velocity as it is forced down the bore. Consequently, the physical principles involving force, work, and energy form the basis of internal ballistics.

Ignition

Shooters who use centerfire firearms have several variables that are under their control, especially if they reload their own ammunition. The type of primer, type and amount of propellant, and the type and seating depth of the bullet are all variables over which the reloader has some control. These are the most important factors in determining the internal ballistics related to firing a shot. Other than selecting the type of ammunition to be fired, the rimfire shooter has little control over the internal ballistics of the firearm. However, an understanding of the basic principles of internal ballistics is helpful when interpreting what is happening as a shot is fired. The discussion presented here makes use of some elementary ideas from physics, but it should be adequate for most purposes. Therefore, in this section we will explore what happens between the time the firing pin strikes the cartridge and the bullet exits from the muzzle.

As a firearm discharges, the first thing that happens is that the sear releases the firing pin (or hammer) as a result of pressure applied to the trigger. From the time the sear is released to the time the firing pin strikes the cartridge is known as the lock time. It is desirable to have a short lock time so there will be as little movement of the firearm as possible while this part of the firing sequence is taking place. Generally, the bolt action rifles that are designed for target shooting have very shot lock times that

Note the dimpled cartridge head used by Federal in the 22 LR Ultra Match rimfire round (now discontinued). Ignition occurs as the firing pin strikes the rim of the case and spreads forward.

measure only a couple of milliseconds. Firing pin design, length of firing pin travel, and tension of the spring that moves the firing pin determine the lock time of a particular firearm. Generally, firearms with exposed hammers that must swing upward as they are released have longer lock times. The lock time is a characteristic of the action of a particular firearm and in some cases there is little that can be done to alter it except by a trained gunsmith. On the other hand, for some rifles modifications can be made by installing certain aftermarket parts. This will be discussed briefly in Chapter 12.

A rimfire cartridge rests in the chamber with the rim against the rear end of the barrel. Rifles designed to deliver the highest level of accuracy have chambers that have slightly smaller dimensions than those of ordinary rifles. This serves to hold the cartridge in more precise alignment with the bore and assures more uniform ignition. As the bolt is closed (regardless of whether the bolt is manually or automatically operated), there must be some clearance between the bolt face and the breech, which is sufficient to accommodate the rim of the cartridge. This distance is known as the headspace. For the 22 LR rimfire cartridge, the headspace is normally in the range of 0.043 to 0.046 inches. Accordingly, headspace is checked by means of two gauges, a so-called "go" or minimum gauge which the bolt should close on fully and a "no go" or maximum gauge which the bolt should not close on. For the 22 LR, the former measures 0.043 inches while the latter measures 0.046 inches.

The rim thickness of most rimfire ammunition is in the range 0.037 to 0.042 inches and averages around 0.040 inches. If the headspace is less than about 0.040 inches, there will be some compression of the cartridge rim as the bolt closes. In autoloaders, this might keep the bolt from closing fully while in bolt-action rifles the force generated as the bolt is turned may be sufficient to compress the cartridge head slightly. If the headspace is excessive, the case can rupture because it is not supported properly.

On the other hand, if the headspace is greater than about 0.048 inches, the cartridge can move forward when impacted by the firing pin, which may give erratic ignition. Consequently, it is desirable to have the headspace be within the range of 0.043 to 0.046 inches. Tests have been conducted in special rifles in which the headspace can be varied by positioning the barrel in the breech and locking it in place. It was found that the best accuracy resulted when the headspace was approximately 0.044 inches. When the headspace was about 0.004 larger this, the shots resulted in groups that were elongated vertically which probably resulted from ignition that was not uniform. Neither the minimum nor maximum necessarily represents the most desirable condition although there is no convenient way to adjust headspace in most rimfire rifles. However, the amount by which the firing pin extends past the bolt face is also important because if the headspace is slightly large but the firing pin extends a few thousandths more from the bolt face it can compensate to give the same degree of crushing of the cartridge rim. The bolt face on a rimfire rifle is recessed or counter bored approximately 0.040 to 0.045 inches and the firing pin protrusion is usually slightly less than that amount so the firing pin does not rest against the edge of the chamber or strike it when the firearm is dry fired without a cartridge in place. These aspects of firearm function concern target shooters who are trying to obtain the maximum accuracy from super accurate rifles, and designers of firearms must consider these factors.

Many rimfire shooters who try to obtain the highest possible accuracy measure the thickness of the rims of their ammunition. In this way, ammunition can be segregated into groups of cartridges that will give more uniform indentation by the firing pin. Other shooters question whether this is effective, but instead weigh unfired rounds and group them in that way to try to obtain maximum uniformity in ammunition. Any means that may result in the highest shot to shot uniformity has probably been tried!

Shooters who install aftermarket barrels on their rifles (see Chapter 12) should at least be aware of the ramifications of headspace and the fact that headspace may be different when a different type of barrel is installed. Some barrel manufacturers such as Green Mountain Rifle Barrel Company produce shims that are actually thin washers having a thickness of 0.002" that can be placed around the shank of a barrel before it is attached to the action, and in this way the headspace can be varied. Of course, this procedure can only increase headspace to correct for instances in which it is too small.

Rim Thickness

As part of the of the study of 22 LR ammunition, I decided to determine the rim thickness for several types of ammunition. Special commercial rim thickness gauges are available for the serious experimenter, but they are not absolutely necessary. A 22 LR cartridge will slip snugly into the neck of a fired cartridge like the 222 Remington or 223 Remington. In this instance, I had available fired 222 Remington cases since I once owned a rifle in that caliber. I mounted the empty case in the chuck of a drill and carefully squared off the mouth by rotating the case against an abrasive wheel. After the case was prepared, I measured its length with a dial caliper and found it to be 1.691 inches. With the empty 222

Remington case between the jaws of the caliper, I set the dial on the caliper to read zero. Then, with a 22 LR round inserted in the neck, I closed the jaws against the rim of the 22 LR and the head of the 222 Remington case. Because the rim thickness is always less than 0.100 inches, I could read the thickness directly on the dial. By this simple procedure, I had a rim thickness gauge that allowed me to read the thickness quickly to three decimal places.

Two dozen types of 22 LR ammunition were selected from the large number of types on hand and the rim thickness of a random sample of 20 cartridges of each type were measured. For all of the cartridges, the rim thickness was never above 0.042 inches or below 0.037 inches. The results obtained are summarized in the accompanying table. In the table, the entry below each rim thickness gives the number of cartridges in the sample of 20 that gave that measurement. For example, with the CCI Velocitor, six cartridges had a rim thickness of 0.040 inches while 14 had a thickness of 0.041 inches.

Although it is not possible to correlate rim thickness with the accuracy displayed by a certain type of ammunition, the data show some interesting facts. First, some types of ammunition have rims

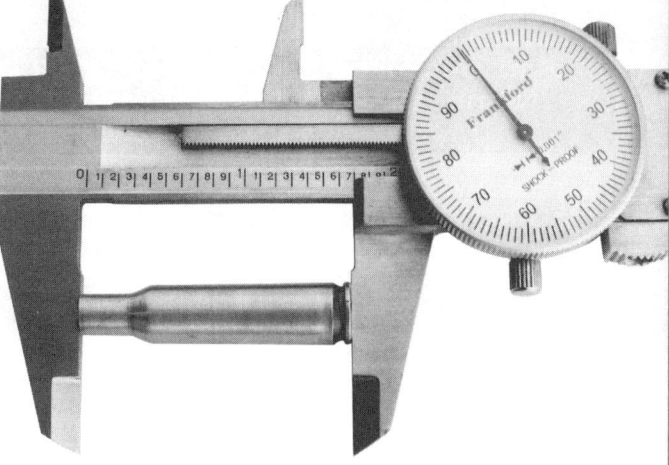

Rim thickness was determined by measuring the length of an empty 222 Remington case then setting the dial to read zero.

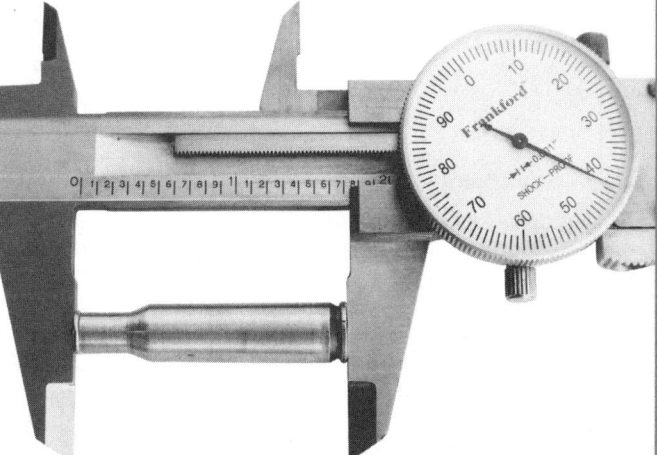

Measuring the length of the 222 Remington case with a 22 LR cartridge inserted in the neck allowed the thickness of the rim to be measured directly. For this cartridge, the rim thickness is 0.042 inch.

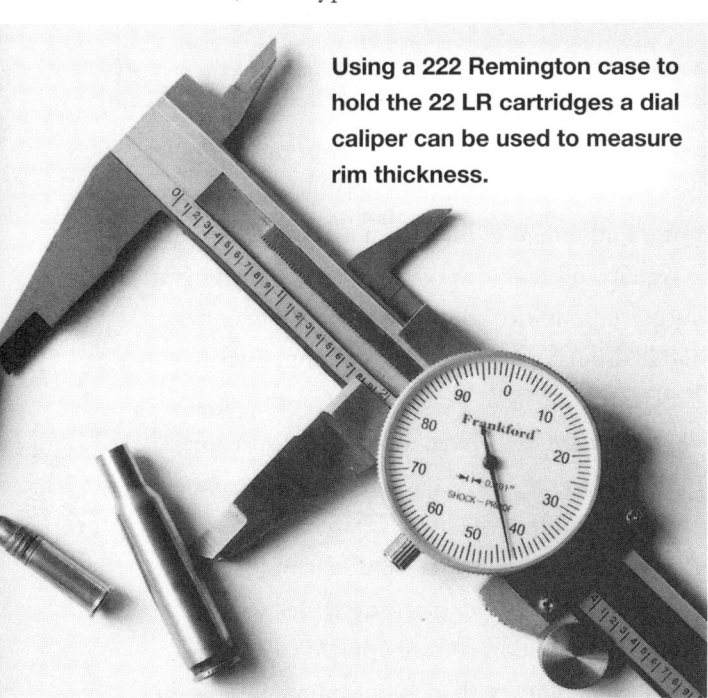

Using a 222 Remington case to hold the 22 LR cartridges a dial caliper can be used to measure rim thickness.

that are very uniform in thickness. For example, the rims of the 20 Federal Ultra Match cartridges all measured 0.042 inches. For some of the other ammunition types (CCI Green Tag and SGB for example), 19 out of the sample of 20 rounds had the same thickness (0.041 inches). In other cases (Remington Club Xtra and Winchester T22), the majority of the rounds had the same thickness and the remainder were very close to that measurement. Second, the data shown in the table reveal that certain types of ammunition have rims that tend to fall toward the maximum thickness. For example, the rims of all cartridges of the CCI ammunition types are in the range 0.040 to 0.042 inches. Rim thickness for other types of ammunition tend to be toward the minimum end of the range. All 20 of the cartridges in the samples of Winchester T22, Remington/

Rim Thickness for 24 Types of 22 LR Ammunition. Entries Indicate the Number of Cartridges Having That Thickness Out of a Sample of 20 Cartridges of Each Type.

Ammunition type	Rim thickness, inches					
	0.037	0.038	0.039	0.040	0.041	0.042
CCI Blazer	0	0	0	0	13	7
CCI Green Tag	0	0	0	1	19	0
CCI Mini Mag	0	0	0	3	17	0
CCI SGB	0	0	0	0	1	19
CCI Standard Velocity	0	0	0	14	6	0
CCI Velocitor	0	0	0	6	14	0
Eley Silhouex	4	9	7	0	0	0
Federal Champion	0	0	2	8	10	0
Federal Gold Medal Target	0	0	0	2	18	0
Federal Ultra Match	0	0	0	0	0	20
Lapua Scoremax	0	0	0	17	3	0
Lapua Super Club	0	0	0	9	11	0
PMC Scoremaster	0	0	0	12	7	1
Remington Cyclone	3	8	9	0	0	0
Remington Golden Bullet H.P.	0	1	7	9	3	0
Remington Match Xtra Plus	0	0	11	9	0	0
Remington Thunderbolt	0	4	9	7	0	0
Remington Target	4	5	8	3	0	0
Remington/Eley Club Xtra	0	16	4	0	0	0
RWS Target Rifle	0	0	4	15	1	0
Winchester Power Point	5	10	4	1	0	0
Winchester Supreme	0	0	0	3	17	0
Winchester T22	5	15	0	0	0	0
Wolf Match Target	0	10	7	3	0	0

Eley Club Xtra, Eley Silhouex, and Remington Cyclone have rims that fall within a range of 0.037 to 0.039 inches. Cartridges of some other types of ammunition show a range of rim thickness that fall toward the middle of the 0.037 to 0.042 inch range.

Whether these differences in rim thickness will manifest themselves in the accuracy given in a particular rifle has yet to be demonstrated conclusively. Undoubtedly, specific rifles will perform better with ammunition for which the rims that tend toward larger thickness while others probably give better accuracy with cartridges having thinner rims. Keep in mind that the headspace in the rifle and how far the firing pin protrudes from the bolt face are also important factors. Uniformity in rim thickness may be more important than whether the rims tend toward minimum or maximum thickness. One thing is certain and that is in the rifles tested, Remington Target ammunition did not give the best accuracy and it also has a large dispersion in rim thickness. Federal Gold Medal Target, CCI Green Tag, and CCI Standard Velocity all have little dispersion in rim thickness and all gave excellent accuracy in most of the rifles tested (see Chapters 13 and 14). Rim thickness is only one factor to consider, but if your rifle doesn't shoot particularly well with the type of ammunition you are using, the data shown in the table indicate that not all ammunition is the same. Other types may perform much better in a particular rifle so some testing should be carried out. A great deal more data is needed before definitive conclusions can be drawn about the relationship between rim thickness and accuracy. Moreover, in no way is a conclusion justified that one type of ammunition is any "better" another. Such a fact can be determined only with respect to a particular firearm by experimentation.

Many competitors believe that better accuracy is achieved if cartridges are sorted by rim thickness and then fired with others having similar thickness. Doubtless, there is some effect but whether is large enough to be seen without firing a very large number of groups is unknown. Some competitors believe that cartridge weight is more important than rim thickness and sort their cartridges that way.

In order to assess the rim thickness of 17 Mach 2 ammunition, the rims of 20 cartridges of each of the two types that are currently available were measured. Since both the Hornady and CCI ammunition are loaded by CCI, it came as no surprise that the rims appear identical. What was a surprise was that for each load all 20 cartridges measured 0.042 inches. Uniformity of this level is normally observed only with the highest quality target ammunition as it the case for Federal Ultra Match and CCI Green Tag. Reports on the 17 Mach 2 indicate that the round is exceptionally accurate and such uniform rim thickness is probably one reason.

Cartridge Weights

As mentioned earlier, the uniformity of cartridges with respect to weight is sometimes considered to be a factor in determining the accuracy of ammunition. One must remember that a cartridge consists of the case, bullet, powder, and primer although the bullet and case comprise most of the weight. When several cartridges are weighed and found to have wide variation, differences may be due to variations in any of the components. In a way, the deviation in the weight of a cartridge from the average weight is meaningless unless a large number of cartridges are considered. However, in another way the uniformity of cartridge weights is meaningful. Uniform cartridge weights indicate that *all* components are assembled into uniform units. Consider two cartridges that have identical weights. This could indicate that the weights of the components in each cartridge are

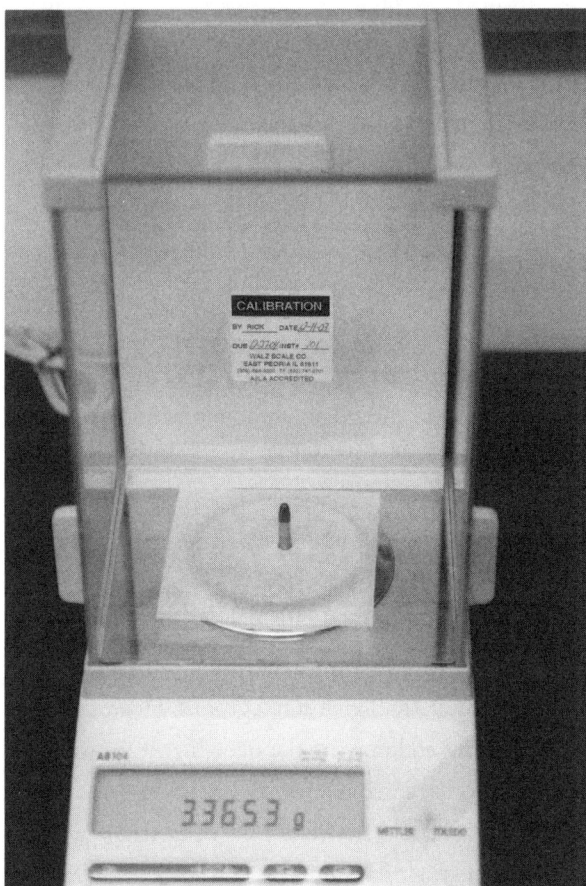

A sensitive balance can detect small differences in cartridge weights.

For a 20-cartridge sample of 17 Mach 2, every cartridge had a rim thickness of 0.042 inch.

Results of Weighing 20 Cartridges of Each Type.

Cartridges	Weight, grams[a]			Std. Dev.[b]
	Highest	Lowest	Average	
CCI Green Tag	3.2986	3.2734	3.2895	0.0074
CCI Standard Velocity	3.3077	3.2500	3.2811	0.0217
CCI Velocitor	3.3397	3.3275	3.3336	0.0040
Federal Gold Medal Target	3.2691	3.2508	3.2577	0.0059
Federal Ultra Match	3.3564	3.3483	3.3521	0.0018
Lapua Super Club	3.3676	3.3290	3.3470	0.0091
PMC Scoremaster	3.3486	3.3149	3.3261	0.0117
Remington/Eley Club Xtra	3.3285	3.2950	3.3089	0.0124
Remington Target	3.3732	3.2988	3.3299	0.0223
Remington Thunderbolt	3.3938	3.3308	3.3623	0.0167
Remington Yellow Jacket	2.9258	2.8358	2.8751	0.0246
Winchester Power Point	3.3692	3.3459	3.3581	0.0074
Winchester T22	3.3361	3.2990	3.3140	0.0134
Wolf Match Target	3.3536	3.3103	3.3304	0.0183

[a] To convert to weight in grains, multiply by 15.432.
[b] Std. Dev. is the standard deviation, a statistical measure of variance.

identical. However, identical weights would result if the case of one cartridge is 0.0050 grams heavier than that of the other but the bullet is 0.0050 grams lighter than that of the other. In other words, weight variations could compensate to yield identical cartridge weights. While this conceivably could occur for any two cartridges, it is almost impossible for it to occur in a sample of 20 cartridges so that differences in weights of the components compensate. In a much more realistic situation, weighing 20 cartridges will show that some cartridges are made from lighter cases and lighter bullets while others will have the opposite situation. Variations in cartridge weights will given an indication of the *overall* uniformity of the cartridges.

The fact that cartridges have uniform weights does not necessarily assure that they will also be highly accurate and give small groups. However, there is value in knowing the overall uniformity of ammunition as long as the data are not used to try to predict accuracy. Wide variations in cartridge weights for a given type of ammunition indicate less control in the manufacturing process or less rigid standards for uniformity.

To determine how several types of 22 LR varied in terms of weight distribution, 14 types were selected and 20 cartridges of each type were weighed on an laboratory balance (which weighs in grams not grains). The cartridges weighed were the first 20 out of the box with no selecting being done. The weights for the 20 cartridges of each type were tabulated and the highest and lowest weights were recorded. For the 20 cartridges of each type, the average weight was calculated and the standard deviation of the weights was determined. Although it is tempting to ascribe weight differences to the lubricant, such difference between individual rounds is small. One of the "greasy" target rounds was wiped off and reweighed only to find that 0.0004 grams of lubricant were removed. The differences in weight between cartridges in the samples are far too large for differences in lubrication to have much effect. The accompanying table shows the results obtained.

The data shown in the table reveal some interesting facts. First, the range of weights obtained for the 20 cartridges and the standard deviation for Federal Ultra Match show it to be unbelievably uniform and have the lowest standard deviation. This is not unexpected given that this ammunition is intended for competitive shooting at the highest levels and sells for about $10 to 11 per box of 50 rounds. Unfortunately, Federal has recently discontinued this ammunition but some is still to be found on dealers' shelves.

Several types of ammunition, such as CCI Green Tag and Velocitor, Federal Gold Medal Target, Lapua Super Club, and Winchester Power Point, have low standard deviations in weight. Perhaps not coincidentally, all of these types are noted for accuracy even though they are not all "target" types. However, the standard deviation for the Wolf Match Target is larger than that of most other types, but that ammunition is known to produce excellent accuracy. In this case, examination of the data showed that three of the 20 cartridges had weights that deviated significantly from the others. When the standard deviation was calculated for the other 17 cartridges in the sample, the value was 0.0141 instead of 0.0183. Wolf rimfire ammunition is produced in Germany by SK-Jagd and the results presented in Chapter 14 show that it gave some of the smallest groups obtained in the tests. Finally, for the cartridges weighed the largest standard deviation found was for the hyper velocity Remington Yellow Jacket which may be one of the reasons this and other hyper velocity loads do not normally give accuracy equal that of other types of ammunition. Keep in mind that hyper velocity ammunition is intended for other purposes so the situation is not as bad as it may at first seem. However, the weight uniformity of CCI Velocitors and Winchester Power Points is outstanding which may also be why these hunting loads gave excellent accuracy with most of the rifles used in the tests.

Is there something about weight uniformity of 22 LR ammunition that is indicative of its accuracy potential? Some competitors believe that there is while others do not. At this point, given the accuracy data shown in Chapter 13 and the data presented here, I would both measure rim thickness and weigh my ammunition and segregate it according to these characteristics if I were competing in events where a difference in bullet placement of 0.01 inches might mean the difference between winning and finishing high. For the vast majority of rimfire users who are engaged in plinking, hunting, and pest shooting, the rifles used are likely not accurate enough to tell the difference between cartridges of the same type that have slightly different weights. As long as a type of ammunition is selected that works well in a particular rifle, the effect produced by variation in cartridge weight is not likely to be detected by a shooter of average ability using ordinary equipment.

Tables that summarize many measurements do not always convey a complete picture of the data analysis. For example, it is helpful to see a graphical comparison of the data for a sample of 20 cartridges of a given type that shows how the weights of the individual cartridges compare to the average weight. To illustrate weight variations for a specific type of ammunition, the deviation from the average was determined for each cartridge in the 20-cartridge sample. Then, for each cartridge, the percent deviation from the average weight was calculated because it is not correct to compare the actual deviations for types of cartridges that have different average weights. That is why the percent deviation (a relative measure) was determined rather than using the actual values for the deviations. After the percent deviations were obtained, a graph was made showing the percent deviation for each cartridge in the 20-cartridge sample. The accompanying figure shows the results of this type of analysis for the ammunition that gave the smallest (Federal Ultra Match) and the largest (Remington Yellow Jacket) standard deviations. Note the difference in the lengths of the bars corresponding to these cartridges. The solid bars represent percent deviations for Ultra Match and the shaded bars represent Yellow Jackets. Short bars mean that the weights of the individual cartridges do not deviate much from the average weight.

Having shown the graph for the most and least

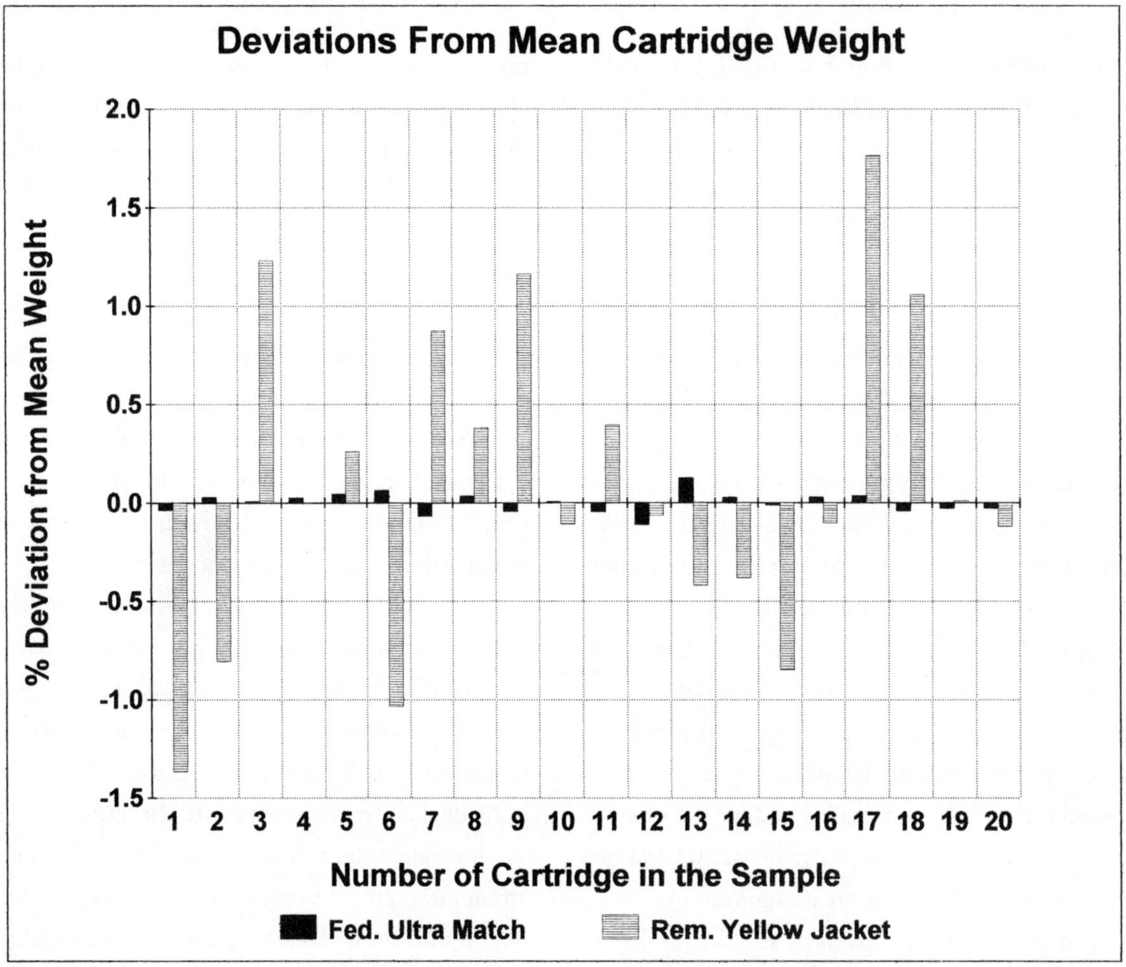

Deviations From Mean Cartridge Weight

Chart: % Deviation from Mean Weight vs. Number of Cartridge in the Sample (1–20), comparing Fed. Ultra Match and Rem. Yellow Jacket.

uniform cartridges of those weighed, it is appropriate to show a comparison of two cartridges that are more typical in respect to weight uniformity. For this comparison, a graph was prepared showing percent deviation of the weights of 20 cartridges from the mean for Winchester T22 and Remington Club Xtra. These types are more typical than are Federal Ultra Match or Remington Yellow Jacket, and the graph shows this. In preparing the graph, the same scale was used so that the characteristics of these types of ammunition can be compared to those shown in the previous graph. Note that the weight variations are greater than for Federal Ultra Match but much less than for Remington Yellow Jackets. Note also that there is not much difference in the lengths of the bars (weight variations) for Remington Club Xtra and those for Winchester T22. This is expected since these are both types of intermediate level target ammunition. The standard deviations for the two types of cartridges are almost identical which is reflected in bars of similar lengths in the graphs.

The graphs show how the weights of the 20 cartridges in each sample are distributed around the average weight with some being higher than the average and some lower. There is no reason to perform this detailed analysis for all 14 types of ammunition, but such a graph shows clearly how differences between the standard deviations of several types of cartridges are determined by the variation in weights for the individual cartridges. The longer the bars, the larger the standard deviation.

Some serious experimenters have weighed cartridges and after grouping them by weight fired them in high precision target rifles. With the highest quality ammunition (such as Federal Ultra Match), grouping by weight made almost no difference. With inexpensive ammunition where the weights were less uniform, grouping cartridges by weight gave smaller

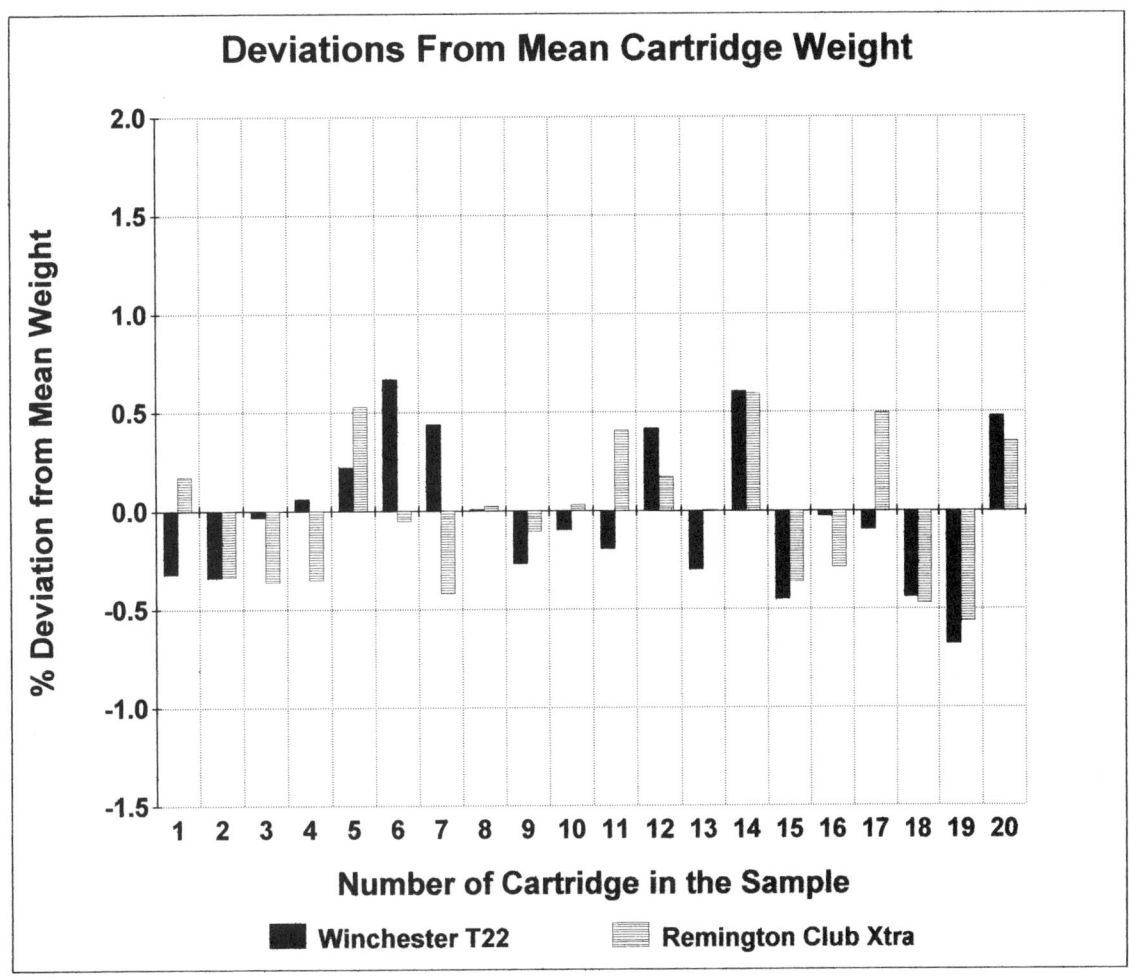

groups when cartridges of similar weight were used. These results are exactly as one would expect. When you look at the weight distribution diagram for Federal Ultra Match, it is clear that segregation of cartridges by weight will not help much because the uniformity is already there. With ammunition having large variations in cartridge weight, it is possible to get a sample of cartridges that is more uniform if they are grouped by weighting. Competitors who already use ammunition of the highest quality are probably wasting time by weighing cartridges. Someone who is trying to achieve the highest accuracy while using a type of cartridge with somewhat larger weight variations could probably do better with cartridges segregated by weight.

Comparing the deviations in weight for the two types of cartridges chosen is not meant to imply that one is "better" than the others because they are designed to serve different purposes. However, the data shown in the table reveal that there can be significant differences in cartridge uniformity when several types of ammunition are studied. If a particular type of ammunition performs satisfactorily in your rifle and does what you expect of it, by all means use it. If you are searching for the ultimate in accuracy, explore all the avenues available, and these include considering not only rim thickness but also cartridge weights. Segregating ammunition with a narrow range of values of these variables may result in some improvement in accuracy.

Another factor that is known to affect the grouping ability of rimfire cartridges is the concentricity. This factor relates to whether the axis of the bullet is aligned with the axis of the case. In other words, if the cartridge does not have concentricity, the bullet will be tipped sideways when the cartridge rests in the chamber. Theoretical studies have been conducted to determine how the grouping ability of the ammunition will be related to the extent to which the bullet and case are not concentric. A special gauge is used to measure the case-to-projectile concentricity. This is an advanced topic that will concern few rimfire shooters. Certainly those who buy ordinary rimfire ammunition and use it for sporting purposes will never have occasion to question this characteristic of their ammunition. However, for those individuals who are concerned with competition at the highest levels, an understanding of the problem is important. For those readers in this category, the excellent article by Frank Tirrell in *Small Caliber News*, Vol. 7, No. 2, Fall 2004, pp. 40-42 will be of great value.

Firing Pin Impact

In rimfire cartridges, the primer is contained in the rim of the case. The firing pin crushes the folded rim which causes the primer to explode which in turn ignites the powder. Smokeless powder burns generating gaseous products which expand rapidly against the base of the bullet. This force applied to the base of the bullet moves it down the barrel with increasing velocity. As the bullet engages the rifling, it is engraved by the lands which causes the bullet to spin. Part of the energy produced by the burning powder is used in deforming the bullet, heating the bullet and barrel, and overcoming friction between the bullet and the barrel. Although the bullet has kinetic energy because of its motion, it also has a smaller amount of energy as a result of its rotation.

There is another aspect of the impact of the firing pin on the cartridge rim that has a bearing on exactly how firing occurs. That factor is the shape of the firing pin and the corresponding shape of the dent that it makes on the cartridge base. If the firing pin hits too far toward the outside of the cartridge or hits inside the rim toward the center of the cartridge, ignition is not as efficient as when the firing pin strikes the cartridge in the optimum manner. When you examine empty cases from cartridges that have been fired in different rimfire rifles, it is clear that there is a considerable difference in precisely how the firing pin strikes the rim. Some firing pins have a wedge-shaped tip while others have rectangular or round tips. Moreover, a rather heavy but reproducible force on the firing pin is necessary to produce uniform shot to shot ignition. When the rifle is held in a horizontal position, the powder rests on the bottom of the case while the firing pin on most rimfire rifles strikes the top edge of the cartridge base. Some of the highest quality target rifles have actions designed to deliver the firing pin blow to the bottom edge of the cartridge base so that the priming mixture is in better contact with the powder. While all of these factors must be considered by engineers when designing a firearm, particularly one designed for the highest level of competition, they are usually beyond the control of the shooter. The vast majority of rimfire shooters will never have occasion to alter these aspects of internal ballistics.

Pressure

Once ignition has occurred, the powder begins to burn generating gas that exerts pressure on the base of the bullet. Owing to the small case volume, rimfire cartridges utilize powder that is fast-burning compared to the powder used in larger centerfire cartridges. The burning powder gives a rapid increase in pressure, and when the pressure inside the case is

    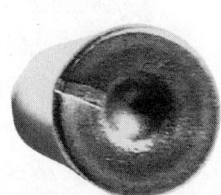

These empty cases show great variation in firing pin dents. The case on the right is a Federal Ultra Match cartridge that has a dimpled case head to control ignition.

sufficiently high, the bullet is forced out of the case. Depending on the design of the firearm, the bullet may already be touching the rifling as is the case in rifles with so-called match chambers. In most ordinary rimfire rifles, there is some small distance between the chamber and where the rifling begins so the bullet must move that distance before it engages the rifling. This distance is known as the free bore of the rifle. When the bullet starts its motion in contact with the rifling, there is greater resistance to the initial movement of the bullet so the pressure rises rapidly. When the rifle has some extent of free bore, the maximum pressure is reached after the bullet is already in motion. The result is that higher velocity can be achieved with a pressure that is still below the design limits of the firearm. This is not much of a factor with rimfire firearms, but free boring is commonly used in magnum centerfire rifles so that the highest velocity can be achieved within prescribed pressure limits. Perhaps the best-known application of the principles related to free bore have been with the Weatherby magnum cartridges. Generally, better accuracy is achieved when the bullet starts out in contact with the rifling so most rimfire match rifles and more expensive sporters are designed that way.

As more of the powder burns, the pressure increases and the bullet is accelerated as it moves along the bore. In a 22 LR cartridge, the small charge of fast burning powder is consumed rather quickly and after that, the bullet velocity may actually decrease as the bullet moves farther along in the barrel. Many tests have been conducted in which the same 22 LR rifle was fired with barrels of varying length (usually by successively shortening the same barrel), and the results of these tests show that the maximum velocity is produced in barrels that are approximately 16 to 18 inches in length. In longer barrels, the velocity decreases after the bullet has traveled farther than that distance down the bore. However, the difference between the velocity produced in a 16-inch barrel and one of 20 inches is only a few feet per second, and the difference is not the same for different types of ammunition. Because of the larger charges of slower burning powder used in the 22 WMR and 17 HMR ammunition, the velocity continues to increase in barrels longer than 16 inches. Accordingly, most rifles in 17 HMR caliber have barrels that are 22 inches in length while those in 22 WMR average around 20 inches. In the very small 17 caliber bore, the volume is small so the confined gas continues to exert pressure on the bullet and the extra two inches of barrel length give some increase in velocity.

The question often arises as to whether an autoloader gives lower velocity than a rifle with a closed breech when the same ammunition is used in both and the barrel lengths are identical. Does the motion of the bolt in the autoloader rob the bullet of some of its velocity? Tests have shown that velocities produced by the bolt-action rifle are usually slightly higher than those produced by the autoloader. However, it is not the motion of the bolt being blown back in the autoloader that is responsible. The bullet has exited the barrel before the bolt has been moved backward a significant amount. The main factor responsible is the difference in chambers of the rifles. In order to accept a variety of types of ammunition and feed them reliably as the bolt slams forward, autoloaders often have chambers that tend toward the maximum dimensions. Bolt action rifles have the cartridges fed by hand and locked in place as the bolt is turned manually. Consequently, bolt action rifles can have tighter chambers than autoloaders and also have the rifling extend back to the front end of the chamber (known as a match-type chamber). The smaller chamber dimensions and the rifling holding the bullet in the cartridge case until the pressure has risen causes the pressure generated in a bolt action to be slightly higher and that is probably responsible for any difference in velocities given by the two types of actions. Only a few autoloaders are built with match type chambers and they are usually target rifles like the Ruger 10/22T and the Thompson/Center

Benchmark. However, the T/C Classic sporter also has a match type chamber.

It is an interesting fact that the majority of types of smokeless propellants have about the same chemical composition and energy content. However, there may be an enormous difference in the burning rates of powders, which controls the rate at which the chemical energy is released. The burning rates of nitrocellulose propellants are determined by particle size, shape of the particles, additives, etc. Since shooters of rimfire ammunition do not reload ammunition (although it can be done), selection of the propellant is not a factor as it is when shooters reload centerfire ammunition. The total energy content of the powder charge is released during the event of firing the cartridge. Much of that energy is lost as heat to the surroundings (the barrel, case, and bullet) and some is carried away as kinetic energy of the moving gases.

The expanding gas generates a force on the base of the bullet that is determined by the pressure (measured in pounds per square inch) and the area of the base of the bullet (measured in square inches). However, unlike the pressure inside a tire, the pressure generated by the expanding gas is not constant. It increases rapidly up to a maximum then decreases as the bullet continues to move. For a 22 LR high-velocity cartridge, the maximum pressure may reach a value as high as approximately 25,000 pounds per square inch (written as 25,000 psi or 25,000 lb/in^2). The maximum pressure generated by 22 WMR and 17 HMR cartridges is not much different, but higher pressure is maintained longer because of the larger charges of slower burning powder used in these rounds. This does not mean that the force acting on the base of the bullet is 25,000 pounds because the area of the base is only a fraction of a square inch. For example, the base of the bullet is circular which means that the area is given by the formula $A=\pi r^2$. For a bullet that is 0.224 inch in diameter, the radius is 0.112 inch so the area is

$$A = \pi r^2 = 3.14 \times (0.112 \text{ inches})^2 = 0.0394 \text{ in}^2$$

Therefore, the maximum force (F) on the base of the bullet is given as the pressure (P) multiplied by the area on which the pressure is exerted.

$$F = P \times A = 25,000 \text{ lb/in}^2 \times 0.0394 \text{ in}^2 = 985 \text{ lb}$$

Although 985 lb may be the *maximum* force on the base of the bullet, the average force is much lower because the maximum pressure is not maintained throughout the entire length of the barrel. Moreover, the net force is lower because part of the force is required to overcome friction, cause the rifling to engrave the bullet, and to increase the rotational velocity of the bullet. If a net force of 985 lb operated on a bullet over a distance of 2 feet, the work done on the bullet (and hence its kinetic energy) would be given as the product of the force times the distance over which it operates.

$$\text{Work} = \text{energy} = E = 2 \text{ feet} \times 985 \text{ pounds} = 1970 \text{ ft lbs}$$

Since the energy of a high speed 22 LR bullet is only about 140 ft lbs, the net force on the base is much lower than 985 lb. In fact, that is the maximum force that would exist at the instant when the pressure is at its maximum value of 25,000 lb/in^2. Throughout most of the time the bullet is in the barrel the pressure is much lower than that value.

The pressure varies in a predictable way. It increases beginning with the explosion of the primer followed by ignition of the powder, which generates a mixture of expanding gases. When the pressure is high enough to overcome the resistance to bullet travel caused by the crimping and friction between the bullet and the inside of the case neck, the bullet starts to move. Continued burning of the propellant causes the pressure to increase as more gas forms. As more of the propellant charge is consumed, the rate at which gas is generated decreases and the pressure is no longer increased. As the bullet moves farther down the barrel, the volume available for the gas to occupy gets larger and the gases are also cooled. Both of these factors cause the pressure to decrease. If a graph is made showing the pressure as it varies with distance of bullet travel, a curve is obtained which shows the pressure rising to some maximum value then decreasing thereafter. The accompanying graph shows this relationship between pressure and the distance the bullet has traveled down the bore. Note that the pressure may reach a peak value of 25,000 lb/in^2, but it is much lower during most of the bullet travel. Therefore, the *average* pressure is well below the *peak* pressure. We will now show in a simple way in which these forces are related to bullet energy.

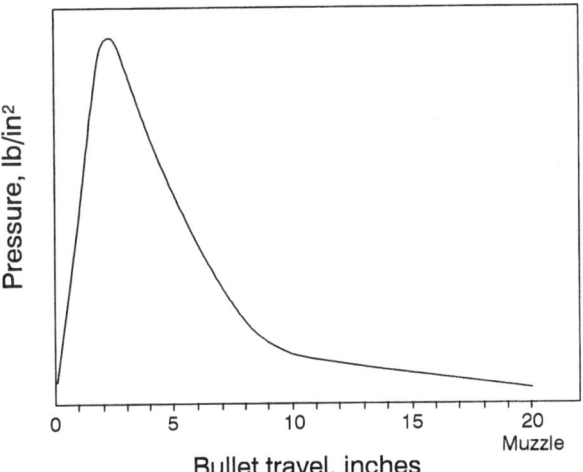

The qualitative relationship between the pressure and the distance the bullet has traveled in a 20-inch barrel.

We can see the importance of these factors are by noting that the kinetic energy of the bullet from a high velocity 22 LR as it leaves the muzzle is approximately 140 ft lbs. Kinetic energy (E) and work (W) have the same units, foot pounds (abbreviated as ft lb), which expresses the amount of work done by a force measured in pounds operating through a distance measured in feet. The multiplication of feet (which is the same dimensionally as one foot) times pounds is how we get the unit ft lb. For example, if the barrel were 2 feet in length, a net force of 70 pounds operating over this distance would involve 140 ft lbs of work or energy which is equal to the energy of the bullet as it leaves the muzzle.

$$E = W = \text{Force} \times \text{Distance} = 2 \text{ feet} \times 70 \text{ pounds} = 140 \text{ foot pounds} = 140 \text{ ft lbs}$$

While the maximum force operating on the base of the bullet may be as much as 985 lb, the *average* force is only a fraction of that value and the average *net* force is lower still. No matter how much total work is done on the bullet by the expanding gases, we know that the new work is only 140 ft lbs because that is how much energy the bullet has when it exits from the muzzle.

One of the simple rules from geometry concerns the area of a rectangle, which is given as the product of the length and the width of the rectangle. This can be written in equation form as

$$\text{Area} = \text{Length} \times \text{Distance} = L \times W$$

The equation that gives energy or work shown above has exactly the same form except that it involves force and distance. Therefore, we can represent the work done as the product of a force and a distance with the product being shown as the area of a rectangle. The accompanying figure shows this representation. However, this simple analogy works only when the force has a constant value. In the case of a projectile being forced down the bore, the force is not constant.

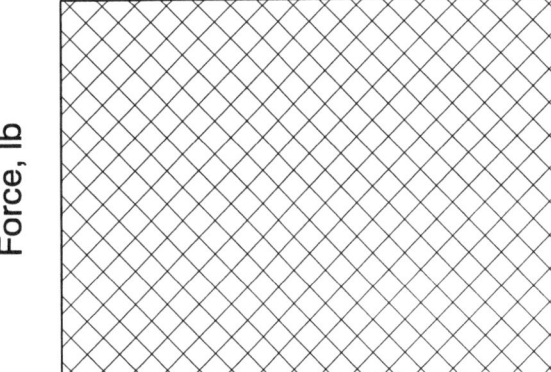

The work by a constant force is given by the product of the force times the distance through which it is applied, W = F x D. This can be expressed as the area of a rectangle for which the area is the product of the length times the width. In this case, the length is the distance and the width is the applied force.

It has been shown that the force on the base of the bullet is given by the pressure multiplied by the area of the base of the bullet. Since the area of the base of the bullet does not change, it is the pressure that is changing as the bullet travels down the barrel. As a result, we could make a graph showing the force on the base of the bullet as a function of distance the bullet has traveled. The result would be a curve that has exactly the same shape as the pressure-distance curve described earlier. Work (or energy) is the product of the net force applied and the distance over which it is applied (the length of the barrel). As shown above, there is no difficulty in performing this multiplication when the force does not change, but in the case of the bullet moving down the barrel, the force is changing. The problem then becomes one known as work done by a variable force. Obtaining the net work done on the bullet by the expanding gases (the energy of the bullet) is not as simple as multiplying a force times a distance to give an area.

under the curve and slice it into small segments (say slices representing one inch of bullet travel) because in those small intervals the force is approximately constant. In other words, the slight curvature in the graph is ignored and within the small slice it is treated as if it were a straight line. The result would be a large number of slices having geometric shapes known as trapezoids for which the areas can be calculated simply. Adding the areas of all of the slices (area segments) would give the total area under the curve. Note that within each slice the product of the average force times the width of the slice (one inch in the example here) gives the work represented by that slice. Therefore, the sum of the areas of all the slices would give the total area under the curve. That area represents the total net work done on the bullet which is the same as its kinetic energy. Thus, it is possible to calculate the energy of the bullet if the pressure is known at several distances along the bore between the chamber and the muzzle.

An interesting phenomenon is observed when two powders having different burning rates are compared. Consider powders A and B with powder A having the faster burning rate. Let us assume that the same

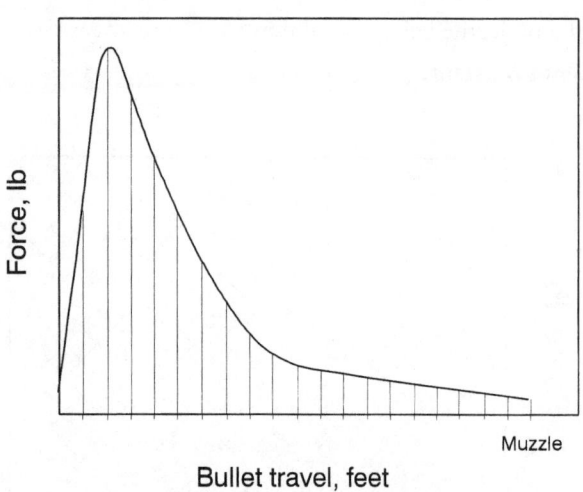

The area under the force curve gives the net work done on the bullet (bullet energy). The area can be considered as a series of slices the area of which can be determined. Adding the areas of the slices gives the total net energy of the bullet.

By appropriate mathematical means, it is possible to determine the area under the force-distance curve even though the force has a different magnitude at each distance. In principle, we could take the area

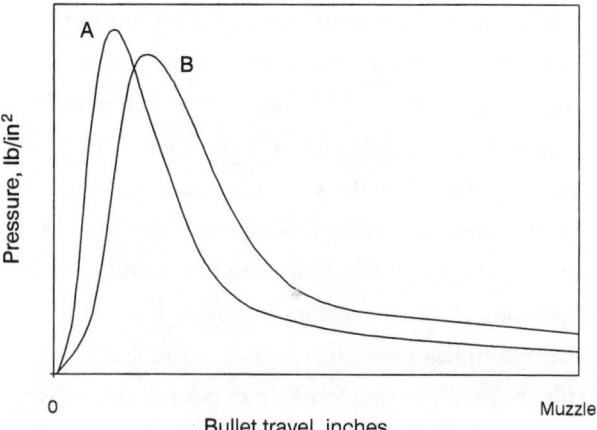

The relationship between pressure and distance of bullet travel for powders A (faster burning rate) and B (slower burning rate). Pressure remains higher for a longer time with powder B which means that more work is done on the bullet giving it a higher velocity. Powder A would produce a higher velocity in a short handgun barrel.

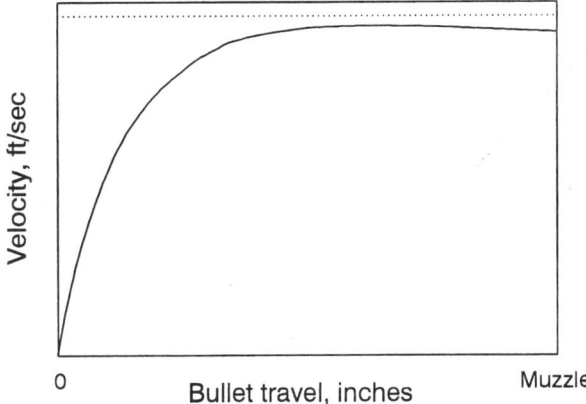

Relationship between velocity and distance the bullet has traveled down a barrel. For the 22 LR, the maximum velocity is reached in about 16 inches of travel.

weight of each powder is loaded in cartridges and then the cartridges are fired. The cartridge loaded with Powder A will produce a higher pressure in a shorter time so the pressure curve will rise to a high value then drop quickly. In fact, it is possible that this peak pressure may be high enough to rupture the cartridge case. When the cartridge containing Powder B is fired, the pressure will rise more slowly, reach a maximum that is lower, and since the powder continues to burn longer, the pressure will remain higher for a longer period of time than in case of the cartridge loaded with Powder A. In addition, since the peak pressure is lower, it may be possible to use an even larger charge of Powder B, which will in turn maintain a higher pressure longer. In other words, the area under the pressure-distance curve will be larger and the resulting bullet velocity will be higher. The accompanying figure shows the relationship between these two situations. This principle is precisely the reason that larger charges of slower burning powders are used to produce high velocities without giving a pressure that is higher than the peak pressure the firearm and case are designed to withstand. Of course, in order to burn the larger charge of slower burning powder efficiently it helps to have a longer barrel.

It has already been explained that the velocity of the bullet in a 22 LR reaches its maximum velocity after traveling approximately 16 inches in the barrel. If we make a graph showing bullet velocity as a function of bullet travel, that curve will reach a plateau at approximately 16 inches and remain constant or decrease slightly as the bullet travels farther in the bore. In other words, the *net* force operating on the bullet is zero because the force on the base is small (the gas has already expanded and cooled) and it is necessary to overcome friction between the bullet and the barrel. The pressure inside the firearm at the instant the bullet leaves the muzzle will be very low. The accompanying graph shows this relationship.

This author once had a Mossberg Model 146 bolt-action 22 LR that had a 26-inch barrel. How well he remembers being told to be especially careful because that big rifle would be dangerous at a greater range than the small single-shot he had used earlier. In truth, the bullet velocity was probably somewhat lower than the short-barreled single shot gave, but no one had a chronograph in those days of innocence and ignorance in rimfire shooting. It was one of those cases where the rifle looked big and the basic statement sounded good so it was probably true. There are many such beliefs that get perpetuated but most rimfire shooters now know better.

The basic principles of propulsion are fairly straightforward, but there is little that can be done to alter the situation. In recent years, bullets for use in centerfire rifles have become available which are coated with molybdenum disulfide to reduce friction as they move down the bore. As a result, higher velocities (but usually less than 10 percent higher) can be achieved. The reloader of centerfire ammunition has another variable that can be brought into play. By selecting a slower-burning propellant, a higher *average* pressure is maintained because the powder burns longer but slower without exceeding the maximum pressure (which is the pressure that represents the limit for a load in a particular firearm). In other words, the pressure still goes up to some maximum value but the slower-burning powder maintains a higher pressure for a longer period of time. This results in a greater average net force on the base of bullet which results in higher velocity. While the shooter using rimfire ammunition has no such option, the engineers do. It is exactly this principle that enables the 17 HMR to achieve its high velocity because a slow burning powder (for a rimfire cartridge) is used.

Rimfire Rifle Velocities

As part of the work carried out in this project, the velocities were measured for several rifle and cartridge combinations. No attempt was made to fire all of the available types of ammunition in every rifle. The idea was to obtain velocities for many types of ammunition in at least one rifle. In most cases, at least 10 rounds (but in some cases as many as 25 to 30 rounds) were fired, and the velocities measured using a Competition Electronics ProChrono Chronograph placed 10 feet from the muzzle. A velocity obtained in this way is known as an instrumental velocity, and it may differ somewhat from the value published by the manufacturer for this particular load. There is some loss in velocity even in the first 10 feet of the bullet's path. The muzzle velocity would be approximately 20 to 25 ft/sec higher than it is at 10 feet. Also, velocity data published by manufacturers are obtained under controlled conditions with barrels measuring 24 inches in length for most cartridges. A particular lot of ammunition may give a velocity that is higher or lower than that specified as being nominal for that particular load. As a result, it is quite common for instrumental velocities to be somewhat different

Instrumental Velocity at 10 Feet for 22 LR Ammunition.					
Velocity, ft/sec in various rifles					
Cartridge	Ruger 77/22	Marlin 25N	Ruger 10/22T	Ruger 10/22	Henry
CCI Green Tag	---	1048 ± 35	---	1047 ± 32	---
CCI Mini Mag	---	1179 ± 43	1176 ± 61	---	---
CCI Std. Vel.	---	956 ± 36	962 ± 35	964 ± 39	---
CCI SGB	1292 ± 52	---	---	1207 ± 50	---
CCI Velocitor	---	1301 ± 51	1316 ± 56	---	---
Fed. G.M. Tgt.	1110 ± 26	1064 ± 41	1051 ±40	1096 ± 31	1096 ± 38
Federal HVHP	---	1304 ± 67	---	---	1251 ± 54
Fed. Lightning	---	1194 ± 48	---	---	---
Federal U. M.	1107 ± 45	---	---	---	---
Lapua Scoremax	1048 ± 31	---	---	---	---
Lapua Sup.Club	1046 ± 37	---	---	---	---
Rem. Club Xtra	---	1049 ± 36	1024 ± 35	---	---
Rem. Game Load	---	1119 ± 55	---	---	---
Rem. Golden	---	1144 ± 49	1209 ± 43	1111 ± 70	1161 ± 51
Remington Tgt.	1153 ± 32	---	1084 ± 35	---	---
Rem. Viper	---	1243 ± 66	---	---	---
Rem. Yel. Jkt.	---	1362 ± 34	---	---	---
Standard Plus	---	---	991 ± 41	1009 ± 26	---
Winchester T22	1116 ± 37	---	1112 ± 37	---	---
Winchester PP	---	1142 ± 50	1174 ± 52	---	1229 ± 42
Winchester SX	---	1150 ± 46	---	1145 ± 66	1119 ± 43
Win. Wildcat	---	1168 ± 52	---	---	---
Wolf M. T.	---	1059 ± 33	---	---	---
Abbreviations: Std. Vel. = Standard Velocity; Fed. = Federal; G.M. Tgt. = Gold Medal Target; HVHP = High Velocity Hollow Point; U.M. = Ultra Match; Sup. = Super; Rem. = Remington; Tgt. = Target; Yel. Jkt. = Yellow Jacket; PP = Power Point; SX = Super-X; Win. = Winchester; M.T. = Match Target.					

from published values. In the table, the average velocity is given followed by the standard deviation (a statistical measure showing uniformity). These values are shown in the form velocity ± standard deviation.

Although there is no need to try to explain every entry in the table, it is possible to make several observations regarding the data. Consider the case of the Federal Gold Medal Target load, which has an advertised velocity of 1080 ft/sec. The velocity of this load was measured in five different rifles as 1110, 1064, 1051, 1096, and 1096 ft/sec with standard deviations ranging from 26 to 41 ft/sec. Clearly, the velocity produced by this load is almost exactly that specified by the manufacturer (and statistically it is the same given the magnitude of the standard deviations). The CCI SGB has an advertised velocity of 1235 ft/sec, and the velocity was determined as 1292 and 1207 in two different rifles. In these cases, the standard deviations were 52 and 50 ft/sec, respectively. Winchester advertises the T22 as having a muzzle velocity of 1150 ft/sec. The velocity at 10 feet from the muzzle was found to be 1116 from a Ruger 77/22 and 1112 ft/sec from a Ruger 10/22T with a standard deviation of 37 ft/sec in each case. This is in almost exact agreement with the published value. Lapua Scoremax has an advertised velocity of 1040 ft/sec for its 48-grain bullet, and the measured velocity is 1046 ft/sec. Numerous other examples of this type of correlation are shown by the data in the table. However, there are some instances in which the instrumental velocity is somewhat lower than the published velocity. Keep in mind that there are lot to lot variations in ammunition so the lot tested may not be among those giving high velocity, and this is normal. Also, some of the testing was conducted at rather low temperature which tends to cause velocity to be lower. Finally, it is the performance in your rifle that counts, not whether the measured velocity is close to that advertised for any load.

The 17 HMR produces high velocities, and this is the reason for its dramatic performance. Several types of 17 HMR were fired through a CZ 452 and a Ruger 77/17 to determine the velocity of 17 and 20-grain bullets. The accompanying table shows the results of these measurements when the chronograph was placed 10 feet from the muzzle. Because all 17 HMR ammunition is manufactured by CCI, velocities of all of the loads with the same bullet weights should be and are identical.

Velocities of 17 HMR loads specified by the manufacturer are 2550 and 2375 ft/sec for the 17- and 20-grain bullets, respectively. The data shown in the table indicate that the advertised velocities are met in all of the loads tested. To well within the standard deviations, velocity of all of the loads with 17-grain bullets are identical as are those of the 20-grain loads. Another observation that can be made is that the velocities are quite uniform. Keep in mind that for a velocity of 2500 ft/sec a standard deviation of 25 ft/sec represents only 1 percent of the velocity. A standard deviation of 1 percent actually represents a high level of uniformity. The two rifles gave average velocities that were well within the standard deviation so it is not possible to assign any significance to a few feet per second higher velocity for one rifle or the other. Clearly, the 17 HMR is a high velocity cartridge that yields dramatic effects on targets and uniform velocities.

Instrumental Velocity at 10 Feet for 17 HMR Ammunition.		
Cartridge	CZ 452 velocity, ft/sec	Ruger 77/17 velocity, ft/sec
CCI TNT (17 gr)	2612 ± 28	2637 ± 28
CCI Game Point (20 gr)	2384 ± 27	2404 ± 40
Federal V-Shok (17 gr)	2612 ± 26	---
Hornady V-Max (17 gr)	2594 ± 29	2577 ± 44
Hornady V-Max (20 gr)	---	2440 ± 29
Remington Premier (17 gr)	2614 ± 23	---

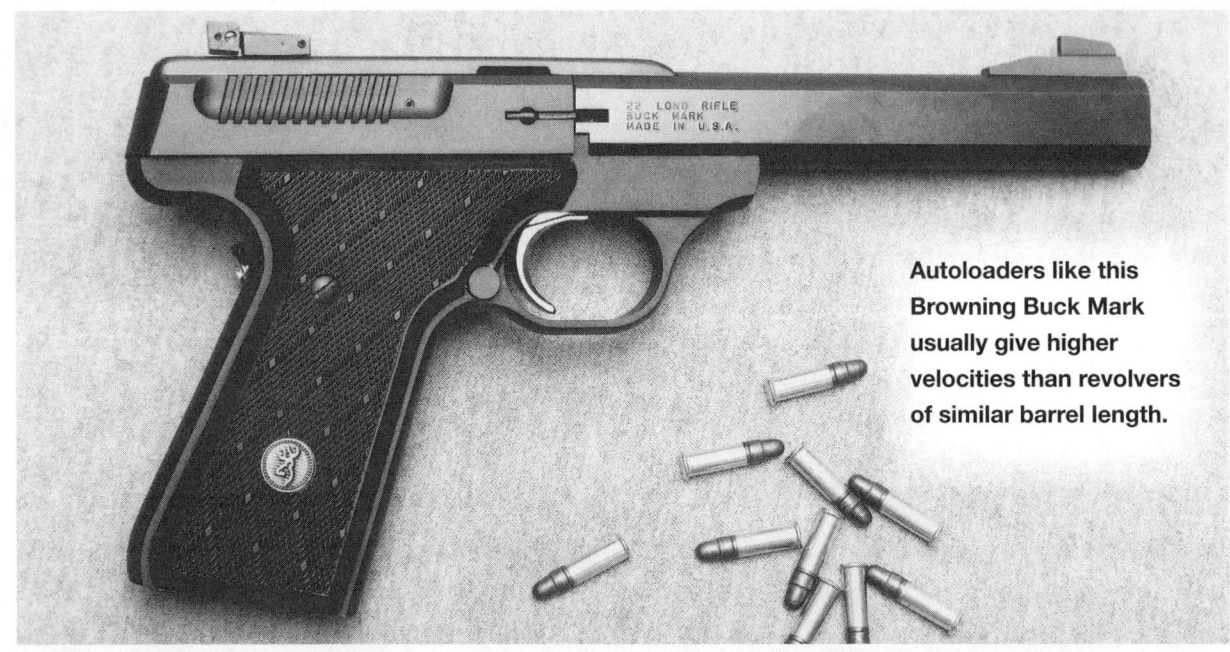

Autoloaders like this Browning Buck Mark usually give higher velocities than revolvers of similar barrel length.

Average Bullet Velocities from Several Handguns.

Cartridge	S&W 2206 4.5"	Brwng. B.M[a] 5.5"	High Std. HB[b] 6.75"	Colt F.S.[c] 4.75"	Colt Bunt.[d] 10"	S&W K-22 6"
Federal HV HP	1061	1129	1114	1034	1020	1076
Remington Golden	944	992	1029	873	886	915
Winchester Power Pt	984	1026	1030	913	875	910
PMC Sidewinder	977	1025	988	864	904	911
Federal Lightning	997	1065	1037	928	926	991
Winchester Wildcat	955	997	1002	860	862	899
Remington Target	853	928	940	868	859	900
Remington Yellow Jacket	1134	1201	------	1101	1137	1117
Remington Viper	1044	1099	------	996	1027	1067
Winchester Super-X HP	1023	1027	1077	964	903	961

[a]Browning Buck Mark; [b]High Standard HB; [c]Colt Frontier Scout; [d]Colt Frontier Scout Buntline

Bullet Velocities from Handguns

With fast burning powders like those used in 22 LR ammunition, the bullet is accelerated rapidly. As a result, most 22 LR cartridges will produce velocities in handguns that are as much as 90 percent of those produced when the same cartridges are fired in rifles. The percentage is somewhat lower when cartridges like the CCI Stinger or Velocitor are considered. Because the gap between the cylinder and barrel allows some gas to escape, revolvers generally give lower velocity than autoloaders that have the same barrel length. In order to show some of these effects, I conducted a series of tests in which several types of ammunition were fired in different handguns. Five-shot strings were fired with the velocity measured at 8 feet from the muzzle. The accompanying table shows the average velocities obtained.

The data shown in the table reveal some interesting trends. First, the velocities produced by the autoloaders are generally higher than those produced by the revolvers. In some cases, even the 4.5-inch barrel of the S&W 2206 resulted in higher velocities than those produced by the 6-inch barreled S&W K-22 revolver. Gas escapes from the gap between the

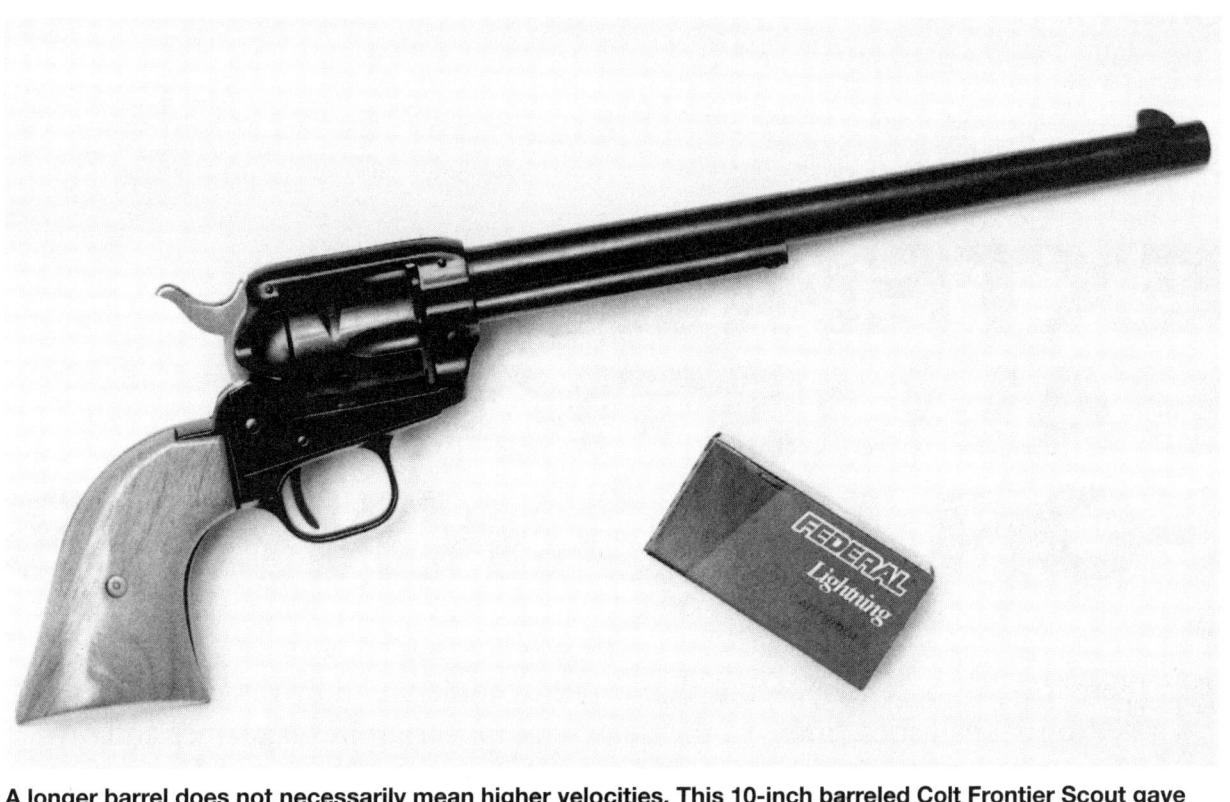

A longer barrel does not necessarily mean higher velocities. This 10-inch barreled Colt Frontier Scout gave lower velocities than did another that had a 4.5-inch barrel.

cylinder and barrel in a revolver so that the pressure on the bullet cannot be maintained at a high enough level to continue to accelerate the bullet, which is retarded by friction. Second, the 5.5-inch barrel of the Browning Buck Mark produced velocities that averaged approximately 50 ft/sec higher than those produced by the 4.5-inch barreled S&W 2206. This difference is typical of what can be expected for a one-inch difference in barrel length when the type of action is the same. Third, the 4.5-inch barreled Colt Frontier Scout gave velocities that are approximately equal to those from the 10-inch barreled version. In a long barreled revolver, gas escaping between the cylinder and barrel reduces the pressure to the point where force on the base of the bullet is not maintained and friction causes the velocity to decrease in the long barrel. This does not happen when a closed breech in an autoloader is involved. Finally, the bullet velocities are considerably lower than the same types of ammunition give in rifles. For example, Remington Yellow Jackets had an average velocity of 1444 ft/sec from a CZ 452 rifle having a barrel length of 20.5 inches, but only 1201 ft/sec (a difference of 16.8 percent) from a 5.5-inch barrel of the Browning Buck Mark. Federal High Velocity hollow points averaged 1315 ft/sec from my 20-inch barreled Winchester 190 but only 1129 ft/sec (a difference of 14.1 percent) from the 5.5-inch barreled Browning Buck Mark. Winchester Super-X hollow points averaged 1160 and 1173 ft/sec from two rifles but only slightly over 1000 ft/sec from the two autoloader pistols. All of these data illustrate the principles described above.

When bullet velocities are measured from handguns, velocities for the 22 WMR and 17 HMR are much lower that they are from rifles (sometimes only 65 to 75 percent as high). The reason is that the magnum loads make use of larger charges of slower burning powders that are not burned as efficiently in short barrels. There is no free lunch.

While it is important to understand the principles of internal ballistics, rimfire shooters can do little to change some of the parameters. The principles set forth in this chapter provide some insight to what happens during the firing process. The next chapter will describe some of the principles of the flight of a bullet.

Chapter 8

EXTERNAL BALLISTICS FOR BEGINNERS

If there is one aspect of shooting that is poorly understood by many shooters, it is external ballistics. Some of the questions appearing in magazines and on Internet sites reveal that the person asking the question has no understanding of the bullet's flight and the factors that influence it. Because there are several variables involved, treating the flight of a bullet as a mathematical problem is a formidable task that requires knowledge of advanced mathematics. Fortunately, this is not necessary, and it is possible to develop a good working knowledge of ballistics without resorting to the use of a lot of mathematics.

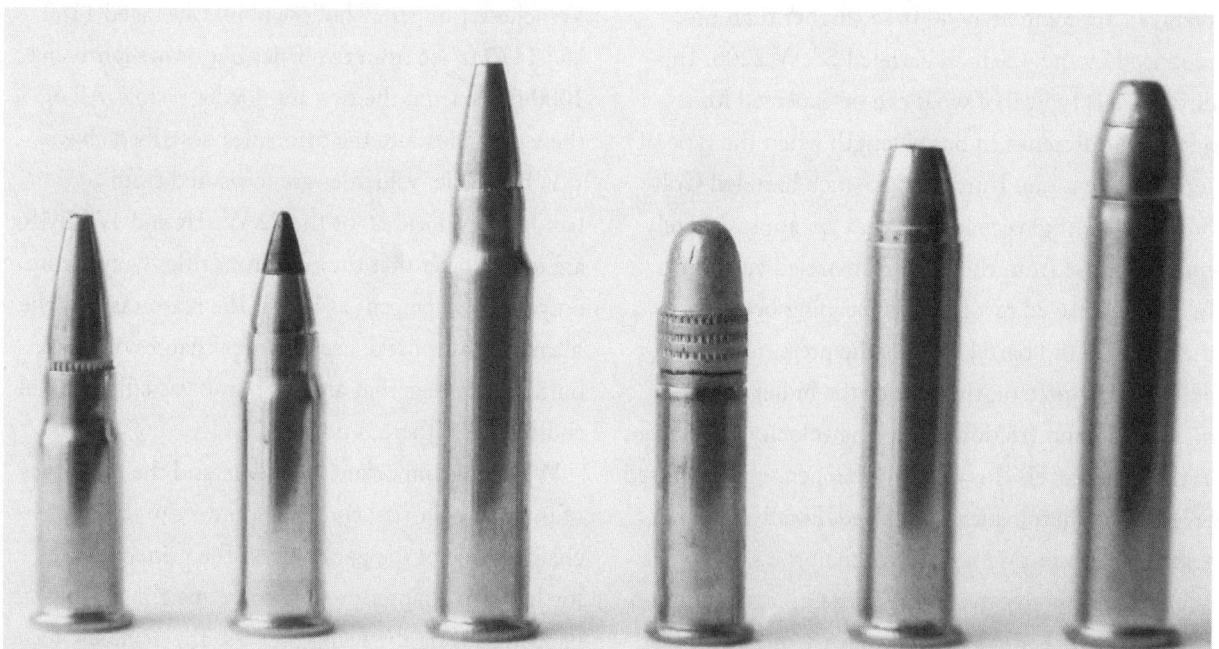

All rimfire shooters need to be concerned with ballistics of their ammunition. Shown are (left to right) the 17 Aguila, 17 Mach 2, 17 HMR, 22 LR, 22 WRF, and 22 WMR.

Forces on Projectiles

In an elementary view of external ballistics, there are only two forces acting on the bullet after it leaves the muzzle. At an advanced level, other forces must be considered, but they are unimportant when describing the path of a bullet over a moderate range. We leave that part of the discussion to the artillery experts and the 1,000-yard competitors (who do not shoot rimfire rifles). The path of a projectile is known as its *trajectory*, and in this section we will consider the trajectories of bullets fired from rimfire rounds.

The first force to be dealt with is air resistance on the bullet. Air is a mixture of gases (oxygen and nitrogen constitute about 99 percent of the atmosphere), which retards an object passing through it. The bullet must push molecules of the gases aside as it passes through the air. At high elevation, the atmosphere is "thinner" (there are fewer molecules in a given volume) so air resistance on the bullet is less than it is at low elevation. Atmospheric pressure depends on the number of molecules in a given volume. At a given elevation, the atmospheric pressure varies slightly depending on the weather conditions. For example, one day the pressure may be 29.92 inches of mercury and the next it may be 29.81 inches. The slight difference in air resistance on a projectile at these atmospheric pressures would not produce a noticeable effect on the trajectory of a bullet except perhaps at extreme ranges. It would take an incredibly accurate rifle to show such a slight difference in trajectory. This would not be true of artillery shells fired at an elevation of 1,000 ft above sea level at a target on the side of a mountain 5 miles away at an elevation of 5,000 ft. Such difficulties need not concern the sport shooter who uses a rimfire rifle.

Air resistance is not the same for all projectiles even those of the same caliber. Moreover, air resistance for a given projectile is not the same at all velocities. The faster a projectile moves, the greater the number of gas molecules it encounters and the greater the air resistance. This will be discussed more fully later.

The ability of a bullet to retain its velocity as it

A comparison of the 17 Mach 2, the 22 LR, and the 17 Aguila. Note the longer case of the 17 Mach 2.

passes through air is designated by a number known as the *ballistic coefficient*. The higher the ballistic coefficient, the better the bullet holds its velocity. Several factors contribute to the ballistic coefficient of a bullet, but the most obvious is the shape. It is easy to see why this is so. A blunt bullet passing through air forces gas molecules sideways at greater angles which means that more of the momentum of the bullet is imparted to the gas molecules being displaced. Therefore, the bullet loses its momentum (and hence its velocity) in passing through air. A pointed bullet also forces gas molecules out of its path, but it can pass through the air while creating less disturbance. The air molecules are not forced outward at angles to the path of the bullet that are as great as when a blunt bullet is involved. Therefore, a sharp pointed bullet loses its momentum (and hence its velocity) less rapidly than does a blunt bullet of the same weight and diameter. A complicating feature that need not concern us here is that the ballistic coefficient is not the same even for the same bullet if the velocity is different. In other words, the ballistic coefficient for a given bullet is not strictly a constant in all velocity ranges. Treating this effect leads into some of the deep topics in the science of ballistics which will not be explored in this book. Some of the references listed in Appendix A should be consulted for a complete study of this topic.

There is a simple way to calculate the ballistic coefficient for a bullet if the loss of velocity is known as the bullet travels between two points. Therefore,

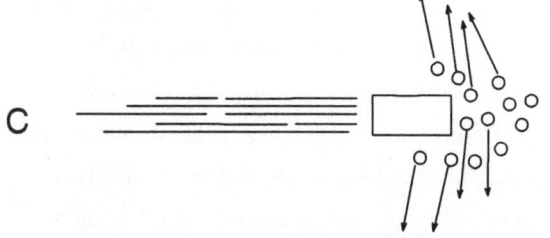

A projectile moving through the air forces molecules out of its path. A sharp pointed bullet (A) can pass through air more easily because the molecules are forces outward at smaller angles to the path. A blunt bullet (B) forced air molecules outward at larger angles which means that they absorb more of the momentum of the bullet than in (A). A very blunt bullet (C) forces air molecules outward at very large angles which results in even greater loss of momentum. Because of this effect, the ballistic coefficient of (A) is high, (B) has an intermediate ballistic coefficient, and (C) has a low ballistic coefficient.

The ballistic coefficient of the 17-grain polymer-tipped bullets used in 17 HMR cartridges is 0.125.

what we need to know is the velocity of the bullet at two points in its trajectory (perhaps at the muzzle and at 100 yards). Ballistics software currently available from many sources (such as suppliers of bullets for reloading centerfire ammunition) enables the user to input the velocity data so that the computer calculates the ballistic coefficient. To provide the data for the discussion presented here, this has been done for many of the available types of rimfire ammunition by taking the velocity data from the tables supplied by the manufacturer. Some surprising facts emerged from the calculations.

The calculated value for the ballistic coefficient of the various polymer tipped 17-grain bullets in 17 caliber turns out to be 0.125, which is determined by the muzzle velocity being 2550 ft/sec and the velocity at 100 yards being 1,900 ft/sec (a loss of 650 ft/sec or 25.5 percent). This is exactly the ballistic coefficient published in various sources. However, some authors have stated that the sharply pointed 17 caliber bullets have a higher ballistic coefficient than those for bullets used in the 22 WMR. If we take the velocity data from CCI tables, the 40-grain bullet from a 22 WMR has a muzzle velocity of 1,875 ft/sec and a remaining velocity at 100 yards of 1,375 ft/sec. Running these data through a program to calculate the ballistic coefficient gives a value of 0.130 which is slightly higher than that for the 17-bullets used in the 17 HMR. The velocity data from the Remington tables for the 33-grain V-Max bullet used in their Premium 22 WMR ammunition shows a muzzle velocity of 2,000 ft/sec and a velocity at 100 yards of 1,495 ft/sec. From these velocities a ballistic coefficient of 0.137 is determined. Even though the bullets used in most 22 WMR ammunition are not sharply pointed, their greater weight keeps them from losing velocity as rapidly as the lightweight 17 caliber bullets. When the 50-grain 22 WMR load from Federal is used as a basis for calculating the ballistic coefficient, a value of 0.158 results. That heavy bullet really holds its velocity well which is indicated by the fact that the remaining energy at

100 yards is 180 ft lbs compared to a value of 130 ft lbs for the high-velocity 30-grain hollow-point load in 22 WMR. The difference in energy is significant especially when hunting larger varmints.

Another surprise arises when ballistic coefficients are calculated for bullets used in the 22 LR ammunition. For example, the CCI ballistics tables for the Velocitor give a muzzle velocity of 1,435 ft/sec and a velocity of 1,112 ft/sec at 100 yards. These values yield a ballistic coefficient of 0.141 for the 40-grain hollow-point bullet. When velocity data for the Federal Gold Medal Target load is used in the calculation, a ballistic coefficient of 0.167 results. When velocities for a considerable number of types of 22 LR ammunition are analyzed, it is found that the 40-grain solid bullets have ballistic coefficients of approximately 0.140-0.160. The 29-grain bullet used in the 22 Short has a ballistic coefficient of only 0.104. For the 32-grain bullet used in the hyper-velocity CCI Stinger, the ballistic coefficient is only 0.100 and a value of 0.106 is found for the 33-grain hollow-point used in Remington Yellow Jacket ammunition. Therefore, the lightweight bullets used in hyper-velocity loads lose velocity more rapidly than the heavier bullets. These facts translate to significantly different energies for the heavy bullets and those used in the hyper-velocity rounds, especially at longer ranges where a varmint may cross paths with the bullet.

Trajectory

Bullets traveling in air follow a curved path, but the line of sight from the shooter's eye to the target is a straight line. When a bullet travels down a straight rifle barrel, it is launched in the direction that the barrel is pointing. In order to take best advantage of the sights, the line of sight and the line of the bore do not exactly coincide. They are slightly closer together at the muzzle than they are at the breech Therefore, if the line of sight to the target is perfectly horizontal, the slightly upward tipped bore (in relation to the line of sight) causes the bullet to be launched in an upward direction that projects it above the horizontal line of sight. The bullet rises to meet the line of sight at some distance, travels above the line of sight, then crosses and falls below the line of sight at some longer distance. The line of sight and the bullet path coincide at two distances. The longer of these distances is usually taken as the sight in distance. The deviation of the bullet path from the line of sight at one-half the range for which the rifle is sighted in is known as the *midrange trajectory*. Because the path of a bullet moving through air is not exactly parabolic, the midrange trajectory is not exactly the same as the maximum deviation from the line of sight. The highest point on the trajectory usually occurs at a distance that is approximately 60 percent of the range for which the piece is sighted in. In other words, when a 22 LR is sighted to hit the point of aim at 70 yards, the highest point on the trajectory is at approximately 40 yards instead of at the midpoint of the path (35 yards).

Most of the popular ballistics programs calculate the *bullet drop*, which is the distance the bullet would fall below the line of the bore at some distance when fired horizontally. This property is determined by the time of flight, and the simple laws of physics enable one to calculate how far an object would fall during that amount of time. This is almost a useless property since shooters do not fire rifles perfectly horizontally while ignoring the sights on the rifle. The whole idea of sighting in at some distance is to optimize the trajectory. This is accomplished by adjusting the sights so that the path of the bullet rises above the line of sight and then meets it at the sight in distance. The overall drop of the bullet

The ballistic coefficients of the light bullets used in hyper-velocity 22 LR ammunition are only about 0.100-0.105 so such bullets lose velocity rapidly.

is immaterial except for the fact that the trajectory (which is useful) is also related to the time of flight. Comparing two bullets that have drops of 4 inches and 8 inches at some range does not mean that the one with the 4-inch drop can be sighted in at a range that is twice the other. It is also meaningless to say that the bullet that gives a drop of 4 inches shoots "twice as flat" as the other. Neither shoots "flat!"

Suppose you want to sight in a rifle so that the bullet path never deviates from the line of sight by more than a certain amount (perhaps one inch). The distance at which the path of the bullet deviates from the line of sight by no more than the specified amount is known as the *point-blank range*. This means that if the target has a size of 2 inches, the path of the bullet must not rise or fall more than one inch from the line of sight when the point of aim is the center of the target. As will be illustrated later, the point-blank range for the standard-velocity 22 LR is approximately 75 yards, the high-velocity about 85 yards, the 22 WMR about 125 yards, and the 17 HMR about 150 yards when an appropriate maximum deviation between the line of sight and point of impact is assumed.

22 Long Rifle

The principles described above will be illustrated by considering several popular rimfire loads, and we will begin with the 22 LR then progress to other cartridges. The trajectory data were obtained by using one of the standard computer programs.

Consider the case of the Federal Gold Medal Target cartridge (Federal Product No. 711B), which gives a muzzle velocity of 1080 ft/sec. If the sights are adjusted

Even though the bullets in these 22 LR cartridges have different shapes, their ballistic coefficients do not differ by much.

so that the bullet strikes the point of aim at 50 yards, the bullet will first cross the line of sight at approximately 18 yards and will strike approximately 0.3 inch high at 25 yards. After crossing the line of sight at 50 yards, the bullet would impact 2.44 inches low at 75 yards. All of this depends on how far the line of sight is above the bore, and that value must be specified when performing ballistic calculations. Typically, the axis of most scopes gives a line of sight that is approximately 1.5 inches above the center of the bore. If the distance between the bore and the line of sight were only 1.3 inches, all of the deviations from the line of sight would be moved up slightly. The effect caused by different sight heights will be demonstrated later. If the sight height were 1.3 inches, the bullet would strike approximately 0.5 inch high at 25 yards when sighted in at 50 yards.

All manufacturers of ammunition provide ballistics tables for their products. However, the ranges specified usually include only 0, 50, and 100 yards when rimfire ammunition is being described. The careful rimfire shooter needs information that provides more details about trajectory at other ranges. Knowing the ballistic coefficient for a bullet and its initial velocity allows the trajectory to be calculated by making use of the ballistics programs that are available from several suppliers of reloading information. The accompanying table shows the results of such calculations for the 22 LR Federal Gold Medal Target ammunition for which the ballistic coefficient of the bullet is taken to be 0.140 and the muzzle velocity is 1,080 ft/sec. These values are characteristic of standard-velocity 22 LR ammunition from other manufacturers. In this example, three different sight in ranges, 50, 60, 70 yards, have been assumed in the calculations to illustrate the effect on trajectory.

The data shown in the table reveal why the common practice of sighting in a 22 LR with standard-velocity ammunition at 50 yards may not be the best plan. Clearly, in this case the bullet rises to a maximum height that is much less than an inch above the line of sight. The point of impact is 0.37 inch high at 30 yards when the rifle is sighted in at a range of 50 yards. When sighting in for squirrel hunting, I usually sight in at 50 yards since I want to be able to hold directly on a very small target and shots at distances greater than 50 yards are uncommon. However, for shooting larger targets (such as ground squirrels sitting vertically) with a 22 LR, it makes sense to sight in with target ammunition at around 60 to 65 yards to give a longer point-blank range. When sighted in this way, the bullet will strike about three-quarters of an inch high at 30 yards and about 0.83 inch high at 40 yards. Unless you are shooting at a very small target with a very accurate rifle, these deviations from the line of sight will not cause misses and the bullet will strike only about an inch low at 70 yards which is about the longest range practical for trying to shoot pests with standard-velocity ammunition. Of course, you could sight in at a range of 100 yards for small-bore competition, but the bullet will strike approximately 3.6 inches high at 50 and 60 yards.

The powerhouse of the 22 LR cartridges is the CCI Velocitor which gives a 40-grain hollow-point bullet a muzzle velocity advertised to be 1,435 ft/sec which corresponds to a muzzle energy of over 180 ft lbs. Even at a range of 100 yards the remaining energy is 110 ft lbs, which is about the same as a standard-velocity, round produces at the muzzle. When using this ammunition on pests and game, we want to sight in the rifle to take advantage of its flat trajectory and power. The results of ballistics calculations that are shown in the table provide the basis for deciding the most advantageous way to sight in when using CCI Velocitors. The ballistic coefficient of this bullet is 0.141.

For most varmint shooting, a deviation of one inch from the line of sight will not cause misses. The data show that it is practical to sight in a rifle shooting Velocitors at a range of 75 yards, which will give a point-blank range of about 85 yards. This is about the maximum practical range for the 22 LR as a varmint rifle.

Keep in mind that game is not shot at the muzzle and that at a range of 50-100 yards the energy may be quite different from that at the muzzle. For example, a high-velocity 22 LR produces about 140 ft lbs at the muzzle, but after the bullet travels 50 yards that has decreased to about 110 ft lbs. A standard-velocity 22 LR produces about 105 ft lbs at the muzzle but the remaining energy at 50 yards is about 90 ft lbs. Note that the high-velocity round has lost 35 ft lbs while traveling 50 yards, but the standard-velocity round has lost only 20 ft lbs in the same interval. Remaining energies at 100 yards are even closer. A hyper-velocity 22 LR that uses a light

Calculated Trajectories for 22 LR Federal Gold Medal Target (R0 is Sight-In Range).

Range, yds.	V, ft/sec	E, ft lb	Deviation from line of sight, inches		
			R0 = 50 yd	R0 = 60 yd	R0 = 70 yd
0	1,080	103	-1.50	-1.50	-1.50
10	1,060	100	-0.57	-0.44	-0.31
20	1,042	96	+0.06	+0.30	+0.58
30	1,025	93	+0.37	+0.73	+1.14
40	1,009	90	+0.35	+0.83	+1.38
50	994	88	0.00	+0.59	+1.27
60	980	85	-0.70	0.00	+0.82
70	967	83	-1.74	-0.95	0.00
80	954	81	-3.16	-2.28	-1.19
90	942	79	-4.94	-3.97	-2.75
100	931	77	-7.10	-6.05	-4.69

weight bullet which has a low ballistic coefficient may produce 160 ft lbs at the muzzle but give a remaining energy of only 90 ft lbs out at 100 yards where the target is. Because it produces a high energy while using a bullet of normal weight, the Velocitor retains its energy advantage even at extended ranges.

22 Winchester Magnum Rimfire

The 22 WMR is a powerful cartridge that is widely used as a varmint load, but it is almost never considered as a target round. For use on varmints, we need to determine the most efficient range for which the rifle should be sighted in. Because there are a variety of bullet weights available in ammunition for the 22 WMR, we need to decide which load is to be used and for purposes of illustration, the Winchester 40-grain jacketed hollow-point will be considered. That load has a muzzle velocity advertised as 1,910 ft/sec with a remaining velocity of 1,330 ft/sec at 100 yards. These velocities correspond to a ballistic coefficient of 0.116 for this bullet. Our procedure is to use this ballistic coefficient and calculate the trajectories that would result when the rifle is sighted in at various distances. The accompanying table shows the results obtained from the calculations when the rifle is sighted in for 75, 100, and 125 yards.

From the table, we see that sighting a 22 WMR rifle in at a distance of 75 yards does not take full advantage of its capabilities. When so sighted, there is maximum deviation of only 0.29 inches from the line of sight at ranges between the muzzle and 75 yards. Such a slight deviation means that the point of impact is almost on the line of sight in this interval, but the bullet would strike 1.30 inches low at 100 yards and 3.79 inches low at 125 yards. Sighting the rifle in at 100 yards gives a deviation from the line of sight of almost exactly one inch at 50 and 75 yards, and the bullet strikes only 2.16 inches below the line of sight at 125 yards. The difference of one inch is small enough that it should not cause misses at shorter ranges, and the point of impact being only 2.16 inches low at 125 would enable hits to be made with regularity on varmints of most sizes. Sighted to hit a point of aim at 100 yards makes a 22 WMR suitable for use as a 125-yard varmint rifle if the accuracy is sufficient.

It might be thought that sighting in a 22 WMR for at 125 yards would be even better. However, the table shows that in order to do that, the bullet would strike 2.27 inches high at 75 yards. Such a deviation would make it necessary to "hold under" at ranges of 50 to 75 yards when shooting at small varmints or even when placing a bullet exactly where you want it on a coyote's head after calling it in to that range.

One of the types of 22 WMR ammunition that has performed well in my rifle is the Remington Premier that fires a 33-grain Hornady V-Max bullet

Calculated Trajectories for 22 LR CCI Velocitors (R0 is the Sight-In Range).					
Range, yds.	V, ft/sec	E, ft lb	R0 = 60 yd	R0 = 70 yd	R0 = 80 yd
0	1,435	183	-1.50	-1.50	-1.50
10	1,396	173	-0.77	-0.70	-0.61
20	1,358	164	-0.22	-0.07	+0.09
30	1,321	155	+0.15	+0.36	+0.61
40	1,287	147	+0.31	+0.60	+0.93
50	1,253	140	+0.27	+0.63	+1.05
60	1,222	133	0.00	+0.43	+0.93
70	1,192	126	-0.50	0.00	+0.59
80	1,164	120	-1.25	-0.67	0.00
90	1,138	115	-2.25	-1.60	-0.85
100	1,114	110	-3.52	-2.80	-1.96

at a published velocity of 2,000 ft/sec. The polymer-tipped V-Max bullet has a ballistic coefficient of 0.137, which is somewhat higher than that of the 40-grain bullets with more rounded profiles. Incidentally, the measured muzzle velocity from my rifle is somewhat higher than 2,000 ft/sec (by about 200 ft/sec!), but the advertised value was used in the calculations. The accompanying table shows the results of the computer calculations for the Remington Premier load.

The results shown in the table indicate that the 33-grain V-Max bullet has a trajectory that has less curvature than that of the 40-grain bullet. With the Remington Premier load, a 22 WMR can be sighted in at 125 yards with the bullet rising no more than about 1.8 inches above the line of sight and striking about 2.5 inches low at 150 yards. If a deviation of no more than 1.4 inches can be tolerated, the rifle can be sighted in at 115 yards, which will give a point of impact that is 0.74 inches low at 125 yards and 3.34 inches low at 150 yards. The Remington Premier load makes the 22 WMR an effective varmint cartridge out to about 140-150 yards, but keep in mind that bullet energy at that distance is only 125 to 130 ft lbs which is about the same as the muzzle energy of a 22 LR high-velocity load.

For larger varmints like foxes and coyotes, the 50-grain hollow-point 22 WMR load from Federal is hard to beat when the range is 100 yards or less. The heavy bullet has a ballistic coefficient of 0.160 so it holds its velocity better than the lighter bullets. However, because the velocity is low with such a heavy bullet, the sight in distance is only 100 yards or less. Performing the trajectory calculations for this load with a sight in distance of 100 yards shows that the bullet would strike 1.31 inches high at 50 yards, 1.41 inches high at 60 yards, 1.33 inches high at 70 yards, hit the point of aim at 100 yards, and strike 1.91 inches low at 120 yards. However, the muzzle energy for this load is approximately 300 ft lbs, but the remaining energy at 100 yards is 186 ft lbs and at 120 yards it is 169 ft lbs. Within its useful range, this is the most powerful rimfire load, and it is effective on the larger species of varmints. Before deciding that this is the load you want to use on such targets, shoot some groups to determine its accuracy in your rifle. Although it is not the most accurate ammunition in my 22 WMR, it is sufficiently

These 22 WMR cartridges are loaded with (left to right) 30-grain hollow-point, 33-grain polymer-tipped, and 50-grain hollow-point bullets. The corresponding ballistic coefficients differ significantly, and the 33-grain and 50-grain bullets

Calculated Trajectories for 22 WMR with 40-Grain Bullet (R0 is the Sight-In Range).

			Deviation from line of sight, inches		
Range, yds.	V, ft/sec	E, ft lb	R0 = 75 yd	R0 = 100 yd	R0 = 125 yd
0	1,910	323	-1.50	-1.50	-1.50
25	1,755	274	-0.25	+0.07	+0.51
50	1,610	230	+0.29	+0.94	+1.81
75	1,475	193	0.00	+0.98	+2.27
100	1,353	163	-1.30	0.00	+1.73
125	1,245	138	-3.79	-2.16	0.00
150	1,155	118	-7.68	-5.73	-3.14
175	1,082	104	-13.20	-10.92	-7.90
200	1,025	93	-20.57	-17.97	-14.51

accurate for use out to 100 yards or so, and it has the highest remaining energy.

17 Hornady Magnum Rimfire

Having considered the trajectories of the 22 LR and 22 WMR, we need to discuss the 17 HMR. Because of its high-velocity, the trajectory of the 17 HMR is quite flat for a rimfire cartridge. Therefore, it is possible to sight in a rifle in this caliber for a rather long range. The calculations for the 17-grain bullet having a ballistic coefficient of 0.125 give the trajectories listed in the table for three different sight-in distances.

The calculated trajectories show that a 100-yard sight in distance does not take full advantage of the trajectory of the 17 HMR cartridge. Between the muzzle and 100 yards there is no more than a 0.33-inch difference between the line of sight and the bullet path. This difference is so small that there is little likelihood of missing even a small target, but with that sighting, the bullet will strike 2.55 inches low at 150 yards and 5.02 inches low at 175 yards. However, if the rifle is sighted in at 125 yards, the bullet will strike no more than 0.89 inch high at any distance between the muzzle and 125 yards and be only 1.43 inches low at 150 yards and 3.73 inches low at 175 yards. If the rifle is sighted in at 150 yards, the bullet will strike 1.70 inches high at 100 yards, which is a larger deviation than one should have for a rifle that is intended for use on small varmints. Therefore, the best compromise is to sight in a rifle chambered for the 17 HMR to hit about three-quarters of an inch high at 100 yards so it will hit the point of aim at 125 yards. If the targets you are shooting will allow you to tolerate a deviation of +1.0 inch, your 17 HMR can be sighted in at approximately 130 yards, which will give a point of impact that is 1.0 inch high at 80 yards. Such a sighting will result in a point of impact that is 3.5 inches low at 175 yards. However, note that the remaining energy is only about 100 ft lbs at 150 yards and only 84 ft lbs at 175 yards, a fact which should lead you to consider the 17 HMR as a varmint cartridge that is suitable for use at ranges of 150 yards or less.

Ammunition in 17 HMR caliber is loaded by CCI and marketed by both Hornady and CCI that utilizes a 20-grain hollow-point bullet that has a muzzle velocity of 2,375 ft/sec. The ballistic coefficient of this hollow-point bullet is 0.125, which happens to be the same as that for the 17-grain polymer-tipped bullet. When this load is sighted to hit the point of aim at 100 yards, the bullet strikes 0.28 inches high at 50 yards, 0.43 inches high at 75 yards, 1.12 inches low at 125 yards, 3.05 inches low at 150 yards, 5.94 inches low at 175 yards, and approximately 10 inches low at 200 yards. Because of the small deviations from the line of sight at intermediate ranges, a rifle firing this load can also be sighted in at 125 yards.

When sighted in at a range of 125 yards, the point of impact is 0.73 inches high at 50 yards, 1.11 inches

Calculated Trajectories for 22 WMR 33-Grain Remington Premier (R0 is the Sight-In Range).				
			Deviation from line of sight, inches	
Range, yds.	V, ft/sec	E, ft lb	R0 = 100 yd	R0 = 125 yd
0	2,000	293	-1.50	-1.50
25	1,868	256	-0.10	+0.25
50	1,742	222	+0.69	+1.38
75	1,622	193	+0.76	+1.79
100	1,509	167	0.00	+1.38
125	1,404	145	-1.72	0.00
150	1,309	126	-4.54	-2.48
175	1,224	110	-8.63	-6.22
200	1,151	97	-14.18	-11.42

high at 75 yards, 0.90 inches high at 100 yards, and 1.70 inches low at 150 yards, 4.36 inches low at 175 yards, and 8.18 inches low at 200 yards. When sighted this way, the bullet is only slightly more than one inch high anywhere along the path to 125 yards and less than 2 inches low at 150 yards. Therefore, the 17 HMR is an effective cartridge for use on small varmints at ranges up to approximately 150 yards, but at that range the remaining energy is only 102 ft lbs which is only slightly higher than 22 LR loads produce at 100 yards and lower than the energy given by the CCI Velocitor 22 LR at 100 yards. While some shooters may stretch the 17 HMR to 200 yards, the remaining energy at that range is almost exactly the same as that given by the 22 Short at the muzzle! That energy is sufficient to dispatch pests but only with precisely placed shots, which is well nigh impossible at 200 yards with bullets that are as susceptible to the influence of wind as are those fired from a 17 HMR (or any other rimfire). There is no free lunch.

17 Mach 2 and 17 Aguila

Having considered the external ballistics of bullets fired from 22 LR, 22 WMR, and 17 HMR cartridges, let us turn our attention to the newest rimfire, the 17 Mach 2 which is sometimes designated as the 17 HM2 or 17 M2. This cartridge uses a 17-grain polymer tipped bullet that is identical to that used in the 17 HMR but with a muzzle velocity of approximately 2,100 ft/sec. A velocity of 2,100 ft/sec is exactly the velocity of the same bullet fired from the 17 HMR after it has traveled approximately 66 yards. Therefore, the velocity and energy of a bullet fired from a 17 Mach 2 over a range 0 to 134 yards will be identical to those characteristics of a bullet fired from a 17 HMR in the interval from 66 to 200 yards. Using a sight in distance of 100 yards and a sight height of 1.5 inches, the trajectory for the 17 Mach 2 was calculated yielding the results shown in the following table.

Calculated Trajectory for 17 Mach 2 with 17-Grain Bullet (Sight in Range = 100 yd).

Range, yds.	V, ft/sec	E, ft lb	Deviation from line of sight, inches
0	2,100	166	-1.50
25	1,946	143	-0.16
50	1,799	122	+0.60
75	1,660	104	+0.71
100	1,530	88	0.00
125	1,411	75	-1.64
150	1,304	64	-4.31
175	1,211	55	-8.19
200	1,134	49	-13.52

With a muzzle velocity that approximates that of a 22 WMR firing the Remington Premier load with 33-grain V-Max bullets, the trajectory of the 17-grain bullets from the 17 Mach 2 is similar to those fired from a 22 WMR. Initial reports on the

Calculated Trajectories for 17 HMR with 17-Grain Bullet (R0 is the Sight-In Range).

Range, yds.	V, ft/sec	E, ft lb	Deviation from line of sight, inches		
			R0 = 100 yd	R0 = 125 yd	R0 = 150 yd
0	2,550	245	-1.50	-1.50	-1.50
25	2,378	213	-0.48	-0.30	-0.06
50	2,212	185	+0.15	+0.52	+1.00
75	2,053	159	+0.33	+0.89	+1.61
100	1,901	136	0.00	+0.74	+1.70
125	1,756	116	-0.93	0.00	+1.20
150	1,620	99	-2.55	-1.43	0.00
175	1,494	84	-5.02	-3.73	-2.05
200	1,378	72	-8.74	-6.99	-5.07

accuracy of rifles firing the 17 Mach 2 indicate that the cartridge is exceptionally accurate. Accordingly, with its trajectory, it should be possible to make hits on small species out to around 125 yards, but at that distance the energy is about the same as that given by the 17 HMR at 200 yards, which is rather anemic (about 75 ft lbs). However, this chapter is concerned with ballistics, and the tiny 17 Mach 2 is an interesting development from that standpoint. Doubtless, there will be those who will shoot animals that should not normally be shot with such a caliber and get one-shot kills because a projectile having an energy at 125 yards that is equivalent to that of a 22 Short at the muzzle will kill a lot of things when placed in a lethal zone. Realistically, the 17 Mach 2 has a flatter trajectory than the CCI Velocitor 22 LR, but it has less energy at all ranges. It remains however that the 17 Mach 2 is a very interesting cartridge that provides outstanding accuracy and flat trajectory from rifles that are identical to those chambered for the 22 LR.

While the 17 Mach 2 was being developed, the 17 Aguila was introduced. This cartridge is based on a standard length 22 LR case necked to hold a 17 caliber bullet. Because powder capacity is slightly less than that of the 17 Mach 2, the velocity is lower and the 17 Aguila utilizes a 20-grain bullet at an advertised velocity of 1,850 ft/sc. While not having specific information on the bullet, the ballistic coefficient was estimated to be 0.125 in order to calculate the trajectory. While not exact, the results of the calculations are sufficiently accurate to show the path of the bullet reasonably well. The accompanying table shows the data generated.

These cartridges are (left to right) the 17 Aguila, 17 Mach 2, and 17 HMR. With their high-velocity, they give trajectory flat enough to make hits possible at relatively long ranges.

Calculated Trajectory for 17 Aguila with 20-Grain Bullet (Sight-In Range = 100 yd).

Range, yds.	V, ft/sec	E, ft lb	Deviation from line of sight, inches
0	1,850	151	-1.50
25	1,713	130	+0.12
50	1,584	111	+1.00
75	1,463	95	+1.01
100	1,352	81	0.00
125	1,255	70	-2.20
150	1,171	61	-5.77
175	1,101	54	-10.94
200	1,045	49	-17.88

In the 17 Aguila we have a cartridge that can literally be substituted for the 22 LR in an enormous number of firearms simply by changing barrels which is not quite the case for the 17 Mach 2. The result may be that the 17 Aguila will achieve popularity in autoloaders, which would otherwise require changes in the bolt and/or recoil spring. In terms of ballistic performance, the 17 Mach 2 has a slight edge owing to its larger capacity case. However, there is very little practical difference, and the 20-grain bullets used in the 17 Aguila should give reliable performance on small game and pests. In terms of trajectory, the 17 Aguila shoots flat enough to make hits possible to a range of almost 125 yards in accurate rifles. The accuracy of the 17 Aguila is reported to be quite good and it should be on a par with the 17 Mach 2 in this regard. Although they are interesting developments, the author does not expect to give up shooting the 22 LR for either the 17 Mach 2 or the 17 Aguila. They are both short on power except for very small animals.

Ballistics Tables

All ammunition makers supply ballistics tables for their ammunition. These tables show the velocity of the bullet at the muzzle and at various ranges. For the 22 LR, the ranges are usually 0, 50, and 100 yards, but may include 25 and 75 yards. For the 17

HMR, the ranges are usually for distances to 200 yards. Also given in ballistic tables is the bullet energy at each of the ranges. It is a simple matter to make use of this information for the particular ammunition being used. However, ballistics tables also include information about bullet trajectory. Such information is usually is presented in terms of the difference between the point of impact and the line of sight. Negative values mean that the bullet strikes below the line of sight while positive values mean that the bullet strikes above the line of sight. Of course, there is some distance for which the rifle is sighted in that the point of aim and the bullet path coincide. The data in the table might be represented as follows for the 22 LR high-speed bullet where the line of sight is assumed to be 1.5 inches above the bore.

Range, yd.	0	25	50	75	100
Height, in.	-1.5	+0.05	0.0	-1.82	-5.8

In hunting situations involving the 22 LR, a deviation of the bullet path from the line of sight should not be more than about 1-1.5 inches. From the data shown above, it can be seen that when the sight in range is 50 yards, the bullet would strike only 0.05 inches above the line of sight at 25 yards. A better plan is to sight in a 22 LR at 65 yards, which puts the bullet about 0.66 inches high at 50 yards and only about 0.83 inches low at 75 yards. So sighted, a 22 LR has a point-blank range of about 80 yards. If the rifle to be used hunting squirrels, its better to have no more than a one-inch deviation because the lethal zone may be about one inch in size. In that case, it is better to sight in at about 65-70 yards so that the bullet is no more than an inch above or below the line of sight to a range of 75 yards. Of course the trajectory for a standard-velocity round is slightly more curved, and the optimum sight in range would be approximately 60 yards.

It is clear that under most circumstances the 22 LR is about a 75-yard cartridge because of its curved trajectory. High-velocity ammunition like the CCI Velocitor will increase the range to 85 to 90 yards. Keep in mind that at a range of 75 yards, the average 22 would probably produce groups of about 1.5 inches so the accuracy becomes a factor also. A shooter who is very good at estimating range and using a rifle that is capable of producing groups of 1.5 inches at 100 yards can make hits at that distance on game that has a fairly large lethal zone. However, the remaining energy is less than 100 ft lbs at that range so the bullet must be placed accurately. If the accuracy is sufficient, using the CCI Velocitor round helps some because it gives a remaining energy of about 110 ft lbs. Also, with a muzzle velocity of approximately 1,400 ft/sec, a rifle firing Velocitor ammunition can be sighted in at 75 yards and the bullet strike only 0.27 inches high at 25 yards, 0.86 inches high at 50 yards, and 2.31 inches low at 100 yards. Therefore, in an accurate rifle, CCI Velocitor ammunition gives an effective range of almost 100 yards. Trying to shoot varmints at distances greater than that involves a lot of luck because even a gentle breeze will move the point of impact a considerable distance. A 10 mph cross wind moves the 17 HMR bullet 3.5 inches at 100 yards, 8.5 inches at 150 yards, and 16 inches at 200 yards. Any bullet fired from a rimfire rifle is affected more by wind than are the heavier bullets fired from most centerfire rifles because the latter have higher ballistic coefficients.

Effect of Sight Height

When ballistics calculations are performed using one of the many computer programs available, the user must specify the height of the line of sight above the bore. Although most scopes have tubes

Scope mounts for use on rimfire rifles come in different heights so that scopes having front bells of different diameter can be accommodated. On the left is the Weaver Tip-Off mount while that on the right is a Beeman mount.

that are one inch in diameter, scope mounts differ in height. Scopes are mounted on the receivers of rifles, but the receiver and the barrel do not have the same diameter. All of these factors contribute to the quantity known as the sight height and in this section we wish to analyze its effect on the calculated trajectory. In order to assess the effect of the sight height, calculations were performed assuming that the sight height is 1.00, 1.25, and 1.50 inches. The results for the standard-velocity 22 LR load are shown in the accompanying table.

Effect of Sight Height (SH) on Trajectory. 22 LR Federal Gold Medal Target, B.C. 0.140, Sight In Range 60 Yards.

Range, yd	Velocity, ft/sec	Energy, ft lb	Bullet path for different sight height		
			SH = 1.00 in.	SH = 1.25 in.	SH= 1.50 in.
0	1,080	103	-1.00	-1.25	-1.50
10	1,060	100	-0.03	-0.24	-0.44
20	1,042	96	+0.64	+0.47	+0.30
30	1,025	93	+0.98	+0.86	+0.73
40	1,009	90	+1.00	+0.92	+0.83
50	994	88	+0.67	+0.63	+0.59
60	980	85	0.00	0.00	0.00
70	967	83	-1.04	-0.99	-0.95
80	954	81	-2.44	-2.36	-2.28
90	942	79	-4.22	-4.10	-3.97
100	931	77	-6.38	-6.22	-6.05

The data show the effects of the height of the line of sight above the bore. In each case the rifle is sighted in at 60 yards. Note that the highest point on the trajectory is 1.00 inch high (at 40 yards) when the sight height is 1.00 inch above the line of sight, but the maximum height of the bullet path is only 0.92 inch above the line of sight if the sight height is 1.25 inches. When the sight height is 1.50 inches, the maximum deviation of the bullet path is 0.83 inch. Likewise, at a range of 80 yards, the point of impact is -2.44, -2.36, or -2.28 when the sight height is 1.00, 1.25, or 1.50 inch, respectively. The higher the line of sight above the bore, the flatter the trajectory appears to be. Of course, the trajectory is exactly the same, but the point of impact deviates slightly from the line of sight because the line of sight is in a different position relative to the bore in the three cases. Note that at 40 yards the difference amounts to only 0.17-inch difference when the sight height

varies from 1.00 to 1.50 inches. At 80 yards, the difference is only 0.16 inch when the sight height varies similarly. For all practical purposes, you will never need to worry whether the center of the scope on your 22 rifle is 1.16 or 1.43 inches above the bore. There is little likelihood that you will ever notice these small differences in the point of impact unless you have a very accurate rifle.

Because the velocity is higher, the trajectory of the 22 WMR is less curved than that of the 22 LR. Therefore, the effect caused by differences in sight height will not be the same as in the case of the 22 LR. To illustrate this, trajectories were calculated assuming that the line of sight is 1.00, 1.25, and 1.50 inches above the bore. The data are shown in the table.

The data in the table show that at a range of 50 yards the difference between the point of impact and the line of sight changes by 0.25 inch as the sight height varies from 1.00 to 1.50 inches. With a rifle that gives one-half inch groups at that range, it is doubtful that a difference of only 0.25 inch would be noted on the basis of one shot. If 10-shot groups

Effect of Sight Height on Trajectory of the 22 WMR, 40-Grain H. P., B.C. = 0.116.

Range, yd	Velocity, ft/sec	Energy, ft lb	Bullet path for different sight height		
			SH = 1.00 in.	SH = 1.25 in.	SH = 1.50 in.
0	1,910	323	-1.00	-1.25	-1.50
25	1,759	275	+0.44	+0.25	+0.06
50	1,617	232	+1.18	+1.05	+0.93
75	1,485	196	+1.09	+1.02	+0.96
100	1,365	165	0.00	0.00	0.00
125	1,258	141	-2.25	-2.19	-2.13
150	1,168	121	-5.88	-5.75	-5.63
175	1,094	106	-11.10	-10.91	-10.72
200	1,036	95	-18.13	-17.88	-17.63

were fired with scopes having center heights above the bore of 1.00 and 1.50 inches, the average point of impact might show the effect of sight height. If the rifle were capable of firing a .5-inch group at 50 yards, the difference in trajectory would be evident, especially if several shots were fired with two different scopes that differed by one-half inch in height.

Having shown how the point of impact varies with height of the line of sight above the bore for the 22 LR and 22 WMR, we will now show the effect on the trajectory of the 17 HMR. As was done for the 22 LR and 22 WMR, it was assumed that the sight height is 1.00, 1.25, or 1.50 inches above the bore. When the calculations are carried out assuming a sight in range of 125 yards, the data shown in the following table were obtained.

\multicolumn{6}{c}{17 HMR, 17-Grain Polymer-Tip Bullet, B.C. = 0.125}					
Range, yd	Velocity, ft/sec	Energy, ft lb	Bullet path for different sight height		
			SH = 1.00 in	SH = 1.25 in	SH = 1.50 in
0	2,550	245	-1.00	-1.25	-1.50
25	2,384	214	+0.09	-0.11	-0.31
50	2,226	187	+0.80	+0.65	+0.50
75	2,070	162	+1.06	+0.96	+0.86
100	1,922	139	+0.83	+0.78	+0.73
125	1,781	120	0.00	0.00	0.00
150	1,648	102	-1.51	-1.46	-1.41
175	1,523	88	-3.82	-3.72	-3.62
200	1,407	75	-7.07	-6.92	-6.77

The data in the table show that when the 17 HMR is sighted in at 125 yards, the point of impact is 1.06 inch high at 75 yards when the sight height is 1.00 inch, but it is 0.86 inch high at that distance when the sight height is 1.50 inches. Again, the trajectory *appears* to be flatter when the sight height is greater. However, it is unlikely that a difference in point of impact of 0.20 inch at 75 yards will ever be noticed. Moreover, even at 200 yards the difference in point of impact is only 0.30 inch, which will clearly be outside the accuracy limits. If you fire enough shots, you might find that the average point of impact is slightly different, but on any individual shot the difference will never be seen. In spite of this, it is still useful to understand the principles involved and how they affect the trajectory.

The number of myths regarding the science of ballistics is surprising. It is all too frequent that someone is overheard making claims regarding a 22 rifle sighted in at 50 yards that still hits right on the point of aim at 100 yards. If the point of aim at 100 yards is hit with a 22 that is sighted in at 50 yards, it is accidental because the bullet should have hit about 7 inches low if the ammunition was of the standard-velocity type. A bullet from the high-velocity 22 should hit about 5 inches low under these conditions. One also hears about some shooter having a 17 HMR sighted in at 100 yards who holds "dead on" a crow at 175 yards and makes a kill. So sighted, the 17 HMR hits about 5 inches low at 175 yards so the crow was having a bad day.

Wind Deflection

When a moving projectile is subjected to a force, some change in its path is produced. The attraction of gravity causes the path of a bullet fired horizontally to be bent toward the earth. Wind blowing across the path of a projectile causes it to be moved laterally on its way to the target. How much the path is bent depends on the wind velocity and the characteristics of the bullet.

If you have ever driven along a highway following a motorcycle you may have observed one of the curious effects produced by a crosswind. The force of the wind on the cyclist causes the cycle to tip into the wind rather than away from it. The same phenomenon happens with a bullet that is subjected to a crosswind. The nose tends to tip into the wind just as an arrow does during its flight. The process can be view in another way by remembering that the area of the bullet is larger toward the base than at the point so the force of the wind is greater in that region of the bullet. Tipping the bullet causes the drag to be altered which results in a curved path for the bullet in a cross wind. This problem is a complex one because there is also an elevation or depression in the path of the bullet which will not be discussed in this elementary treatment. As it turns out, a wind blowing from the right (3 o'clock) causes the bullet to move to the left (9 o'clock) and upward slightly while a wind from the left (9 o'clock) causes the bullet to move to the right (3 o'clock) and down. Although the effect is slight, wind directly opposing the direction of the bullet motion will move the bullet downward while wind in the direction of the bullet path will cause a slight upward movement of the bullet. The reader interested in greater detail of these problems should see the article by Frank Tirrell published in *Small Caliber News*, Vol. 7, No. 1, Spring 2004, pp. 14-20.

Interestingly, it is the extent to which air resistance slows the bullet on its path that determines how much deflection will be produced. If a bullet were to maintain the same velocity after leaving the muzzle, there would be no decrease in velocity as a result of air resistance. In other words, we are considering the bullet to be traveling in a vacuum. If the distance to the target is known, it is a simple matter to calculate the time of flight in a vacuum, T_v. The value of T_v would be the distance (range) divided by the velocity, V. For example, if the range is 100 yards (300 feet) and the bullet has a velocity of 1000 ft/sec, the time of flight, T_v, would be

$$T_v = \frac{\text{Range (ft)}}{\text{Velocity (ft/sec)}} = \frac{300 \text{ ft}}{1000 \text{ ft/sec}} = 0.300 \text{ sec}$$

When fired in air, the bullet experiences a loss in velocity on its way to the target as a result of air resistance. The extent of that loss in velocity is related to the ballistic coefficient of the bullet. Bullets having high ballistic coefficients lose a smaller fraction of their velocity in traveling a given distance than do those having low ballistic coefficients.

The loss in velocity of a bullet as it passes through air is related to the difference between its time of flight in a vacuum and the actual time of flight through the atmosphere. If we call the time of flight in air T_a, the wind deflection is related to the quantity $(T_a - T_v)$. The wind deflection, D, can be expressed by the relationship

$$D = 12 \, W \, (T_a - T_v)$$

In this equation, W is the wind velocity in feet per second and 12 is a conversion factor to convert the deflection in feet to the value in inches. Wind velocity is usually expressed in miles per hour, but since we want to calculate deflection in either feet or inches we need the wind velocity in those units. It is an easy matter to convert from miles per hour to feet/sec because one mile per hour is equivalent to 1.467 ft/sec.

If we consider a 22 LR standard-velocity load firing a 40-grain bullet at 1,080 ft/sec, the time of flight in a vacuum (T_v) to a target 100 yards (300 feet) away would be

$$T_v = \frac{300 \text{ ft}}{1080 \text{ ft/sec}} = 0.278 \text{ sec}$$

Because the bullet loses velocity due to air resistance, the actual time of flight (T_a) is 0.301 sec. Suppose we want to see how much deflection a 5 mph wind coming directly across the path of the bullet would cause. This would be known as a wind from 9 o'clock (or 3 o'clock). By making use of the conversion factor given above, we find that a 5 mph

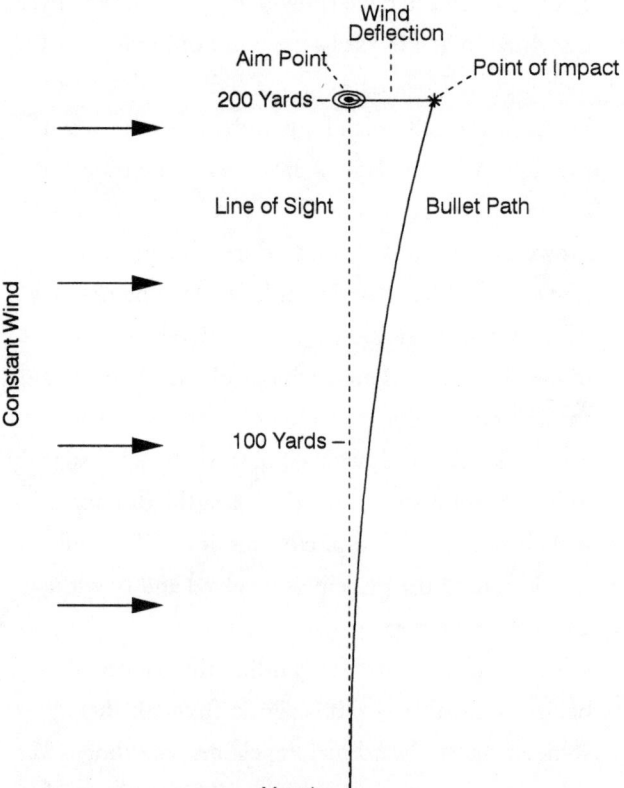

The effect of a constant wind blowing from 9 o'clock. Note that the deflection at 200 yards is more than twice that at 100 yards.

wind is equivalent to 7.335 ft/sec. Therefore, the wind deflection in this case would be

$$D = 12\ W\ (T_a - T_v) = 12 \times 7.335\ (0.301 - 0.278) = 2.02\ \text{inches}$$

This result shows that a standard-velocity 22 LR bullet will be deflected slightly over two inches at 100 yards by a 5 mph cross wind. If the wind were 10 mph, the deflection would be exactly twice as great because the wind velocity, W, is used as a multiplier in the equation.

The question naturally arises as to what would be the deflection if the wind is blowing at an angle to the path of the bullet instead of directly across it. In such a case, the extent to which the bullet will be deflected depends on the angle. If the wind is directly in line with the path of the bullet, the deflection is zero while if the angle is 90 degrees, the deflection is a maximum. If the wind is blowing at an angle to the bullet path, there are two components to the total wind velocity. There is a component of the velocity that is in the direction of the bullet path and a component that is perpendicular to the path. It is the component of the wind velocity that is across the bullet path that determines the amount of deflection. This can be worked out mathematically as a function of angle, but it is not necessary because the accompanying figure shows how to adjust for the angle as it varies from 0 to 90 degrees.

We now know how to compensate for the angle of the wind, but we still have a problem with the actual time of flight. The time of flight in a vacuum is easily obtained by simply dividing the range in feet by the velocity in ft/sec. Calculating the actual time of flight in air is a complex problem that makes use of the ballistic coefficient because that is the quantity that determines air retardation. For the introduction to ballistics presented in this book, it is not necessary to actually calculate the time of flight in air. It is one of the quantities that are contained in the output from calculations performed using the software available from several sources so we will just assume that the value is known.

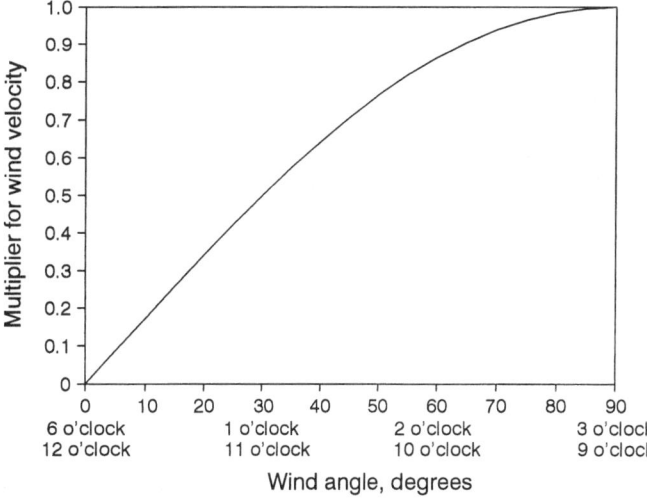

Winds from 3 and 9 o'clock have full effect on the bullet. Winds from other angles have effects given by the multiplier on the vertical axis.

Shooting Uphill and Downhill

When a bullet is fired at an angle upward or downward, the effect of gravity is not the same as it is when the bullet is fired horizontally. When the bullet travels horizontally, the effect of gravity is at right angles to the bullet path so the effect is maximum. If the bullet path is upward, there will be a horizontal component and a vertical component to the motion. Only the component of the velocity in the horizontal direction is affected strongly by gravity. Suppose one were shooting at a crow on a rock ledge that is 50 yards distant and that ledge is 50 yards high. The length of the path of the bullet can be calculated to be 70.7 yards, but it is only the horizontal component of 50 yards that is affected by gravity. Now let us suppose that the rifle is sighted in at exactly 70 yards. Will the bullet strike exactly at the point of aim on the crow? The answer is no because the bullet experiences the effect of gravity over only the horizontal distance, 50 yards. Therefore, the bullet will strike above the point of aim at the target. The effect would be exactly the same if the target were in the bottom of a ravine 50 yards deep and the shooter were at a point 50 yards horizontally and 50 yards vertically from the target.

Clearly, the effect depends on how steep the firing angle is. The bullet drop is related to that angle by the trigonometric function known as the cosine (which is abbreviated cos). The actual bullet drop will be that for same horizontal distance multiplied by the cosine of the angle. For example, in the case above, the angle is 45 degrees and the cosine of that angle is 0.707. Therefore, the bullet drop would be only 0.707 of what it would if the bullet were fired horizontally over a distance of 70 yards. The results show that the bullet will strike higher relative to the point of aim than it would if the shot were at a target on the horizontal plane. It should be apparent that the extent of the error would depend on the firing angle. The accompanying table shows how the bullet drop for shots fired at different angles will be related to the drop when the shot is fired horizontally. The drop for shots fired at each angle is determined by multiplying the amount of drop for a horizontal shot by the multiplier indicated. From the table, it is evident that when firing at a 20-degree angle the drop is 94 percent of what it would be for a shot taken horizontally. Even when the angle is 30 degrees the multiplier is 0.86 so the difference in point of impact will be only slightly above where it would be for a shot taken horizontally. In most cases, the uncertainty in point of impact that is produced by aiming error and the limitation imposed by the accuracy of the rifle will make it unnecessary to adjust the point of aim. However, on those longer shots at steep angles, it must be remembered that the bullet will strike higher than it would if the target were on the same horizontal plane as the shooter.

In this chapter, an introduction to exterior ballistics has been provided with special emphasis on each type of rimfire cartridge. Some of the concepts will be revisited in later chapters as we discuss ways to use rimfire firearms most effectively.

The approach in this chapter has been to try to develop some appreciation and understanding of external ballistics and to explain the factors that affect bullet trajectory. The presentation has only scratched the surface of this important topic, but the basic ideas presented are adequate for practical shooting situations as they apply to rimfire rifles. For a more complete treatment of the subject of ballistics, consult the references listed in Appendix A.

Corrections for Firing at Angles (Up or Down) From Horizontal.

Angle	Multiply by	Angle	Multiply by
0	1.000	50	0.643
10	0.985	60	0.600
20	0.940	70	0.342
30	0.866	80	0.174
40	0.766	90	0.000
45	0.707		

Understanding ballistics comes from conducting a great deal of test firing and keeping good records as the author is doing here.

Chapter 9

RIMFIRE HUNTING TOOLS

Although the tools and techniques employed have changed, hunting is an activity that has been practiced for thousands of years. For well over a century, rimfire firearms have been the choice of many hunters of small game and pests. Today's hunter who plans to use a rimfire firearm probably has the widest range of equipment ever available. This chapter presents an overview of rimfire equipment and ammunition with the hunter in mind. While much of this chapter is written with reference to the use of rifles, the hand gunner can apply the principles equally well. This is as it should be because the use of an accurate handgun for taking small game and pests is entirely appropriate although the ranges will probably be shorter in most cases than if a rifle is used. Also, some of the rimfire handguns (both revolvers and autoloaders) are sold with scope rails in place because they are intended to be hunting arms.

For the small game hunter, an accurate rimfire has long been the chosen tool.

An experienced hunter who uses a rimfire rifle or handgun in his or her sport may simply use the tools that have already been selected with little thought to making changes. On the other hand, someone who is just getting started may benefit from a discussion of some of the guns and ammunition available as an aid to making selections. In this chapter, the conclusions presented are those of the author. Because of the recent introduction of some of the products and the lack of opportunity to use them, the discussion is based on limited experience and testing in some cases. The information and opinions are intended to serve as a guide for hunters who use rimfire firearms.

What Rimfires Can Do

In discussing the use of rimfires for hunting (whether game or varmints), it is necessary to set forth some principles. The first of these deals with the species that can be harvested humanely with a rimfire firearm. A 22 WMR generates approximately 300 ft lbs of energy at the muzzle and a 22 LR approximately half as much. A modern centerfire rifle like the .30-06 Springfield or 7mm Remington Magnum produces as much as 3,000 ft lbs of energy. It is clear that rimfire rifles have very low power compared to centerfire pieces. Therefore, the use of rimfire firearms should be confined to taking small species.

Having said that, it must be pointed out that very large species have been killed with a 22 rimfire. Only a couple of years ago, a woman in Montana killed a grizzly with a 22 LR as it chased her horse in a corral. All manner of large game has fallen to the lowly rimfire. As a young lad, this writer dispatched a large number of hogs with one shot each using a Winchester Model 90 pump firing the 22 Short. The hogs were shot between the eyes at a distance of 10 to 15 feet. When the bullet is placed exactly right, a rimfire will produce death to almost anything. No one is going to advocate using a 22 Short as a deer cartridge although it will certainly kill a deer.

Under hunting conditions, it may not be possible to place the bullet in exactly the right spot so the hunter must use a firearm that will anchor the target with less than ideal bullet placement. Therefore, the firearm must have more power than would be needed to dispatch the species in cases where the bullet strikes perfectly. That does not mean that you need a .338 Winchester Magnum to hunt coyotes. What it means is that the less powerful the rifle used, the more accurately the bullet must be placed in a lethal zone and the more important the choice of ammunition becomes. Shooting ability and sighting equipment also become factors to consider.

Terminal Effects

It doesn't take much energy to make a hole in a piece of paper. Dispatching small game and pests is another matter, and dispatching larger pests is yet a different situation. It is easy to get caught up in the power game and assume that the most powerful cartridge you can get in your rifle is the best choice. That is not always so. There is currently a great deal of interest in hunting with air rifles, and only a few of the most powerful models even approach the power of a 22 Short. One instance to my knowledge involved taking a fox with a 177 caliber air rifle that fires a 7.9-grain pellet at slightly over 900 ft/sec (a muzzle energy of about 14 ft lbs) by placing that pellet precisely between the eye and the ear of the fox. Contrast that airgun with the lowly 22 Short that

Although out of production for 30 years, this Winchester Model 320 performs as well as any current model.

fires a 29-grain bullet at slightly over 1,000 ft/sec (corresponding to a muzzle energy of 70 ft lbs) and you will see just what correctly placing a projectile from a 22 rimfire could do.

Does this make the 22 Short a cartridge to choose for hunting foxes and coyotes? No, but this author has dropped numerous large hogs for the block with a 22 Short placed squarely in the forehead at short range. Keep in mind that there is a great difference between what a particular load will *kill* and what it is suitable for *hunting* with the same load. Hunting involves harvesting animals in a humane way even when the bullet may not be placed *exactly* between the ear and the eye. Field situations may not permit that kind of shot placement.

The theme for the famous book, *Use Enough Gun* by Robert Ruark came about as a result of trying to take a hyena with a 220 Swift that shoots a 40-grain bullet at approximately 4,000 ft/sec. After nine shots in which the frangible bullets simply did not penetrate the tough hyena, Ruark called "*Toa bundouki m'kubwa*" which means "bring out the big gun" in Swahili. He then shot the animal with a 470 Nitro Express. Will a 22 Swift kill a hyena? Absolutely, especially with the bullets that are available today. But penetration of a tough animal can still be a problem. Would a 22 LR kill a hyena? Absolutely, but the bullet would have to be placed exactly right, and a 22 LR certainly should not be used to hunt hyenas. The shooter using a rimfire should select appropriate ammunition for the type of game being harvested. Two factors that are involved in bullet performance can be considered as penetration and rate of energy transfer to the target. A discussion of these factors is presented here.

Penetration

Penetration exhibited by a specific bullet in some medium depends on several factors. The weight, type of construction, and velocity of the bullet are the most important considerations. For a bullet of a given caliber, penetration is generally greater the heavier the bullet. If the bullet does not expand significantly (the typical 40-grain solid point bullet does not expand much in fleshy targets), the diameter of the wound channel is small. A heavier bullet will drive deeper because it has larger mass for the same frontal area even though the heavier bullet will have lower velocity. Tests that I have conducted using heavy 45 caliber, hard-cast handgun bullets that give no expansion have shown that very deep penetration is obtained even though the velocity is only about 800 ft/sec. In 22 LR caliber, the bullets are essentially pure lead, and most solid bullets weigh 40 grains. However, the Lapua Scoremax load utilizes a 48-grain bullet that is loaded to a velocity of 1,040 ft/sec in target-grade ammunition. This load, in rifles tested by this author, exhibits excellent accuracy. A 60-grain bullet at 950 ft/sec is used in the Aguila SubSonic Sniper load. Because of the long, heavy bullet, this load makes use of a case that is significantly shorter than that used in typical 22 LR ammunition in order to meet the restrictions on overall cartridge length. Therefore, the SubSonic Sniper does not work through most actions of semiautomatic firearms.

It can be amazing to see just how deeply a 22 LR can penetrate. This writer has seen autopsy photographs that show a 22 LR fired from a short barrel (the velocity was probably not over 900 ft/sec) penetrated completely through the body of an adult male. For use on small game and pests, the penetration given by solid bullets is excessive because a considerable amount of the energy of the bullet is wasted after the bullet leaves the animal. In order to reduce penetration and cause more of the energy of the projectile to be transferred to the animal, hollow-pointed bullets can be used. The expanding bullets do not penetrate as deeply in animal tissue because they make a wider wound channel.

The 17 HMR has for a good reason quickly become an extremely popular round for taking small varmints. Most of the rifles chambered for the 17 HMR produce excellent accuracy. The sharp-pointed bullets traveling at high-velocity give flat trajectory which makes it easy to hit the target even at ranges of 150 yards or so. However, most negative observations regarding the 17 HMR relate to bullet performance. Within the last few days as this is being written, another writer shared his experiences with the 17 HMR on game. A fox taken in the neck at a range of 50 yards collapsed instantly. A coyote hit in the chest at a similar distance took off for parts unknown. The tiny 17-grain bullet does not give sufficient penetration to be reliable for dispatching such large varmints. However, the 17 HMR was never intended for use on varmints the size of a coyote, except perhaps when head shots are taken at short distances. While there are a lot of cases where the 17 HMR has worked satisfactorily, there are many instances where it has not. It is similar to Ruark's experience when using the 220 Swift on a hyena.

In an effort to reduce the instances where bullets fragment without penetrating sufficiently, CCI and Hornady have introduced ammunition for the 17 HMR that utilizes 20-grain hollow-point bullets of more sturdy construction. With the heavier bullet, the muzzle velocity is only about 2,375 ft/sec, but that is still fast enough to give flat trajectory. It will be interesting to read what people who have used these cartridges on game will report.

The 17-grain polymer-tipped 17 HMR bullet at high velocity is explosive. Tests show that the bullet fragments in many types of test media when the bullet is still traveling at high velocity. However, at ranges of 150 to 200 yards where the velocity is much lower, the bullets often penetrate a varmint without expanding significantly. It is an interesting but significant fact that penetration at longer range is generally deeper than for the same bullet at shorter ranges. Expansion is assured when the velocity is high but when the velocity falls off and expansion is less, penetration is greater. This behavior points out one of the difficulties in designing bullets for use on game. Reliable expansion is needed at long range, but the bullet must not fragment at short range. When small varmints are the targets, fragmentation may actually be desirable so that the bullet expends all its energy on the critter and not on the landscape. It is just that when a caliber as small as the 17 HMR is considered, a coyote is not a small critter.

The most common form of the 22 WMR ammunition is probably that with the 40-grain hollow-point or full-metal-jacket bullet. However, ammunition is also available with hollow-point bullets that weigh 50 grains. Federal produces such a load that is advertised to give a muzzle velocity of 1,650 ft/sec from a rifle with a muzzle energy of 300 ft lbs. From chronograph data, it appears that this velocity is a little optimistic with the measured value being about 75 ft/sec lower from my Ruger 77/22M. However, the heavy bullet holds its velocity well and published data show a remaining energy at 100 yards of 180 ft lbs. Because the velocity is lower, the 50-grain bullets do not expand as violently and as a result give deeper penetration. This provides better performance on larger varmints such as foxes and coyotes. CCI also produced a 22 WMR load with a 50-grain Gold Dot hollow-point for a time, but that load has been discontinued.

In order to stabilize a bullet in flight, the bullet is caused to spin by the rifling in the barrel. The longer the bullet, the higher the rate of rotation required to stabilize the bullet in flight, but the velocity of the bullet is also a factor in determining rotational stability. Barrels for rifles chambered for the 22 WMR are given a rate of twist of 1 turn in 16 inches. With the low velocity of the 50-grain bullets, especially from handgun barrels, stability is marginal and some firearms are not highly accurate with the 50-grain loads. In the two 22 WMR rifles that this author has used, both of the 50-grain loads gave good accuracy.

Ammunition in 17 HMR is available with either 17-grain polymer-tipped bullets or 20-grain hollow-points.

Smash

The essential idea behind shooting animals is to dispatch them cleanly and quickly. In order to do this, part or all of the kinetic energy of the bullet must be used to displace material (tissue, bone, and fluids) in the target. In other words, there must be energy transfer to the target. Any residual energy that remains is lost by virtue of the bullet passing through the target and continuing on its way with considerable velocity. A more desirable situation is for the bullet to expend its total energy on the target. This is one of the reasons that the 17 HMR is devastating to small varmints because the tiny bullet at high velocity disrupts a lot of tissue and seldom exits from the animal. There is no need for a bullet that will penetrate 10 inches of flesh when shooting prairie dogs because after about half that much penetration, the bullet is on the other side of the prairie dog making a furrow in the ground.

Recognizing that rapid transfer of energy is desirable when taking small game and varmints with a rimfire, some means of making the bullet change shape after entry is desirable. One solution to the problem is to make a bullet with a hollow cavity. Upon impact, the walls of the front section of the bullet collapse or rivet giving the bullet a larger diameter. This in turn causes it to displace a larger amount of material which leads to rapid energy transfer to the target. Penetration is less than with a solid-point bullet, but the impact is considerable because the bullet transfers a greater percentage of its energy to the target. Ordinary 22 LR solid bullets weigh 40 grains while the hollow-points are in the 36- to 38-grain range depending on the manufacturer. As a result, the hollow-points have slightly higher velocity, but the difference is negligible.

Because heavy bullets of a given diameter penetrate better than do lighter ones, another technique to give a higher rate of energy transfer is to use lighter bullets pushed at higher velocity. Then, to further increase the rate of energy transfer, the lighter bullet can be a hollow-pointed one. This is exactly the approach taken when the CCI Stinger and long-since discontinued Winchester Expediter rounds appeared in the late 1970s. The Stinger uses a 32-grain hollow-point bullet that reaches a muzzle velocity of about 1,640 ft/sec from a rifle and almost 1,400 ft/sec from a handgun. Remington markets two types of hyper-velocity ammunition, the Yellow Jacket (33-grain hollow-point bullet at 1,500 ft/sec) and Viper (36-grain truncated-cone bullet at 1,410 ft/sec). Federal produces a 22 LR round that utilizes a 31-grain bullet that is given 1,550 ft/sec in a rifle. A hyper-velocity load known as the Super Maximum is available from Aguila, and it gives a 30-grain bullet a muzzle velocity of 1,750 ft/sec. All of these loads are explosive on small species, but the lightweight bullets lose their velocity more rapidly than do the 40-grain solid or 36- to 38-grain hollow-points that are used in regular high-velocity 22 LR loads. As a result, their explosive energy transfer is best utilized at short range. Hyper-velocity ammunition is frequently not as accurate as the high-velocity or standard-velocity types, but may still be quite accurate in some rifles. This should be determined before loading up with hyper-velocity ammunition and going hunting.

In order to give the lightweight bullet the highest

In 22 WMR, ammunition is available with polymer-tipped, soft-point, flat-point, and hollow-point bullets.

possible velocity, CCI uses a heavier powder charge in the Stinger, which is contained in a case that is slightly longer than the usual 22 LR case. In most chambers, this causes no problem, but in rifles that have match chambers the rifling extends to the mouth of the chamber. When a Stinger round is chambered in such a rifle, the case engages the rifling. Since the brass case with the bullet enclosed is not easily deformed, it requires considerable effort to chamber the round as it is forced into the rifling, and it certainly does not do good things to the rifling just in front of the chamber. The instruction manuals that come with some rifles warn against using Stingers in those rifles because they have match chambers. The hyper-velocity ammunition from Remington, Federal, and Aguila is loaded in cases that are the same length as those used for regular 22 LR ammunition.

CCI took a different approach in developing their Quik-Shok ammunition. This load has the same bullet weight and velocity as the Stinger, but the bullet breaks into four segments on impact. This produces a shallow but wide wound channel and virtually guarantees that the total energy of the projectile will be expended on the animal while doing a great deal of damage. However, the Quik-Shok also makes use of a case that is longer than the standard 22 LR case with the attendant chambering problems.

One of the most successful 22 LR high-velocity loads in recent years is the CCI Velocitor. This load uses a bullet that is hollow-pointed but which weighs 40 grains. Muzzle velocity from a rifle is specified as 1,435 ft/sec, which corresponds to a muzzle energy of 183 ft lbs. Moreover, the relatively heavy bullet (for a hollow-point) retains its velocity well and at 100 yards the velocity is 1,112 ft/sec and the remaining energy is 110 ft lbs. This is a higher remaining energy at 100 yards than that of any other 22 LR load. Although the CCI Stinger has a muzzle energy of 191 ft lbs, the lightweight bullet loses its velocity rapidly and the remaining energy at 100 yards is only 90 ft lbs. If you read the stories

The CCI Small Game Bullet (SGB) is an effective round for the small game hunter. The Browning Buck Mark is a very accurate pistol for the handgun hunter.

in magazines concerning varmint hunting with a 22 LR, you will see that the Velocitor ranks high with these hunters. In the experience of this author, the Velocitor gives excellent accuracy in some rifles. Two rifles tested gave an average five-shot group size of less than 1 inch at 50 yards and a couple of others grouped in just over an inch. While this does not rival the accuracy produced by target ammunition, it is fine accuracy for a high-powered hunting round.

Another cartridge that has produced an excellent reputation for effectiveness and accuracy is the Winchester Power Point. It produces a muzzle velocity of 1,280 ft/sec and muzzle energy of 143 ft lbs. In many rifles, the accuracy of Power Points is almost as good as that given by standard velocity ammunition. Some of our rifles tested in this work gave an average of five five-shot groups at 50 yards that was as small as 0.85 inches while others gave an average slightly over one-inch. This is excellent for high-velocity ammunition that is intended primarily for hunting.

Shot Cartridges

The shooter using a 22 LR or 22 WMR has an optional type of ammunition that is not available to the shooter of the 17 HMR. For many years, cartridges have been available from CCI that have a plastic capsule filled with small shot instead of a bullet. Owing to the small volume available, the shot are extremely small so that a sizeable number can be contained in the capsules. In most cases, the shot

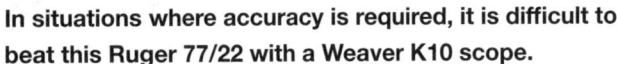

In situations where accuracy is required, it is difficult to beat this Ruger 77/22 with a Weaver K10 scope.

are No. 12 in size (about 0.05 inch in diameter). Instead of using a plastic capsule filled with shot, the 22 LR shot cartridges produced by Winchester and Federal use an extra long case that is crimped at the mouth to hold in the shot. Only CCI produces shot cartridges in 22 WMR caliber. The weight of the shot load in 22 LR is 31 grains while that in 22 WMR is 52 grains, which makes it a potent short-range load. Because there is no way to determine exactly how the dozens of shot will strike, there is always the possibility of some of them bouncing around. It is imperative that safety glasses be worn when shooting rimfire shot cartridges.

Shot cartridges are intended to function as a miniature shot-gun for the smallest of vermin including mice, sparrows, snakes, etc. at very short range. The rifled tube causes the capsule and its contents to spin, which causes the pattern to spread out dramatically at ranges over 15 feet or so. One problem with the shot cartridges is that they do not work reliably through the actions of many firearms so they must often be used in a single-shot mode. Probably the best firearm for using shot cartridges is a revolver where the empty cases need not be removed at all until the cylinder is empty. The length of the case is immaterial as long as it does not protrude from the front of the cylinder.

When shot cartridges are used, it is important to remember that the pattern becomes wide at short distance. Therefore, there is not sufficient pattern density for these loads to be effective at ranges beyond a few feet. Usually, multiple hits with the tiny pellets are required to dispatch small vermin so the range must be kept to around a dozen feet or so at most. The tiny shot are even more effective at ranges less than 6 feet.

Hitting the Target

The small game and varmint hunter who uses a rimfire firearm needs accurate shot placement above all else. A fox or coyote that is brain shot with a 22 Short is going to be dead in very short order while one that is gut shot with a somewhat more powerful rifle like a 22 WMR or 17 HMR will not. This is why the ability to place the bullet accurately is so important to the hunter using a rimfire firearm. Many hunters select a rifle (either target or sporting) that is capable of competition-level accuracy. They then experiment with many types of ammunition to achieve almost unbelievable accuracy. For this type of hunter, it is not unreasonable to dispatch a coyote called to within 75 yards using a rimfire rifle, even one chambered for the 22 LR. To try such shots with an inaccurate (not necessarily the same as inexpensive) rifle with no scope and Super Duper ammunition of limited accuracy *is* unreasonable. It is not the cartridge used that makes hunting a particular species inhumane. Within the limits of accurate bullet placement, the handgun hunter approaches the sport in the same way as the rifleman. In an effort to place bullets more accurately, an increasing number of hunters using handguns are mounting scopes on them.

A very accurate rimfire with a good scope of suitable magnification may produce five-shot groups of one-half inch or less at 50 yards. A rifle that gives only "plinking" accuracy might produce 2-inch or larger groups at 50 yards. I recently read the test results for a 22 rimfire rifle that gave 1 1/2-inch groups at 25 yards. The lethal zone on a squirrel may be only an inch or so in diameter so a rifle that gives only plinking accuracy is *not* a 50-yard squirrel rifle. Neither does the rate of fire ("firepower") have anything to do with the effectiveness of a rimfire rifle that is used as a hunting tool. Although self-defense is a somewhat different matter, it is the first well-placed shot that counts most when hunting. In fact, a fast-firing rifle may encourage a "hose 'em down" mentality. To a disciplined hunter, the type of action employed by the firearm makes little difference because it is accurate shot placement that counts. Accuracy is paramount, but the type of action is totally irrelevant in most cases.

Having said that, it should be pointed out that *generally* bolt-action rifles are more accurate than are those with other types of actions although there are many exceptions. The outstanding Kimber Classic 22 bolt-action must produce a 0.4-inch group at 50 yards to be deemed ready for shipment. Many auto-loading, lever-, and pump-action rifles will deliver 1 1/4 to 1 1/2-inch groups at 50 yards with most types of ammunition. Some of mine will reduce group size to about an inch if the ammunition is chosen carefully. However, two of the most accurate rimfire rifles I own are a Ruger 10/22T target model and a Thompson/Center Classic, both autoloaders. Either will give groups that average well under one-inch at 50 yards with most types of ammunition, and groups of slightly over one-half inch are possible when the most accurate types of ammunition are selected. Individual rifles with *any* type of action *may* deliver outstanding accuracy, but usually even a modestly priced bolt-action rifle may prove to be more accurate than rifles having other action types that cost more. This does not mean that you should not hunt with a rimfire firearm that has some type of action other than a bolt-action. It means that you should determine the accuracy capability of your chosen rifle and ammunition before you hunt live targets. Unless you have exceptional eyesight, it also means that you will need a scope to determine how accurately your rifle will shoot and to place bullets accurately in hunting situations.

The handgun hunter must operate within the limits imposed by the accuracy produced by the combination of gun, ammunition, and sighting equipment. Many rimfire handguns are capable of giving groups of one inch or less at 25 yards and some very accurate models might give groups of 1.5 to 2 inches at 50 yards. Given this level of accuracy, most hunters using handguns should limit their shots to about that distance. If your particular equipment

Shot cartridges are effective on small pests and birds at short ranges. The target on the left was shot at a distance of 6 feet while that on the right was shot at 12 feet. The holes have been circled to increase visibility.

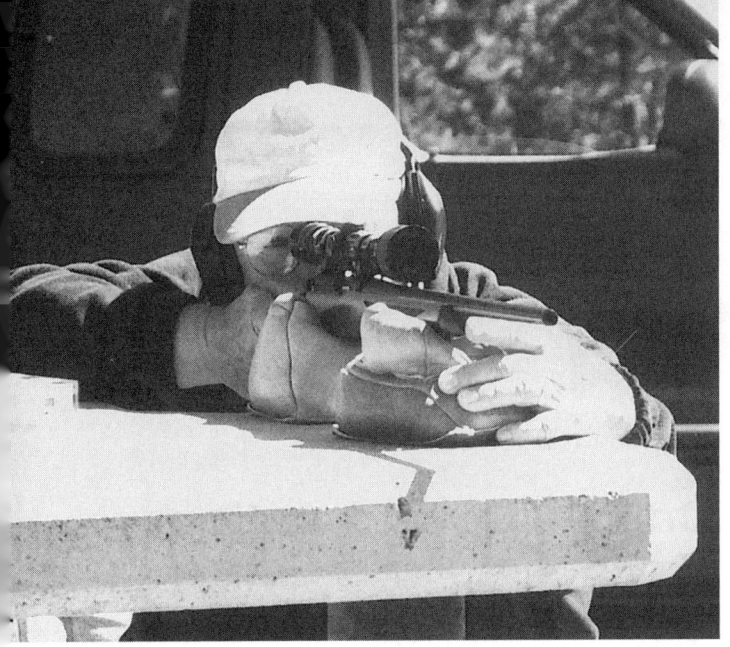

Before setting out to hunt, determine the capability of your rifle and ammunition as the author is doing.

1 inch low at 90 yards. So sighted, the 22 LR has an effective range of approximately 90 yards with the bullet striking no more than an inch above or below the line of sight out to that range.

When using the 22 WMR with 40-grain bullets, it is helpful to know the trajectory that would result when the rifle is sighted in at different distances. The accompanying figure C shows that the most practical

With a good scope, the Ruger 10/22T gives excellent accuracy although it is somewhat heavy for a walking hunt.

will do better and you can shoot well under field conditions, the range might be extended somewhat.

One of the most important factors to consider when hunting is the trajectory of the bullet. We discussed the topic in Chapter 8, but it needs to be revisited here in order to make clear some limitations of rimfire cartridges. Consider a 22 LR that is going to be used with standard-velocity loads or with CCI Velocitors. If the rifle is sighted in at 60 yards in each case, the trajectories will be as shown in the accompanying figure A. Note that the bullet rises slightly less than 1 inch above the line of sight in either case, but the path of the Velocitor is never more than about 0.3 inch above the line of sight. Either bullet will take out a squirrel at any distance out to about 70 yards, at which distance the bullet from the standard-velocity load will strike an inch below the point of aim. As a result, when using standard-velocity ammunition, the 22 LR deviates no more than an inch from the line of sight at 70 yards and should be used within that limit.

Suppose you wish to use CCI Velocitors and sight in so that the bullet will rise no more than 1 inch above the line of sight. The accompanying figure B shows the trajectories that would result when the rifle is sighted in at 60, 70, and 80 yards with Velocitors. Note that when the rifle is sighted in at 80 yards the point of impact is 1 inch high at 50 yards and almost

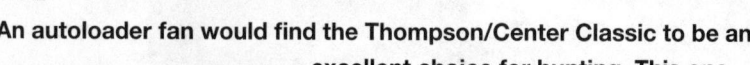

An autoloader fan would find the Thompson/Center Classic to be an excellent choice for hunting. This one has a BSA airgun scope with focusing

If the small game hunter wishes to use a handgun, the Browning Buck Mark has the necessary accuracy. The Weaver 1.5-4X scope is a great asset.

sight-in distance is about 100 yards. When so sighted, the bullet rises just 1 inch above the line of sight at its highest point and strikes less than 2 inches low at 125 yards. Hits can be made on small varmints out to that distance by holding the sights directly on the target.

Because of its high-velocity, the 17 HMR firing a 17-grain bullet gives a trajectory that has less curvature than that of any other rimfire. In order to see how the path of the bullet depends on the distance at which the rifle is sighted in, the accompanying figure D was prepared assuming sight-in distances of 100, 125, and 150 yards. When sighted in at 100 yards, the midrange trajectory is only about one-third of an inch. When sighted in at 150 yards, the midrange trajectory is about an inch and three-fourths, which is a little too much for a rifle that is at its best when used on small varmints. When sighted in at 125 yards, the 17 HMR has a midrange trajectory slightly less than 1 inch, which is about right. In this case, the bullet will strike about 1.5 inches low at 150 yards. This is the most effective sighting for general shooting with the 17 HMR. While the details will not be shown here, the 17 Mach 2 has a trajectory that is not much different from that of the 22 WMR and could be sighted in similarly. The shooter using a rimfire rifle will be more effective when the trajectory of the load used has become very familiar.

Caliber Considerations

The groundhog (or woodchuck) has been a noble varmint for generations. In the west, the marmot (also known as a rockchuck) fills the same role. The largest groundhog that this writer ever took was sitting vertically on the edge of his hole. The distance was about 50 yards, and the high-velocity 22 LR bullet hit him in the chest squarely between the front legs. The groundhog went over backwards and appeared not even to twitch. With shots like this or shots to the head, the 22 LR can be used successfully on groundhogs out to 75 yards or so if the bullet is correctly placed. Although any solid body hit from a centerfire varmint rifle will smash a groundhog or marmot, this is not the case with a 22 LR. The bullet from a rimfire, even a 17 HMR or 22 WMR, must be placed in a lethal zone on the target.

Both the 22 WMR and the 17 HMR give performance that raises the bar significantly compared to a 22 LR. At 100 yards, the remaining energy for the 22 LR is approximately 90 ft lbs. Even with the CCI Velocitor the remaining energy is only about 110 ft lbs at that range. However, with a 40-grain bullet, the 22 WMR has about 155 to 160 ft lbs at 100 yards and the 17 HMR has an energy of 135 ft lbs. Both of these magnum rimfires are legitimate 125-yard groundhog or marmot cartridges in accurate rifles.

As of this writing, there are eight factory loads available for the 17 HMR with six of them utilizing a 17-grain bullet having a nominal muzzle velocity of 2,550 ft/sec. New 20-grain loads from CCI and Hornady have a muzzle velocity specified as 2,375 ft/sec giving a muzzle energy of 250 ft lbs, which is almost the same as the 245 ft lbs produced by the 17-grain rounds. A 50-grain hollow-point 22 WMR load from Federal has 180 ft lbs of energy remaining at 100 yards. Although the trajectory of this load is not as flat as that produced by lighter bullets in 22 WMR, it packs a punch and is perhaps the most effective 22 WMR load for use on larger varmints. A 17 HMR or 22 WMR with any of these rounds far out classes the 22 LR both in energy and flatness of trajectory.

All of this is not meant to imply that the 22 LR is not a useful pest cartridge. Many people like the challenge that arises from the use of a 22 LR instead of a true varmint cartridge of higher power. Extreme accuracy is required, and before you start out, do a great deal of testing with several types of ammunition. As will be described in Chapters 13 and 14, a particular rifle can easily give groups that are twice as large with one type of ammunition as with another. Because bullet placement is vital when using a 22 LR, the hunter needs to know the performance of the ammunition being used. The hunter using a rifle chambered for the 22 WMR or 17 HMR has a little more leeway because of the greater power of these rounds. The user of a 22 centerfire such as the 223 Remington or 22-250 Remington has even more leeway because almost any solid hit with these high-velocity centerfires will put the varmint out of business instantly. Many years ago when the author used a 222 Remington on groundhogs, no groundhog made it anywhere after being hit. The combination of the 222 Remington Model 700 and Weaver K-10 scope made hits almost certain out to 225 yards with the bullets having enough remaining energy to demolish the varmint. On one hunt, I loaned my Mossberg Model 640 Chuckster in 22 WMR to a friend who took three groundhogs with three shots because the bullets were placed correctly. The bullet must be placed accurately in a lethal zone for varmint busting to be humane with a rimfire.

Compared to a 223 Remington or similar calibers, the trajectory of all rimfires is quite curved. A 223 Remington can be sighted to hit the point of aim at 200 yards by being only about an inch high at 100 yards and only about 6 inches low at 300 yards. On the other hand, a 17 HMR firing a 17-grain

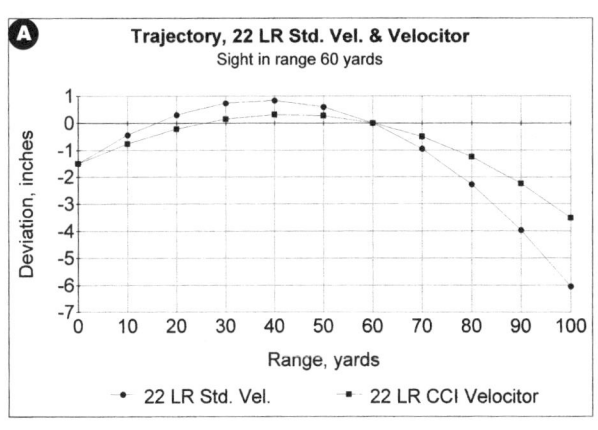

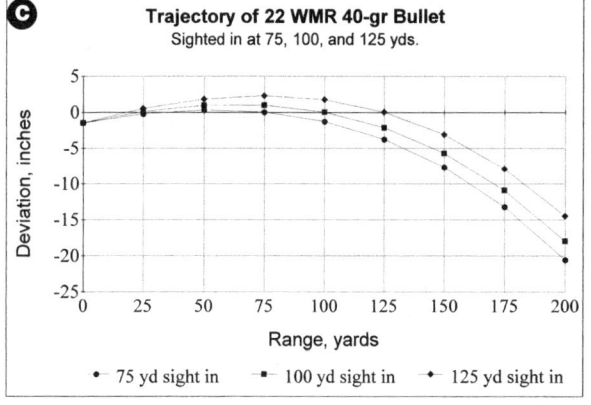

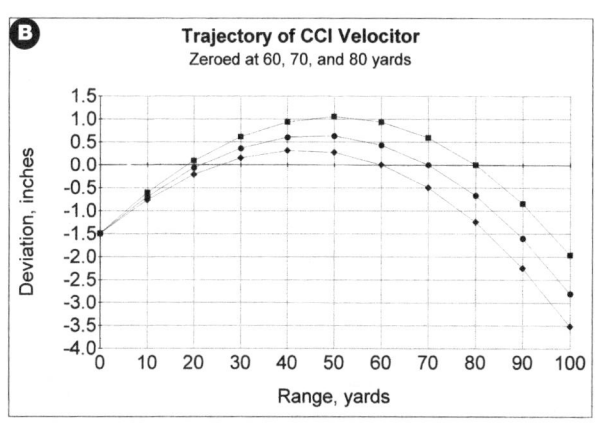

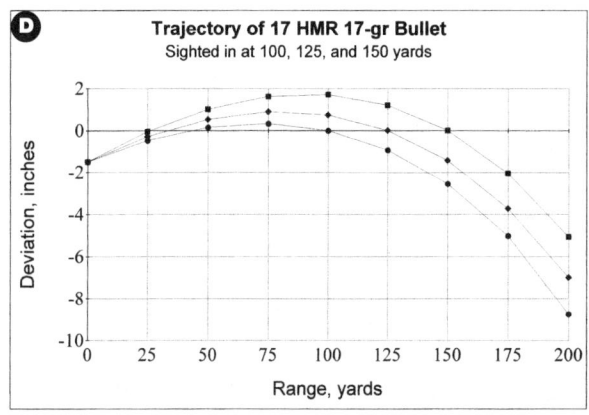

The hunter who wishes to use a rifle chambered for the 17 HMR can get outstanding performance from the CZ 452 American shown here with a Redfield 3-12X scope.

bullet at 2,550 ft/sec sighted to hit the point of aim at 100 yards hits 8.5 inches low at 200 yards. Moreover, at 200 yards, the remaining energy is only 72 ft lbs, about the same as the muzzle energy of a 22 Short! When sighted in at 100 yards, the 17 HMR strikes only 0.1 inch high at 50 yards. A more efficient arrangement is to sight a rifle shooting the 17 HMR to hit approximately 0.5 inches high at 50 yards, which gives a point of impact about 0.75 inches high at 100 yards, a zero at 120 yards, and a point of impact of 1.4 inches low at 150 yards. Such a sighting makes hits possible at almost 175 yards (if the rifle is sufficiently accurate). However, the remaining energy at 175 yards is only 88 ft lbs. In fact, at a distance of slightly over 210 yards, the remaining energy of a 22 LR high speed exceeds that of the tiny 17 caliber bullet from a 17 HMR! Because of its curved trajectory, it would be virtually impossible to hit anything at such long range with a 22 LR. Within the last 48 hours as this is being written a conversation was overheard in a sporting goods store in which the clerk told of killing a coyote at 180 yards with a 17 HMR rifle. I have no doubt that he did it, but such a feat is probably more in the nature of an accident than an indication of the suitability of the 17 HMR for such use.

The 22 WMR has a trajectory that is more curved than that of the 17 HMR, but the heavier bullets of the 22 WMR retain more energy. The 22 WMR can be sighted in at 100 yards with the point of impact being about an inch high at 50 yards, 2.2 inches low at 125 yards, and approximately 6 inches low at 150 yards. At 150 yards, the 40-grain 22 WMR bullet has 15 percent more remaining energy than a bullet from the 17 HMR and it also has a heavier bullet of larger diameter for greater punch. The main advantage of the 17 HMR over the 22 WMR is that the higher velocity results in a flatter trajectory, which makes hits easier at longer ranges especially on small targets.

It is instructive to compare the magnum rimfire cartridges of today with the obsolete 5mm Remington Magnum of the early 1970s. That round fired a 38-grain bullet at 2,100 ft/sec giving a muzzle energy of 372 ft lbs.. Because the bullet is rather heavy

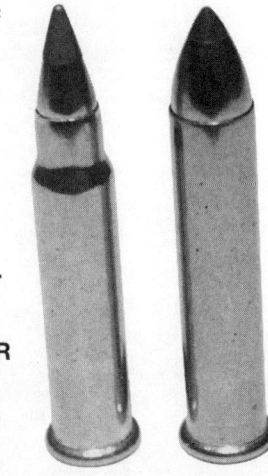

For longer range and greater power than delivered by the 22 LR, the hunter has the choice of the 17 HMR (left) or 22 WMR (right).

The Ruger 77/17 topped with a Weaver V-16 scope can handle many types of varmint hunting.

for a 5mm caliber (0.204" diameter), it holds its velocity well because the ballistic coefficient of the bullet is 0.145. The accompanying figure which is shown on the previous page shows the remaining energy for the 17 HMR, 22 WMR, and 5mm Remington as a function of distance. The 5mm has about the same energy at 200 yards as the 17 HMR does at 100 yards or the 22 WMR does as at 125 yards. While the trajectory has more curvature than that of the 17 HMR, it has less than that of the 22 WMR. The 5mm Remington Magnum was the best of the rimfire magnums, and we can only hope that some manufacturer will see fit to resurrect it or perhaps a 20-caliber round based on a necked down 22 WMR case. With the propellants available today and a Hornady polymer-tipped bullet weighing about 32 to 34 grains, it would be a very interesting development in rimfire ammunition.

When we consider the 17 Mach 2, we face a paradox. The muzzle velocity is 2,100 ft/sec and the ballistic coefficient of the 17-grain polymer tipped bullet is 0.125. The velocity and ballistic coefficient are very similar to those for the 22 WMR, but that is where the similarity ends. A 40-grain bullet from a 22 WMR has almost exactly twice as much energy as the little 17-grain bullet from a 17 Mach 2 at all ranges out to 200 yards! In fact, the CCI Velocitor 22 LR produces *more* energy at the muzzle (183 ft lbs as compared to 166 ft lbs) and at 100 yards (110

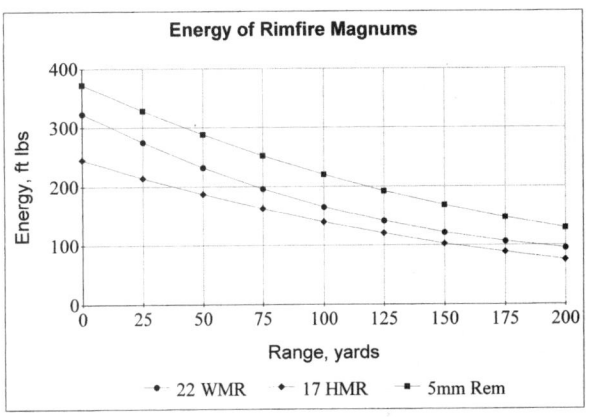

ft lbs as compared to 88 ft lbs). In the 17 Mach 2 we have a cartridge that is extremely accurate which makes hits on small animals possible out to perhaps 125 yards, but at that range the energy is well below that of a high-performance 22 LR and roughly equal to that of a standard velocity 22 LR. At best, it would seem that the 17 Mach 2 should be used on species no larger than ground squirrels which require very little killing or perhaps crows or prairie dogs at ranges so short that the remaining energy is at least 100 ft lbs (about 80 yards). I have absolutely no doubt that many larger species will fall to the 17 Mach 2 and shooters will tell of killing coyotes at considerable distances with it. It will *kill* a coyote, but so will my Webley Patriot air rifle. That does not mean that either is actually suitable for coyote *hunting*. When hunting squirrels at normal ranges (under 75 yards) the 17 Mach 2 will do nothing that can not be done with an accurate 22 LR with

A hunter on a budget can still get excellent performance. In this case, it comes from a Marlin 25N topped with a Weaver K6 scope.

carefully chosen ammunition. The accuracy potential of the 17 Mach 2 cannot be denied, but in power the cartridge duplicates that of the 17 HMR after the bullet from the latter has traveled 65 to 70 yards. If a cartridge with those capabilities excites you, a rifle in 17 Mach 2 caliber might have a place in your future. The same situation exists for the slightly less powerful 17 Aguila.

Several companies offer 22 WMR ammunition loaded with bullets as light as 30 grains. However, the lighter bullets have low ballistic coefficients and they lose velocity rapidly so that the trajectory over a distance of 125 to 150 yards is no flatter and retained energy is less than that of the 40- or 50-grain bullets. The lightweight hollow-point bullets in 22 WMR have large cavities and they are very explosive on small targets at ranges of 100 yards or less. One exception is the Remington Premier load in 22 WMR, which utilizes a 33-grain Hornady V-Max bullet that has a polymer tip similar to those used in 17 HMR ammunition. This bullet has a ballistic coefficient that is higher than that of any of the bullets used in the 17 HMR ammunition, and it much less explosive than the 30-grain hollow-points. With a muzzle velocity specified as 2,000 ft/sec (my chronograph indicates that the actual velocity is higher), this pointed bullet holds its velocity well, and it is quite accurate in my Ruger 77/22M. The Remington Premier has become one of my favorite loads for varmint hunting when using my 22 WMR, but I do not use the explosive 30-grain hollow-point loads to any great extent.

When we come to the 22 LR, the curved trajectory is an even greater problem. The 22 LR high-velocity ammo fires a 40-grain bullet at a nominal velocity of 1,260 ft/sec. In order to zero this load at 100 yards, the bullet must strike approximately 2.7 inches high at 50 yards. This much deviation from the line of sight is unacceptable since it makes accurate bullet placement on small targets difficult because the shooter must "hold under." For the small pests suitable for taking with the 22 LR, the bullet should not deviate more than about an inch from the line of sight. Probably the best plan is to sight a 22 LR to hit about an inch high at 40 yards, be zeroed at 60-65 yards and hit about 2 inches low at 80 yards. This means that the rifleman with an accurate rifle can put a bullet in a small target at approximately 80 yards on a still day. Some shooters with high-quality equipment and the ability to estimate distances accurately can stretch this a bit, but the remaining energy at 100 yards is only about 90 ft lbs. The CCI Velocitor load shoots slightly flatter and has a remaining energy of approximately 110 ft lbs at a range of 100 yards. If the accuracy in your rifle is acceptable, the Velocitor is the most effective 22 LR ammunition available for use on some of the larger species of varmints.

Some types of so-called high-performance or hyper-velocity 22 LR ammunition have become quite popular. One such round is the CCI Stinger, which fires a 32-grain bullet at a muzzle velocity of about 1640 ft/sec which corresponds to an energy of approximately 190 ft lbs. This round gives explosive performance at short range, but the light bullet loses its velocity rapidly so that at 100 yards it has a remaining energy of only 90 ft lbs, about the same as that from most high-velocity 22 LR ammunition. However, the owner's manuals of several rifles warn against using the Stinger in those rifles. If a rifle has a so-called match chamber, the rifling begins at the forward end of the chamber so that the bullet engages the rifling as the round is chambered. The bullet does not have to "jump" to engage the rifling, and this results in greater accuracy. Stingers use a case that is approximately 0.10 inches longer that the standard 22 LR case. When a Stinger is chambered in a rifle having a match chamber, the *case* engages the rifling. This condition can cause difficulties in chambering the cartridge and possible damage to the rifling just ahead of the chamber. Check the owner's manual for your rifle before firing Stingers in your rifle. The CCI load known as the Quik Shok also uses a case that is longer than the standard long rifle case.

While CCI Stinger and Quik Shok rounds use a longer case, the CCI Velocitor round does not. This is the real powerhouse of the 22 LR family. The Velocitor uses a 40-grain hollow-point bullet that leaves the muzzle at a nominal velocity of 1,435 ft/sec and produces a muzzle energy of 183 ft lbs from a 22 LR case of normal length. Even at 100 yards the velocity is 1,112 ft/sec and the energy is 110 ft lbs. In addition, the Velocitor gives very good accuracy in many rifles. If you feel that you want to tackle larger varmints with a 22 LR, by all means test the Velocitor ammunition. However, do not overlook ammunition of lower power that may give target accuracy. Winchester Power Points utilize a 40-grain hollow-point bullet and have become popular for hunting with rimfires because they give excellent accuracy in a wide variety of 22 rifles. Many hunters use highly accurate rifles and target ammunition because it is better to place a bullet having an energy of 100 ft lbs in the lethal zone than it is to place one having an energy of 150 ft lbs outside that zone.

Of the small game animals taken with a 22 LR rimfire, the squirrel is probably the toughest. Given an accurate rifle with good ammunition, squirrels are not difficult to bag. The head offers a target of about an inch in diameter, and the upper body (heart/lung area) perhaps an inch and a half. A good marksman with good equipment should have no trouble hitting such targets at 40 to 50 yards. Rabbits are even easier to kill and offer larger targets. Always remember that a missed shot at a squirrel in a tree sends a bullet on a path to come back to earth a mile or so away. A shot at a rabbit always carries the possibility of a ricochet. Safety must always be paramount when shooting rimfire firearms.

Small pests such as rats, ground squirrels, starlings, crows, etc. offer a challenge to the rimfire shooter only in the areas of marksmanship and hunting skill. Power requirements are secondary. Is it sporting to try to bag larger varmints like groundhogs, marmots, foxes or even coyotes with a rimfire? Perhaps the best answer is the old cliché, "Yes, no, or yes if…" Yes, if the hunter has an accurate rifle/scope/ammunition combination, limits the range, and shows the discipline necessary to make an accurate shot in a lethal zone. It is not uncommon for a varmint hunter to call a coyote to within 50 yards and make a head shot with a 22

The three magnum rimfires are (left to right) the 17 HMR, the 22 WMR, and the obsolete 5mm Remington. In many ways, the 5mm is the best of the three for hunting.

This Remington 597 topped with a 4X scope is an inexpensive but effective hunting tool.

LR. Under these conditions, the 22 LR is adequate. I have recently read of one hunter who has taken almost a dozen coyotes with his Ruger 10/22 with one shot each in this way. The answer to the question posed is definitely "no" if one is talking about taking a sniping shot at 100 to 150 yards or so. Under these conditions, the 22 WMR is just barely an adequate fox or coyote cartridge, but the bullet must still be carefully placed in the anatomy of the varmint.

The 17 HMR is extremely popular. Most 17 HMR rifles give good accuracy and the trajectory is such that it easy to score hits at rather long ranges for a rimfire. Some shooters are attempting to use the 17 HMR in ways it was not intended for. Although many larger varmints have fallen and many more will fall to 17 HMR bullets, it is not a reliable killer on such species. An acquaintance who has taken several coyotes with both 17 HMR and 22 WMR rifles has told me that there is a considerable difference in the effectiveness of the two calibers. He says that coyotes frequently travel some distance after taking a tiny 17 HMR bullet in the chest area, but that the coyotes he has hit similarly with the 22 WMR basically dropped on the spot. Neither the 17 HMR nor the 22 WMR is a great coyote cartridge, but the more powerful 22 WMR with its heavier bullets of larger diameter is better. A 25-caliber rimfire firing a 60-grain bullet at 1,500 to 1,600 ft/sec would be better still, but no such cartridge is currently available. The 25 Stevens Rim Fire cartridge, which has been out of production since 1942, gave a 65- to 67-grain lead bullet a velocity of about 1,200 ft/sec. With a modern loading using propellants available today, a velocity of perhaps 1,500 ft/sec could be produced with a 60- to 65-grain bullet. Such a load would be considerably more effective on larger varmints than any rimfire now available. Even the original load had a good reputation for dispatching small game without destroying much edible meat. For those of us who are interested in sports using rimfire rifles, it would be nice to have such a cartridge as a choice today.

Scopes for Rimfire Hunting

Assuming that you are hunting small game and pests and need to place the shot accurately, a scope is virtually a requirement regardless of whether you are using a rifle or handgun. It certainly is if you buy one of the many rimfire rifles that are marketed with no iron sights installed, a situation that has become common in recent years. Together the rifle and scope essentially constitute the platform for launching bullets accurately to harvest game or dispatch pests. But what type of scope? What power? What type of reticle? How expensive? All of these questions can be perplexing to someone who is selecting the equipment for rimfire shooting sports. Some very inexpensive scopes that can be used on rimfire rifles have tubes that are only three-quarters of an inch in diameter. They are slightly better than no scope, but they are not the type of scope used by serious rimfire shooters who prefer to use scopes of good quality with 1-inch diameter tubes.

Parallax can be illustrated as follows. With your arm extended, point a finger at a distant object and look at your finger and the object with only your right eye. Hold your arm stationary and look at the object with only your left eye. Note how the object appears to have moved. What actually moved was the point of observation. When you look through a scope which has the reticle positioned on a target, the reticle may appear to move on the target as you move your eye from side to side. If so, the scope has parallax error with the target at that distance.

Scopes that are intended for use on centerfire rifles are adjusted to have no parallax at 100 yards. A scope that is intended for use on a rimfire rifle is normally free of parallax at 50 yards. Some scopes that are designed for use on muzzle-loaders or shotguns are corrected for parallax at a distance of 75 yards. Unless the eye is positioned rather far from the axis of the scope, parallax results in a very small sighting error at normal rimfire ranges (25-100 yards). In my youth, I saw some very fine marksmanship produced with a rifle that had a Weaver K4 scope mounted even though the scope was not free of parallax at the usual ranges where 22 rimfires are used. That scope was intended for use on centerfire rifles and was parallax-free at 100 yards, but it made little difference as long as the shooter was careful to place his eye in the same position for each shot.

One type of scope has a front lens (objective) that can be rotated to focus the scope on targets at different distances. This is advantageous for the rimfire shooter who may use a 22 LR rifle on targets at 25 to 75 yards or out to 150 yards if the rifle is a 17 HMR or 22 WMR. However, these adjustable objective, or AO scopes, tend to be rather expensive, but there are exceptions. Some models will be described later.

A question that arises frequently is, "What power scope should I put on my rimfire rifle?" The most logical response is, "What do you plan to do with it? What size targets will you shoot and at what ranges?" For testing the accuracy of ammunition, a scope of 10 to 20 power is not unreasonable. In that case, you want the sighting error to be as small as possible. For most hunting situations, there is no need for a scope having this much magnification even when shooting small varmints at the longest ranges appropriate for using rimfire rifles. A variable scope that is 2-7X or 3-9X in magnification will serve quite well for almost any hunting activity with a rimfire. Of course a 12X or 16X scope will do no harm, especially when ground squirrels at ranges up to 150 yards are the targets for your 17 HMR. My Ruger 77/22 is almost always used with a very old Weaver K10 scope while my Ruger 77/22M has an old Weaver V12 (a 3-12X variable) scope attached. Both of these scopes have adjustable objectives and were bought as used scopes for a fraction of the cost of new scopes of comparable quality. Do not overlook the possibility of finding a good used scope that someone has taken off a rifle to make space for that new high powered, lighted reticle, trajectory compensating model that just had to be mounted. I found two excellent older steel-tube Weaver K6 scopes at a show where the owner had them priced at $60 each. That is a good price for a scope of that quality, but by making an offer of $100 for the pair, I obtained two fine scopes at prices far below those of comparable new scopes. I have also been able to buy three scopes on eBay, but be careful about buying scopes that you cannot look through or check adjustments on.

Marketing specialists have convinced many hunters that there is an enormous advantage to having a high-powered scope with a large objective lens, and

A superb scope for the hunter using a rimfire is the Simmons 3-9X AO shown here mounted on the author's Ruger 10/22T. The scope is the Model 1022T in Simmons' 22 Mag series.

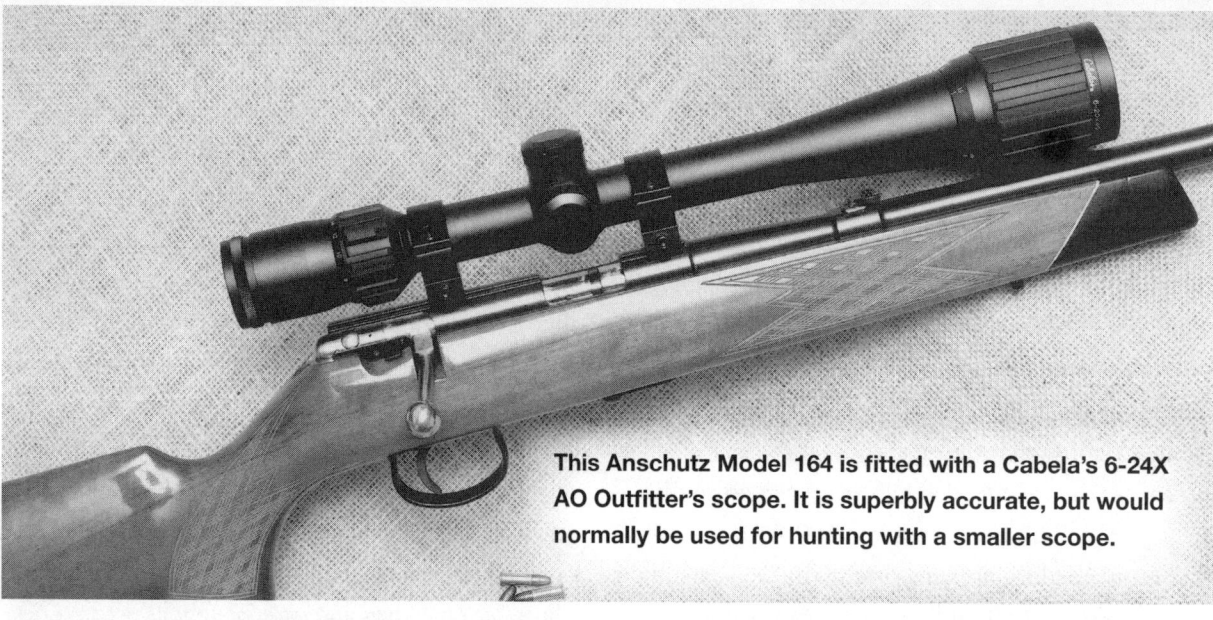

This Anschutz Model 164 is fitted with a Cabela's 6-24X AO Outfitter's scope. It is superbly accurate, but would normally be used for hunting with a smaller scope.

the larger the objective the better. Realistically, such scopes are seldom needed in hunting situations. When using a centerfire rifle to shoot at a crow at 300 yards, high magnification is almost a necessity. However, this author successfully used a 222 Remington with a 4-power Weaver K4 scope as a varmint rifle for many years. I later moved up to a Weaver K10 scope for more accurate shot placement at longer ranges. A large number of crows and groundhogs were taken at ranges up to 225 yards. Rimfire rifles are not 300-yard varmint rifles. The use of a 22 LR should be *at most* about a 90- to 100-yard proposition. The 22 WMR stretches this to 125 to 150 yards, and the 17 HMR is useful to perhaps 25 yards farther. Longer shots are *possible* for the highly skilled, well-equipped shooter, but the average shooter with average equipment should not attempt such feats. The risk of merely wounding the target is too high.

Scopes of variable power are popular even if most of the time they are set on one magnification and left there. Many are 2.5-7X or 3-9X, but the 4-12X, 4-16X, or 6-24X scopes are also common. If the scope is to be used for purposes of testing accuracy where the smallest possible groups are the intent, the scope should have high magnification because a sighting error of 0.1 to 0.2 inches is significant in such shooting. As I write this, I just watched a fly crawling on a target about 100 yards away through a 20X scope. That kind of visibility is an advantage when shooting at small, stationary targets. If the scope is to be used in hunting, lower magnification is satisfactory. It is frustrating to bring a rifle to the shoulder only to find that you must search for the animal because the field of view is so small. It is also very difficult to follow a moving target if the scope has high magnification.

A scope having a maximum power of 7-9X is a good compromise that will serve almost any purpose on a rimfire rifle used for hunting. Even a good quality fixed power 6X scope is a very capable sighting tool, and in the "hunter" class of bench rest target shooting, 6X is the maximum magnification permitted. One of my favorite scopes is the Weaver K6. Many years ago, I witnessed some very fine shooting done with a Winchester Model 75 Sporter and a Model 69A that wore 4-power Weaver K4 scopes. Except when trying to achieve the ultimate accuracy, a scope of high magnification is not necessary. A hunter using a 22 LR for hunting small game and pests within 75 yards or so can do fine work with a good scope of 4 to 6 power. Some rimfire scopes are variables in the 2-7X or 3-9X range, and they represent a good compromise. Such scopes include the Weaver 2.5-7X, the Simmons 3-9X, and 3-9X AO, and the 2.5-7X from Thompson/Center among others. If the range is going to stretch to 150 yards or more by using a 17 HMR or a 22 WMR, a good 3-9X is very useful. Two outstanding scopes are the Weaver 3-9X AO and Simmons 1022T AO both of which are intended for use on rimfire rifles. These scopes have adequate magnification and the advantages of a focusable objective.

Scopes of good quality that are intended for use on air rifles also work well on rimfire rifles. Some such scopes are very ruggedly constructed because they are built to withstand the recoil of break-action air rifles. In those air rifles, a heavy piston lurches forward at the time of firing. When it reaches the forward end of the compression cylinder, it yanks the rifle forward so the scope has to be able to withstand recoil in both directions. Of course, rimfire rifles have almost no recoil backward and none forward so an airgun scope is subjected to much less stress when used on a rimfire rifle. Most of these scopes have adjustable objectives because air rifles are used at ranges from perhaps 10 to 50 yards, and it is necessary to be able to focus sharply on targets over a five-fold variation in distance. Air rifle scopes available from BSA include 4X, 2-7X, and 3-12X models all with AO. Bushnell markets air rifle scopes in 4X, 3-9X AO, and 4-12X AO. My experience with several of the BSA scopes is extensive, especially the 3-12 x 44 AO, which I have also used extensively while testing 22 LR ammunition.

An extensive selection of scopes awaits the handgun hunter. Both fixed and variable power models are available. Scope mounts are produced for almost all popular rimfire handguns, especially those models that would be considered suitable for hunting. For some types of hunting, a good red dot sight might be a better choice, but keep in mind that most of these sights have dots that cover 3 or 4 MOA (about 1.5 or 2.0 inches at 50 yards). That means that the dot itself might cover most of a small critter if the range is 50 to 75 yards. On the other hand, the crosshair of a scope could easily be centered on such a target. In the case of using handguns for hunting small game and pests, it is much more likely that the skill of the hunter under field conditions will be the limiting factor.

Let us look at the facts from the point of view of

Four excellent scopes for use on rimfire hunting rifles are (top to bottom) the Simmons 22 Mag 4X, Simmons 1022T 3-9X AO, Cabela's Pine Ridge 2.5-7X, and Nikon ProStaff 4X.

the rifleman. To hit small species of game and pests, the bullet path should not deviate more than about an inch or an inch and a half from the line of sight. Sighted to hit one inch above the point of aim at 50 yards, the 22 LR high-velocity bullet strikes the point of aim at approximately 65 to 70 yards and falls about 2 inches below the point of aim at 90 yards. Beyond about 80 to 85 yards, it is necessary to "hold over" in order for the bullet to hit within one inch of the point of aim. Unless the range is accurately known, placing the bullet precisely becomes difficult because of the curved trajectory it follows even when assuming that there is no wind deflection. This writer has taken groundhogs at rather long ranges with a 22 LR, but he also stopped trying to do so abruptly after seeing one fall over then crawl into a hole. We must be humane in our sport. There is a large segment of the population that would be quite happy to see all forms of sport hunting banned. We must not give them any additional arguments to use against us as they try to accomplish that goal. Selecting the right equipment and ammunition for the job and being serious enough to take time to develop shooting skills are basic requirements for hunting.

In the 1970s, this Winchester 190 wearing a Weaver 2.5-7X scope would have been well equipped for hunting and varmint shooting. This combination is still a good choice.

Field Accuracy

One of the aspects of hunting that always comes as a surprise when I have not been afield for some time is just how much different things look in the woods than they do on a range. Distances are uncertain. Branches, leaves, bushes, and uneven terrain all combine to give a totally different view from that of looking at a target on a stand 50 yards away. The target is black-on-white and regular in shape while the target I am searching for in the woods is of irregular shape and may blend in with the surroundings.

To prepare for shooting under hunting conditions, try practicing under hunting conditions. If you have access to an area where you can safely shoot at targets on trees or stumps, try putting up some conventional paper targets and shooting them at varying distances using the same positions that you will use when trying to take a squirrel at 50 yards. You may find that the bench rest compensated for more flaws than you would have believed possible. Although the earth is solid, a few feet of swaying, quivering anatomy has a way of producing an unstable shooting platform. After working on conventional targets on stumps or logs, try shooting some targets that are pictures of the animals that you intend to hunt. You can buy targets in the form of squirrels, rabbits, and prairie dogs that are very useful for this purpose. However, you can also find photos of animals in magazines that can be cut out and placed at appropriate distances so that the scale matches the size of the real animal. For example, if you find a squirrel picture that is six inches long, when shot at 25 to 30 yards it would be equivalent to the real animal at perhaps 50 yards.

The idea behind this type of shooting is that an irregularly shaped animal is quite different from those black circles on a white background that most of us shoot so much more often than we do game. The idea is the same as it is for the archer who practices on animal targets rather than the red, blue, gold, and black target faces that are used in target archery. It is absolutely necessary to have a suitable, safe location before you practice rimfire shooting in this way, but such practice will pay dividends when the target is an animal under hunting conditions. You will also get an idea of how proficient you are under field conditions, which is sometimes quite different than on a range.

While position shooting in competition is according to strict rules, the hunter has no such restrictions. By all means lean against a tree for support when shooting while standing. As in target shooting, a sling can be an asset to steady aiming. Take advantage of a convenient stump or log when shooting from a seated position. Remember, the least stable shooting position is standing with no support and shots should be taken in this way only when no other option exists. The hunter using a handgun will at the very least hold the piece with both hands, but it would be much better if some sort of rest could be used.

Hunters who wish to hunt large game will find that taking a squirrel at 50 yards with a rimfire is excellent training for taking larger species at longer ranges. This is no less true for the hand gunner who wishes to move up to hunting large game with a handgun of high power. Handgun hunting is becoming very popular and hunting small game and pests with a rimfire handgun is superb training as well as being a fascinating sport in its own right. Recognizing this, manufacturers are producing more handguns that are delivered with sight rails attached. In this category are some versions of the Browning Buck Mark, Ruger Single Six and Mark III, and the Smith & Wesson Models 22S and 22A autoloaders and Model 617 revolver. It should be no problem to select a suitable handgun for hunting small game and pests.

Although general issues related to safety were discussed in Chapter 2, it is not inappropriate to mention safety here as it relates to hunting. In a recent story on another topic that appeared on the front page of a newspaper, it was described in a sidebar how dangerous hunting is. In 1993, there were a total of 1,199 hunting-related accidents, including 101 fatalities. For 2002, the figures were 850 and 89, respectively. Self-inflicted wounds amount to 39.2 percent of the total while two-person incidents account for 60.5 percent. Contrasted to the number of fatalities from several other sources that were cited in Chapter 2, the number is indeed small considering how many millions of people spend such an enormous amount of time engaging in the sport. However, hunter safety courses are required in many states for a good reason. In the excitement of the chase or stalk, it is easy to forget to watch that muzzle. Gun handling etiquette should be so ingrained in each hunter that it is automatic. There are sidebar writers everywhere that are trying to make a point and generate an image.

Another safety issue is illustrated by this story. It seems as if some bird hunters had taken a break and placed their guns on the ground. Along came an excited bird dog (ever see one that wasn't excited?) and stepped on the trigger area of a shotgun. The dog's weight pushed the safety to the fire position. It also moved the trigger backward slightly and the gun fired. The action should have been open with no shell in the chamber. Anticipate an unsafe condition before it arises. One of the "laws" of human enterprise states that "anything that can go wrong will."

Hunters have been using small-bore rifles for well over a century. Today, such hunters have a wide range of equipment from which to choose. Both rifle and handgun shooters can obtain firearms that will prove completely satisfactory when appropriate sighting equipment and ammunition are selected.

The small game hunter should try to get a steady position as the author is doing here.

For many years, the Smith & Wesson Model 17 K-22 was one of the top choices for the hunter who used a rimfire handgun.

Chapter 10
RIMFIRE MAINTENANCE

Most rimfire firearms are very forgiving when it comes to being neglected. They continue to perform well in spite of the debris and gunk that accumulates as a result of firing. Rimfire ammunition that does not use jacketed bullets employs lubricated lead bullets and a non-corrosive primer so there is little erosion in the barrel. Another factor that contributes to long barrel life is the fact that the powder charges are very small so there is also very little erosion caused by hot gases rushing down the bore. Even with these favorable factors, rimfire rifles and handguns need and deserve some care. Most manufacturers offer models that have stainless steel barrels and actions, and they require even less maintenance. Most rimfire shooters, including this author, actually enjoy tinkering with their guns so cleaning and maintenance is not exactly a chore.

Gun care products are available any from many manufacturers.

Before you make any adjustment or change in your rimfire, read the owner's manual. It is very likely that if you tinker with your firearm you may invalidate the warranty. Do not attempt to alter such things as the trigger pull unless you are fully qualified to do so. The type of activity described in this chapter is limited to cleaning the firearm and making changes in external appearance. At workstations in factories where firearms are assembled, the assemblers have a variety of tools, jigs, and fixtures to orient parts correctly and hold them in place. The home handyman may find it impossible to get something apart or back together without these aids. My advice is don't go beyond your skills and equipment when dealing with your rimfire firearm.

While conducting the firing tests to collect the data that are shown in Chapter 13 and 14, it became apparent that some firearms seem to get messier than others, particularly the autoloaders. It was also found that as groups were fired with a CZ 452 American in 17 HMR caliber, the group size started to increase with some degree of regularity as the number of groups following cleaning increased. After four or five of the five-shot groups were fired, the group size increased by approximately 0.10-0.15 inch. Cleaning the rifle thoroughly caused the group size to be reduced. That observation is in contrast to what has been written by some authors about the small powder charges used in the 17 HMR not causing enough fouling to reduce accuracy. It may not be noted in field use, but on the range the effects were evident. There is also no question that some semiautomatic firearms function much more reliably when the action is kept clean. In this this chapter we will offer some suggestions regarding maintenance that may be of help in keeping your rimfire firearm performing reliably and accurately.

The shooter of a rimfire firearm should be observant. One simple observation that should be made is to inspect fired cases. Carefully note the appearance of the dent made by the firing pin. If the firing pin becomes damaged, the dent will probably reveal some abnormality in terms of depth or shape of the indentation. If the case head is bulged, it may mean that the firearm is developing excessive headspace and needs to be inspected or repaired by a professional. It is not likely that the average shooter will purchase headspace gauges, but if the heads of fired cases are expanded, have the headspace checked by a gunsmith. If the headspace is excessive, ruptured cases could send a spray of gases and debris into the face of the shooter, which is sufficient reason to wear eye protection when shooting any firearm.

Tools

It is not necessary for the rimfire shooter to try to do a great deal of repair or modification on a firearm. However, there will come a time when the rimfire enthusiast will need to remove some part or move a sight. One of the unsightly results of trying to loosen or tighten a screw with the wrong tool is a mangled screw head. Screwdrivers for use on screws in firearms should have the blades ground in such a way that the blade has parallel faces rather than the usual tapered design. When tightening or loosening screws with slotted heads, always use the thickest driver blade that will fit in the slot. I have found that a high quality gunsmith's screwdriver set is one of my most useful accessories. These generally have a handle to which a variety of tips can be attached. Slotted screws were the norm many years ago, but one often encounters Phillips, Allen, or hex head screws, and those with Torx recesses are becoming common on firearms and scope mounts of recent manufacture. Mounting a scope efficiently also requires screwdrivers of high quality if damage to the screws is to be avoided.

Two types of gunsmith's screwdrivers that I have found useful are those marketed by Hoppe's and Pachmayr. The Hoppe's set has a hollow handle in which the tips are stored, and the drive shaft is magnetic to hold the tips securely while working with the tool. Incidentally, the magnetic tip is also useful for locating the tiny screws that fill the holes

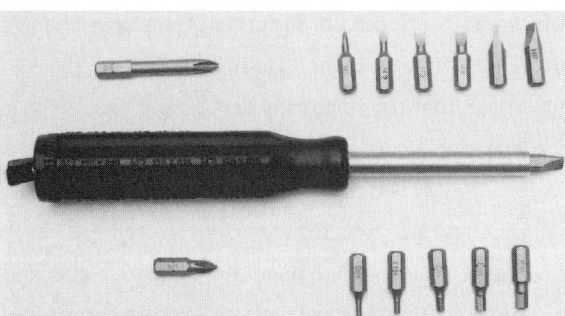

The Hoppe's screwdriver has a hollow handle that provides storage space for the bits.

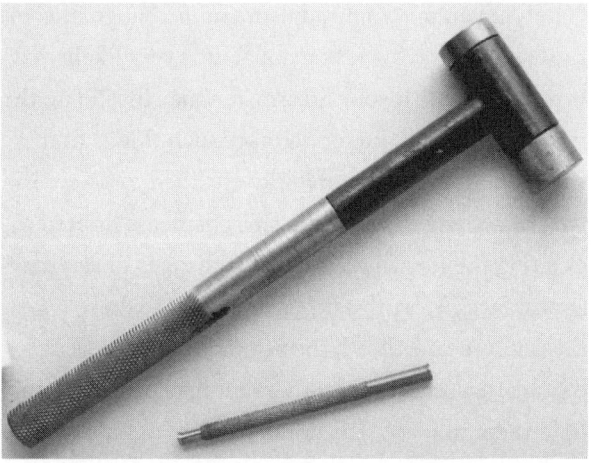

Lyman's gunsmith's hammer is a useful tool that provides three types of striking surfaces.

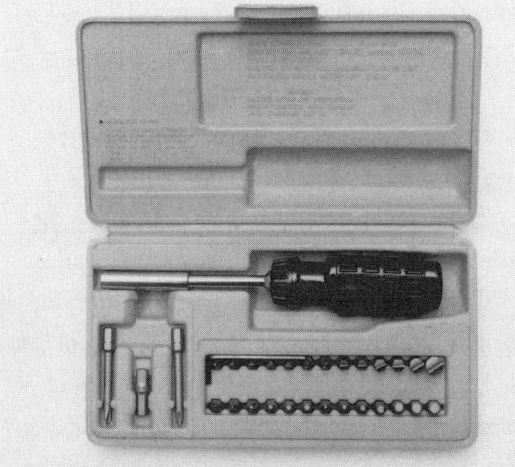

This set from Pachmayr provides an assortment of tips in all popular types.

where mounting screws are placed when attaching a scope. Working outdoors, I have dropped the fill screws in grass or dust with no chance of finding them without a magnet. The screwdriver retrieved them. Tips include blade, Phillips, and hex points each in several sizes. It is a most convenient package. The Pachmayr screwdriver set is a complete outfit that contains the handle and a large number of tips for use with slotted (12 blade sizes are included), hex, Phillips, and Torx headed screws. The whole assembly is contained in a convenient plastic case. Having the right driver for virtually any screw makes it a lot easier to do things to a firearm without causing damage to the screws. In addition to the gunsmith's screwdrivers, two sets of Allen wrenches are kept handy, one in metric sizes (in mm) and one in SAE sizes (fractions of an inch). With these tools, many firearms can be taken apart (and if you are skilled they can also be put back together).

I once had a muzzle-loading rifle that had an adjustable rear sight, but the adjustment screw was very hard to turn. In fact, I ruined one adjustment screw by insisting that I could turn the screw if I applied enough torque. After ruining the screw, I learned that the proper way to move a stubborn screw is to turn it a very slight amount then apply a small amount of thin oil to the threads and turn the screw back to its original position. Then back it out again and turn it slightly farther than the first time then turn it back to its original position and apply oil. This "rocking" motion cleaned out the threads and after working it back and forth instead of simply turning harder to move the screw, it turned easily. On some firearms, it is possible that an accumulation of debris or corrosion may prevent a screw from turning with a reasonable amount of force. Try working the screw back and forth lubricating it as you go in order to avoid damaging the head of the screw. Avoid

A bore light makes it easy to examine the bore.

using undue force when trying to move a screw or pin. There are several solvents that can be of help when loosening parts. One of the most widely used is known as Liquid Wrench®.

Another tool that is handy to have available is the Lyman gunsmith's hammer, which is actually three hammers in one. This hammer has a choice of striking faces made of steel, brass, or Teflon that can be threaded onto the head. One of the three faces is threaded to the end of the hollow handle to form a cap. Inside the handle is stored a brass punch. When it is necessary to move a front or rear sight laterally in its retaining slot, the hammer and brass punch will allow the blows to move the sight without the brass punch marring the blue finish on the steel sight base. The hammer and punch also find other uses when working on firearms. These simple tools form the basis of my kit for tinkering with rimfire firearms.

One of the many useful accessories in any shooter's kit is a bore light. This battery-operated light has a curved piece of plastic rod that directs the beam out from the end of the rod. When the rod is inserted in the bore, looking through the bore at the light makes it possible to see if the bore is clean or where there may be spots of residue that need to be removed. This is a one-size-fits-all light that is equally useful for inspecting the bores of rimfire or centerfire firearms.

Keep in mind that the person who assembled the firearm had available special tools, jigs, and fixtures to hold everything in place as the work progressed. For some firearms, a special tool may be required to perform certain operations. For example, the barrel on a Winchester Model 190 is held to the receiver by a threaded collar that pulls the barrel backward into the receiver. To tighten that collar, a special wrench is required that has an end shaped like a "U" but with the tips bent over. The tips fit in two matching grooves in the retaining collar as the "U" fits around the barrel. This is but one example of a special tool that is needed for removing and attaching a barrel. Even removing the extractor on some rifles requires a special tool.

In the early days of shooting rimfire firearms, the shooter had available only a very meager selection of products for maintaining the firearm. Today, the selection is truly overwhelming. I grew up with the smell of Hoppe's No. 9 Nitro Powder Solvent on my hands, but in looking a catalog from a company that sells shooters supplies I found no less than a dozen different solvents were available from that supplier alone. In fact, there are even more. True, some of them are specifically for removing copper fouling and others are intended for removing lead. Others are intended for general use in cleaning operations. Solvents are available from most of the suppliers of shooting consumables like Hoppe's, Outers, Birchwood Casey and many others. Keep in mind that some of these solutions contain organic solvents that are toxic and potentially harmful, and most are flammable. Follow all safety precautions when using these products.

Over a period that approaches 60 years, I have used more Hoppe's No. 9 cleaning solvent than any other. It is still a fine choice for the rimfire shooter, but it contains nitrobenzene, a toxic solvent that can be absorbed through the skin, and should be used with a lot more care than it was when I did not know better. Another solvent that I have found useful is known as Shooter's Choice, which seems to be an oily solution. Hoppe's Bench Rest-9 is another solvent that does a good job with cleaning most residues out of bores. Many other gun-cleaning solvents are available so by all means try a few to find one that you like to use. If you like to cut cloth into little squares, go right ahead. You will probably find that using commercially available patches is more satisfactory, and they are now readily available in the small size that is appropriate for cleaning 17 caliber firearms. I find that I usually use four or five patches in each bore cleaning session so if you shoot much get a good supply.

The primary tool used in cleaning a firearm is a good cleaning rod. For rimfire firearms today, the rod needs to be useful for both 17 and 22 calibers.

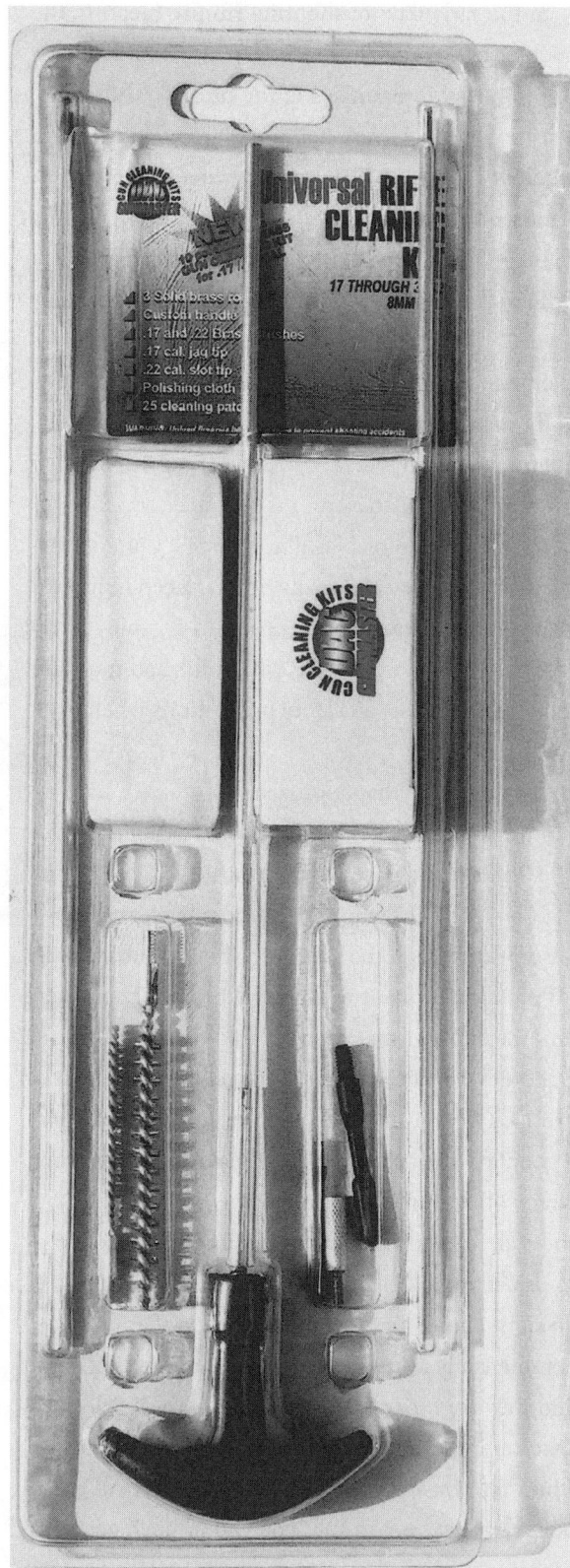

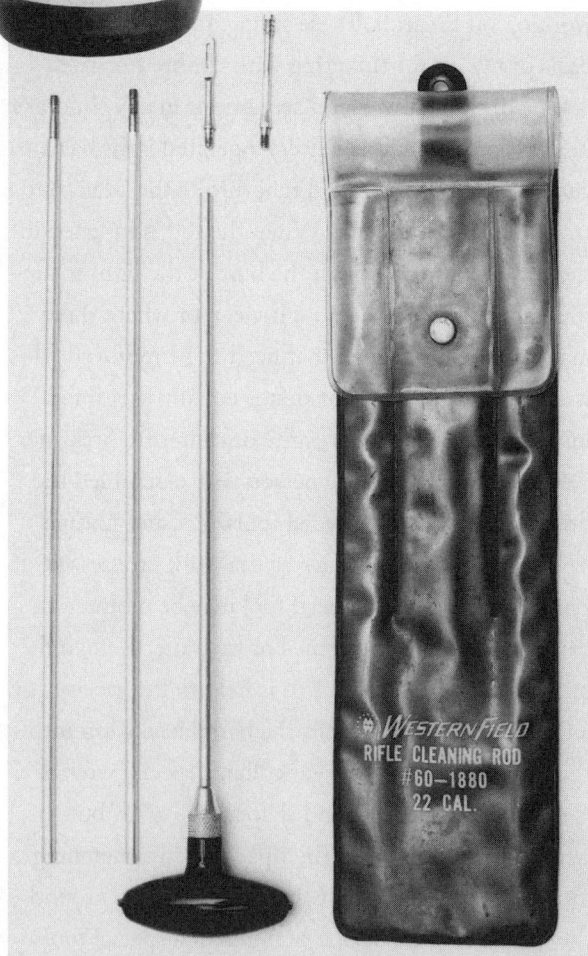

Separate rods for these calibers might be useful, but a surprising number of cleaning rods and cleaning kits that contain rods are available for use with 17 caliber firearms. For cleaning 22 caliber firearms, I always use a rod intended specifically for that caliber. My cleaning rod is a three-section aluminum model that was obtained from Montgomery Ward about 40 years ago. Cleaning rods are made to accept accessories known as jags that screw into

Hoppe's No. 9 solvent is a classic gun care product.

A modern cleaning kit for small bores includes a rod and tips that can be used for both 17 and 22 calibers.

This three-piece cleaning rod has been in use for many years. It is made of aluminum which helps prevent damage to rifling.

the end of the rod. For convenience, most cleaning rods consist of three sections that can be screwed together to make a rod of full length. Long, one-piece rods, sometimes called range rods because of where they are most often found, are available but they are not as convenient as the take-down models. Cleaning rods are most often made of aluminum or brass so that they will not scratch steel barrels. Most cleaning rods have handles that are free to rotate so that as the rod, tip, and patch follow the rifling, the handle can be grasped and moved forward and backward without it rotating. When traveling or in a pinch, I have found that a 1/8-inch dowel rod works well as a one-piece wooden rod for use with 17-caliber rifles. Such small diameter dowels are quite flexible and easily broken unless they are handled carefully.

Techniques

Make absolutely certain that the firearm is unloaded, both in the chamber and in the magazine! Wherever possible, remove the bolt and clean from the breech rather than the muzzle. Rod-end attachments include jags that have ridges or slots to hold a patch as well as brass or nylon brushes. The brushes generally have a twisted wire core into which the bristles are inserted. Although I use such brushes when cleaning centerfire handguns with leaded bores, I almost never use one in cleaning a rimfire firearm. A jag pushing a patch saturated with a solvent through the barrel will thoroughly wet the bore. In order to let the solvent work, set the rifle aside with the muzzle pointing downward or else with the rifle lying flat. If the rifle is placed with the muzzle downward, place some absorbent material under the muzzle to trap excess solvent. Do not set the rifle in such a way that excess solvent can drain downward into the action and stock.

After the solvent has been in the bore for perhaps 15 to 20 minutes, push a clean, dry patch through the bore to remove the dirty solvent and any solid residue. Push a second clean patch through the bore and examine it to see if it is clean. If the second patch indicates that the bore is still not clean, repeat the treatment with a patch saturated with solvent to wet the bore. Allow the solvent to remain in the bore for half an hour or so and repeat the process with the dry patches. Usually a couple of solvent treatments will be sufficient to soak out any residue from rimfire ammunition. In the case of 22 WMR and 17 HMR that fire jacketed bullets, it may be necessary to let the solvent work for a longer period of time to dissolve the copper-based alloy (known as gilding metal) used in the jackets. High velocity ammunition in 22 LR caliber often has copper plated bullets which can leave a copper residue. Sometimes, I just set the rifle in a safe place and leave it overnight to let the solvent work on the residue. In any case, I let the solvent remove the residue rather removing it by abrasion with a brush.

Most rifles that have semiautomatic, lever, and pump actions must be cleaned from the muzzle because there is no way to open the breech to insert a rod.

One of proven products for firearm protection is Sheath from Birchwood Casey.

When inserting a patch in the muzzle, move the rod gently to prevent damage to the crown.

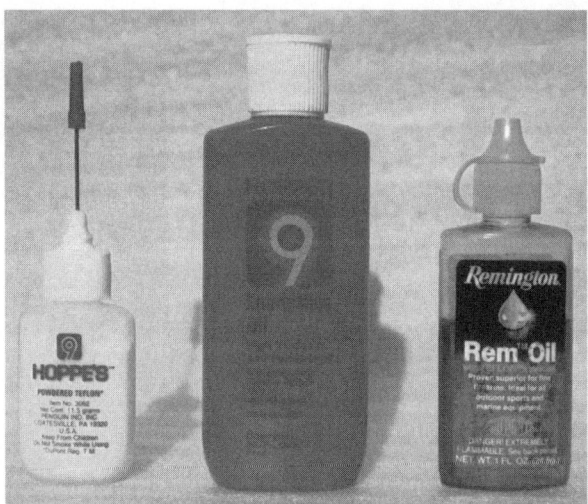

Lubricants come in many forms that are useful for specific applications.

Special precaution must be taken not to damage the rifling at the muzzle. The rifling there is the last part of the barrel to make contact with the bullet, which must depart from the muzzle pointed straight onward rather than being tipped. If done carefully, there is little likelihood that an aluminum or brass rod will damage the steel barrel, but it can happen. One way to prevent the rod from scraping on one side of the bore is to place the tip with the patch on the muzzle then rotate the other end of the rod while applying pressure. When the tip is centered in the bore, the pressure to insert it is the least and the patch can be forced into the bore with the rod scarcely touching the barrel. Even though some authorities say never to clean a rifle from the muzzle, I have no reservation about cleaning my autoloaders that way, but I am also very careful about how the patch is inserted. I also clean muzzle-loading rifles from the muzzle, but I do it carefully.

If the firearm is to be used in the near future, I do not coat the bore with anything. If the firearm is to be stored for a considerable time, I usually run a lightly oiled patch or a patch to which has been applied Birchwood Casey's Sheath® down the clean bore. Tubes containing special gun greases are available for coating the bore if the firearm is to be stored for a very long time or if it is to be stored in an environment that is detrimental to metals. These greases must be swabbed out of the bore before firing the gun.

With most rimfire firearms, there will be some unburned powder and other debris that finds its way into the action. For a bolt action, it is a simple matter to remove the bolt and clean it separately. It is then easy to manipulate a rag inside the receiver to wipe out debris. For autoloader, lever, and pump rifles, the bore can be cleaned as described above, but the action may have to be cleaned by simply opening it and working in the cramped space. Cotton tipped swabs (Q-Tips®) are useful for this work as is a patch moved around with a short section of dowel rod. Some rifles can be partially disassembled (field stripped) for cleaning, but others may have no simple procedures for getting the action apart. It is not possible to give general procedures because there is such a great diversity of types of actions. By all means follow the instructions in your owner's manual for your specific firearm. If you do not, it is possible you may hear something go "boiinng" which will require the services of a gunsmith to fix.

After the bore and action are cleaned, lubricate the parts where metal surfaces must slide while in contact with each other. On bolts, this includes the cocking piece where cam action cocks the rifle as the bolt is opened, trigger pivot points, extractors, etc. It is also a good idea to wipe the bolt itself with a lightly oiled rag. For the actions of autoloaders, pumps, and lever action rifles, lightly oil the moving parts. In order to lubricate some of the hard to reach parts, apply the oil with one of the syringe-type oilers or with a drop of oil on a cotton swab. If the rifle is to be used in extremely cold weather, which could cause the lubricant to stiffen to the point where cycling of the action and ignition become unreliable, use one of the special dry lubricants that are available. In any case, do not oil to excess. A very thin film is all that is required. The owner's manual generally gives information for lubricating a specific type of firearm.

The fact that many rimfire firearms are passed from

generation to generation in good shooting condition testifies to the longevity of these pieces. It has been said that more firearms are ruined by improper cleaning than by neglect. While this may be true, there is merit in using a clean, well cared for firearm. I can still remember the sense of pride that I felt as I cleaned the little Stevens Model 15 single shot that was my first rimfire.

Restore or Refinish?

Before you decide to refinish that old firearm that you inherited from your grandfather, consider the overall situation. No doubt the piece will look better, but that is not the only factor to consider. Highly collectible firearms are usually worth more in their original condition than when they have been refinished. Collectibles have value partially because of their originality and reworked items, while not exactly counterfeits, lose some of their heritage so to speak. In this chapter the discussion that follows involves rimfire firearms that are "users" that do not have any special value as collectibles. For "user" firearms, refinishing usually improves the appearance and thus increases the value somewhat. Of course, it also makes a difference as to who does the refinishing and the quality of the work. Refinishing usually involves buffing off the old blue from the surface and that sometimes makes markings less visible and sharp in their appearance. Too much polishing alters the legibility of the markings to the point that they may not even be legible, especially if the surface was worn and pitted to begin with. In this chapter, the discussion is directed more to keeping your "user" firearms looking good and operating properly rather than professional restoration, which is an entirely different matter. If you are in doubt as to whether an older firearm should be refinished, consult an appraiser or other expert in the field before you do something that may make the firearm look better but be worth less.

Metal Finishing

While spending a few weeks in a campground in the Big Horn National Forest in Wyoming, I became friends with David, the 15-year old son of the campground host. David and Josh, a friend who had come to stay with him for a week, spent a lot of time talking about and using their 22s. David showed up one day with his Ruger 10/22 that had seen considerable service to ask if a section of the barrel could be made to look better. It seems that David had held the rifle in a particular way that placed his hand around the barrel just ahead of the fore end. Sweaty hands have enough saltwater present to remove bluing on steel. For a space of about 6 inches, the barrel on David's rifle was shiny. I assured him that while I could not make it look like new, I could make it look better and keep it from rusting.

As always, I had with me the kit that has a permanent home under the seat of the truck. In the kit, which is housed in a plastic shoe box, are such things as a gunsmith's hammer, a Hoppes gunsmith's screwdriver set, adjustable wrenches, pliers, hack saw, sandpaper, steel wool, pocket knife, ruler, leather, leather punch, etc. This kit has made possible several craft projects and numerous repair jobs during camping trips. So when David wanted the barrel of his rifle to look better, out came the kit. I began by using fine steel wool to remove any layer of oxidized metal and brighten the metal. The barrel was then wiped with a paper towel that had been wet with

Birchwood Casey bluing products include solutions and touch up pens.

Coleman fuel. The reason for this procedure is to remove any oils so that the bluing solution will make contact with bare metal. Commercial solvents are available for removing oils from metal surfaces, but Coleman fuel works well as does the gas line freeze preventative, Heet®.

After the metal surface was clean and oil-free, I applied Birchwood Casey Perma Blue® with a piece of cloth in a back and forth motion. I then let the bluing work for a while, wiped the surface with a damp paper towel, and repeated the bluing process. After a few repetitions, I wiped the barrel with a wet paper towel, carefully dried it, and then wiped the surface with an oil-soaked cleaning patch. The result was not a rifle barrel that looked exactly like a new one, but it certainly looked better than it did when David handed it to me.

The process that I have just described constitutes the steps that are necessary to restore the surface on blued steel. Be sure to have a bright, clean, oil-free surface and follow the directions on the bottle of the bluing solution that you are going to use. By the way, most commercial bluing solutions contain toxic selenium compounds and should be handled carefully. Follow the manufacturer's directions with regard to safety precautions. There are numerous bluing preparations available, and the ones that I have tried have worked well. Birchwood Casey offers bluing preparations in several forms that include the liquid Perma Blue® and Super Blue®. A paste product, Perma Blue® is sold in tubes. If the area to be blued is small, bluing can be applied using a touch-up bluing pen that has a felt tip. Known as the Presto® Gun Blue Pen, this item is also available from Birchwood Casey. Paint pens with felt tips in flat and gloss black are also available for touch up work on black painted surfaces. Complete bluing kits are also available which include the bluing solution, steel wool, degreaser, applicators, etc. needed for the job. Other manufacturers have similar products, but I am more familiar with those described above.

Many firearms have metal parts that are not made of steel. Aluminum and its alloys are frequently used for parts that are not subjected to excessive stress or abrasion. Some parts may also be made of brass, which is coated black. Birchwood Casey offers Aluminum Black® and Brass Black® to restore or touch up these parts. Older firearms and muzzle-loaders often had metal parts that were given a brown finish, and a product known as Plum Brown® is available to match that type of finish. No matter what the type of finish on a metal surface is, there is a product available to restore the finish. Of course, the best practice is to avoid the loss of finish in the first place, and for blued steel alloys keeping the surface oiled or coated with Birchwood Casey Sheath® or an equivalent product from another manufacturer is usually sufficient.

Wood Finishing

If you are like me, you eventually reach the point where you realize that a stock or some portion of it could be made to look better. It may need the finish restored or it may need some reshaping to give a more pleasing shape than the manufacturer was willing to accept. Let me describe both situations in terms of one project.

Touch-up pens are used like any other felt tip pen.

Several years ago, I bought a Marlin 25N bolt action rifle to use as a utility tool. It did not take long to realize that the stock, while having a good overall shape, lacked those little touches that add elegance. The forearm was cut off square. The grip area was plain, and the finish was a muddy brown. I wanted a stock that was shaped like those on sporting rifles and a finish that gleamed. After taking the stock off, the first step involved trying to remove the finish using the usual paint and varnish removers. None of those products even touched the finish known as Mar-Shield® that Marlin applies to its hardwood stocks! That left only one alternative, abrasion, which is also known as sanding. Removing the finish on the Marlin stock took a great deal of time and effort, but I was eventually rewarded by the sight of bare wood. At that point, I was ready for reshaping the stock to

This inexpensive Outers stock finishing kit contains all the items to produce an excellent finish.

For many years, the Marlin 25 has offered good performance in a bolt-action rifle of moderate price.

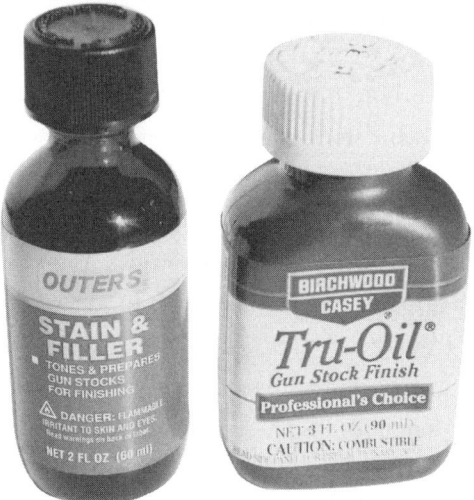

For the stock-finishing project described in the text, Outers stain and filler was used followed by Birchwood Casey Tru-Oil.

produce the desired look. Before you begin to reshape a stock, examine an elegant rifle or at least look at pictures of such rifles so you will have an idea of what you are striving for.

First, I attacked the square end on the forearm with a wood rasp to give it a pleasing rounded look. Next, I began working on the comb by rasping out flutes on the sides. When doing this, be sure that the flutes are directed toward the toe area of the butt and make sure that they are symmetric. Keep the top edges of the flutes sharp and make sure that the

Although the factory magazine for the Marlin 25N holds seven rounds, the shortened magazine holds only four.

bottom sections blend in with the lower section of the stock. The stock now had a fluted comb so the next area to work was the grip. Fine sporting rifles have true pistol grips rather than the type of curved stock found on most inexpensive rifles. To produce such a grip, I used a round wood rasp to remove wood from the area just behind the grip. The sides of the grip were shaped so that they blended in with the bottom portions of the flutes on the comb. The stock now had a pleasing overall shape and had to be prepared for finishing.

Sand, sand, then sand some more is the admonition appropriate when finishing a stock. It is the only way to remove the scratches left by a wood rasp. During the sanding process, you can also make minor changes in the shape so that the areas where wood has been removed blend smoothly with the unmodified areas. Initial sanding was done with medium sandpaper, which was followed by sanding with fine grade paper. Finally, the entire stock was sanded with extra fine paper. The stock was now wetted by rubbing with a damp cloth to raise the grain. This process causes the loose fibers known as "whiskers" to stand and after the stock is dry they can be removed by sanding with extra-fine sandpaper. As a final step in preparing the wood for finishing, the stock was rubbed briskly with 0000 grade (extra fine) steel wool. By this time, the stock was slick.

Walnut has open pores that must be filled and sealed prior to applying the actual finish. This is done with wood filler which is rubbed into the wood. Many types of wood filler are available some of which also contain sealer so that the wood is filled and sealed in one operation. To impart the desired color, a stain may also be applied. The stock on a Marlin 25N is made of hardwood rather than walnut so the process is slightly different. One of the classic stains for stocks on fine rifles is known as French Red. To get that look, I used Outers® Stain and Filler which gives the reddish tone to wood. Hardwoods do not have open pores that readily accept the stain so it may be necessary to apply more than one coat of stain. Having now stained the well-shaped stock, it was time to apply the finish.

Several articles made of wood have come under my hand to be finished. This includes not only gunstocks but also several pieces of furniture. The preparation that I have used most often is Birchwood Casey's Tru-Oil® which gives a beautiful finish to walnut and mahogany, but it also works well on many other types of wood. Having used this product many times, it was the choice for the stock of my Marlin. I apply Tru-Oil® with my fingers. I get a few drops on my hand by covering the mouth of the bottle with my hand and inverting the bottle. The oil is rubbed out to give even coverage over a small area. The process is repeated while making sure that each small area blends smoothly with others where the oil has been applied until the stock has received an even coat. Allow the initial coat to dry completely then rub the stock lightly with 0000 steel wool while being careful not to apply pressure to sharp edges such as along the bottom of the grip or along the flutes in the comb. Additional coats of Tru-Oil® can be applied in exactly the same way to give a hand rubbed, durable finish. I normally apply five or six coats of this fast-drying oil to get a finish with a high gloss. After the last coat is applied, you can decide whether you want a glossy or satin finish. To obtain a satin finish, the stock can be buffed very lightly with 0000 steel wool or by rubbing it with Birchwood Casey's Stock Sheen and Conditioner®. This product is also excellent for removing dirt and oily grime from older stocks to brighten and restore the luster.

The same finishing procedures have been carried out on the stocks of several of my air rifles, and the results have been rewarding. You may not want to remodel a stock, but it can be accomplished with only simple tools and techniques. Just work slowly and make sure that you strive for a smooth, symmetrical appearance. Many newer rifles are furnished with composite or laminated stocks the shapes of which can not be easily altered. They are usually well shaped because it is just as easy to mold a pleasingly shaped stock as it is an ugly one. Others like the new Marlin 925, which is an updated 25N, have stocks that have pressed checkering so you will not want to make extensive changes in them. But many older rifles with stocks that are less than glamorous can be improved with a little work.

It should also be mentioned that after the work on the stock was completed, I grew tired of the magazine protruding from the bottom of the stock just where my hand needed to be to carry the rifle. That problem was solved by sliding the bottom plate off the retaining lips on the bottom of the magazine, removing the follower and spring, and cutting about 1/2-inch off the bottom of the magazine box. The spring was shortened by one full loop, and the bottom edges of the magazine box were turned outward to form lips that would hold the base in place. The shortened magazine fits almost flush with the bottom of the stock and holds four rounds instead of seven. The work that I did on the Marlin does not make it a work of art, but it certainly looks a lot better than the unmodified version. Moreover, instead of having just another Marlin 25N, I now have a unique rifle that I enjoy using even more than I did before.

With a minimum of care and attention, it is easy to keep a rimfire firearm functioning well and looking good. Never before have there been so many fine products available to give the shooter the needed tools and materials for the task.

The author shortened the magazine of his Marlin 25N to fit flush with the stock. Although magazine capacity is reduced, the profile of the rifle is greatly enhanced.

Chapter 11

CHOOSE A RIMFIRE FOR TOUGH TIMES

Firearms have long been an integral part of being in remote places. James Oliver Curwood gave one of the best descriptions of this association in his 1908 adventure novel, *The Wolf Hunters*. Curwood wrote, "Only those who have gone far into the silence and desolation of the unblazed wilderness know just how human a good rifle becomes to its owner. It is a friend every hour of the night and day, faithful to its master's desires, keeping starvation at bay and holding death for his enemies; a guaranty of safety at his bedside at night, a sharp-fanged watch-dog by day, never treacherous and never found wanting by the one who bestows upon it the care of a comrade and friend." Curwood knew how much more effective a rifle is than a handgun, but we will consider both types of firearms. While this was written in a work of fiction, it was written by a man who had experienced such places, and it is an accurate portrayal of the facts in some cases. It would be wonderful if there were more places of silence and desolation available to us today. Perhaps taking a sheep wagon to the high country for the summer is about as good as it gets. Yes, this is still done in some parts of the country.

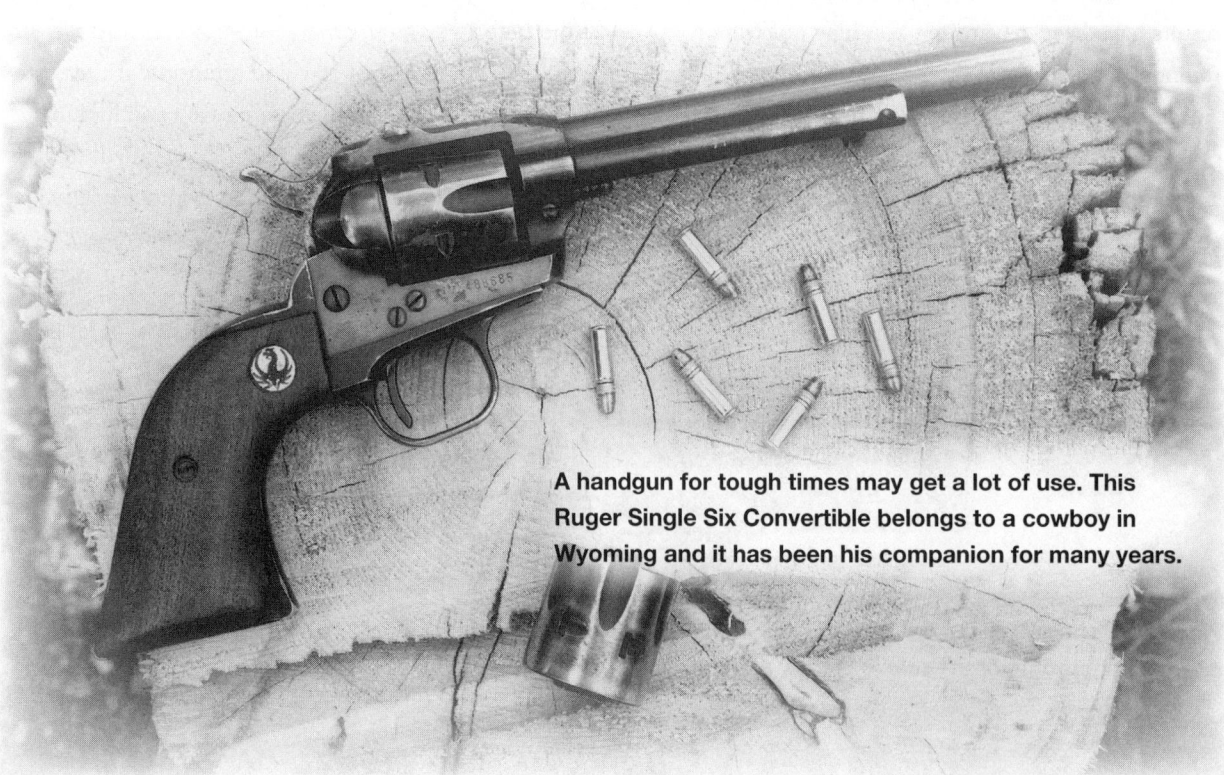

A handgun for tough times may get a lot of use. This Ruger Single Six Convertible belongs to a cowboy in Wyoming and it has been his companion for many years.

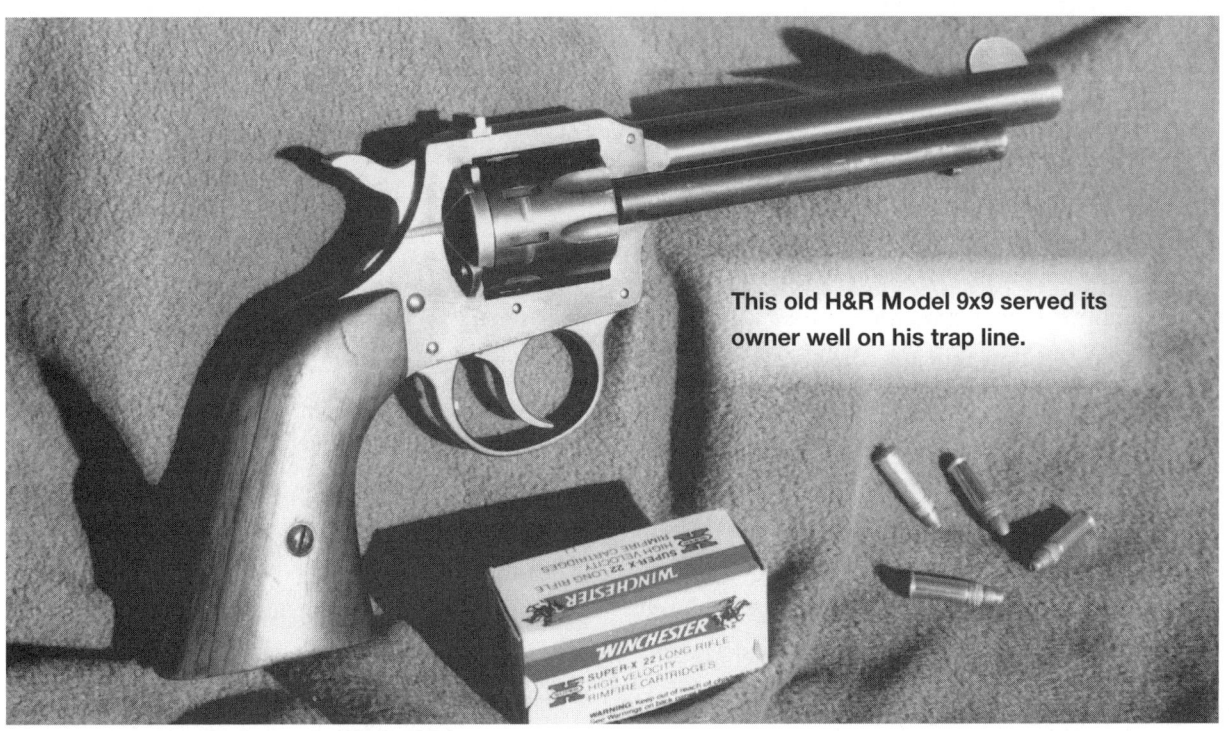

This old H&R Model 9x9 served its owner well on his trap line.

Tough Times

Given the status of the United States and many other countries today, it is unlikely that you will ever find yourself in a survival situation. It has been stated that in the lower 48 states, there is no point that is more than 30 miles from some type of road. However that may be, there is potential value and no harm in maintaining a state of preparedness regardless of where you may be. That is certainly true in some of the more remote areas of the country where you may be many miles from the nearest phone and where those electronic marvels known as cell phones must be transported many miles to get them to a place where they can contact the rest of the world. Under some situations, there is simply no substitute for self-sufficiency. This may mean in the outback, but it may also mean in times of natural disaster or as recent history teaches us, unnatural disaster. It is better to be prepared and not need to be than the other way around.

For many people (including this author) being prepared to deal with whatever arises means being armed when in remote areas. However, being armed in no way eliminates the need for skills that are useful in primitive areas. Knowledge of weather, plants, animals, and geography may also enable you to survive (perhaps even somewhat comfortably) until the situation changes. Whether you consider a firearm as part of your preparation for tough times is up to you. In parts of the west, cowboys still take the cattle herds to high elevation for the summer, and some of those cow camps are rather lonely places. The sight of a herdsman with two or three thousand sheep on the side of a mountain is a beautiful sight that can still be seen in parts of the west. When these intrepid souls head for the high country with the sheep wagon, they know that there is no 911 to call, and the cell phone doesn't work anyway. If coyotes harass the flock, something must be done and not by someone else. If a rattlesnake or a large predator shows up, it may need to be dealt with. Being armed is simply part of that way of life even in the 21st century. It is not about crime statistics or even the Second Amendment, as important as that is. Out there, any day may turn into a tough time so persons there must be ready.

Survival situations are not planned. Someone has said that a "survival knife" is the one you have with you when you have to survive. You do not normally choose a knife then deliberately go out to see if you can survive in a tough situation. In the same way, one does not select a firearm knowing that a survival situation is at hand. You select a firearm as part of your overall program of preparedness knowing that if such a situation arises you have selected your equipment and prepared yourself to deal with that situation. In this chapter, we will discuss various aspects of survival situations and how a rimfire firearm is an appropriate tool. Many books have been written on the subject of survival skills, and the interested reader should consult some of these books to gain knowledge of survival skills. As you will see from these sources, firearms constitute only one aspect of survival equipment. You should be equipped to provide shelter, warmth, and perhaps food as well as protection.

Why a Rimfire?

Compared to most centerfire firearms, rimfires are low-powered. However, it is interesting to note that the 22 Short was developed initially for self-defense! Why not choose something more powerful as a survival tool? Why not select a 44 Magnum handgun or a 30-06 Springfield rifle? There are instances where either of these would be a much better choice than any rimfire firearm. In fact, if you were facing a very large animal bent on having you for a meal, nothing would seem too powerful.

Like it or not, there are very few places where such animals are likely to be encountered today and in many of the places where you might find one, you are not permitted to have a firearm. It is also not likely that you will encounter half a dozen drug-crazed hooligans who are bent on doing you harm all at the same time. In such an instance, I want either a 45 auto or a shotgun rather than a rimfire handgun or rifle, but I would rather have a rimfire firearm than a tiny knife. Much more likely is the fact that the mere presence of a firearm will serve as a deterrent except for the most desperate criminals. Situations where being armed is a good idea do occur even though some segments of the population would tell you to go limp and play dead. Such behavior is not part of my makeup. Of course, any possession of a firearm must be in accord with all applicable laws or you are going to be involved in a lot of paperwork. Unless you have a valid concealed carry permit for the area where you are, a firearm must be clearly visible.

The essence of having a firearm as part of your preparedness for tough times lies in the answer to what purposes you may logically expect it to serve. If you are fishing for salmon in Alaska, a rimfire firearm should not be your chosen companion. There, something more like a 44 Magnum or 454 Casull would be a better choice. Generally, your survival firearm will serve to obtain food, signal for help, and

On the left are 10 rounds of 44 Magnum and on the right are 50 rounds of 22 LR. One reason for selecting a rimfire for tough times is obvious.

possibly for self-protection. In these instances, a rimfire rifle or handgun may be an appropriate choice, but you may need to give some thought to protection from what? One reason why a rimfire firearm is a good choice for long-term tough times situations is that it is possible to store or even carry a substantial amount of ammunition. Even a couple of hundred rounds of 22 rimfire ammunition can be carried more conveniently than can be a box of 25 shells for a shotgun or an equal number of rounds for a centerfire rifle. Another reason for selecting a rimfire is the cost of ammunition. Although some types of low-priced 22 LR ammunition sell for only around $1 per box of 50 rounds, the better types sell for only $2 or $3 per box. While this may seem high, the total cost for a few boxes of the ammunition most appropriate for use in tough times is small, and this is still only a fraction of the cost of ammunition for a centerfire rifle or large caliber handgun.

A firearm selected as a part of a survival package must enable you to obtain food and possibly defend you against attack from species having two or four legs. With regard to obtaining food, a well-placed bullet from a rimfire will quickly dispatch small game such as squirrels, rabbits, raccoons, opossums, turtles, snakes, birds of many types, etc. A well-placed bullet from a rimfire will even dispatch large animals. That is not to imply that the selection of a rimfire for such uses under *sporting* conditions is a wise decision. It is not. However, we are not discussing sporting conditions here, but rather *survival* conditions. In a survival situation, it may even be prudent to be able to procure food without announcing to everything and everyone within three miles that you are there. In this case, a rimfire has a distinct advantage over a high-powered rifle or a large caliber handgun. A powerful airgun would permit taking small species in an even more clandestine manner, but it would not be a good choice for defensive purposes.

It is in the area of defense that a real question arises with regard to the choice of a firearm. Many

The Browning Buck Mark is a durable, reliable pistol that would serve well in tough times.

experts believe that handguns for personal defense begin with the 38 Special and go upward from there. Are they correct? Well, yes and no. For most situations, I want a firearm that is more powerful than any rimfire, but I would be far better off with a rimfire from which I can fire accurately aimed bullets than I would be with a larger-caliber piece that is poorly used. There is no question that a well-placed bullet from a 357 Magnum is much more effective than is an identically placed bullet from a 22 LR. When a rimfire firearm is used in a defense situation, it represents a compromise between low power and ease of use. By placing the bullets in a lethal area, a rimfire can be an effective defense round. As has been described in Chapter 4, several manufacturers produce small rimfire handguns specifically for self-defense. If the adversary being defended against is large, powerful, or can shoot back, one will derive a greater sense of comfort from a larger-caliber handgun, a centerfire rifle, or a shotgun. However, a few years ago, a woman killed a grizzly that was chasing her horse by shooting it with a 22 rifle. She was also fined $1,500 for killing a protected species.

Having spent some summers in mountainous national forest areas, I have often gone afield armed with a 22 rifle or handgun. The region has some mountain lions and black bears but no grizzly bears. Defense in the majority of instances would more likely to be from a rabid skunk or rattlesnake than from a mountain lion. I do not feel particularly well armed with the rimfire but neither do I feel

The Henry U.S. Survival Rifle is easy to assemble and disassemble, and the barrel and action store in the stock.

defenseless. While I have never actually had to use the firearm to keep myself separated from some animal, I believe that there is a very good chance that I could do so if necessary. As far as two-legged predators are concerned, the mere fact that I have a firearm is sufficient to indicate that I would not be easy prey. I once read the story of a game warden who upon starting his job realized that he would have to carry a sidearm. He tried his father's 45-caliber handgun and managed to hit the target once or twice. He switched to his Colt Woodsman 22 LR and fired his usual score in the mid-90s! His sidearm for carry while working quickly became a Colt Woodsman 22. Had he been able to use the 45 equally well, he would have been better protected with it. The truth is that the vast majority of shooters who have limited experience can shoot a rimfire firearm more accurately (and comfortably) than they can a more powerful piece although at a range of a few feet that may be a moot point. The subject of this book is rimfire firearms so we will leave the discussion of other types of firearms to another forum.

Rifle or Handgun?

There is no doubt that a rifle can be fired with greater accuracy and effectiveness than can a handgun under most circumstances. Someone has said that a handgun is the weapon you use until you can get to your rifle. These thoughts would indicate that a rimfire rifle should be chosen for tough times, but there are other factors to consider. First, it is not easy to pick berries, operate a fly rod, or even photograph flowers with a rifle in hand or slung on a shoulder. For certain activities, it is necessary that the survival piece be immediately accessible, but occupy no hands and little space. In such cases,

One of the most popular rifles for tough times is the Ruger 10/22. If the owner wants to modify it, the possibilities are almost endless.

a handgun is a better choice. Moreover, if one is camping or staying in a cabin in a remote area, it is not always convenient to pick up a rifle as you head out to cut an armload of wood. The idea here is that in survival situations, the survival firearm must be readily accessible at all times. Walking 50 yards to a stream for water without it may be just the time you need it and find that you are 50 yards away from it. If you are in a situation where your life may depend on a survival weapon, keep it within arm's length at all times.

For camping in a fixed location for an extended period of time where some supplies can be left in a secure place, a rimfire rifle is a wonderfully effective tool. Some compact models are available that are extremely handy. For example, the Henry 22 Survival rifle has a hollow, removable stock in which the barrel and action can be stored and transported. Even some of the rifles that are not takedown models are compact. One of the primary considerations is that any firearm that may determine your survival must be utterly reliable. A single-shot may suffice, but when "out there" I want to be able to fire repeat shots quickly because a rimfire is none too powerful. Therefore, a repeater of some type is indicated. Bolt-action rifles are generally more accurate than other types, but they also tend to be somewhat larger and heavier. For most types of hunting and self-preservation, fine accuracy is not a requirement.

Rifle Choices

One of the autoloaders in rimfire calibers that has become the standard against which other rifles of this type are judged is the Ruger 10/22 Carbine. This short rifle utilizes a 10-shot rotary magazine that is known to be virtually jam proof. The little carbine is available in a wide range of configurations ranging from blued metal and hardwood stock to stainless steel metal and synthetic stock. The Ruger 10/22 has spawned an incredible number of after market products, and some specialty houses are devoted to selling accessories for this model only. One can obtain a match-grade trigger, a wide range of types of sights, special firing pins, etc. The barrel on the Ruger 10/22 is held in place by a novel arrangement. The bottom of the barrel has a perpendicular cut a short distance from the breech. A bar that fits in the cut

The Marlin Model 60 is a popular 22 autoloader that is reliable and accurate.

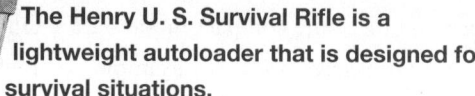

The Henry U. S. Survival Rifle is a lightweight autoloader that is designed for survival situations.

is attached to the front face of the action by two large screws with Allen heads. Removing the barrel is as simple as loosening the two screws and sliding the barrel forward out of the action. For a Ruger 10/22, one can obtain about any type of after market barrel imaginable. After market accessories are dealt with in more detail elsewhere in this book, but the point being made here is that it is possible to configure a Ruger 10/22 to suite almost any taste or use. For many users, that makes the Ruger 10/22 a logical choice for a firearm to be kept at the ready when one is out there. Furthermore, I have seen this fine little carbine with blued metal and a hardwood stock on sale for $139.95 in the recent past although the usual retail price is $160 to $170. The version with stainless steel metal and a composite stock costs about $50 more, but with its overall length of about a yard and its weight of only five pounds, it is hard to imagine a better choice for taking into the outback.

The discussion above is not meant to imply that the Ruger 10/22 is the only choice for a rimfire rifle for tough times. The Remington 597 autoloader is available with a wood or composite stock and a dull matte finish on the metal parts. This rifle also has an excellent reputation for accuracy and dependability although the available aftermarket items do not cover the spectrum of similar items available for the Ruger 10/22. Marlin also offers several variants of the Model 60 autoloader that would be entirely suitable for "out there" wear. One of them is a take down model in which the barrel is attached to the receiver by means of a large knurled ring. This rifle, the Model 70PSS, has a synthetic stock and a stainless steel barrel, and uses a seven-shot clip magazine. Savage also markets several models of rimfire rifles that are autoloaders capable of providing dependable service at low cost. These constitute the Model 64 series that offers just about any combination of stock material and finish on the metal.

A rifle chosen for tough times need not be an autoloader. Some lever and pump action rifles are available, but the range of choices is somewhat limited. Bolt-action rifles abound in rimfire calibers. They range from the inexpensive models available from makers like Marlin and Savage to the elegant sporters from Kimber, Cooper, and Anschutz. In between are models from Ruger, Remington, and CZ. All of these rifles are dependable and some are extremely accurate. I doubt that many people would opt for a rifle that costs $800 to $1,000 to lug around in the outback or to receive the hard knocks of camp

A bolt-action like this Ruger 77/22 is accurate and dependable.

A compact lever-action like this Henry is a convenient, dependable companion in remote areas.

and cabin use. Nor do they have to. Serviceable bolt-action rimfire rifles are available from about $150 on up.

As mentioned earlier, bolt-action rifles tend to accentuate accuracy potential and thus are larger and heavier as a group than are autoloaders. For example, a Ruger 77/22 bolt-action rifle is 39.5 inches long and weighs 6.5 pounds while the 10/22 Carbine is only 37 inches long and weighs 5 pounds. Similarly, a Remington 504 bolt-action rifle is 39.5 inches long and weighs approximately 6 pounds while the 597 autoloader is about the same length but weighs 5.5 pounds. In each of the comparisons given, the bolt-action rifle costs from two to three times as much as the autoloader. The inexpensive bolt-action Marlin 925 and Savage Mark II are available with wood, laminated, or composite stocks and blued or stainless steel metal. They are capable, magazine-fed rifles that are also quite durable.

A lever action rifle such as the Henry H001, Marlin 39A, or the Winchester 9422 would make an excellent little rifle to have available in remote areas. In fact, my Henry lever action is 36.5 inches long and weighs 5.5 pounds so it very convenient to carry. I have always liked the fact that lever action rifles have no bolt handle protruding from the side of the action so they are flat. Regardless of the model chosen, the rifle for tough times must be fitted with a sling so that it can be carried conveniently under a variety of circumstances. Some models come with studs already in place for attaching sling swivels, but swivels can be attached to other rifles.

In the opinion of this writer, a rimfire rifle for tough times should have open sights. There is a trend for rimfire rifles to follow the practice that has become commonplace in recent years with centerfire rifles. When looking recently at several racks of bolt-action centerfire rifles in a large sporting goods store, it was noted with interest that only a small percentage of the rifles had iron sights. Today, it is assumed that the shooter who is going to be using a fine bolt-action rifle will add a scope to the piece to

This stainless steel Smith & Wesson 2206 would be a good choice for taking to remote areas.

An outstanding handgun for survival situations is the Smith & Wesson Model 34, which was known as the Kit Gun.

greatly increase its effectiveness. While that is true in most instances, any rifle that is chosen to have available as a constant companion should have a set of open sights that do not add to the weight and bulk of the rifle. There may also be a scope mounted on the rifle, but far from a shop and range one must have a complete rifle available even if something happens to the scope. Scopes are durable instruments, but it is not at all uncommon for an extra hard bump to do damage to a scope or its mount that cannot be fixed with a Swiss Army knife and duct tape.

Handgun Choices

It is possible for most people to shoot a rifle much, much more accurately than they can any handgun. Having said that, I recall that recently I knocked over four animal silhouettes using five shots at a distance of 50 yards with a revolver. It would have been just as easy to take small animals at a similar distance or to place the bullets within a small area on a larger target. The point is that if one can get within a reasonable distance from the target a handgun can be used to take small game if the shooter is willing to practice and has discipline. Keep in mind that the handgun that is going on long hikes or kept instantly available for long periods of time should not be overly large or heavy. The best choice is a handgun that is accurate, durable, and light to moderate in weight. The fact that the handgun may be only 7 to 10 inches long and weigh 30 to 35 ounces makes it a logical choice as a piece to have available for tough times. For reasons of portability, the handgun for tough times probably will not be equipped with a scope or red dot sight.

Rimfire handguns are available in a wide range of configurations that are based on actions of the single shot, revolver, and autoloader types. For many uses, the long-barreled single shot having a bolt action is a wonderful handgun with which to plink or to shoot small game or pests in a familiar area. However, when restricted to a rimfire, most people would not choose such a piece for general use that may include defense. These specialized pieces simply are not "packin' irons." That leaves the revolvers and autoloaders from which to choose a rimfire for tough times. My personal preference is for a handgun with a barrel neither shorter than about 4 inches and nor longer than 6 inches. My walkabout handgun is usually a stainless steel Smith & Wesson Model 2206 with a 4.5-inch barrel, but my wife and I also have Browning Buck Mark pistols that have 5.5-inch barrels. The extra inch of barrel length results in velocities that are approximately 50 ft/sec higher with most types of ammunition. A difference in velocity of this magnitude will not be noted in general use. For many years, the Smith & Wesson Model 34 Kit Gun was considered to be the ultimate backpacker's 22. Made on the J-frame that Smith & Wesson uses for small revolvers, it had a 4-inch barrel and sights of target quality. This small, six-shot revolver is also referred to as the 22/32 Kit Gun because the J-frame was considered initially

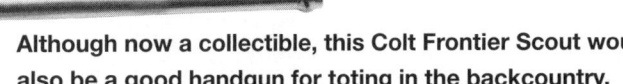

Although now a collectible, this Colt Frontier Scout would also be a good handgun for toting in the backcountry.

This Taurus revolver is utterly dependable and capable of good accuracy.

as the platform for the 32 S&W cartridge. In later years, the Kit Gun was available as the stainless steel Model 63. Weighing only 19 ounces, the Models 34 and 63 are highly prized today for the same reasons as they were in the past; they are small, light, accurate, and dependable. Similar revolvers are available from Taurus in an extensive series of models built on frames of medium size. Particularly attractive are the 4-inch barreled models that are available in blue or stainless steel in either 22 LR or 22 WMR caliber.

For military applications, the advantages of a semiautomatic pistol are obvious. Once the pistol is in play, all the shooter has to do is to pull the trigger to fire successive shots. Pressing the magazine release allows an empty magazine to drop out and a loaded one can quickly be inserted to continue the fray. However, if no additional loaded magazines are available, it takes considerable time to force rounds into the magazine one at a time and then get the loaded magazine back into the piece. Today, the vast majority of law enforcement and military agencies make use of autoloaders. Such an observation should make it clear that men and women who trust their lives to handguns know that semiautomatic pistols are reliable. I have personally fired rimfire pistols hundreds of rounds without a single jam. However, a shooter who stakes his or her life on an autoloader should not go forth with a handgun loaded with a type of ammunition that has not been tested in the piece. Different types of ammunition have bullets with slightly different shapes and dimensions, and the power level varies between standard velocity and high velocity ammunition. A particular autoloader may not function with complete reliability with all types of ammunition. The time to find out is before you are somewhere out there and need a reliable handgun. A look at catalogs from Smith & Wesson, Colt, Kimber, Ruger, Beretta, Walther, Taurus, and others will show that autoloading handguns have become more popular than revolvers.

When selecting a revolver, there are two types from which to choose. Single-action revolvers must be cocked for each shot. Drawing the hammer back causes the cylinder to rotate to align a fresh cartridge with the firing pin. Pulling the trigger discharges the piece, and the hammer must be drawn back to fire another shot. Double-action revolvers can be fired by pulling the trigger, which causes the cylinder to rotate and the hammer to move back simultaneously. When the trigger is pulled fully, the hammer is released and the piece fires. There are two actions involved (rotating the cylinder and moving the hammer) so the revolver is known as a double-action model. Because of the long, heavy trigger pull when shooting in the double-action mode, most shooters will cock the hammer manually and fire in a single-action mode most of the time because the accuracy will be much better.

Double-action revolvers can be fired faster by most shooters than can single-action models. However, except in defensive situations, the difference in rate

A Ruger Mark II is a good choice for use in any situation where reliability and durability are required.

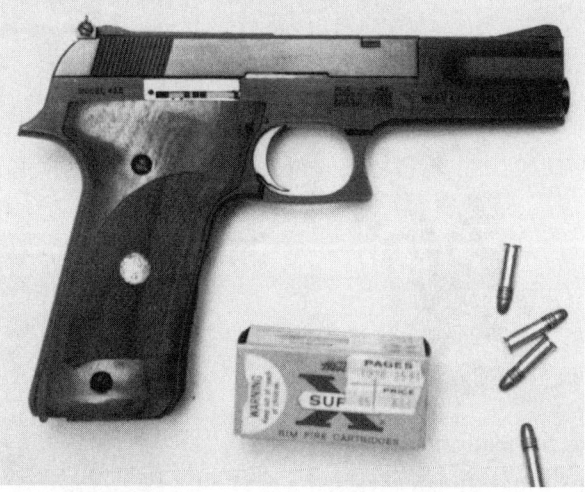

Weighing only about 22 ounces, this Smith & Wesson 422 is easy to carry and reliable.

of fire is likely to be immaterial. If a shooter is using both hands, the hammer can be cocked quickly by using the thumb of the non-shooting hand. It is in the speed of reloading that the double-action revolver has its biggest advantage. Of course, one could argue that by the time the shooter has fired six shots and the problem is still present, it may be time to try something other than reloading.

Revolvers are utterly reliable. Single-action revolvers have few parts and they generally give very long life. Imagine all the cowboys, explorers, and adventurers who roamed the wild places of the earth in days gone by armed with single-action revolvers. The single-action revolvers of today are even more reliable because of advances in design, metallurgy, and manufacturing methods. One could realistically expect a modern single-action revolver to give a lifetime of service. Of course, it is possible to abuse any firearm to the point that it gives problems prematurely. The practice of "fanning" is hard on a single-action revolver. Fanning involves holding the trigger back and quickly and repetitively firing the piece by waving or fanning the shooter's hand across the hammer to pull it back and release it quickly. This places greater stress on the hand that rotates the cylinder and other internal parts.

The double-action revolver that first came into use well over 100 years ago has developed into a precision, durable instrument. Although the revolver can be fired by pulling the trigger, it is possible to achieve greater accuracy by cocking the piece first and then firing. In other words, firing in the single-action mode makes it easier to achieve greater accuracy. However, if necessary a double-action revolver can be placed in action quickly by simply pulling the trigger. This could be an advantage in a defensive situation especially for a shooter who has not practiced extensively with a single-action model. The feats of cowboy action shooters and gunfighters of the old days show that someone who is proficient with a single-action revolver can handle most situations. Having owned and fired both single and double-action revolvers for many years, I find little difference in the speed of the first shot because the piece is cocked as it is raised and brought to bear on the target. The gun is cocked during recoil so that by the time the sights on either type of piece are aligned on the target, the revolver is ready to be fired again. It is when the cylinder is empty and the piece must be reloaded that the user of a single-action revolver is at a severe disadvantage.

A person selecting a revolver for survival situations should handle and fire both single- and double-action models. In this way, the "feel" of the piece can be experienced. One area in which the double-action revolver excels compared to the single-action type is in speed of reloading. When the cylinder latch on a double-action revolver is moved, the entire cylinder rotates out of the frame. Pushing backward on the ejector rod removes all of the empty cases at once so that fresh rounds can be inserted. Pushing the cylinder back into the frame causes the latch to lock it in place and the piece is ready to fire. A single-action revolver has a loading gate on the right hand side at the rear of the cylinder. Using the thumb, this gate is swung outward exposing one chamber in the cylinder. An ejector rod is located in a fixed housing below and to the right hand side of the barrel. Pushing the rod backward forces one empty case out of the cylinder. The ejector rod must be allowed to slide forward and the cylinder turned manually to bring the next chamber into alignment with the ejector rod, which is then pushed to the rear to remove another case. This procedure is repeated until all of the empty cases are ejected and then loaded rounds can be placed in the cylinder one at a time. Through practice, reloading of a single-action revolver can be accomplished fairly quickly, but it is slow compared to reloading a double-action revolver.

One advantage of single-action revolvers like the Ruger Single Six is that they can be obtained with two cylinders. One cylinder is chambered for the 22 LR while the other is chambered for the 22 Winchester Magnum Rimfire. The use of 22 WMR ammunition gives the shooter the option of having a somewhat more powerful handgun while still being able to fire the much less expensive 22 LR for most situations. One drawback to the whole idea of interchangeable cylinders is that one is not going to go walking in the wilderness with the 22 LR cylinder in place and when a situation arises where more power is desired change cylinders at that time. It could happen that while out searching for food (where the 22 LR is appropriate) one could encounter some sort of trouble where the 22 WMR would be a better choice. It is probably a simpler plan to carry the revolver with one cylinder in place while having a supply of ammunition in that caliber and

An older handgun such as this Colt Huntsman can still fulfill the requirements for a handgun for tough times.

not have an extra cylinder along which requires the use of ammunition of a different caliber. The extra cylinder also takes up space and has weight, and there is considerable merit in traveling light.

Over the years, Smith & Wesson has offered some exceptional rimfire revolvers. Some have been target models that had the same dimensions and weight as those in larger calibers. Others mirrored models that were intended for law enforcement use. For example the S & W Model 15 Combat Masterpiece had a rimfire counterpart in the Model 18. The idea was that one could practice with greater comfort and less expense with the rimfire piece to gain proficiency with the duty weapon. Colt offered rimfire models comparable to the Officers Model Match and Diamondback centerfire revolvers. All of these fine rimfire revolvers are no longer manufactured. The trend toward autoloaders in centerfire calibers is also manifested in rimfires. There are currently many more models of autoloaders available than there are revolvers.

Autoloading pistols are available in several types and they will not be discussed in detail here (see Chapter 4). However, a personal preference will be discussed to make a point. The majority of centerfire pistols have a visible hammer. In some cases, firing is only by double-action (DAO) meaning that after each shot the hammer remains "down" until the trigger is pulled again to move the hammer backward and fire the piece. In other cases, the hammer remains cocked after each shot and pulling the trigger only releases the sear to fire the piece. The first shot is fired double-action, but additional shots are fired in the single-action mode. Many autoloaders of the latter type have safeties that also function as decocking levers to lower the hammer when no additional shots are to be fired. Pressing the safety lever downward allows the hammer to fall and strike a large block that prevents it from striking the firing pin. Not only is there an external hammer whose position is clearly visible, but also a safety lever that must be manipulated before the pistol can be fired. This is about as safe as an autoloading pistol gets.

In the case of rimfire pistols, there is no external hammer in most current models, and the safety catch is a small lever on the left hand side of the frame. It is not difficult for the safety lever to be moved as the pistol is withdrawn from a holster or pack, and the shooter is then holding a loaded pistol, which requires only slight pressure on the trigger to fire. In the opinion of many shooters, pistols of this type are not as safe as are the centerfire pistols with visible hammers or either type of revolver. One exception is the Walther P22, which not only has a visible hammer, but also it can be fired double-action for the first shot. This small lightweight pistol has much to recommend it, especially for shooters who like centerfire autoloaders that have external hammers. Any firearm is only as safe as the shooter using it. A responsible shooter with good technique and safe gun handling practices will be a safe shooter with any type of handgun. While I regularly use rimfire pistols having these characteristics, I am fully cognizant of the limitations of a single mechanical safety.

There are many types of semiautomatic pistols in rimfire calibers available to the outdoorsman. One of the pistols that has stood the test of time is the Ruger Mark II that is available in a standard version for sporting use as well as several target configurations for competition. These pistols have been made by the millions, and they have an unsurpassed reputation for dependability and durability. Several versions are available in stainless steel, which is a desirable option for a pistol to be used under harsh conditions.

As this is written in late 2004, the Mark II is being phased out with the introduction of the Mark III models. Another pistol that has become popular is the Browning Buck Mark. Like the Ruger, there are several versions available that have different barrel lengths and finishes. The Buck Mark Standard model is a highly accurate pistol that has excellent adjustable sights. I have had considerable experience with the Ruger and Browning pistols and would unhesitatingly take to the outback with either.

Another pistol that should make an outstanding kit gun is the Walther P22, which is available with barrel lengths of 3.4 and 5 inches. With a polymer frame, the Walther weighs only approximately 20 ounces even with the longer barrel, which has a weight in the form of a fake compensator located at the muzzle. The grip is very short so persons who have large hands will probably have the little finger placed below the grip, but the pistol is extremely compact. The little Walther has dual safety levers located on either side of the receiver in the positions where decocking levers are located on many centerfire pistols. With excellent white dot sights, the Walther would be a convenient choice as a rimfire pistol for tough times.

Smith & Wesson, Beretta, Kimber, Taurus, and many other firms market the ubiquitous rimfire autoloaders. They are fine firearms, and the prospective buyer of a rimfire auto should examine several models to determine what feels best and will meet the buyer's requirements. Many shooters of rimfire autoloaders believe that the Colt Woodsman was the finest 22 auto ever made. Others feel the same way about the Smith & Wesson Model 41. However, a new S&W Model 41 or High Standard pistol or a vintage Colt Woodsman costs some serious money, and such an outlay is not necessary when selecting a handgun for tough times. There is nothing wrong with them, but they are too exquisite for rough use as kit guns. If the outdoorsman wishes to select one of these elegant models, more power (or money!) to him or her. They are fine shooters. This discussion is not meant to be a complete product review, but rather an indication that the choice of a rimfire firearm for tough times is rather large (see Chapter 4).

Caliber

Except for a few highly specialized pistols chambered for the 22 Short, there are really only four rimfire calibers available in handguns. Of these, the 22 LR is by far the most common with many more models available in that caliber. The 22 WMR has never been very popular in handguns. For a time Smith & Wesson has produced a double-action revolver in that caliber, and an autoloader known as the Automag II has been available. Volquartsen markets a long-barreled autoloader in 22 WMR that is intended to have a scope mounted and to be used as a varmint gun. Colt produced the single-action rimfire revolver known as the Frontier Scout for many years and many of them were offered with an additional cylinder in 22 WMR. Ruger has done this for many years with the popular Single Six Convertible model. Today, the selection of handguns chambered for the 22 WMR is only a fraction of what is for 22 LR guns. Taurus produces an extensive line of excellent revolvers. A 4-inch barreled version is available in blue or stainless steel in either 22 LR or 22 WMR caliber. Actual retail price for a box of 22 WMR cartridges is around $6-7 depending on the brand and type so cost of ammunition is also a factor.

I am going to show some of my prejudice with what follows in this paragraph, but right or wrong it is the opinion of this writer. If there is one caliber that makes little sense to me as a handgun caliber except in single-shot guns with long barrels it is the 17 HMR. Before you go ballistic, let me explain my thinking on the subject. At the current time, the 17 HMR ammunition lists for about $12 per box of 50 and actually retails for $9 to $11 per box. This prices it out of the plinking category for many shooters including me. In a handgun with 4- or 6-inch barrel suitable for convenient carrying, the velocity is much lower than the 2,500-2,600 ft/sec achieved in rifles. The performance of a tiny 17-grain bullet is dependent on its high velocity, which simply isn't produced in most handgun barrels. That is why some of the models offered in 17 HMR have barrels in the 10-12 inch range. It has been demonstrated that at fairly long ranges where the velocity has dropped to about half the muzzle velocity, bullet performance of the 17 HMR is questionable in terms of expansion even when fired from rifles. It behaves more like an ice pick than the explosive little round that it is when the bullet velocity is over 2,000 ft/sec. The 22 WMR drives a 40-grain bullet at over 1,400 ft/sec and produces nearly 200 ft lbs of energy is a more effective handgun cartridge. In addition, the 22 WMR ammunition is available with full-metal-jacketed bullets for situations where deep penetration is needed or damage to pelts must be kept to a minimum, and shot cartridges are available in 22 WMR for dispatching small pests. True, a 17 HMR handgun gives velocities high enough that a flat trajectory results making it possible to hit ground squirrels at longer ranges. A scope would almost certainly be necessary to find out. I have no problem with this type of equipment for the pest hunter, but for a survival firearm it seems out of place. A bullet from a 17 Mach 2 at the muzzle represents the same power level as a 17 HMR without 20 to 25 percent of its velocity so the same comments apply. There are many gas stations in remote areas that sell the 22 LR, but they probably do not have 17 HMR or 17 Mach 2 ammunition on the shelves.

I own and use firearms in 22 WMR and 17 HMR calibers. In rifles, they perform in a different league than the 22 LR. So much of that additional performance is lost when the rimfire magnum cartridges are used in handguns that they may not be worth the additional expense, noise, and uncertainty in availability. The 22 WMR makes some sense when used in single-action revolvers by swapping cylinders, but there is nothing to swap a 17 HMR cylinder for except another 17 caliber of lower power, the 17 Mach 2. As a stand-alone handgun cartridge, it is interesting and useful as a varmint cartridge but I do not want to pack one in the backcountry. I think that if one wants something other than the 22 LR or the 22 LR/22 WMR combination, a 38 Special or 357 Magnum makes a lot of sense. The guns are no larger than most of those in rimfire calibers, ammunition can be bought as cheaply as for a 17 HMR, effective shot cartridges are available, and with some loads a much larger degree of smash can be delivered to the target. The main drawback to centerfire handguns for a extended use that it is not so easy to carry several hundred rounds of ammunition. When the cost and availability of ammunition and other factors considered, selecting the 22 LR as my handgun for tough times makes a lot of sense. However, the reasons underlying my selection may be different than for yours so you may arrive at a different conclusion.

Ammunition

When selecting equipment for tough times, consider that while you may be taking squirrels with head shots at 25 yards you may also be trying to keep something much larger away from you. Under the latter circumstances, you should load your rimfire with the most potent ammunition available as long as it gives the necessary accuracy for other chores. Personal preference may be showing here, but I do not want ammunition for tough times that makes use of a very light bullet at high velocity because penetration is very low. Such ammunition is fine for taking ground squirrels, starlings, crows, or other fragile species, but not for doing damage to the internal organs of large species.

Keep in mind that a 40-grain high velocity bullet from a handgun barrel of average length moves at around 1000 ft/sec and generates approximately 100 ft lbs of energy at the muzzle. A high performance load such as the CCI Velocitor or Remington Yellow Jacket will probably exceed this by a small amount. If you want to shoot something a little more exotic, the Lapua Scoremax makes use of a 48-grain bullet. The velocity is given as 1,040 ft/sec from a rifle and would not be more than perhaps 900 ft/sec from a handgun, but the heavy bullet would penetrate very well. In fact, at handgun velocities the standard 40-grain solids penetrate very well. Trajectory is not much of a factor for a survival handgun because shots would almost always be taken at short ranges. Survival situations are not those where a scoped handgun has its greatest utility, and using open sights the average shooter should limit shots to ranges under 50 yards or so. If you try shooting some groups at 50 yards with most handguns, you may limit your shots at game to well under the 50-yard mark.

When the cost and availability of ammunition and other factors were considered I have selected the 22 LR as my handgun for tough times. If circumstances allow a rifle to be chosen, almost any high velocity ammunition that gives suitable accuracy in that rifle is satisfactory. The CCI Velocitor and Winchester Power Point are two high velocity hollow-point rounds that have given outstanding accuracy in several of my rifles. For use in all possible situations in remote areas, a few boxes of high velocity ammunition with solid bullets would also be required. With the emphasis being on obtaining as much power as possible, it is easy to overlook the fact that standard velocity ammunition often gives better accuracy. From a handgun, the difference in velocity between standard velocity and high velocity ammunition is almost always less than 100 ft/sec. When identical barrel lengths are involved, bullet velocities from semiautomatics are usually higher than those given by revolvers, part of which is due to the gap between the cylinder and the barrel. As a result, a semiautomatic firing standard velocity ammunition will give approximately the same velocity as a revolver firing high velocity ammunition. For hunting purposes, I would generally try several types of ammunition and select a type that my handgun fed reliably through the action and shot best.

If you are using a rifle or handgun in 22 WMR, the 40-grain jacketed hollow-points will perform as well as any other type of ammunition. I especially like the Federal 50-grain hollow-point load, but it may not give the best accuracy and the point of impact is often 2 to 3 inches from where the 40-grain bullets hit at a range of 50 yards. It is better to pick one load that performs well, become familiar with it, and stick with it. One additional factor for selecting 40-grain loads for the 22 WMR is that you have a choice of identical loads with hollow-point or full metal jacket bullets.

The user of a 22 LR handgun also has the option of the CCI Stinger, SGB, and Quik Shok cartridges. The Stinger and Quik Shok bullets are quite fast and the latter breaks into four pieces on impact. However, both of these types of ammunition utilize cases that are longer than those in ordinary 22 LR rounds, and some autoloaders do not feed them reliably. This is not a factor when they are used in revolvers. In 22 LR caliber, the Power Point from Winchester is a good choice. It utilizes a 40-grain hollow-point bullet and gives excellent accuracy in most rimfire rifles and handguns. However, almost any of the high velocity solids will give good performance. The cost of ammunition in 22 LR is around $2 to $3 per box, which makes it possible to practice a lot. Finally, don't overlook the fact that shot cartridges are available in 22 LR and 22 WMR calibers. These can be of use when trying to get rid of rodents or pest birds at short ranges.

The idea of surviving in some remote area while being armed with only a knife and a few matches is intriguing. No doubt there are some who can successfully do that, but just in case I am not among them, I want at least a 22 handgun and a supply of ammunition. On the other hand, I have never actually been faced with a tough situation of that type, but I would rather be prepared and not need to be than the other way around. It is known as preventative medicine or a strategic strike force, depending on your point of view.

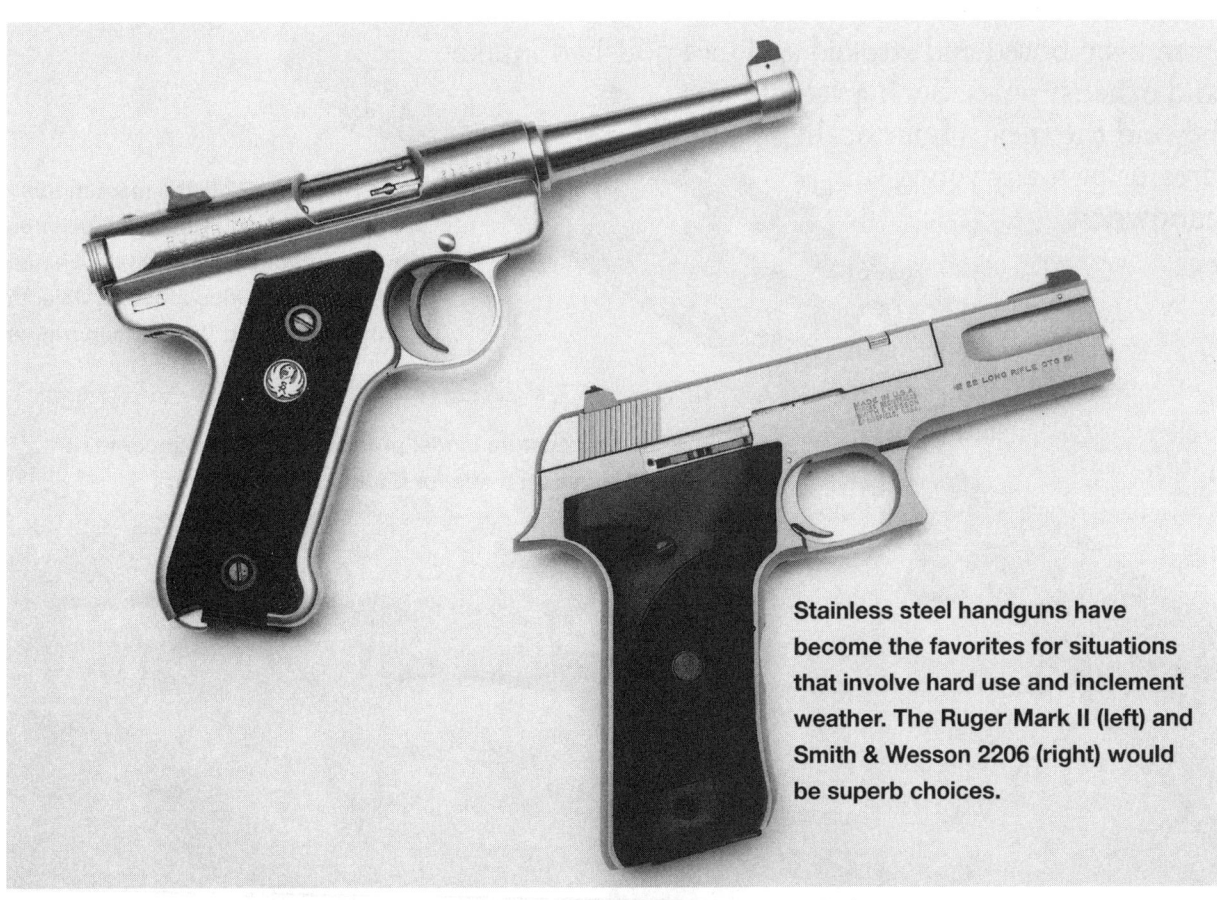

Stainless steel handguns have become the favorites for situations that involve hard use and inclement weather. The Ruger Mark II (left) and Smith & Wesson 2206 (right) would be superb choices.

Chapter 12
ACCESSORIES, ACCURACY, AND COMPETITION

Many years ago, the owners of automobiles found it exciting to modify their vehicles. Such modifications were aimed at improving the performance of the machine or perhaps making it look better (a result that was dubious in many instances). Automotive supply houses offered everything from fender skirts to camshafts for most cars. Most of the acquaintances of the author simply did not have available the funds to take advantage of the opportunities to obtain such merchandise. The coin of the realm came from odd jobs like sweeping floors at night or picking peaches in the summer. If the car ran at all, it was left as it was because keeping fuel in the tank was the primary concern. But there were many more affluent owners who bought intake manifolds so that two or three carburetors could be attached. A three-quarter race camshaft may have been installed, and dual exhausts were almost mandatory. The engine may have even been bored and stroked and had polished intake and exhaust ports. Such a vehicle was beyond the means but not the dreams of many young car owners.

The Ruger 10/22 is the most modified rimfire in history. This 10/22 belongs to the author's son, Keith, and it has a Hogue overmolded stock, a Majestic Arms barrel, and Volquartsen trigger.

This stock is a custom model produce by Altius Handcrafted Firearms for use on a rifle for biathlon competitors.

Each hobby area has its following. Today, computers have become the nemesis of many hobbyists, and the available aftermarket peripherals are endless. In days gone by, the author spent many hours perusing the catalogs and magazines that dealt with firearms. It was possible to buy stocks, sights, triggers, and other items to change the appearance and perhaps the performance of many firearms. It was with great interest that items such as Timney and Canjar triggers, Fajen stocks, and Marble's sights were studied. Never mind that a rifle to accept such items was not at hand. Eventually, a Mauser 98 came along and the work began with a semi-inletted Bishop stock. The military bolt handle was cut off and a Jaeger bolt handle with a neat ring of checkering around the knob replaced it. A Redfield Sourdough front sight and a Lyman 48 peep sight replaced the military hardware. With the metal reblued, the result was a rather attractive sporting rifle. As is the case with other young men (or those who are young at heart), along came a single-action revolver and the Mauser went in trade.

In those days long ago, most cars stayed "stock" for several reasons. Today, most rifles stay "stock" because they function satisfactorily that way. Some models have been made by the millions so there is a substantial market for items to use with these rifles. The result is that there is a huge aftermarket industry in specialty parts for firearms, especially rimfire models. Some of the items are for cosmetic changes while others are designed to enhance the performance of the piece. In this chapter, we will briefly explore this area of the rimfire shooting sports. Keep in mind that aftermarket products often enable the owner of a rifle or handgun in one form to change it to another. There is less reason to do this with some models because the number of options offered by the manufacturer is so large. It is possible to buy most rimfire rifles with almost any choice of stock material and metal finish initially. However, the aftermarket items are not restricted to simply choices in stock and metal finishes.

Stocks

One of the most commonly replaced items on a rimfire rifle is the stock. For certain models (particularly the Ruger 10/22), the range of optional stocks is enormous. Perusal of the catalogs from suppliers such as Midway USA, Cabela's, Natchez Shooter Supply and many others will reveal that the selection of available stocks includes models with all sorts of configurations and compositions. The selection is so vast that only a few examples will be mentioned here. The outstanding Hogue Overmolded stock with rubber pebbled grip surfaces is a perennial favorite for good reasons. They provide outstanding feel and controllability combined with durable construction at a price of only $59.95 from most sources. Other options include the low cost synthetic stocks from manufacturers such as Ram Line, Butler Creek, and others. Some of the black stocks from Butler Creek sell for around $55, but they are also available with an attached bipod for about $30 more. Advanced Technology produces the Fiberforce stock that sells $54.99 from Midway USA. This is a skeletonized model with an open grip area in the stock. CoreLite produces a synthetic stock for the Ruger 10/22 that sells for about $45 in black or about $70 in camo finish.

On the other end of the scale are stocks from Bell & Carlson with one model being a target-type stock that features an adjustable butt plate and comb. This composite stock sells for approximately $185. Also near the upper end of the price range is the composite stock from Volquartsen, which has a price of over $200. Fajen produces a selection of stocks for the Ruger 10/22 that includes several thumb-hole models that sell for around $160 and up depending on composition. Some models are offered as unfinished stocks for about $120 so the owner can do the finial finishing to produce the desired result. Midway also offers a large number that include a stock and barrel combination with prices in the $200 to $250 range. Folding skeleton stocks are also available for the Ruger 10/22, but be advised that these are not legal in all areas.

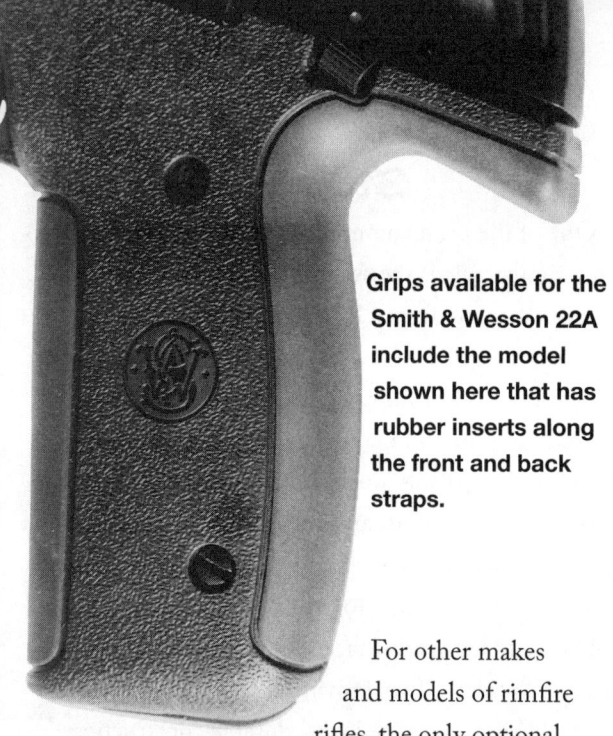

Grips available for the Smith & Wesson 22A include the model shown here that has rubber inserts along the front and back straps.

For other makes and models of rimfire rifles, the only optional stocks available may be those from the firearm manufacturer. For example, the owner of a Marlin rimfire rifle will not find an aftermarket stock available from most stock makers. The author has been told that the cost of preparing the molding equipment for a particular stock runs up in the six-figure range so the manufacturer must limit the number of models available. Many shooters who have Marlin rimfire rifles have a range of options available directly from the Marlin Firearms Company. The stocks available include black synthetic, black/gray laminated, brown laminated, and camo versions, but not all types are available for all rifle models. These stocks are priced competitively with those available from aftermarket sources. For example, the black synthetic stocks are available for the bolt-action rifles in 22 LR and 22 WMR calibers as well as the Model 60 and 70 autoloaders for $48.25. A black/gray laminated stock is available for all variants of the Model 60 for a price of $72.45. The brown laminated stock is available for most of the current bolt-action rifles as well as all of the variants of the Model 60 autoloader for a price of $55.70. If you own a Marlin rimfire rifle and want to change the appearance and functionality of the piece, it is quite possible that the stock you want is available from Marlin. This is a particularly desirable option for the owner of an older gun that has a damaged stock or one that is in poor shape because a new stock will dress up the rifle in short order. A stock known as the Advanced Technology Fiberforce model for the Marlin 60 series autoloaders is available from Midway USA for $54.99.

Shooters of rimfire handguns also have many options to help them get a grip on things. Grips are popular items to replace because the process is so easy. In many cases only a screw or two holds the panels to the frame. No doubt some shooters change the grips on handguns simply to improve the looks. For example, a pair of staghorn grip panels on a single-action revolver makes a considerable change its appearance.

In recent years, handguns leaving the factories have much better grips than those of a generation ago. Gone are most of the slick wood or plastic grips that were so common. Replacing them are grips produced by aftermarket grip makers such as Hogue and Uncle Mike's who supply grips to firearm manufacturers. Most of these grips have been available as aftermarket items for many years, but in some cases the handguns are shipped from the factory with them already installed. The primary reason is that the Hogue and Uncle Mike's grips are made of rubber and give a good purchase in the hand. The grip afforded by the rubber surface is augmented by raised bumps, finger grooves, and imprinted checkering. Grips such as these are especially effective when handling a handgun in cold weather. The Smith & Wesson Models 22A and 22S are available with several options in grips. Three of the choices involve grips made of hard plastic either with or without thumb rest. The option is also available for grips made of plastic that have rubber inserts along the front and rear surfaces. The fourth option is a large target style grip made of laminated wood. Any of these grips can be added as aftermarket options for the Model 22A and 22S pistols if the owner wishes to change grip style. My own preference is for the soft grip option with rubber inserts because it is compact but still gives an excellent feel.

Barrels

A practice that was virtually unheard of in my younger days is now quite common. I am talking about switching barrels on a rimfire rifle. Rifles that have barrels threaded to the action or locked in place by a transverse pin are not amenable to barrel swapping by the average shooter. A competent gunsmith can replace any barrel, but this chapter is aimed at the typical rimfire shooter. The rimfire rifles that are ordinarily considered as candidates for barrel replacement are those manufactured by Sturm, Ruger & Co. The Model 10/22 has spawned a number of aftermarket industries because the design of the rifle allows the barrel and many other parts to be replaced easily. Less popular is barrel swapping for the Models 77/22, 77/22M, and 77/17 the barrels of which are attached to the action in a manner that is similar to that used on the 10/22. Let me say quickly that there is nothing wrong with the barrels made by Sturm, Ruger & Company for these models. There is nothing wrong with a two-barrel carburetor, but swapping the intake manifold for one that would allow a four-barrel carburetor to be used was a fairly common activity some years ago. Analogous comments could be made about camshafts and rifle barrels.

The primary motivation for changing barrels on a firearm is to enhance accuracy. In some cases, there is a change in appearance, weight, and durability, but accuracy is the most important issue. This section is not devoted entirely to the Ruger 10/22, but it will probably seem like it. In the rimfire rifle category, the ultimate in versatility with regard to aftermarket accessories is the Ruger 10/22.

Modifying a Ruger 10/22 by replacing the factory parts with parts from other manufacturers (known as "tricking out" the rifle) is extremely popular. If you want to verify that, go to the eBay web site and type "Ruger 10/22" in the search blank. When the search is made, you will see a bewildering array of items that are offered for auction. Interestingly, there are always numerous factory barrels and stocks available because many people want only the rifle action to use as the starting point for building a custom 10/22. Because the Ruger 10/22 in 22 WMR and 17 HMR calibers are becoming popular, many of the aftermarket items produced for the 22 LR version are also available for rifles in the magnum calibers.

Much of the basis for the ease of modification of a Ruger 10/22 lies in the way in which the barrel is attached to the action. A few rimfire rifles have barrels that are threaded into the actions. These include the Thompson/Center semiautomatic rifles and the CZ bolt-action models. The vast majority of inexpensive 22s have barrels that are fitted friction tight in the receiver then locked in place by a pin that extends through the front ring of the receiver while passing through a groove in the barrel extension. Barrel attachment on the Ruger 10/22 is unique. A large slot is cut across the bottom of the barrel, and a bar fits in the cut. The bar has two holes that have large Allen-headed screws that pass through them and thread into the front face of the action. Tightening these screws pulls the barrel backwards so that the barrel is drawn tightly against the action. Removing the barrel is as simple as removing two screws. However, it should be kept in mind that the receiver on a Ruger 10/22 is made of an

A Majestic Arms Aluma-Lite barrel is attached by placing the retaining block in the notch in the bottom of the barrel and tightening two screws.

Removing the barrel from a Ruger 10/22 Carbine requires loosening the two large screws as shown.

aluminum alloy so it would be possible to strip the threads if too much torque is applied to the locking screws. The screw holes in the rather soft receiver are subject to wear if the barrel is removed and attached frequently.

Aftermarket barrels for the Ruger 10/22 (and to a lesser degree the bolt-action 77 series) span the range from around $125 to well over $300 depending on the metal and manufacturer. Some of the finest barrels are produced by Lilja Precision Rifle Barrels of Plains, Montana. Lilja produces a 21-inch stainless steel barrel for both the 22 LR and the 22 WMR versions of the 10/22. A 23-inch stainless steel barrel is produced for the Ruger 10/17. These barrels are priced at $315 and $340, respectively, but they represent the epitome in replacement barrels for the Ruger semiautomatic rifles. As is the case with many other replacement barrels, the Lilja barrels are cylindrical with a 0.920-inch diameter.

Green Mountain Rifle Barrel Company of Conway, New Hampshire produces barrels having an outstanding reputation for accuracy. Configurations are available in blue and stainless steel with both smooth and fluted surfaces. Prices range from around $90 to $140 with the fluted stainless steel model being the most expensive. Also available from Green Mountain are blue and stainless steel fluted barrels for the 10/22 in 22 WMR. These have retail prices of approximately $120 and $140, respectively. However, a section of about six inches at the muzzle end has a diameter of 0.925 inches, which gives the effect of a muzzle weight. This barrel can be used with the factory stock, but it is a heavier barrel that provides greater stability for offhand shooting.

Volquartsen Custom Ltd. of Carroll, Iowa, produces several barrels for the Ruger 10/22. One series of barrels is of the tensioned type with carbon sleeves surrounding the barrel itself. These barrels retail for around $230. Volquartsen barrels are also available with a built in compensator at the muzzle with retail prices of approximately $270. Volquartsen produces another interesting barrel for the 10/22

The Majestic Arms Aluma-Lite barrel has a steel inner barrel surrounded by aluminum. It is light in weight but very accurate.

that has a contour that matches that of the factory barrel throughout most of the length then widens to 0.920 inch. Volquartsen barrels have a strong following among varmint hunters and an unsurpassed reputation for accuracy. Another Volquartsen product involves the 22 Short, which produces less back thrust on the bolt than does a 22 LR. As a result, most autoloaders chambered for the 22 LR will not cycle properly with 22 Short cartridges even if the difference in length does not cause feeding problems. Shooters of Ruger 10/22 rifles can convert them to fire 22 Short cartridges by installing aftermarket accessories from Volquartsen. The kit includes a different bolt as well as a barrel chambered for 22 Short.

Majestic Arms, LTD of Staten Island, New York produces an interesting barrel for the Ruger 10/22. This barrel, known as the Aluma-Lite, is of the dual composition type. It features an inner steel barrel produced by famed barrel maker Lothar Walther that is surrounded by an outer sleeve made of aircraft-grade aluminum permanently bonded to the inner barrel. With an outside diameter of 0.920 inch and an overall length of 17 inches, the barrel weighs only 24 ounces. As a result, it is possible to obtain a barrel having the dimensions of a target barrel but having the light weight of a barrel of sporting contour. The Aluma-Lite barrel, which retails for approximately $150, has a target crown that is beveled inward to the muzzle to protect the muzzle. Accuracy data obtained with this barrel will be presented in Chapter 13.

Lothar Walther produces a blued barrel for the Ruger 10/22 that has the profile of a standard factory barrel throughout most of its 16-inch length so it can be used with a factory stock. A few inches from the muzzle, the barrel widens to a diameter of 0.980 inch, which results in built in muzzle weight. This fine barrel is available from Hornet Products of Sarasota, FL.

Butler Creek also produces barrels for the Ruger 10/22, which are 20 inches long and are constructed of 416 stainless steel although blued steel barrels are also available. These have 0.920-inch diameter and retail for about $160 and $180, respectively. Adams & Bennett produces a series of barrels for the Ruger 10/22. They measure 18 inches in length and are available in blue and stainless steel with either cylindrical or fluted configurations having 0.920-inch diameter. Prices range from about $90 for the blue cylindrical model to about $170 for the fluted stainless steel version with a built in compensator. A 20-inch blue model is also available in 22 WMR caliber.

Butler Creek produces a series of barrels that have a slender stainless steel barrel that is surrounded by a hollow cylinder of carbon fiber. These barrels are light in weight yet relatively unaffected by temperature. All are 0.920 inches in diameter, and lengths are 18 and 20 inches for the 22 LR barrels, 18 inches for the 22 WMR barrels, and 20 inches for the 17 HMR barrels. The barrels described by no means constitute a complete list of the available options.

In addition to the Ruger 10/22, the other rifle that is capable of considerable alteration is the bolt-action Ruger 77 in both the standard and magnum forms. Moreover, because most of the dimensions of the 17 HMR and 22 WMR cases are identical, it is convenient to convert a 77/22M to a 77/17 simply by changing barrels. Not only can that be done for the magnum version, but also a 77/22 can be converted to a 17 Mach 2 rifle by changing barrels. Several barrel options are available, but two of them are the barrels produced by Green Mountain Rifle Barrel Company and Volquartsen. Both produce barrels in 17 HMR that can be interchanged with the factory barrels on the Ruger 77/22M. The Green Mountain barrels are available in a 20 inch fluted stainless steel model with a diameter of 0.920 inches and as a 22-inch octagonal blue sporter model. These barrels retail for about $170 and $200, respectively. Additional information on the octagonal sporter weight barrel in 17 HMR can be found in Chapter 13.

Volquartsen produces 17 HMR barrels for the Ruger 77/22M bolt-action in two forms. The first is a stainless steel cylindrical barrel of 0.920 inches diameter while the second is a tensioned barrel enclosed in a carbon fiber sleeve. These barrels retail for about $220 and $230, respectively. The aftermarket barrels described do not represent an inclusive list, but they are representative of those

The barrel on a Smith & Wesson 22A is unlocked by pushing inward on the latch at the front of the trigger guard.

available. Generally speaking, barrels on rimfire rifles produced by Marlin, Savage, Winchester, Browning, Thompson/Center, Kimber, Anschutz, and others are not user interchangeable.

High quality barrels in 22 LR, 22 WMR, and 17 HMR are produced for Ruger rifles by Jarvis, Inc. of Hamilton, MT. However, Jarvis also produces barrels for the Remington 597 rifles.

Generally, owners of rimfire handguns have the barrel that came on the gun with no possibility for making changes other than by a gunsmith or returning the gun to the factory. There are some notable exceptions to this restriction. The Smith & Wesson Models 22A and 22S are available from the factory with 4-, 5.5-, or 7-inch barrels. However, because of the design of the pistol, it is a simple matter to remove the barrel and its accompanying sight rail (as is done during field stripping). Barrels in all three lengths are available from Smith & Wesson if the owner wishes to change the barrel from one length to another. The same pistol can be fitted with a 7-inch barrel for target work or one of 4-inch length for general use.

Another barrel switching option exists for the Walther P22, which is available with barrels measuring 3.4 and 5 inches in length. The barrels are easily changed by loosening two Allen headed screws, and barrels in either length are available from the manufacturer. In fact, one available option for purchasers of new Walther P22 pistols includes barrels in both lengths as part of an optional kit.

Owners of Browning Buck Mark pistols also have the possibility of changing barrels by purchasing an additional barrel as a part available from the factory. The Buck Mark Standard pistol has a 5.5-inch barrel, but other versions have different barrel lengths. Because the barrel is attached to the frame by two large screws, it is possible to interchange barrels easily. Extra barrels are available from Browning's Parts Department at (800) 322-4626.

In addition to rifle barrels, Volquartsen also produces match barrels for Ruger Mark II and Mark III pistols. Volquartsen produces an extensive line of semiautomatic rifles consisting of nine models.

Triggers

In addition to barrel quality, trigger action is a factor that has an impact on accuracy. A long, raspy trigger pull is not conducive to reproducible let off which in turn is not conducive to small groups. There are essentially two ways in which to improve trigger action. First, the entire trigger can be replaced if an aftermarket trigger is available for that particular rifle. The problem is one of availability because many rimfire rifles simply are not amenable to trigger replacement. This includes the vast number of autoloaders, pumps, and lever actions. Relatively few bolt-action rimfire rifles have an aftermarket trigger option available. Part of the reason lies in the area of economics. It is unlikely that most shooters who have $150 rifle would spend about half that amount simply to replace the trigger. Moreover, there is also the feeling of why should the trigger be replaced when barrels, stocks, and other items are going to have to be left as originals. This argument does not apply to the Ruger 10/22 because it is possible to replace everything except the receiver with aftermarket items.

Most notable in terms of trigger replacement are the Ruger 10/22 autoloader and 77 bolt-action series. Outstanding among the options available for the 10/22 and 10/22 magnum are the triggers from Volquartsen known as Trigger Guard 2000. These are available as complete, drop-in units for about $199.95 for either the 22 LR or magnum version, and they represent the highest quality components for individuals seeking to produce the ultimate autoloader. Although these units include the complete trigger assembly, individual parts such as the sear, hammer, springs, and shims can be purchased. Jard of Sheldon, Iowa produces aftermarket triggers for both the Ruger 77/22 and 10/22 rifles. Other trigger kits for these rifles produced by Moyers are available from Midway

USA. Cabela's markets the sear and spring kit produced by Timney for the Ruger 77/22 rifle. As if these options were not enough, many firms offer gunsmith services that include trigger work. Among this list is Clark Custom Guns of Princeton, Louisiana.

In recent years, Rifle Basix has produced replacement triggers for bolt-action rifles made by Marlin and Savage in addition to those for the Ruger 77 series. Marlin adopted an improved trigger mechanism known as the T-900 Fire Control System, and all of the current bolt-action models make use of that trigger. The system also includes a redesigned safety. However, Marlin personnel have informed the author that the T-900 trigger cannot be installed as an aftermarket option on earlier models such as the 25N. Moreover, Marlin does not endorse the replacement of triggers on older bolt-action rifles with any aftermarket trigger. Replacement triggers for both the pre-2004 and 2004 (which have the T-900 trigger) Marlin bolt-action rifles are available from Rifle Basix for $79.95. A similar model is available for Savage bolt-action rifles. Both of these trigger units make use of the factory safety.

Sights

Perhaps no area involves a greater aftermarket industry than does sighting equipment. Sights are so important and of universal concern to shooters that Chapter 5 is devoted to that subject. Regardless, sights constitute such a broad area that some additional observations will be made here. Because scopes and red dot sights were covered in Chapter 5, the discussion here will concern other issues related to sights. Many fine rifles are produced and marketed with no sights mounted on the barrels. It is anticipated that these rifles will be fitted with appropriate scopes so the receivers are either drilled and tapped or grooved to accept scope mounts. It is anticipated that these rifles will never wear "open" or "iron" sights.

If the only concern were with accuracy, a scope of high magnification would be mounted on the firearm and other factors would be subjected to fine-tuning. There are, however, cases in which the suitability and durability of the sighting equipment become more important than accuracy. Should the owner wish to do so, the factory sights can be replaced with others because aftermarket sights are available in many configurations from several producers. On most rimfire rifles, the rear sight is attached by means of the sight base fitting tightly in a dovetail groove on top of the barrel. In order to install a different sight, the original must be removed by driving it laterally out of the groove. In most cases, the width of the dovetail groove is a standard width so sights from other producers will fit satisfactorily. It is a different matter with front sights. In many cases, the sights are also attached by means of a dovetail groove, but in others one or more screws attach the front sight. If you wish to attach sights that attach differently, you will need the services of a gunsmith to drill and tap holes or to attach the sight base by brazing, silver soldering, or other means. Keep in mind that it is possible to attach almost any

Some handguns have sights mounted in a dovetail groove and can be replaced by other models that have correct height.

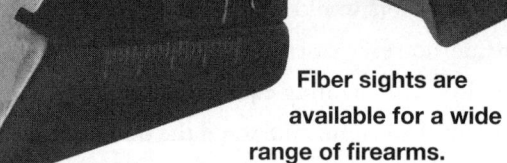

Fiber sights are available for a wide range of firearms.

Aftermarket sights are available in a wide range of styles. The white bead front and folding rear sights shown here are from Lyman.

type of sight to a rifle or handgun, but it is not always as simple as tightening a screw.

Williams Gun Sight Company produces an extensive line of sights known as Firesights, which feature fiber optic inserts. Models include front sights on ramps as well as open rear sights with fiber optic inserts on either side of the notch. Lyman Products Corporation has produced sights for generations. Lyman produces not only open sights, but also peep sights and target front sights with removable inserts. Suppliers such as Midway USA, Brownell's, and Numrich have many types of sights available. Bob's Gun Shop of Royal, Arkansas offers a wide assortment of sights many for older guns from several manufacturers. Handgun sights are available in an impressive array from manufacturers such as Millett, Trijicon, Novak, and others. These are just a few of the suppliers of aftermarket sights.

The owner of a Ruger 10/22 has the option of fitting the rifle with several types of sights that cannot be mounted conveniently on other types of rimfire rifles. For example, a peep sight is produced that mounts in two of the holes on top of the receiver where the scope base is normally attached. A rear and front sight pair known as the Zephyr Sighting System consists of a rear sight with protective ears that have an aperture mounted between them and a front sight that has a post encircled in a small circular hood. The effect is similar to that given by some types of military sights. Williams Firesights are also available for specifically to fit the Ruger 10/22. Specialty firms that produce aftermarket items for the Ruger 10/22 produce other types of sights.

It is appropriate to include a caution in regard to replacement sights. Most rear sights have a rather limited range of adjustment for elevation. If the front sight is too low or too high, it will not be possible to move the rear sight enough to allow the sights to be adjusted properly. The height of the front and rear sights must be matched appropriately. Before you invest in replacement sights, make sure that the front and rear sights are compatible in terms of height.

Accuracy

Before addressing the topic of enhancing accuracy, we need to explain what accuracy is. Two terms that are often used interchangeably are accuracy and precision. When applied to the capabilities of rifles, they are often used incorrectly. A shooter who fires a small group often remarks about the "accuracy" of the rifle used. However, the ability of a rifle to place shots close together is really a measure of its precision. When a quarterback places the football right on target we say that he is an accurate passer, which is the correct use of the word. Suppose as a practice drill three tires are set up 25 yards away from the quarterback and he is attempting to throw a football through the middle tire. If he consistently throws the ball through the tire on the left, his passing shows poor accuracy but good precision.

Suppose a particular type of bullet is advertised as weighing 40.0 grains. If 10 of the bullets have weights ranging from 43.3 to 43.5 grains with an average of 43.4 grains, the bullet weights show good precision because they are all close to the same value. However, with regard to weight, the bullets show poor accuracy because the weight is not very close to the desired weight of 40.0 grains. Therefore, the bullets show good precision but poor accuracy in regard to weight. It is rather like an archer who sticks six arrows in an area the size of an apple at 50 yards, but the cluster is in the lower left hand corner of the target rather than in the center of the target. The precision is good, but the accuracy is poor.

When groups are fired at 50 yards to try to obtain the smallest possible cluster of bullet holes in the target, it is actually precision that is being determined. In many instances, it doesn't matter whether the group is precisely in the center of the target or not because that can be corrected by changing the sights. However, if the cluster measures three inches across, the rifle is not capable of a high degree of precision. Although not a correct usage of the word, we speak of the accuracy of a rifle to denote that it is capable of producing small groups. That practice will be continued here, but it is important to know the difference.

There are several factors that determine the ability of a rifle to produce small groups. Some of these factors are identifiable in terms of critical dimensions and closeness of fit. Others are intangibles. The author once damaged a rear sight and called the rifle maker to obtain another. The model had been discontinued for some time but the helpful customer service representative said that there was a sight on a barrel that was not attached to a rifle. He said that all of the dimensions of the barrel were well within specification, but for some reason the barrel would not group and so it had not been used to build a complete rifle. Such is sometimes the case. A barrel that otherwise seems normal just does not shoot well.

The finish of bore is an important consideration.

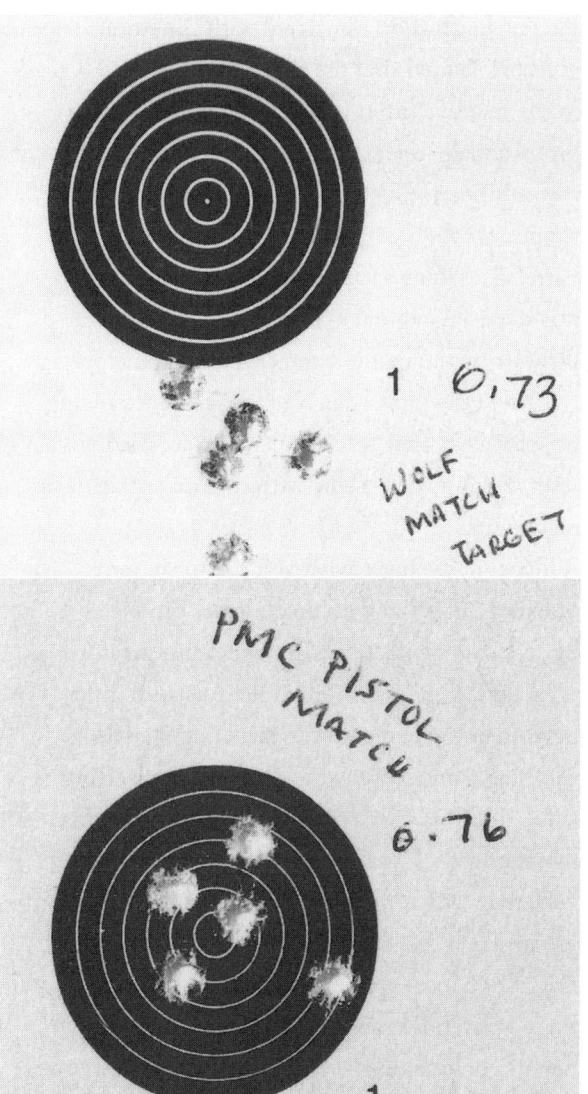

The group at the top shows good precision but poor accuracy. The bottom group shows good accuracy and good precision.

Some barrels are mirror smooth and free from defects. However, the author once bought a centerfire rifle that had been produced by one of the most famous makers. Eager to test the rifle, a scope was mounted and a few sight in shots were fired. Then, the truth became known. The rifle would not group for sour apples. After thoroughly cleaning the bore, the bore light revealed rather large machine marks that ran around the bore throughout its length. Somehow, the barrel had not been properly finished inside the bore. A call to the dealer led to a request to bring the rifle in for examination and testing in the gunsmith shop associated with the store. The gunsmith stated that the rifle needed to be returned to the manufacturer. True to the reputation of a professionally operated customer service department, it was acknowledged that the rifle had somehow slipped through with a defective barrel and a new barreled action was attached to my stock because it was a special laminated one that I wanted to keep. Otherwise, the manufacturer would have simply replaced the whole rifle. Needless to say, knowing how the customer service operation works, I have no reservation buying a rifle with that manufacturer's name on it.

Generally, you get what you pay for in terms of barrel quality and accuracy. Rifles produced by certain manufacturers are widely known for their performance. For example, Anschutz rifles have an enviable record for garnering medals in shooting competition at the highest levels. Rimfire rifles produced by Cooper Firearms of Montana must produce extremely small groups before being declared ready for shipment. Kimber has a required group size of 0.4-inch for a Classic 22 in order for the rifle to meet specifications. Rifles from both of these prestigious makers are shipped with the test targets enclosed in the boxes with the rifles. Barrels produced by these firms are made from high quality materials with the application of rigid quality control. It should also be mentioned that the cost of such rifles is commensurately high.

Can you get a rifle that shoots accurately for a modest price? The answer is sometimes yes. The author once bought an inexpensive bolt-action 22 that would place the first shot or two exactly at the point of aim. After a couple of shots, the subsequent shots would string out vertically. After installing a barrel band, the shots strung out somewhat less, but there was no obvious solution to the problem. If you examine the data shown in Chapter 13, you will see that the inexpensive Marlin 25N gave composite group averages of less than one inch with several types of ammunition. While not indicative of the kind of accuracy given by an Anschutz, Cooper, or Kimber, an average of five five-shot groups that measures less than one inch is not bad at that range. For many years, the one-inch group at 50 yards has been sort of a standard for 22 rimfires. If you read the test results published in magazines for rimfire products, you will see that groups produced by "ordinary" rifles are frequently in the 1 to 1.5-inch range or larger. Groups in the .75- to 1-inch range indicate a rather high level of performance while those in the half-inch range or less are rare except for target rifles and high quality sporting rifles. Of course, the ammunition chosen always plays a major role in determining accuracy.

What degree of accuracy do you need or expect? Having worked with a sizeable number rimfire rifles over a span of many years, I have developed some feeling for accuracy. The rifles studied have ranged from very inexpensive single-shot models to inexpensive repeaters (having bolt, lever, and semiautomatic actions) to moderately expensive sporting rifles and finally to a Winchester 52D target rifle. I have learned not to expect one-hole groups from most rimfire rifles, but neither do I expect a rifle to give a random pattern measuring six inches across at 50 yards. All of the rifles that I have ever shot fall between these extremes. For the moment, I will refrain from discussing the phenomenal Winchester 52D because it is simply the most accurate rimfire rifle I have ever fired. Period. Now, let us discuss the other types.

Most of the inexpensive repeating rifles of my experience would give groups measuring two inches or smaller at 50 yards with most types of ammunition. With a few types of ammunition, such as Remington Vipers, the groups might be as large as three inches. Generally such rifles would give groups of 1.5 inches or less with some of the ammunition that performed best in a particular rifle. Occasional groups smaller than one inch were obtained, and an average of 1.25 inches is typical. Most of the inexpensive repeating rifles fall into this category.

Some of the better performing inexpensive repeaters (such as the Ruger 10/22 Carbine, Henry Lever Action, and Marlin 25N gave groups that were smaller than 1.5 inches with almost any type of ammunition and as small as one inch with the ammunition that performed best in that model. In other words, these rifles consistently gave groups in the 1.0- to 1.5-inch range but with some ammunition groups of one inch or slightly less were produced.

Repeaters tested by the author that have given the best accuracy include the Ruger 77/22, CZ 452 American, Thompson/Center Classic, Ruger 10/22T, and Winchester 320. These rifles gave groups that average less than one inch with almost all types of ammunition with individual groups running one-half inch or smaller. With the most compatible types of ammunition, each of these rifles gave an average group size that was not much larger than a half inch. Any difference in the accuracy of the rifles listed is totally insignificant. Having read almost everything written about the Remington 504 bolt-action sporter, it appears that the rifles listed will approximately equal the accuracy the 504 normally gives. None of these rifles will match the accuracy of a Kimber Classic, Cooper 57M, or an Anschutz 1710 nor should they be expected to. These fine sporting rifles will consistently give groups that average one-half inch or smaller at 50 yards.

One should not lose sight of the fact that for almost any use other than formal competition, a 22 rimfire rifle that will give groups of half an inch or less at 50 yards is an accurate rifle. Having tested many rimfire rifles and read the results of tests for many more, it has become apparent that an inexpensive 22 LR that consistently groups in less than one inch is performing about as well as can be expected. My experience with rifles in 22 WMR caliber is much more limited in terms of the number of rifles tested. My Ruger 77/22M will consistently give groups in the 0.60 to 0.75 inch range with most types of ammunition. Both my Ruger 77/17 and my wife's CZ 452 rifles in 17 HMR will give groups averaging close to one-half inch with occasional groups of 0.3 to 0.4 inch.

The question arises as to whether accuracy can be improved by aftermarket items. The answer is undoubtedly yes, but only at a price. Installing a new barrel (on models where it is possible for the user to do so) will cost from $100 to $200 or perhaps even more. If the barrel has a different configuration than the original, a new stock may be required or the original may have to be modified to accept the aftermarket barrel. Replacement of the trigger assembly can cost from $80 to $200 although replacing only the sear and other parts can cost less. It is easy to invest several hundred dollars in aftermarket items in addition to the original price of the rifle. The result is likely to be a rifle that will give one-half inch groups at 50 yards. However, the same amount of money might well have bought a new rifle that would have given one-half inch groups right out of the box. But there is something to be said for having a somewhat unique rifle that you have developed. Improvements in accuracy occur in small increments by doing a lot of little things right.

There is a tendency to fall into the pattern of thinking, "If I only had a … (you can fill in the blank), my groups would improve." My suggestion is that before you go too far in aftermarket items, try tweaking some things. First, make sure that everything is clean and tight. If you have one of the Ruger models that allows the barrel to be interchanged, make sure that the screws are tight (but not overly so for the 10/22) that hold the barrel to the action. In terms of accuracy, some of my rifles are very sensitive to the tension of the screws that hold the stock to the barreled action. Check the tightness of the screw(s) and try shooting groups with a different screw tension. My Ruger 77/17 seems to function best when the screws are tight, but not overly so. Scope mounts seem to have a way of loosening themselves so make sure that the screws are tight.

If aftermarket items are not available to produce the rifle of your dreams, there are many custom shops such as Altius Handcrafted Firearms operated in West Yellowstone, Montana by Marc Sheppard who specializes in biathlon rifles.

Having taken care of some of the mechanical aspects, experiment with different types of ammunition. My Ruger 10/22 Target gave 5-shot groups at 50 yards that averaged 0.45 inch with SK Jagd. Standard Plus ammunition and groups were twice that size with CCI Green Tag. Both types of ammunition are of very high quality, but the rifle works better with the Standard Plus. In my wife's CZ 452 American, the average group size was 0.54 inch with Federal Ultra Match and twice that size with Federal Gold Medal Target. Rimfire rifles give drastically different accuracy with different types of ammunition. If you experiment with many types of ammunition, it is possible that your rifle may give a level of accuracy that will meet your requirements without any modification of the rifle.

As this is being written in late 2004, I know where there is an unusual rifle in the gun rack of a sporting goods store. The previous owner had the rifle built with all of the bells and whistles imaginable. No expense was spared because the owner wanted to win a certain benchrest competition. A special barrel was mounted on a fully tricked out action with a custom trigger and all sorts of other items. The stock is precision made of metal. By the time the project was complete, the owner had spent approximately $2,500 on the rifle. After winning the particular benchrest competition, the owner decided that he had had enough of the sport and sold the rifle (at a great loss). The point is that it is possible to build a rifle that will achieve almost any desired level of accuracy, but before you do so make sure that you understand the costs involved. You may decide that the level of accuracy that will be satisfying to you can be obtained with less expense by starting with a different rifle. Regardless, the aftermarket items are available for some rifles to convert them into almost anything you desire.

Holding Steady

Steady holding of a rifle requires a weight distribution with considerable weight toward the muzzle end. Let me illustrate the reason for this with a simple illustration. Suppose you pick up an 8-pound iron ball with one hand and let your arm hang down. Rotate the ball by simply turning your hand back and forth. Note how easy it is to twist the wrist and rotate the ball. Suppose now that you have an 8-pound dumbbell in your hand and you rotate your wrist. It is more difficult to rotate than the 8-pound ball, but it is still easy to rotate eight pounds in this way. Finally, suppose you have an 8-pound bar that is four feet in length. Try rotating your wrist with this weight and note the difference. Rotation of the bar is much harder to start and stop because part of the weight is far from your hand, the pivot point. If you had a long rod that weighs 2 pounds and it had a 3-pound weight on each end, the total weight would still be 8 pounds, but it would be still harder to rotate because the weights are far from the center of rotation, your hand. The four systems have the same total weight but different moments of inertia.

What does all this have to do with holding a rifle steady? A rifle that has a long, heavy barrel resists small movements better than one that has a short, slender barrel. The heavy barrel has more weight farther from the center of rotation, which is usually a point (the pivot point) somewhere between your hands. There is a reason why target rifles have barrels that measure up to 28 inches in length and nearly an inch in diameter. That much mass in the shooting platform (the shooter and the rifle) means that the muzzle will not waiver as much as a result of small unbalanced forces due to twitches, jerks, and muscle tension. As a member of a small bore team, the author used a Winchester Model 52D that weighed approximately 11 pounds which was designed for steady holding and accuracy. A 6-pound sporter with a slender barrel cannot be held as steady.

These principles also apply to rifles used for other shooting activities. Some rifles have such short, slender barrels that for all practical purposes most of the mass is in the action and stock between the shooters hands. It is very difficult to hold such a rifle steady in the standing position because it requires so little force to cause the muzzle to dance around. Furthermore, if a scope is mounted, it is also positioned on the rifle between the shooter's hands. Such a rifle is not conducive to steady holding. Contrast that rifle with a lever action rifle with a 20-inch barrel of medium weight that has a full-length magazine tube below the barrel. If most people tried to hold each of the rifles steady in a standing position they would be amazed at how much difference there is in the movement of the muzzle. Short, light rifles are convenient to carry, but they are not conducive to steady holding. Target rifles are not normally short or light and for good reasons. Depending on the weight restrictions and rifle design, weights may be added to the muzzle, which also helps to reduce wobble.

To some extent, the same principles apply to handguns. Certain pistols have receivers that are heavy, but tapered barrels that are rather light in

The Browning Buck Mark is a high-quality pistol that has superb weight distribution as a result of its heavy barrel.

weight. Most of the weight in such a pistol rests directly above the shooter's hand, and the pistol requires very little force to cause the muzzle to move. Other pistols, especially those intended for target shooting, have longer, heavier barrels so they have a "weight forward" design. Some models even have a provision for adding muzzle weights. Muzzle motion is less pronounced with such a pistol. Formal target shooting requires a one-hand, extended arm position, which leaves the piece very mobile. In such shooting, the weight-forward condition produced by a 5.5- to 7.5-inch heavy barrel makes it much easier to hold the pistol steady.

Some shooters may sit at a shooting bench with sandbag rests and shoot almost any rifle or pistol well. The supports offset the instability caused by an unfavorable weight distribution. However, on the firing line or in the woods, it is an entirely different situation. Any firearm chosen for target shooting or for hunting (where shots must often be taken from a standing position) should be evaluated with respect to its handling characteristics. It is often not a case of difference in weight of two firearms, but rather a difference in weight distribution. At various times, I have verified how much more accurately I can fire a certain 32-ounce pistol than another that weighs 36 ounces because the former has a heavy barrel on a light action while the latter pistol has the opposite characteristics.

In recent years, silhouette shooting has become a popular sport for rimfire, centerfire, and air rifles.

Competition

A shooter who enjoys using rimfire rifles and handguns has a variety of competitive sports in which he or she can participate. These include the formal disciplines of three-position (prone, kneeling, and standing) shooting on indoor and outdoor ranges. Competition on indoor ranges is usually conducted at 50 feet while in outdoor competition targets are normally shot at 50 yards or meters, and at 100 yards. A typical match consists of firing from three positions (prone, kneeling, and standing) with one shot fired at each bull. Targets for use on the 50-foot range consist of 10 bulls. A "possible" score for a three-position match would be 300 points. In some matches, the sitting position is also used so 400 points are possible. Other forms of competition involve shooting only from a prone or standing position. Getting all of the points possible in a given position or the entire match is known as shooting a "possible." Competition is held on many levels, and to some extent, equipment requirements and rules depend on the level of the competition. This situation also exists for pistol competition. Competition at the highest levels requires cutting-edge equipment, which is reflected in the cost. Although the specific rules for position shooting will not be given here, they can be found on the web site http://www.nrahq.org/compete/smallbore.asp which is linked to the National Rifle Association and can be accessed through http://www.nrahq.org.

The United States Rimfire Association (USRA) sanctions a series of benchrest competitions at a variety of levels. Known as IR50/50, the course of fire consists of 25 shots for record at 50 yards or 50 meters within a time limit of 30 minutes. In order for contestants to be using similar equipment, rifles are grouped in three categories. These are known as the Sporter Class (rifle and scope must weigh 7.5 pounds or less and the scope must be 6.5-power or less), 10.5-pound class, and the 13.5 pound class. The scopes used in the Sporter Class are typically high-quality 6X models produced by Burris, Leupold, Weaver, and other makers. Although some of the rifles described in Chapter 13 could be used in low level competition, at the higher levels the vast majority of the rifles are custom built. Some of the most frequently encountered actions include the Anschutz 54, Sako, Remington (40X and 541), or similar high quality types. Custom barrels are frequently those made by Douglas, Lilja, Hart, Walther, and Shilen. This is the ultra high precision sport in rimfire shooting. The rules are very specific and detailed which leads to a rather long document. It can be found at http://www.ir5050.com/rules.html.

In IR50/50 contests, one shot is fired at each target with the circles representing 10, 9, etc. Inside the 10-ring is a small "X" ring which can be used to separate the scoring. For example, a perfect score for 25 shots would be 250 with all shots touching the X ring. This is listed as 250 25X. Two competitors could have all shots touching the 10-ring for a score of 250, but the shooter having the higher number of shots touching the X-ring would be the winner. In other words, 250 14X wins over 250 13X.

In a form of benchrest shooting known as Barnyard Benchrest, the rifles used must be factory rifles that retail for no more than $300 and the ammunition used must sell for no more than $3 per box. A scope of not over 6-power is allowed. This sport is intended to enable shooters to compete even though they have not invested a few thousand dollars in equipment. Even with these restrictions on equipment, the grouping ability normally runs under one-half inch and sometimes well under that size. Some of the rifles described in Chapter 13 could be used in this event.

Another sport that has become more popular in recent years is the biathlon which involves skiing over a course and stopping to shoot at targets placed at stations along the course. This is a demanding sport because the elapsed time is determined by skiing ability and how long it takes to fire at the targets. However, shooting ability is also important. Accurate placement of a bullet after the physical stress of skiing requires a great deal of skill, conditioning, and practice.

Finally, shooting at metal plates having the shapes of animals constitutes silhouette competition. As in all other shooting sports, there are restrictions on the equipment used so that shooters compete on an equal basis. The rifle must weigh not more than 10 pounds, 2 ounces including sights. There are numerous other restrictions on the rifle that include a maximum barrel length of 30 inches and specific measurements and shapes for stocks. In a category known as the Hunting Rifle division, the rifle must not weigh more than 8.5 pounds including sights. Any type of sight may be used and scopes may be of any magnification. The silhouettes are placed at different ranges, and they have different sizes, which makes for varying levels of difficulty. Matches may be conducted with ranges in yards or meters. Ranges (in either meters or yards) for the different silhouettes are as follows: chicken, 40; pig, 60; turkey, 77; and ram, 100. Firing is from the standing position. Details of small-bore silhouette competition can be found on the web site www.scssa.org.

The silhouette shooter has available ammunition designed specifically for that sport.

Ancillaries for competing in different rimfire sports are many and varied. In some cases, it is essential that the competitor have a special shooting jacket and glove, a mat for use in the prone position, a spotting scope, a sling for the rifle, etc. Because many of these are described in the rules for the particular type of shooting event, they will not be covered in more detail in this chapter. Rules for some types of competition include specific information on the types of ancillary equipment that is permitted. While one may compete for fun in a variety of competitive events, successful competition at a high level is much more specialized in terms of the discipline itself and the necessary equipment.

As described above, there are several types of shooting events that can be enjoyed by the rimfire shooter. All of these sports provide opportunities for the shooter of rimfire rifles and handguns to compete at the local, regional, and in some cases, international levels. If you have an interest in one or more of these types of shooting, find out where competition is being held and go watch the event. Note the techniques, ammunition, and equipment being used by successful competitors. You will learn a great deal about the sport as well as the level of funding and dedication you will need to be successful.

Chapter 13
EVALUATIONS OF SOME CURRENT RIMFIRE RIFLES

Previous chapters have dealt with safety, ballistics, hunting, and numerous other aspects of the use of rimfire rifles and handguns. Discussion of performance has been kept to a level that gives only an indication of what can be expected from certain rifles. No general evaluation of the performance of several rifles has been given which would show how they compare. This chapter is intended to provide concrete evidence on the performance of current rimfire rifles, and Chapter 14 deals with some vintage models. Chapters 15 and 16 are devoted to currently produced and vintage handguns, respectively. No manufacturer supplied any of the rifles or ammunition used in this research so there is no "payback" in terms of making any product look good. What is presented is simply the facts as they emerged during the tests.

Evaluating the performance of several rifles with many types of ammunition requires a lot of time spent at the bench. The author's wife, Kathy, is testing her CZ 452 in 17 HMR caliber.

The Study

Performance is what separates a Super Bowl contender from a last place team. It is what determines the winner of the Winston Cup in NASCAR, and it is what gives one golfer the green jacket at the Master's tournament. Many shooters are vitally interested in the performance of various firearms. In fact, some gun and shooting magazines devote a great deal of space to presenting product review information that is at least partially based on evaluations of the performance of the firearms. A book that is concerned with rimfire firearms should present information of the performance of several models. Because of the enormous number of models of rimfire rifles available, only a few representative models could be tested. If your favorite rifle is not included, it is simply because we did not have one available. Keep in mind that two rifles that are nominally identical may perform differently. Another specimen might give results that are different than those presented.

Performance of rifles is primarily concerned with accuracy. Rate of fire, longevity, and looks have little to do with the performance of a rifle for most sporting purposes. It is the ability to place the bullet at the desired spot that makes a particular rifle suitable for the purpose it is employed. In this chapter, we will present the results of accuracy tests obtained with several rifles that are representative of those currently being manufactured. We will also describe these models in some detail in order for this chapter to serve as a sort of buyer's guide or user's guide.

Today, certain rifles have become (or are becoming) benchmarks against which other rifles are judged. For example, the Ruger 10/22 is the most popular autoloader currently produced if not of all time. A huge after market industry has sprung up around this rifle, and it is probably the most widely modified firearm in history. Upon encountering a used Winchester 190 autoloader from the 1970s, a prospective buyer might logically ask, "How does it

The author's Marlin 25N with reworked stock (left) and his wife's unmodified rifle are dependable and accurate.

compare to a Ruger 10/22?" Is it to be compared to a tricked out 10/22 or just the standard model in original configuration? The same comparison might be made between a Remington Nylon 66 or some other out of production autoloader. In the case of bolt-action rifles, the Ruger 77/22 is one of the current standards, and the new Remington 504 is becoming another. How do some of the bolt-action rifles of a generation ago compare in performance to these current models? In this chapter and the one following, we seek to answer these questions by examining the performance of current rifles and a

Accuracy Results for the Marlin 25N with Bushnell Banner 3-9X Scope.

Ammunition	Smallest	Group size, inches Largest	Average
High-velocity			
CCI Mini Mag	1.00	1.60	1.31
CCI Velocitor	0.82	1.10	0.99
Federal High Velocity H.P.	1.02	1.65	1.34
Federal Lightning	0.85	2.09	1.32
Remington Game Load	0.93	1.71	1.19
Remington Golden H.P.	1.09	1.66	1.29
Winchester Power Point	0.89	1.39	1.17
Winchester Super-X	1.13	1.70	1.31
Winchester Wildcat	0.68	1.47	1.22
			Overall Av. 1.24
Standard-velocity			
CCI Green Tag	0.56	0.98	0.77
CCI Standard Velocity	0.69	1.53	1.07
Federal Target (711B)	0.79	0.97	0.90
PMC Match Rifle	0.86	1.61	1.34
PMC Scoremaster	1.00	1.39	1.18
Remington Target	0.89	1.41	1.14
Winchester Supreme	0.55	1.14	0.89
Winchester T-22	0.64	1.34	1.04
Wolf Match Target	0.67	0.89	0.78
			Overall Av. 1.01

few of those that are gone from production but not forgotten.

In order to test rifle accuracy, it essential that a scope be used in order to decrease the sighting error. In the tests conducted, there was no attempt (nor was it possible) to use identical scopes on all the rifles. The scopes used represent those that might be appropriate for a particular rifle, and the magnification was sufficient to assure that sighting error was not responsible for the results obtained. In each case, group sizes were measured by determining the distance between the centers of the two widest holes. Test firing on this scale was carried out over an extended time period. As a result, temperature and wind conditions were not uniform nor could they be for all the tests.

Marlin 25N (925)

Among the inexpensive bolt-action rimfire rifles, those produced by Marlin have been some of the most successful. There are models that utilize tubular and detachable box magazines that have been produced for many years. The Marlin Model 25N was the box magazine version, but the 2004 catalog lists this model as the Model 925 because it utilizes the new 900 Series trigger mechanism. Except for cosmetic appearance, comments made about the 25N also apply to the current Model 925.

The Marlin Model 25N is a full-size 22 that is sturdy and dependable. It has a 22-inch barrel that is pinned to the receiver, and it features Marlin's Micro-Groove rifling. The hardwood stock has a rather plain appearance although the Mar-Shield® finish is durable and gives a new meaning to the word! However, the stock on the Marlin 25N can be reshaped to give a more pleasing profile and I have done that to mine (see Chapter 10). The current Model 925 has pressed checkering on the grip and forearm. While the forend on the Model 25 is cut square, the 925 has a rounded forend.

Sights on the Model 25N consist of a square-topped post on a ramp and a fully adjustable rear

The Ruger 10/22 is available in several configurations. Shown are (top to bottom) the Carbine, Target, and Rifle models.

sight. Elevation adjustment is made by sliding a stepped ramp while windage adjustment requires the sight to be moved laterally in the dovetail groove. With a square notch in the rear sight blade and the square-topped post, a good sight picture is afforded. The receiver is grooved so that scope mounts can be easily attached. The safety is located on the right hand side at the rear of the receiver. The detachable magazine holds seven rounds, but I wish that it didn't. With that capacity, the magazine is long enough that it protrudes from the bottom of the stock by an inch or so which makes it awkward to carry the rifle while holding it at its natural balance point. This is a durable, no-frills rifle, and one that I have used with satisfaction for many years.

Many shooters of rimfire rifles including me do not have one of the elegant sporting rifles that cost upwards of $500. A Marlin 925 currently sells for around $150 so the question naturally arises as to what type of performance one can expect from this basic rifle. Exhaustive tests were conducted to find out. In the tests, ammunition was used which is representative of all types. The types ranged from the $10.00 per box Federal Ultra Match (recently discontinued) to Federal Lightning (now named Champion) that I bought for $0.99 per box. For the tests, a Bushnell Banner 3-9X scope was mounted on the rifle. The accompanying table shows a summary of the results obtained when using both standard-velocity target loads as well as high-velocity hunting types of ammunition.

The results shown in the table indicate that one can expect groups to average about 1 inch with standard-velocity types and around 1.25-inch with high-velocity ammunition. As a check on the results, second specimen was found to give almost identical results with a selection of the ammunition types. Is a Marlin 25N a worthy companion for the small game and pest shooter? I believe that the answer is clearly affirmative. Numerous rimfire rifles are available that will not match the performance of a Marlin 25N, and many of them cost considerably more. Certainly the user of a Marlin 25N should try different types of ammunition to determine what works best in his or her rifle, but that is true of all rimfire shooters.

Ruger 10/22 Carbine

Introduced in 1964, the Ruger 10/22 Carbine is one of the most frequently encountered rimfire firearms. Over 4 million of these rifles have been produced, and they are available in several versions that have different stock material or metal finish. The most common version has an 18.5-inch barrel, a hardwood stock, and a barrel band that encircles the forearm and the barrel. With a length of 37 inches and a weight of about 5 pounds, this is a compact, handy firearm. In 1997, the 10/22T was

The author's son, Keith, has a lightweight tack-driver. His Ruger 10/22 has a Majestic Arms barrel with an aluminum shroud and a Lothar Walther steel insert. The stock is the Hogue Overmolded model.

introduced which has a heavy hammer forged barrel that measures about 0.920" without taper. This target version is available with blued metal and laminated stock or with stainless steel and synthetic stock. In 2004, a new variant of the 10/22 was produced which is called the 10/22 Rifle because it has a 20-inch barrel and a slimmer stock without the familiar barrel band. The most attractive version of the 10/22 is known as the Sporter model, and it has a checkered walnut stock of good shape.

The housing for the action of the Ruger 10/22 is made of an aluminum alloy. In order to attach a scope, a scope rail is attached to the top of the receiver by four screws. Two types of rails are available. The first is a flat-topped rail that has grooves along the sides where clamp-type mounts can be attached. New in 2004 is a scope rail that not only has grooves along the sides, but also it has grooves across the bar which allow rings known as Weaver type to be attached. The latter rail thus provides greater versatility in terms of the number of types of mounts that can be used.

One distinguishing characteristic of the Ruger 10/22 is the rotary magazine that holds 10 rounds of 22 LR. Because the magazine is laterally thick, the magazine well in the stock is wide which makes the overall stock thick. The result is that the rifle is almost as thick as it is high which gives it a round, chunky appearance and feel when the standard stock is in place. In order to improve the feel and looks, I installed a Hogue rubber over molded stock. The result is a short, handy little rifle that has to be handled to be appreciated, and it has become my favorite walk about rifle.

Although the Ruger 10/22 has several unusual features, perhaps the most unique is the method used to attach the barrel to the receiver. The barrel has a cut out section across the bottom near the breech. A mating block fits in the slot and it attaches to the face of the action by two large Allen headed screws. Tightening the screws pulls the barrel extension into the action and locks it in place. Because only two screws must be removed, the barrel can readily be removed and an aftermarket barrel produced by one of many suppliers can be installed. In fact, the design of the Ruger 10/22 is such that several parts are replaceable by someone with a modest amount of manual dexterity. Barrels chambered for the 17 Mach

2 are available for the Ruger 10/22. However, the 17 Mach 2 cartridge causes the bolt to be driven to the rear at a velocity that is higher than that produced when a 22 LR is fired in the rifle. Knowledgeable people in the industry have told me that installing a 17 Mach 2 barrel on a 10/22 will cause the standard action to be ruined after a few hundred shots. Rebarreling a Ruger 10/22 to 17 Mach 2 is not as simple as unbolting one barrel and replacing it with another.

A bewildering array of aftermarket parts and accessories are available for the Ruger 10/22. One can buy barrels in numerous configurations, stocks, triggers, sears, hammers, etc. that can be used to configure a 10/22 in almost any way. Several companies produce items essentially for the 10/22 alone as aftermarket industries. The Ruger 10/22 Carbine tested was of "stock" configuration except for having a scope attached. The accompanying table shows the results of the accuracy testing.

Accuracy of the Ruger 10/22 is quite good for a short, light rifle that is intended for general use. It is certainly qualifies the 10/22 for hunting and pest control with most types of ammunition as long as the range is around 60 yards or less. The accuracy shown by the CCI Standard-velocity and the SK Jagd. Standard Plus is truly outstanding for this type of rifle. Sighted to hit a point of aim at approximately 60 yards, either of these loads would make it possible to pick off varmints out to around 75 yards. The 10/22 Carbine model gave the smallest groups with SK Jagd. Standard Plus ammunition as did the 10/22T. Clearly, Ruger autoloaders like this ammunition so you should try it in your Ruger if you are looking for top accuracy.

The Ruger 10/22 is one of the most successful sporting firearms ever produced. It has an outstanding reputation for reliability, durability, and accuracy. In fact, the Ruger 10/22 has become a true icon among American firearms. If you do not like the appearance of the chunky little carbine, you can modify it to almost any form you desire. Although

With a stainless steel barrel and laminated stock, this Ruger 10/22 is a versatile and dependable rifle.

the 10/22 has a list price of $250, the usual retail price is around $160-$175. If anyone wants a compact semiautomatic, it is safe to say that the Ruger 10/22 should be given very serious consideration.

Since a large number of shooters using Ruger 10/22 Carbines do not leave them in the stock configuration, I decided to follow suit at least up to a point. Of the large number of aftermarket options available, I choose a Majestic Arms Aluma-Lite barrel and a Hogue Overmolded Stock. The Aluma-Lite barrel has a steel insert produced by Lothar Walther that is encased in an aluminum cylinder that measures 0.920 inches in diameter. The Hogue stock that is intended for use with target barrels of that diameter fits perfectly. The combination is a compact, lightweight rimfire. However, the old saying, "Pretty is as pretty does", seems to apply so the obvious way to find out was to start shooting.

In order to obtain small groups, one must be able to see the target clearly. Attaching a 4-16X Weaver Classic using Leupold Rifleman mounts made sure that the bull could be seen in detail. To test the modified 10/22, I selected a few types of target ammunition because the barrel is made to match standards and there is no advantage to getting good groups when excellent groups are possible. The results obtained are shown in the accompanying table.

The accuracy obtained with the Aluma-Lite barrel shows what is possible when a Ruger 10/22 is modified even to a modest extent. I am not sure that I could get much better accuracy than this because of vision problems. There is no question that this is an extremely accurate barrel when match ammunition is used. Would the accuracy be as good with hunting loads? Probably not with most types, but the Remington Game Load performed extremely well. However, a hunting load will not accomplish any more than a well-placed bullet from a target load that is traveling with slightly lower velocity but placed with greater accuracy. The Ruger/Aluma-Lite/Hogue combination is capable of putting the bullet in the desired spot on the target.

Ruger 10/22 Target

A number of rimfire disciplines are best enjoyed when using a rifle that is a "target" model. Several manufacturers produce such rifles, which usually employ the same action as the "standard" model but use a special heavy barrel. Ruger responded to this demand in 1996 with the 10/22T featuring a heavy hammer forged barrel that is 20 inches in length which results in a rifle weighing 7.5 pounds. No sights are provided so this rifle is intended for use with a scope. My specimen is the version that has a richly blued barrel and laminated stock, but another version with a stainless steel barrel and synthetic stock is available. Operating characteristics of the 10/22T are identical to those of the 10/22 Carbine model discussed above. Whether by design or accident I do not know, but my 10/22T has a better trigger pull than my Carbine model. In fact, it is as

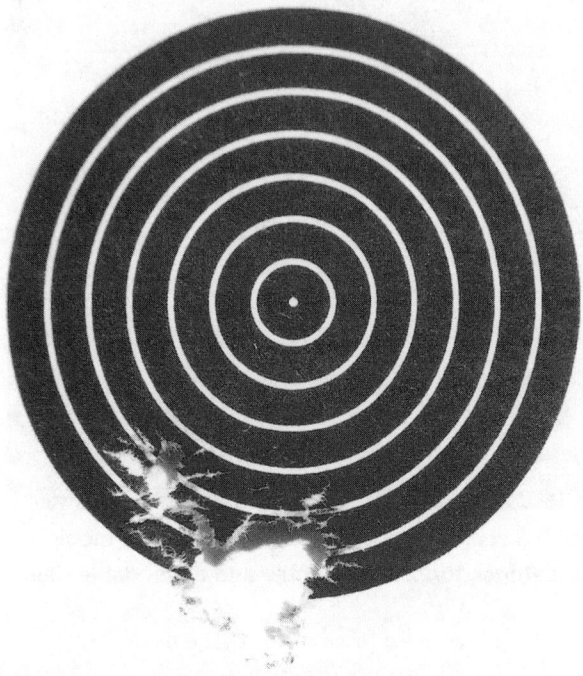

This 0.44 inch five-shot group was fired at 50 yards with the author's Ruger with a Majestic Arms barrel using Lapua Super Club ammunition. Four shots produced one ragged hole.

Accuracy Results for the Ruger 10/22 Carbine with BSA 3-12X Scope.			
Ammunition	Smallest	Group size, inches Largest	Average
CCI Green Tag	0.69	1.53	1.08
CCI Standard Velocity	0.65	1.10	0.88
Federal Target (711B)	0.95	2.00	1.47
Remington Golden H.P.	0.99	1.79	1.39
SK Jagd. Standard Plus	0.53	0.94	0.78
Winchester Super-X H.P.	0.68	1.88	1.31
Winchester Super-X solid	0.90	1.67	1.18
			Overall Av. 1.16

Accuracy Results for the Ruger 10/22 with Aluma-Lite Barrel and Weaver V-16 Scope.

Ammunition	Smallest	Group size, inches Largest	Average
Eley Target	0.49	0.85	0.68
Lapua Super Club	0.43	0.69	0.49
Remington Game Load	0.41	0.64	0.55
Wolf Match Target	0.45	0.84	0.67

Overall Av. 0.60

good as can be found on any other autoloading rifle I own.

Testing of a target model should be carried out with a scope worthy of this potential level of accuracy. In this case, the scope used was a Cabela's Outfitter 6-20X model with AO so the scope could be focused sharply and corrected for parallax at 50 yards. The accompanying table shows the results obtained.

The data given in the table show that a Ruger 10/22T is capable of fine accuracy. An average group size of 0.45 inch for five five-shot groups was obtained with SK Jagd. Standard Plus ammunition, and Lapua Super Club also performed well giving an average group size of only 0.66 inch. The Ruger 10/22 Carbine model also gave its best accuracy with the SK Jagd. Standard Plus ammunition. Interestingly, the 10/22T performed better with CCI Standard Velocity ammunition than it did with the more expensive CCI Green Tag. This was also the case with the 10/22 Carbine. My 10/22T has not been modified in any way so I am not sure what a modified specimen would do, but it would be fun to find out! With the rifle weighing 7.5 pounds, adding a scope raises the weight to 8.5 pounds or more. This somewhat heavy for a walking rifle, but for still hunting or calling varmints a Ruger 10/22T is a fine choice.

The Ruger 10/22T has a heavy hammer-forged barrel, and it gives superb accuracy.

Ruger 10/22 Rifle

Since its introduction in 1964, a seemingly endless number of variants of the Ruger 10/22 have appeared. These differed primarily in the type of barrel steel and in the stock material and configuration. In 2004, Ruger introduced the Model 10/22 Rifle, which has a 20-inch barrel and a smooth hardwood stock that does not have a barrel band. With a stock that is slimmer than that on the 10/22 Carbine and has a better-shaped comb, the 10/22 Rifle has a very pleasing appearance. It is amazing how much difference in appearance an inch and a half in barrel length and a slimmer stock makes. The cover of this book is graced with a photo of the Ruger 10/22 Rifle. One departure from the 10/22 Carbine deals with the open sights. On the 10/22 Rifle, the front sight is a square-topped post and the rear sight has a matching square notch. The sight picture is much better than that given by a round bead in a notch. In fact, it

With the superb Simmons 3-9X AO scope attached, the Ruger 10/22 Rifle gave excellent accuracy.

Accuracy Results for the Ruger 10/22 Target with Cabela's Outfitter 6-20X Scope.

Ammunition	Smallest	Group size, inches Largest	Average
CCI Green Tag	0.54	1.14	0.93
CCI Standard Velocity	0.45	0.96	0.68
CCI Velocitor	0.55	1.57	1.10
Federal High Velocity H.P.	0.69	1.32	1.13
Federal Target (711B)	0.77	0.91	0.84
Lapua Super Club	0.52	0.82	0.66
Remington Club Extra	0.68	0.92	0.82
RWS Rifle Match	0.55	1.15	0.85
SK Jagd. Standard Plus	0.36	0.50	0.45
Winchester Power Point	0.64	0.93	0.75
Winchester T-22	0.57	1.08	0.82

Overall Av. 0.83

Accuracy Results for the Ruger 10/22 Rifle with Simmons 3-9X AO Rimfire Scope.

Ammunition	Smallest	Group size, inches Largest	Average
CCI Green Tag	0.49	1.00	0.83
CCI Standard Velocity	0.55	1.48	0.99
Remington Game Load	0.55	1.30	1.00
Remington/Eley Target	0.54	0.86	0.68
Wolf Match Target	0.78	1.26	0.99

Overall Av. 0.90

is possible with the factory sights on the 10/22 Rifle to achieve rather high accuracy.

Mechanical features and function of the 10/22 Rifle are exactly like those of the Carbine and Target models discussed earlier. Therefore, they do not need to be reviewed, and we can progress directly to the results of accuracy testing which are shown in the table.

The accuracy demonstrated by the Ruger 10/22 Rifle is outstanding. For the five types of ammunition tested, not one gave an average group size of over one inch. For all of the groups with these five types of ammunition, 67 percent measured under one inch. While this does not mean that the 10/22 Rifle is as accurate as a high priced sporting rifle, it does mean that this rifle is a good choice for a wide range of activities that could include hunting small game and varmints as well as plinking.

With a suggested price of $275, the 10/22 Rifle is often found at retail at a price of approximately $200. To this author, the 10/22 Rifle makes all of the desirable features of the 10/22 Carbine available in a considerably more handsome firearm. It would be a nice touch if the rifle were produced with sling swivel studs. The model known as the Ruger 10/22 Sporter has a checkered walnut stock, but the forend is squared off and the barrel is the same 18.5-inch unit that is available on the Carbine. As a real eye catching sporter, the 20-inch barreled 10/22 Rifle could be offered with a checkered walnut stock shaped just like the hardwood stock that is standard on the rifle. Such a version would be, in the opinion of the author, the most attractive format ever offered for the 10/22. Even without these characteristics, the Ruger 10/22 Rifle is a handsome rifle that is also very capable.

The Marlin Model 60 is a classic American autoloader. There is a reason why more than 4 million of these rifles have been produced.

Marlin 60

Arguably the most popular semiautomatic 22 rifle ever made, the Marlin Model 60 is one of the best bargains in the rimfire field. As this is written, a Marlin Model 60 is available in one of the large "marts" for under $120 in the "basic blue and hardwood" configuration. This rifle has been produced by the millions. Basically, the Model 60 is a 19-inch barreled semiautomatic with a tubular magazine that holds 14 rounds of 22 LR. Not too many years ago, the Model 60 was offered with a 22-inch barrel and a magazine that held 17 cartridges.

This inexpensive rifle has several desirable features. First, it has a hold open device that holds the bolt half way open after the last shot. Second, the Model 60 has a cross bolt safety of generous size located behind the trigger. Third, the receiver is grooved for easy attachment of scope mounts. Fourth, with its receiver having a rounded back, the Model 60 has sleek styling, and it has a well-shaped stock. Moreover, with an overall length of 37.5 inches and weight of 5.75 pounds, the rifle is very convenient to hold and carry. The tubular magazine gives the rifle the "weight forward" feeling that allows for steady holding. Fifth, the Model 60 has a square-topped post front sight on a ramp and an adjustable rear sight with a square notch. This sighting equipment permits a good sight picture to be established.

One of the things about the Marlin 60 that has changed over the years is the number of options in stocks and metal finishes. The Model 60 can be obtained with blued metal and either hardwood or camo stock. Stainless steel metal parts combined with hardwood, composition, or laminated stock make up other available options. The variant with the blued metal and hardwood stock represents the lowest price option.

The Marlin Model 60 has been a staple in the rimfire market for many years. It has been offered not only as a Marlin but also carrying the labels of other retail chains. For many years, this was a common practice for stores like Sears, Wards, Western Auto,

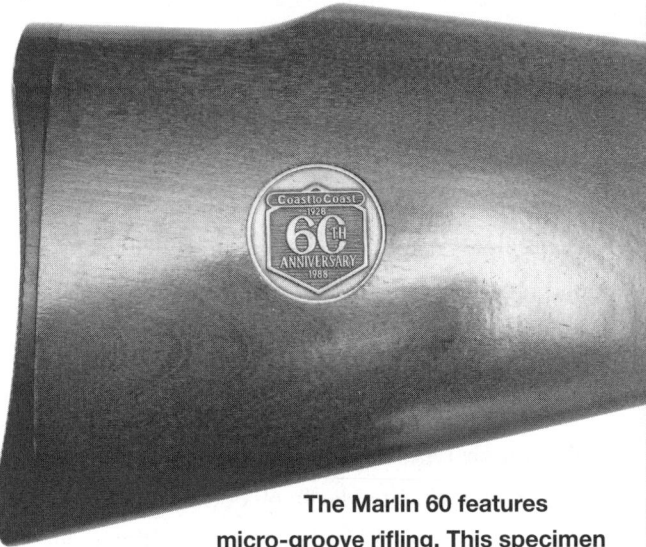

The Marlin 60 features micro-groove rifling. This specimen is designated as Mod. 6088CC which denotes a Model 60 produced in 1988 for Coast to Coast stores.

Accuracy Results for the Marlin Model 60 Rifle with a 3-12X BSA Scope.			
Ammunition	Smallest	Group size, inches Largest	Average
CCI Green Tag	0.83	1.50	1.04
Federal Target (711B)	0.63	1.39	1.11
Remington Game Load	0.66	0.93	0.82
Winchester Power Point	0.97	1.56	1.25
Winchester T22	0.77	1.19	0.93
Wolf Match Target	0.62	1.07	0.92
			Overall Av. 1.01

and hardware stores who did not produce their own firearms. My, how times have changed! The Model 60 tested in this work was produced for the 60th anniversary of Coast to Coast hardware stores, and it carries an inlayed medallion to denote the occasion. It should also be remembered that the magazine-fed Models 70, 795, and 7000 (target version) are essentially the Model 60 with a different means of holding cartridges.

Testing this American classic began by attaching a BSA 3-12X AO airgun scope with a Beeman mount. A few shots were fired to sight in the rifle, and it was the tested for accuracy at 50 yards using six types of ammunition. It should be mentioned that these tests were conducted at Buffalo, Wyoming in December. The temperature was approximately 35 ºF, and because of having no sandbags along, a makeshift support was used on the concrete shooting bench. Consequently, conditions were somewhat less than ideal for accurate shooting. The accompanying table shows the results obtained.

When testing rimfire rifles, one is never sure which types of ammunition will perform best, but the attempt is made to find a few kinds that give good accuracy. In the case of the Marlin 60, three of the six types of ammunition gave average group sizes of under one inch, and the Remington Game Load gave an average group size of only 0.82 inch. All of the six types of loads gave individual groups of under an inch. The Marlin 60 does not seem to be quite as finicky with regard to ammunition as are some autoloaders. In fact, an aggregate group size of 1.01 inches is very good for a rifle of this type. I have other 22 rimfire rifles, but the Marlin 60 showed that it is the only rifle I really need for most small game hunting and plinking.

The accuracy results given by the Marlin Model 60 show that this rifle is capable of fine accuracy with certain types of ammunition. In fact, I do not know of another inexpensive rimfire autoloader that will give better performance. To see if my experience with the Model 60 is typical, I spent some time reading comments posted on the Internet at various sites devoted to rimfire shooting. What I found was amazing. Almost every comment from a user of a Model 60 praised the accuracy of this rifle. Some of the comments by users indicated that the Model 60 is even more accurate than the results that I obtained. When you realize that a Marlin Model 60 with blue metal and wood stock sells for under $120 at a large "mart", it is clear that it is possible to get into rimfire shooting very inexpensively. Even when a good scope is added the total cost can be less than $200, and Remington Game Load is an inexpensive type of ammunition. However, as the data show, this combination is capable of producing excellent results. Keep in mind that the Marlin Model 60 is produced in several combinations of metal and stock finish so one is not restricted to a single version of this fine rifle. For many rimfire shooters, one of the versions of the Marlin Model 60 could well be all the rifle needed. I like inexpensive firearms that give performance well beyond their cost, and the Marlin Model 60 certainly belongs in that category. This rifle is a true American icon.

Accuracy Results for the Remington 597 with BSA 4X Scope.			
Ammunition	Smallest	Group size, inches Largest	Average
CCI Standard Velocity	0.72	1.17	1.00
Federal Target (711B)	0.89	1.85	1.34
Remington/Eley Target	0.44	1.14	0.81
Remington Golden H.P.	0.80	1.43	1.14
Winchester T-22	1.24	1.72	1.57
			Overall Av. 1.17

Remington 597

Autoloaders are the most popular type of 22 rifle so it is natural that there should be a large number of models available. In 1959, Remington broke new ground in rimfire autoloaders with the introduction of a model known as the Nylon 66. This rifle had a tube located in the butt stock, which held 14 rounds. This was not a new approach to housing the magazine in a rimfire, but what was new was the fact that the stock was made of a plastic known as Zytel. Moreover, most of the rifle was made of structural nylon that needed no lubrication and very little maintenance. Even the receiver was made of nylon but it had a thin sheet of metal surrounding it. After the Nylon 66 was discontinued in 1987, the next mass-produced Remington autoloader was the Viper 522 which was produced for several years. As is so often the case in firearm development, the Viper was a transitional piece that led to the Remington 597. The Model 597 is actually a family of rifles that includes variants with different metal finishes and stock compositions in 22 LR caliber. Not content with offering rifles in one caliber, magnum models have appeared that are chambered for the 22 WMR and 17 HMR although they cost much more than those in 22 LR caliber.

The Remington 597 has several attractive features. First, it is reasonably light, but it has enough weight to hold steady. Second, the Model 597 has a metal magazine that is easier to load than those on other clip fed models. The clip has a bright orange follower which makes it easy to see when the last cartridge has been removed. Third, the bolt rides on dual rails and operates very smoothly. This rifle has been fired fewer than 20 rounds when the testing was initiated, and the action became noticeably smoother during the firing. With a couple of shots early in the testing, ejection of the empty case was not complete because the action was stiff and the round being fired was a low powered one. After that, ejection and feeding were flawless. The stock on the Model 597 has a forearm of generous width that allows it to rest on sandbags in steady manner.

The Remington tested belongs to a brother who has a 4X BSA scope mounted. Because the rifle was sighted in and was going to be used with that scope, it was tested that way. Therefore, the sighting error was somewhat larger than in cases where a scope of higher power was used. In spite of that, the Remington 597 gave the excellent results shown in the accompanying table.

Like all other rimfire rifles, the Remington 597 shows preferences in ammunition. Impressive accuracy was obtained with the Remington/Eley Target with the average group size being only 0.81 inch with only a 4X scope used on the rifle. CCI Standard Velocity gave an average group size of only an inch. There is no question that the Model 597 is capable of better accuracy when fully broken in and with a scope of higher magnification attached. Under the conditions of the tests, the results are excellent with the composite group size being only 1.17 inches. Keep in mind that the Remington 597 sells for around $150 and the BSA scope used is available at one of the large "marts" for around $25 including a mount. This is an inexpensive combination that delivers performance that is entirely adequate for plinking or small game hunting. While the range of aftermarket goodies available for the Remington 597 is not as extensive as that for the Ruger 10/22, it is a growing industry. The Remington 597 is, as it deserves to be, a very popular 22 autoloader.

Thompson/Center Classic

I think that the Thompson/Center (T/C) Classic autoloader and the bolt-action Remington 504 are perhaps more indicative of the health of the rimfire market than any other rifles. The T/C autoloader retails for around $300 while the Remington that lists for $710 normally retails for about $600. These rifles were introduced to meet the demand for high quality sporting rifles that were sought by

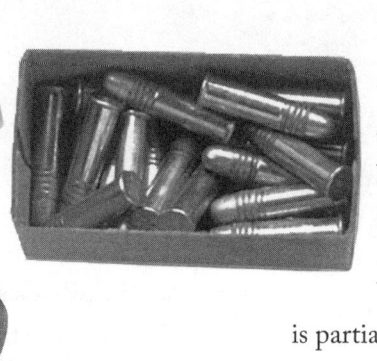

One reason for the outstanding accuracy of the T/C Classic is that the barrel is threaded into the steel receiver.

serious rimfire shooters. Neither fits in the category of plinking rifles although either could meet that criterion admirably. No, these rifles are intended for use by rimfire shooters who take their sport seriously.

The T/C Classic is a true sporting rifle albeit a semiautomatic. High quality rimfire sporting rifles have traditionally had bolt-actions although this is by no means a requirement. The T/C is a rather robust rifle that has a solid feel when you pick it up. One reason is that unlike most autoloaders that have a receiver made of aluminum alloy, the T/C Classic has a steel receiver. Moreover, the 20-inch match-grade barrel is of generous weight, and it is threaded into the receiver in the way traditionally used for centerfire rifles. Such construction is unusual in a rimfire rifle, but it gives a rigid barrel/action unit, and that is partially responsible for the fine accuracy of the T/C Classic.

The T/C Classic has a very well shaped walnut stock, but it is not checkered. Another version of the Classic, known as the Silver Lynx, is available that has a composite stock and stainless steel barrel and action. Sights on the Classic are unusual in that they make use of fiber optic inserts. The front sight has a green fiber optic insert that rides along the top of the post while the square-notched rear sight has fiber optic inserts on either side of the notch. The inserts appear as glowing dots when viewed from the rear, and aligning the dots aids in getting the front and rear sights in proper relationship. Frankly, I do not care for such sights and would prefer simply a square-topped post front and square notch in the rear sight, but it is a matter of taste. I never fire at

One of the most elegant autoloaders is the Thompson/Center Classic. It is also one of the most accurate autoloaders.

Accuracy Results for the Thompson/Center Classic with 3-12X Redfield Scope.			
Ammunition	**Smallest**	**Group size, inches Largest**	**Average**
CCI Green Tag	0.66	1.08	0.88
CCI SGB	0.54	1.20	0.81
CCI Velocitor	0.70	1.24	0.93
Federal Target (711B)	0.75	1.06	0.87
Remington/Eley Club Extra	0.41	0.74	0.62
Remington Golden H.P.	0.87	1.18	1.03
Remington Target	0.76	1.75	1.33
SK Jagd. Standard Plus	0.34	0.85	0.63
Winchester Power Point	0.70	0.95	0.81
Winchester T-22	0.77	1.25	1.05
Wolf Match Target	0.41	1.10	0.86
			Overall Av. 0.89

targets when the light is so dim that these optical gimmicks are needed. In dim light a scope would be a better choice. The receiver of the Classic is drilled and tapped to attach Weaver-type bases so the receiver is not grooved as are many on rimfire rifles. A detachable five-shot magazine is standard. The safety is a lever located on the right hand side of the receiver with red and green indicators on the top edge of the stock.

In addition to the Classic and Silver Lynx, T/C also produces a target model known as the Benchmark which has an 18-inch heavy barrel and a laminated target style stock. A 10-round magazine is supplied with this version.

Because the T/C Classic is at home in a variety of situations where a rimfire rifle is used, it was tested with a wide variety of ammunition types. The accompanying table shows the results of the accuracy testing.

Overall accuracy of the T/C Classic is outstanding for an autoloading sporting rifle. With a match grade barrel that has a match chamber, it is not surprising that this rifle delivers fine accuracy with target ammunition. Especially fine accuracy was delivered by Remington/Eley Club Extra and SK Jagd. Standard Plus loads. However, Winchester Power Points gave an average group size of only 0.81 inch, and the largest average group size (only 1.05 inches) was obtained with Winchester T-22. The composite group size of 0.89 inch indicates accuracy that is comparable to that produced by some bolt-action sporters. It is especially noteworthy that even with the wide variety of ammunition types employed, none of the types performed poorly in the T/C. I suspect that this is due in part to the fact that because of its rigidity the barrel and action assembly simply is not affected by minor differences in ammunition.

Numerous jams occurred during the test firing. Ejection was positive, but as the bolt moved forward it frequently took the top round in the magazine forward into the bottom of the barrel breech or into the top edge at the front of the magazine. The nose of the cartridge did not come up at the correct angle. It was found that the spring in this particular magazine seemed not to have sufficient force to raise the nose of the cartridge upward enough for it to move into the chamber. A call to T/C to explain the problem led quickly to a new magazine which is clearly constructed in a different manner and which has a much stiffer spring. Apparently, the magazines now produced are somewhat different from those made early in the production of this fine rifle. There is no defect in the design, and it is an outstanding rifle.

For shooters who want a fine sporting rifle but who do not choose a bolt-action, the T/C Classic is a superb choice. While not strictly a target rifle, it would be quite at home in the woods hunting squirrels or on the prairie shooting pests.

Henry

I grew up in an era when western movies were a significant form of wholesome entertainment. It would have been impossible for me to grow up not liking single-action revolvers and lever-action rifles. While I have had the former for many years, the lever-action rimfire rifle escaped my clutches until comparatively recent times. While both Marlin and Winchester have produced lever-action rifles in

The Henry Lever-action performed very well in the tests and always fed and ejected reliably.

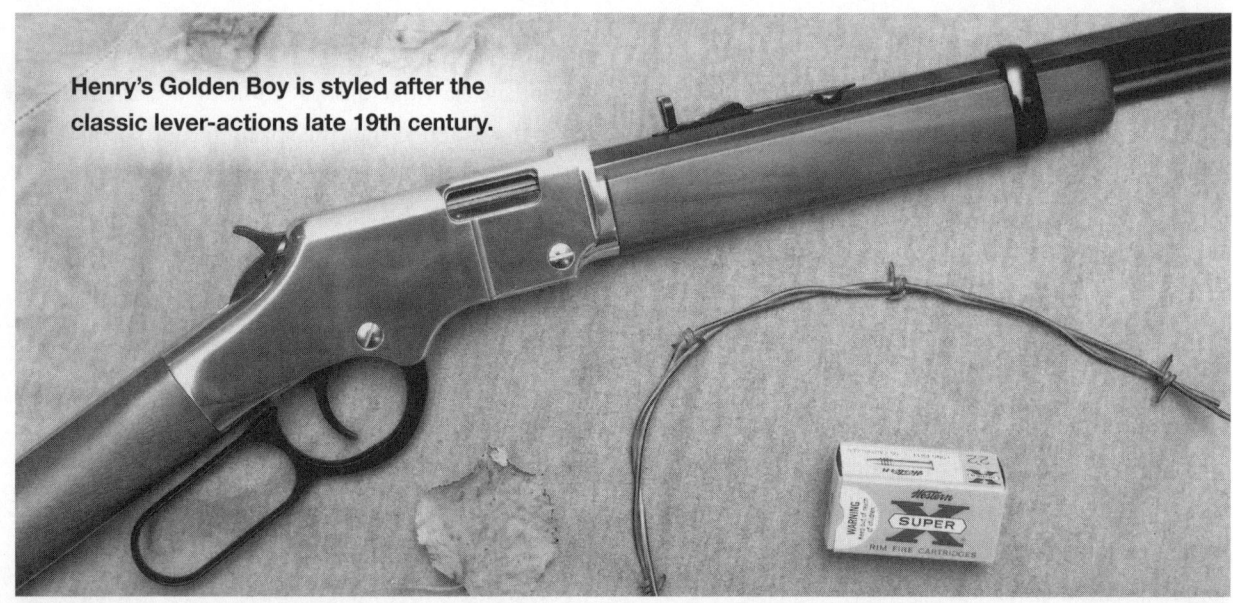

Henry's Golden Boy is styled after the classic lever-actions late 19th century.

Accuracy Results for the Henry Lever Action with Weaver 2.5-7X Scope.

Ammunition	Smallest	Group size, inches Largest	Average
CCI Standard Velocity	0.79	1.79	1.18
Federal High Velocity H.P.	1.29	2.07	1.73
Federal Target (711B)	0.82	1.67	1.20
Remington Golden H.P.	1.38	1.78	1.56
Winchester Power Point	0.83	1.36	1.09
Wolf Match Target	0.73	1.77	1.25

Overall Av. 1.34

rimfire calibers for many years, it is neither of these that produced the lever-action rifle to be described here. No, it was the Henry Repeating Arms Company of Brooklyn, NY that produced that rifle. List price of the Henry is $269.95, but in one of the large "marts" it retails for just under $200.

I had looked at the Henry over the years, but for some reason had never added one to the collection. Traditional styling is evident in the Henry, but it is not just to be looked a—this rifle is for shooting. The Henry has a steel barrel that measures 18.25 inches in length and a weight of 5.25 pounds. The grooved receiver on the Henry is made of an alloy that has been given a durable black finish. The Henry is fitted with a walnut stock and forearm, which are made of very good wood on most of the specimens that I have examined. A tubular magazine that holds 15 rounds of 22 LR resides under the barrel. Sights on the Henry consist of a hooded post on a ramp front sight and a square notch in a blade rear sight. The rear sight can be adjusted for elevation by sliding a stepped ramp under the blade. Windage is adjusted by drifting the sight laterally in the retaining notch. Like older lever-actions, the Henry has a safety notch position for the hammer but no other safety.

To test the Henry, a Weaver 2.5-7X rimfire scope was mounted. This superb scope is compact and fits well on the little Henry. The results of the accuracy testing are shown in the accompanying table.

While the Henry will not win any benchrest competition, the accuracy is actually quite good for this type of rifle. Many plinking rifles give five-shot groups that measure around 2 inches and the Henry beats that with all of the types of ammunition tested. In fact, with Winchester Power Points, the average group size is slightly over one inch. This suits me just fine because the Power Point is one of my favorite hunting loads, and with this ammunition the Henry

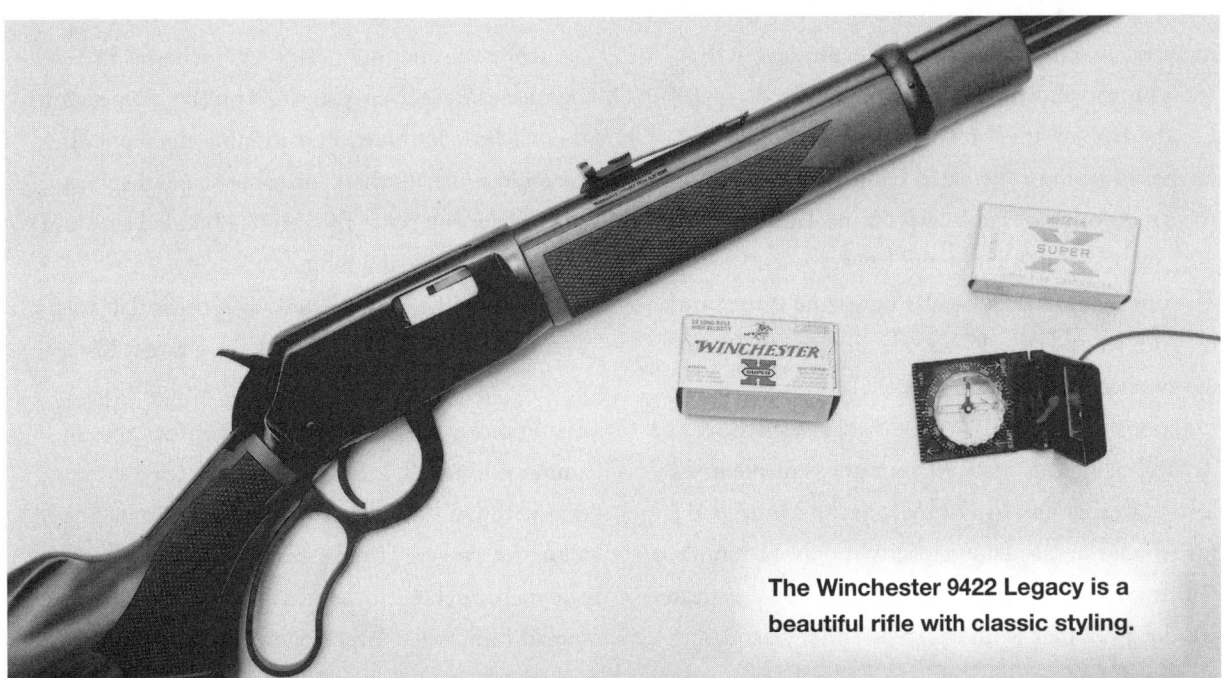

The Winchester 9422 Legacy is a beautiful rifle with classic styling.

Accuracy Results for the Winchester 9422 Legacy with a Leupold 2.5-7X Scope.			
Ammunition	Smallest	Group size, inches Largest	Average
CCI Standard Velocity	0.52	0.79	0.69
CCI SGB	0.85	1.46	1.22
Federal High Velocity H.P.	0.53	1.42	1.03
Lapua Super Club	0.59	1.33	0.94
Remington Game Load	0.89	1.52	1.17
Winchester Power Point	0.68	1.54	1.12
			Overall Av. 1.03

is certainly a 50-yard squirrel and pest rifle. Because of its beautiful styling and excellent handling qualities, my Henry is destined to be one of my two favorite rifles for woods roaming. I may even set up shop and try to call in a predator while using the rifle that has my favorite action type.

Functioning of the Henry during the tests was impressive. There was positive and crisp movement of the empty case and cartridge every time the lever was cycled. Empty cases were ejected vigorously every time. The Henry is a fine rifle, and I couldn't be happier with mine.

Winchester 9422

The production of lever-action rifles bearing the Winchester name is well into its second century. One model, the Model 94, has been in continuous production for well over a century. Not only is the rimfire lever-action being described here a Winchester, but it also has the distinction of being the only rimfire rifle produced by that famous company for many years. Gone are the pump, semiautomatic, and bolt-action models that were produced throughout the 1970s. Perhaps one reason for their passing is that in 1972 Winchester introduced the Model 9422, and the rifle has been very successful, not that it much of a surprise given the popularity of the legendary Model 94 centerfire rifle. However, in early 2005, Winchester announced that production of the Model 9422 was being terminated.

The most recent offerings in the Model 9422

included two basic models, the Traditional with a straight grip and the Legacy with a curved grip. On the Legacy, the forend extends an inch or so farther in front of the barrel band than it does on the Traditional. Barrel length on the Traditional is 20.5 inches while that on the Legacy is 22.5 inches. The under-the-barrel tubular magazine is the same on both rifles so the 15-round capacity of 22 LR ammunition is common to both. Of course, the functions and controls are identical as well. Both the Traditional and Legacy versions are available in 22 WMR caliber and in 17 HMR as the Model 9417 for which the magazine capacity is only 11 rounds.

If there is one word that describes the Winchester Model 9422 that word has to be either classic or elegant. Come to think of it, both descriptors are appropriate. Unlike many rimfire rifles, the receivers are made from forged steel that is highly polished and brightly blued. The receivers carry the grooves that are now almost universal for attaching scope mounts. Barrels and magazine tubes are also very well finished. Stocks on most of the recently produced rifles that I have examined are made of very good walnut, and the cut checkering is done with a high level of technique. The end result is that the appearance of Model 9422 is the equal of many (if not most) centerfire rifles. Such elegance comes at a price, and the manufacturer's suggested price for the 22 LR caliber Traditional version is $479 while in the magnum calibers it is $515. Suggested prices for the Legacy are $512 for the 22 LR and $551 for the magnums. Retail discounts lower these figures somewhat, but these are not inexpensive rimfire rifles.

Sights on the Model 9422 are conventional. The front sight is a hooded bead on a ramp while the rear sight is the familiar notched blade which can be adjusted for elevation by means of a stepped ramp and for windage by drifting the sight laterally in its dove tail retaining notch. Other than the usual safety notch that is common to many firearms with exposed hammers, there is no safety on the Model 9422.

For accuracy testing, a Leupold Vari-X II 2.5-7X scope was mounted on the Winchester 9422. Because the receiver is so short on the lever-action, there is little latitude in positioning the scope. The Leupold fit better than any other scope that was available at the time. The results obtained are shown in the accompanying table.

In testing the Winchester 9422, the intent was to use ammunition that ranges from target loads to some of the popular types used for hunting. The Winchester 9422 handled all of the types of ammunition well. It is particularly gratifying to see that with CCI Standard-velocity and Lapua Super Club the average group sizes were smaller than one inch. Such performance should dispel the wide spread rumor that lever-action rifles are capable of only mediocre accuracy. Moreover, the composite group size for all six types of ammunition is just over an inch. If you like lever-action rifles but have heard that they may not be accurate, the data show that if you are willing to experiment with several types of ammunition, you should be able to find a couple of types that will give good accuracy. For my use, it would be hard to imagine a finer rifle for the person who stalks the woods.

Not coincidentally, the resemblance of the Model 9422 to the legendary Model 94 is unmistakable. But this rimfire is more than just a classic in terms of its appearance. Made of high quality materials, this is a durable and functional rifle that is right at home in the woods or fields. It is a superb hunting rifle, especially for the hunter who uses a lever-action centerfire for hunting large game. The cost of a Model 9422 is not trivial, but many of the better bolt-action rimfire rifles are in a comparable price range. I may have somehow avoided owning a lever-action rimfire for most of my life, but that deficiency is corrected now.

As the manuscript for this book is being finished in early 2005, Winchester has just announced that the Model 9422 lever-action is being discontinued. Undoubtedly, some of these fine rifles will be on dealers' shelves for some time, and some special issue versions will probably appear. In production for over 30 years, the Model 9422 provided a superb alternative to those rimfire shooters who wanted an elegant rifle but did not want it to be a bolt-action.

Ruger 77/22

In 1983, Ruger responded to a demand for a high quality rimfire rifle by introducing a bolt-action sporter in 22 LR caliber. This elegant rifle had a checkered walnut stock, a 20-inch barrel, and utilized a 10-round rotary magazine. Like the Ruger 10/22 autoloader, the 77/22 bolt-action is a little thick in the midsection because of the large rotary magazine, but in side view, this is one of the trimmest bolt-action rifles around. At the time it was introduced, the Ruger 77/22 may well have been the most elegant rimfire sporter produced in the United States, and some would say that it still ranks high on the list.

The 2004 Ruger catalog list four variants of the 77/22. They consist of the combinations of blue metal with walnut stock, stainless steel with synthetic stock, and low glare stainless with laminated stock all without sights. The stainless steel with synthetic stock variant is also offered with open sights. The open sights consist of a bead on a post front sight and an excellent folding rear sight. My 77/22 was made many years ago when walnut-stocked version could be obtained with sights.

Let me describe the mechanical features of the 77/22. First, the action is robust, really robust. The bolt is of the two-piece type with the rear half rotating while the front section simply moves forward and backward. Turning the rear section as the bolt handle is lowered into locked position causes two locking lugs to move into recesses in the action. The front section of the bolt has dual extactors. At the rear of the bolt on the left-hand side is a rotating wing-type safety that can be placed in three positions. When the safety is in the rearmost position, both the trigger and bolt are locked. Moving the safety forward into the middle position keeps the trigger locked, but allows the bolt to be opened. In the forward position, the rifle can be fired.

The barrel is attached to the receiver on the Ruger 77/22 in a manner similar to that used on the 10/22. A notch in the bottom of the barrel has a mating block that is attached to the front of the receiver by means of two large Allen headed screws. Therefore, it is not difficult to remove and replace a barrel.

However, when the factory

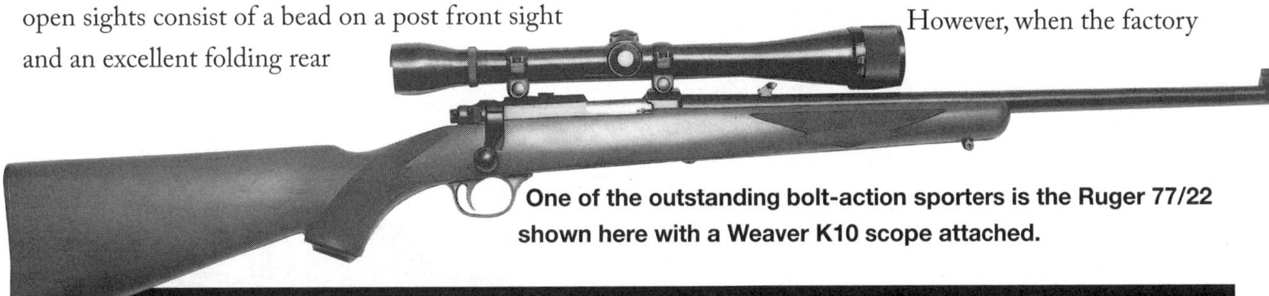

One of the outstanding bolt-action sporters is the Ruger 77/22 shown here with a Weaver K10 scope attached.

Accuracy Results for the Ruger 77/22M with Weaver V12 Scope.

Ammunition	Smallest	Group size, inches Largest	Average
CCI Maxi Mag G.D. (50 gr)	0.71	1.40	1.08
CCI Maxi Mag H.P.	0.57	0.72	0.65
CCI TNT	0.63	1.01	0.77
CCI 22 WRF	0.37	0.78	0.63
Federal JHP (50 gr)	0.70	1.31	0.99
Federal TNT (30 gr.)	0.48	1.03	0.72
PMC Predator PSP	1.26	2.75	1.41
Remington Premier (V-Max)	0.62	0.81	0.73
Winchester Dynapoint	0.72	1.55	1.07
Winchester Super-X H.P.	0.57	0.89	0.78
Winchester Supreme	0.88	1.53	1.21

Ruger's 77/22M is an outstanding rifle chambered for the 22 WMR cartridge. The author's rifle wears an old Weaver V-12 scope.

barrel is replaced by one of the many aftermarket barrels that are available, it is necessary to make sure that the headspace is not excessive. Of course, the replacement barrel need not be chambered for the 22 LR, and barrel swapping to make the rifle a 17 Mach 2 is popular. As long as the headspace is satisfactory, there is no problem with the bolt-action like that encountered with excessive bolt speed that can occur when a barrel chambered for the 17 Mach 2 is installed on the 10/22 autoloader.

The expected level of accuracy from a fine rimfire sporting rifle is always high so the tests with the Ruger 77/22 were undertaken with enthusiasm. In order to see the target clearly, I mounted an old 10-power Weaver K-10 scope on the rifle and set forth to test the rifle with several types of ammunition. The results obtained are shown in the accompanying table.

I find the results of the tests with the Ruger 77/22 to be among the most interesting obtained in this entire project, and several conclusions can be drawn. First, like all other rimfire rifles used in these tests, the Ruger 77/22 did not like the Remington Target ammunition. This was the only type of ammunition that gave an average group size of over one inch. Second, the Lapua Scoremax performed extremely well, giving an average group size of only 0.60 inch.

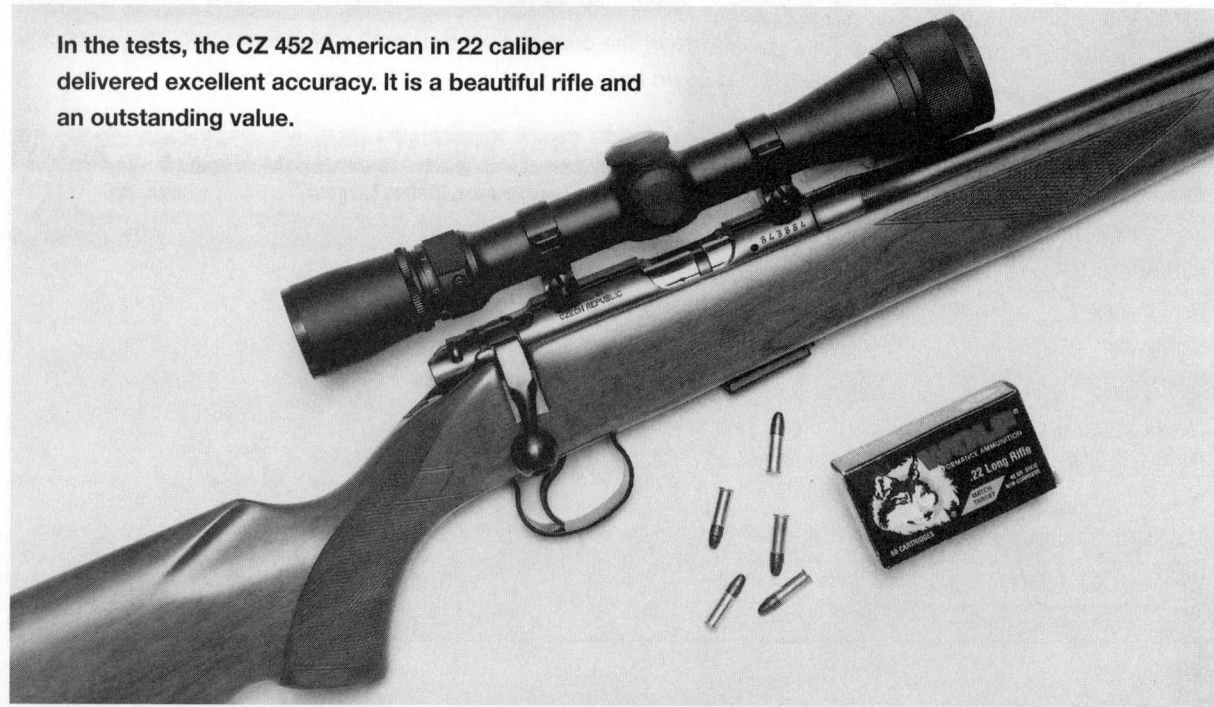

In the tests, the CZ 452 American in 22 caliber delivered excellent accuracy. It is a beautiful rifle and an outstanding value.

This load utilizes a 48-grain bullet at a modest velocity of 1040 ft/sec, and it is intended for hunting and silhouette applications. In this rifle, the Scoremax would be an excellent choice for accurately placed shots on predators that have been called in to modest ranges. Outstanding accuracy was also exhibited by several other types of ammunition. Third, one aspect of accuracy that I find pleasing is that CCI Velocitors gave excellent accuracy with the average group size being only 0.84 inch. With the Velocitor giving a remaining energy of 110 ft lbs at 100 yards, I am particularly interested in knowing that the accuracy is high enough to take advantage of this powerful load. Finally, an aggregate group size of only 0.85 inch is outstanding. Having read everything published on the recently introduced Remington 504, it seems that the Ruger 77/22 will give about equal accuracy, but the Ruger sells for a considerably lower price.

If I had to start deleting rimfire rifles from the safe, the Ruger 77/22 would be about the last to go. It is supremely reliable, its accuracy is predictable, and its appearance is classic. It is an outstanding rimfire that is a superb choice for hunting and pest control. Yes, I love shooting this rifle having the obsolete Weaver K10 scope mounted with its fine crosshair reticule. If I place the crosshairs where they should be and squeeze the trigger while holding steady, I am always confident that the bullet will go where I want it to. What more can one ask from a rifle?

CZ 452 American (22 LR)

Czeska Zbrojovka, abbreviated as CZ, produces a variety of firearms in their plant that they proclaim to be the largest small arms factory in the world. Among the rimfire rifles produced by this manufacturer is the outstanding Model 452 American, a classic bolt-action sporting rifle that is

Accuracy Results for the CZ 452 American 22 LR Tasco Mag IV 6-24X Scope.

Ammunition	Smallest	Group size, inches Largest	Average
CCI Green Tag	0.60	1.15	0.79
CCI Mini Mag	0.61	0.99	0.91
CCI SGB	0.80	1.09	0.95
CCI Standard Velocity	0.55	1.53	0.94
CCI Velocitor	0.86	1.43	1.13
Eley Target	0.32	0.61	0.51
Federal High Velocity H.P.	0.56	1.12	0.81
Federal Target (711B)	0.90	1.26	1.07
Federal Ultra Match	0.39	0.67	0.54
Lapua Super Club	0.41	0.62	0.57
PMC Match Rifle	0.64	1.14	0.76
PMC Scoremaster	0.77	1.29	0.97
Remington Golden H.P.	0.55	1.02	0.83
Remington Game Load	0.46	0.84	0.66
Remington Target	0.77	1.40	1.08
RWS Rifle Match	0.31	0.94	0.69
Winchester Power Point	0.68	0.94	0.83
Winchester Super-X H.P.	0.62	1.05	0.82
Winchester Supreme	0.51	0.96	0.67
Winchester T-22	0.44	1.00	0.67
Wolf Match Target	0.32	0.68	0.55

Overall Av. 0.80

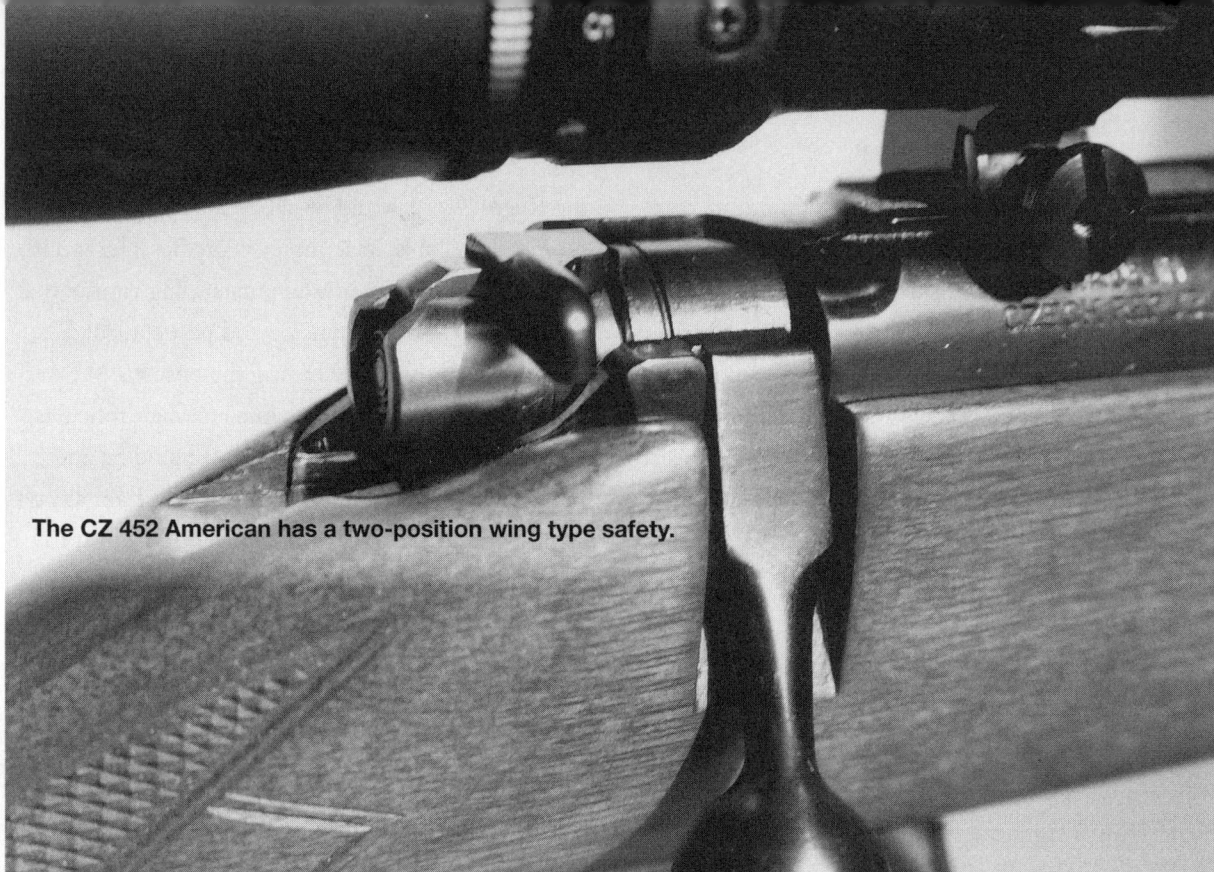

The CZ 452 American has a two-position wing type safety.

available in 22 LR, 17 HMR, and 22 WMR calibers. This rifle has a well-shaped, checkered walnut stock and highly polished and blued metal parts but is sold without sights. The receiver is grooved for attaching scope mounts.

The basic bolt-action is used as the starting point for several other rifles that include the heavy-barreled CZ 452 Varmint, a Mannlicher stocked CZ 452 FS, the longer barreled European-style stocked CZ 452 Lux, and the CZ 452 Silhouette which has a synthetic stock. There are also three versions that are known as the Training Rifle, the Scout which is a youth rifle on a smaller scale, and the CZ 452 Style which has a synthetic stock and nickel finished metal parts. The CZ 452 is available in a configuration for almost any taste in bolt-action rifles. The finish on the metal parts of most of the CZ rifles that I have examined is quite good. Bolts are very well machined and highly polished. The trigger guard and floor plate assembly is highly polished, and the magazine fits almost flush with the bottom of the stock on rifles in 22 LR caliber. Because of the larger cartridges in 22 WMR and 17 HMR calibers, the magazines of rifles in these calibers protrude from the bottom of the rifle by almost an inch. Magazine capacity is five rounds in all three calibers.

Accuracy of the CZ 452 rifles in enhanced by the fact that the barrel is threaded into the forged steel receiver. Barrels are hammer forged and are lapped. While some rimfire rifles may feel cheap and flimsy, the CZ 452 is sturdy and robust. These rifles are constructed of high quality materials in the traditional way. The safety on the CZ 452 is of the wing type and it is located at the rear of the bolt. Unlike the Ruger 77 series, the CZ has a two-position safety which blocks the firing pin not just the trigger. The trigger is adjustable for weight of pull. Operation of the CZ 452 is positive and precise. Retail prices for the CZ 452 vary slightly with caliber, but is generally in the $325 to $400 range.

Having examined the rifle in detail, it was with considerable anticipation that accuracy testing was begun. The results obtained are summarized in the accompanying table. Although a scope of high magnification was used, it has a rather thick crosshair reticule so the high magnification is not as much of an advantage as it might be.

During the testing of the CZ 452, the farther we

progressed into accuracy testing the more interesting the results became. Since my wife did all of the firing with her CZ, the result was that a total of 22 different types of 22 LR ammunition were tested because she was enjoying her new rifle so much. She also liked getting smaller groups than I was getting with most of my rifles! The data show that the CZ 452 produces superb accuracy with most types of ammunition. Four types of target ammunition produced groups that averaged less than 0.60 inch. I measured so many groups that were simply a ragged hole that I almost tired of the work. Such outstanding accuracy was not limited to target ammunition. Remington Game Loads produced an average group size of only 0.66 inch and Winchester Power Points gave an average of only 0.83 inch. The aggregate average group size of 0.80 inch was slightly smaller than that produced by any other 22 LR tested in the study. However, it must be kept in mind that the Ruger 77/22 was tested with a 10X scope while the CZ 452 had a 24X scope in place. Now, just wait until we get 24X scopes on both rifles!

Although lacking the aftermarket modifications possible with the Ruger 77/22, the CZ 452 is fully its equal in accuracy. There may be no more capable sporting rifle available in its price range. You can spend a lot more money before you gain much in accuracy

Ruger 77/22M

The outstanding Ruger 77/22 had been in production for several years when Ruger introduced the version chambered for the 22 WMR, the Model 77/22M. This rifle became popular with varmint hunters who wanted more range and a more potent tool than afforded by any 22 LR. Currently, there are four versions of the 77/22M that include blued metal and walnut stock, stainless steel and synthetic stock (with or without sights) and a low glare stainless steel and laminated stock. Mechanical features and operation of the rifles are identical to those described in detail for the 77/22 that was discussed earlier so that information will not be repeated here. One slight difference is that the rotary magazine holds nine rounds of 22 WMR while that for the 22 LR rifles holds 10 rounds.

My 77/22M is fitted with a scope that is a true classic. It is one of the old steel-tubed Weaver scopes made in El Paso, TX. This scope, known as the Model V12, is a 3-12X variable that has the AO feature. If memory serves correctly, I bought the scope for $40 in a gun shop in Bismarck, ND several years ago. Since the rifle/scope combination has been used for several years, it was with some degree of anticipation that I began the accuracy testing that led to the data shown in the accompanying table.

The data shown in the table indicate that with

Accuracy Results for the Ruger 77/22 with Weaver K-10 Scope.			
Ammunition	Smallest	Group size, inches Largest	Average
CCI Green Tag	0.65	0.85	0.72
CCI SGB	0.66	1.00	0.95
CCI Velocitor	0.71	0.99	0.84
Federal Target (711B)	0.55	1.03	0.80
Federal Ultra Match	0.53	0.99	0.77
Lapua Scoremax	0.46	0.82	0.60
Lapua Super Club	0.68	1.27	0.90
Remington Target	0.69	2.04	1.31
Winchester T-22	0.49	1.04	0.75
Winchester Supreme	0.56	1.01	0.86
			Overall Av. 0.85

several types of ammunition the Ruger 77/22M produces groups of about three-quarters of an inch or less. The smallest groups were given by CCI Maxi Mags with 40-grain hollow-point bullets with the average group size being 0.65 inch. In my rifle, the Winchester Supreme seemed to give four shots almost in one hole but the groups always seemed to have one flyer. Both of the identical Federal and CCI TNT loads gave very good accuracy with groups from 0.72 to 0.77 inches. Because of the wide variety of loads that includes both 22 WMR and 22 WRF, a composite group size is meaningless so it is not included.

If you have read Chapter 7 dealing with ballistics, you will know why I will continue to use the Federal 50-grain load for larger varmints when the range is 100 yards or less. It has excellent retained energy because the heavy bullet has a high ballistic coefficient. The CCI 50-grain Gold Dot load has been discontinued, but it did not give best accuracy in my rifle. There have been reports that bullets as heavy as 50-grains are not stabilized by a 1:16 twist because of the lower velocity. That seems strange in view of the fact that the velocity is even lower when this ammunition is fired from a handgun. I have not seen any evidence of a lack of stability, but the fact remains that neither of the 50 grain loads produces best accuracy in the 77/22M tested.

Perhaps the biggest surprise was how well the CCI ammunition in 22 WRF caliber performed in the 77/22M. Logic would dictate that this shorter cartridge would be less accurate because the bullet has to "jump" to engage the rifling just as when a 22 Short is fired in a 22 LR chamber. If you check the data, you will find that the 22 WRF is just as accurate as anything else in the 77/22M tested! However, the point of impact was almost 6 inches below where the 40-grain 22 WMR bullets hit so do not go hunting using 22 WRF ammunition without sighting in first. Also, the 50-grain bullets hit the target about 3 inches below where the 40-grain bullets hit.

One load that should be immensely popular in the 22 WMR is the Remington Premier that utilizes a 33-grain Hornady V-Max polymer-tipped bullet. Although the advertised velocity for this load is 2000 ft/sec, my chronograph indicated that this is low by almost 10 percent! The bullet has a ballistic coefficient of 0.137, which is higher than the value of 0.125 for the highly praised 17-grain V-Max bullet used in the 17 HMR. Calculations show that the Remington Premier load shoots flat and retains its velocity and energy better than the 30-grain hollow-points used in some 22 WMR ammunition. Although the velocity is lower, the 33-grain V-Max bullet from a 22 WMR has considerably more energy than any 17 HMR load at all ranges (about 25 percent more at 150 yards). However, the Remington Premier sells for about $10 per box (which is almost identical to the price of the "premium" 17 HMR ammunition).

For most of my shooting with the 22 WMR, I use the 40-grain hollow-points of the CCI Maxi Mag or Winchester Super-X type. They give good accuracy, and the bullets have reasonably high ballistic coefficients.

If you have read articles that deal with the 17 HMR, you have seen a lot of hype about how much more accurate the 17 HMR is than the 22 WMR. Although the results of testing 17 HMR rifles will follow this discussion, it is appropriate to make some observations here in relation to the 22 WMR. Some people who write articles about the 17 HMR seem to have forgotten that all currently available 17 HMR ammunition is manufactured by the same company, CCI, and that it is all "premium" ammunition that makes use of premium bullets. The price of the 17 HMR ammunition reflects that situation. Of course, it should be more uniform that most 22 WMR ammunition which is made by numerous companies using components that in many instances are by no means "premium." It may also be that manufacturing tolerances are held slightly closer in the case of 17 HMR firearms. Please do not misunderstand. My Ruger 77/17 is slightly more accurate than my 77/22M, but it is a comparison of apples with oranges with the obvious differences that exist in ammunition.

In a published test by a careful experimenter using identical 17 HMR and 22 WMR rifles made by Cooper, it was reported that there was almost no difference in accuracy. I do not believe that there is a great deal of difference in inherent accuracy between the two cartridges, but there is a difference in quality of ammunition in most cases. With its heavier bullets of larger diameter, the 22 WMR is a better choice when dealing with larger varmints. With its small bullets at higher velocity, the 17 HMR is a better choice for small varmints at extended ranges. If you have a Ruger 77 in one of the calibers, you can add an aftermarket barrel and change to the other because the actions and magazines are identical.

Ruger 77/17

If there is one cartridge that has taken the shooting world by storm, it is the 17 HMR. The bottlenecked cartridge utilizes a 22 WMR case necked down to hold a 17 caliber bullet. Initial loads featured a 17-grain Hornady V-Max bullet, and with the polymer tip it is a very attractive cartridge. With a generous charge of slow-burning (for a rimfire) powder, a muzzle velocity of 2,550 ft/sec could be reached. There are eight loads in 17 HMR currently available, and I have worked extensively with six of them. Six of the eight have 17-grain bullets (four polymer-tipped and one hollow-point) while two make use of 20-grain hollow-point bullets. As of this writing, all 17 HMR ammunition is loaded by CCI regardless of the color of the polymer tip on the bullet.

The Ruger 77/17 in 17 HMR caliber is right at home in prairie dog country. The scope is a Weaver Classic V-16.

Accuracy Results for the Ruger 77/17 with Weaver V-16 Classic Scope.			
Ammunition	Smallest	Group size, inches Largest	Average
CCI Game Point (20 gr.)	0.65	0.85	0.72
CCI TNT	0.38	0.90	0.67
Federal V-Shok	0.33	0.75	0.57
Hornady V-Max	0.49	0.63	0.53
Hornady XTP (20 gr.)	0.42	1.01	0.75
Remington Premier	0.50	0.84	0.63
			Overall Av. 0.65

Ruger has produced rifles in 17 HMR caliber from the beginning. One reason is that they already produced rifles in 22 WMR so all it took was a 17 caliber barrel. As a result, Ruger offers the bolt-action Model 77/17, the autoloader Model 10/17, and the lever-action Model 96/17 which are the tiny bore companions to the small bore 22 WMR rifles. The 77/17 tested has a synthetic stock with blued barrel and action. Because the action and mechanical features of the 77/17 are identical to those of the 77/22M, we will progress directly to the test results, which are shown in the accompanying table. The rifle was equipped with a new 4-16X Weaver Classic V-16 scope with AO. This is not a book about scopes, but I love this one!

Before discussing the results obtained in the

(Photo courtesy: U. S. Fish and Wildlife Service)

accuracy tests, it should be mentioned that this particular rifle was very sensitive to the tension on the two screws that hold the barreled action to the stock. Initially, it was found that some groups tended to be strung out vertically with one or more flyers increasing the size of the groups to 0.7 to 0.8 inches. Tweaking the tension on the screws reduced this tendency somewhat so that smaller groups were generally obtained. Whether or not this tendency is present in Ruger 77/17 rifles having walnut stocks I do not know.

Several conclusions can be drawn from the data shown in the table. First, there is no great difference in accuracy shown by the different types of ammunition. What a surprise considering that all of the types are loaded by CCI! While I have seen results reported which show phenomenal groups attributed to 17 HMR rifles and I did get some such groups, it seems to me that an aggregate group size of a little over one-half inch is not too bad considering that all firing was conducted outdoors with a substantial breeze in some cases. Second, as expected, there was no measurable difference in point of impact regardless of which type of ammunition was being used. There is a difference of only 3 grains in bullet weight, the muzzle velocities differ by only 200 ft/sec, and the bullets all have almost identical ballistic coefficients. This rifle has the accuracy to be a 150-yard pest rifle and the high-velocity necessary to give a sufficiently flat trajectory to that distance.

Being of an experimental frame of mind, I simply had to switch barrels on the 77/17. The aftermarket barrel that I chose is the 22-inch tapered octagonal barrel from Green Mountain Rifle Barrel Company. Since I have always favored rifles of the classic style, I wanted to remove the synthetic stock, but needed a walnut stock to replace it. After consulting with almost everyone who sells aftermarket stocks, I found that most sell aftermarket stocks for almost everything except the Ruger bolt-action rimfires. Where was I to find one but on eBay. Someone had taken the checkered walnut stock off a 77/22M (probably to replace it with something ugly), and I bought it which also necessitated buying a trigger guard assembly. With my special 77/17 complete, I tested the accuracy of CCI 20-grain Game Point and 17-grain Federal V-Shok ammunition. The average group sizes were 0.54 and 0.48 inch, respectively. Groups were tight clusters because the tendency to experience flyers was eliminated. While the accuracy obtained was slightly better with the Green Mountain barrel, the improvement is slight. Was the new barrel worth it? From the point of view of cost, probably not, but as I said, I am an experimentalist. If you have a 77/17 that does not group the way you think it should, try changing the tension on the stock screws before you give up.

The Ruger 77/17 is a trim, attractive, sturdy rifle. It has become on of my most frequent companions when searching for pests to eliminate, but it will never accompany me when squirrel hunting. The bullets are simply too destructive. Do I like the 17 HMR? Absolutely, but it should be used where its tiny bullets at high-velocity are most appropriate.

CZ 452 American (17 HMR)

As part of its rimfire product line, CZ produces several rifles chambered for the 17 HMR. In general, the variations described in the section dealing with the CZ 452 in 22 LR caliber are also available in 17 HMR. Like the 22 LR rifle, the 17 HMR has the barrel threaded into the action, has a beautiful checkered walnut stock, and excellent polishing and bluing of metal parts. It is truly a beautiful sporter, but one could wish that the magazine did not protrude quite so far from the bottom of the stock. Having discussed the operation of the 22 LR version of this rifle, we will proceed directly to the results obtained during accuracy testing.

As in the case of the results from the Ruger 77/17, all types of ammunition gave overall group sizes that differ very little, which is expected since they are all produced by CCI. Any difference is likely due to the small differences that result from different manufacturing lots. The aggregate average group size of only 0.59 inch represents a high degree of accuracy by this fine rifle. I suppose someone will want to compare the results from the Ruger with those from the CZ, but the aggregate average from the CZ being 0.06 inch smaller than that obtained with the Ruger 77/17 is totally insignificant. One flyer expanding a group by about 0.2 inch could account for this difference. For all practical purposes, the Ruger 77/17 and CZ 452 give equal accuracy. The CZ sells for slightly less, but the Ruger comes with a set of rings for scope mounting. A choice between the two rifles might come down to what you want to do with it after you have used it for a while. If you want to tinker with it, the Ruger is more versatile because of the possibility to interchange barrels. The CZ is a fine rifle that is usually found at retail for under $400. There are less expensive 17 HMR caliber rifles available and they may match the accuracy of the CZ. I know no other rifle in its price range that can match both the accuracy and looks of the CZ 452 American.

In this chapter, the results of a great deal of work with some of the current models of rimfire rifles has been presented. No attempt was made to include all of the models available nor would it have been possible to complete such a comprehensive task in one lifetime. However, the rifles selected for study include some of the inexpensive bolt-action and autoloader models as well as some of the higher priced models. In that way, the selection is broad enough to show what to expect in terms of performance from many of the fine rimfire rifles produced by several manufacturers. Not only do the results of the study show the performance of the rifles, but also the characteristics of numerous types of ammunition are clearly seen. If you have not conducted extensive accuracy tests with your rimfire rifle, study the tables shown in this chapter to see just how important the selection of ammunition is. With some different types of ammunition, your favorite rimfire rifle may perform much better than you thought possible.

(Photo courtesy: U. S. Fish and Wildlife Service)

An elegant CZ 452 American in 17 HMR was selected by the author's wife as a rifle for small varmints. It delivered outstanding accuracy.

Accuracy Results for the CZ 452 American with Redfield 3-12X Scope.

Ammunition	Smallest	Group size, inches Largest	Average
CCI Game Point (20 gr.)	0.23	0.84	0.61
CCI TNT	0.54	0.72	0.62
Federal V-Shok	0.35	0.56	0.48
Hornady V-Max	0.39	0.66	0.56
Hornady XTP (20 gr.)	0.27	0.78	0.61
Remington Premier	0.54	0.72	0.68
			Overall Av. 0.59

Chapter 14
SHOOTING SOME VINTAGE RIMFIRE RIFLES

Because rimfire rifles utilize ammunition that is relatively low in power, firing a large number of shots does not produce a lot of wear and tear on the equipment. The majority of rimfire rifles have parts that are robust in view of the size and power of the cartridges they fire. As a result, a good rimfire rifle will literally last for generations if it is given reasonable care. Some models that are no longer available were produced in enormous numbers, and they are widely available as used rifles from a variety of markets. Many of them are by no means worn out, and they are often available at very reasonable prices. In producing this book, it became apparent that while there is an excellent selection of current rimfire models, some attention should be given to a few of the models that have been out of production for a time to see how they perform.

There are rifles and there are special rifles. To the author, the Winchester Model 90 was a true companion many years ago.

The Model 90 inherited by the author is chambered for the 22 Short only.

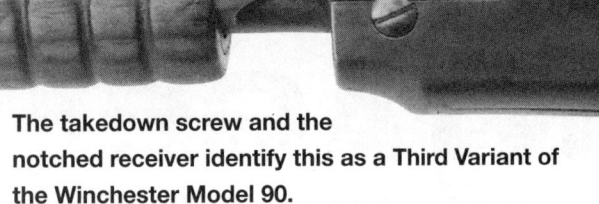

The takedown screw and the notched receiver identify this as a Third Variant of the Winchester Model 90.

In using the term vintage, we mean any rimfire rifle that has not been produced for a few years rather than those that are old enough to be officially called antiques. By so doing, the range of models that could be included is exceedingly large because there have been literally hundreds of different rimfire models produced. This chapter is in no way meant to be encyclopedic in its coverage. The rifles tested are those that are readily available to us from private sources. No attempt was made to obtain rifles from museums or other collections for testing. As a result, the selection of rifles is of necessity limited, but several types of rifles are included. The idea is simply to take several representative rimfire rifles that are in regular service and to present information for some of them that may be useful to a prospective buyer who is searching for a used rifle. The results will provide a basis for comparing some older models to those in current production. It is appropriate to begin the presentation with a discussion of the rifle that started my rimfire experience.

Winchester 90

A large percentage of rimfire shooters have some special rifle with which they identify in a personal way. It may have been their first rifle, one that was a special gift, or one that commemorates some special occasion. For others, it may be the rifle that they grew up with. In my case, it is a rifle that came into the family when I was but a young lad. A great uncle who was a dentist gave the rifle, a Winchester Model 90 pump chambered for the 22 Short, to my father. However, my grandfather thought that his brother must have meant the rifle for him because it went to his house rather than ours. I cannot remember ever seeing my grandfather fire the rifle. I never heard the story of how my great uncle came to have the rifle. He may have had it since younger days or it may have come to him as payment from a patient who could not pay his dental bill.

By the mid-1940s, the rifle had made its way to our house but my father, being a shotgun man, almost never fired the rifle. My brothers and I made up for that. For some reason, the old pump sort of became my rifle in terms of use. From the age of 10 or 12, I carried that rifle an incredible number of miles and hours. After school, the rifle accompanied me to the large tracts of timber that forested the area along a sizeable river. Sometimes, it was with me when I went to the woods to build a little fire and wait for dusk while watching the leaves fall from the trees. Since we lived in a rural (almost remote) area, the meat for the winter was home processed. I became the designated shooter and many hogs were dropped with a single 22 Short to the forehead.

After leaving home and graduating from college, the rifle spent several years with me as my only 22. Eventually, I got another rifle and took the old Winchester pump back to Dad. About three years ago as this is written, Dad passed on and eventually it came time to make arrangements for some of his property. By drawing lots, my oldest brother got the first pick and he took the 20-gauge double gun that had belonged to Dad. I got the second pick, and without hesitation I picked up the Winchester pump. The gun is essentially worn out, but I spent so much time with that rifle in my younger days that I wanted to have it around to pass on to my son sometime. If this story sounds familiar, you are among the very large number of shooters who have a special relationship with some rimfire rifle. If this introduction seems somewhat long, it is because my relationship with this rifle spans three score years.

Introduced in 1890, the Winchester pump was produced until 1941 by which time approximately 750,000 had been made. If not the most famous pump rifle of all time, it is certainly one of the most famous. The serial number on my rifle indicates that it was made in 1920. There were three variants of the Model 90 over the 50 years of its manufacture. The first variant was a solid-frame model, but the second and third variants were takedown models. Receivers of the three models differ in the nature of the breech bolt. The first variant had solid sidewalls with the breech bolt moving back and forth between the walls. The second model had the same type of breech bolt, but it was a takedown model. The third variant had a breech bolt with forward lugs that locked into recesses at the top edges of the receiver sidewalls. Eventually, the Model 90 gave way to the Model 62, which has a similar appearance except for having a round barrel. The Model 62 was produced from 1932 to 1958.

This section is actually about two Winchester Model 90 rifles. The second is one belonging to my brother that is chambered for the 22 Winchester Rim Fire, which was introduced in 1890 with the rifle chambering it. Serial number correlation for this rifle indicates that it was made in 1910.

Like other pump-action rimfire rifles, the Model 90 has a tubular magazine and an external hammer. Operating the slide action moves a cartridge from the magazine while cocking the hammer. Forcing the slide forward moves the cartridge into the chamber. There is no safety except for a safety notch that is engaged by drawing the hammer back slightly. Sights on the Model 90 consist of an open rear sight with a notch and a bead front sight. There is no provision for mounting a scope because the breech bolt rises out of the receiver as it moves backward.

Shooting these vintage Winchesters did not involve a complete set of accuracy tests. Emphasis was on the functioning of the rifles and just plinking at a few targets from a range of 25 yards. Ammunition in 22 Short consisted of CCI, Remington, and Winchester solid high-speed rounds. In 22 WRF, ammunition included the CCI and Winchester loads. These rifles still work and would be suitable for fun and games. Taurus has produced the Model 62 pump rifles that are similar to the Winchester Model 62, and Henry also produces a pump with a visible hammer. Taurus also produces the Model 72 pump that is available in 22 WMR and 17 HMR calibers. The point is, the visible-hammer pump rifle has been an enduring design, and rifles of this type are still available as new guns.

Working with the old Winchester Model 90 that belonged to my father brought back a lot of memories. It was really getting reacquainted with an old friend.

Browning SA-22

One of the most enduring designs in rimfire rifles is the little semiautomatic invented by John M. Browning. Known as the Browning Semi Automatic 22 (or simply the SA-22), it may well be the most slender, streamlined rifle made. There is no tube under the barrel and no magazine that sticks out of the bottom of the action. The SA-22 does make use of a tubular magazine, but it is located in the stock. Other semiautomatic 22s including the Winchester Models 74, 03, and 63 had similar cartridge reservoirs. For many years, the SA-22 was offered in both 22 Short and 22 LR calibers, but only the 22 LR version is currently available. In addition, the SA-22 is a take down model with the barrel being held to the receiver by means of a large knurled ring located at the junction of the barrel and action. Although the Browning SA-22 is still produced by Miroku in Japan, the rifle tested in this work is an older model that was made in Belgium where Fabrique Nationale manufactured this model from 1914 to 1976. It clearly merits vintage status even though there is an

These are two of the fine Browning Semi Automatic rifles that were made in Belgium.

Unlike most autoloading 22s, the Browning Semi Automatic (SA-22) ejects empty cases from the bottom.

Cartridges are loaded through the port in the side of the stock of the SA-22.

equivalent model currently produced.

Unique to the Browning SA-22 is the fact that empty cases are ejected from the bottom of the action. There are no openings on the sides of the receiver. Moving the breech bolt to the rear to load the first cartridge is accomplished by pushing backward on the ridge located on the bottom of the bolt. A port on the right-hand side of the stock allows cartridges to be inserted into the magazine. Turning the flanged end that is located in a recess in the butt plate unlatches the magazine tube. The magazine tube can then be drawn out from the butt plate so that the loading port is open. Magazine capacity of the SA-22 is 11 rounds. The version that is chambered 22 Shorts holds 16 rounds. Weight of the SA-22 is 5 pounds 3 ounces and it measures 37 inches in length. These dimensions make

Elegant touches such as the engraved receiver made the Browning SA-22 one of the most sought after rimfire autoloaders of all time.

it one of the most portable rimfire rifles around.

Operation of the SA-22 is straightforward. After loading, the bolt is pulled back to the rear and released which moves a cartridge from the magazine to the breech. A cross bolt safety is located in the rear part of the trigger guard.

Characteristic of other Browning firearms, the SA-22 is offered in several grades that vary in the extent of engraving and gold inlay work. The suggested price of the SA-22 in Grade I is $519 while the highly ornate Grade VI lists for $1,112. Sights on current production rifles consist of a bead front sight and a folding leaf rear. For many years, the SA-22 has been produced with a grooved receiver for attaching a scope. However, this rifle was intended to be a compact companion in the woods while wearing the sights that came on it. Even the stock design is really more compatible with the use of iron sights.

Shooting the little Browning SA-22 made it clear why this rifle has been considered to be a classic for many years. It is so compact and weighs so little that it is a superb choice for the shooter who wants a 22 for those precious times while traveling light in the woods. Moreover, the fact that it is a takedown model makes it an appropriate choice for travel as long as all regulations are obeyed.

With fit and finish that are outstanding, the Browning SA-22 is a compact, attractive rifle that bespeaks of days gone by. It would not seriously challenge the accuracy of most of the rifles described

The magazine tube in the SA-22 is contained in the stock. The latch is turned which unlocks the tube so it can be drawn out.

in the last chapter, but it doesn't have to. The shooter who selects the SA-22 is going to make the selection based on other criteria. It is in these other areas that the SA-22 is a true classic.

Winchester 190

The Winchester Model 190, an autoloader with a tubular magazine under the barrel, was introduced in 1967 and discontinued in 1980. A deluxe model produced with a stock of higher grade of wood with pressed checkering was known as the Model 290. It was produced from 1963 to 1977. The models 190 and 290 were basically identical except for stock and sights. Accordingly, the Model 190 was basically a plain model introduced after the Model 290 had

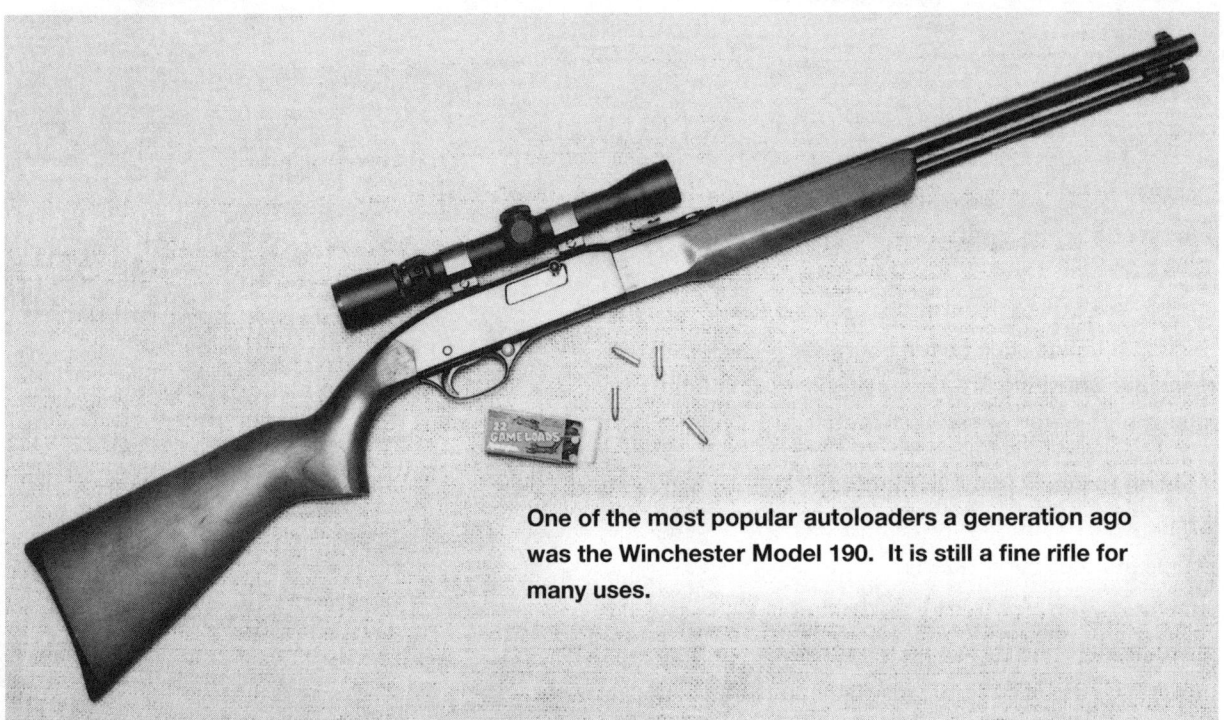

One of the most popular autoloaders a generation ago was the Winchester Model 190. It is still a fine rifle for many uses.

Accuracy Results for the Winchester 190 with a Weaver 2.5-7X Rimfire Scope.

	Group size, inches		
	Smallest	Largest	Average
CCI Standard Velocity	0.36	1.22	0.97
Federal High Velocity H.P.	0.92	1.68	1.31
PMC Scoremaster	0.55	1.48	1.21
Remington Game Load	1.00	1.59	1.23
Wolf Match Target	1.10	2.24	1.75

been in production for several years. The 200 series of rifles also included a lever-action Model 250 and a slide action Model 270, but they were never as popular as the autoloader models. A lever-action Model 255 was chambered for the 22 WMR. Production for the series was well over 2 million units, the majority of them the Model 190 and 290 autoloaders. Because of the sheer number of rifles produced, the Model 190 and 290 are frequently encountered as used rifles. Prices tend to be in the $100 to $150 range depending on condition. I always wanted a Model 190 or 290 in the 1970s but never got one. For some reason, this rifle has always had pleasing lines, but of course this is a subjective judgment.

Operation of the Winchester 190 requires the bolt to be pulled back to the rear and allowed to move forward to load a cartridge in the chamber. The safety is of the cross bolt type, and it is located in the front of the trigger guard. When the bolt is drawn to the rear, pushing the bolt handle inward locks the bolt open although the bolt does not remain open after the last shot. Cocking the rifle and allowing the bolt to go forward facilitate cleaning a Winchester 190. Driving the large plastic pin located above the trigger out of the receiver allows the trigger/hammer group to be removed from the bottom of the receiver. If desired, the breech bolt can be removed (carefully! because of the tension of the recoil spring), but be aware that threading the recoil spring back onto its guide is not always easy to do.

While the Winchester 190 is a competent, dependable rifle, it and others of its general configuration are not known as tack driving machines. In order to get an idea of its accuracy potential, a limited series of tests was performed in which five five-shot groups were fired at 50 yards with a Weaver 2.5-7X Rimfire scope mounted on the rifle. The results are summarized in the accompanying table.

Accuracy of the Winchester 190 is adequate for

This Winchester 69A Target model is a beautiful rifle with classic styling. It was and is an outstanding performer.

The magazine release on the 69A was a recessed button on the left-hand side of the stock. The flush fitting magazine gave the rifle clean lines.

the uses to which a rifle of this type is likely to be put. It has sufficient accuracy for plinking and for hunting small game or pests to ranges of 50 yards or so. It is important to note that with the CCI Standard Velocity ammunition, the average group size was less than one inch, which is quite good for an inexpensive autoloader. The data shown in the table also point the importance of trying several brands and types of ammunition in your rifle if you want to bring out its best accuracy. My tests with many rifles have shown that there seems be a greater difference in accuracy produced by ammunition of different types when in fired autoloaders than when the same types are tested bolt-action rifles. It is interesting to note that the accuracy displayed by the Winchester 190 when using Wolf Match Target ammunition was not as good as with other types. That load has given outstanding accuracy in several other rifles, but for some reason this autoloader did not seem to shoot well with it. On the other hand, my Thompson/Center Classic performs very well with the Wolf ammunition.

The accuracy of the Model 190 is comparable to that of other lightweight autoloaders, lever-actions, and slide-actions. In all of the firing, the rifle proved to be reliable and no malfunctions occurred. While performance of the Model 190 was not spectacular, it is a competent rifle that can sometimes be found at low prices. There does not seem to be much of a demand for the 190 and 290 rifles (and many other older autoloaders), and I am sure that part of the reason is the enormous popularity of the Ruger 10/22 with all of its after market possibilities for customization. The low priced Marlin Model 60 and the Remington Model 597 are also available as new rifles for about the same price as a used Winchester 190 in good condition. Although the Winchester 190 is not my most accurate rifle (or even my most accurate autoloader), I have always had a fondness for this model. Its sleek appearance and the fact that it is a Winchester 22 have made it a favorite plinking rifle for me. If you want to obtain a Winchester 190 or 290, it should not difficult because with over 2 million produced they are seen in racks of used guns.

Winchester 69A

The idea of a bolt-action rifle that offers a high level of performance at a reasonable price has been an attractive one for many years, and numerous models were introduced over the years to meet the demand. One of the most successful of these was the Winchester 69 and 69A. The Model 69 cocked on closing the bolt while the 69A cocked as the bolt was opened. The action of the 69A is superb. The fit and finish of the bolt were very good. In fact, the action was identical to that used on the Model 75 Sporting and Target rifles. The Model 69 remained in the catalogs from 1935 to 1963 with a total of 355,363 rifles being produced. Good used Model 69s are not hard to find, but while I bought mine new in the mid-1950s for about $32, used specimens now sell for around $275 and up. The reason is simple. The Winchester 69A offered and still offers outstanding accuracy. In terms of performance, a 69A can hold its own with the majority of 22s produced today.

In addition to the open-sighted model, target and match versions of the Winchester 69A were produced that had a hooded ramp front sight and a peep sight. They were budget priced target rifles for beginning shooters or club use. Rifles produced late in the production period had grooved receivers for mounting a scope.

The Winchester Model 69A made use of a five-shot detachable box magazine that was released by pushing inward on a recessed metal button on the left hand side of the stock. Optional 10-round magazines were also available. Barrel length on the Model 69A was 25 inches and weight was approximately six pounds. The walnut stock was generally of good quality with full-size dimensions.

Although the author no longer has a Winchester 69A in the cabinet, a brother does. This rifle is a beautiful target specimen that has a Lyman peep sight attached. For testing, a BSA 3-12X airgun scope was mounted on the rifle. The temperature was around the 30-degree mark with a rather stiff breeze at 10 o'clock. Only limited testing of the Winchester Model 69A was conducted because the conditions were hardly ideal for shooting groups. In spite of the weather when Wolf Match Target ammunition was used, five five-shot groups measured in the range 0.53 to 0.78 inch with an average size of 0.63 inch. With Federal Gold Medal Target, the average group size was slightly more than an inch, and it was around that with other types of ammunition. What would the 69A give on an ideal day using the most compatible ammunition? I do not know, but this rifle can definitely hold its own with the majority of bolt action sporters produced today except perhaps for some of the very expensive models. We can only hope that Winchester will see fit to once again produce a rifle to replace the 69A and the Model 320 described later in this chapter.

Ithaca Saddle Gun

The 22 LR caliber long gun in terms of length of production is the lever-action Marlin Model 39A and its predecessor. Probably the most famous name in lever-action rifles is that of Winchester. The newcomer among the producers of lever-action rimfires is Henry whose factory is located in

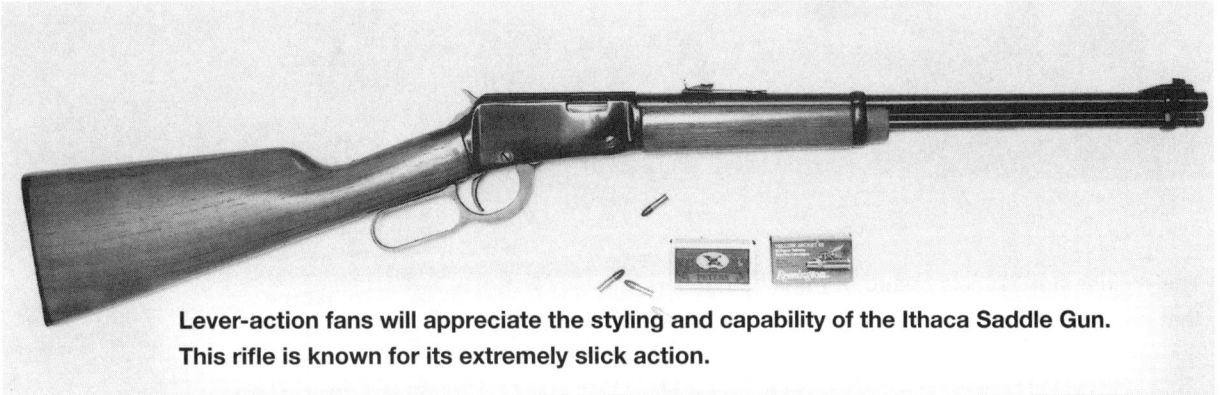

Lever-action fans will appreciate the styling and capability of the Ithaca Saddle Gun. This rifle is known for its extremely slick action.

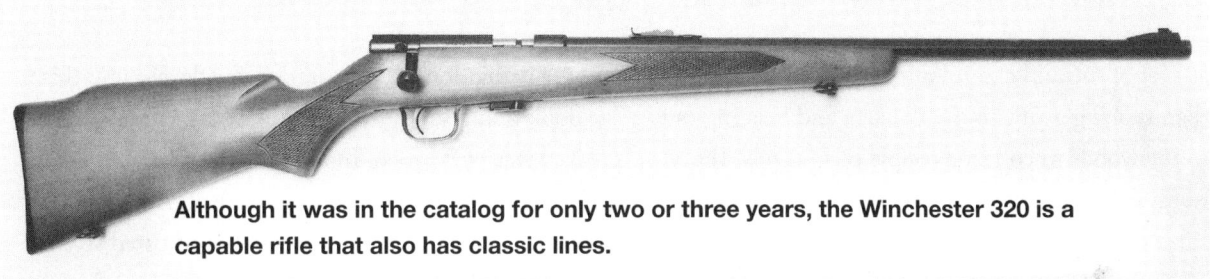

Although it was in the catalog for only two or three years, the Winchester 320 is a capable rifle that also has classic lines.

Brooklyn, NY. With all these other players in the game, you may be surprised to find that none other than Ithaca, the famous maker of shotguns, marketed one of the slickest lever-action rimfires although Erma Werke in Germany produced the rifle. A lever-action look alike was known as the Model 49, but it was actually a single-shot rifle. A fake magazine tube under the barrel was merely a cosmetic feature. The lever behind the trigger actually operated a falling block that allowed a single round to be loaded (this is known as a Martini-type action). Produced from 1961-1978, the Model 49 had a visible hammer and the appearance of a lever-action repeater, but looks can be deceiving.

Produced from 1973 to 1978, the Ithaca Model 72 Saddle Gun has an 18.5-inch barrel and a tubular magazine below the barrel. The rifles were available in both 22 LR and 22 WMR calibers. A deluxe version having an octagon barrel and a silver-colored receiver was produced for a couple of years in the mid-1970s.

Most of the features of the Ithaca Model 72 are characteristic of other lever-actions. It has a full-length tubular magazine under the barrel and a hammer with a safety notch but no other safety. Operation is simply a down-then-up swing of the lever to eject an empty case, cock the hammer, and move a cartridge into the chamber. That operation with the Ithaca 72 is unbelievably smooth and positive. The rifle operated flawlessly. It is a pleasant rifle to shoot and would make a nearly ideal rifle for plinking and hunting small game for the shooter who prefers a lever-action rifle.

Although the Ithaca 72 has been out of production for many years, the currently produced Henry is a very similar rifle. If you examine a collectible Ithaca that isn't for sale or the price of this collectible is too steep, get a Henry. It is also a fine rifle (see Chapter 13).

Winchester 320

While the Winchester 69A offered excellent performance in an inexpensive sporting rifle in a bygone era, the demand for bolt-action rifles was decreasing. Autoloaders had become the hot tickets

The Winchester 320 is a beautifully finished rifle that has a magazine that fits almost flush with the bottom of the stock.

as rate of fire and can rolling became more common than tucking a rifle under the arm and heading out to the woods to collect a couple of squirrels. The result was that not many new bolt action rimfire rifles were introduced in the turbulent times of the 1960s and 1970s and most were none too successful. One rifle that was introduced was a real gem known as the Winchester Model 320. The Model 320 has a walnut stock that is very well shaped and has pressed checkering and sling swivels. This slick bolt-action rifle made use of a five-shot magazine that has a magazine release located behind the magazine itself. A grooved receiver made attaching a scope a simple proposition. The polishing and bluing on the Model 320 is excellent for a rifle that was a relatively inexpensive model. The trigger guard assembly is especially beautifully shaped and polished.

The factory sights consist of an adjustable rear sight and a bead front sight on a ramp. Produced only from 1971 to 1974, the total production was very small for a rimfire rifle. A single shot Model 310 was also available. In the early 1970s, the Model 320 was available for $57.95 and it was a bargain. Used rifles are now seen priced in the $300 range. When one considers that a new Ruger or CZ bolt action of comparable quality retails for $350 to $450, it does not seem that the price of a Model 320 is too outrageous.

It was only as the enormous amount of testing was being done in preparation for developing this book that a serious evaluation of my Winchester 320 was performed. In order to see what this rifle was capable of, I mounted a 6-20x40 AO Cabela's Outfitter scope, and the scope was adjusted so that the shots hit near the point of aim at 50 yards. After selecting the ammunition to be fired, the initial firing was carried out with the Wolf Match Target. With the high magnification of the Cabela's scope, it was possible to see the holes as they appeared in the target and even watch some of the bullets in flight. As usual, five five-shot groups were fired. What is this? My, the groups look small! When the groups were measured, it was found that they were 0.87, 0.48, 0.76, 0.95, and 0.58 inches with an average group size of only 0.73 inches! And now you see why the Winchester Model 320 is still a very desirable rifle. It follows in the tradition of the Model 69A and Model 75 sporters that are well known for their accuracy. A summary of the accuracy data obtained using several types of ammunition in the Model 320 is shown in the following table.

As the data show, the Winchester Model 320 that went out of production in 1974 is an extremely accurate rifle. One of the most publicized rimfire rifles in recent years is the Remington 504 and rightfully so. From data presented in all of the published tests on that rifle, and I have read almost all of them, it appears that the Winchester 320 will match the accuracy of the Remington 504. Please do not misunderstand. The Remington is a fine, accurate sporter that offers outstanding performance, but so is the Winchester 320. Just so you do not think that I am singling out the Remington, it should be mentioned that the performance of my Winchester 320 almost exactly duplicates that of my Ruger 77/22 and that of my wife's CZ 452. All of these bolt-action models offer outstanding performance and appearance. However, if you already have one of these models, don't rush out to get one of the others thinking that you are going to obtain a quantum leap in accuracy.

At the time of testing the Model 320, approximately 35 to 40 types of ammunition were on hand. There simply wasn't time to test every type of ammunition in all of the rifles so some selection had to be made. The Winchester 320 was not tested with some of the very low-end ammunition with which it probably would not perform quite as well. It should be noted that the ammunition tested does include some of the high-velocity hunting types.

It is the opinion of this author that there has been an increase in interest in high-performance rimfire rifles. The fine Ruger 77/22 has been available since 1984. Although some very accurate autoloaders are available, the production of bolt-action rifles like the Remington 504, Kimber 82, CZ 452, Anschutz 1416,

Accuracy Results for the Winchester 320 with 6-20X Cabela's Outfitter Scope.

Ammunition	Group size, inches		
	Smallest	Largest	Average
CCI Green Tag	0.50	0.82	0.68
CCI SGB	0.70	1.02	0.85
CCI Standard Velocity	0.48	0.80	0.72
CCI Velocitor	0.79	2.21	1.39
Eley Target	0.44	1.19	0.88
Federal Target (711B)	0.62	0.84	0.76
Federal Ultra Match	0.58	0.88	0.76
Lapua Super Club	0.36	0.84	0.67
Remington Target	0.61	1.04	0.85
Winchester Power Point	0.63	0.95	0.81
Winchester Super-X H.P.	0.51	0.90	0.81
Winchester Supreme	0.55	1.17	0.82
Winchester T-22	0.64	1.37	1.00
Wolf Match Target	0.48	0.95	0.73
		Overall Av.	0.84

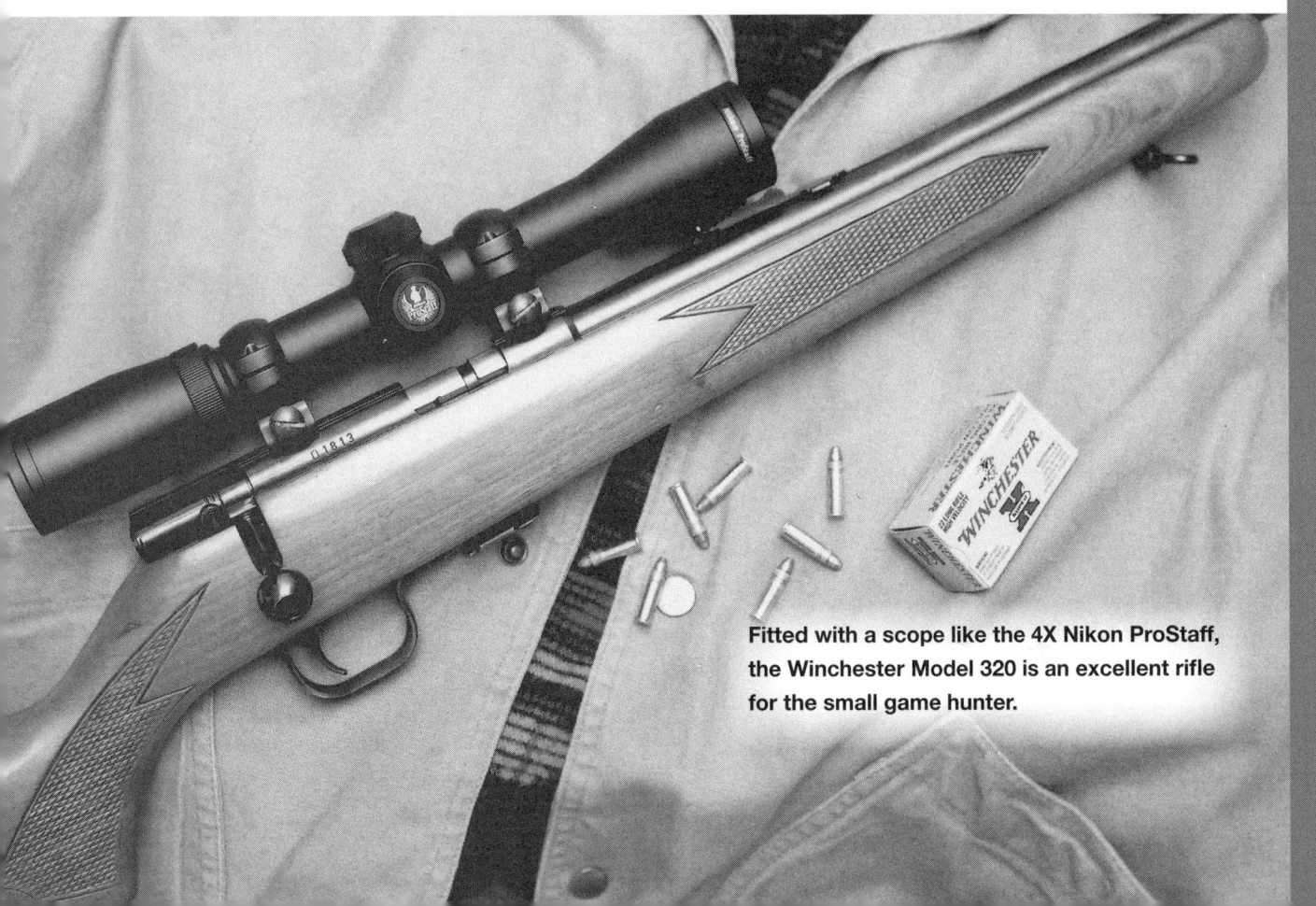

Fitted with a scope like the 4X Nikon ProStaff, the Winchester Model 320 is an excellent rifle for the small game hunter.

Sako Finnfire, and others indicates that the classic rimfire sporting rifle is not dead. It is my fervent hope that Winchester will once again produce a bolt-action model to join this elite group, and this wish has been expressed to the appropriate personnel. A brief reintroduction of the classic Winchester 52 Sporting Rifle was made in 1993 with a copy made in Japan, but I am talking about a model that would compare to the Model 75 Sporter or the Model 320 described here. I believe that such a rifle selling in the $400 to $500 range would capture a significant segment of the market. The bottom line is that the Winchester 320 showed that it could hold its own with most other rimfire sporting rifles produced today.

Daisy 2201, 2202, and 2203

The Daisy name is one of the most widely recognized names in the shooting sports. The only problem is, it is always associated with airguns. However, it has not always been so. Daisy Manufacturing Company (now known as Daisy Outdoor Products) entered the field of firearm production in 1968 with the introduction of the VL system that used caseless ammunition. A small cylinder of solid propellant was attached to the base of the bullet, and it was ignited upon firing by a blast of compressed air. Although the rifles firing caseless ammunition were discontinued quickly, the air compression system became the basis for the Daisy PowerLine 880 air rifle that was introduced in 1972.

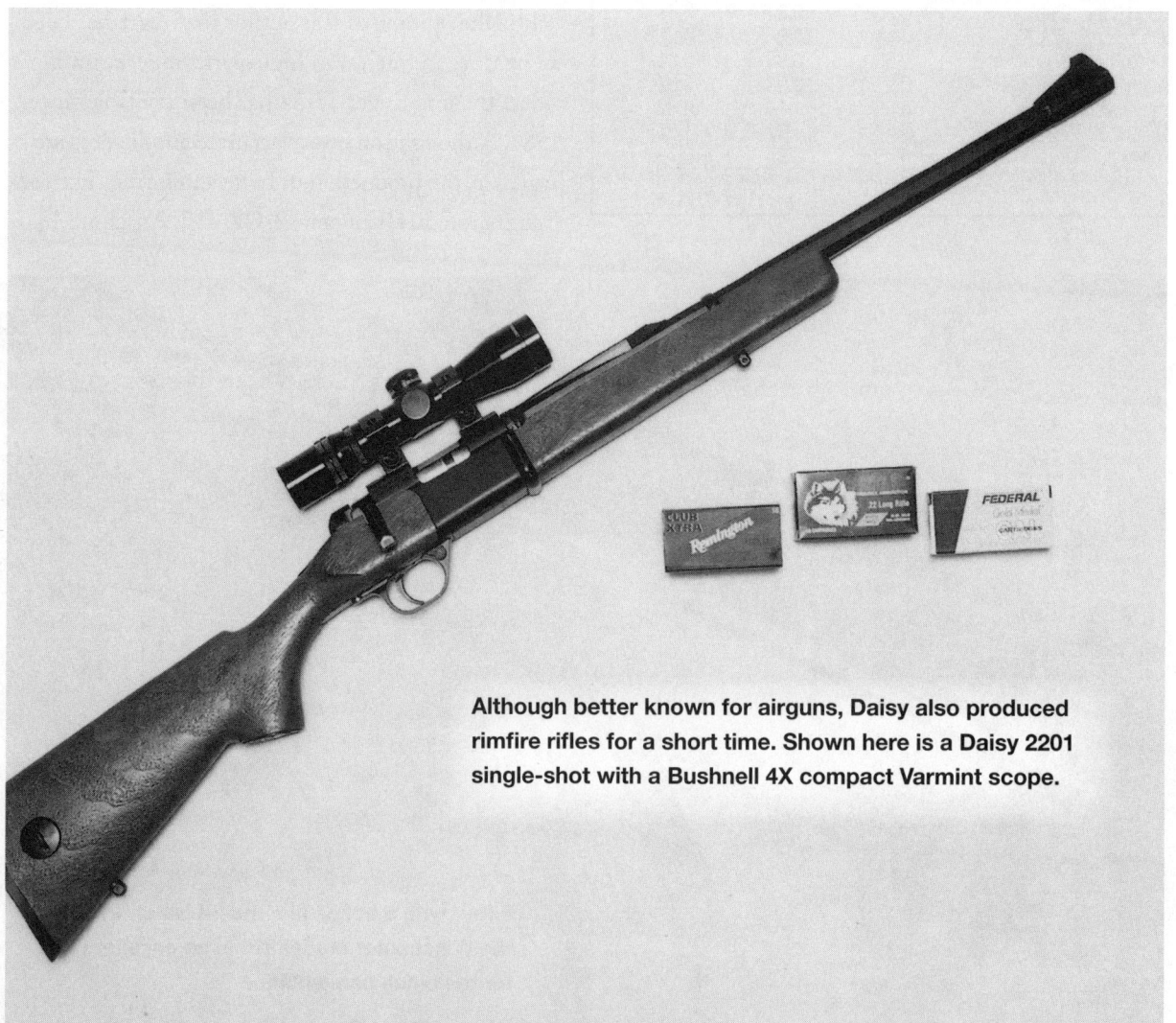

Although better known for airguns, Daisy also produced rimfire rifles for a short time. Shown here is a Daisy 2201 single-shot with a Bushnell 4X compact Varmint scope.

When disassembled, the Daisy 2201 consists of three major parts. The front swivel stud attaches the forearm to the barrel.

That model was Daisy's first multi-pump air rifle. However, it is not the VL system or air rifle that is of interest here.

In 1987, Daisy bought parts for a small single-shot bolt-action 22 rimfire from Iver Johnson. The assembled rifle was known as the Daisy Model '08, and it was sold through Wal-Mart stores. About 30,000 units were marketed. In 1988, Daisy reentered the firearm field with the introduction of three models known as the Legacy, which included a bolt-action single-shot, a bolt-action repeater using a rotary magazine holding 10 rounds, and a semiautomatic that uses a detachable magazine that holds seven rounds stacked. There were, in fact, two versions of each of the models that differed in the type of stock material.

The Models 2201 and 2211 were the single-shot rifles with polymer and hardwood stocks, respectively. The Models 2202 and 2212 were the bolt-action repeaters, and the 2203 and 2213 were the autoloaders with stock materials designated as in the case of the single-shot models. All of the models have two-piece stocks that have studs for attaching sling swivels, and all of the models were discontinued in 1991.

The Daisy Legacy rifles have a number of unique features. For example, the barrels consisted of a steel inner barrel

A flange that is threaded into the receiver pulls the barrel into the action.

encased in a black composite material that has an octagonal surface. The barrels are held to the receiver by means of a knurled locking nut that engages a flange on the breech end of the barrel. The locking nut which screws into the receiver has four holes in the knurled surface of its outside edge that allow a special wrench to be used to turn the locking ring. On the bolt-action models, the forearm is held to the barrel by means of the front swivel stud.

The Daisy Legacy autoloader models have no bolt handle for cycling the action. A rod that is attached to the bolt protrudes from the front end of the forearm. Pushing the rod backward forces the action open. A similar arrangement has been used over the years on a number of autoloaders, both rimfire and center fire. For example, the actions on the Winchester Models 03 and 63 were cycled in this way.

A choice of hardwood or plastic stock models was offered for the Daisy rimfires. One unique feature of the plastic stocked versions is that pressing inward on a large button on the right hand side of the stock and pulling the butt plate outward can change the stock length. The front sight is molded as part of the composite barrel shroud. The rear sight is fully adjustable in a unique way. Elevation is adjusted by loosening a screw and sliding the rear sight forward or backward on a stepless inclined ramp. The sight blade can be moved laterally to adjust windage after a locking screw is loosened. The receiver is made of die cast metal and has grooves for attaching scope mounts. While many of these features themselves are unique, there is more. The entire trigger assembly can be removed by pressing upward on a button located just behind the trigger guard and sliding the trigger assembly down and backward. The sear serves as the bolt stop so the bolt can be slid out after the trigger assembly is removed.

In order to see what the Daisy Legacy would produce in terms of accuracy, I mounted a BSA 3-12X airgun scope on my Daisy 2202. Firing was conducted at 50 yards with Wolf Match Target ammunition, which has shown outstanding accuracy in a variety of other rifles. My Daisy gave groups that averaged 1.5-inches! Other types of ammunition gave groups in the 1.5- to 2.0-inch range which is not bad considering that this very light weight, small rifle is a take-down model. Daisy rimfire rifles were intended for use as plinking rifles. If I were to restrict my shots to 40 to 50 yards, the Daisy could also be used for hunting and pest shooting. Prices for used Daisy Legacy rifles have escalated in recent years, as they have become collectibles.

Remington 541T

There has been so much written about the new Remington 504 bolt-action sporter that it might be possible to overlook some of the other fine sporting rifles that Remington produced over the years. To this author, one of the most elegant was the Model 541, which was available as the 541S sporter and the 541T target model. The major difference between the two versions is in the stock. The stock on the 541T was made with a target styling and without some of the embellishments found on the sporter. For example, the 541S has a forearm tip and grip cap made of dark colored rosewood. It also has a beautiful checkering pattern on the grip and forearm.

Mechanical features of the target and sporter models are identical. Most notable are the multiple lug lockup at the middle of the bolt and the outstanding trigger. A crisp, light let off characterizes the trigger action that initiates a very fast lock time. This makes for controllable, predictable firing. A five-shot detachable box magazine was employed that sometimes drew condemnation because it was made of plastic. The fact that it did not fit flush with the bottom of the stock did not endear it to many critics. Barrel length is 24 inches on either model. Both versions of the Remington 541 are drilled and tapped to accept scope bases, but the receiver is not grooved.

During the firing tests, the chamber was loaded in single shot fashion. It was noted that some types of ammunition were difficult to load because of the

The Remington 541 is a beautiful sporter that is also well known for accuracy.

very tight chamber that has dimensions of a target rifle.

It was particularly difficult to single load CCI Green Tag rounds in the rifle.

The rifle tested belongs to a nephew of the author and was purchased as a new rifle. It is clearly marked 541T on the barrel but has the elegant stock of the 541S sporter. A call to Remington showed that the serial number of the rifle corresponds to a 541T, but the stock is not of the target type. The sporter models are normally marked 541S. Several possible scenarios were given as to how the barrel marking and the stock are at variance, but the actual reason is not known. However, it is not a major issue because the barrel and action of the 541T and 541S are identical, and it is only the stock that makes one the target version while the other is a sporter. The rifle being discussed is clearly the sporter and will be called a 541S regardless of which model number is on the barrel.

Fit and finish of the Remington 541S are outstanding. Highly polished and deeply blued, the barrel and action are beautifully finished. The stock has the high gloss finish like that found on centerfire models like those in the 700 BDL series. No sights adorn the barrel because the rifle is intended to be used with a scope attached.

Firing of the Remington 541S was conducted with a 3-9X Leupold Vari-X II scope attached. The temperature was approximately 30 degrees and there was a 5 to 10 mph wind blowing from 10 o'clock. The weather offered very difficult conditions under which to test accuracy, but some five-shot groups were obtained on targets at a range of 50 yards. It was found that Wolf Match Target, CCI Green Tag, and Federal Gold Medal Target gave average group sizes of around an inch, but these results do not indicate the true capability of this fine rifle. With the most compatible ammunition, the Remington 541S should produce groups of about half that size.

Produced from 1986 until 1999, the Remington 541S has long been one of my favorite sporting rifles. Although the author has not tested a Remington 504, several specimens have been examined, and the 541S seems to be a more elegant rifle. It would be even more elegant in appearance if the plastic magazine did not protrude from the bottom of the stock. If I had my choice between a new Remington 504 and a new 541S, I would choose the 541S. It is that good.

The plastic magazine that protrudes from the bottom of the stock is one feature that many lovers of the Model 541 could do without.

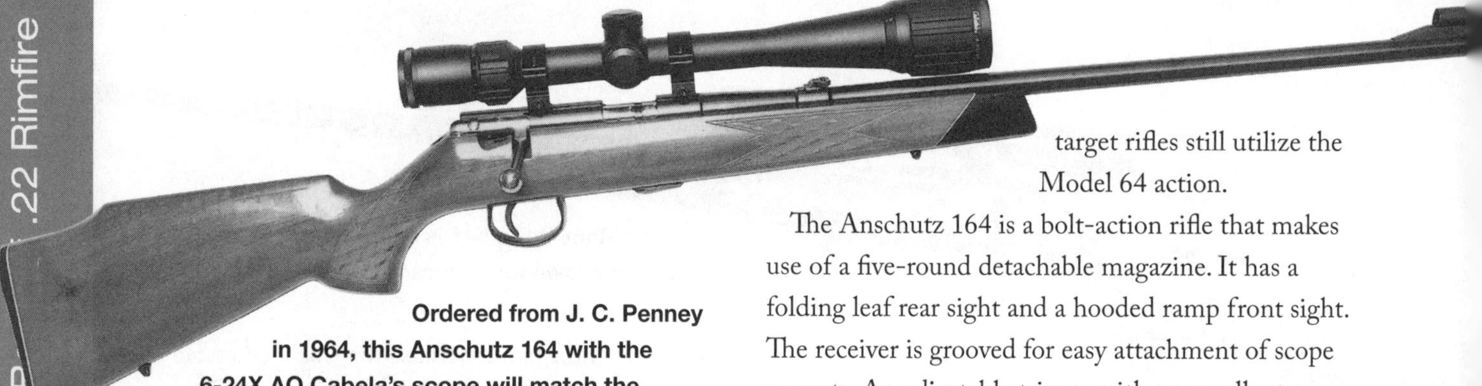

Ordered from J. C. Penney in 1964, this Anschutz 164 with the 6-24X AO Cabela's scope will match the performance of almost any rimfire produced today.

Anschutz 164

In the 1960s, an agreement was reached between Anschutz GmbH of Ulm, Germany and the Savage Arms Corporation under which Savage would market Anschutz rifles in the U.S. In 1964, it was possible to order the Anschutz Model 164 from J. C. Penney. The rifle, a small-tube scope, and a padded case constituted a package for which the price was $87. Having only a very inexpensive bolt-action rifle at that time that did not shoot at all well, I ordered an Anschutz 164. Several Anschutz sporters and target rifles still utilize the Model 64 action.

The Anschutz 164 is a bolt-action rifle that makes use of a five-round detachable magazine. It has a folding leaf rear sight and a hooded ramp front sight. The receiver is grooved for easy attachment of scope mounts. An adjustable trigger with an excellent crisp let off is another desirable feature. The stock is of European walnut and has a skip line checkering pattern on the grip and forearm, and the tip of the forearm is made of a contrasting dark wood. An Anschutz 164 is a handsome sporting rifle in all respects.

The Model 164 was available for only a few years before the Model 1416 replaced it. Of course, the Gun Control Act of 1968 meant the end of ordering firearms from Sears, J. C. Penney, or Montgomery Ward, and the changing socioeconomic climate led to the termination of firearm sales by such stores. Gone are the store brands like J. C. Higgins and

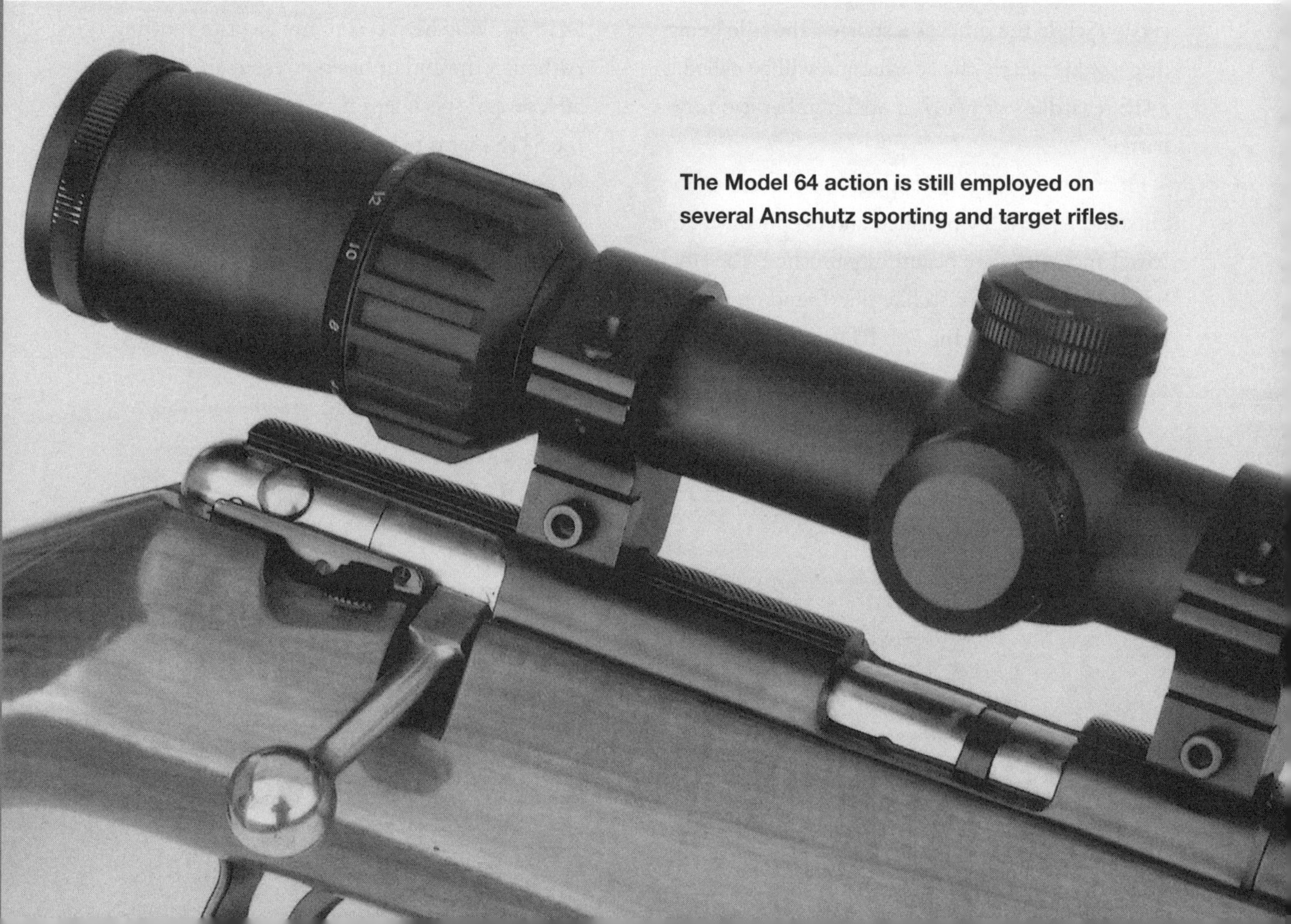

The Model 64 action is still employed on several Anschutz sporting and target rifles.

Ted Williams from Sears and the Western Field brand from Montgomery Ward. In fact, gone is Montgomery Ward.

As I was growing up, the Winchester Model 52 was the finest target rifle available for rimfire competition. It was with a Model 52D that I competed as a member of an Air Force ROTC team that established an enviable record. However, inroads were being made into the Model 52's dominance, and those inroads were being made by Anschutz among others. The Winchester Model 52 has been out of production since about 1979. Now, Anschutz is a dominant force in the production of rimfire rifles for formal competition at the highest levels. All this is meant simply to point out that the Anschutz name on any rifle carries with it the connotation of high performance.

I was always impressed with how a bullet from the Anschutz 164 always went where it was supposed to when I did my part. Strange as it may seem, comprehensive accuracy tests were never conducted with the rifle until it became necessary to assemble data for this book. At that point, a Cabela's Outfitter 6-20X scope was mounted on the rifle. With several types of target and match ammunition, the Anschutz delivered ragged holes measuring about one half inch. This rifle will hold its own against most of the sporting rifles produced today and will give better accuracy than some that cost considerably more.

Although it would have been interesting to test a large number of rimfire rifles from the past, one must work with the tools and time available. Hopefully, this chapter will give some appreciation of the level of accuracy of a variety of rifles as well as their features and operating procedures. If you have an older rimfire rifle that you would like to shoot, make sure that it is safe and that everything works as it should. Try several types of ammunition, and you may find that the performance you desire from a rimfire rifle has been in the gun cabinet all along.

Long known for rifles having outstanding fit and finish, the gleaming trigger guard and floor plate of this Model 164 reflect traditional Anschutz quality.

Chapter 15

EVALUATIONS OF SOME CURRENT RIMFIRE HANDGUNS

Rimfire handguns are among the most popular firearms in the world. One of the reasons for this popularity is that shooting a rimfire handgun is just plain fun. Another is that one can use a rimfire handgun to build skill that transfers to a different firearm for hunting or protection. The versatility of a rimfire handgun has been explored in other chapters of this book. However, an additional factor to consider is that it is possible to do a great deal of shooting for a modest amount of money after the handgun has been purchased.

As has been explained elsewhere in this book, the global term "handgun" applies to any short firearm that can be operated with one hand. When such firearms were single-shot muzzle-loading pieces, the term pistol seems to have been applied, but it was later applied to double-barreled handguns and eventually to those with multiple chambers. It is not inappropriate to use the term pistol in a general way rather than just applying it to semiautomatic handguns. The issue is rather like applying the term "long gun" only to shotguns since the traditional use of the word "gun" was applied only to one having a smooth bore. Moreover, the term "gun control" is now applied in some circles to airguns, which are not even firearms!

A rimfire autoloader such as the Smith & Wesson 2206 (left) enables a shooter to practice with a firearm of the same general type as a centerfire such as the Smith & Wesson 4506 (right).

The number of types of rimfire handguns that are available from all of the manufacturers is large. The number of variants of all these models is enormous. In any project of reasonable size that is to be completed in one lifetime, the number of pieces studied must of necessity be limited. A phrase used by football coaches is "going with what got us here" and in this case it means using handguns that are readily available. As a result, a limited number of handguns were evaluated but with the notion that these models are representative of the available selection.

Accuracy

Someone has said that it is not necessary to eat a whole pie in order to tell if is delicious. In the same way, it is not necessary to fire a large number of groups each consisting of many shots in order to assess the overall performance of a handgun. One of the reasons is that the accuracy obtained from any handgun is dependent on the ability of the shooter to a far greater degree than it is with a rifle. The author has had only one eye that performed anywhere near normal for most of his lifetime. In recent months, the deterioration of the gel lining of the good eye has deteriorated leaving large lumps of gelatinous material that result in blurring in certain areas of vision. This can be compensated for when testing rifles by making use of a scope of high magnification and a steady rest, but it is really hampers accurate shooting of a handgun.

Vision is only one factor in firing a handgun with the ultimate accuracy as a goal. The size of the shooter's hands, the size and shape of the grip, and the quality of the trigger action all enter into the picture. In this work, it was deemed appropriate to fire each handgun with several types ammunition in order to test the functioning and general handling characteristics of each gun. To determine the true accuracy potential, it is necessary to use a machine rest or mount a scope on the handgun. The inherent accuracy of many handguns is impressive, but most shooters cannot approach this level of accuracy without the use of a scope. Perhaps this is why an increasing number of handguns wear scopes and some models are sold with rails permanently attached for mounting a scope. Because a handgun moves at the moment the sear is released, trigger action is vital

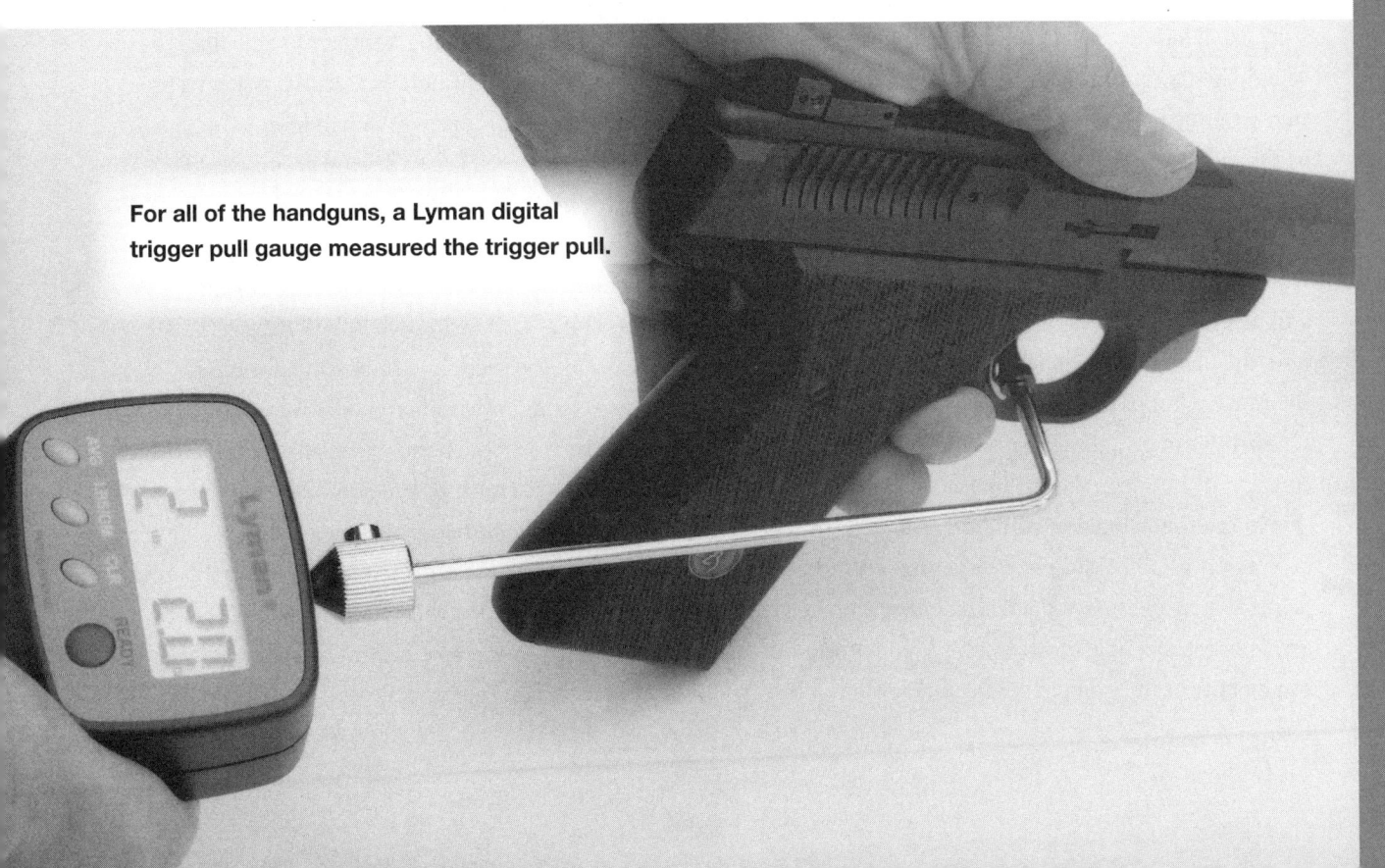

For all of the handguns, a Lyman digital trigger pull gauge measured the trigger pull.

Testing the accuracy of a handgun requires better sights than the usual open sights. In this case, a Weaver 1.5-4X handgun scope was mounted on a Smith & Wesson 22A.

to determining consistent accuracy. For the pistols tested, the trigger pull was measured by means of a Lyman Digital Trigger Pull gauge.

When a handgun is fired, even one with recoil as light as that produced by a rimfire cartridge, the muzzle jumps. To allow for this movement of the gun as the bullet is moving down the bore, the sights do not "look" along the same line as the line of the bore. In fact, the bore points below the line of sight so that when the muzzle rises during recoil the bullet path will meet the line of sight at the target. Consequently, how the handgun is gripped will affect how much the muzzle jumps and where the bullet strikes. Uniformity in gripping the pistol is essential to consistent shooting. The author once demonstrated this in the following way while shooting a Smith & Wesson K-38 Masterpiece target revolver. After firing several sighting shots with hands propped across a rest, a couple of shots were fired with the square butt of the grip resting firmly on the top of the bench. This prevented the muzzle from rising in a normal way, and the shots hit two or three inches lower than the previous group, which has nothing to do with the outstanding accuracy of this fine handgun. A consistent hold is essential when trying to produce small groups with a handgun.

To begin the tests, I fired several groups at 25 yards with my 18-year-old Browning Buck Mark. Firing with my hands propped across a rest, the groups measured about 2 to 2.5 inches with the smallest being 1.19 inches when Winchester T22 ammunition was used. It is impossible for me to shoot any handgun with better accuracy than that because I can't see any better. Similar results were obtained with a Smith & Wesson 22A. Are the handguns capable of better accuracy? Most assuredly!

To demonstrate these principles, a Weaver 1.5-4X Classic handgun scope was mounted on the scope rail of a Smith & Wesson 22A using the new Weaver Quad Lock rings. The process took all of a minute

With a Weaver 1.5-4X handgun scope attached, the Browning Buck Mark delivered outstanding accuracy.

or so because the S&W 22A has a permanently attached scope rail. It took a few shots to get the points of aim and impact close together but the process was simple because the adjustments on the scope worked perfectly. After sighting in, the first five-shot group at 25 yards with Winchester T22 ammunition measured 0.68 inches! Immediately it became apparent that in order for me to do accurate shooting with any handgun it must be fitted with a scope. It is such a realization that shows why the sizes of groups reported from testing handguns are relatively meaningless in many cases. Consider taking a rifle that is incredibly accurate and testing ammunition by firing groups at 50 yards using open sights. In such a case, what is being tested is the sighting ability (vision) of the shooter, not the accuracy of the rifle. Knowing this, I have elected not to fire groups with each of the handguns described and to report groups size as some sort of indication of the accuracy potential of these guns. Only if the sighting error is minimized with a scope would such data be meaningful. The discussion will be more directly concerned with other characteristics.

Having made that decision; let me return to describing the true accuracy potential of two handguns. The first is the Smith & Wesson 22A described above. During an extended period of testing, it became apparent that applying a firm, uniform grip for such a long period of time caused my hand to become fatigued and shaky. In general, the groups showed an increase in size the longer the shooting continued even with the same type of ammunition. By looking through the scope and trying to keep the crosshairs in place, the increase in shaking was obvious. Even with this problem, the average size of five-shot groups using Wolf Match Target ammunition was only 0.69 inches at a range of 25 yards. With CCI Standard Velocity, the groups averaged almost exactly one inch in size and with Federal Match Target the average was slightly over an inch. Interestingly, the groups were fired in that order, and the increase in group size is the result of fatigue in the shooting hand. My wife took the S&W 22A and fired three five-shot groups with Federal

High Velocity hollow-points with the first measuring only 0.39 inch. As she continued firing, there was a general increase in group size.

What is the ultimate accuracy of the Smith & Wesson 22A? With one group measuring only 0.39 inches and the average of three others being only 0.69 inches (before hand fatigue became a problem) it must surely be around half an inch or less at 25 yards with some types of ammunition. Even by testing in this way the ultimate accuracy has not been determined, but this is a very accurate pistol. Having never cared for scopes on handguns, it was now clear that one would be required if I ever wanted to do accurate shooting with a handgun.

The next experiments were conducted with a Browning Buck Mark after mounting the Weaver 1.5-4X scope on it. In order to mount a scope on the Buck Mark it is first necessary to attach a scope rail. The rail used was one produced by B-Square, and it can be attached after removing the rear sight and top strap on the action. The rail mounts along the top of the frame and is attached by removing two large screws, one that holds the top of the barrel to the front end of the frame and the other that is located at the rear of the frame. With the scope rail placed on top of the frame, the screws are replaced to attach it.

Firing a few shots allowed the scope to be sighted in and testing was initiated. Groups with Federal Gold Medal Target measured approximately an inch for five shots at 25 yards. Groups obtained using CCI Green Tag were similar in size. Switching to Wolf Match Target produce groups measuring 0.79 and 0.91 inches. The Buck Mark is capable of even better accuracy, but shooting conditions were not ideal at the time of the tests. Once again it was demonstrated that the accuracy shown by any handgun is dependent on the ability to achieve a steady, consistent rest and grip. The Browning Buck Mark demonstrated a level of accuracy that would make it a superb choice for a small game hunter who goes afield with a handgun. Based on later tests,

additional information on the accuracy of this fine pistol will be given in the next section.

The accuracy demonstrated by scoped handguns is truly remarkable when compared to the limited accuracy indicated by firing them with conventional open sights. A Ruger Mark II 22/45 with a 5.5-inch bull barrel belonging to my brother has a 2X Bushnell scope mounted. With it he has produced 7/8-inch 10-shot groups at 25 yards using the bulk-pack Federal High Velocity hollow-points. When five-shot groups are fired, even smaller groups are regularly obtained. This combination has become his choice when hunting squirrels with a handgun.

With scopes attached, the three handguns described will regularly give groups that measure well under an inch at 25 yards. Does this level of accuracy show the ultimate capability of these models? Not at all. They were fired without the aid of a machine rest and as the pull on the trigger approaches three or four pounds, the movement of the crosshairs on the target shows the shaking clearly. After conducting the tests described in this section, I believe that most of the handguns described in this chapter are capable of groups that measure no more than half an inch or so. That is why the usual procedure of shooting several groups and reporting average group sizes was not followed in determining some level of accuracy that does not represent anything but a vision and hand test.

Browning Buck Mark

Introduced in 1985, a Browning Buck Mark has been in regular use by the author since soon after that time. The Buck Mark is the culmination of a series of semiautomatic pistols that included the Nomad and Challenger models from the 1960s and 1970s. The Challenger went through several versions designated as Challenger I, II, and III. With the introduction of the Buck Mark in 1985, the Challenger III was discontinued.

The Buck Mark Standard originally had black composite grips, which gave way to grips made

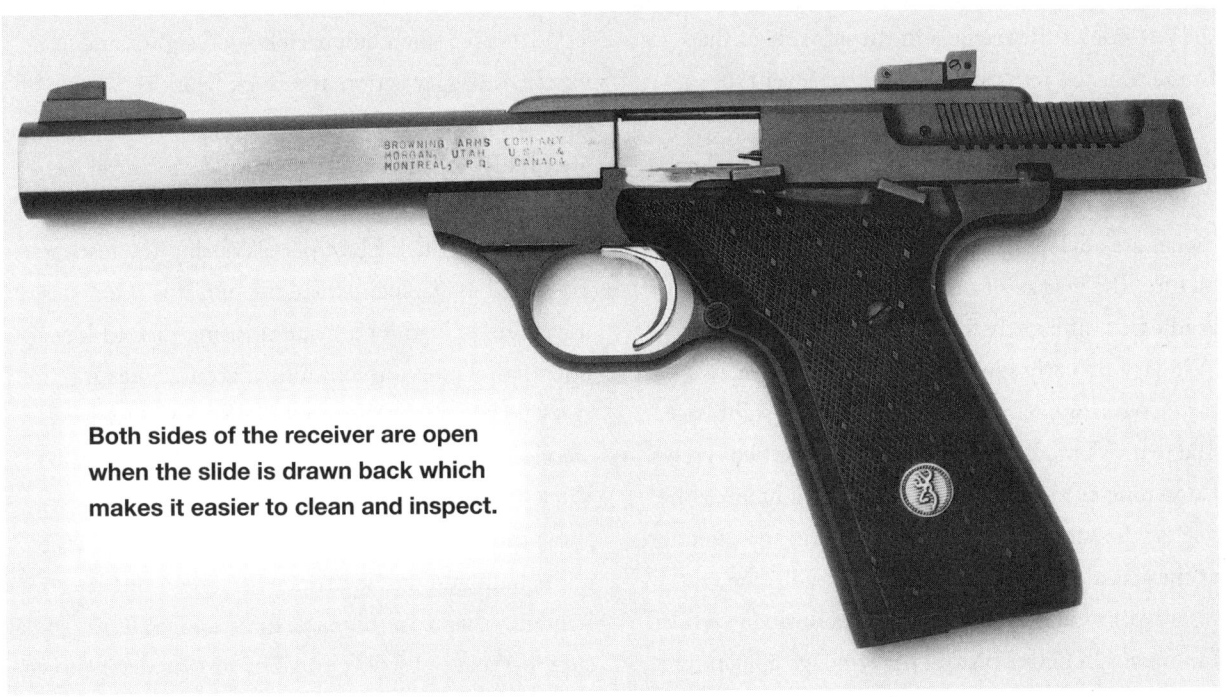

Both sides of the receiver are open when the slide is drawn back which makes it easier to clean and inspect.

of rubber in 1991. In 1987, the Buck Mark Plus version with smooth grips of laminated wood was introduced. It is this model that my wife selected after some experience with my Buck Mark. Several versions of the Buck Mark have been produced in the intervening years. The Buck Mark has a 5 1/2-inch heavy barrel with a recessed crown. One of the unique features of the Buck Mark is that the slide operates within the frame so that the top of the frame does not move during firing. As a result, the rear sight remains stationary, and the action is open on both sides when the slide is drawn backward. The front sight is a square topped blade of generous width while the rear sight is fully adjustable.

Other versions in the Buck Mark series include the Buck Mark Micro which has a 4-inch barrel and is available in either blue (suggested price $310) or nickel finish (suggested price $360). The Buck Mark Plus has laminated wood grips while the Buck Mark Classic Plus (suggested price for either is $379) has rosewood grip panels. The Buck Mark Plus Nickel has a nickel finish and laminated wood grips (suggested price of $415). These three variants also have a fiber optic insert in the front sight post. The Buck Mark Challenge (suggested price $346) is distinguished by its round, lightweight barrel and checkered walnut grip panels. The result is a 25-ounce pistol with many of the desirable features of the Buck Mark. The Buck Mark Camper has a tapered round barrel with a matte finish and with a suggested price of $279. It is the least expensive Buck Mark.

As if the seven variants described above were not enough, there are three Buck Mark pistols in the series that are intended for more serious target pursuits. The variant known as the Bullseye has a 7.5-inch fluted bull barrel and weighs 36 ounces and can be had with composite grips (suggested price $454) or laminated rosewood grips (suggested price $586). Two versions known as the 5.5 Target (weight 35.5 ounces) and 5.5 Field (weight 35 ounces) are also available (list price is $496 for either). These versions have a full-length sight rail attached for mounting scopes or red dot sights. These pistols are capable of rifle-like accuracy.

The two Buck Mark pistols tested were a standard model of early production and a more recent vintage Buck Mark Plus. Controls on all versions of the Buck Mark are identical. The release for the 10-round magazine is a button located behind the trigger on the left side of the frame. On the left side of the frame near the rear can be found the lever type safety, and just ahead of it is the slide release button. A hold-open device on the Buck Mark keeps the slide in the rear position after the last shot is fired. Sights are adjustable and provide an excellent sight picture. The rear sight on current Buck Mark pistols is adjusted differently than those on early models. Windage on early specimens was adjusted by two tiny screws, one on either side of the rear sight base. The rear sight is held tightly between the two screws. Loosening the screw on one side and tightening the one on the other moves the rear sight in the direction of the screw that was loosened. Invariably, the rear sight works loose on my Buck Mark during extended shooting. On newer pistols, the windage adjustment is a single screw with click stops.

Trigger action on the Buck Marks tested is outstanding. Mine has a crisp release with a pull of 2.75 pounds with absolutely no creep. The Buck Mark Plus belonging to my wife has a somewhat stiffer trigger with let off requiring a pull of 3.5 pounds without noticeable creep. The trigger action of these pistols is as good as on any pistol that is not a full-fledged target model. Although it has a listed weight of 34 ounces, my Buck Mark actually weighs only 31.9 ounces on a postal scale. With the slightly heavier wood grips, my wife's Buck Mark weighs 32.7 ounces.

With a 5.5-inch bull barrel, good sights, and excellent trigger action, the Buck Mark is capable of outstanding accuracy. The barrel has flat sides that are highly polished while the top of the barrel has a matte finish. There was only one failure to cycle with either of the Buck Mark pistols during the testing. A 10-round magazine is standard, and it is the easiest magazine to load for any autoloading pistol I have operated. Some of the results of accuracy testing the Buck Mark with a Weaver 1.5-4X scope attached were discussed earlier in this chapter. However, the Buck Mark was tested extensively at 25 yards to show the level of accuracy that one can expect from a fine handgun that is fitted with a high quality handgun scope. In this case, the scope used was the superb Weaver 1.5-4X. The data obtained are shown in the accompanying table.

Accuracy Results for the Browning Buck Mark with a Weaver 1.5-4X Scope.

Ammunition	Group size, inches[a]		
	Smallest	Largest	Average
CCI Pistol Match	0.63	1.75	1.01
Federal High Velocity H.P.	0.52	0.98	0.79
PMC Pistol Match	0.55	0.82	0.72
PMC Scoremaster	0.88	1.46	1.15
Remington Golden H.P.	1.57	2.02	1.73
Winchester T22	1.75	2.61	2.04
Wolf Match Target	0.73	1.03	0.87
		Overall Av.	1.19

[a]At 25 yards.

The safety locks the slide on the Buck Mark and it cannot be placed "on" unless the pistol is cocked.

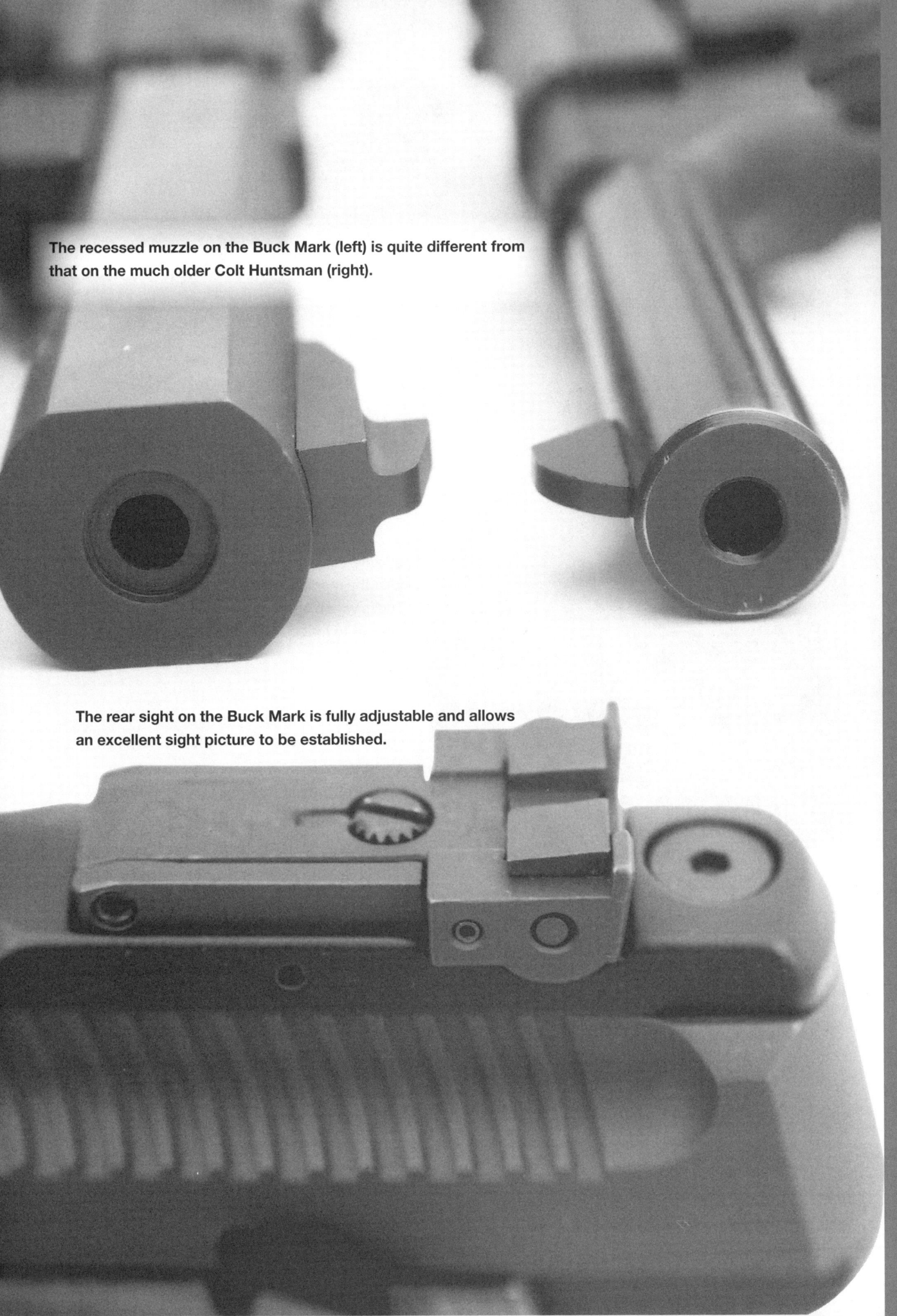

The recessed muzzle on the Buck Mark (left) is quite different from that on the much older Colt Huntsman (right).

The rear sight on the Buck Mark is fully adjustable and allows an excellent sight picture to be established.

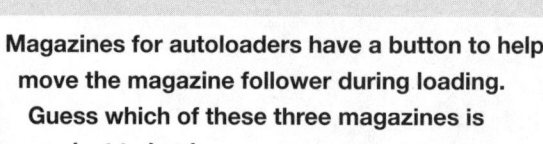

Magazines for autoloaders have a button to help move the magazine follower during loading. Guess which of these three magazines is easiest to load.

This small five-shot group at 25 yards is typical of those given by the Browning Buck Mark with a scope attached.

The data summarized in the table indicate that the Browning Buck Mark is a very accurate handgun. Of course, tested under similar conditions so are several others. When fired from a steady rest with a scope attached, handguns are about as accurate as some rifles. This should come as no surprise since accuracy is not determined by barrel length. The scope removes the necessity for trying to align the rear sight, front sight, and target, which are at different distances from the shooter's eye. When that problem is overcome, handguns can be extremely accurate. As with all other types of rimfire firearms, the Buck Mark showed preferences in ammunition. Perhaps even more than the rifle shooter, the handgun hunter should test several types of ammunition to find types that give best accuracy because bullet placement is more important than is a small increment in velocity.

Suffice it to say, the Buck Mark has accuracy that will match the shooting ability of almost anyone.

The grip on the Buck Mark is of comfortable size and contour. The trigger is correctly placed and the shape is comfortable for the finger. Overall, it is a pleasant piece without some of the annoying little nuances that plague some models. Outstanding in fit and finish, accurate, and reliable, the Browning Buck Mark is a superb handgun. It would be difficult to find a more capable pistol in the same price range.

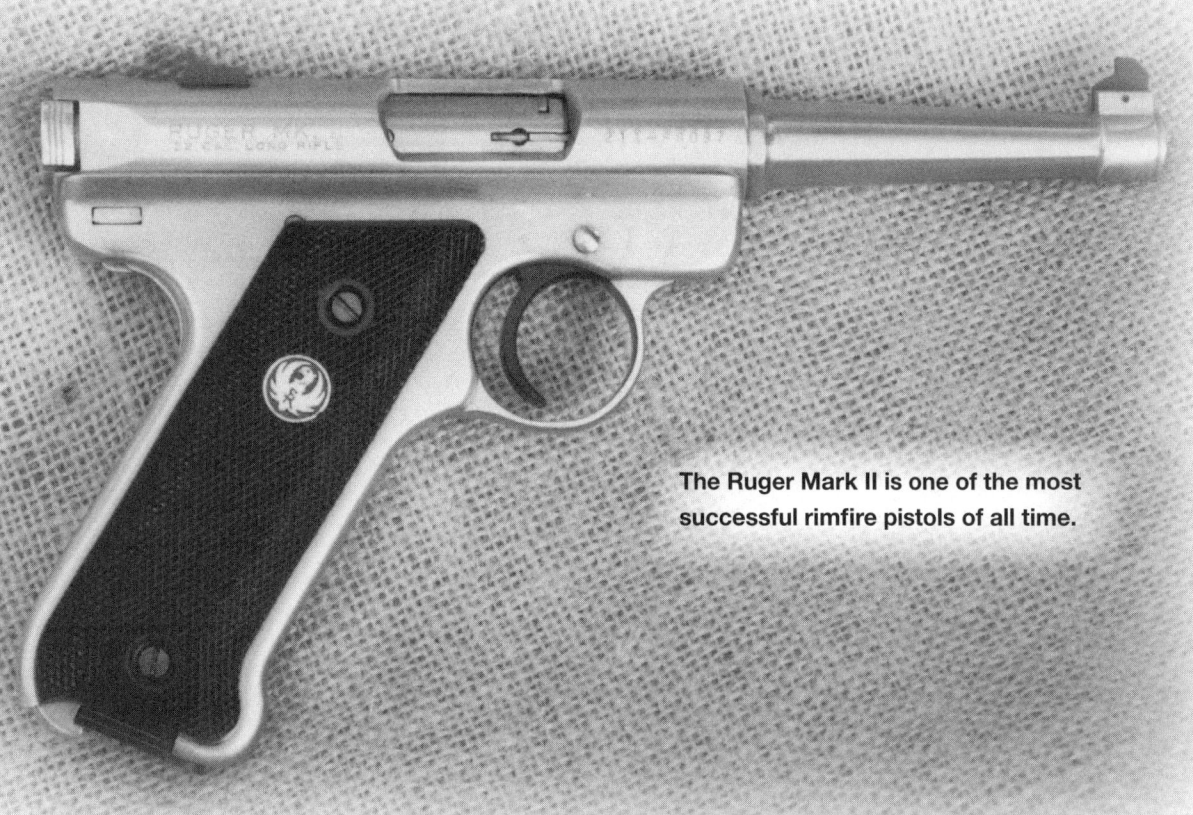

The Ruger Mark II is one of the most successful rimfire pistols of all time.

Ruger Mark II

In 1949, Sturm, Ruger, & Co. introduced a semiautomatic pistol that has become one of the most successful rimfire pistols of all time. The initial version was known as the Standard Model and it had a retail price of $37.50 at the time. The author owned one of those early pistols in his late teen years, but before long it was traded for something that had a special interest at the time. I do not remember what it was. A couple of years later, a target version having a 6 7/8-inch barrel was introduced. In 1982, an improved pistol known as the Mark II was produced. It differed only slightly from the original model, most notably in changes to the safety that allowed the bolt to be drawn back with the safety "on" and a slight change in the rear of the receiver that allowed a better grip on the grooved areas of the bolt. Production of over 3 million pistols indicates something of the popularity of the Ruger line, which includes many variants that differ in barrel length, sights, and type of steel. Finally, in November 2004 production was shifted to the new Mark III series.

A more complete discussion of the Mark II variants and the new Mark III was given in Chapter 4.

The Ruger Mark II tested was the stainless steel Standard model with a 4 5/8-inch barrel with fixed sights. In some ways, this variant has the most pleasing looks of all Ruger rimfire autoloaders in the opinion of this author. Operating the pistol is straightforward for anyone who is somewhat knowledgeable about 22 semiautomatic pistols. Like many of the older pistols, the magazine release on the Mark II is located on the bottom of the grip. Pushing the catch backward releases the 10-round magazine. The magazine release on the new Mark III pistols is a button on the left hand side of the frame just behind the trigger. Loading the magazine with cartridges requires some degree of hand strength because the Ruger makes use of a strong spring, and the button for pushing the magazine follower down is small. Inserting the magazine into the grip and pushing it upward causes it to be latched in position. The bolt remains open after the last shot is fired, and the

On the Ruger Mark II, the safety is located on the left-hand side of the frame below the receiver. The bolt can be pulled back with the safety on.

safety is located on the left hand side of the frame as is the bolt release. Drawing the bolt to the rear and releasing it allows it to move forward taking the top round in the magazine into the chamber. Trigger pull on the Mark II was measured as 3.5 pounds with almost no creep.

During testing, the Ruger Mark II performed flawlessly which came as no surprise since that has been the reputation of this pistol for many years. It feeds, fires, and ejects regularly with any type of ammunition. The Browning Buck Mark is a substantial, sturdy handgun in all regards, but in comparison the Ruger Mark II seems as if it is built like a tank. This is not meant to imply that the Buck Mark is in any way flimsy because it definitely is not. It is just that with its heavy tubular receiver, the Ruger Mark II (or the newer Mark III) is very robust. Long life and reliability have been the trademarks of the Ruger autoloaders for many

The Ruger Mark II has the magazine release on the bottom of the grip, but on the newer Mark III it is located behind the trigger.

years. The author did not find the Ruger quite as steady on target as was the Buck Mark because of the difference in weight distribution. However, that a subjective issue that might strike other shooters differently.

Outwardly, the Ruger Mark II and Mark III have some resemblance to the famous Luger. To the author, there is no more attractive rimfire pistol available. For most shooting, the models with fixed sights are adequate, but many shooters will opt for one of the variants with adjustable sights. As a general "carry" gun, I would select the fixed model with a short barrel, but for hunting small game and pests, I would select one of the versions that can readily have a scope attached. The Mark III Hunter would meet the expectations of any handgun hunter and will last almost forever in the process.

Ruger Super Single Six Convertible

The Ruger Single Six was first offered in 1953 with 4 5/8- or 5 1/2-inch barrel options. The original model had a loading gate that was a flat disk with a thumbnail notch for opening. The author had one of theses early versions (now collectible of course), but before long another firearm needed to have part of its price covered by a trade-in. Later, another Single Six came to the author in December 1958 so the author's experience with the Ruger Single Six goes back almost half a century. From 1960 to 1972 the Single Six Convertible was offered with both 22 LR and 22 WMR cylinders.

In 1973, the so-called New Single Six resulted from Ruger's modernization of the single-action revolver. The loading gate was connected to the

With an interchangeable cylinder chambered for the 22 WMR, the Single Six Convertible is a versatile, reliable handgun.

cylinder bolt so that when the loading gate was opened the cylinder could be rotated for loading without the hammer being drawn back to the "half-cock" notch. Also, a transfer bar mechanism was included that prevented the hammer blow from being transmitted to the firing pin unless the transfer bar was moved into its upward position behind the firing pin which occurs only when the trigger is pulled to the rear. As has been discussed earlier in this book, this was a great safety measure. A wide range of options regarding barrel lengths, type of steel, and sights were offered as is the case to this time.

Single-action revolvers represent the ultimate simplicity in terms of operation. The loading gate is opened, the cylinder is rotated to load each chamber, and the loading gate is closed. Drawing the hammer back cocks the revolver and causes the cylinder to turn to index the next chamber for firing. After pulling the trigger and firing a shot, cocking the hammer rotates the cylinder to align the next chamber. When all shots have been fired, the loading gate is opened and empty cases are ejected one at a time by pushing back on the ejector rod and rotating the cylinder.

The Super Single Six Convertible used in this testing has a 6.5-inch barrel and the adjustable rear sight common to this model. With the square-topped post on a ramp and the square notched rear sight, the sight picture afforded is about as good as with any rimfire handgun. Loading and functioning are predictable and reliable.

With considerable experience with both rimfire and centerfire autoloaders, the author has found them to be extremely reliable, especially the centerfire models. However, some (if not most) rimfire autoloaders are somewhat finicky about feeding certain types of ammunition. This was experienced in testing some of the pistols described in this chapter. When it comes to a revolver, if the round goes into the cylinder, it will fire. Only a faulty round (several of which were found in conducting the tests with rifles) will cause a misfire. In keeping with this, no misfires were experienced with the Single Six nor were they expected. It is this type of reliability and the safety that accompanies the visible hammer that makes a revolver so appealing and comforting. In this regard, the Ruger Single Six is unsurpassed.

How accurate is a Ruger Single Six? It is accurate enough to meet or exceed any requirement of this author. To determine the ultimate accuracy, a scope would have to be mounted on the gun and that the author refuses to do. A classic single-action revolver is going to remain that way because that is the way it is going to be carried and used. Some shooters seem to shoot better with an autoloader than with a revolver, but the author has never found much difference. It is probably more a matter of shaky hands and vision in my case although competitors at a high level virtually always use an autoloader in rimfire competition. The Ruger Single Six remains a superb choice for plinking and comfort in remote areas.

Ruger Mark II 22/45

As popular as the Ruger Mark I and II pistols are, there are still those who would like something different. One objection voiced by many handgun shooters is that the grip angle on some guns does not match some preconceived notion of what it ought to be. My opinion is that

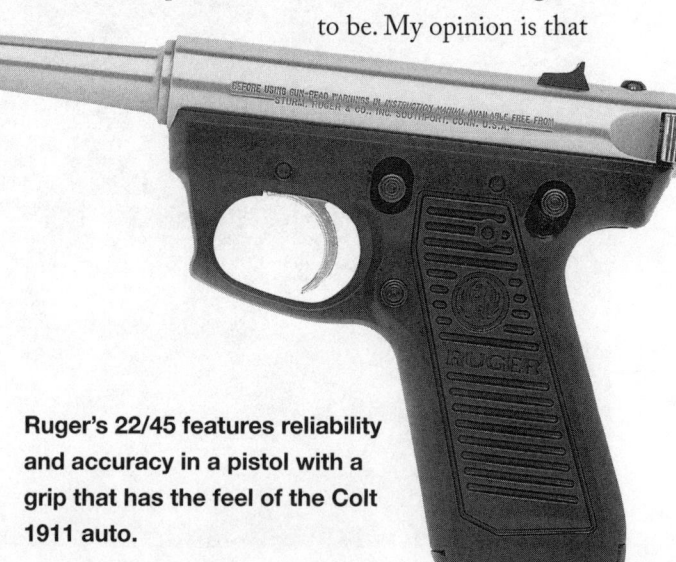

Ruger's 22/45 features reliability and accuracy in a pistol with a grip that has the feel of the Colt 1911 auto.

The Smith & Wesson 22A is a versatile handgun that is capable of fine accuracy. Optional sighting equipment can easily be mounted on the permanently attached rail.

except in unusual cases, the shooter will adjust to any reasonable grip angle. Many shooters, the author not being one of them, feel that the grip angle of the Colt Model 1911 represents perfection. Accordingly, Ruger produced a version of its famous semiautomatic known as the 22/45 in which the grip matches the size and angle of the famous Colt 1911 45 ACP. Introduced in 1992, the Model 22/45 has a polymer grip frame, and the push-button magazine release functions in a manner similar to that of the Colt 1911.

Four variants of the Model 22/45 are listed in the 2004 Ruger catalog. These include a stainless steel model having a standard weight 4.75-inch barrel and fixed sights (weight is 28 ounces). Two other versions are blue and stainless steel guns that have 5.5-inch bull barrels and adjustable sights (weights are 35 ounces). The fourth option is a blued model having a 4-inch bull barrel, adjustable sights, and a weight of 31 ounces. The 22/45 has a safety that is located in essentially the same place as it is on the Mark II. List prices for the 22/45 pistols range from $290 to $380. The variants of the Ruger 22/45 have much in common with the Mark II (described earlier) and current Mark III models, but weigh less because of having a polymer frame.

With a 2X Bushnell scope attached, the author's brother has used this Ruger 22/45 regularly to hunt small game. It is utterly reliable and the accuracy is outstanding. If one is addicted to the grip design of the Colt 1911 45 ACP autoloader, the Ruger 22/45 should be the rimfire pistol of choice. It has been so pleasing to the author's brother that several rimfire handguns have come and gone, but the 22/45 has remained. That should tell you where it ranks in the estimation of a serious shooter.

Smith & Wesson Model 22A

As discussed in Chapter 1, the Smith & Wesson name has been associated with rimfire firearms since the earliest days. In the mid-1900s, the reputation of Smith & Wesson was carried on by the medium- and larger-frame revolvers in calibers like 357 Magnum, 44 Magnum, and 45 Colt. Later, the introduction of a novel 9mm double-action pistol, the Model 39, came about as the general interest in semiautomatic handguns was growing. This led to the present lineup of pistols that includes many that are designed for law enforcement and defensive uses. However, the Smith & Wesson name appears on a series of popular rimfire pistols as well as on the legendary Model 41 target pistol. There are actually two series of 22 pistols that share most characteristics of design except the metal used in the frame. The two series are the 22A which was introduced in 1996 and the 22S which was introduced in the following year. The 22S series is made of stainless steel while the 22A pistols have frames made of aluminum alloy. Contrasted with pistols having the classic Colt and High Standard appearance, the Smith & Wesson pistols

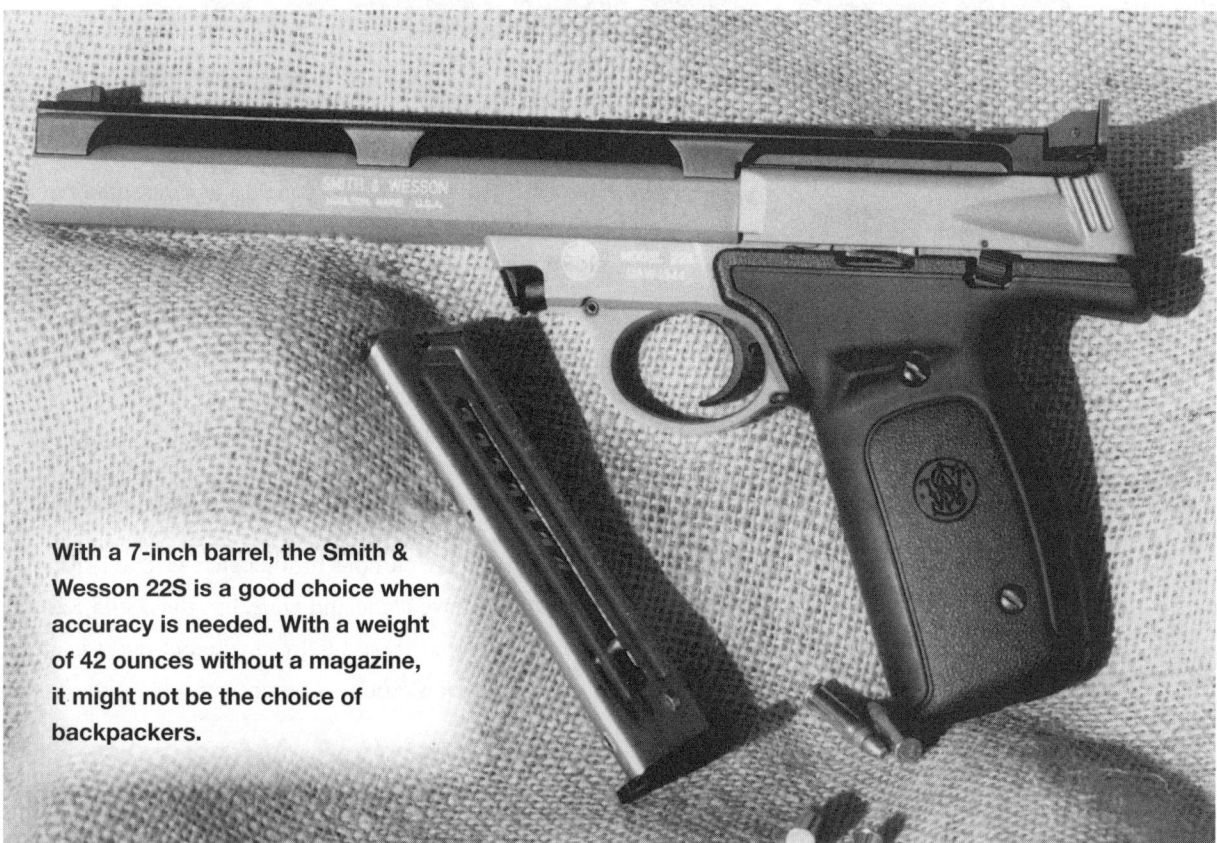

With a 7-inch barrel, the Smith & Wesson 22S is a good choice when accuracy is needed. With a weight of 42 ounces without a magazine, it might not be the choice of backpackers.

have a modern look, but not as radically so as do the Beretta rimfire offerings.

In designing the 22A and 22S series, Smith & Wesson kept the rear sight from moving back with the slide by having a sight rib that serves as the top of the action. Therefore, the rear sight is stationary with the slide moving below it in the same way as in the Browning Buck Mark. However, the Smith & Wesson pistols have a full-length sight rib permanently mounted on the barrel and action. The rear sight rests in a cut out area at the end of the rib. The sight rib has four lateral notches in it where Weaver-type scope rings can be attached. Although all 22A and 22S pistols have adjustable sights, they are also set up for easily attaching a complete array of aftermarket sights.

The pistol used in this evaluation is the

Pressing inward on the checkered button in front of the trigger initiates takedown.

Model 22A with a 5.5-inch barrel although other variants have 4- or 7-inch barrels. With a 5.5-inch barrel, the 22A is 9.5 inches long and weighs 32 ounces (without magazine) so it is not a compact model. Being made of stainless steel, the 22S models average almost 10 ounces heavier. The alloy frame of the 22A is finished with a black coating, and the pistol has composite grips with rubber inserts along the front and back edges of the grip frame. The grip is hand filling, but not too large, and the grip has an excellent feel. Another 22A pistol is available with full coverage camo finish, and wood grips are available on one variant. Pistols in the 22S series are available having 5.5-inch or 7-inch barrels with choices of grips. Smith & Wesson produces grips for the 22A and 22S that are made of hard plastic with or without the rubber inserts, a plastic grip with thumb rest, and a large target grip of laminated wood. As aftermarket items, barrels in 4, 5.5, and 7-inch lengths and grips of different style can be purchased for installation on any 22A or 22S.

Sights on the S&W 22A are standard in that the front sight is a square-topped post and the rear is a blade with a square notch. The rear sight is fully adjustable for windage and elevation by means of slotted screws. The sights permit a good sight picture to be established. Other controls are standard with the safety and slide release levers located on the left hand side of the frame. One feature that is different from most rimfire auto pistols is the magazine release, which is located in a recess along the front edge of the grip frame. This is a holdover from the design of the earlier 2206, 422, and 622 models. This allows the grip to have a clean appearance with the bottom of the magazine flush with the bottom of the grip. Although the S&W 22A looks a little unusual with a rather large sight rail installed along its top edge, the pistol handles well and has good weight distribution.

Trigger action on the 22A requires a soft take up motion after which the let off occurs with a pull that measures 4.1 pounds. It is almost like a two-stage trigger in its operation except that during the first stage the pull gets greater and the trigger moves backward. Overall trigger action is good on my specimen, but the pull should be about a pound lighter. The rather small trigger has a sharp front edge at the bottom, which dug into my finger, and it became uncomfortable during extended shooting. Although the magazine of the 22A has a protruding knob to help in moving the magazine follower downward, it still requires considerable effort to compress the magazine spring. It is not the easiest magazine to load. Two or three failures to feed were experienced during testing with standard velocity ammunition. High velocity ammunition cycled regularly, and this behavior is in accord with the experience of other shooters with these pistols. They function better with full power ammunition.

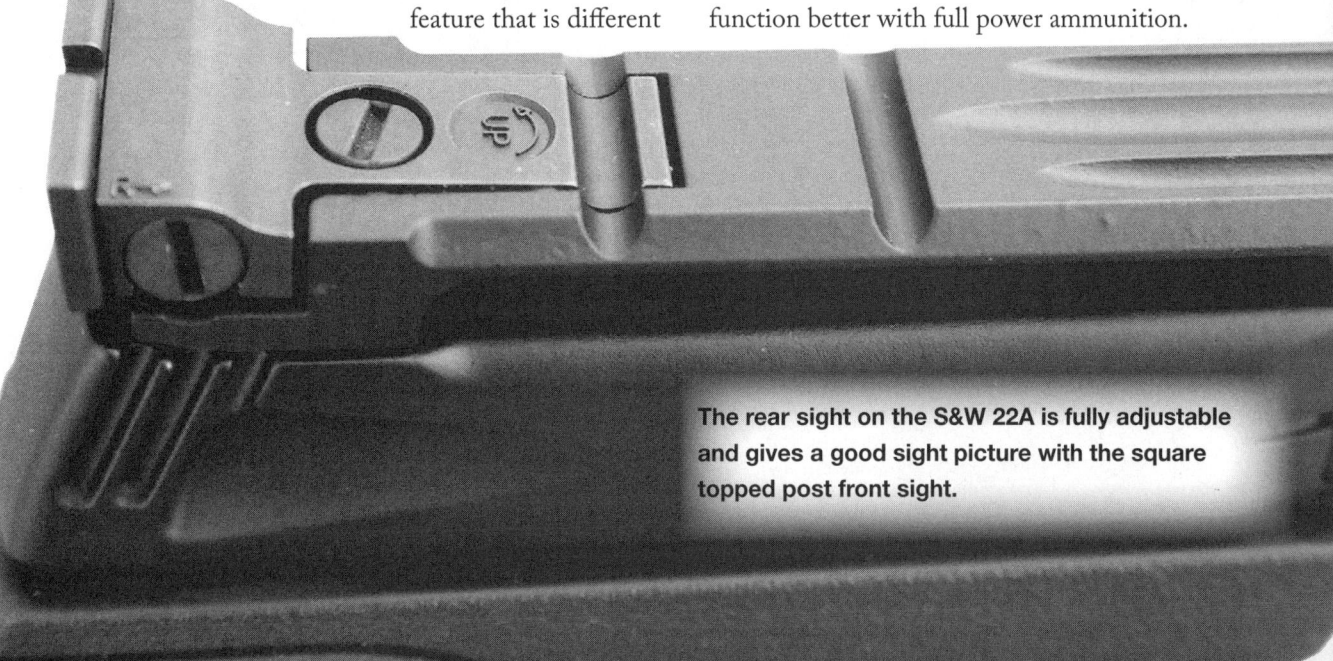

The rear sight on the S&W 22A is fully adjustable and gives a good sight picture with the square topped post front sight.

One minor irritation with the Model 22A involved the sight rail. One of the popular optical sights for a handgun is the Simmons red dot sight that comes with its own mounting base. The base has two Weaver-style cross bolts with one of them in a slot so the spacing between the cross bolts can be varied. In spite of this latitude, it was not possible to mount the sight on the rail of the S&W 22A because of the spacing between the lateral grooves in the scope rail. This is no more a fault of the 22A than it is of the mounting base on the red dot sight.

Overall, the Smith & Wesson 22A is a substantial pistol that gives excellent performance. With a manufacturer's suggested price of $313, it is normally found at a retail price of approximately $250 and at this price it represents a good value. With the 5.5-inch barrel or an optional one of 7 inches, the 22A or the stainless 22S would be a good choice for the hunter with small game and varmints in mind. The superb accuracy of a 22A with a scope mounted was described earlier in this chapter.

Walther P22

Two of the most recognizable pistols of all time are the Walther P-38 of World War II fame and the Walther PPK, which is nearly 75 years old. The firm of Carl Walther also has produced some elegant rimfire sporting rifles in the past. Target rifles for the competitive shooter have also carried the Walther name. Although the PPK and PPK/S models live on, Walther is probably best known at this time for the famous P99 centerfire pistol that is intended primarily for law enforcement and military use. The P99 exhibits numerous innovative features one of which is that the rear portion of the grip is removable so that inserts of different thickness can be attached to change the grip profile. Another novel feature is that the decocking lever is flush with the top of the action near the rear sight and is activated by pushing it downward into the receiver. The P99 is offered with many options in 9mm and 40 S&W calibers.

The P99 also serves as the design

The safety on the S&W 22A and 22S is located where it can be conveniently operated by the thumb for right-handed shooters.

Even with a 5-inch barrel, the Walther P22 is a compact, lightweight pistol with several novel features.

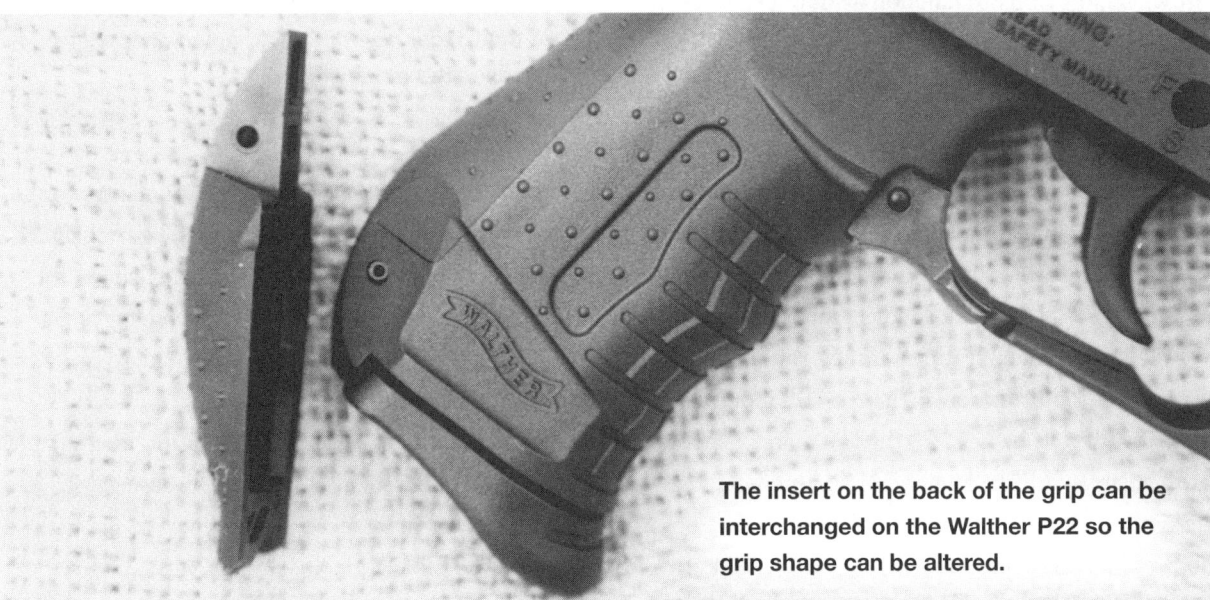

The insert on the back of the grip can be interchanged on the Walther P22 so the grip shape can be altered.

model for the CO_2-powered 177 caliber pellet pistol known as the CP99. Another offspring of the centerfire P99 is the P22, which is the subject of this evaluation. Although outwardly resembling the P99, the P22 has some important differences. First, it has a visible hammer and functions in the way that is customary for double-action pistols. When the safety is off, the first shot can be fired in the double-action mode while succeeding shots are fired single-action, or the pistol can be cocked manually and all shots fired single-action. Second, the P22 has dual safety levers that are located on either side at the rear of the receiver. Third, the magazine release consists of a lever that is contoured to match the trigger guard, and it is located along the sides at the rear part of the trigger guard. Pulling downward on either portion of the lever releases the 10-round magazine. The P22 also has a key lock that is located on the right side of

Dual safety levers are provided on the Walther P22. However, they do not function as decocking levers.

As on the Walther P99, the magazine release on the P22 is a lever that forms an integral part of the trigger guard. Pulling down on the lever releases the magazine.

the frame just above the trigger. Integrated locks of this type are appearing on an increasing number of handguns including the new Ruger Mark III. The Walther P22 also has a loaded chamber indicator.

While the general features of the Walther P22 have been listed above, there is still more to describe. Barrels having lengths of 3.4 and 5 inches are available with the longer barreled models designated as "target" models and those with shorter barrels called "standard" models. However, as a result of the lightweight polymer frame, both models weigh 20 ounces or less. The target pistols have a nonfunctioning "compensator" that serves as a barrel weight. Sights on both models consist of a post with a white dot insert and a rear blade with dots on either side of the notch giving the "three dot" type of sight that is popular on modern pistols. Walther offers a bridge type mount that clamps around the barrel to the sight rail, which constitutes an integral part of the frame in front of the trigger guard. Also offered is a laser sight that clamps to the sight rail so that it fits nicely under the barrel ahead of the trigger guard. As a really unique feature, the short and long barrels are readily interchangeable so one is not permanently linked to a standard or target model.

Pistols with each of the barrel lengths are available in three finishes. The first is an all-black surface. Other options include a black polymer frame with a silver-gray slide and a black slide with an olive drab grip frame. The latter is known as the "military" version in keeping with the designations applied to the P99 pistols.

The Walther P22 can be fired either single- or double-action. As a result, the trigger action of the P22 is not quite as good as that of the Browning Buck Mark, but it is acceptable nonetheless. In single-action mode, the let off was crisp at a pull measured as 5.0 pounds. The owner's manual states that the trigger pull in single-action firing is 4.85

With increased safety in mind, the Walther P22 has a key lock on the right hand side of the receiver. A slotted key is necessary to turn the lock.

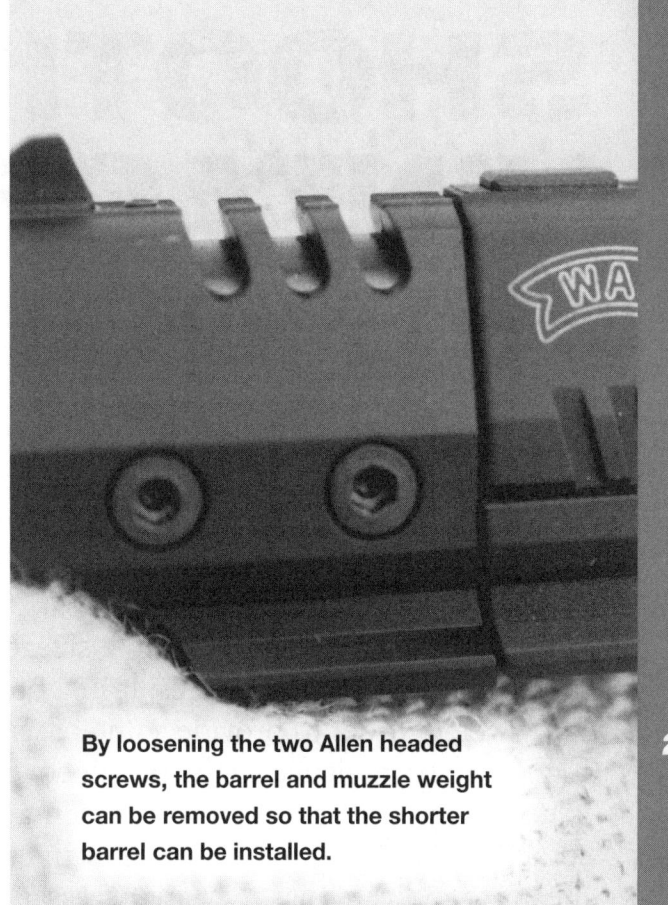

By loosening the two Allen headed screws, the barrel and muzzle weight can be removed so that the shorter barrel can be installed.

pounds so it is quite close to the specified pull. It is the double-action pull for the P22 that is impressive. To fire in the double-action mode, a smooth pull of only 9.5 pounds was required. Overall, trigger action is quite good for a double-action model.

One could wish that the designers of the P22 had made the safety levers also function as decocking levers as is the case on many centerfire autoloaders. The only way in which the P22 can be decocked is by carefully holding the hammer while pulling the trigger to the rear and letting the hammer down slowly.

Compact but capable, the Walther P22 is a rimfire pistol with many innovative features. The 3.4-inch barreled pistols are so small and light that they are comparable to many of the so-called pocket pistols that have been produced over the years. While the short-barreled version would make a good hiking piece, even the 5-inch barreled pistol is small and weighs only about 20 ounces. It would also be very convenient to carry, and the longer barrel would give slightly higher velocity, and it could also be fired more accurately as a result of the longer sight radius. In firing, the Walther P22 functioned reliably and gave good accuracy for a pistol of this type. With a barrel of either length, the P22 is an effective handgun for plinking, camping, and trail wear.

Carrying the legendary Walther name and marketed by means of an alliance between Walther and Smith & Wesson, the P22 is an interesting piece. Retail prices are in the $300 to $400 range depending on barrel length and other options.

Of necessity, a limited number of handguns have been described in this chapter. In most cases, the guns selected are representative of an extensive number of similar models. Therefore, this chapter gives an overview of a larger number of the available rimfire handguns. From compact autoloader to long barreled single-action revolver, there is a rimfire handgun to suite almost any taste and budget.

Chapter 16

SHOOTING SOME VINTAGE RIMFIRE HANDGUNS

According to history, the first rimfire firearm was a small handgun chambered for the original 22 Short cartridge. The number of handgun models produced in the intervening century and a half is staggering. Companies that came on the scene and flourished for a time were many, and most of them have been defunct for many years. To try to produce a review of all the rimfire handguns ever produced or even a sizeable fraction of that number would be a prodigious task that would result in a book (make that a large book!) on the subject. However, in order to provide some basis for comparison with current models and to give some guidance to the prospective buyer of a vintage rimfire handgun, it is necessary to evaluate a few representative models. This chapter is devoted to some rimfire handguns that are not in current production, but this in no way is meant to indicate that they are necessarily antique firearms which is a different subject altogether. Along with the discussion of some of these handguns, historical information and notes will be given that relate to other models that are similar. In terms of the enormous range of vintage handguns produced, the sampling here is of necessity quite limited.

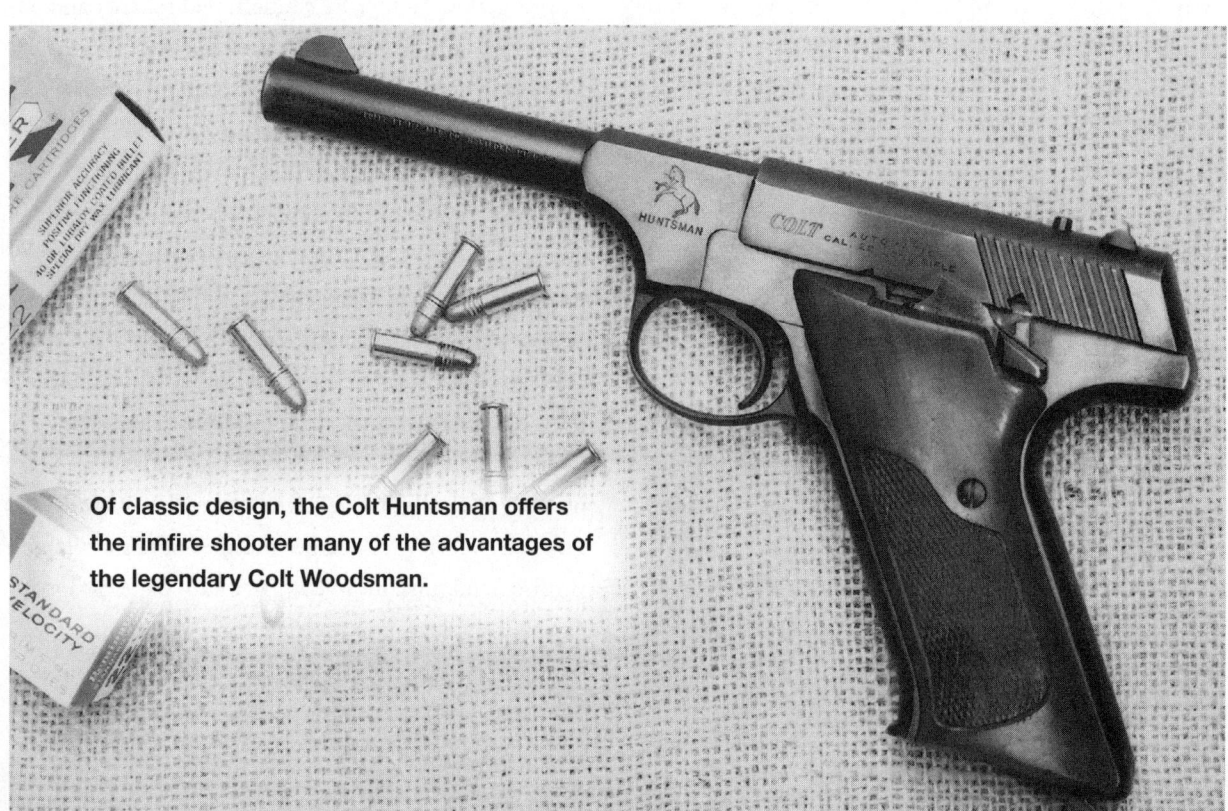

Of classic design, the Colt Huntsman offers the rimfire shooter many of the advantages of the legendary Colt Woodsman.

The magazine release on the Colt Huntsman is located on the bottom of the grip.

As was explained in the last chapter, the accuracy of a handgun is much more a function of who is shooting it than in the case of a rifle. Resting a rifle across sandbags on a sturdy bench and aligning the reticule of a scope of high magnification on a target removes much of the human element. Therefore, thorough testing of several rifles to establish their accuracy capability and to test ammunition is justified. In testing the vintage handguns, it was felt that there was no need for an extensive series of accuracy tests. The idea behind the work was not to try to establish a baseline of accuracy for comparisons between models, but rather to show that these models are still functional, capable pistols. Accordingly, each pistol was fired with several types of ammunition to check function and collect data on velocity (see Chapter 7). It was deemed sufficient for the purposes intended to examine each gun with regard to handling characteristics and function and to conduct limited firing.

As on the Colt Woodsman, the safety on the Huntsman locks the slide. The safety must be off before the slide can be withdrawn.

Colt Huntsman

Colt introduced a 22 autoloader in 1915 that was to become one of the premier pistols of that type. With approximately 700,000 pistols produced over a period of 62 years, this pistol underwent a great many improvements and alterations. The pistol was known as the Colt Woodsman although the initial model was known as the 22 Caliber Colt Automatic Pistol, Target Model. The Woodsman name began to be used around 1927, and it lasted for about 50 years. The 4.5-inch barrel length was introduced in 1933. A heavy barrel version introduced in 1938 was known as the Match Target Woodsman, and 4.5- and 6-inch barrels were available. Throughout the early years of the author's shooting experience, the Colt Woodsman was one of the most highly regarded pistols for target shooting. However, the Woodsman and the later Match Target Woodsman were quite expensive for that time period. They are even more so now.

Responding to the demand for a lower priced pistol for general use, Colt introduced the Challenger in 1950. Unlike the Woodsman that had outstanding adjustable sights, the Challenger was a fixed-sight model. After a few years in production, the Challenger gave way to the Huntsman. This model was offered with 4.5- and 6-inch barrels and fixed sights. Approximately 100,000 Huntsman pistols were produced between 1955 and 1977. Early variants had black plastic grips but later pistols like the one described here were produced with checkered walnut grips. Like the Challenger, the Huntsman did not have a device to hold the bolt open after the last shot was fired.

While the Colt Huntsman was regarded as a sort of budget priced Woodsman, it was a fine handgun with many desirable features. The checkered walnut grips were comfortable and attractive. The traditional high polish and exquisite bluing were unmistakably Colt. With the 4.5-inch barrel, a Huntsman weighs only about 29.3 ounces. The 10-round magazine unlatches at the bottom of the grip. Trigger action on the Huntsman is reminiscent of those found on many older semiautomatic pistols. The trigger broke cleanly and reproducibly at 3.0 pounds with no creep and overall trigger action was about as good as that for any of the semiautomatic pistols tested. One feature of the Huntsman and many of the other older semiautomatic rimfire pistols that makes one cringe a bit is that the safety must be taken "off" in order to pull back the slide. This means that the shooter is holding a loaded pistol in the "ready" position as the slide is drawn back, and special care is advised.

During the firing tests, the Huntsman performed just as it did when it was new. It fed reliably with all types of ammunition and gave good accuracy even though the sights are not adjustable. Colt no longer produces a rimfire semiautomatic, so older models have risen in value. A Huntsman in good condition will cost as much as a new Ruger or Smith & Wesson model, but it would be a good choice for most rimfire shooting. While the Huntsman is not the equal of the Woodsman, it is nonetheless a fine pistol.

A large button allows the magazine follower to be drawn downward for easy loading of the Colt Huntsman's magazine.

Smith & Wesson 2206

Manufactured from 1957 until the present time, the Smith & Wesson Model 41 is one of the premier rimfire target pistols. While there is always a steady, small demand for such pistols, models for more general use (and lower price since the list price of the Model 41 is just over $1000) are much more popular. In 1987, Smith & Wesson introduced a new model identified as the Model 422, and this was followed by the Model 622 in 1990. Both models were offered with 4.5 and 6-inch barrels with either fixed or adjustable sights. The adjustable sight versions were called Target models. The difference between the 422 and 622 models is in the finish. Both were made with aluminum frames and steel slides, but the 422 has a blued finish while the 622 has a satin finish resembling stainless steel. Weights of the 422/622 pistols are 21.5 and 23.5 ounces, respectively, for the 4.5 and 6-inch barreled pistols. Later, 3-inch barreled versions known as the Sportsman were introduced.

Based on the success and performance of the 422/622 pistols, the all steel Model 2206 was introduced in 1990. Versions were available which had barrel lengths of 4.5 and 6 inches. Weights were 35 and 39 ounces, respectively, so these were hefty, durable handguns. As in the case of the 422 and 622, the 2206 with adjustable sights is designated as a Target model. The 2206 uses a simple blowback principle with only the rear portion of the slide moving. However, one radical point of departure that separates the 2206 from most other autoloaders is the fact that it uses a barrel that is mounted as low as possible in the frame. The idea behind this procedure is that the focus of the recoil is as close to top of the hand as possible which helps reduce the effect of recoil to give less muzzle jump. The barrel is retained

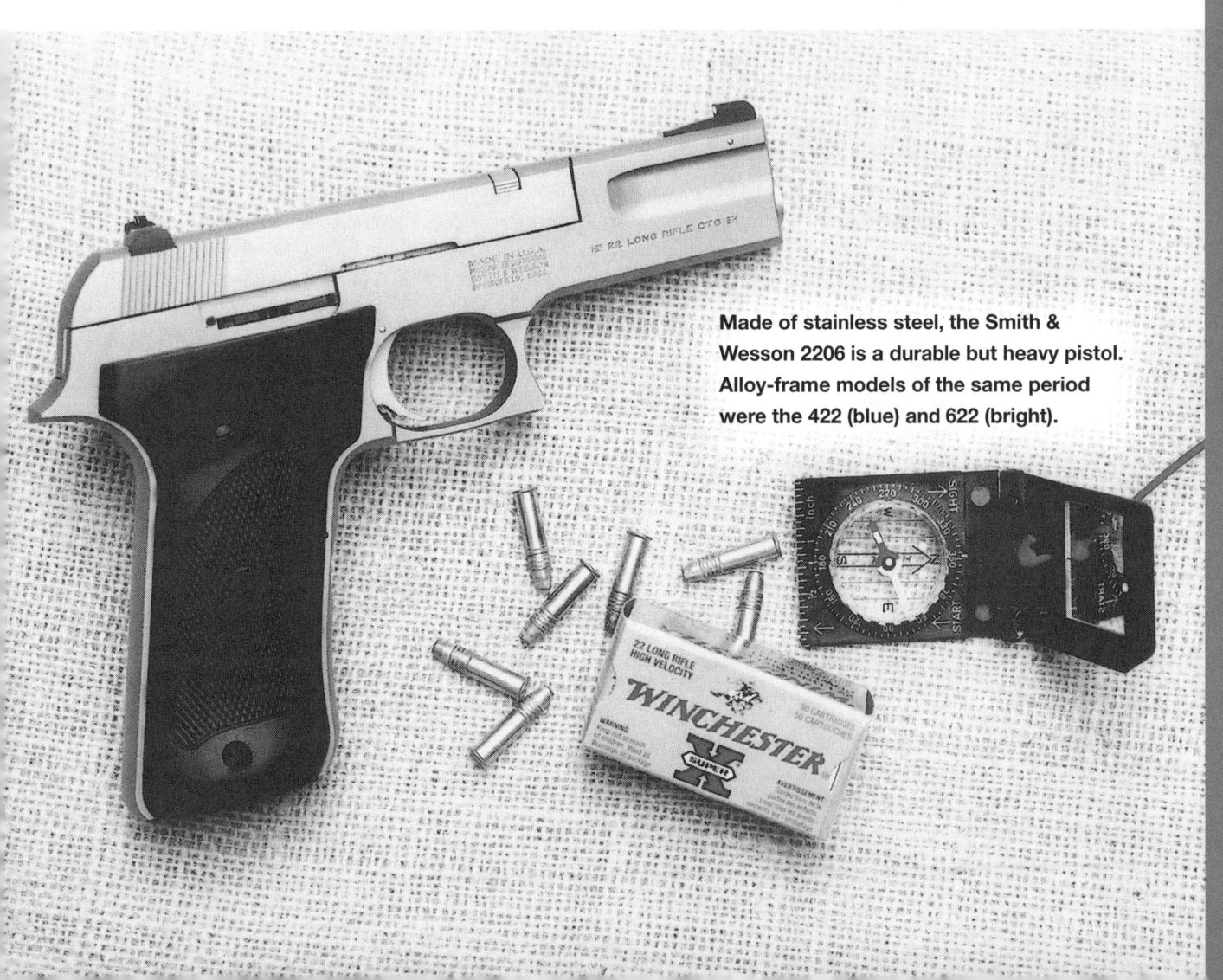

Made of stainless steel, the Smith & Wesson 2206 is a durable but heavy pistol. Alloy-frame models of the same period were the 422 (blue) and 622 (bright).

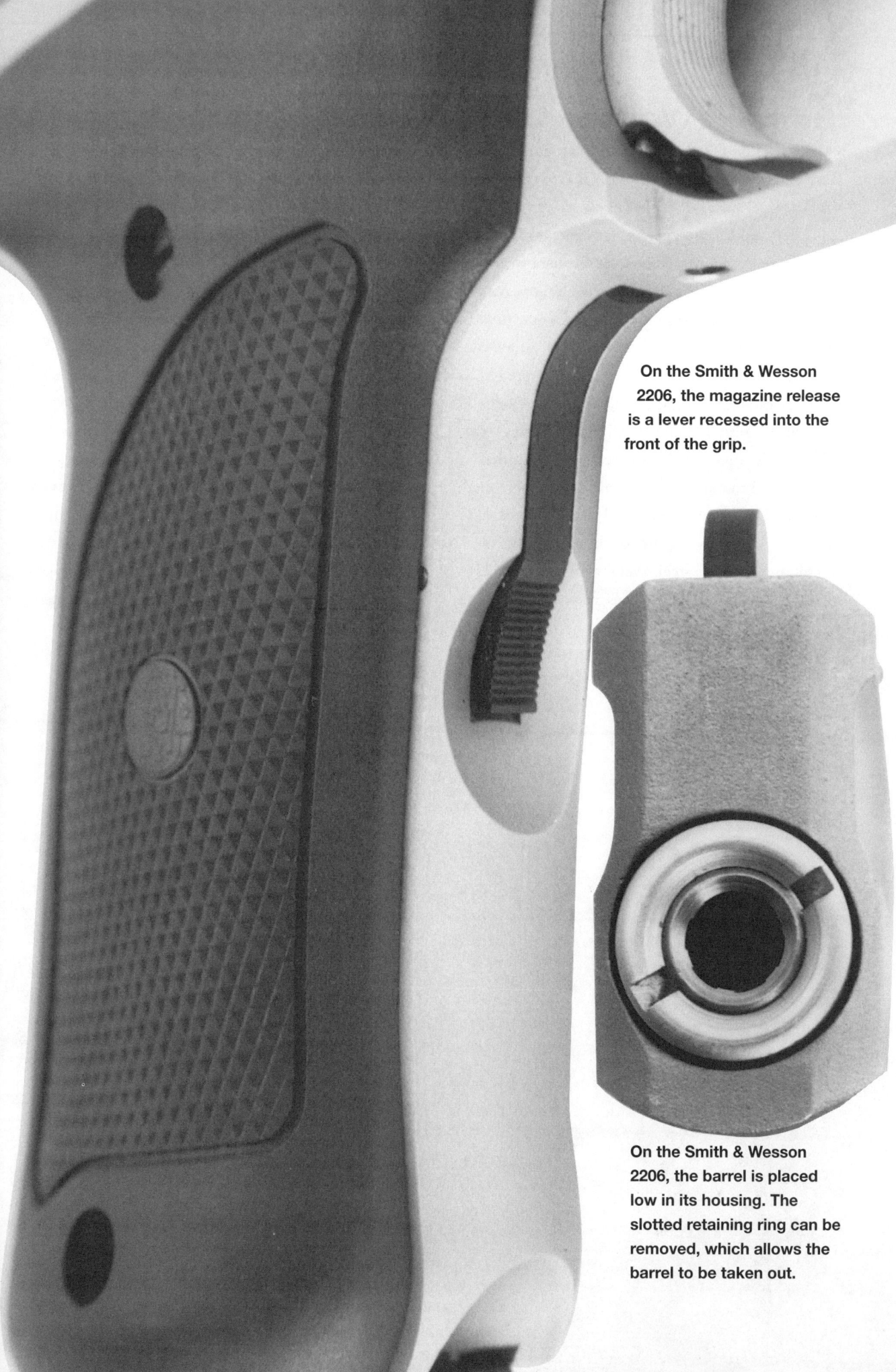

On the Smith & Wesson 2206, the magazine release is a lever recessed into the front of the grip.

On the Smith & Wesson 2206, the barrel is placed low in its housing. The slotted retaining ring can be removed, which allows the barrel to be taken out.

in the frame by a slotted, recessed sleeve and is easily removed.

The Model 2206 makes use of the same 10-round magazine that is used in the S&W Model 41. Unlike most autoloading pistols, the 2206 has a magazine release that is located in a recess on the front of the grip. It might seem that one could inadvertently press the latch and drop the magazine, but I have never had that happen. The hand simply wraps around the grip without making much contact with the latch, which requires a substantial force to release. The safety lever is located on the left side of the frame at the rear. A stop is provided which holds the slide open after the last shot. One attractive feature of the 2206 is that the pistol will not fire with the magazine removed. This is a valuable safety feature because if the magazine is removed, a forgotten round in the chamber cannot be fired.

The front edge of the trigger guard is curved to assist when a two-hand hold is applied. An adjustable trigger stop is provided for controlling overtravel. It is a setscrew with an Allen head located in the bottom of the rear portion of the trigger guard. The Lyman trigger pull gauge showed that the trigger broke cleanly with a pull of 4.7 pounds on the 2206 tested.

The 2206 digested all types of ammunition without hesitation or stoppage as it always has. Discontinued in 1996, a Model 2206 can sometimes be found for an attractive price. Although the models having adjustable sights are generally preferable, the pistol tested shot very close to the point of aim. While others may have need of a rimfire handgun with better accuracy, I have found the 2206 to shoot quite well. With my eye problems, I have to use a handgun with a scope to shoot much better. For the intended uses of the Model 2206, it would be difficult to find a current model that would be more appropriate. It has been a trusted and faithful companion for many years in many places. As described in Chapter 11, it has been a frequent choice for a rimfire for tough times.

The safety lever on the Smith & Wesson 2206 is conveniently located on the left side of the frame and operates independently of the slide.

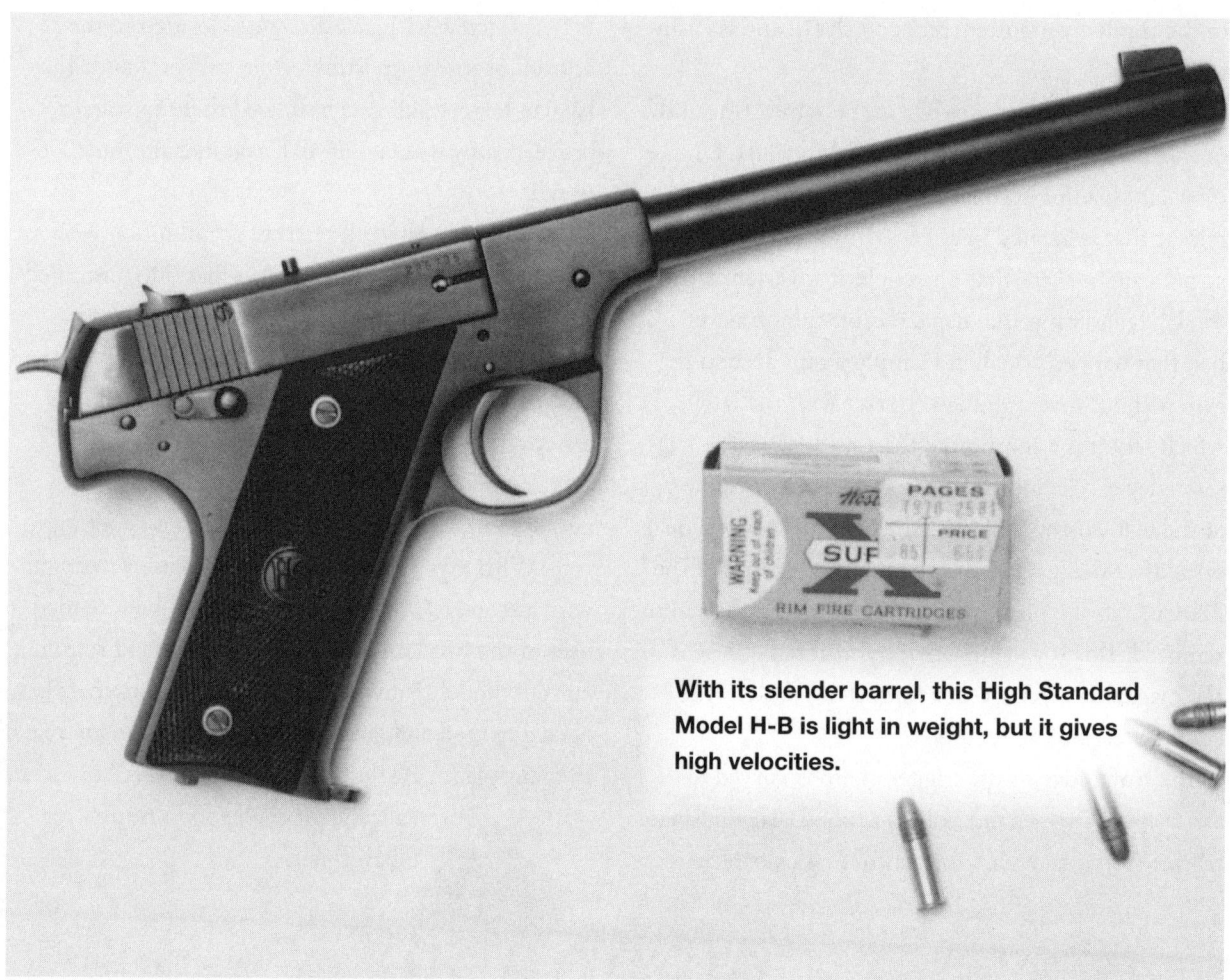

With its slender barrel, this High Standard Model H-B is light in weight, but it gives high velocities.

High Standard H-B

Founded in 1926, the High Standard Manufacturing Company in New Haven, Conn., produced rimfire handguns for many years. In 1932, High Standard purchased the Hartford Arms and Equipment Company. Over the years, High Standard, which was first located in New Haven, moved to Hamden, Conn. then to East Hartford. In 1984, High Standard ceased production of handguns due in no small measure to the enormous popularity of lower priced models like the Ruger Standard Mark I and the later Mark II and some of the lower-priced models from Smith & Wesson and Colt. But there were many fans of High Standard pistols that mourned their passing, and as will be explained later, it is hard to keep a good product out of the marketplace.

Over the years, High Standard autoloaders were produced in an enormous range of variants. Some of the early models were designated as the Models B, C, A, D, and E. Almost concurrently, other models were designated as the H-D, H-E, H-A, and H-B with the letter H denoting that the model has a visible hammer. The most popular barrel lengths were 4.5 and 6.5 inches, but not all models had the same barrel diameter. There were also other differences between the models in details regarding sights, grips, etc. Eventually, High Standard produced pistols for the U.S. government for military training. Some of these pistols had the letters "US" after the model designation. One model, the H-D Military, was also sold to the civilian market. About half a century ago, a friend of the author had an H-D Military model with a 6.5-inch barrel that he could shoot with great skill. His use of that handgun to hunt squirrels demonstrated just how effective a handgun could be in the hands of a careful hunter.

As strange as it may seem at this time, some of the models that had visible hammers did not have an external safety. The hammer functioned as it does on a revolver, which also has no external safety. The High Standard Model H-B Second Model described in this section was produced from 1949 to 1954. As with almost all of the other models, it had a magazine that held 10 rounds and checkered grips made of black hard rubber. The Model H-B exhibited the outstanding trigger pull that is sometimes found on older semiautomatics.

Only limited firing tests were conducted with the Model H-B, but the 6.5-inch barrel produced high velocities (see Chapter 7). This particular specimen failed to feed a few times because the cartridge was not forced into the chamber fully. The pistol seemed to have a weak recoil spring, which was another reason that only limited testing was conducted. Although highly prized by collectors, many of the older High Standard pistols are still capable of fine performance. Later models such as the Sport King were trim, versatile handguns that would make excellent companions for today's outdoorsman.

In 1993, High Standard Manufacturing Co., Inc., of Houston, TX began producing handguns that emulate to a high degree some of the earlier models. Two of the new versions are the High Standard Trophy and the Victor. These are target pistols that can be obtained with sights or scope rails in place. List prices for these models range from $540 to $689 depending on options selected. Although not one of the largest producers of rimfire handguns, pistols carrying the High Standard name are once again available.

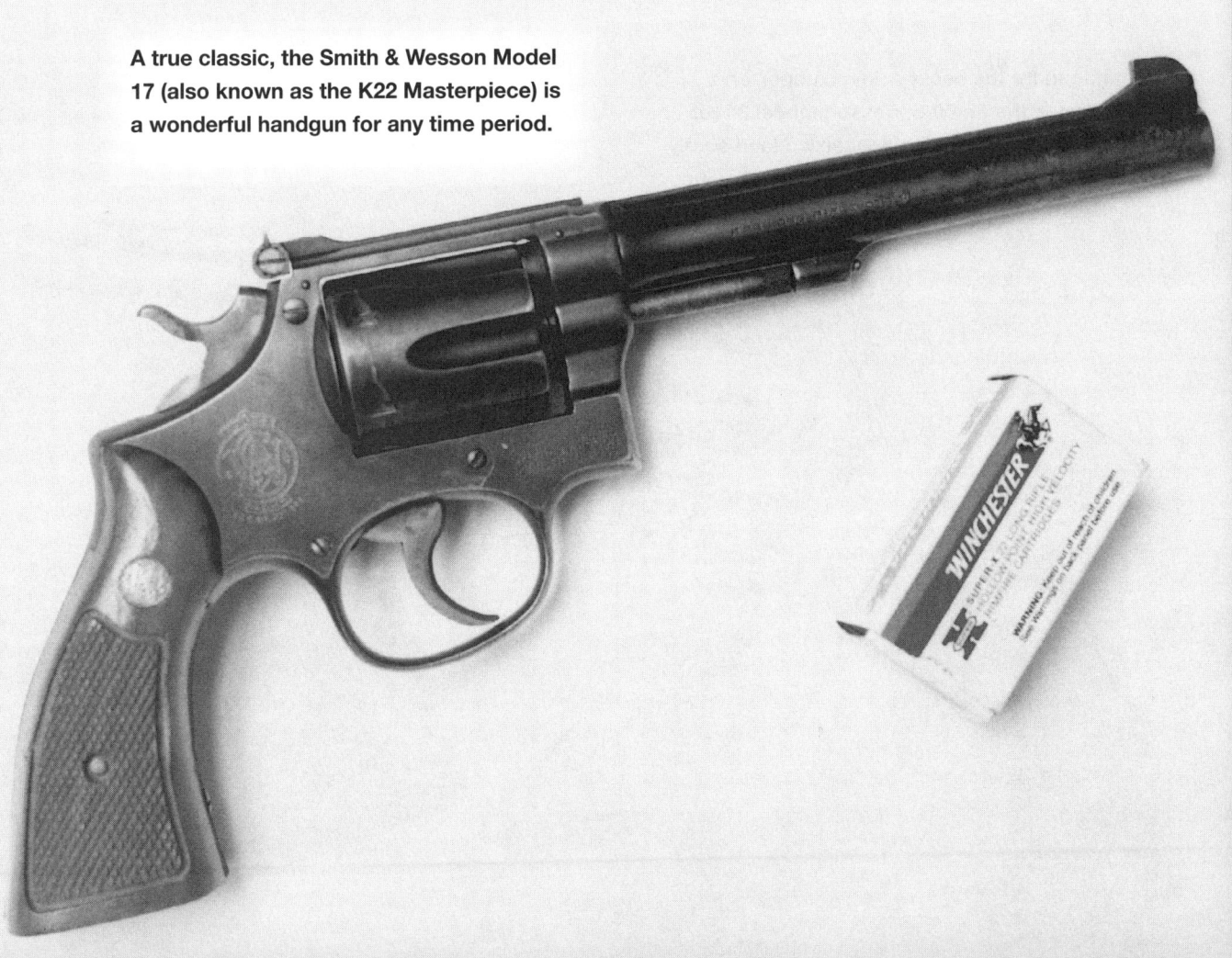

A true classic, the Smith & Wesson Model 17 (also known as the K22 Masterpiece) is a wonderful handgun for any time period.

Smith & Wesson K-22

In 1899, Smith & Wesson introduced a double-action revolver that was destined to become one of the most successful firearms of all time. Known as the S&W First Model, it was chambered for the then-new 38 Special cartridge, and the mid-sized frame was of an appropriate size for that round. The S&W revolver frame of that size is now known as the K-frame. For about 100 years, Smith & Wesson has produced revolvers with frames of four sizes. The smallest is the J-frame, the midsize is the K-frame, slightly larger is the L-frame, and the large frame used for magnum calibers is the N-frame. The new 500 S&W is produced on an even larger size frame known as the X-frame.

In a long evolutionary process, the initial 38 Special revolver came to be known as the Military and Police model, and when Smith & Wesson began to designate models numerically in 1958, the highly successful revolver became known as the Model 10. The K-frame became the basis for many other models such as the Model 15 Combat Masterpiece with a 4-inch barrel and target sights. While some of the other K-frame models are interesting and important, it is the series of target revolvers known as the Masterpiece series that is relevant here. The K-38 Masterpiece (38 Special caliber) was known as the Model 14 while the K-22 Masterpiece (22 LR caliber) was known as the Model 17. The Model 18 was a 22 LR version that was a companion piece to the Model 15 Combat Masterpiece. Some of these models underwent evolutionary changes, but they were eventually discontinued. Currently, Smith & Wesson produces the Model 617 which is built on the K-frame, but it is made of stainless steel and has a full length lug under the barrel. The current Model 617 is a fine handgun that is considerably heavier than the K-22.

Over the years, the K-22 was available with 4-, 6-, and 8.38-inch barrels with the 6-inch length being

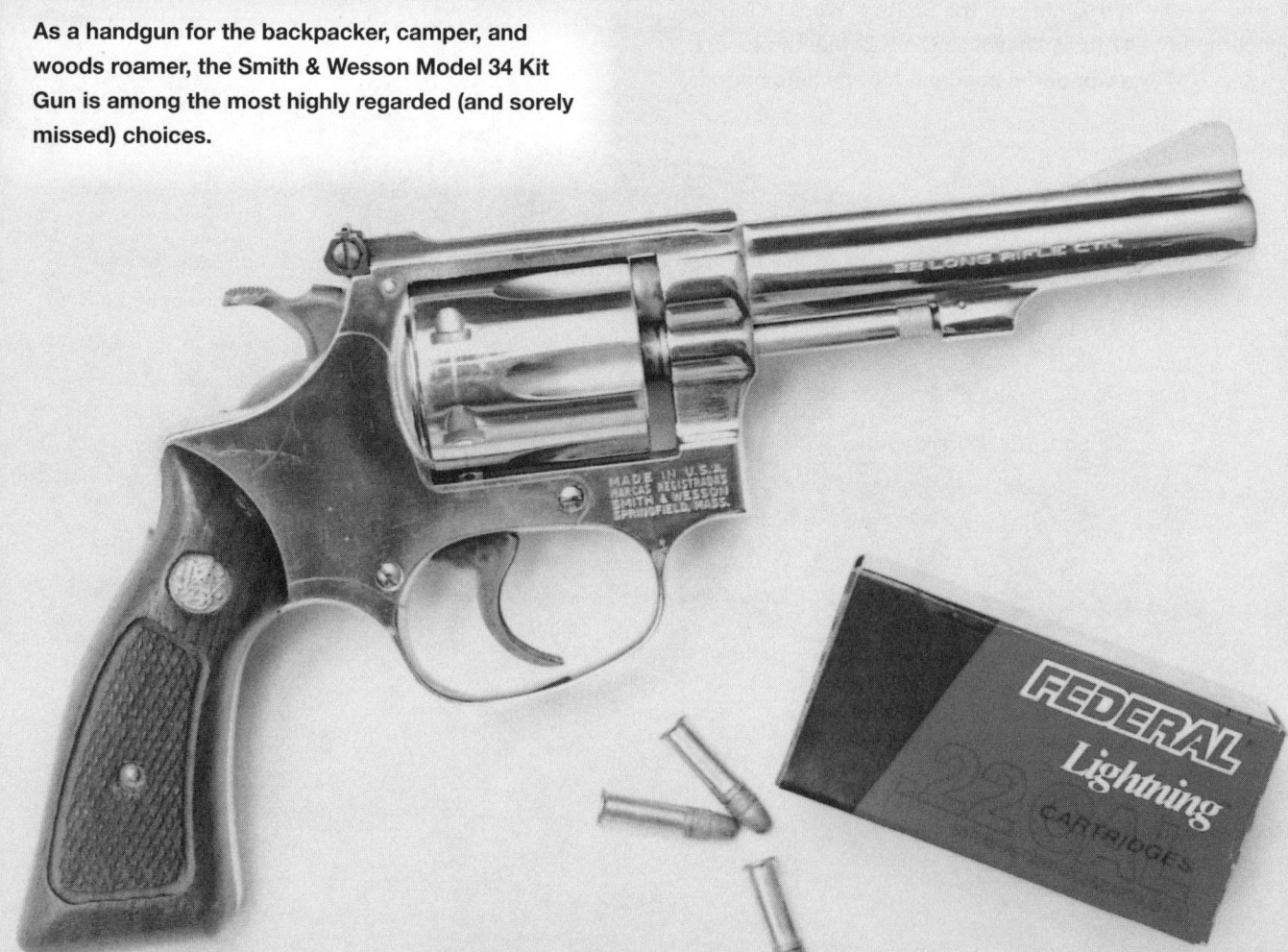

As a handgun for the backpacker, camper, and woods roamer, the Smith & Wesson Model 34 Kit Gun is among the most highly regarded (and sorely missed) choices.

the most popular. Many options were available including target grips as well as target hammers and triggers. Realizing that most target shooters would cock the gun for each shot, one version was offered as a single-action-only gun. Needless to say, the Masterpiece series were highly regarded arms that were widely used in target competition. The square topped post and fully adjustable rear sights are the equal of those on any currently produced handgun. As autoloaders became more popular, the demand for these fine revolvers decreased and most of the options were no longer offered. Another group of shooters that became interested in the K-22 were the small game hunters who chose to hunt with handguns. A K-22 was and still is one of the best choices for this type of activity. Trigger pull on the K-22 is crisp and predictable which is fully consistent with the intended use of these fine guns.

As Smith & Wesson makes changes in a particular model, the new variants are indicated by a number following the basic model number. For example, the 15-3 designation indicates the third variant of a Model 15 Combat Masterpiece. The designation can be found by opening the cylinder and looking at the yoke where the serial number and model designation appear. The K-22 evaluated belongs to the author's brother, and it is old enough that it does not have this type of designation. A call to Smith & Wesson allowed a check of the serial number to be made which showed that this gun was produced in 1951, several years before models were designated numerically. However, in spite of its age, the K-22 performed admirably. It is completely dependable and displayed good accuracy. With the addition of a good holster, the old S&W K-22 would be a superb choice for the outdoorsman who needs a reliable rimfire handgun, and being several ounces lighter than the current Model 617 would make it even more desirable. A safer, more dependable, better performing 22 revolver than the Smith & Wesson K-22 has never been made in my opinion.

Smith & Wesson Model 34 Kit Gun

As this is being written in 2004, rimfire autoloaders are much more popular than are revolvers, but it has not always been so. While each type of action has its advantages and disadvantages, one of the most useful rimfire handguns is a compact, sturdy revolver with target sights and good action. There are several reasons for this. First, a revolver can be loaded with the Short, Long, or Long Rifle cartridges, and it is ideal for making use of shot cartridges. Semiautomatics will not feed all of these types of ammunition. Second, it is the belief of the author that revolvers are inherently safer than semiautomatic pistols. Whether a revolver is loaded or not can be ascertained instantly. Third, when carried in a holster, there is much less chance of the hammer on a revolver being moved back accidentally than there is for the small safety lever on a semiautomatic being moved from the "safe" position. In fact, I almost never carry a holstered autoloader that has no external hammer with a round in the chamber. With modern revolvers, the transfer bar is not moved upward so that the blow of the hammer is transmitted unless the trigger is pulled back. With all of these factors considered, what is the ideal rimfire handgun for general use?

There are many shooters who believe that the Smith & Wesson Model 34, also known as the Kit Gun, is about as close as you can get to the ultimate in a rimfire utility handgun. It was referred to as the Kit Gun because it was appropriate to include with the camping kit, fishing kit, or hunting kit, not because it was purchased as parts and assembled later. Introduced in 1935, the original model was known as the 22/32 Kit Gun because it utilized the small J-frame of the 32 Hand Ejector model. In 1953, the later version of the Kit Gun that became known as the Model 34 when model numbers were assigned was available with a barrel of 2- or 4-inch length and a weight of about 22 ounces. The front sight is a serrated ramp of 0.10-inch thickness while the rear sight is a square notch blade that can be adjusted for windage and elevation. Over the years, both round and square butt models were available in blue or nickel finish. From 1955-1974, a variant with a weight of 14.5 ounces was produced with an aluminum frame and cylinder and a 3.5-inch barrel.

While the Kit Guns of early manufacture (1935-1953) are highly prized as collectibles, the later versions are highly prized as shooters. This is still one of the most practical rimfire handguns ever made for the hiker, camper, or outdoorsman. As part of the testing program reported here, the near mint nickel-plated specimen belonging to my brother was made available for testing (unfortunately not for purchasing).

Superb in fit and finish, the Kit Gun performed with excellence. I must admit, however, that I cannot fire it as accurately as I can a Browning Buck Mark autoloader which weighs about 10 ounces more and has a heavy barrel. But in every other aspect, the performance of the Kit Gun would be difficult to improve on. Being a revolver, it can readily accept any 22 LR ammunition from shot cartridges to CCI Stingers with no question as to whether feeding will be reliable. There is no more versatile rimfire handgun than a good revolver. This and many other S&W revolvers perform flawlessly now just as they have for many years.

In spite of its many desirable attributes, the Kit Gun in the form tested is no longer available. What is available is the Smith & Wesson Model 317 that has an alloy frame and cylinder. It is an 8-shot revolver that is available with a 3-inch barrel and adjustable HVIZ® (fiber optic) sights. Weighing only 11.9 ounces, it ought to be a fine backpacker's or camper's gun, but there is one problem. It has a manufacturer's suggested price of $636, which even at retail amounts to approximately $525 according to my dealer. This is approximately twice as much as several autoloader models cost. Therein lies one of the reason why rimfire autoloaders are currently much more popular than revolvers. Given a choice at a comparable price, I would select the Kit Gun over any rimfire autoloader as a trail gun.

Ruger Single Six

Sturm, Ruger and Company produced its first handgun model in 1949. That handgun was the original autoloader that continues in production today in a highly evolved form known as the Mark III. In 1953, Ruger introduced the single-action revolver known as the Single Six. It was very similar in many respects to the original Colt Peacemaker (Single-Action Army) that was introduced in 1873. Unlike the Colt, which had a rounded loading gate, the loading gate of the Ruger Single Six was a flat piece of metal with a curved notch to be engaged by the thumb nail when opening the gate. This author bought one of those early models with the flat loading gate and used it until something else caught his youthful fancy (the identity of which can not be remembered at this time). As in the case of many other items, the early models, which were traded off without regret at the time, have become collectibles and command a premium in price. These become the pieces known as "I wish I had that one back" which afflicts many shooters. But wisdom comes to those who think so I got another Single Six with the rounded loading gate in 1958. Recounting my experiences associated with this handgun over so many years would fill a small volume.

In 1957, the loading gate was redesigned to resemble the rounded loading gate of the Colt single-action revolvers. However, the Ruger single-action revolvers suffered from some of the same deficiencies as the early Colt models. Most important of these flaws is that when the hammer is down, the firing pin rests against a cartridge that is in alignment with it (the chamber at the "top" of the cylinder). A blow to the hammer could cause the revolver to fire accidentally. Drawing the hammer back slightly allows it to engage a safety notch. However, even the safety notch on the hammer that was designed to

This three-screw or "old model" Ruger Single Six and the author became companions in 1958. They are still close friends.

hold the hammer back slightly away from the firing pin could not be relied upon to prevent accidental discharge when a heavy blow struck the hammer. To circumvent this problem, it was common practice to carry the piece with only five rounds loaded in the cylinder with the empty chamber being directly below the hammer. Another problem was that the hammer had to be drawn back to half cock to release the cylinder lock so that the cylinder could be rotated during the loading process. After loading, the hammer had to be drawn back to full cock and held with the thumb as the trigger was pulled and held back so that the hammer could be let down. The result was that during the loading process, the shooter was dealing with a cocked, loaded revolver. These aspects applied to both Colt and Ruger single-action revolvers. Ruger revolvers with this older type of action have three screws visible on the right hand side of the frame. Accordingly, they are known as "three-screw" models, but Ruger refers to them as "old model" single-action revolvers.

In 1973, Ruger introduced a redesigned single-action revolver that circumvented the problems described above. The "new model" revolvers make use of a transfer bar to transmit the blow of the hammer to the firing pin. The transfer bar is raised between the hammer and firing pin as the trigger is pulled. Therefore, unless the trigger is pulled to the rear, a blow to the hammer merely forces it forward against the frame and cannot cause the piece to discharge. Moreover, the loading gate is linked to the cylinder in such a way that opening the gate releases the cylinder lock and allows the cylinder to be rotated. In that way, the cylinder can be loaded with the hammer in the down position. The new model revolvers can be carried with all six chambers loaded and they can be loaded without having to go through the process of moving the hammer in any way. Clearly, the new model Ruger single-action revolvers are much safer than the older models. For many years, Sturm, Ruger & Co. has offered a free upgrade for the three screw revolvers. It requires that the gun be sent to the factory for fitting the new parts, but the old parts are returned with the modified gun so nothing is lost in terms of the collector value of the gun. For the purposes of this project, the pre-1973 three screw models are vintage revolvers.

Ruger single-action revolvers have an enviable reputation for durability and reliability. Although some versions have fixed sights, excellent adjustable sights are standard on most of the new Ruger single-actions, and they provide a good sight picture. On the old model tested, the front sight is the familiar semicircle with a square top and serrations on the back edge. The rear sight has a square notch of suitable size. There is no provision for elevation adjustment, but windage can be adjusted by moving the rear sight laterally in its retaining dovetail. With virtually any type of ammunition, this handgun has always shot as nearly to the point of aim as I can discern. The sights have never been found lacking for my purposes, and they have never been adjusted.

Trigger action on my old Ruger Single-action is unbelievably good with absolutely no creep and a let off at 2.8 pounds. Of all the handguns tested, only the trigger action of my Browning Buck Mark is this good. One rarely finds a trigger with these characteristics today except on target models. In my younger days, the revolver was disassembled and internal surfaces were polished with crocus cloth. The action is as smooth as that of any single-action revolver produced today.

When the hammer is drawn back and the trigger is pulled, the Single Six fires every time no matter what type of ammunition resides in the chambers. It is this kind of behavior that makes a single-action revolver so reliable. It is also the reason why single-action revolvers are still chosen for carry in remote areas by many knowledgeable people. True, the single-action is an outmoded design for uses such as military and law enforcement work. But as a handgun for tough times, the single-action is still a viable option.

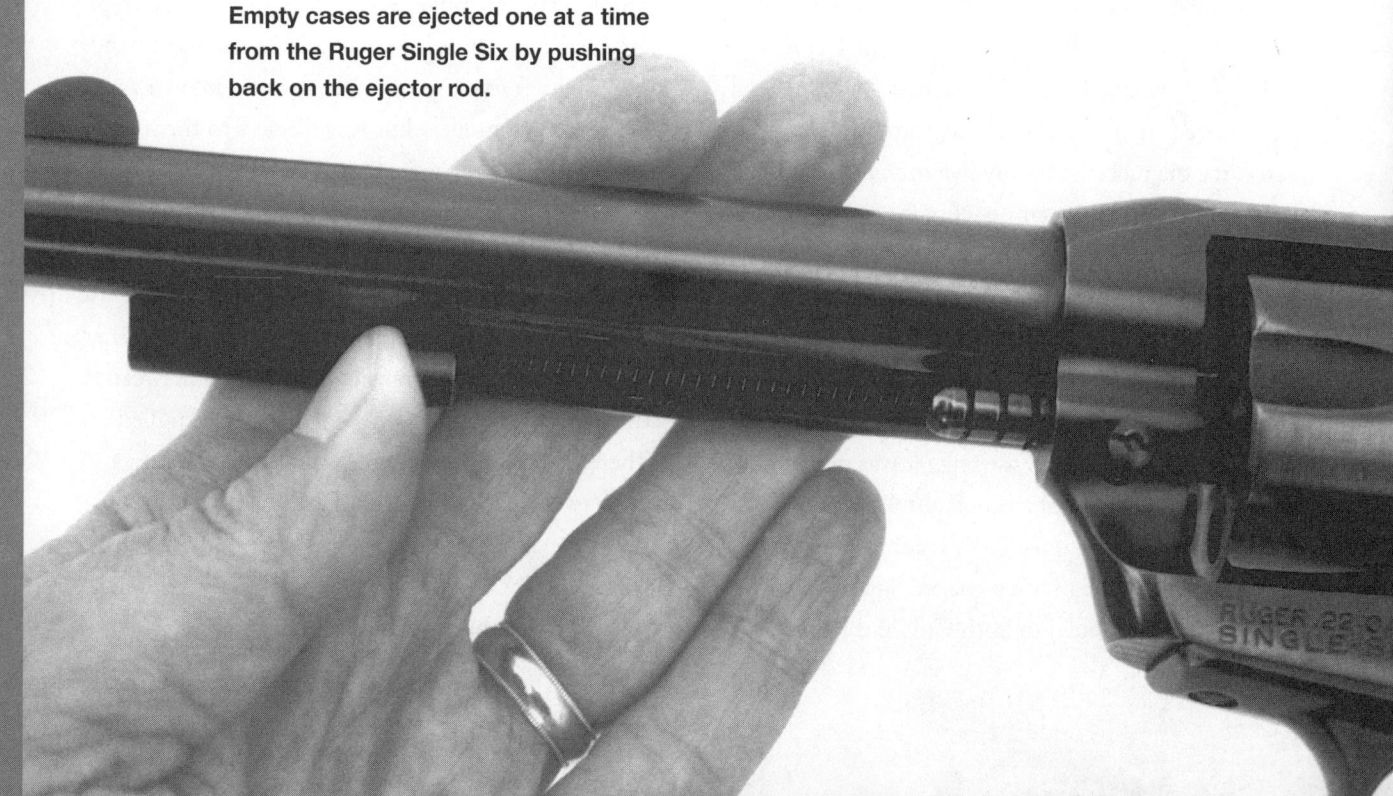

Empty cases are ejected one at a time from the Ruger Single Six by pushing back on the ejector rod.

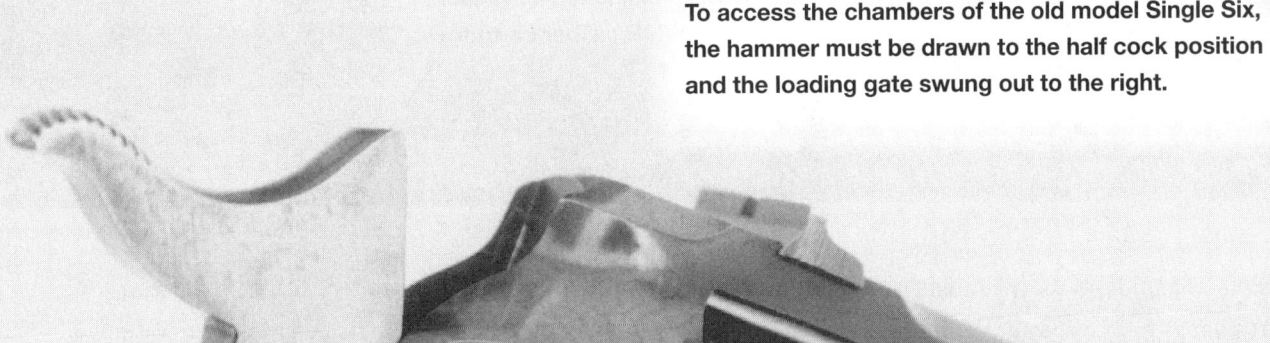

The Colt Frontier Scout (left) and the old model Ruger Single Six (right) function in similar ways.

To access the chambers of the old model Single Six, the hammer must be drawn to the half cock position and the loading gate swung out to the right.

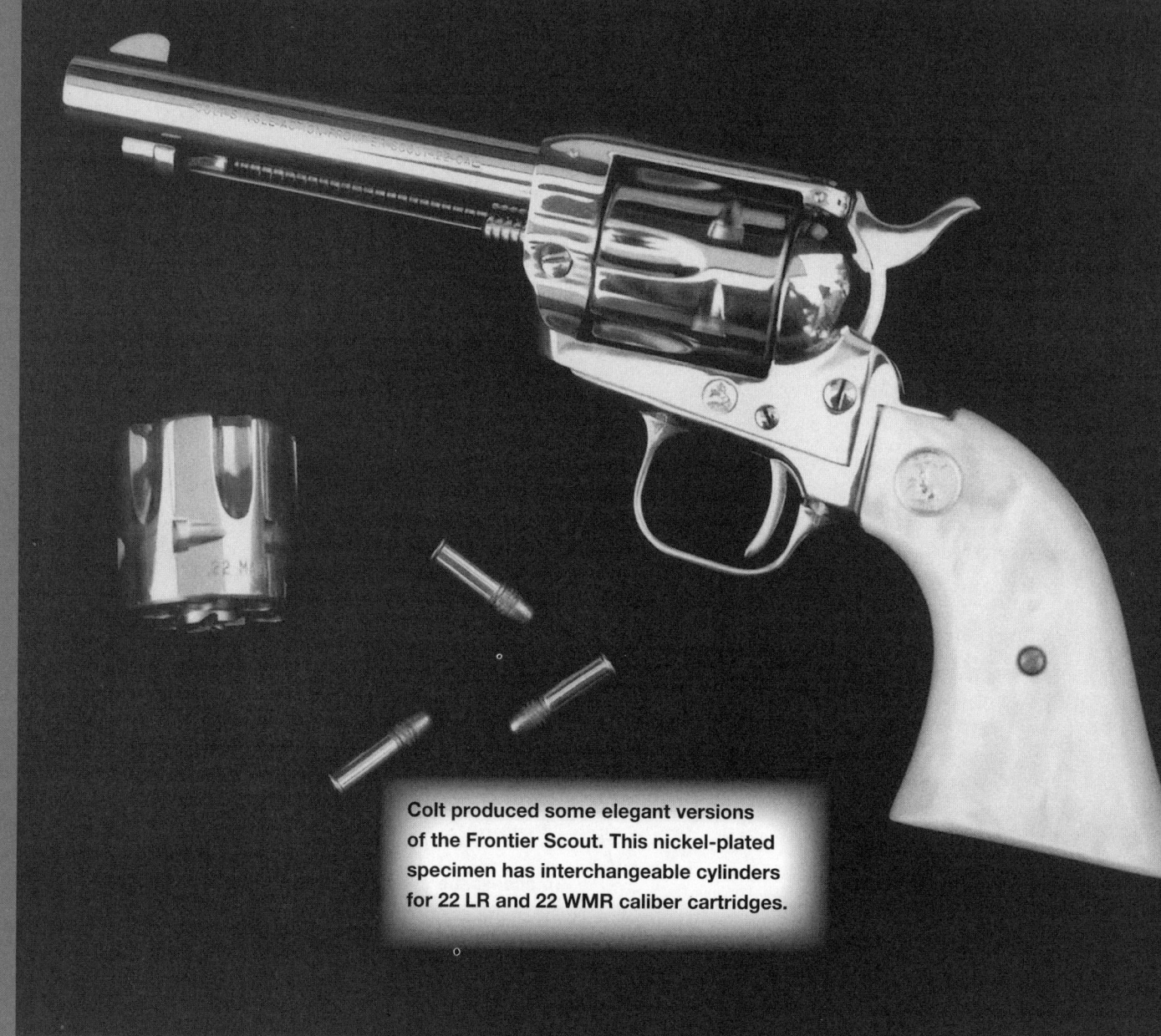

Colt produced some elegant versions of the Frontier Scout. This nickel-plated specimen has interchangeable cylinders for 22 LR and 22 WMR caliber cartridges.

Elsewhere in this book is pictured an old Single Six that belongs to a cowboy in Wyoming. It has been carried on foot, on horse, and on ATV countless hours and miles. It is a working gun, and it still works even though it has very little blue left on it and the grip panels are chipped. I seriously doubt that the owner of that gun would be interested in trading it for most of the modern autoloaders.

The old Single Six described and pictured here had not been used much in recent years as I had become infatuated with other models. In order to collect some thoughts on the gun, it was carefully examined and tested. There is something special about the look, feel, and pointing qualities of a single-action revolver.

It was like getting reacquainted with an old friend. For many years, the Single Six described here was my only handgun, and it always performed well. It would still meet any need that I could have for a rimfire handgun.

Colt Frontier Scout

With the most recognizable revolver ever made being the Colt Single-action Army model of 1873, there has always been an interest in single-action revolvers. The legendary Colt has such an aura of romance and respect that it generates interest in a similar gun chambered for rimfire calibers. This interest led to the introduction of the Ruger

Single Six in 1953 and introduction of the Colt Frontier Scout in 1957. In later years, both models were produced with an optional cylinder that was chambered for the 22 WMR. The Frontier Scout was produced with several barrel lengths that included 4.75 and 9.5 inches. Currently, Ruger produces several single-action rimfire models, and Heritage Manufacturing produces revolvers with interchangeable cylinders in 22 LR and 22 WMR calibers in both blue and stainless steel.

The Frontier Scout used an aluminum alloy frame and was produced in several variants over the years of its production. In 1970, Colt produced another rimfire single-action known as the Peacemaker, and it remained in production until 1977. It had a steel frame that was case hardened, and the Peacemaker was marketed with an additional cylinder in 22 WMR. The cylinders chambered for the 22 LR were fluted, but those chambered for the 22 WMR were not. A later version, known as the New Frontier, had a steel frame and adjustable sights. Barrel lengths on the Peacemaker and New Frontier models were 4.38, 6 and 7.5 inches. When taken as a series, the various Colt single-action rimfire models have been offered in a wide variety of barrel lengths and sight options. Numerous commemorative models have also been produced. Some were offered with nickel finish, gold accents, and ornate wooden cases which made them beautiful collectibles.

Operation of a Frontier Scout follows that of the famous Single-action Army. Drawing the hammer back to the half cock position releases the cylinder so it can be rotated. Opening the loading gate exposes a chamber into which a cartridge can be inserted. Rotating the cylinder one-sixth of a revolution exposes another chamber, and so on, until all of the chambers can be loaded. With revolvers of this type, a blow to the hammer can cause the revolver to fire. As discussed earlier, Ruger modified its single-action revolvers in 1973 by incorporating a transfer bar that is in position to allow a blow from the hammer to be transmitted to the cartridge only when the trigger is pulled to the rear.

The two Frontier Scouts tested have barrels measuring 4.75 and 9.5 inches (see Chapter 7). The 4.75-inch barreled specimen is a solid old gun with

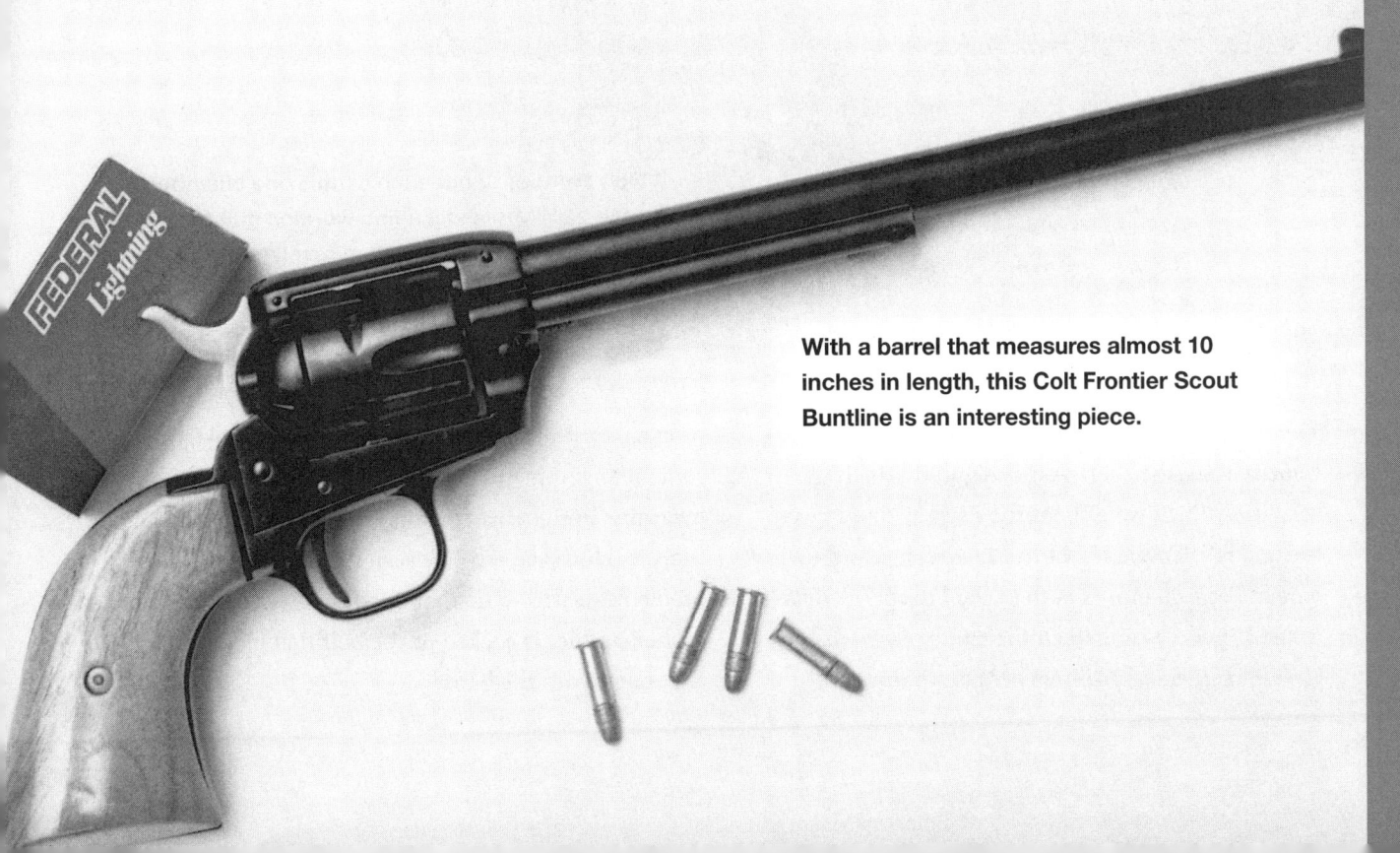

With a barrel that measures almost 10 inches in length, this Colt Frontier Scout Buntline is an interesting piece.

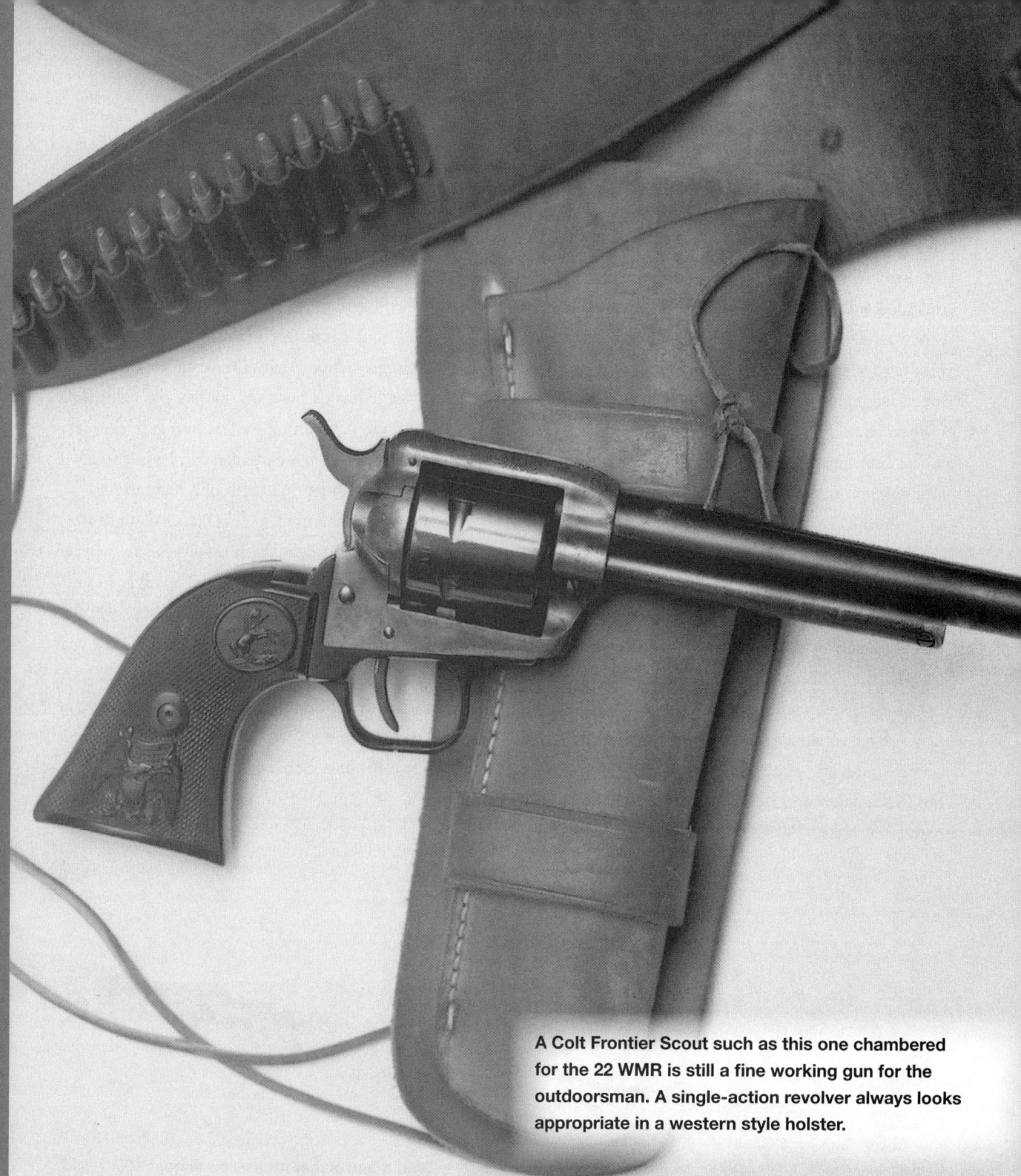

A Colt Frontier Scout such as this one chambered for the 22 WMR is still a fine working gun for the outdoorsman. A single-action revolver always looks appropriate in a western style holster.

a close fit between the cylinder and barrel. In the velocity tests, the short-barreled gun routinely gave velocities which were about the same as those given by the Frontier Scout that has a barrel nearly 5 inches longer. Performance of both of the Frontier Scouts is just as good as was when the guns were new. This is characteristic of revolvers because there are no problems with feeding cartridges which can plague some semiautomatics when chamber edges get rough, magazine lips get bent, recoil springs weaken with age, etc. However, revolvers can be plagued with problems related to the hand that rotates the cylinder as the hammer is cocked or the bolt that locks it in alignment with the barrel.

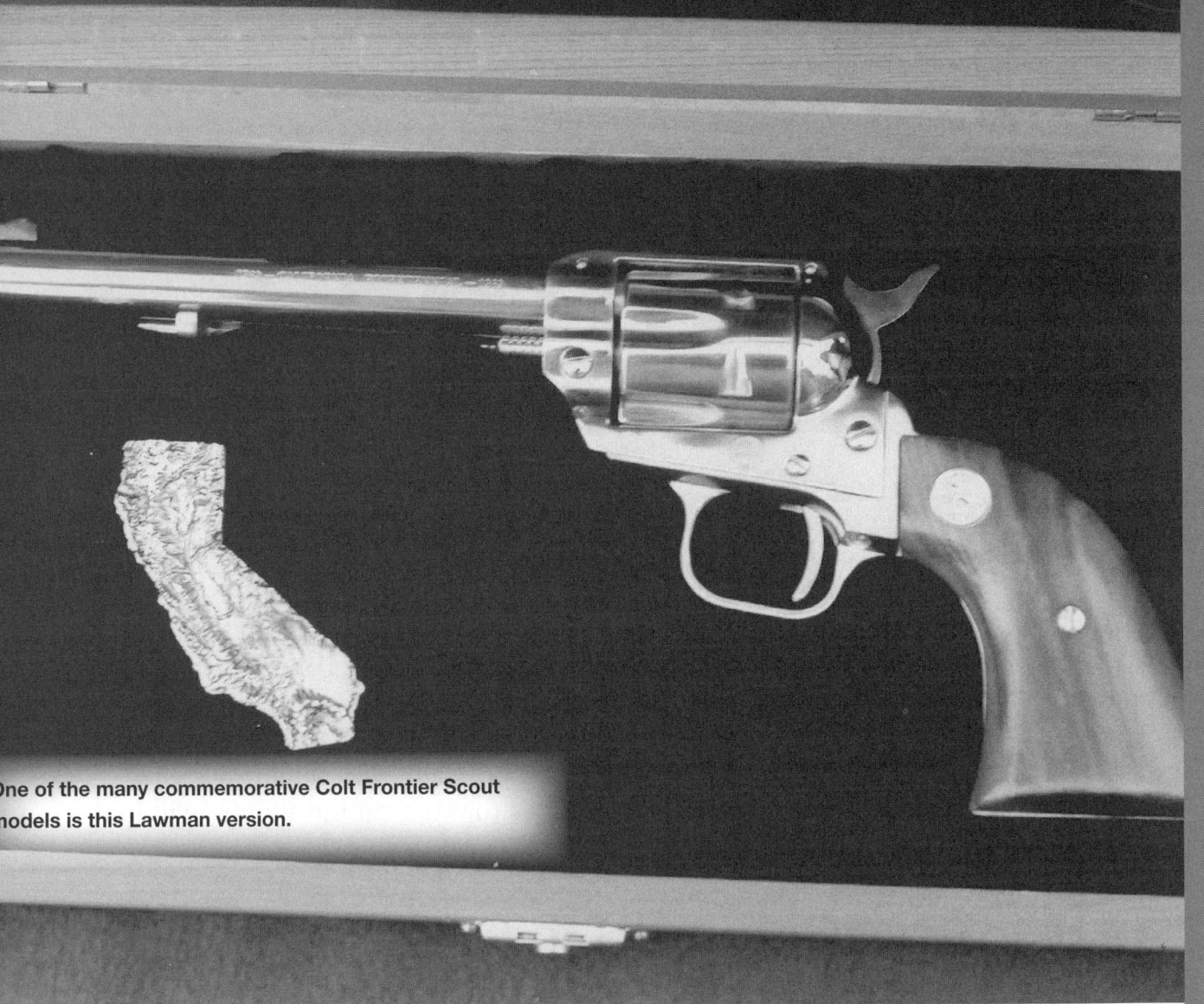

One of the many commemorative Colt Frontier Scout models is this Lawman version.

The crude sights on the Frontier Scouts made accurate shooting impossible, but for short-range work these handguns would perform admirably. Moreover, with its aluminum alloy frame, the Frontier Scout is a lightweight handgun that carries and like other single-actions points very well. If one is searching for a single-action rimfire to carry as a trail gun, the Frontier Scout would be a good choice. Unfortunately, these models are also quite collectible so prices have risen in recent years. A Frontier Scout in good condition is often found for about $400 or so which exceeds the retail price of a new Ruger Single Six or Bearcat model.

Evaluating the vintage handguns described in this chapter made it clear that these models can perform just as well as current models, but some current models have additional safety features. Should you select a vintage rimfire handgun for general use? If a specimen is found in good condition at a reasonable price, there is no reason not to select it for a variety of uses. However, the prospective buyer of a rimfire handgun should examine current models along with the older ones to make sure that the handgun chosen has the required feel and handling characteristics. Remember also that new firearms come with a warranty while the assurance program for used firearms (if any) depends on the dealer. Although models like the Colt Woodsman and Frontier Scout and the Smith & Wesson K-22 and Kit Gun are no longer produced, they are not difficult to find if you should decide you must own one. However, there are also many choices at comparable prices among the current models for the rimfire handgunner.

Appendix A

SUGGESTIONS FOR FURTHER READING

In the process of dealing with firearms and the shooting sports, many people develop a thirst for additional information. This interest may be directed toward some narrow aspect of the shooting sports or may simply reflect the desire for a broader appreciation of the field. The following bibliography lists references that may prove useful as you seek to improve your knowledge of rimfire firearms and ammunition. The literature dealing with the shooting sports is extensive so some selection was required. For example, even though they contain information on shooting, there is no need to list books that deal specifically with double barreled shotguns, so the books described are some of those that the rimfire shooter will find most helpful.

Arnold, Dave, *Handguns 2005, 16th Ed.*, Krause Publications, Iola, WI (2004) (888) 457-2873. www.krause.com. A valuable resource for users of all types of handguns, including rimfires.

Barber, John L., *The Rimfire Cartridge in the United States and Canada*, Thomas Publications, Gettysburg, PA (2000). A history of rimfire cartridges.

Barnes, Frank C., *Cartridges of the World*, 7th Edition, Krause Publications, Iola, WI (2003). www.krause.com. The standard reference on both current and obsolete metallic cartridges.

Datig, Fred A., *Cartridges for Collectors*, Vol. 2, Pioneer Press, Union, TN (1999). Illustrated dictionary of rimfire cartridges. Out of print but sometimes available through dealers who specialize in hard to find books.

Fadala, Sam, *The Book of the Twenty-Two: The All-American Caliber*, Stoeger Publishing Company, South Hackensack, NJ (1989). A general reference work on the 22 caliber that covers both rimfire and center fire calibers.

Fears, J. Wayne, *The Complete Book of Outdoor Survival*, Krause Publications, Iola, WI (2000). (888) 457-2873 www.krause.com A complete guide to the skills necessary for survival and safety in outdoor situations.

Forker, Bob, *Ammo & Ballistics II*, Safari Press, Huntington Beach, CA (2003). A comprehensive book devoted to ammunition and ballistics.

Geiger, D. F., *22 Caliber Handguns: A Shooter's Guide*, Andrew Mowbray, Inc., Lincoln, RI (2003). A general introduction to the use of rimfire handguns.

Hatcher, Julian S., *Hatcher's Notebook*, Odysseus Editions Firearms Classics, NRA, Fairfax, VA (1996). This book is an essential reference on ballistics and a wide range of subjects dealing with arms and ammunition.

Houze, Herbert G., *The Winchester 52: Perfection in Design*, Krause Publications, Iola, WI (1997). www.krause.com. The Winchester Model 52 target rifle is probably the most famous small-bore target rifle ever made. This book covers the evolution of the Model 52 throughout its period of production.

Lachuk, John, *The Gun Digest Book of the .22 Rimfire*, DBI Books, Northfield, IL (1978). A book dealing with all aspects of rimfire shooting by a highly regarded author in the field. As with all such books, the models change although there is a wealth of information presented that is not related to specific models. Long out of print, it still can be found by some dealers in hard to get books. Digest Books are now published by Krause Publications, Iola, WI.

Long, Duncan, *The Ruger .22 Automatic Pistols, Standard/Mark I/Mark II Series*, Paladin Press, Boulder, CO (1989). www.paladin-press.com. A reference work on the ever- popular Ruger pistols.

Long, Duncan, *The Sturm, Ruger 10/22 Rifle and .44 Magnum Carbine*, Paladin Press, Boulder, CO (1988). www.paladin-press.com. A small book devoted to the Ruger semiautomatic rifles.

Madis, George, *Winchester Dates of Manufacture*, Art and Reference House, Brownsboro, TX (1984). This little book contains a lot of information on Winchester firearms, serial numbers, and dates of manufacture.

Matunas, Edward, *.22 Rimfire*, Peterson Publishing Company, Los Angeles, CA (1984). This is a special publication that was part of the Guns & Ammo Action Series. An excellent reference that deals with all aspects of rimfire firearms and ammunition. It contains a large amount of information, but many of the firearms discussed are no longer available.

McCann, John D., *Build the Perfect Survival Kit*, Krause Publications, Iola, WI (2004) (888) 457-2873. www.krause.com. Information on how to assemble a survival kit for numerous types of activities.

McCoy, Robert L, *Modern Exterior Ballistics*, Schiffer Publishing Co., Atglen, PA (1999). A valuable resource for shooters who want to develop their expertise in ballistics.

Nonte, George C., and Jurras, L. E., *Handgun Hunting*, Winchester Press, New York, NY (1975). Although the emphasis is on hunting with center fire handguns, there is a great deal of information that would be useful the small game hunter using a rimfire handgun.

Quest for Rimfire Accuracy http://members.com.net/benchrest/rimfire_notes.html. This website is devoted to information for serious rimfire shooters. Topics posted by experts include equipment, ammunition, and techniques. Highly recommended for the shooter who wants to learn.

Ramage, Ken, *Gun Digest 2005*, Krause Publications, Iola, WI (2004). Billed as "the world's greatest gun book" it has 558 pages to back up that claim. The 59th edition of a classic, it contains numerous articles on a plethora of subjects in addition to a complete catalog section. Also included is a huge section on periodicals and books dealing with guns and shooting. A highly recommended resource.

Rees, Clair, *Optics Digest*, Safari Press, Huntington Beach, CA (2005). A complete book devoted scopes, binoculars, rangefinders, and spotting scopes.

Schwing, Ned, *2004 Standard Catalog of Firearms*, 14th Edition, Krause Publications, Iola, WI (2003). An enormous volume that contains an enormous amount of information on firearms and their values.

Schwing, Ned, *Winchester Slide Action Rifles*, Krause Publications, Iola, WI (2004). A reference work on the Models 1890, 1906, 61, and 62 Winchester rimfire rifles. For serious collectors of rimfire Winchester rifles, this book gives an enormous amount of information.

Serven, James E., *Colt Firearms 1836-1960*, Wolfe Publishing Company, Prescott, AZ (1991). A historical book that contains a lot of information of older models of Colt handguns, both black powder and cartridge.

Stebens, Henry M., Shay, Albert J. E., and Hammond, Oscar R., *Pistols: A Modern Encyclopedia*, The Stackpole Company, Harrisburg, PA (1961). Although many of the models discussed are no longer in production, this book is a worthwhile reference on all subjects related to handguns.

Traister, John E., *Gunsmithing at Home: Lock, Stock, & Barrel*, 2nd ed., Stoeger Publishing Company, Accokeek, MD (1996). Although this book deals with gunsmith work, it also contains a wealth of information on maintenance, tools, finishing, etc.

White, Mark, *The Ultimate Ruger 10/22 Manual and User's Guide*, Paladin Press, Boulder, CO (2000). www.paladin-press.com. This book presents a great deal of information on the performance and modification of the most popular autoloader in 22 LR caliber, the Ruger 10/22.

Wilson, R. L., *Ruger and His Guns*, Simon & Schuster, New York, NY (1996). In addition to chronicling the Ruger Company, this lavishly illustrated book contains a great deal on the design and development of Ruger firearms as well as historical information and serial numbers.

Wilson, R. L., *Winchester: An American Legend*, Random House, New York, NY (1991). A noted author provides a history of Winchester firearms in this beautifully illustrated "coffee table" book. A valuable resource for anyone interested in Winchester firearms.

Wood, J. B., *The Gun Digest Book of Firearms Assembly/Disassembly Part III. Rimfire Rifles*, Krause Publications (1994). A highly respected gunsmith gives step-by-step instructions for taking apart and putting together a large number of rimfire rifles. Many of the techniques described are useful for working on firearms other than those specifically covered.

Workman, W. E., *The Ruger 10/22*, Krause Publications, Iola, WI (1994). A complete reference work that covers variations, markings, and advertising material from the introduction of the Ruger 10/22 in 1964 to the time of publication. A must for serious 10/22 buffs.

Workman, W. E., *Know Your Ruger 10/22 Carbine*, Blacksmith Corp., Chino Valley, CA (1991). Reference data on the Ruger 10/22.

Appendix B

SOURCES FOR THE RIMFIRE SHOPPER

Aimtech Mount Systems, P.O. Box 223, Thomasville, GA 31799 (229) 226-4313 www.aimtech-mounts.com. Sells scope mounts for a wide variety of firearms.

Aguila Ammunition, Centurion Ordnance, Inc. 11614 Rainbow Ridge, Helotes, TX 78023 (210) 695-4602 www.aguilaammo.com.

Altius Handcrafted Firearms, 125 Madison Ave., West Yellowstone, MT 59758 (406) 646-9222 www.altiusguns.com. A source for the serious rimfire shooter. Custom built biathalon and sporting rifles and other gunsmith services by Marc Sheppard.

J. G. Anschutz GmbH & Co. KG, P.O. Box 1128, D-89001 Ulm, Germany (800) 534-3150 www.anschutz-sporters.com. Manufacturers of an extensive line of high quality rimfire rifles.

B-Square, P. O. Box 11281, Fort Worth, TX 76110-0281 (800) 433-2909 www.b-square.com. Maker of an extensive line of scope mounts.

Bald Eagle, 101-J Allison St., Lock Haven, PA 17745 (570) 748-6772 www.baldeaglemachine.com. Products include a rim thickness gauge.

Beretta USA Corp., 17601 Beretta Drive, Accokeek, MD 20607 (800) 636-3420 www.berettausa.com. Manufacturer of a com. plete line of handguns including several rimfire models.

Bianchi International, P.O Box 9015, Temecula, CA 92589 (800) 477-8545 www.bianchi-intl.com. Producer of an extensive line of holsters.

Birchwood Laboratories, Inc., 7900 Fuller Road, Eden Prairie, MN 55344 (800) 328-6156. www.birchwoodcasey.com. Producers of a full line of gun care products, targets, and other supplies for the shooter.

Bob's Gun Shop, P. O. Box 200, Royal, AR 71968 (501) 767-1970 www.gun-parts.com. A supplier of parts including sights.

Bo-Mar Tool & Mfg. Co., 6136 State Hwy. 300, Longview, TX 75604 (903) 759-4784 One of the leading producers of handgun sights.

Boyds' Gunstock Industries, Inc., 25376 403 Rd. Ave., Mitchell, SD 57301 (605) 996-5011 www.boydboys.com. A producer of aftermarket stocks in many configurations

Brownells, 200 South Front St., Montezuma, IA 50171 (800) 741-0015 www.brownells.com. Supplier of tools, accessories, and parts in a bewildering array.

Browning Arms, One Browning Place, Morgan, UT 84050 (800) 333-3288 www.browning.com. Producers of lever-action and semiautomatic rimfire rifles.

BSA Optics, Southwest 47th Avenue, Suite 914, Ft. Lauderdale, FL 33314 (954) 581-2144 www.bsaoptics.com. Markets an extensive line of scopes.

Burris Company, Inc., 331 E. 8th St., Greeley, CO 80631 (970) 356-1670 www.burrisoptics.com. Producer of high quality scopes.

Bushnell, 9200 Cody, Overland Park, KS 66214 (888) 838-1449 www.bushnell.com. A supplier of an extensive line of scopes.

Butler Creek, P.O. Box 1690, Oregon City, OR 97045 (800) 948-1356 www.butler-creek.com. A large supplier of aftermarket item such as stocks and barrels.

Cabela's, One Cabela Drive, Sidney, NE 69160 (800) 237-4444 www.cabelas.com. A supplier of an enormous range of supplies for shooters both through catalog and retail sales.

CCI/Speer, 2299 Snake River Ave., Lewiston, ID 83501 (866) 286-7436 www.cci-ammunition.com. Manufacturer of a full line of rimfire ammunition.

Clark Custom Guns, Inc., 336 Shootout Lane, Princeton, LA 71067 (318) 949-9884 www.clarkcustomguns.com. Producer of products and services for enhanced accuracy.

Clerke International Arms, 101 Bacon St., Raton, NM 87740 www.clerkebarrels.com. Producer of aftermarket barrels and other items.

Colt's Manufacturing Co., P.O. Box 1868, Hartford, CT 06144-1868 (800) 962-2658 www.colt.com. A source of information and service for Colt handguns.

Competition Electronics, 3469 Precision Drive, Rockford, IL 61109 (815) 874-8001 www.competitionelectronics.com. Manufacturer of chronographs.

Cooper Firearms of Montana, P.O. Box 114, Stevensville, MT 59870 (406) 777-0373 www.cooperfirearms.com. Manufacturer of elegant sporting rifles.

CZ USA,
P. O. Box 171073, Kansas City, KS 66117-0073 (800) 955-4486 www.cz-usa.com. Marketer of the outstanding CZ rimfire rifles produced in the Czech Republic.

Custom Shooting Technologies, Inc.,
P.O. Box 43280, Louisville, KY 40253 (502) 797-3380 www.cstmtech.com. Producer of aftermarket parts for the Ruger 10/22.

DMPS, Inc.,
3312 12th St., St. Cloud, MN 56304 (800) 578-3767 www.dmpsinc.com. Maker of a unit to convert an AR-15 to 22 LR.

Dynamit Nobel-RWS Inc.,
81 Ruckman Road, Colster, NJ 07624 (201) 767-7971 www.dnrws.com. Producer of high quality ammunition.

Eley Limited, P.O. Box 705,
Witton, Birmingham, B6 7UT, England www.eley.co.uk. Manufacturer of many types of rimfire ammunition including high quality target loads.

Excel Industries,
4510 Carter Court, Chino, CA 91710 www.excelarms.com. Maker of the Accelerator semiautomatic in 22 WMR and 17 HMR calibers.

Federal Cartridge Co., 900 Ehlen Drive, Anoka, MN 55303-7503 (800) 322-2342 www.federalcartridge.com. Producer of many types of rimfire ammunition.

Freedom Arms, Inc.,
314 Highway 239, Freedom, WY 83120 (307) 883-2468 www.freedomarms.com. Producer of single-action handguns including small rimfire models.

GALCO International Ltd.,
2019 W. Quail Ave., Phoenix, AZ 85027 (623) 474-7070 www.usgalco.com. One of the large producers of handgun holsters.

Gold City Gun & Cartridge Co., LLC,
162 Lumpkin County Parkway, Suite 10, Dahlonega, Georgia 30533 (706) 864-1205 www.22ammo.com. Advertised as 22 ammo from around the world, this is a source for an incredible range of rimfire ammunition.

Graf & Sons, Inc.,
4050 S. Clark St., Mexico, MO 65265 www.graf.com. A catalog store of almost everything related to shooting.

Green Mountain Rifle Barrel Co. Inc.,
153 W. Main St., Conway, NH 03818 (603) 447-1095 www.gmriflebarrel.com. Makers of aftermarket barrels for rimfire rifles.

GunMate, P.O. Box 1690,
Oregon City, OR 97045 (800) 471-4999 www.gunmate.com. Manufacturer of holsters and related items.

Gunslick,
P.O. Box 39, Onalaska, WI 54650 (800) 635-7656 www.gunslick.com. Source for a wide range of gun care products.

H&R 1871, LLC,
60 Industrial Rowe, Gardner, MA 01440 (978) 632-9393 www.hr1871.com. Maker of firearms including single shot rimfire rifles.

Henry Repeating Arms Company,
110 8th Street, Brooklyn, NY 11215 (718) 499-5600 www.henryrepeating.com. Maker of several models of rimfire rifles including several lever-action models.

Heritage Manufacturing, Inc.
4600 N.W. 135 Street, Opa Locka, FL 33504 www.heritagemfg.com. Manufacturer of single-action revolvers with 22 LR and 22 WMR cylinders.

High Standard Mfg. Co.,
5200 Mitchelldale, No. E17, Houston, TX 77092-7222 (713) 462-4200 www.highstandard.com. Manufacturer of semiautomatic pistols.

Hogue Grips, P. O. 1138,
Paso Robles, CA 93447 (800) 438-4747 www.getgrip.com. Producer of a wide range of handgun grips and stocks including the rubber over molded models.

Hoppe's, P.O. Box 1690,
Oregon City, OR 97045 (800) 962-5757 www.butler-creek.com. Produces an extensive line of shooter's supplies including gun care products, finishing materials, and targets.

Hornady Manufacturing Co.,
Box 1848, Grand Island, NE 68802-1848 (800) 338-3220 www.hornady.com. Manufacturer of reloading equipment, ammunition, and supplies. Developer of the 17 HMR and 17 Mach 2 calibers.

Hornet Products, P.O. Box 1664,
Sarasota, FL 34230 (941) 359-1319 www.hornetproducts.com. Supplier of a wide range of aftermarket products for the Ruger 10/22 and 77/22 rifles and Mark II pistols. Products include Green Mountain, Lothar Walther, and Volquartsen barrels.

Hunter Co., Inc., 3300 W. 71st Avenue, Westminster, CO 80030 (303) 427-4626 www.hunterCompany.com. Producer of leather goods and holsters.

J. A. Ciener, 8700 Commerce St., Cape Canaveral, FL 32920 (321) 868-2200 www.22lrconversions.com. Produces a 22 LR conversion unit for the AR-15.

Jard, Inc., 2737 Nettle Ave., Sheldon, IA 51201 (712) 324-7409 www.jardinc.com. Producer of aftermarket triggers for many rifles including Ruger 77/22 and 10/22.

Jarvis, 1123 Cherry Orchard, Hamilton, MT 59840 (406) 961-4392 www.jarvis-custom.com. Maker of high quality aftermarket custom barrels.

Keystone Sporting Arms, Inc.,
8920 State Route 405, Milton, PA 17847 (800) 742-0455 www.cricket.com. Maker of the Cricket line of youth rifles.

Kimber, One Lawton Street,
Yonkers, NY 10705 (800) 880-2418 www.kimberamerica.com. Maker of high quality bolt action sporting rifles.

Kleen-Bore, Inc., 16 Industrial Parkway, Easthampton, MA 01027 (413) 527-0300 www.kleen-bore.com. Supplier of products for gun cleaning and maintenance.

Kramer Handgun Leather,
P. O. Box 112154, Tacoma, WA 98411 (800) 510-2666 www.kramerleather.com. A supplier of an extensive line of holsters and other leather goods.

Kuehl Precision Firearms,
P.O. Box 260, Labadie, MO 63065
(314) 330-2666 www.
kuehlprecisionfirearms.com.
Manufacturer of a unit to convert an
AR-15 to 22 LR.

Les Baer Custom, Inc.,
29601 34th Ave.,
Hillsdale, IL 61257 (309) 658-2716
www.lesbaer.com. A source of sights for
many handguns.

Leupold,& Stevens,
14400 N.W. Greenbrier Parkway,
Beaverton, OR 97006
(503) 526-1400 www.leupold.com.
Manufacturer of high quality scopes and
mounts.

Lilja Precision Rifle Barrels, Inc.,
P.O. Box 372, Plains, MT 59859
(406) 826-3084 www.riflebarrels.com.
Producer of high quality replacement
barrels.

Lock, Stock, and Barrel Shooting Supply,
Inc., P.O. Box B, Valentine, NE 69021
(800) 228-7925 www.lockstock.com.
Comprehensive supplier of shooting
accessories.

Lyman Products Corporation,
475 Smith St., Middletown, CT 06457
(800) 225-9626 www.lymanproducts.com.
Maker of trigger pull gauge, gunsmith
tools, etc.

Majestic Arms, LTD.,
101-A Ellis Street,
Staten Island, NY 10307
(718) 356-6765 www.majesticarms.
com. Producer of the Aluma-Lite barrels
designed by Dino Longueira with a
steel insert in an aluminum sleeve. Also
produces a kit to make stripping the Ruger
Mark II pistol easier and a takedown rifle.

Marlin Firearms,
100 Kenna Drive, P.O. Box 248,
North Haven, CT 06473-5621
www.marlinfirearms.com. One of the
largest manufacturers of rimfire rifles.

Midsouth Shooters Supply,
770 Economy Dr., Clarksville, TN 37043
(800) 272-3000
www.midsouthshootersupply.com.
A supplier of all types of accessories for
shooters.

Midway USA,
5875 W. Van Horn Tavern Road,
Columbia, MO 65203 (800) 243-3220
www.midwayusa.com. One of the largest
catalog com. panies that offers a wide range
of aftermarket item, scopes, grips, etc.

Millett Sights,
16131 Gothard St.,
Huntington Beach, CA 92647
(800) 645-5388 www.millettsights.com.
Supplier of sighting equipment including
scopes, red dot sights, rings, and bases.

Natchez Shooter Supply, Inc.,
P.O. Box 182212, Chattanooga, TN 37422
www.natchez.com. (800) 251-7839 Mail
order firm with a com. plete range of items
related to the shooting sports. Includes
scopes, grips, stocks, etc.

National Rifle Association,
11250 Waples Mill Road, Fairfax, VA
22030-9400 (800) 642-3888
www.nra.org The source of an incredible
amount of information on shooting sports
and the organization most visible in
supporting Second Amendment rights.

North American Arms, Inc.,
2150 S. 950 E, Provo, UT 84606-6285
(800) 821-5783 www.naaminis.com.
Maker of small revolvers in rimfire calibers.

Numrich Gun Parts Corporation,
226 Williams Lane, P.O. Box 299, West
Hurley, NY 12491 www.e-gunparts.com.
One of the largest suppliers of parts for
firearms.

Oehler Research, Inc.,
P.O. Box 9135, Austin, TX 78766 (800)
531-5125 www.oehler-research.com.
Manufacturer of chronographs.

Outers, Route 2, P.O. Box 39,
Onalaska, WI 54650 (800) 635-7656
www.outers-guncare.com. Markets an
extensive line of gun care products.

Pachmayr,
475 Smith Street, Middletown, CT 06457
(800) 423-9704 www.pachmayr.com.
Maker of an extensive line of aftermarket
grips for handguns.

PMC Ammunition,
Boulder City, NV 89005 (702) 294-0025
www.pmcammo.com. Supplier of an
extensive line of rimfire ammunition.

Power Custom, Inc.,
29739 Hwy. J, Gravois Mills, MO 65037
(573) 372-5684 www.powercustom.com.
Marketer for many accessories for Ruger
10/22 and 77/22 rifles.

Remington Arms Co.,
870 Remington Drive, P.O. Box 700,
Madison, NC 27025 (800) 243-9700
www.remington.com. Producer of firearms
for almost 200 years and an extensive line
of ammunition.

Rifle Basix,
P. O. Box 23593, Charlotte, NC 28227
(704) 556-1939 www.riflebasix.com.
Manufacturer of triggers for a variety of
rifles including rimfires.

Rimfire Benchrest Association,
5609 Lantana Avenue,
Charlotte, NC 28212 (704) 536-8210 rba.
benchrest.net The association that is the
governing body for the sport of benchrest
shooting.

Rogue Rifle Company, Inc.,
1140 36th Street N Suite B,
Lewiston, ID 83501 (208) 743-4355
www.roguerifle.com. Makers of the
Chipmunk line of youth rifles and
accessories.

Safariland Ltd., Inc.,
3120 E. Mission Boulevard,
P.O. Box 51478, Ontario, CA 91761
(909) 923-7300 www.safariland.com.
Producer of holsters.

Savage Arms, Inc.,
118 Mountain Road, Suffield, CT 06078
www.savagearms.com. Manufacturer of an
extensive line of bolt action, semiautomatic,
and single shot rimfire rifles.

Shilen,
205 Metro Park Boulevard,
P. O. Box 1300, Ennis, TX 75119
(972) 875-5318 www.shilen.com.
A producer of highly regarded barrels and triggers.

Shooter's Choice,
15050 Berkshire Industrial Parkway,
Middlefield, OH 44062
(440) 834-8888 www.shooters-choice.com.
Marketer of gun care products.

Shooting Chrony, Inc.,
3840 E. Robinson Rd.,
PMB 298, Amherst, NY 14228
(800) 385-3161 www.shootingchrony.com.
Maker of chronographs.

SIGARMS,
18 Industrial Drive, Exeter, NH 03833
www.sigarms.com. Producer of pistols that include the Trailside 22 LR.

Simmons Outdoors Corporation,
201 Plantation Oak Drive,
Thomasville, GA 31792 (800) 285-0689
www.simmonsoptics.com. Supplier of an extensive line of scopes and other optical sights.

Sinclair International,
2330 Wayne Haven St.,
Fort Wayne, IN 46803 www.sinclair.com.
Offers a wide range of products such as rests, sandbags, bipods, cleaning rods and supplies, and com. petition receiver sights

Small Caliber News,
Technology Media Ventures,
11220 Hilltop Road SW,
Baltic, OH 43804 (330) 897-0614
www.smallcaliber.com. A magazine devoted to shooting small caliber (both centerfire and rimfire) rifles.

Smith & Wesson,
2100 Roosevelt Avenue,
P.O. Box 2208,
Springfield, MA 01102-2208
(800) 331-0852
www.smith-wesson.com. Manufacturer of a wide variety of handguns for sporting, military, and law enforcement uses. Also markets Walther firearms. Originators of the 22 rimfire cartridge.

Sturm, Ruger & Co., Inc.,
Lacey Place, Southport, CT 06890 and 200 Ruger Road, Prescott, AZ 86301
(928) 541-8820 www.ruger.com.
Manufacturer of an extensive line of rimfire rifles in bolt, lever, and semiautomatic types.

Superior Products,
355 Mandela Parkway, Oakland, CA
(707) 585-8329 www.slip2000.com.
Producer of the Slip 2000 line of gun care products.

Tasco,
9200 Cody, Overland Park,
KS 66214 (800) 221-9035 www.tasco.com.
Markets a com. plete line of rifle scopes and red dot sights.

The Woodchuck Den, Inc.,
11220 Hilltop Road SW,
Baltic, OH 43804 (330) 897-0614
www.smallcaliber.com. A supplier of shooting accessories of all types.

Trijicon, Inc.,
49385 Shafer Ave.,
P. O. Box 930059, Wixom, MI 48393-0059
(800) 338-0563 www.trijicon.com.
A manufacturer of scopes, red dot sights, and metallic sights.

Triple-K Mfg. Co., Inc.,
2222 Commercial St.,
San Diego, CA 92113 (619) 232-2066
www.triplek.com. Manufacturer of holsters, especially for single-action revolvers.

Tristar Sporting Arms,
1814-1816 Linn Street, N.
Kansas City, MO 64116
www.anschutz-sporters.com. Importer of Anschutz rimfire rifles.

Uncle Mikes,
P.O. Box 1690, Oregon City, OR 97045
(800) 845-2444 www.butlercreek.com.
Marketer of grips, sling swivels, holsters, and other accessories.

United States Rimfire Association
IR50/50, 318 Wright Drive,
Selma, AL 36701 (334) 875-1980
www.ir5050.com. The association devoted to rimfire shooting sports.

Volquartsen Custom Ltd.,
24276 240th Street,
P.O Box 397, Carroll, IA 51401
www.volquartsen.com. Manufacturer of aftermarket barrels, triggers, and other items as well as com. plete rifles, especially autoloaders in rimfire calibers.

Weaver,
201 Plantation Oak Drive,
Thomasville, GA 31792 (800) 285-0689
www.weaveroptics.com. Producers of many types of scopes including some specifically for rimfire rifles.

Williams Gun Sight Company, Inc.,
7389 Lapeer Rd, Box 329,
Davison, MI 48423 (800) 530-9028
www.williamsgunsight.com. Manufacturer of sighting equipment including peep sights.

Winchester Ammunition,
427 N. Shamrock, East Alton, IL 62024
(618) 258-3599 www.winchester.com.
One of the largest manufacturers of rimfire ammunition.

Wolf Performance Ammunition,
1225 N. Lance Lane, Anaheim, CA 92806
(888) 757-9653. www.wolfammo.com.
Supplies a wide range of ammunition including some outstanding rimfire target loads made in Germany.

(Courtesy: U. S. Fish and Wildlife Service/Photo by Dave Menke)

Appendix C
SOURCES FOR HUNTING INFORMATION

Alabama Department of Conservation
and Natural Resources
64 North Union Street
Montgomery, AL 36130
(334) 242-3465
www.dcnr.state.al.us/agfd

Division of Wildlife Conservation
P.O. Box 25526
Juneau, AK 99802-6197
(907) 465-6197
www.state.ak.us/local/akpages/fish.game/wildlife

Arizona Game and Fish Department
2221 West Greenway Road
Phoenix, AZ 85023-4312
(602) 942-3000
www.gfd.state.az.us

Arkansas Game & Fish Commission
#2 Natural Resources Drive
Little Rock, AR 72205
(800) 354-4263
www.agfc.state.ar.us

California Department Fish & Game
1416 9th Street
Sacramento, CA 95818
(916) 227-2244
www.cfg.state.ca.us

Colorado Division of Wildlife
1313 Sherman Room #718
Denver, CO 80203
(303) 297-1192
http://wildlife.state.co.us/

Connecticut Department of
Environmental Protection
Wildlife Division
79 Elm Street
Hartford, CT 06106-5127
(800) 424-3105
http://dep.state.ct.us/pao/

Delaware Division of
Fish and Wildlife
89 Kings Highway
Dover, DE 19901
(302) 739-4431
dep.state.ct.us/burnatr/wildlife

Florida Department of Game and
Freshwater Fish
620 South Meridian Street
Tallahassee, FL 32399-1600
(850) 488-4676
www.state.fl.us/gfc

Georgia Department of
Natural Resources
Wildlife Management Division
2111 Highway 278
Social Circle, GA 30025
(770) 918-6416
www.ganet.org/dnr/

Idaho Department of Fish and Game
P.O. Box 25
Boise, ID 83707
(208) 334-3700
www.state.id.us/fishgame

Illinois Department of
Natural Resources
524 South Second Street, Room 210
Springfield, IL 62701
(217) 782-2965
www.dnr.state.il.us/ildnr/

Indiana Department of
Natural Resources
402 West Washington Street
Indianapolis, IN 46204
(317) 232-4080
www.dnr.state.in.us

Iowa Department of
Natural Resources
Wallace State Office Building
Des Moines, IA 50319-0034
(515) 281-5145
www.dnr.state.ia.us

Kansas Parks and Wildlife
900 SW Jackson Street, Suite 502
Topeka, KS 66612-1233
(785) 273-6740
www.kdwp.state.ks.us

Kentucky Department of
Wildlife Resources
#1 Game Farm Road
Frankfort, KY 40601
(502) 564-4336
www.state.ky.us/agencies/fw/kdfwr.htm

Louisiana Wildlife & fisheries
P.O. Box 98000
Baton Rouge, LA 70898
(504) 765-2980
www.wlf.state.la.us

Maine Department of Inland
Fisheries & Wildlife
285 State Street
41 State House Station
Augusta, ME 04333-0041
(207) 287-2571
webmaster_ifw@state.me.us

Maryland Department of
Natural Resources
Wildlife Division
580 Taylor Avenue, E-1
Annapolis, MD 21401
(401) 260-8540
www.dnr.state.md.us/huntersguide

Massachusetts Department
Fisheries and Wildlife
Field Headquarters
Westboro, MA 01581
(508) 792-7270, ext. 110
www.state.ma.us/dfwele/

Michigan Department of
Natural Resources
4590 118th Avenue, Route 3
Allegan, MI 49010
(517) 373-1230
www.dnr.state.mi.us

Minnesota Department of
Natural Resources
500 Lafayette Road
St. Paul, MN 55155-4026
(651) 296-4506
www.dnr.state.mn.us

Mississippi Department of Wildlife
2906 North State Street
Jackson, MS 39205
(800) 546-4868
www.mdfo.state.ms.us

Missouri
Department of Conservation
P.O. Box 180
Jefferson City, MO 65102
(573) 751-4115
www.dnr.state.mo.us

Montana
Department of Fish,
Wildlife, and Parks
1420 East 6th Avenue
Helena, MT 59620
(406) 444-2535
http://fwp.state.mt.us/

Nebraska Game and Parks
2200 North 33rd Street
Lincoln, NE 68503
(402) 471-5003
www.ngpc.state.ne.us

Nevada Division of Wildlife
P.O. Box 10678
Reno, NV 89520
(702) 688-1500
www.ndw.state.nv.us

New Hampshire
Fish and Game Department
2 Hazen Drive
Concord, NH 03301
(603) 271-3211
www.wildlife.state.nh.us

New Jersey
Division of Fish, Game, and Wildlife
P.O. Box 400
Trenton, NJ 08625-0400
(609) 292-2965
www.state.nj.us/dep/fgw

New Mexico
Department of Game and Fish
P.O. Box 25112
Sante Fe, NM 87504
(505) 827-7911
www.gmfs.state.nm.us

New York
Department of Environment
Conservation
Wildlife Division
50 Wolfe Road
Albany, NY 12233
(518) 457-3521
www.dec.state.ny.us/

North Carolina
Wildlife Resources Commission
512 North Salisbury Street
Raleigh, NC 27640
(919) 662-4370
www.ncwildlife.org/

North Dakota Game and
Fish Department
100 N. Bismarck Expressway
Bismarck, ND 58501-5095
(701) 328-6300
www.state.nd.us/gnf/hunting

Ohio Division of Wildlife
1840 Belcher Drive
Columbus, OH 43224
(614) 265-6300
www.dnr.state.oh.us/odnr/wildlife/hunting

Oklahoma Division of Wildlife
1801 North Lincoln Boulevard
Oklahoma City, OK 73152
(405) 521-3853
www.odr.state.ok.us

Oregon Department of
Fish and Game
P.O. Box 59
Portland, OR 97207
(503) 872-5270
www.odfg.state.or.us

Pennsylvania Game Commission
2001 Elmerton Avenue
Harrisburg, PA 17110
(717) 787-4250
www.pgc.state.pa.us

Rhode Island
Fish and Wildlife
Oliver Steadman Government Center
480 Tower Hill Road
Wake Field, RI 02879
(401) 789-3094
www.state.ri.us

South Carolina
Department of Natural Resources
Wildlife Division
P.O. Box 167
Columbia, SC 29202
(803) 734-3843
www.dnr.state.sc.us

South Dakota
Department of Game, Fish, and Parks
523 East Capitol
Pierre, SD 57501
(605) 773-3485
www.state.sd.us

Tennessee
Wildlife Resource Agency
Ellington Agricultural Center
Nashville, TN 37302
(615) 781-6580
www.state.tn.us

Texas
Parks and Wildlife
4200 Smith School Road
Austin, TX 78744
(512) 389-4820
www.tpwd.state.tx.us/hunt

Utah
Wildlife Resources
1594 West, North Temple, Suite 2110
Salt Lake City, UT 84114-6301
(801) 538-4700
www.nr.state.ut.us

Vermont
Department of Fish and Wildlife
103 South Main Street, 10 South
Building
Waterbury, VT 05671-0501
(802) 241-3700
www.dnr.state.vt.us/fw/fwhome

Virginia
Department of Game and Inland
Fisheries
P.O. Box 11104
Richmond, VA 23230-1104
(804) 367-1000
www.dgif.state.va.us

Washington
Department of Fish and Wildlife
600 Capitol Way North
Olympia, WA 98501-1091
(360) 902-2464
http://wdfw.wa.gov/

West Virginia
Department of Natural Resources
Wildlife Division
1900 Kanawha Boulevard East
Capital Complex, Building 3
Charleston WV 25305
(304) 558-3380
www.wvdnr.state.wv.us

Wisconsin
Department of Natural Resources
Box 7921
Madison, WI 53707
(608) 266-2621
www.dnr.state.wi.us/

Wyoming
Game and Fish Department
5400 Bishop Boulevard
Cheyenne, WY 82006
(307) 777-4600
http://gf.state.wy.us/